DATE DUE

DEMCO 128-5046

SOMETHING ABOUT THE AUTHOR®

Something about
the Author *was named
an "Outstanding
Reference Source"
the highest honor given
by the American
Library Association
Reference and Adult
Services Division.*

ISSN 0276-816X

SOMETHING ABOUT THE AUThOR®

**Facts and Pictures about Authors
and Illustrators of Books for Young People**

EDITED BY
KEVIN S. HILE

VOLUME 86

GALE

STAFF

Editor: Kevin S. Hile
Managing Editor: Joyce Nakamura
Publisher: Hal May
Contributing Editors: Alan Hedblad and Diane Telgen
Assistant Editor: Marilyn O'Connell Allen

Sketchwriters/Copyeditors: Linda R. Andres, Shelly Andrews, Joanna Brod,
Ronie-Richele Garcia-Johnson, Mary Gillis, Janet L. Hile, Laurie Hillstrom,
Motoko Fujishiro Huthwaite, David Johnson, J. Sydney Jones, Julie Karmazin,
Sharyn Kolberg, Thomas F. McMahon, Pamela J. Nealon-LaBreck, Susan Reicha,
Pamela L. Shelton, and Mel Wathen

Research Manager: Victoria B. Cariappa
Project Coordinator: Cheryl L. Warnock
Research Associates: Tamara Nott, Michele P. Pica, Tracie Richardson, and Norma Sawaya
Research Assistants: Alicia Biggers and Michelle Lee

Permissions Manager: Marlene S. Hurst
Permissions Specialists: Margaret A. Chamberlain and Maria Franklin
Permissions Associate: Rita Velazquez

Production Director: Mary Beth Trimper
Production Assistant: Deborah Milliken

Graphic Services Manager: Barbara J. Yarrow
Image Database Supervisor: Randy Bassett
Macintosh Artist: Sherrell Hobbs
Scanner Operator: Robert Duncan
Photography Coordinator: Pamela A. Hayes

Library of Congress Catalog Card Number 72-27107

ISBN 0-8103-9372-7 ISSN 0276-816X

Printed in the United States of America

10 9 8 7 6 5 4 3 2 1

Contents

Authors in Forthcoming Volumes

Below are some of the authors and illustrators that will be featured in upcoming volumes of *SATA*. These include new entries on the swiftly-rising stars of the field, as well as completely revised and updated entries (indicated with *) on some of the most notable and best-loved creators of books for children.

Alan Baillie: A Scottish-born Australian author of young adult books, Baillie is a former journalist who turned his hand to writing young adult novels often set in Asia, such as *Little Brother* and *The China Coin,* or Australia, including *Hero* and *Songman.*

Natalie Bober: Bober is a respected author of biographies for young readers who has won awards for such books as *Abigail Adams: Witness to a Revolution* and *A Restless Spirit: The Story of Robert Frost.*

Mary Alice Downie: One of Canada's best-known authors and editors of children's books, Downie often writes stories set in Canada during the colonial era, and she has also published retellings of folktales from Europe and Asia.

*Mary Elting: Elting's prodigious output of nonfiction for children covers a wide variety of topics, ranging from archaeology to zoology, in dozens of books published over the last fifty years.

Roy Fuller: An English poet, novelist, and critic, the late Fuller was best known for his verses for adults, but he also wrote a number of well-received novels and poetry collections for children, including *The World through the Window, Catspaw,* and *Seen Grandpa Lately?*

*Sheila Ellen Green: Writing under the name Sheila Greenwald, Green is an illustrator and author who has become popular for her ''Rosy Cole'' stories, which chronicle the adventures of a pre-teen girl as she endures the typical trials of adolescence.

*Helen V. Griffith: With a style that has been characterized by one critic as ''quiet, poetic, and subtly powerful,'' Griffith has been praised for both her picture and her chapter books, from *Mine Will, Said John* to the more recent *Grandaddy's Stars.*

Bill Harley: Harley, a talented storyteller and musician who is also a commentator for National Public Radio's *All Things Considered,* has recorded many of his delightful vignettes about growing up on books and tapes.

Paul Jennings: A bestselling author of books for children in their early teens in his native Australia, Jennings writes short story collections about the bizarre and supernatural aimed at encouraging reluctant children to read.

Kate and Jim McMullan: The husband-and-wife team has created several award-winning picture books, including *The Noisy Giants' Tea Party, Nutcracker Noel,* and *Hey, Pipsqueak!*

*Mary Rayner: Rayner has written and illustrated many picture books for children, but she is most widely recognized for her stories featuring the Pig family, which have won her honors such as the 1987 Parents' Choice Award for *Mrs. Pig Gets Cross and Other Stories.*

*Miriam Schlein: Winner of seven Outstanding Science Trade Book for Children citations for her nonfiction for young readers, along with numerous other awards, Schlein is best known for her books for beginning readers that introduce children to interesting animals and dispel common myths about them.

Kate Spohn: Using pencil and oils, Spohn illustrates her simple yet original picture books that sometimes feature highly unusual characters, such as anthropomorphized fruit in *Introducing Fanny* and *Fanny and Margarita: Five Stories about Two Best Friends.*

*Denys James Watkins-Pitchford: Best known for his children's books written under the pseudonym ''BB,'' the late Carnegie Medal-winning English author and illustrator turned a lifelong fascination for nature into a library of works that have delighted readers since the 1930s.

Introduction

Something about the Author (*SATA*) is an ongoing reference series that deals with the lives and works of authors and illustrators of children's books. *SATA* includes not only well-known authors and illustrators whose books are widely read, but also those less prominent people whose works are just coming to be recognized. This series is often the only readily available information source on emerging writers and artists. You'll find *SATA* informative and entertaining, whether you are a student, a librarian, an English teacher, a parent, or simply an adult who enjoys children's literature for its own sake.

What's Inside SATA

SATA provides detailed information about authors and illustrators who span the full time range of children's literature, from early figures like John Newbery and L. Frank Baum to contemporary figures like Judy Blume and Richard Peck. Authors in the series represent primarily English-speaking countries, particularly the United States, Canada, and the United Kingdom. Also included, however, are authors from around the world whose works are available in English translation. The writings represented in *SATA* include those created intentionally for children and young adults as well as those written for a general audience and known to interest younger readers. These writings cover the entire spectrum of children's literature, including picture books, humor, folk and fairy tales, animal stories, mystery and adventure, science fiction and fantasy, historical fiction, poetry and nonsense verse, drama, biography, and nonfiction.

Obituaries are also included in *SATA* and are intended not only as death notices but also as concise overviews of people's lives and work. Additionally, each edition features newly revised and updated entries for a selection of *SATA* listees who remain of interest to today's readers and who have been active enough to require extensive revisions of their earlier biographies.

Two Convenient Indexes

In response to suggestions from librarians, *SATA* indexes no longer appear in every volume but are included in alternate (odd-numbered) volumes of the series, beginning with Volume 57.

SATA continues to include two indexes that cumulate with each alternate volume: the Illustrations Index, arranged by the name of the illustrator, gives the number of the volume and page where the illustrator's work appears in the current volume as well as all preceding volumes in the series; the Author Index gives the number of the volume in which a person's Biographical Sketch or Obituary appears in the current volume as well as all preceding volumes in the series.

These indexes also include references to authors and illustrators who appear in Gale's *Yesterday's Authors of Books for Children, Children's Literature Review,* and the *Something about the Author Autobiography Series.*

Easy-to-Use Entry Format

Whether you're already familiar with the *SATA* series or just getting acquainted, you will want to be aware of the kind of information that an entry provides. In every *SATA* entry the editors attempt to give as complete a picture of the person's life and work as possible. A typical entry in *SATA* includes the following clearly labeled information sections:

- *PERSONAL:* date and place of birth and death, parents' names and occupations, name of spouse, date of marriage, names of children, educational institutions attended, degrees received, religious and political affiliations, hobbies and other interests.

- *ADDRESSES:* complete home, office, electronic mail, and agent addresses, whenever available.

• *CAREER:* name of employer, position, and dates for each career post; art exhibitions; military service; memberships and offices held in professional and civic organizations.

• *AWARDS, HONORS:* literary and professional awards received.

• *WRITINGS:* title-by-title chronological bibliography of books written and/or illustrated, listed by genre when known; lists of other notable publications, such as plays, screenplays, and periodical contributions.

• *ADAPTATIONS:* a list of films, television programs, plays, CD-ROMs, recordings, and other media presentations that have been adapted from the author's work.

• *WORK IN PROGRESS:* description of projects in progress.

• *SIDELIGHTS:* a biographical portrait of the author or illustrator's development, either directly from the biographee—and often written specifically for the *SATA* entry—or gathered from diaries, letters, interviews, or other published sources.

• *FOR MORE INFORMATION SEE:* references for further reading.

• *EXTENSIVE ILLUSTRATIONS:* photographs, movie stills, book illustrations, and other interesting visual materials supplement the text.

How a SATA Entry Is Compiled

A *SATA* entry progresses through a series of steps. If the biographee is living, the *SATA* editors try to secure information directly from him or her through a questionnaire. From the information that the biographee supplies, the editors prepare an entry, filling in any essential missing details with research and/or telephone interviews. If possible, the author or illustrator is sent a copy of the entry to check for accuracy and completeness.

If the biographee is deceased or cannot be reached by questionnaire, the *SATA* editors examine a wide variety of published sources to gather information for an entry. Biographical and bibliographic sources are consulted, as are book reviews, feature articles, published interviews, and material sometimes obtained from the biographee's family, publishers, agent, or other associates.

Entries that have not been verified by the biographees or their representatives are marked with an asterisk (*).

Contact the Editor

We encourage our readers to examine the entire *SATA* series. Please write and tell us if we can make *SATA* even more helpful to you. Give your comments and suggestions to the editor:

BY MAIL: The Editor, *Something about the Author,* Gale Research, 835 Penobscot Bldg., 645 Griswold St., Detroit, MI 48226-4094.

BY TELEPHONE: (800) 347-GALE

BY FAX: (313) 961-6599

BY E-MAIL: CYA@Gale.com@Galesmtp

Acknowledgments

Grateful acknowledgment is made to the following publishers, authors, and artists whose works appear in this volume.

JEZ ALBOROUGH. Illustration from *Cuddly Dudley* by Jez Alborough. Walker Books, Ltd., 1993. Copyright © 1993 by Jez Alborough. Reprinted by permission of Walker Books, Ltd. / Illustration from *Running Bear* by Jez Alborough. Random House, 1985. Copyright © 1985 by Jez Alborough. Reprinted by permission of Random House, Inc. / Illustration from *Where's My Teddy?* by Jez Alborough. Walker Books, Ltd., 1992. Copyright © 1992 by Jez Alborough. Reprinted by permission of Walker Books Ltd.

RACHEL ANDERSON. Cover illustration from *The Bus People* by Rachel Anderson. Henry Holt and Co., Inc, 1989. Copyright © 1989 by Rachel Anderson. Reprinted by permission of Henry Holt and Co., Inc. / Cover illustration by Elyse Feldman from a jacket of *Paper Faces* by Rachel Anderson. Henry Holt and Co., Inc., 1991. Jacket illustration copyright © 1993 by Elyse Feldman. Reprinted by permission of Henry Holt and Co., Inc. / Portrait of Rachel Anderson by Kenneth Saunders. Courtesy of *The Guardian*.

MESHACK ASARE. Illustration from *Cat in Search of a Friend* by Meshack Asare. First American Edition 1986 by Kane/Miller Book Publishers. American text copyright © 1986 by Kane/Miller Book Publishers. All rights reserved. Reproduced by permission of the publisher.

SALLY BAHOUS. Portrait of Sally Bahous. Reproduced by permission.

BARBARA BARTHOLOMEW. Illustration by Yuri Salzman from *The Great Gradepoint Mystery* by Barbara Bartholomew. Macmillan Publishing Company, 1983. Copyright © 1983 by Yuri Salzman. All rights reserved. Reproduced by permission of the artist.

BARBARA BAUMGARTNER. Portrait of Barbara Baumgartner. Reproduced by permission.

SARAGAIL KATZMAN BENJAMIN. Cover illustration by Marylin Hafner from *My Dog Ate It* by Saragail Katzman Benjamin. Holiday House, 1994. All rights reserved. Reproduced by permission of the publisher. / Portrait of Saragail Katzman Benjamin from a jacket of *My Dog Ate It*. Holiday House, 1994. Courtesy of Holiday House, Inc.

ELISABETH BERESFORD. Portrait of Elisabeth Beresford. Reproduced by permission.

EMILIE BOON. Illustration from *1 2 3 How Many Animals Can You See?* by Emilie Boon. Copyright © 1987 by Emilie Boon. Reproduced by permission of the publisher, Orchard Books, New York. / Illustration from *Peterkin's Wet Walk* by Emilie Boon. Copyright © 1983 by Emilie Boon. All rights reserved. Reproduced by permission of William Heinemann Ltd.

BERKELEY BREATHED. Illustration from *A Wish for Wings That Work: An Opus Christmas Story* by Berkeley Breathed. Little, Brown & Company, 1991. Copyright © 1991 by Berkeley Breathed. All rights reserved. Reprinted by permission of Little, Brown & Company. / Illustration from *Penguin Dreams and Stranger Things* by Berke Breathed. Little, Brown & Company, 1985. Copyright © 1985 by The Washington Post Company. All rights reserved. Reproduced by permission of Little, Brown & Company. / Illustration from *Red Ranger Came Calling: A Guaranteed True Christmas Story* by Berkeley Breathed. Little, Brown & Company, 1994. Copyright © 1994 by Berkeley Breathed. All rights reserved. Reproduced by permission of Little, Brown & Company. / Portrait of Berke Breathed by Jody Boyman. Copyright © Jody Boyman.

STEVEN K. BRUST. Cover illustration by Jim Burns from *Agyar* by Steven Brust. Tor Books, 1993. All rights reserved. Reproduced by permission of Tom Doherty Associations. / Cover illustration by Kinuko Craft from *Taltos* by Steven Brust. Ace Books, 1988. All rights reserved. Reproduced by arrangement with The Berkley Publishing Group. / Cover illustration by Jim Gurney from *Cowboy Feng's Space Bar and Grille* by Steven Brust. Ace Books, 1990. All rights reserved. Reproduced by arrangement with The Berkley Publishing Group.

JACK BUSHNELL. Portrait of Jack Bushnell. Reproduced by permission.

RAYMOND CARROLL. Photograph of Edward Stettinius (with Harry Truman) from *The Future of the United Nations*. UN/DPI Photograph. Courtesy of the United Nations.

MARY M. CERULLO. Portrait of Mary Cerullo by Arthur A. Cerullo. Reproduced by permission.

GRACE CHETWIN. Illustration from *Jason's Seven Magical Night Rides* by Grace Chetwin. Bradbury Press, 1994. Copyright © 1994 by Grace Chetwin. All rights reserved. Reprinted by permission of Simon & Schuster Books for Young Readers. / Portrait of Grace Chetwin by Allison MacGuffin. Reproduced by permission.

DOROTHY CLEWES. Illustration by Sofia from *The Runaway* by Dorothy Clewes. Coward-McCann, Inc., 1957. All rights reserved. Reproduced by permission of the author. / Jacket illustration by Justin Todd from *Storm over Innish* by Dorothy Clewes. Thomas Nelson Incorporated, 1972. All rights reserved. Reproduced by permission of the author. / Jacket illustration by Loretta Trezzo from *Missing from Home* by Dorothy Clewes. Harcourt Brace Jovanovich, Inc., 1975. All rights reserved. Reproduced by permission of the author.

/ Portrait courtesy of Dorothy Clewes.

NANTZ COMYNS-TOOHEY. Portrait of Nantz Comyns-Toohey from *The Legend of Blazing Bear*. Windswept House Publishers, 1992. Reprinted by permission.

SARA CORRIN. Illustration by Errol Le Cain from *Mrs. Fox's Wedding* by Sara and Stephen Corrin. Doubleday and Company, 1980. Copyright © 1980 by Sara and Stephen Corrin. Illustrations copyright © 1980 by Errol Le Cain. Reproduced by permission of Doubleday, a division of Bantam Doubleday Dell Publishing Group, Inc. / Cover illustration by Gerald Rose from *Laugh out Loud: More Funny Stories for Children*. Edited by Sara and Stephen Corrin. Faber and Faber, 1972. Illustrations copyright © Faber & Faber Limited, 1972, 1989. All rights reserved. Reprinted by permission of Faber & Faber Limited. / Portrait courtesy of Sara and Stephen Corrin.

STEPHEN CORRIN. From a cover of *Stories for 7-Year-Olds*. Edited by Sara and Stephen Corrin. Faber & Faber, 1964. This collection © Faber & Faber Limited 1964. All rights reserved. Reprinted by permission of Faber & Faber Limited.

MARY SHURA CRAIG. Illustration by Adrienne Adams from *The Nearsighted Knight* by Mary Francis Shura. Alfred A. Knopf, 1964. / From a cover of *Gentle Annie: The True Story of a Civil War Nurse* by Mary Francis Shura. Scholastic, 1991. Illustration copyright © by Scholastic Inc. Reproduced by permission. / Illustration by Jacqueline Rogers from *Don't Call Me Toad!* by Mary F. Craig. Copyright © 1987 by Mary Francis Shura. All rights reserved. Reprinted by permission of The Putnam & Grosset Group. / Illustration by Susan Swan from *Chester* by Mary Francis Shura. Copyright © 1980 by Mary Francis Shura. Reprinted by permission of The Putnam & Grosset Group. / Illustration by Ted Lewin from *The Search for Grissi* by Mary F. Shura. Copyright © 1985 by Mary Francis Shura. All rights reserved. Reprinted by permission of The Putnam & Grosset Group. / Portrait of Mary Francis Shura. Reprinted by permission of The Literary Estate of Mary Francis Shura.

A. C. CRISPIN. Cover illustration by Doriau from *Songsmith* by A. C. Crispin. Copyright © 1992 by Andre Norton, Ltd. and A. C. Crispin. Reprinted by permission of Tom Doherty Associates.

JOHN ARTHUR CUNLIFFE. Illustration by Celia Berridge from *Postman Pat and the Mystery Thief* by John Cunliffe. Andre Deutsch Limited, 1982. Illustrations copyright © 1982 by Celia Berridge and Ivor Wood. Reproduced by permission of Scholastic Ltd. / Illustration by Alexy Pendle from *The Great Dragon Competition and Other Stories* by John Cunliffe. Andre Deutsch, 1973. All rights reserved. Reproduced by permission of Scholastic Ltd. / Jacket illustration by Fritz Wegner from *Giant Kippernose and Other Stories* by John Cunliffe. Andre Deutsch, 1972. All rights reserved. Reproduced by permission of Scholastic Ltd.

JOHN LITTLEDALE de HAMEL. Portrait of Joan Littledale de Hamel. Reproduced by permission.

LISA DESIMINI. Cover illustration by Lisa Desimini from *My House* by Lisa Desimini. Henry Holt and Company, 1994. Copyright © 1994 by Lisa Desimini. All rights reserved. Reproduced by permission of Henry Holt and Company, Inc. / Illustration from *Moon Soup* by Lisa Desimini. Text and illustrations copyright © 1993 by Lisa Desimini. Reprinted by permission of Hyperion Books. / Portrait of Lisa Desimini by Matt Mahurin from a jacket of *My House* by Lisa Desimini. Henry Holt and Co., Inc., 1994. Reprinted by permission of Henry Holt and Co., Inc.

LYNLEY DODD. From an illustration in *Hairy Maclary's Scattercat* by Lynley Dodd. Gareth Stevens, 1988. Reproduced by permission of the publisher. / Portrait of Lynley Dodd. Reproduced by permission.

MARY LEE DONOVAN. Illustration by Kimberly Bulcken Root from *Papa's Bedtime Story* by Mary Lee Donovan. Alfred A. Knopf, Inc., 1993. Illustrations copyright © 1993 by Kimberly Bulcken Root. All rights reserved. Reproduced by permission of Random House, Inc.

PHILIPPE DUPASQUIER. Illustration from *The Great Escape* by Philippe Dupasquier. Copyright © 1988 by Philippe Dupasquier. Reprinted by permission of Houghton Mifflin Company. / Portrait of Philippe Dupasquier by Richard Mewton. Reproduced by permission of *Books for Keeps*.

NORBERT EHRENFREUND. Illustration by Chris Costello from *You're the Jury* by Norbert Ehrenfreund and Lawrence Treat. Copyright © 1992 by Norbert Ehrenfreund and Lawrence Treat. Reproduced by permission of Henry Holt & Company, Inc.

JEANNETTE EYERLY. Jacket illustration by Ilse Koehn from *Escape from Nowhere* by Jeannette Eyerly. J. B. Lippincott Company, 1969. All rights reserved. Reproduced by permission of the publisher. / Illustration by Emily Arnold McCully from *The Seeing Summer* by Jeannette Eyerly. J. B. Lippincott, 1981. Illustrations copyright © 1981 by Emily Arnold McCully. All rights reserved. Reproduced by permission of the publisher. / Jacket illustration by Ellen Raskin from *A Girl Like Me* by Jeannette H. Eyerly. J. B. Lippincott. Reproduced by permission of the publisher. / Jacket illustration by Ellen Thompson from *Someone to Love Me* by Jeannette Eyerly. J. B. Lippincott, 1987. Jacket art copyright © 1987 by Ellen Thompson. Jacket copyright © 1987 by Harper & Row, Publishers, Inc. All rights reserved. Reproduced by permission of the publisher. / Portrait of Jeannette Eyerly. Reproduced by permission.

CLIFF FAULKNOR. Cover illustration by Gerald Tailfeathers from *The White Calf* by Cliff Faulknor. Little, Brown & Company. Reproduced by permission of the author. / Portrait of Cliff Faulknor by Tops Photo Studio. Reproduced by permission.

GARY L. FISHER. Illustration by Jackie Urbanovic from *The Survival Guide for Kids with LD* by Gary L. Fisher and Rhoda Woods Cummings. Free Spirit Publishing, 1990. All rights reserved. Reprinted by permission of the publisher.

SIMON FRENCH. Portrait of Simon French from a jacket of *Change the Locks* by Simon French. Ashton Scholastic, 1991. Copyright

THOMAS S. OWENS. From a cover of *Collecting Baseball Cards* by Thomas S. Owens. The Millbrook Press, 1993. Cards used on cover copyright © and reproduced with permission of Action Packed Cards, LBC Sports, Inc.; Mother's Cookies; Pacific Trading Cards, Inc. All rights reserved. Reproduced by permission of the publisher. / Portrait of Thomas S. Owens. Reproduced by permission.

DAWN PETERSON. Portrait of Dawn Peterson. Reproduced by permission.

KIN PLATT. Jacket illustration by Fred Marcellino from *Brogg's Brain* by Kin Platt. Lippincott, 1981. Reprinted by permission of HarperCollins Publishers. / Portrait of Kin Platt. Reproduced by permission of Kin Platt.

ALISON PRINCE. Jacket illustration by Toby Gowing from *How's Business* by Alison Prince. Four Winds Press, 1987. All rights reserved. Reproduced by permission of the illustrator. / Illustration by Alison Prince from *The Type One Super Robot* by Alison Prince. Four Winds Press, 1986. Copyright © 1986 text and illustrations by Alison Prince. All rights reserved. Reproduced by permission of the author. / Illustration by Leonard Shortall from *The Red Jaguar* by Alison Prince. Atheneum, 1972. Illustrations copyright © 1972 by Leonard Shortall. All rights reserved. Reprinted by permission of Atheneum Books for Young Readers, an imprint of Simon & Schuster. / Portrait of Alison Prince by Ben Parry. Reproduced by permission.

A. K. RAMANUJAN. Cover illustration by Meera Dayal Deshaprabhu from *The Interior Landscape: Love Poems from a Classical Tamil Anthology*. Translated by A. K. Ramanujan. Oxford University Press, Delhi, 1967. Reproduced by permission of Oxford University Press. / Photograph by Jean Grant. Details from Rajasthani storyteller's scroll, courtesy of Joan Erdman. From a cover of *Folktales from India: A Selection of Oral Tales from Twenty-two Languages*. Edited by A. K. Ramanujan. Pantheon Books, 1991. All rights reserved. Reproduced by permission of Joan Erdman.

MARGRET REY. From an illustration in *Curious George and the Dinosaur*. Edited by Margret Rey and Alan J. Shalleck. Houghton Mifflin Company, 1989. All rights reserved. Reproduced by permission of Houghton Mifflin Company. / Illustration by H. A. Rey from *Curious George Flies a Kite* by Margret Rey. Houghton Mifflin Company, 1958. Copyright © 1958 by Margret E. Rey and H. A. Rey. Copyright © renewed 1986 by Margret E. Rey. Copyright assigned to Houghton Mifflin Company in 1993. All rights reserved. Reproduced by permission of Houghton Mifflin Company. / Illustration by H. A. Rey from *Curious George Goes to the Hospital* by Margret and H. A. Rey. Houghton Mifflin Company, 1966. Copyright © 1966 by Margret E. Rey and H. A. Rey. Copyright assigned to Houghton Mifflin Company in 1993. All rights reserved. Reproduced by permission of Houghton Mifflin Company. / Illustration by H. A. Rey from *Pretzel* by Margret Rey. Harper & Row, Publishers, 1944. All rights reserved. / Portrait of Margret Rey. Reproduced by permission.

JOANNE ROCKLIN. Illustration by Diane De Groat from *Jace the Ace* by Joanne Rocklin. Illustration copyright © by Diane De Groat. Reprinted by permission of Macmillan Publishing Company, a division of Simon & Schuster, Inc. / Illustration by Julie Downing from *Sonia Begonia* by Joanne Rocklin. Macmillan Publishing Company, 1986. Illustration copyright © 1986 by Julie Downing. Reprinted by permission of Macmillan Publishing Company, a division of Simon & Schuster, Inc. / Portrait of Joanne Rocklin courtesy of Joanne Rocklin.

BARBARA ROGASKY. From a cover of *Smoke and Ashes: The Story of the Holocaust* by Barbara Rogasky. Holiday House, 1988. All rights reserved. Reproduced by permission of the publisher.

MICHAEL J. ROSEN. Jacket by Victoria Chess from *The Greatest Table* by Michael J. Rosen. Harcourt Brace & Company, 1994. Cover illustration copyright © 1994 by Victoria Chess. Reprinted by permission of Harcourt Brace & Company. / Cover illustration by Aminah Brenda Lynn Robinson from *Elijah's Angel* by Michael J. Rosen. Harcourt, 1992. Reprinted by permission of Harcourt Brace & Company. / Portrait of Michael Rosen. Copyright © Will Shively.

DAVID SALTZMAN. Illustration by David Saltzman from *The Jester Has Lost His Jingle* by David Saltzman. The Jester Co., Inc., 1995. All rights reserved. Reproduced by permission of the publisher. / Portrait of David Saltzman. Copyright © and ™ by The Jester Co., Inc. All rights reserved. Reproduced by permission of the publisher.

SANDY EISENBERG SASSO. Illustration by Phoebe Stone from *In God's Name* by Sandy Eisenberg Sasso. Jewish Lights Publishing, 1994. Illustrations copyright © 1994 by Phoebe Stone. All rights reserved. / Portrait of Sandy E. Sasso by Larry Seidman. Reproduced by permission of Laurence Seidman Photography.

MARGARET M. SCARIANO. Jacket illustration by Terrence Fehr from *Illiteracy in America* by Edward F. Dolan and Margaret M. Scariano. Franklin Watts, 1995. All rights reserved. Reproduced by permission of the publisher. / Portrait of Margaret M. Scariano. Reproduced by permission.

CECILIE EUGENIE SEED. From an illustration in *Place among the Stones* by Jenny Seed. Tafelberg Publishers, Ltd., 1987. Reproduced by permission of the publisher. / Portrait of Cecilie Eugenie Seed. Reproduced by permission.

SEAN SHEEHAN. Portrait of Sean Sheehan. Reproduced by permission.

BARBARA SHOUP. Portrait of Barbara Shoup by Drew Endicott. Reproduced by permission.

DICK SMOLINSKI. Portrait of Dick Smolinski. Reproduced by permission.

SUE STOPS. Portrait of Sue Stops. Reproduced by permission.

JOAN TATE. Jacket illustration by Judith Gwyn Brown from *Ben and Annie* by Joan Tate. Doubleday & Company, Inc., 1973. Copyright © 1974 by Joan Tate. Illustrations copyright © 1974 by Judith Gwyn Brown. Used by permission of Doubleday, a division of Bantam Doubleday Dell Publishing Group, Inc. / Portrait of Joan Tate. Reproduced by permission.

CAROLYN KOTT WASHBURNE. Portrait of Carolyn Kott Washburne. Reproduced by permission.

NICKI WEISS. Portrait of Nicki Weiss. Reproduced by permission.

JILL WHEELER. Portrait of Jill Wheeler. Reproduced by permission.

MARGARET WILLEY. From a cover of *The Melinda Zone* by Margaret Willey. Dell Publishing, 1993. All rights reserved. Reproduced by permission of Dell Publishing Co., Inc., a division of Bantam Doubleday Dell Publishing Group, Inc. / Portrait of Margaret Willey by Rosemary Willey. Reproduced by permission.

KEN YOUNG. Portrait of Ken Young. Reproduced by permission.

MALCAH ZELDIS. Illustration by Malcah Zeldis from *Martin Luther King* by Rosemary L. Bray. Greenwillow Books, 1995. Illustrations copyright © 1995 by Malcah Zeldis. All rights reserved. Reproduced by permission of William Morrow and Company, Inc. / Portrait of Malcah Zeldis. Reproduced by permission.

BENJAMIN ZEPHANIAH. Portrait of Benjamin Zephaniah. Reproduced by permission.

SOMETHING ABOUT THE AUTHOR®

ALBOROUGH, Jez 1959-

■ Personal

Born November 13, 1959, in Kingston-upon-Thames, Surrey, England; son of John Warmen (an accountant) and Cecily (a librarian; maiden name, Gathercole) Alborough; married Rikke Buhl (a therapist), July 18, 1987. *Education:* Norwich School of Art, degree in graphic design, 1981. *Religion:* "I am religious but have no religion."

■ Addresses

Home—24-26 Nottingham House, Shorts Gardens, London WC2H 9AX, England.

■ Career

Writer and illustrator.

■ Awards, Honors

Runner-up, Mother Goose award, 1985, for *Bare Bear;* Graphics for Children prize (with others), Bologna Children's Book Fair, 1987, for *The Great Games Book.*

■ Writings

FOR CHILDREN; SELF-ILLUSTRATED

Bare Bear, Benn, 1984.
Running Bear, A. & C. Black, 1985.
Willoughby Wallaby, Walker Books, 1986.

Poor old bear's soaked

In Alborough's self-illustrated book *Running Bear,* Polar Bear's morning jog ends on a chilly note when he falls into the icy ocean.

The Grass Is Greener, A. & C Black, 1987, published as *The Grass Is Always Greener,* Dial, 1987.
Esther's Trunk, Walker Books, 1988.
The Tale of Hillary Hiccup, Macmillan (London), 1988.
The Candle's Story ("Featherby House Fables"), Gollancz, 1988.

"MY TED!" gasped the bear. "A BEAR!" screamed Eddie.

While searching the woods for his lost teddy bear, a young boy is startled to find a real bear looking for the very same thing. (Illustration by the author from *Where's My Teddy?*)

The Clock's Story ("Featherby House Fables"), Gollancz, 1988.
The Umbrella's Story ("Featherby House Fables"), Gollancz, 1988.
The Mirror's Story ("Featherby House Fables"), Gollancz, 1988.
Cupboard Bear, Walker Books, 1989.
Beaky, Houghton, 1990.
Archibald, Macmillan, 1991.
Shake before Opening (poems), Hutchinson, 1991.
Where's My Teddy? Candlewick Press, 1992.
Cuddly Dudley, Candlewick Press, 1993.
Clothesline, Candlewick Press, 1993 (published in England as *Washing Line,* Walker Books, 1993).
Hide and Seek, Candlewick Press, 1994.
It's the Bear!, Walker Books, 1994, Candlewick Press, 1995.
There's Something at the Mail Slot, Candlewick Press, 1995.

Also author of *Wordoodles* (poems), Aurum, and of unpublished book, *Mabel at the Table.*

ILLUSTRATOR

Pat Thomson, *Can You Hear Me, Grandad?*, Gollancz, 1986.
Oscar Wilde, *The Canterville Ghost,* Oxford University Press, 1987.
Dick King-Smith, *Martin's Mice,* Gollancz, 1988.

Contributing illustrator to *The Great Games Book,* A. & C. Black, 1985.

■ Sidelights

Jez Alborough's picture books for young children feature rhyming texts and exaggerated drawings of animal characters in humorous scenarios that teach simple lessons to preschoolers. Alborough usually includes silly or ridiculous incidents in his picture books, and critics note that his cartoon-like drawings emphasize the humorous intent of his words, with his use of color in particular garnering applause. While Alborough's plots are sometimes faulted as overly conventional, critics invariably find his illustrations apt, vibrant, and appealing to children.

Alborough has published several books with bears as the central character. His first book, *Bare Bear,* follows a polar bear home, where he strips down to his pink skin after removing sunglasses, boots, and finally his fur coat. The story is told in simple, two-line rhymes, and to convey the arctic setting the artist relies on cool blues, whites, and dark shadows that reviewers found fitting. A *Publishers Weekly* critic praised the work for its "peculiar slapstick brand of humor that little kids adore." In *Running Bear,* a sequel to *Bare Bear,* Polar Bear decides to lose weight by jogging, but slips into the ocean instead and comes home with a cold. Although Janet E. Fricker of *School Library Journal* found some of Alborough's exaggerated illustrations unpleasant, and felt that children unfamiliar with *Bare Bear* would find this story confusing, she allowed that "*Running Bear* is colorfully illustrated and sometimes humorous."

Where's My Teddy? is another of the author's self-illustrated picture books to feature a bear. An "irresistible bedtime story," according to *Publishers Weekly, Where's My Teddy?* tells the story of Eddy, a little boy who ventures into some dark and scary woods to search for his lost teddy bear. While he finds a giant-sized teddy bear that a real bear has lost, and mistakes it for his own grown large, a bear finds Eddy's teddy bear and thinks his own toy has shrunk. The two meet, realize their mistakes, exchange teddy bears, and the book ends with each tucked into his own bed with his own stuffed toy. Martha Topol of *School Library Journal* praised Alborough's rhyming text, adding that "[readers'] fear of the unknown and the ensuing visual absurdity will keep them riveted." *Kirkus Reviews* focused on the effectiveness of Alborough's illustrations: "The striking, expressive watercolors are just right for this satisfying, nicely symmetrical tale."

The Grass Is Always Greener features sheep in a story based on the old adage, "The grass is always greener on the other side." Thomas, the lead sheep, decides that the grass on top of the hill in the next pasture must be fresher than that in his own field, and convinces all the other sheep to go there, except Lincoln Lamb, who can't be bothered to stop playing. Once the sheep get to the hill, they decide that a beautiful green pasture in the distance must have even better grass, but when they get there, they see Lincoln and realize it is the pasture where they started. While noting that the book is not a particularly original portrayal of the old saw, John Philbrook of *School Library Journal* praised Alborough's illustrations: "Color is nicely used . . . : vivid

greens and lighter pastels make the countryside come alive."

Alborough's *Beaky* explores the theme of identity for preschoolers. In this picture book, a bird's egg falls from a tree and Beaky is hatched, but in the absence of others like him on the forest floor, he doesn't know who he is. A passing frog helps him until a beautiful song draws Beaky into a tree where he discovers a large version of himself—a bird of paradise. Although Heide Piehler called this plot "contrived and well worn" in her *School Library Journal* review, a *Publishers Weekly* critic commented: "It is an uplifting moment when Beaky discovers his true identity and soars above the treetops."

Cuddly Dudley employs Alborough's signature wordplay to tell the story of a penguin who is so cute that his family always wants to hug and kiss him. Dudley finally runs away in an attempt to get some peace but encounters a man who feels the same way about him, so he returns home. Reviewers enjoyed Alborough's action-packed illustrations more than the somewhat conventional story, although Christine A. Moesch of *School Library Journal* thought "the images of lots of snuggly penguins might appeal to children."

Alborough has also earned praise for his entertaining rhymes. In *Archibald* the author and illustrator tells of a man inordinately proud of his red hair who loses it one day and is teased by the friends whom he had earlier slighted. *Junior Bookshelf* reviewer R. Baines found this "a lively and enjoyable read" that is "enlivened by being told in rhyming couplets." Alborough's book of poems, *Shake before Opening,* covers such topics of interest to youngsters as body parts, animals, school, and other everyday subjects with humor, rhymes, and sketchy drawings. Alborough "uses rhyme expertly," according

An adorable penguin finds it nearly impossible to get some rest and relaxation in Alborough's self-illustrated *Cuddly Dudley.*

to a critic for *Junior Bookshelf,* who concludes: "If you need a lift, a grin on your lips, then this jumpy, hoppity book will do the business."

Alborough once commented: "I write to awaken and realize the child in myself, and hopefully to do so in those who read my books. To me, 'the child' is that part of oneself which is still innocent, heartful, mindless, and unaffected by upbringing and the conditioning of society. When I see some people read my books, I can see the child shining through, and I am happy."

■ Works Cited

Baines, R., review of *Archibald, Junior Bookshelf,* October, 1991, p. 200.
Review of *Bare Bear, Publishers Weekly,* August 17, 1984, p. 59.
Review of *Beaky, Publishers Weekly,* July 27, 1990, p. 231.
Fricker, Janet E., review of *Running Bear, School Library Journal,* October, 1986, p. 154.
Moesch, Christine A., review of *Cuddly Dudley, School Library Journal,* April, 1993, p. 90.
Philbrook, John, review of *The Grass Is Always Greener, School Library Journal,* November, 1987, pp. 85-86.
Piehler, Heide, review of *Beaky, School Library Journal,* October, 1990, p. 84.
Review of *Shake before Opening, Junior Bookshelf,* December, 1991, p. 247.
Topol, Martha, review of *Where's My Teddy?, School Library Journal,* August, 1992, p. 132.
Review of *Where's My Teddy?, Kirkus Reviews,* July 1, 1992, p. 845.
Review of *Where's My Teddy?, Publishers Weekly,* July 6, 1992, p. 54.

■ For More Information See

PERIODICALS

Bulletin of the Center for Children's Books, September, 1992, p. 4.
Christian Science Monitor, November 6, 1992, p. 11.
Junior Bookshelf, December, 1987, p. 267; August, 1990, p. 164; April, 1993, p. 56.
Kirkus Reviews, November 1, 1987, p. 1569.
Publishers Weekly, April 12, 1993, p. 61.
School Librarian, May, 1990, p. 58; February, 1993, p. 14; May, 1995, p. 57.
School Library Journal, January, 1985, p. 62.
Times Educational Supplement, September 16, 1988, p. 32; March 30, 1990, p. B10; March 29, 1991, p. 23.*

*   *   *

ANDERSON, Rachel 1943-

■ Personal

Born March 18, 1943, at Hampton Court, Surrey, England; daughter of Donald Clive (a writer and military historian) and Verily (a writer; maiden name, Bruce) Anderson; married David Bradby (professor of

RACHEL ANDERSON

Theatre Studies at University of London), June 19, 1965; children: Hannah, Lawrence, Nguyen Thanh Sang (adopted son), Donald. *Education:* Attended Hastings School of Art, 1959-60. *Politics:* Socialist. *Religion:* Church of England. *Hobbies and other interests:* Children, drinking, talking, gardening.

■ Addresses

Home—Lower Damsels, Cromer Northrepps, Norfolk NR27 0LJ, England.

■ Career

Writer. Chatto & Windus Ltd., London, England, publicity assistant, 1963-64; affiliated with editorial department of *Women's Mirror,* London, 1964; *Good Housekeeping* magazine, London, children's book page editor/reviewer, 1979-89. Worked variously as a nursemaid, cleaning woman, van driver, gardener, and as broadcaster for BBC *Woman's Hour.*

■ Awards, Honors

Runner-up for Guardian Award, 1978, for *Moffatt's Road;* Medical Journalists' Award, 1990, for *For the Love of Sang;* Guardian Award, 1992, for *Paper Faces;* Times Educational Supplement/Nasen Award, 1994, for *Jessy and the Long-Short Dress;* Eastern Arts Writers' Bursary, Tyrone Guthrie Centre (Ireland), 1995.

■ Writings

FOR CHILDREN; FICTION

Moffatt's Road, illustrated by Pat Marriott, J. Cape, 1978, Merrimack Book Service, 1980.
Little Angel Comes to Stay, illustrated by Linda Birch, Oxford University Press, 1983.

Winston's Wonderful Weekend, Lion Books, 1983.
Tim Walks, illustrated by Trevor Stubley, CIO Publishing, 1986.
Little Angel, Bonjour, illustrated by Birch, Oxford University Press, 1987.
The Boy Who Laughed, Macmillan, 1989.
Jessy Runs Away, illustrated by Shelagh McNicholas, A. & C. Black, 1989.
Best Friends, illustrated by McNicholas, A. & C. Black, 1991.
Happy Christmas, Little Angel, illustrated by Birch, Oxford University Press, 1991.
Tough as Old Boots, illustrated by Birch, Methuen, 1991.
When Mum Went to Work, Oxford University Press, 1992.
Jessy and the Long-Short Dress, illustrated by McNicholas, A. & C. Black, 1994.
Jessy and the Bridesmaid's Dress, illustrated by McNicholas, Lion Books, 1994.
Princess Jazz and the Angels, Methuen, 1995.
Letters from Heaven, Methuen, 1996.

FOR CHILDREN; TRANSLATOR

The Cat's Tale, Oxford University Press, 1985.
(With husband, David Bradby) *Renard the Fox,* illustrated by Bob Dewar, Oxford University Press, 1986.
Wild Goose Chase, Oxford University Press, 1986.
Little Lost Fox, Oxford University Press, 1992.

FOR YOUNG ADULTS; FICTION

The Poacher's Son, Oxford University Press, 1982.
The War Orphan, Oxford University Press, 1984.
French Lessons, Oxford University Press, 1988.
The Bus People, Oxford University Press, 1989, Holt, 1992.
Paper Faces, Oxford University Press, 1991, Holt, 1993.
The Working Class, Oxford University Press, 1991.
Black Water, Oxford University Press, 1994, Holt, 1995.
The Doll's House, Oxford University Press, 1995.

FOR ADULTS

Pineapple (novel), J. Cape, 1965.
The Purple Heart Throbs: A Survey of Popular Romantic Fiction, 1850-1972 (literary criticism), Hodder & Stoughton, 1974.
Dream Lovers (semi-autobiographical), Hodder & Stoughton, 1978.
For the Love of Sang (autobiographical), Lion Books, 1990.

OTHER

Also author of radio play, *Tomorrow's Tomorrow,* 1970; author of children's musical, *Fairy Snow and the Disability Box,* 1981. Contributor of articles to *Observer, Good Housekeeping, Homes & Gardens, Times* (London), *Weekend Telegraph, Punch, Guardian,* and other magazines and newspapers in England.

■ Sidelights

Rachel Anderson once told *SATA:* "I was brought up in a literary family and felt incapable of doing anything else so I had to be a writer. I am a practicing Christian in an essentially heathen age. I speak French and Italian; main interests are domestic bliss, travel and peace."

Both of Anderson's parents were writers, and she began her career by typing manuscripts for her mother, Verily Anderson. Having no intention of following in either parent's footsteps, she began in journalism, concentrating on what she held to be significant aspects of the modern world: jazz festivals, the merits of disposable cardboard furniture, the etiquette of marriage, and interviews with film and pop stars.

Anderson also worked for BBC Radio, on magazines, and for publishing firms. Her early writing efforts included articles, radio scripts, short stories, and several newspaper and magazine columns. Her first children's book was not written until she was in her mid-thirties; instead, she published *Pineapple,* which she referred to in *Something about the Author Autobiography Series* (*SAAS*) as "a short and very silly novel," as well as a semiautobiographical documentary called *Dream Lovers,* and a study of popular romantic fiction that included some six hundred novels.

When she was twenty-two, the same summer her first novel was published, Anderson married David Bradby. While expecting their first child, the couple moved to Scotland so that David could start his first "real" job as a junior university lecturer in French. They eventually had three more children, and Rachel continued to work as a free-lance journalist while raising them.

"Like parents everywhere, I told made-up stories to my children, but I also told them to my neighbors and nieces and nephews, and to my children's friends if they sat still," the author recounted in *SAAS.* "I told them at bedtime, also on buses, in the dentist's waiting room, in the car in traffic jams, in the dark, on the beach, when they were ill, when they were well. I told them stories about themselves as other people, about their toys, about birds and insects, about rivers, about food and bad dreams, about burglaries and lost socks, about teeth falling out and grazed arms.

"And, like most storytellers, I made them up on the spur of the moment, and they ended when the moment passed.

"Some authors say that this is how they began, with the stories they told for their children. In my case, this was not true. None of those told stories were intended to become public or published, nor have they. They were transitory tales, vanishing stories, long since forgotten, at least by me and probably by the people they were invented for."

The family later moved to the cathedral city of Canterbury, then to France. They spent a spring in Venice,

Italy, and a year in Nigeria. There David worked at the University of Ibadan, while Anderson had a brief career as a television actress on Western Nigerian Television. *Moffatt's Road,* her first book for children, was set in Nigeria. *Moffatt's Road* "fits into none of the usual categories and belongs to no recognisable age-group," and is also "neatly characterised [and] beautifully written," according to a *Junior Bookshelf* contributor.

In 1980 Anderson and her family adopted Nguyen Thanh Sang, a mentally-disabled nine-and-a-half-year-old Vietnamese orphan who had been found on the pavement in Saigon and spent five years in an orphanage in England. "At the time Sang came to us," she wrote in *SAAS,* "I was at work on a book which is essentially about rural life in a gamekeeper's labouring family in East Anglia in the early 1900s. Into this story crept an unexpected character, Jonas, who can't sit up, can't speak, can't do anything except lie in a wooden box beside the grate. He has no function in the plot except to be loved by his hard-worked country mother as much, if not more, than she loves her numerous other children.... Writing about Jonas was, perhaps, a first tentative step towards being able to absorb and face up to the reality that Sang was a Jonas." Zena Sutherland, writing for the *Bulletin of the Center for Children's Books,* refers to that book, *The Poacher's Son,* as "a

In this 1989 collection of stories, Anderson reveals the hopes and longings of a busload of mentally challenged students.

finely-crafted novel that testifies vividly to the rigidity of the class system."

Three years later, Anderson wrote *The War Orphan,* which is set in Britain and Vietnam. It's the story of Simon, an English school boy whose insulated life is disrupted when his family adopts Ha, a Vietnamese war orphan. "I'd like to have been able to say that I wrote *The War Orphan* to show Sang that I knew, cared, and understood what he had endured," the author related in *SAAS.* "He is proud of his contribution to the book in so far as I was able to involve him. But he will never be able to read it to himself, nor understand it being read aloud to him."

"'The War Orphan' is not a pretty story with an antiseptic plot, but it is a terrific example of realistic fiction, the kind likely to make your heart pound, make you furious, make you cry. It will even make you think," states Kristiana Gregory in the *Los Angeles Times Book Review.* The critic calls it "a powerful tool to help teens—adults, too—better understand our culture, to care about those who are different."

Anderson's next book for young adults, *French Lessons,* follows Ben and his sister Maris as they are summoned to Nice, France, to meet their father's intended bride and her spoiled, bratty daughter. Peter Reading, in the *Times Literary Supplement,* calls it an "amusing and moving story." In *Junior Bookshelf,* a critic likewise finds it "a remarkably powerful book. The French background is strongly and lovingly detailed."

The Bus People focuses on eight children, each burdened with a mental or physical handicap. Each chapter describes a different "fruitcake," as their bus driver lovingly describes them, and reveals their individual fears and dreams. Writing in *School Library Journal,* Constance A. Mellon notes that "with its rich prose and unforgettable characters, *The Bus People* is more than a good book about disability. It is—quite simply—a good book." In a review for *Junior Bookshelf,* a writer calls it a "warm, understanding and affectionate novel which will bring a sympathetic reader alternately to laughter and tears."

Reviewers especially appreciated Anderson's next book for young adults. *Paper Faces* is "an absorbing and distinctive story," writes Louise L. Sherman in *School Library Journal.* Although it's hard to imagine that anyone would want World War II to continue, it's the only life young Dot has ever known. Having endured air raids, bombings, and the death of her baby brother, her greatest fear now is the return of the father she has never known. In *School Librarian,* Sue Rogers remarks, "The characters are marvelously observed and believable," and predicted it would be "an award-winner of the future." Ellen Fader notes of the Guardian Award-winner in *Horn Book:* "This is a perceptive novel of character that holds a reader's attention from beginning to end." And a *Junior Bookshelf* reviewer adds, "This is a wonderfully-penetrating study of a little under-privileged girl, a child of her time and her place, but one with depth of resources."

Among her children's books, Anderson is especially proud of the "Jets" series, a collection of books featuring Jessy, a Down's Syndrome child, written for children who are beginning to read simple stories alone. *Jessy Runs Away,* the first in the series, is reviewed in *Junior Bookshelf* as a "simple, agreeably told story [that] depicts the difficulties of incorporating a mentally handicapped child into family life." Writing in the *Times Literary Supplement,* Stephanie Nettell calls it "an amusing and sensible little book." Next in the series is *Best Friends,* in which Jessy becomes jealous of her sister's new best friend. In her *School Librarian* review of the book, Lucy Love points out that the book's visual format "makes this series one of the most appealing for new readers."

Referring again to her inspiration, Anderson stated in *SAAS,* "Adopting our fourth child had an apocalyptic effect on our household, on our extended family, and on the number of hours a day I could sit peacefully writing at my desk. It also had a fundamental effect on what I write about." As she once told *SATA:* "My son can't read and thinks books are boring, real life more interesting. Thus, he is radically changing my views about whether books and literacy are so important.... Sang's presence has opened up for all of us the whole world of handicapped children, and how much simple and unsophisticated joy they create if you're prepared to see it."

■ Works Cited

Anderson, Rachel, essay in *Something about the Author Autobiography Series,* Volume 18, Gale, 199, pp. 19-38.

Review of *The Bus People, Junior Bookshelf,* December, 1989, p. 288.

Fader, Ellen, review of *Paper Faces, Horn Book,* March/April, 1994, p. 196.

Review of *French Lessons, Junior Bookshelf,* August, 1988, p. 203.

Gregory, Kristiana, review of *The War Orphan, Los Angeles Times Book Review,* June 29, 1986, p. 11.

Review of *Jessy Runs Away, Junior Bookshelf,* June, 1989, p. 117.

Love, Lucy, review of *Best Friends, School Librarian,* November, 1991, p. 143.

Mellon, Constance A., review of *The Bus People, School Library Journal,* January, 1993, p. 96.

Review of *Moffatt's Road, Junior Bookshelf,* June, 1978, p. 146.

Nettell, Stephanie, review of *Jessy Runs Away, Times Literary Supplement,* June 9, 1989, p. 648.

Review of *Paper Faces, Junior Bookshelf,* August, 1991, p. 167.

Reading, Peter, review of *French Lessons, Times Literary Supplement,* June 24, 1988, p. 716.

Rogers, Sue, review of *Paper Faces, School Librarian,* August, 1991, p. 103.

Sherman, Louise L., review of *Paper Faces, School Library Journal,* December, 1993, p. 134.

A young girl fears the changes that the end of World War II will bring to her already unstable life in this 1991 tale. (Cover illustration by Elyse Feldman.)

Sutherland, Zena, review of *The Poacher's Son, Bulletin of the Center for Children's Books,* April, 1983, p. 141.

■ For More Information See

PERIODICALS

Booklist, July, 1983, p. 1398; September 1, 1986, p. 56; December 15, 1987, p. 700; November 1, 1993, p. 518; March 15, 1994, p. 1357.

Book Report, September, 1986, p. 30; May, 1993, p. 45; May, 1994, p. 42.

Books for Keeps, September, 1987, p. 23; May, 1992, p. 32; July, 1992, pp. 6, 14, 24; January, 1994, p. 24; March, 1994, p. 14; May, 1994, pp. 13, 17.

Books for Your Children, Spring, 1985, p. 21; Summer, 1989, p. 25; Spring, 1990, p. 23; Summer, 1994, p. 21.

Bulletin of the Center for Children's Books, October, 1986, p. 21; October, 1992, p. 35; November, 1993, p. 74.

Children's Literature in Education, March, 1994, p. 41.

Growing Point, January, 1985, p. 4368; January, 1987, p. 4723; November, 1989, p. 5234; July, 1991, p. 5548, p. 5551.

Horn Book, August, 1980, p. 403; August, 1983, p. 449; January, 1993, p. 88.

Junior Bookshelf, February, 1985, p. 33; October, 1991, p. 210; April, 1993, p. 50; April, 1994, p. 61.

Kirkus Reviews, September 15, 1987, p. 1387; November 15, 1992, p. 1438; December 1, 1993, p. 1519.

Library Talk, March, 1994, p. 48.

Magpies, July, 1992, p. 31; November, 1993, p. 27.

Observer (London), January 20, 1974, p. 25; November 28, 1982, p. 31.

Publishers Weekly, November 9, 1992, p. 87; November 8, 1993, p. 77.

Punch, April 17, 1985, p. 29.

School Librarian, June, 1985, p. 154; February, 1987, p. 40; February, 1989, p. 19; May, 1989, p. 57; February, 1990, p. 17; May, 1994, p. 71.

School Library Journal, August, 1980, p.60; March, 1984, p. 168; October, 1986, p. 185; February, 1988, p. 76.

Spectator, January 26, 1974, p. 107.

Times Educational Supplement, April 7, 1989, p. B12; September 13, 1991, p. 43; November 8, 1991, p. 32; February 12, 1993, p. 12; November 12, 1993, p. R3.

Times Literary Supplement, June 10, 1965, p. 469; February 15, 1974, p. 153; November 30, 1984, p. 1375.

Voice Literary Supplement, December, 1993, p. 26.

Voice of Youth Advocates, December, 1993, p. 286.

*   *   *

ARAUJO, Frank P. 1937-

■ Personal

Born May 8, 1937, in Bakersfield, CA; son of Frank P. (a sheep rancher/cowboy) and Clarice G. (an international banker; maiden name, Illizalliturri) Araujo; married Mary A. Juncker (an elementary school teacher), July 2, 1994; children: Frank P. III. *Education:* U.C. Berkeley, A.B., 1959, M.A., 1963; U.C. Davis, Ph.D., 1970. *Politics:* Democrat. *Religion:* Roman Catholic. *Hobbies and other interests:* "Folklore, structure of myth and archetype."

■ Addresses

Home—1016 Galleon Way, Sacramento, CA 95838. *Office*—P.O. Box 4476, Davis, CA 95617-4476.

■ Career

Diablo Valley College, Pleasant Hill, CA, instructor, 1970-72; Washington State University, Pullman, assistant professor, 1978-81; University of Wyoming, Laramie, associate professor, 1984-86; National University, Sacramento, CA, adjunct professor, 1987—. Consultant, international economic development projects. *Military service:* U.S. Navy, 1959-62; lieutenant. *Member:* Society of Children's Book Writers and Illustrators, American Anthropological Association.

■ Writings

Nekane, the Lamina & the Bear: A Tale of the Basque Pyrenees, illustrated by Xiao Jun Li, Rayve Productions, 1993.

The Perfect Orange, illustrated by Li, Rayve Productions, 1994.

■ Work in Progress

Dragon Water, a picture book, with illustrations by Li; continuing folklore research.

■ Sidelights

Frank P. Araujo told *SATA,* "My primary interest in writing children's books and stories stems from a desire to stimulate children's imaginations, and at the same time, give voice to the child in myself. The world of the child is one of discovery and wonder, and the universe of the story (especially the folktale) is one fraught with meaning, mystery, and adventure. Both ambits reflect and, in their turns, are reflected by the primitive elements resident in our own being. Writers write. Illustrators draw. Children learn. When L. Frank Baum was asked why he wrote *The Wizard of Oz,* he replied, 'To please a child.'"

■ For More Information See

PERIODICALS

Booklist, February 1, 1994, p. 1007.

Bulletin of the Center for Children's Books, March, 1994, p. 214.

Five Owls, March, 1994, p. 86.

Publishers Weekly, December 13, 1993, p. 70.

School Library Journal, May, 1994, p. 106.*

*   *   *

ASARE, Meshack (Yaw) 1945-

■ Personal

Surname pronounced "*Ah*-suh-ree"; born September 18, 1945, in Nyankumasi, Ghana; son of Joseph Kwaku (an accountant) and Adjoa (a trader; maiden name, Adoma) Asare; married Rose Tachie Menson (a bank clerk), 1969; children: Akosua (daughter), Kwajo (son), Kofi, Kwaku. *Education:* Attended University of Science and Technology (Kumasi, Ghana), University of Wisconsin—Madison, and School of Journalism and Television (Berkshire, England). *Politics:* "Universalism." *Religion:* Christian.

■ Addresses

Office—c/o Educational Press and Manufacturers, P.O. Box 9184, Airport, Accra, Ghana.

A lonely cat tries to locate a strong, protective ally among the other animals in Meshack Asare's self-illustrated *Cat in Search of a Friend.*

■ Career

Teacher in elementary school in Tema, Ghana, 1966-68; Lincoln Community School, Accra, Ghana, teacher, 1969-79; Educational Press and Manufacturers, Accra, art director and illustrator, 1979—. Artist, illustrator, and designer; has made sculptures for the government and for public buildings. *Member:* Ghana Association of Artists.

■ Awards, Honors

National Book Award (Ghana), 1980, for *Tawia Goes to Sea;* Noma Award for publishing in Africa, 1982, for *The Brassman's Secret.*

■ Writings

SELF-ILLUSTRATED CHILDREN'S FICTION

Tawia Goes to Sea, Ghana Publishing (Accra), 1970, Panther House, 1972.

I Am Kofi, Ghana Publishing, 1972.

Mansa Helps at Home, Ghana Publishing, 1972.

The Brassman's Secret, Educational Press (Accra), 1981.

The Canoe's Story, Three Brothers and Cousins (Accra), 1982.

Chipo and the Bird on the Hill: A Tale of Ancient Zimbabwe, Zimbabwe Publishing House (Harare), 1984.

Cat in Search of a Friend, Kane/Miller (Brooklyn, NY), 1986 (originally published as *Die Katze sucht sich einen Freund,* Verlag Jungbrunen [Vienna], 1984).

Halima, Macmillan (London), 1992.

The Frightened Thief, Heinemann (London), 1993.

OTHER

(With others) *Ghana Welcomes You,* Valco, 1968.

(Illustrator) Alero and Cecile McHardy, *Akousa in Brazil,* 1970.

Seeing the World, Ghana Publishing, 1975.

(Illustrator) Tony Fairman, reteller, *Bury My Bones But Keep My Words: African Tales for Retelling,* Harper-Collins (London), 1991, Puffin Books, 1994.

Also author of playlets *Ananse and Wisdom* and *The Outdooring,* and of play *The Hunter.* Contributor of articles on Ghanian culture to magazines.

■ Sidelights

A native of the west African country of Ghana, Meshack Asare "is an imaginative storyteller and talented artist who skillfully weaves cultural traditions and daily realities of life into picture stories for African children," Nancy J. Schmidt comments in *Twentieth-Century Children's Writers.* His picture books portray both everyday activities of children and folkloric stories from the oral tradition, with his illustrations giving his works an African context. In his award-winning book *The Brassman's Secret,* Asare combines the two types of tales when a boy, after helping his father craft some goldweights, falls asleep and learns of the goldweight's history in a dream. Other stories tell of the fisherfolk of southern Ghana (*Tawia Goes to Sea* and *The Canoe's Story*), the Great Bird of Zimbabwean legend (*Chipo and the Bird on the Hill*), and the everyday lives of young Africans (*I Am Kofi* and *Mansa Helps at Home*). Children in America may be familiar with Asare's *Cat in Search of a Friend,* a folktale in which a cat seeking protection discovers her own strength, or his illustrations for Tony Fairman's folktale collection *Bury My Bones But Keep My Words.* Whatever their subjects, according to Schmidt, "Asare's picture stories skillfully incorporate the cultural content of specific African settings in a manner that makes them widespread in their appeal to African children regardless of their cultural background."

Asare once commented: "Sometimes it is hard to tell what I am, but I like to think that I am an Artist. I feel that is a better way to think of myself, because then everything I am doing is art. . . . I sculpt and draw and design beautiful things. That is creativity. I enjoy doing those.

"But writing is different. My work in writing is very important to me. I consider writing to be a kind of construction; precisely, a kind of construction that bridges the gaps to reality—for even dreams and imagination are, in fact, reality. There are no dreams without images. Neither is there imagination without images. And, for that matter, no thought. Writing creates images. That is why it is so important. It creates images of time and life. Writing enables one to perceive the depth and roundness of civilization. It does not simply record it and enrich it.

"Who needs help in perceiving reality more than young people? The world is too complex to be perceived in its wholeness. . . . But there is a part of the world that is unchanging, unaffected and perhaps [permanent] in value. It is the warmth of knowing that there is something about you that the other person appreciates, something that everyone has a feeling for. It is a very exclusively human 'something' that universally communicates—and appeals. It is this 'something' that I try to write about."

■ Works Cited

Schmidt, Nancy J., "Meshack Asare," *Twentieth-Century Children's Writers,* 4th edition, St. James Press, 1995, pp. 37-38.

■ For More Information See

PERIODICALS

Emergency Librarian, January, 1992, p. 61.
Publishers Weekly, December 14, 1992, p. 57.
School Library Journal, March, 1987, p. 140.*

B

SALLY BAHOUS

BAHOUS, Sally 1939-

■ Personal

Born April 29, 1939, in Tiberias, Palestine; daughter of Elias Saleh (a biologist) and Carolyn (a math professor; maiden name, Rogers) Bahous; married Delmas James Allen (a college president), July, 5, 1958; children: Carrie Allen Simmons, James Saleh Allen, Sudie Allen Henn. *Education:* University of North Carolina, A.B., 1960; University of North Dakota, M.A., 1974; University of Toledo, Ph.D., 1984. *Politics:* Palestinian. *Religion:* Melkite.

■ Addresses

Home—P.O. Box 1123, Dahlonega, GA 30533. *Office*—English Department, North Georgia College, Dahlonega, GA 30597.

■ Career

American University of Beirut, Beirut, Lebanon, instructor, 1964-67; Georgia State University, Atlanta, professor, 1986-87; North Georgia College, Dahlonega, currently faculty member of the English department.

■ Writings

Sitti and the Cats: A Tale of Friendship, illustrated by Nancy Malick, Roberts Rinehart, 1993.

■ Work in Progress

Mustapha and the Watermelon; Leila.

■ Sidelights

Sally Bahous told *SATA,* "Because I grew up an Arab in Palestine during World War II, I grew up knowing that life was not always easy and that humans need an inner world into which they can escape. My inner world was of stories that everyone in our family village told: fairy tales and proverbs, real life adventures and histories. Every house in our village was like a modern television channel. Our imaginations were our televisions and the story tellers were the producers. When, years later and miles away, my husband and I learned that we were to become grandparents, I decided to write down in English for our unborn grandchild some of those fairy tales that had taught me so well how life should be lived in the world our imagination creates. *Sitti and the Cats: A Tale of Friendship* is the tale I recorded in English from the ancient Palestinian tradition of folklore which so enriched my own life. Katie, our grandchild, loves

Sitti and now, in the first grade, can read it herself. Since Katie's birth, we have been blessed with Will and Sudie James, and for the two of them I have written *Mustapha and the Watermelon* and *Leila,* which I hope to get into the mail for publication soon."

■ For More Information See

PERIODICALS

Booklist, November 15, 1993, p. 627.
Horn Book Guide, spring, 1994, p. 105.
School Library Journal, April, 1994, p. 116.

*   *   *

BARTHOLOMEW, Barbara 1941-

■ Personal

Born August 25, 1941, in Beckham County, OK; married Keith Bartholomew (a computer manager), January 22, 1964; children: Trudy, Jay, Brooke, Shayne. *Education:* Oklahoma University, B.A., 1965. *Politics:* Independent. *Religion:* Baptist. *Hobbies and other interests:* Foster parenting.

■ Addresses

Home—200 Farms Rd., McKinney, TX 75069.

■ Career

Freelance writer and editor. Former newspaper reporter and business editor. Contributed to the development of the *Wishbone* television series, PBS-TV. *Member:* Society of Children's Book Writers and Illustrators.

■ Awards, Honors

Golden Medallion Award for best young adult romance novel of the year, Romance Writers of America, 1984, for *Julie's Magic Moment.*

■ Writings

FOR YOUNG PEOPLE

The Cereal Box Adventures, Chariot Books, 1981.
Flight into the Unknown, Chariot Books, 1982.
The Great Gradepoint Mystery, Macmillan, 1983.
Something Special, G. K. Hall, 1984.
The Timekeeper, Signet Books, 1985.
Child of Tomorrow, Signet Books, 1985.
When Dreamers Cease to Dream, Signet Books, 1985.

Contributor of short stories to magazines, including *Seventeen, Cricket,* and *Highlights for Children.*

YOUNG ADULT ROMANCE NOVELS

Anne and Jay, Signet Books, 1982.
Julie's Magic Moment, Signet Books, 1983.
Mirror Image, Signet Books, 1983.
Someone New, Signet Books, 1984.
Lucky at Love, Signet Books, 1985.

■ Sidelights

Barbara Bartholomew is the author of a variety of books for young adults, including a mystery, a science fiction-fantasy trilogy, and several romance novels. One of her books, *Julie's Magic Moment,* received the Golden Medallion Award from the Romance Writers of America as the best young adult romance novel of 1984.

The Great Gradepoint Mystery, published in 1983 as part of the "Microkid Mystery" series, follows the adventures of a group of junior high school computer whizzes. The story begins as an anonymous stranger known as Mr. Smith challenges two junior high schools to compete to see which can maintain the highest gradepoint average over the course of a semester. The reward for the winning school is $100,000, which Ricky Foster and his friends decide would help build a state-of-the-art computer center at South Street Junior High. All the students study hard to beat their rivals at Dickson Junior High, but their grades mysteriously go down. Ricky concludes that someone is tampering with the school's computer system, and he sets off to find the culprit by using the high-powered system at his father's company. In the process he discovers ALEC, an artificial intelligence that has been created through a comput-

Convinced someone has invaded his school's computer system, Ricky Foster enlists the aid of ALEC, an electronic personality, to pursue the culprit in Barbara Bartholomew's *The Great Gradepoint Mystery.* (Illustration by Yuri Salzman.)

er glitch. With ALEC's help, Ricky and his friends solve the mystery. In a review for *School Library Journal*, Drew Stevenson called *The Great Gradepoint Mystery* "a fast-moving story with likable characters and well-placed surprises."

Bartholomew published a trilogy of books in 1985 with time travel as their theme: *The Timekeeper, Child of Tomorrow,* and *When Dreamers Cease to Dream.* All three books feature sixteen-year-old Jeanette Lacy and her twelve-year-old brother Neil, who live with their father and a new stepmother and stepsister in Dallas. In *The Timekeeper,* Neil has problems adjusting to his newly expanded family, so he runs away. Jeanette finally finds him in the basement of an abandoned house, just as he steps on some eerie, glowing stones and disappears. She follows him, and the siblings find themselves transported through time to a bizarre, alternate-world Dallas of 1858. There they meet seventeen-year-old Jesse, who is also able to travel through time and decides to accompany them home. Instead, the trio are transported into the future, where all individual actions are strictly controlled by the Guardians and time travel is forbidden. They finally find their way back home again, but then Jeanette realizes that Jesse may still be stuck in the wrong time period. In *Child of Tomorrow,* Jeanette goes back to rescue Jesse and discovers that one of her friends, Amy, has actually been sent from the future. In the third book of the trilogy, *When Dreamers Cease to Dream,* Jeanette and Neil continue their time travels in order to help Amy and to answer their own questions about the world. A *Kliatt* reviewer called *The Timekeeper* "a good, fast-moving story—a real mind and imagination stretcher," while a *Junior Bookshelf* reviewer noted that the series "should make compulsive reading" for young adults.

Bartholomew has also written several popular romance novels for young adults. *Mirror Image* tells the story of sixteen-year-old identical twins, Brooke and Adrienne, who could not be more different. Brooke is quiet, bookish, and slightly overweight, while Adrienne is charming, vivacious, and pretty. Their parents, worried about their development, send the girls to their great-aunt's farm in Oklahoma for the summer. At first, the city twins have a difficult time adjusting to life in the country. Before long, however, Brooke develops a love of horses and the outdoors. She also has continual arguments with a neighbor boy, Brett, that eventually turn into romance. Even though she is still not like her sister, "by the end of the summer Brooke has discovered that she is a special person," according to Becky Johnson Xavier in *Voice of Youth Advocates.* Writing in *Booklist,* Ilene Cooper commented that "Bartholomew makes the most of a rural setting," adding that the book would appeal to "readers who like horse stories" as well as those who enjoy romance novels.

In *Julie's Magic Moment,* Julie faces the challenge of going to a new high school. Though she is naturally shy, she decides to change her personality and acts as if she is outgoing and bubbly. As a result, she manages to win the leading role in the school play, gain the favor of the popular crowd, and attract the attention of the school football hero, Todd. When she is no longer able to keep up her facade, however, her new "friends" drop her and it is uncertain whether she will keep her part in the play. Finally, with her friend Pete standing by her, Julie is able to succeed with her true personality. Writing in *Voice of Youth Advocates,* Anne Frost stated that "Bartholomew shows a keen insight into the feelings and concerns of teenage girls. They will enjoy this book."

■ Works Cited

Cooper, Ilene, review of *Mirror Image, Booklist,* July, 1983, p. 1398.

Frost, Anne, review of *Julie's Magic Moment, Voice of Youth Advocates,* June, 1984, p. 95.

Stevenson, Drew, review of *The Great Gradepoint Mystery, School Library Journal,* December, 1983, p. 81.

Review of *The Timekeeper, Child of Tomorrow,* and *When Dreamers Cease to Dream, Junior Bookshelf,* April, 1986, p. 74.

Review of *The Timekeeper, Kliatt,* fall, 1985, p. 20.

Xavier, Becky Johnson, review of *Mirror Image, Voice of Youth Advocates,* October, 1983, p., 196.

■ For More Information See

PERIODICALS

Children's Book Review Service, April, 1984, p. 94.
Growing Point, May, 1986, p. 4617.
Kliatt, spring, 1984, p. 4; spring, 1985, p. 4.
School Library Journal, December, 1985, p. 97.
Voice of Youth Advocates, December, 1982, p. 28; October, 1985, p. 263; December, 1985, p. 323.

* * *

BAUMGARTNER, Barbara 1939-

■ Personal

Born September 9, 1939, in Wilmington, DE; daughter of I. Fletcher (a research chemist) and Elsie (a homemaker; maiden name, Hansen) Walker; married Alex Baumgartner, 1963 (divorced, 1989); children: Kirsten Margaret. *Education:* Oberlin College, B.A., 1961; Drexel University, M.S., 1968; attended Union Institute, 1994—. *Religion:* Episcopalian. *Hobbies and other interests:* Storytelling, folksinging, and quilting.

■ Addresses

Home—P.O. Box 48424, Philadelphia, PA 19144-8424. *Office*—Free Library of Philadelphia, 1901 Vine St., Philadelphia, PA 19103.

■ Career

Free Library of Philadelphia, Philadelphia, PA, children's librarian, 1968-78, 1984-86, area children's specialist, 1986-89, community services librarian, 1990—; Chestnut Hill College, Rosemont College, University of

BARBARA BAUMGARTNER

Pennsylvania, and Temple University, adjunct instructor in storytelling and children's literature, 1980-83, 1991—. Conductor of storytelling workshops throughout greater Philadelphia. *Member:* National Storytelling Association, Patchwork Storytelling Guild (president, 1986-92; treasurer, 1992—).

■ Writings

Crocodile! Crocodile! Stories Told around the World, illustrated by Judith Moffatt, Dorling Kindersley, 1994.

■ Work in Progress

A collection of folktales with the theme of gold, for Dorling Kindersley; another collection of folktales; a manual of storytelling workshops; and a handbook of therapeutic storytelling.

■ Sidelights

Barbara Baumgartner made a discovery during the many years she spent working with children as a librarian and storyteller. She found that she "really enjoyed *telling* the story (as opposed to reading it aloud)." Performing one of her favorite stories, Richard Chase's "Sody Saleratus," for many young audiences eventually inspired Baumgartner to combine it with five other stories in *Crocodile! Crocodile! Stories Told around the World.*

A collection of read-aloud tales from China, India, Puerto Rico, and both the Native American and Appalachian traditions of North America, *Crocodile! Crocodile!* features many of Baumgartner's favorite animal characters in a book that *School Library Journal* reviewer Ronald Jobe praised for its "direct, easily recalled style."

"Storytelling is the most important part of the work that I do and is also my avocation," Baumgartner told *SATA,* "People often ask how I became a storyteller. My interest in stories really began in my childhood, because my mother often read aloud to us. I grew up in a small town north of Wilmington, Delaware. I was the oldest of four girls, and we often had lots of chores to do, helping our parents by feeding the chickens, mowing the lawn, picking blueberries and cherries in the summer. I also spent my summers reading lots of books. My mother frequently took us to the Wilmington Public Library, and I liked to walk along the shelves and pick out my own books. When I was eight years old, my Grandfather Walker gave me a collection of *Grimm's Fairy Tales,* which I read many times. That same year my Grandmother Walker gave me *On the Banks of Plum Creek,* by Laura Ingalls Wilder. That was another of my favorite books, and I went on to read all of the 'Little House' books.

"While I loved reading *Grimm's Fairy Tales,* no one in my family told folktales or fairytales. They did tell lots of personal stories, such as the time that my father was naughty when he was little or how my mother's brothers made fun of her when her pie crust was tough. I began to hear other people tell stories when I went to Girl Scout camp and I told stories, such as 'The Gingerbread Boy' and 'The Three Bears,' to children when I was baby-sitting. When I worked as a camp counselor, I liked to tell ghost stories at the evening campfire."

Evening campfires gradually gave way to library reading circles, and since then Baumgartner's pleasure in reading aloud has grown steadily stronger. "As I began working with children in libraries . . . I began to observe other storytellers, attend storytelling workshops and conferences. I always try out new stories with groups of children and adults."

■ Works Cited

Jobe, Ronald, review of *Crocodile! Crocodile! Stories Told around the World, School Library Journal,* August, 1994, p. 149.

■ For More Information See

PERIODICALS

Booklist, July, 1994, p. 1938.
Horn Book, fall, 1994, p. 338.
Kirkus Reviews, June 1, 1994, p. 772.
School Librarian, November, 1994, p. 144.

BELLOLI, Andrea P. A. 1947-

Personal

Born November 16, 1947, in New York; daughter of Willi (an attorney) and Selma (an art historian; maiden name, Podnus) Pfeiffenberger; children: Sabina E. Aran. *Education:* Vassar College, B.A. (summa cum laude), 1968; University of California—Los Angeles, M.A., 1976.

Addresses

Home and office—5 Hosford House, 48 Devonshire Rd., London SE23 3SU England.

Career

Managing editor and editor in chief at various museums, including Detroit Institute of Arts, Los Angeles County Museum of Art, and J. Paul Getty Museum, 1978-92; Macmillan Publishers, London, England, editor, 1992-93; Prestel-Verlag, New York and London, editorial director and consulting editor, 1993—. *Member:* International Association of Art Museum Publishers (chair, 1991-92), London Library.

Awards, Honors

Charles Montgomery Prize; George Wittenborn Award; *Parenting Magazine* Certificate of Excellence, 1994, for *Make Your Own Museum: An Activity Package for Children.*

Writings

FOR CHILDREN

Make Your Own Museum: An Activity Package for Children, illustrated by Keith Godard, Ticknor & Fields, 1994.

OTHER

Oriental Ceramics from the Collection of Justice and Mrs. G. Mennan Williams, Detroit Institute of Arts, 1980.
(With E. Savage-Smith) *Islamicate Celestial Globes,* Smithsonian Institution Press, 1986.
Guide to the Museum and Its Gardens, J. Paul Getty Museum, 1990.

Advisory board member, *History of Photography,* 1992-93.

Work in Progress

An introduction to the history of world art for children.

For More Information See

PERIODICALS

Publishers Weekly, October 17, 1994.
School Library Journal, January, 1995.
Voice of Youth Advocates, February, 1995.

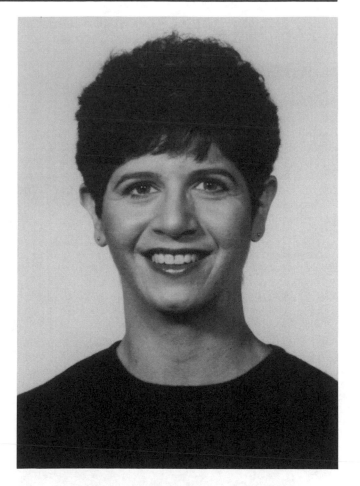

SARAGAIL KATZMAN BENJAMIN

BENJAMIN, Saragail Katzman 1953-

■ Personal

Born July 13, 1953, in Omaha, NE; daughter of Daniel (a mobile home manufacturer) and Ruth (a craft gallery owner; maiden name, Goldberg); married Scott Paul Benjamin (an attorney), December 26, 1983; children: Joshua, Aaron. *Education:* Sarah Lawrence College, B.A., 1975.

■ Addresses

Home and office—27 Kewanee Rd., New Rochelle, NY 10804. *Agent*—Marilyn Epstein Weintraub, 196 Mitchell Rd., Somers, NY 10589 (print rights); Gary Salt, Paul Kohner, Inc., 9169 Sunset Blvd., Los Angeles, CA 90069 (dramatic and film rights).

■ Career

New York metropolitan area entertainer, musician, and singer, 1977—. Teaching artist, Lincoln Center Institute, 1986-87; music workshop leader, primarily for nursery school children, 1990—. Has a one-woman children's music show called "A Joyful Noise." *Member:* Dramatists Guild, Authors League of America,

Society of Children's Book Writers and Illustrators, BMI-Lehman Engel Musical Theater Workshop.

■ Writings

My Dog Ate It, Holiday House, 1994.

Author of children's songs included on the album *A Joyful Noise.* Also author of children's songs "Goodnight," *We Like Kids Songbook,* Good Year Books, 1992; "Take Good Care of the Earth," *Songs for the Earth,* Good Year Books, 1992; "My Little Car"; and "Chocolate Chip Cookies." Contributor to *Long Island Parenting News.*

PLAYS

The Furnished Room (one-act musical; for adults), first produced in New York City, 1984.
The DYBBUK (musical), presented in part at Merkin Hall, New York City, 1992.

Also author of *The Alexandria Municipal Reading Library,* a children's musical, produced in New York City and in schools in Texas.

In this 1994 tale, Danny Wilder plans to flunk the fifth grade to avoid entering middle school. (Cover illustration by Marilyn Hafner.)

■ Work in Progress

A new children's book and a new adult musical theater piece.

■ Sidelights

"Fear of success has never been a problem for author Saragail Katzman Benjamin," notes Lynn Thompson in her *Oodles of Fun Magazine* review of Benjamin's first children's book, *My Dog Ate It.* Since moving from her native Omaha to study music and theater at New York's Sarah Lawrence College in 1971, Benjamin has enjoyed a considerable amount of success in both fields, including the publication of numerous songs and articles and the staging in New York City and Texas of *The Alexandria Municipal Reading Library,* her children's musical based on the true story of a boy who started his own library.

Another of Benjamin's musical pieces, *The Furnished Room,* was included in a workshop presentation of seven "ten-minute musicals" at San Francisco's Climate Theatre in 1990. In his *San Francisco Examiner* review, Scott Rosenberg notes that the piece "uses an O. Henry yarn as the jumping-off point for a moody saga of self-destructive romantic obsession, with a kick of 'Sweeney Todd'-like menace." He also refers to the work as "probably the most hauntingly successful of the pieces here."

It was an ad in *Variety,* in which a production company sought ideas for a fantasy show aimed at kids, that led to Benjamin's entree into the book world. When her two-page outline was rejected, she wisely decided to expand the concept and sent a twenty-page version out to other television production companies. While she was not successful in her television quest, it was this concept that became the basic story line for her first book, *My Dog Ate It.* Thanks to her extremely supportive husband, Scott, she was able to juggle writing and caring for her two sons, then two and a half years and six months old.

Her agent, Marilyn Epstein Weintraub, is also an Omaha native. They attended school together and, when Benjamin approached Weintraub with *My Dog Ate It,* Weintraub was taking a hiatus from her work as a contracts manager for Harper and Row. Little did they know just how much dedication and persistence lay ahead.

In his *Omaha World-Herald* column in which he announced the publication of Benjamin's book, Robert McMorris noted that, "Once upon a time aspiring novelists were advised by instructors to accept rejection slips as an inevitable consequence in the struggle for recognition. The lesson," he added, "was to try, try again." McMorris cited Margaret Mitchell as an example, pointing out that she sent the manuscript for *Gone with the Wind* to sixteen different publishers before it was accepted. Benjamin would have been delighted with only sixteen rejections. After receiving rejection slips from forty publishers, *My Dog Ate It* was bought by Holiday House, a major children's publisher.

In addition to setting aside the time necessary to write her books, Benjamin fills her schedule with speaking engagements at various schools, penning articles on parenting for *Long Island Parenting News,* and composing children's songs. Her tunes have been included in Good Year Books' anthologies of children's songs.

■ Works Cited

McMorris, Robert, "Try, Try Again," *Omaha World-Herald,* March 16, 1994, p. 13.

Rosenberg, Scott, "Enter the Mini-musical," *San Francisco Examiner,* February 13, 1990.

Thompson, Lynn, review of *My Dog Ate It, Oodles of Fun Magazine,* October, 1994, pp. 14-15.

■ For More Information See

PERIODICALS

Children's Book Review Service, May, 1994, p. 116.
Kirkus Reviews, March 15, 1994, p. 392.
Publishers Weekly, April 18, 1994, p. 63.
School Library Journal, May, 1994, p. 112.

* * *

BERESFORD, Elisabeth

■ Personal

Born in Paris, France; daughter of J. D. (a novelist) and Evelyn (Roskams) Beresford; married Maxwell Robertson (a sports commentator), 1949; children: Kate, Marcus. *Education:* Attended schools in Brighton, Sussex, England. *Hobbies and other interests:* Reading, photography, surfing, gardening, "and not working, if at all possible."

■ Addresses

Home—Alderney, Channel Islands. *Agent*—Juvenilia, Avington, Winchester, Hampshire, SO21 1DB, England.

■ Career

Writer; freelance journalist, beginning 1949; radio broadcaster. *Wartime service:* Radio operator in Women's Royal Naval Service during World War II.

■ Writings

FOR CHILDREN

The Television Mystery, Parrish (London), 1957.
The Flying Doctor Mystery, Parrish, 1958.
Trouble at Tullington Castle, Parrish, 1958.
Cocky and the Missing Castle, illustrated by Jennifer Miles, Constable (London), 1959.
Gappy Goes West, Parrish, 1959.
The Tullington Film-Makers, Parrish, 1960.

Two Gold Dolphins, illustrated by Peggy Fortnum, Constable, 1961, illustrated by Janina Domanska, Bobbs-Merrill, 1964.
Danger on the Old Pull 'n Push, Parrish, 1962, White Lion, 1976.
Strange Hiding Place, Parrish, 1962.
Diana in Television, Collins (London), 1963.
The Missing Formula Mystery, Parrish, 1963.
The Mulberry Street Team, illustrated by Juliet Pannett, Friday Press (Penshurst, Kent), 1963.
Awkward Magic, illustrated by Judith Valpy, Hart-Davis (London), 1964, published as *The Magic World,* illustrated by Domanska, Bobbs-Merrill, 1965, revised edition published as *Strange Magic,* illustrated by Cathy Wood, Methuen, 1986.
The Flying Doctor to the Rescue, Parrish, 1964.
Holiday for Slippy, illustrated by Pat Williams, Friday Press, 1964.
Game, Set, and Match, Parrish, 1965.
Knights of the Cardboard Castle, illustrated by C. R. Evans, Methuen (London), 1965, revised edition illustrated by Reginald Gray, 1976.
Travelling Magic, illustrated by Valpy, Hart-Davis, 1965, published as *The Vanishing Garden,* Funk (New York), 1967.
The Hidden Mill, illustrated by Margery Gill, Benn (London), 1965, Meredith Press (New York), 1967.
Peter Climbs a Tree, illustrated by Gill, Benn, 1966.
Fashion Girl, Collins, 1967.
The Black Mountain Mystery, Parrish, 1967.
Looking for a Friend, illustrated by Gill, Benn, 1967.
The Island Bus, illustrated by Robert Hodgson, Methuen, 1968, revised edition illustrated by Gavin Rowe, 1977.
More Adventure Stories (includes *The Mulberry Street Team*), Benn, 1967.
Sea-Green Magic, illustrated by Ann Tout, Hart-Davis, 1968.
David Goes Fishing, illustrated by Imre Hofbauer, Benn, 1969.
Gordon's Go-Kart, illustrated by Gill, McGraw (New York City), 1970.
Stephen and the Shaggy Dog, illustrated by Robert Hales, Methuen, 1970.
Vanishing Magic, illustrated by Tout, Hart-Davis, 1970.
Dangerous Magic, illustrated by Oliver Chadwick, Hart-Davis, 1972.
The Secret Railway, illustrated by James Hunt, Methuen, 1973.
Invisible Magic, illustrated by Gray, Hart-Davis, 1974.
Snuffle to the Rescue, illustrated by Gunvor Edwards, Kestrel (London), 1975.
Beginning to Read Storybook, Benn, 1977.
Toby's Luck, illustrated by Doreen Caldwell, Methuen, 1978.
Secret Magic, illustrated by Caroline Sharp, Hart Davis, 1978.
The Happy Ghost, illustrated by Joanna Carey, Methuen, 1979.
The Treasure Hunters, illustrated by Carey, Elsevier Nelson (New York), 1980.
Curious Magic, illustrated by Claire Upsdale-Jones, Elsevier Nelson, 1980.

ELISABETH BERESFORD

The Four of Us, illustrated by Trevor Stubley, Hutchinson (London), 1981.
The Animals Nobody Wanted, illustrated by Carey, Methuen, 1982.
(Adapter) *Jack and the Magic Stove* (folktale), illustrated by Rita van Bilsen, Hutchinson, 1982.
The Tovers, illustrated by Geoffrey Beitz, Methuen, 1982.
The Adventures of Poon, illustrated by Dinah Shedden, Hutchinson, 1984.
The Mysterious Island, illustrated by Carey, Methuen, 1984.
One of the Family, illustrated by Barrie Thorpe, Hutchinson, 1985.
The Ghosts of Lupus Street School, Methuen, 1986.
Emily and the Haunted Castle, illustrated by Kate Rogers, Hutchinson, 1987.
Once upon a Time Stories, illustrated by Alice Englander, Methuen, 1987.
The Secret Room, illustrated by Michael Bragg, Methuen, 1987.
The Armada Adventure, Methuen, 1988.
The Island Railway, illustrated by Maggie Harrison, Hamish Hamilton (London), 1988.
Rose, Hutchinson, 1989.
Charlie's Ark, Methuen, 1989.
The Wooden Gun, Hippo (London), 1989.
Tim the Trumpet, Blackie (London), 1992.
Jamie and the Rola Polar Bear, illustrated by Janet Robertson, Blackie, 1993.
Lizzie's War, illustrated by James Mayhew, Simon & Schuster (London), 1993.
Rola Polar Bear and the Heatwave, illustrated by Robertson, Blackie, 1994.
The Smallest Whale, illustrated by Susan Field, Orchard Books, 1996.
Lizzie's War, Part II, illustrated by Mayhew, Simon & Schuster (London), 1996.

"THE WOMBLES" SERIES; FOR CHILDREN

The Wombles, illustrated by Margaret Gordon, Benn, 1968, Meredith Press, 1969.
The Wandering Wombles, illustrated by Oliver Chadwick, Benn, 1970.
The Invisible Womble and Other Stories, illustrated by Ivor Wood, Benn, 1973.
The Wombles in Danger, Benn, 1973.
The Wombles at Work, illustrated by Gordon, Benn, 1973, revised edition illustrated by B. Leith, 1976.
The Wombles Go to the Seaside, World Distributors (London), 1974.
The Wombles (play; adaptation of her own stories), produced in London, 1974.
The Wombles Annual, 1975-1978 (four volumes) World Distributors, 1974-77.
The Wombles Book (includes *The Wombles* and *The Wandering Wombles*), Benn, 1975.
Tomsk and the Tired Tree, illustrated by Gordon, Benn, 1975.
Wellington and the Blue Balloon, illustrated by Gordon, Benn, 1975.
Orinoco Runs Away, illustrated by Gordon, Benn, 1975.
The Wombles Gift Book, illustrated by Gordon and Derek Collard, Benn, 1975.
The Snow Womble, illustrated by Gordon, Benn, 1975.
The Wombles Make a Clean Sweep, illustrated by Wood, Benn, 1975.
The Wombles to the Rescue, illustrated by Gordon, Benn, 1975.
Tobermory's Big Surprise, illustrated by Gordon, Benn, 1976.
Madame Cholet's Picnic Party, illustrated by Gordon, Benn, 1976.
Bungo Knows Best, illustrated by Gordon, Benn, 1976.
The Wombles of Wimbledon (includes *The Wombles at Work* and *The Wombles to the Rescue*), Benn, 1976.
The MacWomble's Pipe Band, illustrated by Gordon, Benn, 1976.
The Wombles Go round the World, illustrated by Gordon, Benn, 1976.
The World of the Wombles, illustrated by Edgar Hodges, World Distributors, 1976.
Wombling Free, illustrated by Hodges, Benn, 1978.

Also author of *The Wombles* (screenplay), 1971; author of sixty television scripts for *The Wombles* (series), from 1973.

NOVELS; FOR ADULTS

Paradise Island, Hale (London), 1963.
Escape to Happiness, Hale, 1964, Nordon (New York City), 1980.
Roses round the Door, Hale, 1964, Paperback Library (New York City), 1965.
Island of Shadows, Hale, 1966, Dale (New York City), 1980.
Veronica, Hale, 1967, Nordon, 1980.
A Tropical Affair, Hale, 1967, published as *Tropical Affairs,* Dell (New York), 1978.
Saturday's Child, Hale, 1968, published as *Echoes of Love,* Dell, 1979.
Love Remembered, Hale, 1970, Dale, 1978.

Love and the S.S. Beatrice, Hale, 1972, published as
    Thunder of Her Heart, Dale, 1978.
Pandora, Hale, 1974.
The Steadfast Lover, Hale, 1980.
The Silver Chain, Hale, 1980.
The Restless Heart, Valueback (New York City), 1982.
Flight to Happiness, Hale, 1983.
A Passionate Adventure, Hale, 1983.

OTHER

(With Nick Renton) *Road to Albutal* (play), produced in
    Edinburgh, Scotland, 1976.
(With Peter Spence) *Move On,* BBC Publications, 1978.
The Best of Friends (play), produced in the Channel
    Islands, 1982.

Also contributor of short stories to magazines.

■ Sidelights

Elisabeth Beresford has achieved her greatest success as
a writer through the creation of the "Wombles," a small
race of creatures that inhabit her "Wombles" series of
books for children. In over twenty-five books, this hard-
working, fun-loving family, who lives by the motto
"make good use of bad rubbish," uphold old-fashioned
virtues and introduce children to the more modern
value of conservation.

Beresford was born in Paris, France, where her father,
novelist J. D. Beresford, was living at the time. She
returned to England and was educated in British
schools. "Having a novelist for a father and two
brothers who were successful writers, I was brought up
in a world of books," Beresford once recalled to *SATA,*
"so it seemed natural that I should become a writer
too." She started off working as a journalist and
eventually became a radio and television reporter for
the BBC, a job that took her from the Outback in
Australia to the jungles of South America. "Which, of
course, all make wonderful backgrounds for books," she
explained. "I've also met some extraordinary and unusual people; from goldminers to royalty, from Dukes to
derelicts."

Names like Bulgaria, Tobermory, Orinoco, Tomsk, and
Yellowstone seem more inclined to be part of a geogra-
phy lesson than a cast of characters for a series of
children's books, but in the case of the "Wombles,"
characters are most certainly what they are. Beresford's
furry creatures, who live in burrows underneath the
London suburb of Wimbledon and who take their
names from an atlas, are led by Great Uncle Bulgaria,
introduced to young readers for the first time in 1969's
The Wombles. As ardent collectors of things, words, and
knowledge, Wombles are expert recyclers, intelligent,
and, as Ginger Brauer observes in *Library Journal,*
"generally superior in virtues to [humans] ... with
whom they don't normally associate." In the over
twenty books that followed—from *The Wombles at
Work* and *Wellington and the Blue Balloon* to *Wombling
Free,* the crowning book of the series—Beresford's
engaging characters go beyond merely illustrating moral

tales about picking up garbage and conserving natural
resources. Their inventiveness and positive approach to
many of society's growing problems have drawn praise
from critics, and the author's sprightly prose keeps
young readers interested. With the Wombles, Beresford
"has done more than graft human characters on to
animals," notes Margery Fisher in *Growing Point.*
Instead the author "has created a new race, as consistent
and plausible as the hobbits of Tolkien, whose likeness
to ourselves is only one aspect of their existence."

The illustrations for Beresford's "Wombles" books were
inspired by the puppetry magic of Ivor Wood, who
designed the marionette figures used in the popular
television series *The Wombles;* most of the books in the
series have depicted Wood's original puppet characters—like Bungo, Tomsk, and Wellington—in vivid
illustrations by Margaret Gordon. The Wombles have
become somewhat of a legend in children's literature.
The stories have been translated into twenty languages
and made into both films and a television series.

Although less widely known, Beresford has written
many other novels for children that include both fantasy
and adventure. Beresford "shares in some degree the
dilemma of [Arthur] Conan Doyle," contends Marcus
Crouch in *Twentieth-Century Children's Writers.* Explaining that Conan Doyle's character of Sherlock
Holmes "hung around his neck like a dead weight,"
forcing him to continue writing fiction featuring that
famous detective long after he wanted to, Crouch goes
on to say, "Beresford invented the Wombles.... There
can be no doubt that, in writing these gently humorous
tales, she is sharing with readers her own warm affection
for these curious creatures. But, in achieving a run-away
success with the Wombles, Beresford has distracted
attention from her other, and not less important,
writing."

The Animals Nobody Wanted is just one of Beresford's
books of real-life adventure focusing on the concerns of
young readers. Sharing the theme of conservation with
the Wombles books, this 1982 novel tells about Rosa
and Paul, who go on a seaside vacation and meet
Granny Campbell, an old woman who lives in run-down
Ballig Fort near the sea. Granny is dedicated to caring
for the oil-soaked seabirds she finds near her door, as
well as other sick animals who are gathered up by a local
boy named Midge. Rosa and Paul bring their city-bred
instincts for commerce to the aid of Granny and her
animal hospital, gathering support from the nearby
townspeople and getting funding for the woman's humanitarian efforts. "Elisabeth Beresford knows how to
tell a good story and this one is nicely constructed [and]
pleasantly readable," D. A. Young writes in *Junior
Bookshelf.*

In *The Adventures of Poon* Beresford portrays the
problems of an average family in dealing with a disabled
child. Poon is profoundly deaf; when she is taken by her
social worker to a farm in the country to allow her
mother a chance to rest, Poon tries to run away. It's then
that her adventures begin: in her quest for independence

she helps the police by discovering an important piece of evidence in a police investigation into cattle rustling, uncovers a flint axehead for a local archaeologist, and, along the way, learns to cope with her own sense of isolation from people and to enjoy her new surroundings. In a *School Librarian* review, Sheila Armstrong comments that the characters are "likeable and amusing" but not idealized, and adds that Poon's adventures "are told with a lighthearted and sure touch."

Being uprooted and having to cope with a whole new set of people and circumstances is a situation that many children—not only those who are hearing-impaired or otherwise disabled—have to deal with sometime in their childhood, and it provides the subject of Beresford's 1988 novel *The Island Railway* as well. When Police Sergeant Stafford is transferred from a busy town to a small, scantily populated island off the English coast, his son Thomas is not thrilled. Grudgingly, he seeks the friendship of Matthew, whose father is a fisherman, and together the two boys explore the small island with the help of Matthew's dog. When they find an old engine and a pair of abandoned railcars left behind after a local quarry shut down years before, the boy's stick-to-itiveness inspires the entire community—including a cantankerous elderly neighbor who alone has the knowledge to get the old engine moving again—to help set up a railroad on the island. "Beresford always fills her tales with vigorously drawn characters and this new story is no exception," commented Fisher in *Growing Point.* "Here is a most believable group of people linked in an unusual enterprise."

In Beresford's books, the everyday world can often stray into the realm of the fantastic, often at the most unpredictable times. Quite ordinary children can suddenly find themselves experiencing quite out-of-the-ordinary things. "One of the many wonderful things about children is that *they* still live in a world where anything is possible," Beresford told *SATA,* "and the words 'once upon a time' can make it all happen." In the author's "Magic" books that began in 1964 with the publication of *Awkward Magic,* she weaves a spell of various impossibilities. In this first novel, for example, Beresford's characters journey through time. On his first day of school vacation, Joe finds a stray dog cowering in the basement of the flat where he lives with his father's landlady. When the dog states quite clearly that it has no intention of taking a dip in some warm, soapy water after Joe brings it in, readers know that amazing adventures are in store. The dog, who is actually an ancient griffin, has been sent from Antiquity to recover a lost treasure. Along the way, Joe and the Griffin gain an ally in Grace, a young girl who lives in the mansion where the treasure is finally located. "Beresford has the happily offhand, confident way with magic with which Edith Nesbit conducted her tales," comments *Growing Point*'s Fisher in her review of the book's 1986 update, titled *Strange Magic.* The critic adds that "comic fantasy is one of the trickiest outlets for imagination, demanding discipline, moderation, lightness of touch and complete confidence, all of which Elisabeth Beresford certainly has."

In a *Booklist* review of *Travelling Magic* and *Invisible Magic,* Denise M. Wilms likewise praises the author as "a skillful writer, so her stories flow smoothly, with well-developed scenes and spritely dialogue." In the former book, Kate and her younger brother Marcus befriend curious Mr. Trevellick, a magician from ancient Britain. *Invisible Magic* is the story of a young boy who encounters the snobbish but transparent Princess Elfrida-of-the-Castle (or is she just a scullery maid?) while bicycling around in a park near his home. Mr. Patrick, the local librarian, becomes the children's confidante as Roy, Elfrida, and Roy's dog, Bouncer, make several journeys back through time to Elizabethan England to search for the enchanter, Old Wickery, who made her invisible in the first place.

In 1978's *Secret Magic,* Beresford showcases her skills in the story of two boys who run a vegetable stand in the local farmer's market for their great uncle. When they discover a scruffy-looking cat haunting the market, they first react as typical boys and try to shoo it away. Then it starts to speak in its own defense and turns out to be a chatty, three-thousand-year-old Sphinx who was banished from his home for his talkativeness. The trio link up with a girl who possesses a magic locket, and, of course, magic adventures follow. "Very well written indeed," B. Clark writes in *Junior Bookshelf,* "this is first-class reading." *Curious Magic,* published in 1980, repeats the time-travel motif as young Andy Jones comes to realize a striking similarity between the Mr. Dunk he knows as a neighbor on the island where he is spending his winter vacation, a Mr. Donkey from Roman days, and a Mr. Dunker from the Tudor period. The reason he knows so many people from ages past? His neighbor, the "white witch" Mrs. Tressida, and her niece Ella practice a form of magic that carries the three in and out of ages past to experience British history first-hand. *Curious Magic* "is warmed by humour and sharpened by the unexacting and intriguing shifts in time which Andy, a responsive but not over-emotional lad, takes in his stride," according to Fisher of *Growing Point.*

Although she has been a successful author for most of her adult life, Beresford is quick to note that it hasn't gotten any easier. "I hate typing the dreaded words 'Chapter One' as I find writing very hard work and will think up a dozen good reasons for *not* sitting down at the typewriter," she once confessed. "But one of the great bonuses is getting letters from children all over the world who sometimes just put 'The Wombles, England' on the envelope." "My pet peeve is the people who say, 'Of course I could write a book if I had the time,'" she once confessed. "If I had a sunny day for every time that's been said to me I should live in a world of perpetual sunshine." Despite her professed difficulty with writing, Beresford's love of her craft has inspired many others—including her own children: daughter Kate has written several children's books and son Marcus is a sports journalist.

"Children (and adults) write to me from all over the world," Beresford once told *SATA,* "and quite often they seem to know more about my books than I do. I particularly like listening to children, because—fortunately—they still go on believing that anything is possible and that all kinds of adventures are just around the next corner. And when I put something funny into a story and it makes me laugh I know it will make a lot of children laugh. And there's no better sound in the world than children laughing."

■ Works Cited

Armstrong, Sheila, review of *The Adventures of Poon, School Librarian,* September, 1984, p. 233.

Brauer, Ginger, review of *The Wombles, Library Journal,* March 15, 1970, p. 1192.

Clark, B., review of *Secret Magic, Junior Bookshelf,* December, 1978, p. 298.

Crouch, Marcus, "Elisabeth Beresford," in *Twentieth-Century Children's Writers,* 4th edition, edited by Laura Standley Berger, St. James Press, 1995, p. 88.

Fisher, Margery, review of *The Snow Womble* and others, *Growing Point,* January, 1976, p. 2785.

Fisher, Margery, review of *Curious Magic, Growing Point,* July, 1980, p. 3716.

Fisher, Margery, review of *Strange Magic, Growing Point,* July, 1986, p. 4641.

Fisher, Margery, review of *The Island Railway, Growing Point,* January, 1989, p. 5096.

Wilms, Denise M., review of *Travelling Magic* and *Invisible Magic, Booklist,* March 15, 1978, p. 1185.

Young, D. A., review of *The Animals Nobody Wanted, Junior Bookshelf,* August, 1982, p. 138.

■ For More Information See

PERIODICALS

Growing Point, November, 1975, p. 2746; March, 1979, p. 3467; July, 1981, p. 3910; July, 1982, p. 3931; May, 1987, p. 4800; September, 1988, p. 5026; November, 1989, p. 5234.

Horn Book, August, 1965, p. 390.

Junior Bookshelf, December, 1988, p. 287; February, 1990, p. 34; April, 1994, p. 54.

Publishers Weekly, May 1, 1967, p. 56.

School Librarian, March, 1979, p. 34; December, 1982, p. 329.

School Library Journal, May 15, 1967, pp. 55, 74; August, 1980, p. 60; March, 1981, p. 140.

Times Educational Supplement, August 7, 1987, p. 19.

Times Literary Supplement, June 6, 1968, p. 584; June 15, 1972, p. 684; April 6, 1973, p. 386; July 11, 1975, p. 763; December 5, 1975, p. 1446; August 19-25, 1988, p. 917.

*   *   *

BISSET, Donald 1910-1995

■ Personal

Born August 30, 1910, in London, England; died August 10, 1995; married wife, Nancy, 1946 (divorced); children: one son. *Education:* Attended Warehousemen,

Clerks, and Drapers School, Addington, Surrey, England. *Hobbies and other interests:* Horseback riding.

■ Career

Author and illustrator of children's books. Radio, television, and stage actor; appeared with the National Theatre and Royal Shakespeare Theatre companies; appeared in the television film *Henry VIII,* New York, and in *The Great Waltz,* Drury Lane Theatre, London, both 1971. *Military service:* British Royal Artillery, 1940-46; became lieutenant.

■ Writings

CHILDREN'S FICTION; SELF-ILLUSTRATED

Anytime Stories, Faber, 1954, Transatlantic, 1955.
Sometime Stories, Faber, 1957.
Next Time Stories, Methuen, 1959.
This Time Stories, Methuen, 1961.
Another Time Stories, Methuen, 1963.
Talks with a Tiger, Methuen, 1967.
Nothing, Benn, 1969.
Time and Again Stories, Methuen, 1970.
Tiger Wants More, Methuen, 1971.
Father Tingtang's Journey, Methuen, 1973.
The Adventures of Mandy Duck, Methuen, 1974.
"Oh Dear," Said the Tiger, Methuen, 1975.
The Lost Birthday, Progress Publishers, 1976.
The Story of Smokey Horse, Methuen, 1977.
This Is Ridiculous, Beaver, 1977.
The Adventures of Yak, Methuen, 1978.
What Time Is It When It Isn't?, Methuen, 1980.
Johnny Here and There, Methuen, 1981.
The Joyous Adventures of Snakey Boo, Methuen, 1982.
Sleep Tight, Snakey Boo!, Methuen, 1985.

CHILDREN'S FICTION

Little Bear's Pony, illustrated by Shirley Hughes, Benn, 1966.
Hullo Lucy, illustrated by Gillian Kenny, Benn, 1967.
Kangaroo Tennis, illustrated by Val Biro, Benn, 1968.
Benjie the Circus Dog, illustrated by Val Biro, Benn, 1969.
Upside Down Land, Progress Publishers, 1969.
Barcha the Tiger, illustrated by Derek Collard, Benn, 1971.
Yak and the Sea Shell, illustrated by Lorraine Calaora, Methuen, 1971.
Yak and the Painted Cave, illustrated by Lorraine Calaora, Methuen, 1971.
Yak and the Buried Treasure, illustrated by Lorraine Calaora, Methuen, 1972.
Yak and the Ice Cream, illustrated by Lorraine Calaora, Methuen, 1972.
Jenny Hopalong, illustrated by Derek Collard, Benn, 1973.
Yak Goes Home, illustrated by Lorraine Calaora, Methuen, 1973.
The Happy Horse, illustrated by David Sharpe, Benn, 1974.
Baby Crow Learns to Fly, Benn, 1975.

Hazy Mountain, illustrated by Shirley Hughes, Kestrel, 1975.

(With Michael Morris) *Paws with Numbers,* illustrated by Tony Hutchins, Intercontinental Books, 1976.

Paws with Shapes, illustrated by Tony Hutchins, Intercontinental Books, 1976.

Journey to the Jungle, Beaver, 1977.

The Hedgehog Who Rolled Uphill, Methuen, 1982.

Just a Moment!, Methuen, 1987.

Ogg, illustrated by Amelia Rosato, Methuen, 1987.

Upside Down Stories, Puffin, 1987.

Please Yourself, Methuen, 1991.

OTHER

Also author of *Cornelia and Other Stories,* 1980. Writer for the animated television series *Yak,* 1971. Bisset's books have been translated into sixteen languages.

■ Sidelights

"All my books are modern fairy stories—animistic in concept—and, on the surface, nonsensical, but nevertheless they have meanings (varied)," British children's author and illustrator Donald Bisset told Stephanie Nettell in *Twentieth-Century Children's Writers.* This formula led to a successful career during which Bisset produced nearly forty children's books. Nettell praised Bisset's "spiky little childlike drawings," engaging use of language, and appealing characters, concluding that "innocence is the essential quality of all Donald Bisset's work—a pure, shining, quite unselfconscious innocence that finds a delighted response in a small child's mind and has an extraordinary *cleansing* effect in an adult's." Liz Waterland described the reaction of a group of young children to Bisset's *Upside Down Stories* in *Books for Keeps:* "They fell about with laughing and then fought to read them themselves. A palpable hit!"

Bisset's work includes many collections of nonsense animal stories for very young children, one of which is *The Hedgehog Who Rolled Uphill.* In addition to the title character, this book features an elephant who has trouble sleeping and a crocodile who loves to sing. "The author's lively style makes the book ideal for reading aloud," according to a *British Book News* reviewer. Writing in the *Times Educational Supplement,* Will Harris noted that Bisset's stories "somehow capture the freshness and illogicality and zest of a child's imagination."

The Joyous Adventures of Snakey Boo, which features illustrations by Bisset, is told in short episodes that incorporate jokes, puzzles, and rhymes. The title character is a snake who is the captain of a steamboat, *Foley Bridge,* which really wants to be a houseboat. Snakey Boo's crew consists of a number of other animals with funny problems and habits. In a review for the *Times Literary Supplement,* Nettell stated that Bisset's "voice speaks from the page as captivatingly as his drawings." Bisset continued the adventures of Snakey Boo in 1985 with *Sleep Tight, Snakey Boo!*

■ Works Cited

Harris, Will, "Once Upon a Time ...," *Times Educational Supplement,* June 18, 1982, p. 28.

Review of *The Hedgehog Who Rolled Uphill, British Book News,* autumn, 1982, p. 18.

Nettell, Stephanie, review of *The Joyous Adventures of Snakey Boo, Times Literary Supplement,* January 31, 1986, p. 126.

Nettell, Stephanie, "Donald Bisset," *Twentieth-Century Children's Writers,* 4th edition, St. James Press, 1995.

Waterland, Liz, review of *Upside Down Stories, Books for Keeps,* March, 1988, p. 17.

■ For More Information See

PERIODICALS

Books for Keeps, January, 1986, p. 14.

British Book News, March, 1986, p. 27; June, 1987, p. 11.

Growing Point, May, 1981, p. 3875; April, 1983, p. 73.

Junior Bookshelf, August, 1980, p. 172; October, 1981, p. 193.*

*   *   *

BOON, Emilie (Laetitia) 1958-

■ Personal

Surname is pronounced "bone"; born December 31, 1958, in the Netherlands; immigrated to United States; naturalized citizen; daughter of Gerard K. (an economist) and Emilie E. (a teacher and homemaker; maiden name, Krul) Boon. *Education:* Royal Academy of Visual Arts, Diploma in Graphic Design, 1981.

■ Addresses

Home—325 East 80th St., Apt. 5H, New York, NY 10021.

■ Career

Graphic design apprentice for Vorm Vijf, The Hague, Netherlands, and Stadium Kommunikatier Vormgeving, Lisse, Netherlands, both 1980-81; freelance graphic designer for Dutch publishers and for the Dutch postal service, 1981-83; writer and illustrator of children's books, 1983—.

■ Writings

SELF-ILLUSTRATED CHILDREN'S BOOKS

Peterkin Meets a Star, Random House, 1984.

Peterkin's Wet Walk, Random House, 1984.

Belinda's Balloon, Knopf, 1985.

It's Spring, Peterkin, Random House, 1986.

1 2 3 How Many Animals Can You See?, Orchard Books/F. Watts, 1987.

Peterkin's Very Own Garden, Random House, 1987.

Hannah's Helpers, Doubleday, 1993.

During a rainstorm, Peterkin and his two friends, a rabbit and a hedgehog, seek shelter under a large mushroom. (Illustration by the author from *Peterkin's Wet Walk.*)

ILLUSTRATOR

Ruth McCarthy, *Katie and the Smallest Bear,* Knopf, 1985.
Joyce Dunbar, *A Bun for Barney,* Orchard Books, 1987.
Dunbar, *A Cake for Barney,* Orchard Books, 1987.
Harriet Ziefert, *Daddy, Can You Play with Me?* Puffin, 1988.
Ziefert, *Mommy, Where Are You?* Puffin, 1988.

■ **Sidelights**

As an illustrator, Emilie Boon has garnered praise for her attractively colored, uncluttered pictures of friendly animals and small children. As a storyteller, her work is considered ideal for both very young children and first readers due to its clarity, repetition, and reassuring messages. Boon attributes her interest in publishing books for children to her unusual childhood. Born in Holland, Boon moved with her family first to California and then to Mexico, where the warm, sunny climate contrasted greatly with that of her native country. "After graduating from the American high school in Mexico," Boon once revealed, "I moved back to Holland and enrolled in art school, opting for the practical career of graphic design, instead of painting. The gloomy Dutch climate contrasted with the brightness of California and Mexico, and magnified my sunny childhood in my mind. This, together with my love for color, animals, reading, and working with the printed word,

probably influenced me most to become a children's book illustrator."

Boon's picture books for young children and first readers have delighted reviewers with their simple, reassuring stories and clear, brightly colored illustrations. Characterized as cheerful and bold, Boon's illustrations keep background detail to a minimum, lending them an uncluttered, cartoon-like quality that critics often felt the youngest of children would find appealing. Her simple, repetitive stories have been deemed ideal for both infants and children learning how to read.

Boon has written several picture books featuring Peterkin, a little boy with two friends, a rabbit and a hedgehog. Together the three have a variety of small adventures in which helping each other and learning little lessons play an important part. In *Peterkin Meets a Star*—a "simply charming" story according to Jill Bennett of *Books for Keeps*—Peterkin captures a star but decides to set it free when he realizes it cannot live anywhere but in the sky. Often reviewed with *Peterkin's Wet Walk,* in which Peterkin and his friends take shelter under a large mushroom during a rainstorm, both books were praised as charming fantasies. "Both stories," commented *School Library Journal*'s Lynda Riell, "will give children a sense of order and belonging." "No one should miss Boon's prize," enthused a *Publishers Weekly* reviewer of *Peterkin's Wet Walk,* "or the companion book, equally irresistible, *Peterkin Meets a Star.*"

Also in this series are *It's Spring, Peterkin* and *Peterkin's Very Own Garden.* In her *School Library Journal* review, Liza Bliss recommended the former title, in which Peterkin helps a baby robin back into its nest, as "an uncluttered, gentle story featuring object recognition and action without hyperactivity." In *Peterkin's Very Own Garden,* Peterkin and his friends plant a garden but must find a way to keep all the other animals from eating the little plants. Although *School Library Journal* critic Gale W. Sherman found Boon's resolution made for only an "average" story, she nonetheless praised Boon's "pleasant, uncluttered watercolor illustrations." In another *School Library Journal* article, however, Jeanne Marie Clancy called this an "excellent" choice for story hour.

One of Boon's earlier solo efforts, *Belinda's Balloon,* tells the story of a bear family having a picnic. When Lucy buys her younger sister a balloon, a sudden wind floats the two of them into the air. Lucy rescues her sister with the help of three balloons and the two enjoy a treat in the high branches of a tree before floating back down to earth. While Susan Denniston, writing in *School Library Journal,* felt this work lacked "pizzazz," Jane Doonan recommended *Belinda's Balloon* in the *Times Literary Supplement* for its "strong sensory appeal," which made the book "accessible to the youngest child."

Boon's counting book, *1 2 3 How Many Animals Do You See?* uses going to school as its theme. As Rabbit walks to school, his friends join him one by one, until there are

Boon's self-illustrated counting book *1 2 3 How Many Animals Do You See?* **follows the adventures of a host of forest creatures.**

ten. Zena Sutherland of *Bulletin of the Center for Children's Books* noted that this effort offered "nothing unusual in format, concept, or visual presentation," though she found it "perfectly pleasant." "Toddlers will like this one, and beginning readers will enjoy it too," averred Lucy Young Clem in *School Library Journal,* adding praise for Boon's "endearing but not saccharine" illustrations. Boon is also the author of *Hannah's Helpers,* a storybook about a group of farm animals who help mother by cleaning the house, though they wake the baby in the process. *School Librarian* contributor Cliff Moon recommended this work for "read-aloud and join-in sessions with infants."

Although she is now an American citizen living in New York, Boon once noted that "it was in London, where I moved after earning my diploma from the academy in The Hague, where I first started to write and illustrate my own children's books. The charm of London and the English countryside was a great source of inspiration for my work. Equally so were the snowy villages nestled in

the Swiss mountains which I loved and still love to visit. My dream is to go to Japan in wintertime and travel through the snow country there."

■ Works Cited

Bennett, Jill, review of *Peterkin's Wet Walk* and *Peterkin Meets a Star, Books for Keeps,* January, 1986, p. 12.

Bliss, Liza, review of *It's Spring, Peterkin, School Library Journal,* December, 1986, p. 80.

Clancy, Jeanne Marie, review of *Peterkin's Very Own Garden, School Library Journal,* July, 1989, p. 35.

Clem, Lucy Young, review of *1 2 3 How Many Animals Do You See? School Library Journal,* November, 1987, pp. 86-87.

Denniston, Susan, review of *Belinda's Balloon, School Library Journal,* December, 1985, pp. 67-68.

Doonan, Jane, "Amiable Beginnings: Picture Books 2," *Times Literary Supplement,* March 29, 1985, p. 351.

Moon, Cliff, review of *Hannah's Helpers, School Librarian,* August, 1993, p. 101.

Review of *1 2 3 How Many Animals Do You See?, Kirkus Reviews,* July 15, 1987, p. 1066.

Review of *Peterkin's Wet Walk, Publishers Weekly,* January 20, 1984, p. 88.

Riell, Lynda, review of *Peterkin Meets a Star* and *Peterkin's Wet Walk, School Library Journal,* May, 1984, p. 62.

Sherman, Gale W., review of *Peterkin's Very Own Garden, School Library Journal,* September, 1987, p. 160.

Sutherland, Zena, review of *1 2 3 How Many Animals Do You See?, Bulletin of the Center for Children's Books,* September, 1987, pp. 3-4.

■ For More Information See

PERIODICALS

Growing Point, November, 1983, p. 4167; September, 1985, p. 4504; March, 1987, p. 4764.

Junior Bookshelf, December, 1983, p. 233; February, 1987, p. 15.

Kirkus Reviews, July 15, 1987, p. 1066.

Publishers Weekly, July 10, 1987, p. 66.*

*   *   *

BREATHED, Berke
See BREATHED, (Guy) Berkeley

*   *   *

BREATHED, (Guy) Berkeley 1957-
(Berke Breathed)

■ Personal

Surname rhymes with "method"; born June 21, 1957, in Encino, CA; son of John William Breathed (an oil equipment executive) and Martha Jane (Martin) de Varennes; married Jody Elizabeth Boyman (a photographer), May 10, 1986. *Education:* University of Texas at Austin, B.A., 1980. *Politics:* "Middle-winger." *Religion:* Agnostic. *Hobbies and other interests:* Power boating, travel, racquetball, animals of all shapes and sizes.

■ Addresses

Office—Washington Post Writers Group, 1150 15th St. N.W., Washington, DC 20071-0002. *Agent*—Esther Newberg, International Creative Management, 40 West 57th St., New York, NY 10019.

■ Career

Freelance writer and illustrator, 1980—. University of Texas at Austin, photographer and columnist for *Daily Texan* (school newspaper) 1976-79; *Washington Post* Writers Group, Washington, DC, syndicated cartoonist and writer, 1980—. Creator of comic strips "Bloom County," 1980-89, and "Outland," 1989-1995.

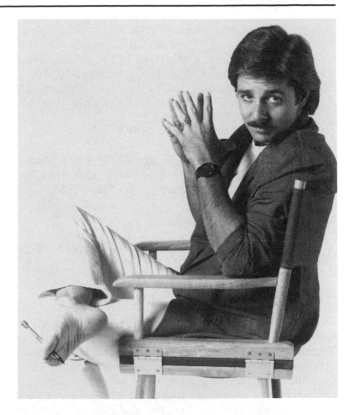

BERKELEY BREATHED

■ Awards, Honors

Harry A. Schweikert Jr. Disability Awareness Award, Paralyzed Vets of America, 1982, and Pulitzer Prize for editorial cartooning, 1987, both for "Bloom County"; Fund for Animals Genesis Award, 1990, for "focusing on animal welfare issues."

■ Writings

FOR CHILDREN; SELF-ILLUSTRATED

A Wish for Wings That Work: An Opus Christmas Story, Little, Brown, 1991.

The Last Basselope: One Ferocious Story, Little, Brown, 1992.

Goodnight Opus, Little, Brown, 1993.

Red Ranger Came Calling: A Guaranteed True Christmas Story, Little, Brown, 1994.

COMIC STRIP COLLECTIONS; UNDER NAME BERKE BREATHED

Bloom County: Loose Tails, Little, Brown, 1983.

'Toons for Our Times: A Bloom County Book of Heavy Metal Rump 'n' Roll, Little, Brown, 1984.

Penguin Dreams, and Stranger Things, Little, Brown, 1985.

Bloom County Babylon: Five Years of Basic Naughtiness, Little, Brown, 1986.

Billy and the Boingers Bootleg, Little, Brown, 1987.

Tales Too Ticklish to Tell, Little, Brown, 1988.

Night of the Mary Kay Commandos: Featuring Smell-O-Toons, Little, Brown, 1989.

Classics of Western Literature: Bloom County, 1980-1989, Little, Brown, 1990.

Happy Trails, Little, Brown, 1990.
Politically, Fashionably, and Aerodynamically Incorrect: The First Outland Collection, Little, Brown, 1992.
The Romantic Opus n' Bill, Little, Brown, 1994.
His Kisses are Dreamy—But Those Hairballs down My Cleavage!: Another Tender Outland Collection, Little, Brown, 1994.
One Last Peek, Little, Brown, 1995.

Author and artist of comic strips "Bloom County," 1980-89, and "Outland," 1989-1995; also author and artist of "Opus Goes Home," *Life,* May, 1987.

■ Adaptations

A Wish for Wings that Work was adapted as an animated television special, 1991.

■ Sidelights

Since he began writing and illustrating the popular and satirical "Bloom County" comic strip in 1980, Berkeley Breathed has become one of the country's most popular newspaper cartoonists, winning the 1987 Pulitzer Prize for editorial cartooning. After 1989, when he retired the curious cast of characters that inhabited "Bloom County," Breathed continued writing and illustrating "Outland," a cartoon that appeared weekly in the Sunday comics until March 1995. In addition, he has created a number of picture books that have been popular with both children and adults.

Breathed was born June 21, 1957, in Encino, California. After graduating from high school, he decided to go to the University of Texas at Austin. "I ended up doing a comic strip because it was the most effective way to make a point and get people listening," Breathed told an interviewer in *Comics Journal,* recalling his college days. Confessing to being the proud owner of an overactive imagination, Breathed found his creativity to be an asset when he began working for the *Daily Texan,* his college school paper, in 1976. "I was a writer for the paper, an avid photographer, and a columnist. I loved the idea of expressing myself in a mass medium ... [and] when you drew a figure next to your words, it had an element of attraction for people that was unimaginable to me at the time."

During his senior year of college, Breathed began to approach newspaper syndicates—companies that market articles, columns, and cartoons to a wide variety of newspapers at the same time—with samples of his work in the hope that he could find a new outlet for his cartoons. While the syndicates didn't express any interest at first, a year later he got a call from Al Leeds of the *Washington Post,* who commissioned the young cartoonist to create a new comic strip for the paper. "Bloom County" was born, and debuted in newspapers in 1980.

To make its irreverent points, "Bloom County" boasted an illustrious cast of characters: the scruffy Bill the Cat, who constantly "Ack!"'s up hairballs, Opus the over-anxious penguin, and several humans who include lowlife lawyer Steve Dallas, scientific whiz-kid Oliver Wendell Jones, disabled Vietnam veteran Cutter John, wimpy ten-year-old Michael Binkley, and the ever-gloomy child-entrepreneur Milo Bloom. Touted by many critics as the "comic strip of the '80s," Breathed's creation gained a strong readership and he received many letters—from loyal fans and offended detractors alike.

Breathed's "Bloom County" saga spawned several anthologies, including 1987's *Bloom County Babylon: Five Years of Basic Naughtiness,* and *Billy and the Boingers Bootleg* and *The Night of the Mary Kay Commandos,* both published in 1988. In the omnibus volume *Bloom County Babylon,* the first five years of the series are encapsulated, reminding fans of the comic strip how each of the characters, as well as the strip's overall sarcastic slant, developed. Breathed "quickly hit his stride," noted Charles Solomon in the *Los Angeles Times Book Review,* "and turned his strip into something unique." Solomon also praised Breathed's strong characterizations, his improved artistic abilities, and the barbed wit that made "Bloom County" "one of the funniest and most relevant strips" in the newspaper.

Billy and the Boingers Bootleg followed soon after, featuring all-new antics of the "Bloom County" gang. Poking fun at everything from movie stars and espionage rings to heavy metal music—Bill the Cat and his band The Boingers doing a feral rendition of "Death-tongue" are among those brought to life by a pen heavily inked with satire—*Billy and the Boingers Bootleg* was sought out by Breathed's growing fans. By *Tales Too Ticklish to Tell,* Bill the Cat had traded in his amplified guitar for a microphone, a teleprompter, and a hat to pass as the televangelist "Fundamentally Oral Bill." Conversion of all of "Bloom County" quickly follows; just as quick is its "deconversion" when the entire list of comic characters decides to go on strike, demanding an end to crowded conditions in their small strip in the newspaper.

The strip was published in almost 1,200 newspapers across the country and throughout the world before the final segment was published in August of 1989. "A good comic strip is no more eternal than a ripe melon," Breathed was quoted as saying in *Newsweek.* "The ugly truth is that in most cases, comics age even less gracefully than their creators. 'Bloom County' is retiring before the stretch marks show."

The Night of the Mary Kay Commandos and *Happy Trails* were published in 1989 and 1990 respectively; they allowed fans who had only followed the comic sporadically to fill in the gaps on the Bloom County gang's doings. The 1988 election sees Bill the Cat and Opus the penguin (not surprisingly) beaten at the polls, while steps must be taken to break failed candidate Opus's mom out of Mary Kay Cosmetics, where she is in peril of being used for cosmetic testing. *Happy Trails,* the last of the "Bloom County" books, while considered by the *Los Angeles Times Book Review*'s Solomon to be

The "anxiety closet" was one of the many ways Breathed spoofed modern life in his Pulitzer Prize-winning comic strip "Bloom County." (Illustrations by the author from *Penguin Dreams and Stranger Things*.)

"uneven," was a fitting end to the series. The characters indulge in one last round of sarcasm during a theatrical "wrap" party celebrating the end of their long-running performance and, in the bittersweet final strip, Opus the Penguin abandons his regular haunts and, suitcases in hand, walks off the edge of the page.

Fortunately for Breathed fans, scarcely a month later he hit the presses with a new comic strip. Called "Outland," the new comic, unlike its predecessor, was featured only once each week, in the Sunday color supplements. Although it contained a different cast of characters, the first anthology of "Outland" comics, *Politically, Fashionably, and Aerodynamically Incorrect: The First Outland Collection,* showed, from its very title, that "Outland" was covering the same territory—and stepping on the same sets of toes—as "Bloom County" had.

The character of Opus the penguin was also saved from extinction after the demise of the "Bloom County" series when Breathed cast him in a starring role in the first of several books he has written and illustrated for children. In 1991's *A Wish for Wings that Work: An Opus Christmas Story,* Breathed tells of the penguin's desire to use his wings the same way other birds do—to actually fly. He gets his wish in a roundabout way after his swimming skills get Santa and his sleigh full of goodies out of a lake after a piece of the sleigh's harness snaps. While some reviewers expected the sarcasm of the original comic strip and found it lacking, others felt the book was appropriate for young readers: a *Publishers Weekly* reviewer praised *A Wish for Wings that Work* as "a work that little ones will love for its own magic and logic." Breathed's first book for children was also adapted as an animated television special in 1991.

In *The Last Basselope: One Ferocious Story,* a book intended for more sophisticated readers, the sturdy penguin and his friends end up in the dark, creepy forest in a search for a ferocious and legendary beast. With vivid, full-color, full-page airbrushed illustrations as opposed to the black and white "comic strip" format, *The Last Basselope* lets readers follow Opus the "Great and Famous Discoverer" and his comrades—characters from "Outland" and even that Breathed favorite, Bill the Cat—as they hunt down and corner the terrible Basselope, only to discover ... a quiet basset hound burdened with a set of ten-times-too-large antlers and an allergy to dandelions. Ilene Cooper of *Booklist* praised Breathed's "dramatic, full-color" illustrations as "eye-popping" but believed the story "falls curiously flat." Lisa Dennis, however, noted in *School Library Journal* that older children will appreciate the author's "delightfully sarcastic and sophisticated" humor while younger readers may enjoy the book's "sheer silliness."

In *Goodnight Opus,* a 1993 parody of Margaret Wise Brown's classic children's story *Goodnight Moon,* the author-illustrator inks scenes of Opus listening to a favorite bedtime story read by his grandmother. When sleep and a vivid imagination carry Opus away on a fantastic journey through the night, the world breaks into blazing color courtesy of artist Breathed. Opus joins such fantastic creatures as a pillow with a balloon for a head and a purple snorklewacker on a flying three-wheeler as they voyage to see the cows of the Milky Way; the trio visits everyone from Abe Lincoln to the tooth fairy during the trip. While Lisa Dennis commented in *School Library Journal* that the book is "less sarcastic than that of his cartoon collections ... mak[ing] the book accessible to a wide age range," other reviewers still detected the presence of Breathed's incorrigible humor. Fellow cartoonist Gahan Wilson raised both hands in mock alarm at Breathed's good-

Although Breathed stopped writing "Bloom County" in 1989, his beloved characters—such as Opus the penguin—still appeared in his later books, including 1991's *A Wish for Wings That Work*. (Illustration by the author.)

natured twist on the innocent *Goodnight Moon* and joked in the *New York Times Book Review* that *Goodnight Opus* "is so well disguised as a children's book that I suspect it will be purchased and actually read aloud to children by many people who would, if they understood it, burn the thing on sight.... I highly recommend this book."

A young disbeliever gives Santa one last chance in *Red Ranger Came Calling: A Guaranteed True Christmas Story,* published as a tribute to Breathed's father in 1994. The book takes place in 1939, when nine-year-old "Red" Breathed lives for the day when he will be the proud and rightful owner of an Official Buck Tweed Two-Speed Crime-Stopper Star-Hopper bicycle. When he is sent to spend Christmas with his aunt at her island

home he knows that all pleas to his now-absent parents have been wasted—his only hope now lies with a mysterious toothless old man who may or may not be Santa Claus. Floating old men who look suspiciously elf-like and the granting of a small wish make Red suspect the old fellow is for real, and he makes his demands; when Christmas morning dawns and there's no cycle in site, he figures it's just another case of being let down by grownups. The surprise ending "reaffirm[s] a reader's belief in the spirit that is Santa," according to a *Publishers Weekly* reviewer. *Booklist* critic Carolyn Phelan hailed Breathed's "extraordinary full-color illustrations [that] seem three-dimensional," and concluded that *Red Ranger Came Calling* is "a most original Christmas book."

"The imagery of children's books (i.e. Dr. Seuss books, *The Phantom Tollbooth* by Norman Juster, and others) has had a long and overlooked influence on my approach to comic strips," the author once commented. Now, his own books for children have expanded Breathed's admirers to include many young readers who laugh at the playfulness of his imaginative characters. For his ever-growing numbers of adult fans, the laughter they experience is directed as much towards themselves: their politics, beliefs, concerns, and worries are acted out through the antics of characters like Opus, Bill the Cat, and Milo Bloom. As Breathed told Gail Buchalter in *People:* "If someone sticks my comic strip on their refrigerator door, it's like that person [is] saying: 'This is my life; he's writing about me.'"

■ Works Cited

Breathed, Berke, "Interview: Can Breathed be Taken Seriously?," *Comics Journal,* October, 1988.

Breathed, Berke, remarks in *Newsweek,* May 15, 1989.

Buchalter, Gail, "Cartoonist Berke Breathed Feathers His Nest by Populating 'Bloom County' with Rare Birds," *People,* August 6, 1984.

Cooper, Ilene, review of *The Last Basselope: One Ferocious Story, Booklist,* December 12, 1992, p. 735.

Dennis, Lisa, review of *The Last Basselope: One Ferocious Story, School Library Journal,* January, 1993, p. 73.

Dennis, Lisa, review of *Goodnight Opus, School Library Journal,* January, 1994, p. 82.

In his self-illustrated 1994 book, *Red Ranger Came Calling,* Breathed retells a favorite childhood story about the Christmas his father got a Red Ranger bicycle from a mysterious stranger.

Phelan, Carolyn, review of *Red Ranger Came Calling: A Guaranteed True Christmas Story*, *Booklist*, October 1, 1994, p. 325.

Review of *Red Ranger Came Calling: A Guaranteed True Christmas Story*, *Publishers Weekly*, September 19, 1994, p. 28.

Solomon, Charles, review of *Bloom County Babylon: Five Years of Basic Naughtiness*, *Los Angeles Times Book Review*, October 5, 1986, p. 5.

Solomon, Charles, review of *Happy Trails*, *Los Angeles Times Book Review*, April 15, 1990, p. 14.

Wilson, Gahan, review of *Goodnight Opus*, *New York Times Book Review*, December 5, 1993, p. 72.

Review of *A Wish for Wings That Work: An Opus Christmas Story*, *Publishers Weekly*, July 25, 1991, p. 52.

■ For More Information See

PERIODICALS

Booklist, November 15, 1987, p. 527; December 1, 1988, p. 608; November 1, 1989, p. 512; January 1, 1994, p. 832.

Kirkus Reviews, August 1, 1991, p. 1018.

Kliatt, January, 1987, p. 59; January, 1990, p.49.

Los Angeles Times, November 26, 1987.

New York Times Book Review, November 13, 1994, p. 40.

Publishers Weekly, September 27, 1993.

School Library Journal, October, 1991, p. 27.

Time, May 15, 1989, p. 77; December 25, 1989.

Washington Post Book World, April 24, 1983; August 24, 1986; August 23, 1987.

*   *   *

BRUST, Steven K. (Zoltan) 1955-

■ Personal

Born November 23, 1955, in St. Paul, MN; son of William Z. (a professor) and Jean (Tilsen) Brust; married; wife's name, Reen, December 29, 1974; children: Corwin Edward, Aliera Jean and Carolyn Rocza (twins), Antonia Eileen. *Education:* Control Data Institute, Programming Certificate (with honors), 1976; attended University of Minnesota—Twin Cities. *Politics:* "Trotskyist." *Religion:* "Materialist." *Hobbies and other interests:* Cooking, Shotokan Karate, fencing, Hungarian culture.

■ Addresses

Home—3248 Portland Avenue S., Minneapolis, MN 55407. *Agent*—Valerie Smith, Route 44-55, RD Box 160, Modena, NY 12548.

■ Career

Employed as systems programmer, 1976-86, including Network Systems, New Brighton, MN, 1983-86; full-time writer, 1986—. Former actor for local community theater; rock 'n' roll drummer; drummer for Middle-Eastern and Oriental dancers; folk guitarist, banjoist, singer, and songwriter. *Member:* Science Fiction Writers of America, Interstate Writers Workshop, Minnesota Science Fiction Society (executive vice-president), Pre-Joycean Fellowship.

■ Writings

SCIENCE FICTION AND FANTASY NOVELS

Jhereg, Ace Books, 1983.
To Reign in Hell, Steel Dragon, 1984.
Yendi, Ace Books, 1984.
Brokedown Palace, Ace Books, 1985.
Teckla, Ace Books, 1986.
The Sun, the Moon, and the Stars, Armadillo Press, 1987.
Taltos, Ace Books, 1988.
Cowboy Feng's Space Bar and Grille, Ace Books, 1990.
Phoenix, Ace Books, 1990.
The Phoenix Guards, Tor Books, 1991.
(With Megan Lindholm) *The Gypsy*, Tor Books, 1992.
Agyar, Tor Books, 1992.
Athyra, Ace Books, 1993.
Five Hundred Years After, Tor Books, 1994.
ORCA, Ace Books, 1996.

Work represented in anthologies, including *Liavek Anthology*, 1985.

■ Work in Progress

A book about "the viscount of Adrilaukha, Freedom, and Necessity (with Emma Bull)."

■ Sidelights

In the realms of science fiction and fantasy, Steven K. Brust's fans have become accustomed to discovering exciting, strange yet believable new worlds. "It is very easy to cheat when writing fantasy—to say 'This is magic, it just works,'" Brust once commented. "But if one is able to avoid this trap, one has the power to work real magic with the story. For me, magic must be either an alternate set of physical laws, used to express something about how we view our tools, or else a metaphor for Mystery, or the Unknown, or whatever."

Brust's Hungarian ancestry is evident in many of his books, especially his popular five-book series that chronicles the adventures of Vlad Taltos, a warlock and hired assassin educated by a swordsman and a sorceress, who carries out assignments on behalf of the Dragonlords of the Dragaeran Empire.

In *Jhereg*, the first book in the series, young Vlad is left to fend for himself when his father dies. He quickly discovers that his early education comes in handy when he has to rely on his own cunning and wit to survive among the powerful Dragaerans. In his *Booklist* review, Roland Green notes that "the book features intelligent world building" and "good handling of the assassin character."

Brust uses flashbacks to establish the chronology and setting of *Yendi,* the second book in the series, which is actually a prequel. Here, readers discover how Vlad has risen through the ranks from his start as a small-time mobster to his current status as a major criminal. *Yendi* also chronicles the romance and courtship of Vlad and Cawti, the Dagger of the Jhereq, who would become his wife. Roland Green, again in *Booklist,* says that *Yendi* "is as intelligent, witty, and generally well written as its predecessor."

The next book in the series, *Teckla,* picks up where the first, *Jhereg,* left off. In this outing, Vlad becomes involved in a revolution against the Dragaeran Empire along with the Teckla, the empire's lowest class of citizens. During the rebellion, Vlad finds himself in the role of Cawti's protector, which only exacerbates their rocky relationship.

The chronology of the series shifts again as the fourth novel, *Taltos,* goes back to Vlad's early life. Writing about *Taltos* in *Voice of Youth Advocates,* Carolyn

ACE · 0-441-18200-3 · [$5.99 CANADA] · $4.99 U.S.
STEVEN BRUST
author of JHEREG,
YENDI, and TECKLA
TALTOS
In which we learn
what really happened
when Vlad found himself walking
the Paths of the Dead

This 1988 work, the fourth in a series about warlock Vlad Taltos, follows Vlad as he walks the Paths of the Dead. (Cover illustration by Kinuko Craft.)

Caywood states that "This is one of the four novels of Taltos which will be of interest to the fantasy fan who discovers any one of them."

Phoenix, the latest story of the series, once again finds Vlad embroiled in revolution and upheaval. This novel, which *Voice of Youth Advocates* reviewer Caywood describes as "more somber and more straightforward" than Brust's previous four, finds Vlad questioning his life-long beliefs and occupation. Caywood adds that fans may be disappointed by the introspective nature of this book but that "readers who are willing to follow the author's lead will discover that his conclusion has added depth to the entire series."

The Dragaeran Empire is not the only fantasy world Brust envisions in rebellion and turmoil. *To Reign in Hell,* published just after *Jhereg,* takes place in Heaven where some of the angels are in the midst of their own revolution. "There are many fantasy novels that are thinly disguised Christian metaphors," Brust once stated. "So I wrote *To Reign in Hell,* which is a Christian metaphor that is really a thinly disguised fantasy novel." In *Voice of Youth Advocates,* critic Janet R. Mura applauds *To Reign in Hell* and declares that Brust "has created an engaging story with consummate skill and ability."

Another of Brust's tales derived from Hungarian folklore is *Brokedown Palace,* a story of magic and determination set in a crumbling palace on the banks of the river of Faerie and concerning four brothers who share power in the land of Fenario. Jean Kaufman, writing in *Voice of Youth Advocates,* remarks, "The author creates a land where magic is expected if not really loved." Kaufman goes on to refer to the book as "a sophisticated and rewarding fantasy."

In *The Sun, the Moon, and the Stars,* a retelling of a Hungarian folktale in the idiom of modern fantasy, Brust once again writes about brothers, this time three, who are on a quest to return the sun, moon, and stars to the sky, thereby bringing light to the world. Interestingly, Brust uses the folktale in this case as the framework for a novel depicting the struggle of five young artists to achieve the impossible. A reviewer for *Library Journal* explains how the author utilized his "Fantasist" conventions and generated a book that is "recommended for general fiction and fantasy collections."

With *Cowboy Feng's Space Bar and Grille,* in which a fiendish paranoiac called the Physician decides to destroy his native planet in order to stop the spread of a deadly illness called Hags disease, Brust shows that he can write science fiction as well as fantasy. The setting is Feng's, a bar and grille that features Jewish cooking, a dance floor, and the ability to travel through time and space. *Publishers Weekly* notes that "Brust's fantasy landscape seems truer than the backdrops of many realistic novels" and, in *Voice of Youth Advocates,* Mary R. Voors calls the work "a compelling and humorous science fiction novel."

A traveling intergalactic saloon is the setting for this 1990 novel. (Cover illustration by Jim Gurney.)

The Phoenix Guards is set in Dragaera, the same world that was home to Vlad Taltos in Brust's earlier books. Though *Publishers Weekly* notes that this book "shares the wit and exuberance of the Taltos books," don't expect to find Vlad here; it is one thousand years earlier. Even its sequel, *Five Hundred Years After,* is set too early for Vlad to make an appearance. "Full of flamboyant action and arch dialogue, this latest adventure in Brust's popular 'Dragaeran' novels pits sword against sorcery in classic swashbuckling style," according to a critic for *Library Journal.*

In *The Gypsy,* a collaborative effort between Brust and Megan Lindholm, a sinister being called Fair Lady reaches out from a parallel universe seeking to extend her shadowy dominion through magic, corruption, and murder. Opposing her is a cast of magical archetypes fronted by the Gypsy. *Publishers Weekly* calls it "a powerful and memorable fantasy" and Scott Winnett, in *Locus,* notes that it is "an exciting fantasy/mystery crossover," referring to Brust's and Lindholm's work as "one of the best jobs yet combining these contrasting genres. The marriage of the two genres is near-perfect."

Brust created something of a puzzle in *Agyar,* an impressively wrought modern vampire/redemption yarn. The novel is presented as a bunch of bits and pieces, like a diary, written by John Agyar, an amateur with time on his hands and an old Royal typewriter, in the abandoned house he's staying in. The pieces of the puzzle are shaped by the author's first person point of view; the clues lie more in what he doesn't say than what he does. Agyar's secret is pretty obvious, but Brust tantalizes, holding off on a firm confirmation for much of the novel. Eventually the puzzle pieces fall together, as events come to a head.

In *Locus,* reviewer Carolyn Cushman considers *Agyar* "a different vampire novel, a striking contemporary dark fantasy." A piece in *Kirkus Reviews* notes that the work is "compact, understated, and highly persuasive. Brust accomplishes with a wry turn of phrase or a small flourish what others never achieve despite hundreds of gory spatters." And in the *Washington Post Book World,* Robert K. J. Killheffer refers to *Agyar* as "good, fast-moving, intelligent fun."

"There appears to be a split in literature between work with strong story values and nothing else, and work that has depth and power but no story values," Brust has said. "The stuff I enjoy reading most can be read as

In this dark fantasy tale, a drifter finds himself drawn to two women, one of whom seeks his destruction. (Cover illustration by Jim Burns.)

simple entertainment but rewards more intense reading as well. Since I try to write the sort of stories I like to read, that is what I attempt to do in my own work. Science fiction is a category that allows and even encourages this, which is one of the reasons I write it."

■ Works Cited

Review of *Agyar, Kirkus Reviews,* December 15, 1992, p. 1517.

Caywood, Carolyn, review of *Taltos, Voice of Youth Advocates,* August, 1988, p. 137.

Caywood, Carolyn, review of *Phoenix, Voice of Youth Advocates,* February, 1991, p. 361.

Review of *Cowboy Feng's Space Bar and Grille, Publishers Weekly,* December 8, 1989, p. 50.

Cushman, Carolyn, review of *Agyar, Locus,* February, 1994, p. 75.

Review of *Five Hundred Years After, Library Journal,* March 15, 1994, p. 104.

Green, Roland, review of *Jhereg, Booklist,* July, 1983, p. 1387.

Green, Roland, review of *Yendi, Booklist,* September 15, 1984, p. 108.

Green, Roland, review of *Phoenix, Booklist,* November 1, 1990, p. 504.

Review of *The Gypsy, Publishers Weekly,* May 25, 1992, p. 43.

Kaufman, Jean, review of *Brokedown Palace, Voice of Youth Advocates,* June, 1986, p. 86.

Killheffer, Robert K. J., review of *Agyar, Washington Post Book World,* May 2, 1993, p. 8.

Mura, Janet R., *To Reign in Hell, Voice of Youth Advocates,* February, 1986, p. 393.

Review of *The Phoenix Guards, Publishers Weekly,* August 2, 1991, p. 66.

Review of *The Sun, the Moon, and the Stars, Library Journal,* March 15, 1987, p. 93.

Voors, Mary R., review of *Cowboy Feng's Space Bar and Grille, Voice of Youth Advocates,* June, 1990, p. 113.

Winnett, Scott, review of *The Gypsy, Locus,* September, 1992, p. 37.

■ For More Information See

PERIODICALS

Analog: Science Fiction/Science Fact, September, 1987, p. 159; December, 1992, p. 161; June, 1993, p. 160.

Booklist, February 15, 1986, p. 851; April 1, 1987, p. 1180; March, 1988, p. 1098; August, 1991, pp. 2108, 2110; June 15, 1992, p. 1811; March 1, 1994, pp. 1185, 1188.

Bookwatch, June, 1993, p. 2.

Kirkus Reviews, March 1, 1987, p. 338; September 1, 1991, p. 1121; May 15, 1992, p. 641; February 15, 1994, p. 179.

Kliatt, April, 1990, p. 22; November, 1993, p. 14; July, 1994, p. 13.

Library Journal, September 15, 1991, p. 117; February 15, 1993, p. 196.

Locus, July, 1991, p. 33; October, 1991, p. 44; July, 1992, p. 47; April, 1993, p. 46; August, 1993, p. 44; March, 1994, p. 35; April, 1994, p. 47; May, 1994, p. 47.

Magazine of Fantasy and Science Fiction, December, 1987, p. 35.

Publishers Weekly, March 4, 1983, p. 97; June 1, 1984, p. 63; November 22, 1985, p. 50; March 27, 1987, p. 36; February 14, 1994, p. 83.

Science Fiction Chronicle, December, 1987, p. 46; July, 1990, p. 37; June, 1992, p. 33; December, 1992, p. 38; February, 1994, p. 28; June, 1994, p. 39.

Voice of Youth Advocates, December, 1990, p. 269; April, 1991, p. 10; April, 1992, p. 40; December, 1992, p. 320; February, 1993, p. 345; August, 1994, p. 154.

* * *

BUSHNELL, Jack 1952-

■ Personal

Born November 28, 1952, in Grand Rapids, MI; son of John H. (a biology professor) and Judith (a hospital administrative assistant; maiden name, Clark) Bushnell; married Jennifer Shaddock (an English professor), 1992; children: Zachary. *Education:* University of Colorado, B.A., 1974; Rutgers University, M.A., 1978, Ph.D., 1983. *Hobbies and other interests:* Tennis, softball, "biologizing," birding, farming, baseball, and writing.

JACK BUSHNELL

■ Addresses

Home and office—RR2, Box 239, Eleva, WI 54738. *Agent*—Kendra Marcus, Bookstop Literary Agency, 67 Meadow View Rd., Orinda, CA 94563.

■ Career

Rutgers University, New Brunswick, NJ, assistant professor and lecturer, 1974-84; DMB&B Advertising, New York City, senior account planner, 1984-88; Geer, DuBois Advertising, New York City, vice-president, 1988-92; Nabisco Foods, New Jersey, associate manager of business information, 1992-93; University of Wisconsin, Eau Claire, adjunct assistant professor, 1994-95; full-time writer, 1993—. *Member:* Society of Children's Book Writers and Illustrators, National Storytelling Association, The Loft, Phi Beta Kappa.

■ Writings

FOR CHILDREN

Circus of the Wolves, illustrated by Robert Andrew Parker, Morrow, 1994.
Sky Dancer, illustrated by Jan Ormerod, Morrow, 1996.

OTHER

Also author of *Midnight Run, Bayou Song, Great Grandfather's Farm, White Deer, The World According to Jumping Spiders,* and *Exploring the Aurora Borealis.* Literary essays include "Where is the Lamb for a Burnt Offering?," *The Wordsworth Circle,* 1981; "Maggie Tulliver's Stored Up Force," *Studies in the Novel,* 1984; and "The Daughter's Dilemma" (a scholarly book review), *Configuration,* 1994.

■ Work in Progress

Adult short stories, *Tales from Mother Goose.*

■ Sidelights

Jack Bushnell told *SATA:* "I have been writing at least since I was eight years old and I don't think I ever made a conscious decision to be a writer. It just happened, like it does for most writers, I suspect. But I have been *very* conscious about what I try to *do* when I create. In my fiction and nonfiction for children and adults, I am concerned with the magical and the mythic, in how the natural world and human behavior become surprising and poignant and full of meaning if we just look at them a certain way. Growing up with a biologist father no doubt contributed to my perceptions of the world, as well as to my general understanding of and appreciation for nature and this web of life. But being a father myself has probably had the most profound impact on who I am and how I see. I have learned a great deal from my son, Zachary, about honesty and wonder and love. All of my children's books begin as stories to him, and *everything* I write benefits from what he has taught me.

"I am a fantasist and a storyteller. I imagine lives and situations for myself all the time. I create narratives for myself and others, and when they seem especially surprising or true, I write them. But I am also a dedicated stylist, in love with the music of prose."

Bushnell's first children's book, *Circus of the Wolves,* is an almost mythic tale of a black timber wolf who is captured by a circus trainer and tamed to become part of a troupe of performing wolves. But the wolf, named Kael, yearns for his freedom and, prompted by his trainer, teaches the entire troupe to howl. When the wolves howl, the audience is "drenched by sound … caught in the rush of mountain night music, a downhill rush that deepened and grew grander with each note." Several reviewers appreciated Bushnell's work. A *Kirkus Reviews* critic commented that *Circus of the Wolves* is "poetically told … deeply felt and genuinely dramatic," while *Booklist*'s Carolyn Phelan found the story to be written with "grace and restraint."

■ Works Cited

Bushnell, Jack, *Circus of the Wolves,* Morrow, 1994.
Review of *Circus of the Wolves, Kirkus Reviews,* April 1, 1994.
Phelan, Carolyn, review of *Circus of the Wolves, Booklist,* April 1, 1994.*

C

CARROLL, Raymond 1924-

■ Personal

Born August 10, 1924, in Brooklyn, NY; son of Raymond J. (a politician) and Margaret (a social worker; maiden name, McCarthy) Carroll; married Anne Starck, 1954 (divorced 1979); children: Paul, Suzanne. *Education:* Hamilton College, B.A., 1948; graduate study at Johns Hopkins School of Advanced International Studies, 1949-51. *Politics:* "Usually Democrat." *Religion:* None.

■ Addresses

Home—New York, NY.

■ Career

Cadmus Book Store, Washington, DC, owner, 1953-55; Editors Press Service, New York City, designer of promotional material, translator from Spanish, and newspaper columnist, 1955-61; *Newsweek,* New York City, associate editor, 1961-69, general editor, 1969-81, also chief of United Nations Bureau; freelance writer, 1981—. *Military service:* U.S. Army Air Forces, 1943-46. *Member:* Amnesty International, English-Speaking Union.

■ Writings

JUVENILE

Anwar Sadat, F. Watts, 1982.
The Palestine Question, F. Watts, 1983.
The Caribbean: Issues in U.S. Relations, F. Watts, 1984.
The Future of the United Nations, F. Watts, 1985.

OTHER

Family Encyclopedia of American History, Reader's Digest Association, 1975.
The Story of America, Reader's Digest Association, 1975.
America's Fascinating Indian Heritage, Reader's Digest Association, 1978.

Consumer Advisor: An Action Guide to Your Rights, Reader's Digest Association, 1984.

Also author of *Funk and Wagnalls Encyclopedia Yearbook,* and of articles for periodicals.

■ Sidelights

A journalist for twenty-five years, Raymond Carroll worked as general editor at *Newsweek,* writing and editing articles in the foreign affairs department. For ten years he was the magazine's United Nations correspondent. "In twenty years as a writer, reporter, and editor at *Newsweek* I learned to deal with an enormous variety of subject matter, to work quickly under pressure, and to tell a story accurately, clearly, and colorfully," Carroll commented. "Most of my assignments concerned foreign affairs, but from week to week I never knew what area of the world I would be covering. It might be Vietnam or South Africa one week, the Middle East or Northern Ireland the next. Then, on occasion, I would find myself assigned to such strange precincts as American politics or the world of international adventure.

"Covering the United Nations, which I did from time to time, was sometimes an exhilarating experience. Among the people I met and in some cases interviewed were such Middle East figures as Egypt's Anwar Sadat, Jordan's King Hussein, Israel's Golda Meir, and Palestine Liberation Organization chief Yasser Arafat, such diverse leaders as Sweden's Olaf Palme, Cambodia's Prince Sihanouk, and Uganda's infamous Idi Amin, and such varied American ambassadors as George Bush [later to become president of the United States], Pat Moynihan, and Andy Young."

Now a freelance writer, Carroll has written four historical/political books for young readers. *Anwar Sadat* follows the Egyptian leader's childhood, military training and career, up to and including his assassination and his succession by Hosni Mubarak. Reviewing the book for the *School Library Journal,* Symme J. Benoff called Carroll's citations of Sadat's own writings "enlightening" and recommended that libraries purchase this title.

As U.S. President Harry Truman (left) looks on, Secretary of State Edward Stettinius signs the official charter of the United Nations in a photograph from Raymond Carroll's *The Future of the United Nations.*

In his 1983 *The Palestine Question,* Carroll "succeeded in presenting the political history of the region from all points of view, without taking sides," according to Benoff, again writing for the *School Library Journal.* A review in *Booklist* by Denise M. Wilms called Carroll an "evenhanded, lively reporter," and commended his bibliography for listing "several important adult works" and indicating "their respective biases."

Wilms also reviewed Carroll's 1984 release, *The Caribbean: Issues in U.S. Relations,* which emphasizes the struggle between democracy and communism in that region. "A summary chapter reiterates the Caribbean's

status as a strategically important region," she observed, "and cites the need for a more coherent U.S. foreign-aid and policy approach." A review by Virginia B. Moore in *Voice of Youth Advocates* called the book an "easily readable, factual, and timely presentation," and noted Carroll's inclusion of the roles of "Columbus, African slaves, Asian indentured laborers, Winston Churchill, Jamaica's Norman Manley, Fidel Castro, and U.S. presidents including Kennedy and Reagan" in shaping Caribbean history.

In *The Future of the United Nations,* published in 1985—a book Julie Burwinkel, writing for *Book Report,* called "an excellent overview"—Carroll examines the United Nations' origins and purpose, including the emphasis of its ideals as well as documented criticisms and failures. His treatment of these criticisms was noted by reviewer Linda Callaghan in *Booklist,* where she wrote that Carroll's "terse, clear narrative examines the various viewpoints and explains areas under attack."

"How I became interested in foreign affairs is difficult to say," Carroll has noted. "Spending time in the Pacific (Guam, Okinawa, and Japan) during my military service in World War II probably played a role. Then, at Hamilton College, a history professor named Graves (called 'Digger,' of course) steered me toward graduate studies at the School of Advanced International Studies of Johns Hopkins University, chiefly because an old friend of his was a leading professor there. As a result of this background, my writing has been concerned primarily with foreign affairs, but I have also written on subjects as diverse as America's pre-history, Eskimos, and consumer problems.

"The books I've written are meant for high-school readers, though some of the volumes find their way into general bookstores and college libraries. They are not in any sense textbooks; they are readable, concise supplementary reading. I must say I have been delighted to receive many letters from high-school students, teachers, and principals who have read my books and responded favorably."

■ **Works Cited**

Benoff, Symme J., review of *Anwar Sadat, School Library Journal,* November, 1982, p. 96.
Benoff, Symme J., review of *The Palestine Question, School Library Journal,* November, 1983, p. 130.
Burwinkel, Julie, review of *The Future of the United Nations, Book Report,* March/April, 1986, p. 48.
Callaghan, Linda, review of *The Future of the United Nations, Booklist,* December 15, 1985, p. 624.
Moore, Virginia B., review of *The Caribbean: Issues in U.S. Relations, Voice of Youth Advocates,* April, 1985, p. 59.
Wilms, Denise M., review of *The Palestine Question, Booklist,* June 15, 1983, p. 1336.
Wilms, Denise M., review of *The Caribbean: Issues in U.S. Relations, Booklist,* December 1, 1984, p. 521.

■ **For More Information See**

PERIODICALS

Book Report, January, 1984, p. 55.
School Library Journal, May, 1985, p. 100; January, 1986, p. 73.*

MARY M. CERULLO

CERULLO, Mary M. 1949-

■ **Personal**

Born September 6, 1949, in San Francisco, CA; daughter of George R. (an engineer) and Kathleen (a homemaker; maiden name, Waltz) Moore; married Arthur Cerullo (an attorney), August 19, 1973; children: Christopher, Margaret. *Education:* Tufts University, B.S. (cum laude), 1971; Boston University, M.Ed., 1981. *Avocational interests:* Hiking, biking, camping with family and friends.

■ **Addresses**

Home—101 Highland Rd., South Portland, ME 04106.

■ **Career**

RISE (Resources in Science Education), owner and consultant to schools and environmental organizations, 1988—; founder of Feral Press. Maine Mathematics and Science Alliance, communications coordinator. *Member:* Gulf of Maine Marine Education Association (president), Maine Writers and Publishers Association.

■ **Awards, Honors**

Outstanding Marine Educator of 1992, National Marine Education Association; Outstanding Science Trade Books for Children citations, National Science Teachers Association/Children's Book Council, for *Sharks: Challengers of the Deep* and *Lobsters: Gangsters of the Sea.*

■ **Writings**

Sharks: Challengers of the Deep, illustrated by Jeffrey L. Rotman, Dutton/Cobblehill, 1993.

Lobsters: Gangsters of the Sea, illustrated by Rotman, Dutton/Cobblehill, 1994.
Coral Reef: A City That Never Sleeps, Dutton/Cobblehill, 1996.

■ Work in Progress

A children's book on octopuses; a handbook for teachers on using children's literature to teach science.

■ Sidelights

Mary M. Cerullo told *SATA:* "At thirteen, I decided to become an oceanographer because adults were always asking me, 'What do you want to be when you grow up?' If they were asking, I figured I was supposed to have my future planned out. I studied through high school and college preparing for a career in oceanography. I put off six or more years of graduate school and started working at the New England Aquarium in Boston. It was there that I discovered I was really a dilettante, not a scientist, and that I preferred learning a little about a lot of different subjects rather than specializing in one narrow field of study.

"I love collecting children's books on science, both fact and fiction. I keep finding new favorite authors, including Joanna Cole, Patricia Lauber, and Lynne Cherry. One of the things I enjoy most is helping elementary teachers use children's trade books to teach science."

The author added, "Although I teach and write about other areas of science, I am most intrigued by ocean life, partly because so little is known about even the most popular (or infamous) animals of the sea, such as sharks, octopuses, dolphins, and whales. I found when I was researching *Sharks: Challengers of the Deep* that scientists couldn't even agree on how many species of sharks there are, let alone about their behavior, how long they live, and their number of offspring. Part of the reason I wrote the book was to dispel some of the prejudices against sharks that portray them as blood-thirsty man-eaters."

Sharks: Challengers of the Deep is filled with information about sharks' anatomy, habits, reproduction, survival, and behavior, including the fact that out of 350 species of sharks, only 5-10 percent are potential man-eaters, and the fact that a "good sized shark may go through 20,000 teeth in ten years."

Cerullo's second book explores the world of the crustacean known as "the gangster of the sea" because of its aggressive and territorial nature. *Lobsters: Gangsters of the Sea* not only explores the creature's physical characteristics, life cycle, courtship, and breeding, it also goes into great detail about the lobster industry and lobster consumption. According to *Kirkus Reviews,* the text is "spiced with plenty of the odd facts" including that lobsters at one time were "'poverty food' ... served to children, to prisoners, and to indentured servants."

Cerullo told *SATA:* "After more than twenty years of writing and teaching about the ocean, I recently became a certified scuba diver. My first open ocean dive was in the Bahamas, in the company of ten Caribbean reef sharks. I sat on the ocean floor almost breathless as sharks swarmed around a diver handing out fish scraps and then silently glided over my head. At one point, I turned around to discover a shark watching me from ten feet away. I looked at it, it looked at me. It blinked first (with a nictitating membrane) and swam off."

■ Works Cited

Cerullo, Mary M., *Sharks: Challengers of the Deep,* Cobblehill, 1993.
Review of *Lobsters: Gangsters of the Sea, Kirkus Reviews,* February 15, 1994.

■ For More Information See

PERIODICALS

American Scientist, November, 1994, p. 568.
Appraisal: Science Books for Young People, fall, 1993, p. 14.
Booklist, January 15, 1993, p. 887; March 1, 1994, p. 1254.
Horn Book, January/February 1994.
Kirkus Reviews, December 15, 1992, p. 1569.
School Library Journal, February, 1993, p. 96; March, 1994, p. 226; January, 1996, p. 115.
Science Books and Films, April, 1993, p. 84; August, 1994, p. 176.

*   *   *

CHETWIN, Grace

■ Personal

Born in Nottingham, England; immigrated to the United States, 1964; daughter of Charles William and Ada (Fletcher) Chetwin; married Arthur G. Roberts (a professional tennis player); children: Claire, Briony. *Education:* University of Southampton, B.A. (with honors).

■ Addresses

Home and office—37 Hitching Post Lane, Glen Cove, NY 11542. *Agent*—Jean V. Naggar, Jean V. Naggar Literary Agency, 336 East 73rd St., New York, NY 10021.

■ Career

High school English and French teacher in Auckland, New Zealand, in 1950s and 1960s; high school English teacher and department head in Devon, England, in 1960s; director of drama group in Auckland in 1970s; writer, 1983—; founder of Feral Press, 1995. Directed her own dance company in New Zealand for four years; producer of amateur plays and operas.

GRACE CHETWIN

■ Writings

FOR YOUNG ADULTS

On All Hallow's Eve, Lothrop, 1984.
Out of the Dark World, Lothrop, 1985.
Gom on Windy Mountain, Lothrop, 1986.
The Riddle and the Rune, Bradbury, 1987.
The Crystal Stair: From the Tales of Gom in the Legends of Ulm, Bradbury, 1988.
The Starstone, Bradbury, 1989.
Collidescope, Bradbury, 1990.
Child of the Air, Bradbury, 1991.
Friends in Time, Bradbury, 1992.
The Chimes of Alyafaleyn, Bradbury, 1993.
(Self-illustrated) *Jason's Seven Magical Night Rides,* Bradbury, 1994.

PICTURE BOOKS

Mr. Meredith and the Truly Remarkable Stone, illustrated by Catherine Stock, Bradbury, 1988.
Box and Cox, illustrated by David Small, Bradbury, 1990.
(Self-illustrated) *Rufus,* Feral Press, 1995.

OTHER

The Atheling: Volume I of the Last Legacy (adult), Tor, 1987.

Contributor to textbook, *Battling Dragons: Issues and Controversy in Children's Literature,* edited by Susan Lehr, Heinemann, 1995.

■ Adaptations

Rufus has been recorded on audio cassette.

■ Sidelights

Grace Chetwin is best known as the author of fantasy and science fiction books for young adults. Chetwin's first two books feature two sisters, Meg and Sue. *On All Hallow's Eve* tells the story of the sisters' recent emigration to the United States from England, Meg's dislike of her new home, and her struggle to deal with Kenny, a classmate who is a tease and a bully. Meg gets her revenge by humiliating Kenny at a Halloween party. When Meg and Sue run for home, they find themselves caught in a different world and time, and they must fight a battle that pits good against evil. Writing in *Booklist,* reviewer Barbara Elleman stated: "The children's adventures . . . contain enough chilling effects to keep readers immersed in the struggle."

Sisters Meg and Sue appear again in Chetwin's second novel, *Out of the Dark World,* a book Karen P. Smith, writing in *School Library Journal,* called "an unusual science fiction fantasy which combines Welsh lore with modern-day computer technology." In this complicated fantasy, Meg materializes the spirits of Peter Saltifer, an abrupt, outspoken Welshman, and the infamous enchantress Morgan le Fay to help her save her dying cousin from forces of evil.

Chetwin's fantasies have been influenced by European folktales, especially the four books in her series about the wizard Gom. Gom is the tenth son of woodcutter Stig and his wife, a mysterious woman who disappeared on the day of Gom's birth, leaving him only a rune, or magic stone. By his tenth birthday, Gom is small and dwarf-like, has three moles on his chin, and can communicate with animals. His strange powers lead him to a hidden cache of gold where he meets Dismas Skeller, whom Kathleen Brachmann in *School Library Journal* called "as evil a gold-seeking malefactor as ever trod his way across the pages of a fantasy." When Stig dies, Gom sets off for Far Away to find his mother, his heritage, and his destiny.

During his quest for the gold, Gom discovered that his mother was really Harga the Brown, a great wizard. In the second book of the series, *The Riddle and the Rune,* Gom uses the stone, his only clue to his mother's existence, to reunite the pair. However, the reunion is short-lived. In *The Crystal Stair: From Tales of Gom in the Legends of Ulm,* Harga is called off to do battle against the destruction of Ulm; Gom must become a wizard himself to be of any help, and his mother leaves him with the names of three wizards who might become his mentor. *Voice of Youth Advocates* contributor Barbara Evans stated that "the story is well-written and the action exciting."

The final book of the series, *The Starstone,* finds Gom at odds with Folgan, his reluctant mentor. Eventually Gom finds himself on his own, having to use Harga's old notebooks to complete his education in order to thwart the evil Katak's plans to take over the world of Ulm. In the midst of this cosmic struggle between good and evil, the teenage Gom finds a love interest. Anne Raymer, writing in *Voice of Youth Advocates,* called *The Star-stone* a "pure fantasy adventure where a young boy comes of age through a fight with phantom and flesh enemies," and Ruth S. Vose in *School Library Journal* stated that "followers of Gom's adventures will devour this new addition to his story."

In 1989 and 1990, Chetwin digressed from her fantasy writing and created two picture books. *Mr. Meredith and the Truly Remarkable Stone* has its roots in the old "Fisherman and His Wife" tale. The story, told with "a chanting, dancing rhythm," according to a critic in *Publishers Weekly,* begins on a day when young Mr. Meredith trips over an old stone which seems remarkable to him. He brings it home to his greenhouse and invites his friends over to view his find. Then the setting does not seem to do the stone justice, so he builds a larger edifice to house it. This pattern continues even after the stone is forgotten altogether—until old Mr. Meredith trips over it once again and gives it a simple home on his bedroom windowsill. According to Chetwin, the tale is "a metaphor for honoring the nucleus of a creative idea, an allegory about how humble an original idea can be, a reminder that we should never forget the origins of what we do."

The title characters in *Box and Cox,* Chetwin's second picture book, come from a Victorian vaudeville routine. Mr. Box and Mr. Cox both rent a room from the portly Mrs. Bouncer. What they do not know is that they have both rented the same room. When Mr. Box leaves for his night job, Mrs. Bouncer runs in, clears away his messy belongings, and installs the super-neat Mr. Cox's possessions in their tidy places just before he arrives home for supper. This routine continues until both Cox and Box ask Mrs. Bouncer for her hand in marriage—and she accepts. When the two men discover the double deception, they pack up and leave. Mrs. Bouncer, upset at first, soon hangs out a sign: "Single Room to Rent." In her critique in the *New York Times Book Review,* Moira Hodgson claimed the book had "all the elements of a good classic farce: split-second timing, a tightly structured plot and instantly recognizable archetypes."

Chetwin returned to fantasy for young adults in a book Lesa M. Holstine, writing in *Voice of Youth Advocates,* described as "a riveting story of time travel in which three civilizations collide." *Collidescope* tells the story of Hahn, a cyborg (a bionically-enhanced human being) from the future, Frankie, a present-day Long Island teenager, and Sky-fire-trail, a Delaware Indian of pre-Colonial America. When these three, traveling from different points in time, do meet, they manage to offer each other help, solace, and friendship in what Susan L. Rogers of *School Library Journal* called "fast-paced, action-packed pursuits through time and space." Chetwin explained to *SATA* that *Collidescope* is "an examination of what humanity is, of what makes a human being."

The time travel theme continues in *Friends in Time,* which tells of Emma Gibson, a lonely sixth grader who suddenly finds a friend in Abigail Bentley, a ten-year old

who has been mysteriously transported to the present from 1846. The action in *The Chimes of Alyafaleyn* takes place in a different world all together: a world where floating golden spheres, called "heynim," control the weather and have healing powers. Because of her ability to attract these spheres away from their rightful owners, young Caidrun is forced to suppress her talents. When she grows older and runs off to take her revenge, her only friend, Tamborel, sets out to find her. A contributor in *Kirkus Reviews* labeled the book a "soft-edged romantic fantasy," and an "entertaining, if far-fetched, love story."

A different sort of relationship is the foundation for Chetwin's 1994 work, *Jason's Seven Magical Night Rides.* Eleven-year-old Jason is being raised by his mother, but he longs to know what it would be like to have a father in his life. One night, a mysterious stranger appears and offers him seven rides on famous mythical horses, including Pegasus, Chiron the centaur, and the Trojan Horse. As a *Kirkus Reviews* critic noted, "each episode teaches the fatherless boy a bit about maturity and responsibility." This is a running theme throughout Chetwin's works: characters all go through obstacle-laden paths and feelings of failure, inadequacy, shame,

A fatherless eleven-year-old boy finds himself fighting side-by-side with ancient heroes in Chetwin's self-illustrated work *Jason's Seven Magical Night Rides.*

anger, guilt, and loneliness, only to come out at the end stronger, more confident, and worthy of even greater adventures.

In 1995, Chetwin produced her first book for Feral Press, a publishing company she founded. *Rufus,* Chetwin told *SATA,* "deals with loss and honesty." In the work, a child's beloved pet dies. "The child keeps her dignity by acknowledging the loss and deciding on her own if she wants to accept a new animal," Chetwin said.

■ Works Cited

Brachmann, Kathleen, review of *Gom on Windy Mountain, School Library Journal,* May, 1986, p. 89.

Review of *The Chimes of Alyafaleyn, Kirkus Reviews,* October 29, 1993.

Elleman, Barbara, review of *On All Hallow's Eve, Booklist,* October 15, 1984, p. 304.

Evans, Barbara, review of *The Crystal Stair: From the Tales of Gom in the Legends of Ulm, Voice of Youth Advocates,* June, 1988, p. 95.

Hodgson, Moira, review of *Box and Cox, New York Times Book Review,* July 1, 1990.

Holstine, Lesa M., review of *Collidescope, Voice of Youth Advocates,* April, 1990, p. 37.

Review of *Jason's Seven Magical Night Rides, Kirkus Reviews,* April 15, 1994.

Review of *Mr. Meredith and the Truly Remarkable Stone, Publishers Weekly,* March 10, 1989, p. 87.

Raymer, Anne, review of *The Starstone, Voice of Youth Advocates,* October, 1989, p. 220.

Rogers, Susan L., review of *Collidescope, School Library Journal,* May, 1990, p. 122.

Smith, Karen P., review of *Out of the Dark World, School Library Journal,* January, 1986, pp. 64-65.

Vose, Ruth S., review of *The Starstone, School Library Journal,* June, 1989, p. 103.

■ For More Information See

PERIODICALS

Horn Book, November/December, 1986, pp. 743-744; May/June, 1990, p. 321.

Kirkus Reviews, February 1, 1988, p. 168.

Publishers Weekly, January 29, 1988, p. 418.

School Library Journal, August, 1989, p. 116; July, 1992, p. 72.

Voice of Youth Advocates, December, 1986, p. 234; August, 1991, p. 178; October, 1992, p. 236.

Washington Post Book World, May 13, 1990, p. 18.

Wilson Library Bulletin, June, 1993, p. 112.

*   *   *

CLEWES, Dorothy (Mary) 1907-

■ Personal

Born July 6, 1907, in Nottingham, England; daughter of Frank and Annie Gertrude Parkin; married Winston David Armstrong Clewes (a writer), 1932 (died, 1957). *Education:* Attended private school in Nottingham, and University of Nottingham. *Religion:* Church of England. *Hobbies and other interests:* Travel.

■ Addresses

Home—Soleig, 1 Kings Ride, Alfriston, East Sussex BN26 5XP, England. *Agent*—Curtis Brown, 162-168 Regent St., London WIR 5TB, England.

■ Career

Secretary and dispenser to a physician in Nottingham, England, 1924-32; writer. Speaker at schools and libraries in England and the United States. *Wartime service:* Drove an ambulance during World War II. *Member:* PEN (member of executive committee), Society of Authors, National Book League.

■ Awards, Honors

Junior Literary Guild award, 1957, for *The Runaway.*

■ Writings

FICTION; FOR YOUNG PEOPLE

The Rivals of Maidenhurst, Nelson (London), 1925.

The Cottage in the Wild Wood, illustrated by Irene Hawkins, Faber (London), 1945.

The Stream in the Wild Wood, illustrated by Irene Hawkins, Faber, 1946.

The Treasure in the Wild Wood, illustrated by Irene Hawkins, Faber, 1947.

The Wild Wood (contains *The Cottage in the Wild Wood* and *The Stream in the Wild Wood*), illustrated by Irene Hawkins, Coward McCann (New York City), 1948.

The Fair in the Wild Wood, illustrated by Irene Hawkins, Faber, 1949.

DOROTHY CLEWES

Henry Hare's Boxing Match, illustrated by Patricia W. Turner, Chatto & Windus (London), 1950, Coward McCann, 1950.

Henry Hare's Earthquake, illustrated by Patricia W. Turner, Chatto & Windus, 1950, Coward McCann, 1951.

Henry Hare, Painter and Decorator, illustrated by Patricia W. Turner, Chatto & Windus, 1951.

Henry Hare and the Kidnapping of Selina Squirrel, illustrated by Patricia W. Turner, Chatto & Windus, 1951.

The Adventure of the Scarlet Daffodil, illustrated by R. G. Campbell, Chatto & Windus, 1952, as *The Mystery of the Scarlet Daffodil,* Coward McCann, 1953.

The Mystery of the Blue Admiral, illustrated by J. Marianne Moll, Coward McCann, 1954, Collins (London), 1955.

The Secret, illustrated by Peggy Beetles, Hamish Hamilton (London), 1956, Coward McCann, 1956.

The Runaway, illustrated by Peggy Beetles, Hamish Hamilton, 1957, illustrated by Sofia, Coward McCann, 1957.

Adventure on Rainbow Island, illustrated by Shirley Hughes, Collins, 1957, as *Mystery on Rainbow Island,* Coward McCann, 1957.

The Jade Green Cadillac, illustrated by Shirley Hughes, Collins, 1958, as *The Mystery of the Jade Green Cadillac,* Coward McCann, 1958.

The Happiest Day, illustrated by Peggy Beetles, Hamish Hamilton, 1958, Coward McCann, 1959.

The Old Pony, illustrated by Peggy Beetles, Hamish Hamilton, 1959, Coward McCann, 1960.

Hide and Seek, illustrated by Peggy Beetles, Hamish Hamilton, 1959, Coward McCann, 1960.

The Lost Tower Treasure, illustrated by Shirley Hughes, Collins, 1960, as *The Mystery of the Lost Tower Treasure,* Coward McCann, 1960.

The Hidden Key, illustrated by Peggy Beetles, Hamish Hamilton, 1960, Coward McCann, 1961.

The Singing Strings, illustrated by Shirley Hughes, Collins, 1961, as *Mystery of the Singing Strings,* Coward McCann, 1961.

All the Fun of the Fair, illustrated by Juliette Palmer, Hamish Hamilton, 1961, Coward McCann, 1962.

Wilberforce and the Slaves, illustrated by Peter Edwards, Hutchinson (London), 1961.

Skyraker and the Iron Imp, illustrated by Peter Edwards, Hutchinson, 1962.

The Purple Mountain, illustrated by Robert Broomfield, Collins, 1962, as *The Golden Eagle,* Coward McCann, 1962.

The Birthday, illustrated by Juliette Palmer, Hamish Hamilton, 1962, Coward McCann, 1963.

The Branch Line, illustrated by Juliette Palmer, Hamish Hamilton/Coward McCann, 1963.

Operation Smuggle, illustrated by Shirley Hughes, Collins, 1964, as *The Mystery of the Midnight Smugglers,* Coward McCann, 1964.

Boys and Girls Come out to Play, illustrated by Jane Paton, Hamish Hamilton, 1964.

The Holiday, illustrated by Janet Duchesne, Hamish Hamilton, 1964, Coward McCann, 1964.

Guide Dog, illustrated by Peter Burchard, Hamish Hamilton, 1965, Coward McCann, 1965; as *Dog for the Dark,* White Lion (London), 1974.

Red Ranger and the Combine Harvester, illustrated by Peter Edwards, Hutchinson, 1966.

Roller Skates, Scooter and Bike, illustrated by Constance Marshall, Hamish Hamilton, 1966, illustrated by Sofia, Coward McCann, 1966.

A Boy Like Walt, Collins, 1967, Coward McCann, 1967.

A Bit of Magic, illustrated by Robert Hales, Hamish Hamilton, 1967.

A Girl Like Cathy, Collins, 1968.

Adopted Daughter, Coward McCann, 1968.

Upside-Down Willie, illustrated by Edward Ardizzone, Hamish Hamilton, 1968.

Special Branch Willie, illustrated by Edward Ardizzone, Hamish Hamilton, 1969.

Peter and the Jumbie, illustrated by Robert Hales, Hamish Hamilton, 1969.

Fire-Brigade Willie, illustrated by Edward Ardizzone, Hamish Hamilton, 1970.

Library Lady, illustrated by Robert Hales, Chatto Boyd & Oliver (London), 1970, as *The Library,* illustrated by Reisie Lonette, Coward McCann, 1971.

Two Bad Boys, illustrated by Lynette Hemmant, Hamish Hamilton, 1971.

The End of Summer, Coward McCann, 1971.

Storm over Innish, Heinemann, 1972, Nelson (Nashville), 1973.

A Skein of Geese, illustrated by Janet Duchesne, Chatto Boyd & Oliver, 1972.

Ginny's Boy, Heinemann, 1973.

Hooray for Me, illustrated by Michael Jackson, Heinemann, 1973.

Wanted—a Grand, illustrated by Robert Micklewright, Chatto & Windus, 1974.

Missing from Home, Heinemann, 1975, Harcourt, 1978.

Nothing to Declare, Heinemann, 1976.

The Testing Year, Heinemann, 1977.

The Adventures of Willie (includes *Upside-Down Willie, Special Branch Willie,* and *Fire-Brigade Willie*), illustrated by Caroline Crossland, MacRae (London), 1991.

NONFICTION; FOR CHILDREN

Guide Dogs for the Blind, photographs by Louis Klemantaski, Hamish Hamilton, 1966.

(Editor) *The Secret of the Sea: An Anthology of Underwater Exploration and Adventure,* illustrated by Jeroo Roy, Heinemann, 1973.

NOVELS; FOR ADULTS

She Married a Doctor, Jenkins (London), 1943, as *Stormy Hearts,* Arcadia (New York City), 1944.

Shepherd's Hill, Sampson Low (London), 1945.

To Man Alone, Jenkins, 1945, Arcadia, 1945.

A Stranger in the Valley, Harrap (London), 1948.

The Blossom on the Bough, Harrap, 1949.

Summer Cloud, Harrap, 1951.

Merry-Go-Round, Hodder & Stoughton (London), 1954.

I Came to a Wood, Hale (London), 1956.

OTHER

Contributor to *The Eleanor Farjeon Giftbook.* Contributor to magazines and annuals for children.

■ Adaptations

The Adventure of the Scarlet Daffodil and *Operation Smuggle* were adapted for British television.

■ Sidelights

English author Dorothy Clewes has written many books for children of all ages—from pre-school to young adult—in a career that has spanned over three decades. From the popular "Willie" books to well-liked teen novels that include *Storm over Innish* and the thrilling *Missing from Home,* her books have pleased both British and American readers with their interesting settings, intriguing subjects, and likeable, well-drawn characters.

Born Dorothy Mary Parkin on July 6, 1907, Clewes was raised in Nottingham, England. "I have always written, as long as I can remember," Clewes once told *SATA*—"fairy stories and animal stories for newspapers and magazines when I was in my earliest teens, a full length school novel when I was 18." She attended a private school in Nottingham before going on to study chemistry and medicine at the University of Nottingham. After college, she worked for her family's doctor in Nottingham while putting the finishing touches on her first novel, *The Rivals of Maidenhurst,* a story about life at a girl's private school that was published in 1925. Clewes continued her work as a physician's secretary for nine years and drove an ambulance and worked in a nursery during World War II.

In 1932 she married Winston Clewes, a prolific writer of short stories, novels, and plays for radio and television. Winston encouraged his new wife to devote herself to writing on a full-time basis; Clewes eventually began to intersperse children's writing with her light romantic novels at the suggestion of her agent. She wrote nine romantic novels, including *Shepherd's Hill, To Man Alone,* and *The Blossom on the Bough,* before deciding to focus her attention on creating children's books. When her husband passed away in 1957, Clewes's work helped her to deal with the loss. "I suppose this all began as a fascinating hobby," she once explained, "began to be a lucrative one, and then, when my husband died, I decided to use it as a serious career. I miss very much the discussions and criticisms he used to give, as he was a writer in a quite different field so that we could read each other's work quite objectively."

Several years after her husband's death, Clewes was working on a story about smuggling along the South of England near the English Channel coast. She fell in love with the area, left her home in London, and moved to the old smuggling village of Alfriston, Sussex—the same town where she had set her story. It would be in this new home that Clewes would write many of her popular

The Runaway, **winner of the 1957 Junior Literary Guild award, is about an English girl who contemplates running away from home after she moves from the city to the country, but she decides not to after making new friends.** (Illustration by Sofia from *The Runaway.*)

books, including *Roller Skates, Scooter and Bike, The Library,* and *Special Branch Willie.*

Special Branch Willie is one of three books featuring Willie, a likeable young lad who was featured in *Upside-Down Willie,* published in 1968. When the reader is introduced to the enthusiastic Willie, he has decided that he will join the circus; but the only acrobatic trick he knows is a handstand, so he practices it constantly. When we next meet up with him in *Special Branch Willie,* the fickle lad has changed his mind and now longs to be a policeman. When he gets the chance to use the emergency number after he discovers a small fire, the attention and praise given him by the hardworking firemen cause Willie to change his career goals again; he wants to be a fireman! Hoses and ladders and soaked parents come into play in *Fire-Brigade Willie,* as the boy's excessive enthusiasm causes mischief—but also teaches him that wanting something isn't enough, that time and hard work are also needed to do things well. Clewes tells Willie's stories in a "direct, simple and entirely gripping" manner, in the words of a *Times Literary Supplement* reviewer. The three books about Willie were reissued as *The Adventures of Willie* in 1991.

Clewes has always had a special knack for knowing what interests young boys. In *Roller Skates, Scooter and Bike,* curious young boys Kay, Rory, and Gerald investigate a new road going through their small town; after ducking for cover during a sudden rainstorm, they return to find that two of their means of transportation have disappeared. During their attempt to solve the mystery and get their scooter and bicycle back, the three boys meet up with a band of gypsies, a butcher, a baker, and the local rag-man. Quick-witted Kay, Rory, and Gerald are also featured in several other books by Clewes, including *The Branch Line* and *The Old Pony.*

In *The Library,* two older brothers come under the sway of their little sister as six-year-old Ginny gets a card at the town's brand new library. She tries to get big brothers Dudley and Charlie interested in books rather than the gang of tough kids they've been spending their time with, and finally hooks them into helping with a library display on fishing. When valuable fishing rods are stolen from the display, Ginny's brothers are among the suspects. Her efforts to prove their innocence and get them to read more books engages young readers in a story where "family relationships are warm and realistic, particularly those between Ginny and her brothers," according to a *Bulletin of the Center for Children's Books* reviewer.

"I take most of my material from first-hand experience and information," Clewes once explained to *SATA.* "I like a real background in my stories and feel that coming fresh to the experience myself adds a freshness to my writing." The real background of *Guide Dog* is the result of the research she did in the breeding, training, and use of seeing-eye dogs. In the story, nineteen-year-old Roley Rolandson is blinded for life after a package explodes near his face during his part-time job delivering mail at the post office. With his dreams of becoming a doctor destroyed, Roley becomes bitter and depressed, but two friends encourage him to get a seeing-eye dog. Efforts like those of Roley in learning to use his canine compass are further studied in Clewes' *Guide Dogs for the Blind,* as she describes the work of the British Guide Dogs for the Blind Association and the way in which a strong bond is established between a sightless human and a trained guide dog.

Guide Dog is but one of many books that Clewes has written for older teen readers. One of her most popular novels for this age group is 1972's *Storm over Innish,* which takes place on a remote island off the coast of Ireland. In the novel, Letty Ward and her family have moved to Innish when her brother dies tragically. Her parents' relationship begins to fall apart; they fight constantly while each tries vainly to cope with the loss, and fifteen-year-old Letty is left alone to deal with her own grief. When a young man is discovered washed up into a shoreline cavern, the lives of both Letty and her parents are transformed. Obviously well-educated despite being confused by temporary amnesia, the enigmatic young man prompts Letty's mother, a well-known artist, to continue to paint and engages her father, a retired Oxford don, in conversations that reawaken his

intellectual faculties. When the young man recalls that he is John O'Neil, a member of an old Innish family, he returns to the mainland school where he is enrolled as an art student, and he and Letty make plans to one day reunite. *Storm over Innish* was praised by *Publishers Weekly* for its "engrossing plot against a sharply realistic background of land and sea."

While *Storm over Innish* had its moments of mystery, Clewes's *Missing from Home,* set in southern France, is a full-fledged mystery novel. Clara and Maxwell Grant have moved from England with their parents to live in the beautiful French countryside. But things fall apart after their father, an art teacher, experiences a mid-life crisis and runs off with a spoiled young student, leaving his wife Sara to fall into alcoholic depression. Plotting to force their father's return by running away from home, Clara and Maxwell leave for an ancient campsite in the nearby hills. There they meet up with Louis, the seemingly amiable son of their family housekeeper, who promises to help them but actually plots, along with an even more dastardly accomplice, to extort money from the Grant parents for their children's return. Meanwhile, Mr. Grant has second thoughts about leaving his wife and family and returns to help search for the

An injured boy, washed up on the shore of a private island, changes the lives of Letty and her parents in this 1973 novel.

children who are now *really* missing from home. A sequel to the popular *Missing from Home, The Testing Year* describes what happens to the kidnapper Louis after he is released from prison. Resolving to "go straight" and getting a job at a local vineyard, he is manipulated by fellow kidnapper Pierre to become involved in Pierre's quest for revenge until the intervention of girlfriend Carrie keeps him from resuming the criminal path.

Clewes' other books for older teens include *A Boy like Walt, Adopted Daughter,* and 1976's *Nothing to Declare.* In the first novel, published in 1967, Norma's conservative, snobbish parents prohibit her from going out with "a boy like Walt," a garage mechanic who, although he hangs out with the fast-driving crowd, is basically a hard-working young man. When he and friend Trevor decide to "borrow" an expensive car to impress Norma's parents, they find themselves involved in grand auto theft and worse. Meanwhile, Norma's shallow older brother is pushed by his parents' unreasonable expectations to do something that ultimately disgraces the family far more than Norma's relationship with Walt.

Clewes examination of how the actions and expectations of parents can distort the lives of their children is also seen in 1968's *Adopted Daughter.* After her mother dies, Cathy, an adopted teen, goes to live with her adult sister Dale, and rebels against Dale's strictness by sneaking out to visit a new boyfriend. The problems in the household are compounded when Cathy learns of her other siblings' dysfunctional relationships, and the fact that she has inspired a secretive relationship between her fourteen-year-old niece and a middle-aged man. Cathy has been curious about her natural parents ever since her mother died, and now her curiosity becomes an obsession. When she discovers that Dale is, in fact, her natural mother, her feelings of confusion grow even worse until she is able to come to terms with her relatives and her situation.

Feelings of not belonging are also common to Clewes' *The End of Summer.* After her widowed father remarries, seventeen-year-old Elizabeth runs away to London. Bad luck follows her both on the job and in her romantic life, and it isn't until her stepmother comes to the rescue that Elizabeth begins to take control of her life.

Throughout her writing career, Clewes has been praised by critics for the lack of condescension in her books for young people. Her realistic characters and vivid settings have continued to engage the imagination of both elementary and high school-aged children. "I do not find that English and American readers are so different," Clewes explained to *SATA,* "and try and write an honest and unsentimental book, not pointing morals but leaving them there for children to find for themselves. I don't think I have ever written down, and don't really subscribe to the idea of children's books and adult books being in a strongly emphasized category—a good children's book I feel should be interesting to an adult, and vice versa."

In a desperate attempt to force their separated parents to reunite, a brother and sister run away from home, not knowing their plan would lead them into a web of intrigue. (Cover illustration by Loretta Trezzo.)

■ Works Cited

Review of *Fire-Brigade Willy, Times Literary Supplement,* August 14, 1970, p. 909.

Review of *The Library, Bulletin of the Center for Children's Books,* April, 1971, p. 120.

Review of *Storm over Innish, Publishers Weekly,* November 19, 1973, p. 61.

■ For More Information See

BOOKS

Twentieth-Century Children's Writers, 4th edition, St. James Press, 1995, pp. 217-19.

PERIODICALS

Bulletin of the Center for Children's Books, November, 1967; February, 1974; February, 1978.

Horn Book, August, 1965, pp. 394-95; August, 1967, p. 474; February, 1969, p. 58.

Junior Bookshelf, April, 1977, p. 107; June, 1978, p. 150.

School Library Journal, June 15, 1966, pp. 3256-57; May 15, 1971, p. 1801; November, 1978, p. 58.

Times Literary Supplement, November 17, 1966, p. 1053; November 24, 1966, p. 1087; December 11, 1970, p. 1459; July 14, 1972, p. 814; March 29, 1974, p. 326; July 5, 1974, p. 720.

* * *

COMYNS, Nantz
See COMYNS-TOOHEY, Nantz

* * *

COMYNS-TOOHEY, Nantz 1956-
(Nantz Comyns)

■ Personal

Born January 3, 1956, in Portland, ME; daughter of William and Helen (Dewey) Comyns; married Paul Toohey (in computers), May 10, 1986; children: Brendan, Trevor. *Education:* University of South Maine, B.F.A. (cum laude); University of Pennsylvania, M.F.A. (sculpture), 1982. *Religion:* "Life." *Hobbies and other interests:* Skiing, family, skating.

■ Addresses

Home—P.O. Box 2042, West Scarborough, ME 04074.

■ Career

Sculptor and gallery director; touring artist through the Maine Arts Commission. Has worked at Philadelphia Museum of Fine Art and University of Pennsylvania Archaeological Museum; designed and produced Please Touch Museum, Philadelphia, PA, 1982. *Exhibitions:* Work exhibited in galleries and museums throughout New England. Exhibitions include "Innerscapes," Bath Performing Art Center, Bath, ME, 1985; "Emerging Maine Artists," Barn Gallery, Ogunquit, ME, 1989; "Furs, Feathers and Fins," Maine Art Gallery, Wisscassette, ME, 1993.

■ Awards, Honors

National Museum Association grant, 1980, for developing exhibit on Mesopotamia.

■ Illustrator

(Under name Nantz Comyns) Sis Boulos Deans, *Chicka-dee-dee-dee: A Very Special Bird,* Gannett, 1987.

Deans, *Emily Bee in the Kingdom of Flowers,* Gannett, 1988.

Deans, *The Legend of Blazing Bear,* Windswept House, 1992.*

NANTZ COMYNS-TOOHEY

CORRIN, Sara 1918-

■ Personal

Born August 25, 1918, in London, England; daughter of Jacob and Fanny (Shereshevsky) Nirenstein; married Stephen Corrin (a writer and translator), October, 1938; children: Evelyn, Julia Corrin Nightingale. *Education:* University of London, Teacher's Certificate (with distinction), 1956, Advanced Diploma in Child Development, 1963. *Politics:* Socialist. *Religion:* "Humanist."

■ Addresses

Home—10 Russell Gardens, London NW11 9NL, England.

■ Career

Primary school teacher, 1956-63; University of London, London, England, teacher of child development course, 1963-64; primary school teacher, 1964-65; Hertfordshire College of Higher Education, Watford, England, lecturer, 1965-67, senior lecturer in education, 1967-83. Writer, 1964—. *Wartime service:* Women's Home Army, 1943.

■ Awards, Honors

Best Picture Book of the Season citation, *New Yorker* magazine, 1984, for *Mrs. Fox's Wedding;* Premio "Critici in Erba," Bologna, 1990, for *The Pied Piper of Hamelin.*

■ Writings

FOR CHILDREN; WITH HUSBAND, STEPHEN CORRIN

(Reteller) *Mrs. Fox's Wedding,* illustrated by Errol Le Cain, Doubleday, c. 1980.
(Reteller) *The Pied Piper of Hamelin,* illustrated by Le Cain, Faber, 1987, Harcourt, 1989.
Classic Fairy Tales, Faber, 1987.

EDITOR WITH STEPHEN CORRIN

Stories for Seven-Year-Olds and Other Young Readers, illustrated by Shirley Hughes, Faber, 1964.
Stories for Six-Year-Olds and Other Young Readers, illustrated by Hughes, Faber, 1967.
Stories for Eight-Year-Olds and Other Young Readers, illustrated by Hughes, Faber, 1971.
A Time to Laugh: Thirty Stories for Young Children, illustrated by Gerald Rose, Faber, 1972, published as *A Time to Laugh: Funny Stories for Children,* 1985.
Stories for Five-Year-Olds and Other Young Readers, illustrated by Hughes, Faber, 1973.
Stories for Under-Fives, Faber, 1974.
Stories for Tens and Over, Faber, 1976.
More Stories for Seven-Year-Olds and Other Young Readers, illustrated by Hughes, Faber, 1978.
Stories for Nine-Year-Olds and Other Young Readers, illustrated by Hughes, Faber, 1979.
The Faber Book of Modern Fairy Tales, illustrated by Ann Strugnell, Faber, 1981.

SARA and STEPHEN CORRIN

Once upon a Rhyme: One Hundred One Poems for Young Children, illustrated by Jill Bennett, Faber, 1982.
Round the Christmas Tree, illustrated by Bennett, Faber, 1983.
The Faber Book of Christmas Stories, illustrated by Bennett, Faber, 1984.
Pet Stories for Children, illustrated by Bennett, Faber, 1985, published as *The Puffin Book of Pet Stories,* Puffin, 1987.
Imagine That!: Fifteen Fantastic Tales (fairy tales), illustrated by Bennett, Faber, 1986.
The Faber Book of Favourite Fairy Tales, illustrated by Juan Wijngaard, Faber, 1988.
More Stories for Under-Fives, illustrated by Vanessa Julian-Ottie, Faber, 1988.
Laugh out Loud: More Funny Stories for Children, illustrated by Rose, Faber, 1989.
The Faber Book of Golden Fairytales, illustrated by Peter Melnyczuk, Faber, 1993.

■ Work in Progress

An anthology for young adults.

■ Sidelights

Since the 1960s, Sara Corrin and her husband Stephen have edited numerous collections of stories and poems for children. The Corrins' books are suitable for children in age groups ranging from under five to ten and older. Beginning in 1964 with *Stories for Seven-Year-Olds and Other Young Readers,* they have presented read-aloud stories such as James Thurber's "Many Moons," Charles Dickens's "The Magic Fishbone" (both in *Stories for Eight-Year-Olds and Other Young Readers*), and Rudyard Kipling's "The White Seal," along with Greek myths and folktales (all in *Stories for Nine-Year-Olds and Other Young Readers*).

Critics have praised the Corrins for dividing their collections into various age groups, making it easy for teachers and parents to choose appropriate stories. In *Stories for Under-Fives,* for instance, the Corrins compile stories that contain "a foundation of security so that very young children won't become alarmed," as *Books and Bookmen* contributor Lavinia Learmont noted. Similarly, *Stories for Tens and Over,* which Margery Fisher of *Growing Point* called a "sensible collection," includes tales that will "satisfy young readers some way into the 'teens."

Fourteen years after their first book was published, *More Stories for Seven-Year-Olds and Other Young Readers* appeared; this "new addition to their praiseworthy collection," according to Colin Mills in the *Times Literary Supplement,* has "a wider thematic and geographical range," and includes tales from Ireland, Greece, Russia, Italy, and Canada. *Stories for Nine-Year-Olds and Other Young Readers* encompasses stories by such notable writers as Gerald Durrell, James Thurber, Saki, Rudyard Kipling, and Jack London. *Junior Bookshelf* critic G. Bott called it a "varied and pleasing collection, suitable for a range of reading abilities." In a review for the *Times Literary Supplement,* Joy Chant praised the book "whole-heartedly" and noted that the majority of tales "are concerned either with high-spirited farce, or with the triumph of wit over power; both themes especially appealing at the age of nine."

The Corrins combined two variants of a Brothers Grimm tale to produce a picture book entitled *Mrs. Fox's Wedding,* published in 1980. In a *New Yorker* review, Faith McNulty called this story of Widow Fox's painstaking search for a new husband "one of the best picture books of the season." This work was followed by a new edition of humorous tales called *A Time to Laugh: Thirty Stories for Young Children,* which includes such familiar characters as Pooh, Mrs. Pepperpot, and Brer Rabbit, and *Once Upon a Rhyme: 101 Poems for Young Children,* which Peter Neumeyer of the *School Library Journal* described as containing "poems children do like, rather than ones adults think they should."

These collections were followed by *Round the Christmas Tree,* sixteen short stories (by authors such as Ruth Sawyer, Alison Uttley, and V. H. Drummond) with Christmas as their central theme. Neil Philip, writing for the *Times Educational Supplement,* called the stories well suited for "that warm and pleasurable transaction which takes place between the seated adult and the child on the knee." The theme of the Corrins' next collection was one of children's favorite subjects: pets. *Pet Stories for Children* includes such characters as dogs, cats, ponies, hamsters, giraffes, a kangaroo, an owl, a crocodile, a goat, and a jackdaw. Stories include Joan Aiken's retelling of Edgar Allan Poe's poem of Arabel and the raven, Adele Geras's tale of children and friendship, "The Christmas Cat," and the Russian story "Katya, the Crocodile and the School Pets." In Fisher's review for *Growing Point,* she deemed *Pet Stories* a "useful book altogether for wet days, primary school libraries and for parents looking for something to read aloud to restless children."

The collection of pet stories was followed in 1986 by *Imagine That!: Fifteen Fantastic Tales,* which a *Kirkus Reviews* critic called a "small, well-chosen collection." This international group of tales includes one about a wife who tricks her husband into marrying her four times; one about a princess who is ugly every day but Sunday searching for a prince who is handsome every day but Sunday; and several about people who are granted wishes and use them foolishly. Renee Steinberg's review in *School Library Journal* called these tales "excellent for read-alouds, storytelling, and creative dramatics."

In reviewing the Corrins' next work for *Children's Book Review Service,* T. R. Hollingsworth called their retelling of *The Pied Piper of Hamelin* a "classic," while *Booklist* critic Ilene Cooper noted that the Corrins' version "has a special panache" and is "chronicled with both drama and humor." Reviewers also praised the authors for ending the book with an epilogue about what really

happened in the small German town of Hamelin. The Corrins again turned to fairy tales in two collections: *The Faber Book of Favourite Fairy Tales,* and *The Faber Book of Golden Fairytales. Books for Keeps* contributor Fiona Walters called the former "a stunning book," while *Junior Bookshelf* critic R. Baines called the latter collection of twenty-six stories concerning gold a "well chosen and interesting" book containing some "robust yarns."

"I have an unquenchable desire to share great yarns and beautiful tales with children, whose imaginations feed on these wondrous stories," Sara Corrin once said. "They speak to children at the deepest level and make a direct and intuitive appeal to the imagination. The stories we tell arise out of the human condition, hence their universal appeal. Our books include translations from the Grimms, Charles Perrault, Alexandr Afanasyev, and Antoine Galland (whose French translations brought the *Arabian Nights* to Europe and the West)."

■ Works Cited

Baines, R., review of *The Faber Book of Golden Fairytales, Junior Bookshelf,* December, 1993, p. 230.

The Corrins served as editors for this collection of fifteen humorous stories. (Cover illustration by Gerald Rose.)

After her husband dies, Mrs. Fox must deal with a seemingly endless line of suitors in the Corrin's retelling of *Mrs. Fox's Wedding*. (Illustration by Errol Le Cain.)

Bott, G., review of *Stories for Nine-Year-Olds and Other Young Readers*, *Junior Bookshelf*, June, 1980, p. 126.

Chant, Joy, review of *Stories for Nine-Year-Olds and Other Young Readers*, *Times Literary Supplement*, December 14, 1979, p. 129.

Cooper, Ilene, review of *The Pied Piper of Hamelin*, *Booklist*, April 1, 1989, p. 1380.

Fisher, Margery, review of *Stories for Tens and Over*, *Growing Point*, November, 1976, p. 3003.

Fisher, Margery, review of *Pet Stories for Children*, *Growing Point*, November, 1985, p. 4516.

Hollingsworth, T. R., review of *The Pied Piper of Hamelin*, *Children's Book Review Service*, July, 1989, p. 146.

Review of *Imagine That!: Fifteen Fantastic Tales*, *Kirkus Reviews*, November 1, 1986, p. 1648.

Learmont, Lavinia, review of *Stories for Under-Fives*, *Books and Bookmen*, November, 1975, p. 60.

McNulty, Faith, review of *Mrs. Fox's Wedding*, *New Yorker*, December 1, 1980, p. 219.

Mills, Colin, review of *More Stories for Seven-Year-Olds and Other Young Readers*, *Times Literary Supplement*, September 29, 1979, p. 1085.

Neumeyer, Peter, review of *Once Upon a Rhyme: 101 Poems for Young Children*, *School Library Journal*, January, 1983, p. 73.

Philip, Neil, review of *Round the Christmas Tree*, *Times Educational Supplement*, December 16, 1983, p. 20.

Steinberg, Renee, review of *Imagine That!: Fifteen Fantastic Tales*, *School Library Journal*, April, 1987, p. 93.

Walters, Fiona, review of *The Faber Book of Favourite Fairy Tales*, *Books for Keeps*, November, 1990, p. 25.

■ For More Information See

PERIODICALS

Booklist, November 1, 1979, p. 452.
Books and Bookmen, May, 1974, p. 107.
Horn Book, April, 1983, p. 177.

Junior Bookshelf, August, 1976, pp. 222-23; August, 1986, p. 146.
School Library Journal, October, 1983, p. 178; March, 1986, p. 158.
Times Educational Supplement, January 6, 1989, p. 26; July 1, 1994, p. R2.

* * *

CORRIN, Stephen

■ Personal

Born in Tredegar, Wales; son of Joseph and Rebecca Corrin; married Sara Nirenstein (a writer and lecturer), October, 1938; children: Evelyn, Julia Corrin Nightingale. *Education:* Studied French language and literature at University of Wales and Institut Francais, London, England.

■ Addresses

Home—10 Russell Gardens, London NW11 9NL, England.

■ Career

Bookseller prior to World War II; Kilburn Grammar School, London, England, head of modern languages, 1944-70. Lecturer on children's literature; consultant to British Broadcasting Corp. *Military service:* British Army, 1942-45.

■ Awards, Honors

Best Picture Book of the Season citation, *New Yorker* magazine, 1984, for *Mrs. Fox's Wedding;* Premio "Critici in Erba," Bologna, 1990, for *The Pied Piper of Hamelin.*

■ Writings

FOR CHILDREN

The Fantastic Tale of the Plucky Sailor and the Postage Stamp, Faber, 1958.
(Reteller with wife, Sara Corrin) *Mrs. Fox's Wedding,* illustrated by Errol Le Cain, Doubleday, c. 1980.
(Reteller with Sara Corrin) *The Pied Piper of Hamelin,* illustrated by Le Cain, Faber, 1987, Harcourt, 1989.
(With Sara Corrin) *Classic Fairy Tales,* Faber, 1987.

Also reteller of *Tales from Hans Andersen,* illustrated by Edward Ardizzone, 1989.

EDITOR WITH SARA CORRIN

Stories for Seven-Year-Olds and Other Young Readers, illustrated by Shirley Hughes, Faber, 1964.
Stories for Six-Year-Olds and Other Young Readers, illustrated by Hughes, Faber, 1967.
Stories for Eight-Year-Olds and Other Young Readers, illustrated by Hughes, Faber, 1971.
A Time to Laugh: Thirty Stories for Young Children, illustrated by Gerald Rose, Faber, 1972, published

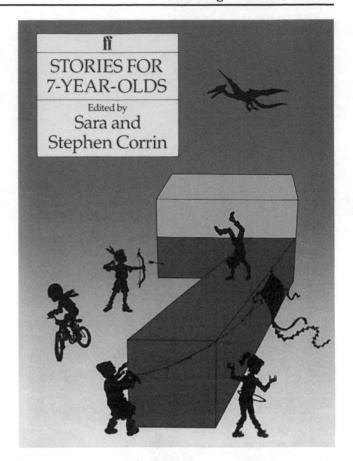

This set of tales, chosen by the Corrins especially for readers around the age of seven, includes works by the Brothers Grimm and Rudyard Kipling.

as *A Time to Laugh: Funny Stories for Children,* 1985.
Stories for Five-Year-Olds and Other Young Readers, illustrated by Hughes, Faber, 1973.
Stories for Under-Fives, Faber, 1974.
Stories for Tens and Over, Faber, 1976.
More Stories for Seven-Year-Olds and Other Young Readers, illustrated by Hughes, Faber, 1978.
Stories for Nine-Year-Olds and Other Young Readers, illustrated by Hughes, Faber, 1979.
The Faber Book of Modern Fairy Tales, illustrated by Ann Strugnell, Faber, 1981.
Once upon a Rhyme: One Hundred One Poems for Young Children, illustrated by Jill Bennett, Faber, 1982.
Round the Christmas Tree, illustrated by Bennett, Faber, 1983.
The Faber Book of Christmas Stories, illustrated by Bennett, Faber, 1984.
Pet Stories for Children, illustrated by Bennett, Faber, 1985, published as *The Puffin Book of Pet Stories,* Puffin, 1987.
Imagine That!: Fifteen Fantastic Tales (fairy tales), illustrated by Bennett, Faber, 1986.
The Faber Book of Favourite Fairy Tales, illustrated by Juan Wijngaard, Faber, 1988.
More Stories for Under-Fives, illustrated by Vanessa Julian-Ottie, Faber, 1988.

Laugh out Loud: More Funny Stories for Children, illustrated by Rose, Faber, 1989.
The Faber Book of Golden Fairytales, illustrated by Peter Melnyczuk, Faber, 1993.

OTHER

(Translator from French) Mircea Eliade, *The Forge and the Crucible,* Rider & Co., 1961.
(Translator from French) Victor Smirnoff, *The Scope of Child Analysis,* Routledge & Kegan Paul, 1971.
(Translator from French) Jean Lohisse, *Anonymous Communication,* Allen & Unwin, 1973.

Also translator from Russian of *Katya and the Crocodile;* translator of *Ardizzone's Andersen.* Contributor to *Vallentine's Encyclopedia.* Contributor of reviews to periodicals, including *Daily Telegraph, Guardian, Punch, Times Educational Supplement, Times Literary Supplement,* and the London *Times.*

■ **Work in Progress**

An anthology for young adults.

■ **Sidelights**

Stephen Corrin commented: "My main interests, other than children and human behavior, are philosophy and linguistics. I engage in voluminous exchanges of correspondence with leading world thinkers, including Noam Chomsky, John Searle, Arthur Koestler, and Dame Iris Murdoch (for over fifteen years). My motto is: 'View everything with irreverence other than cruelty and waste.'"

For more information on the works of Stephen Corrin, see the joint sidelights in the entry for Sara Corrin in this volume.

■ **For More Information See**

PERIODICALS

Books, April, 1989, p. 12.
Books for Keeps, November, 1990, p. 25.
Booklist, April 1, 1989, p. 1380.
Growing Point, November, 1985, p. 4515.
Junior Bookshelf, June, 1988, p. 135; December, 1993, p. 230.
Kirkus Reviews, October 1, 1980, p. 1292; November 1, 1986, p. 1648.
New Yorker, December 1, 1980, p. 219.
New York Times Book Review, September 10, 1989, p. 32.
School Library Journal, November, 1989, p. 135; February, 1994, p. 18.
Times Educational Supplement, January 6, 1989, p. 26; July 1, 1994, p. R2.

* * *

CRAIG, M. F.
See CRAIG, Mary (Francis) Shura

CRAIG, M. S.
See CRAIG, Mary (Francis) Shura

* * *

CRAIG, Mary
See CRAIG, Mary (Francis) Shura

* * *

CRAIG, Mary S.
See CRAIG, Mary (Francis) Shura

* * *

CRAIG, Mary (Francis) Shura 1923-1991 (M. F. Craig, M. S. Craig, Mary Craig, Mary S. Craig, Mary Francis Shura; pseudonyms: Alexis Hill, Meredith Hill)

■ **Personal**

Born February 27, 1923, in Pratt, KS; died of injuries sustained in a fire in her apartment, January 12, 1991, at the Loyola University Medical Burn Center in Maywood, IL; daughter of Jack Fant and Mary (Milstead) Young; married Daniel C. Shura, October 24, 1943 (died June 13, 1959); married Raymond Craig, December 8, 1961 (divorced, 1984); children: (first marriage) Marianne, Daniel Charles, Alice Barrett; (second marriage) Mary Forsha. *Education:* Attended Maryville State College, 1940-43.

■ **Career**

Freelance writer. Girl Scouts of America, public relations director, 1960-61. Creative writing teacher at various universities, including University of Kansas and California State University; lecturer and participant in workshops, including Mystery Writers Workshops, 1986-88. Had weekly book review program, WOI-TV, Ames, IA, 1976. *Member:* Authors League of America, Authors Guild, Mystery Writers of America (Midwest regional vice-president, 1983-84; general awards chairman, 1988; member national board of directors; president, 1990-91), Women in Communication, Children's Book Writers of America, Crime Writers of Great Britain, Children's Reading Round Table (Chicago).

■ **Awards, Honors**

Simple Spigott was named to the 100 Best List, *World Book Encyclopedia,* 1960; *The Nearsighted Knight* was named to the Best Books list, *New York Times,* 1963; citation for outstanding contribution to children's literature, Central Missouri State University, 1974; Lillian Steinhauer Award, New York Poetry Forum, 1976; Pinetree Award, 1983, for *Chester;* Carl Sandburg Award, Friends of the Chicago Public Library, 1985, for

MARY SHURA CRAIG

The Search for Grissi. Seven of her books for young readers were chosen as Junior Library Guild selections.

■ Writings

JUVENILE FICTION; UNDER NAME MARY FRANCIS SHURA

Simple Spigott, illustrated by Jacqueline Tomes, Knopf, 1960, illustrated by Sarah Garland, Hamish Hamilton, 1967.
The Garret of Greta McGraw, illustrated by Leslie Goldstein, Knopf, 1961.
Mary's Marvelous Mouse, illustrated by Adrienne Adams, Knopf, 1962.
The Nearsighted Knight, illustrated by James Spanfeller, Knopf, 1965.
Run Away Home, illustrated by N. M. Bodecker, Atheneum, 1965.
Shoefull of Shamrock, illustrated by N. M. Bodecker, Atheneum, 1965.
A Tale of Middle Length, illustrated by Peter Parnall, Atheneum, 1966.
Backwards for Luck, illustrated by Ted CoConis, Knopf, 1967.
Pornada, illustrated by Erwin Schachmer, Atheneum, 1968.
The Valley of the Frost Giants, illustrated by Charles Keeping, Lothrop, 1971.
The Seven Stone House, illustrated by Dayle Payson, Holiday House, 1972.

The Shop on Threnody Street, Grosset & Dunlap, 1972.
Topcat of Tam, illustrated by Charles Robinson, Holiday House, 1972.
The Riddle of Raven's Gulch, illustrated by Salem Tamer, Dodd, 1975, published as *The Riddle of Raven's Hollow,* Scholastic, 1976.
The Season of Silence, illustrated by Ruth Sanderson, Atheneum, 1976.
The Gray Ghosts of Taylor Ridge, illustrated by Michael Hampshire, Dodd, 1978.
The Barkley Street Six-Pack, illustrated by Gene Sparkman, Dodd, 1979.
Mister Wolf and Me, illustrated by Konrad Hack, Dodd, 1979.
Chester, illustrated by Susan Swan, Dodd, 1980.
Happles and Cinnamunger, illustrated by Bertram M. Tormey, Dodd, 1981.
My Friend Natalie, Scholastic, 1982.
Eleanor, illustrated by Susan Swan, Dodd, 1983.
Jefferson, illustrated by Susan Swan, Dodd, 1984.
Jessica, Scholastic, 1984.
The Search for Grissi, illustrated by Ted Lewin, Dodd, 1985.
Marilee, Scholastic, 1985.
Tales for Dickens, Scholastic, 1985.
The Josie Gambit, Dodd, 1986.
Don't Call Me Toad!, illustrated by Jacqueline Rogers, Dodd, 1987.
Gabrielle, Scholastic, 1987.
The Sunday Doll, Dodd, 1988.
Diana, Scholastic, 1988.
Darcy, Scholastic, 1989.
The Mystery at Wolf River, Scholastic, 1989.
Polly Panic, Putnam, 1990.
Gentle Annie: The True Story of a Civil War Nurse, Scholastic, 1991.
Winter Dreams, Christmas Love, Scholastic, 1992.

JUVENILE FICTION; UNDER PSEUDONYM MEREDITH HILL

The Silent Witness, Scholastic, 1983.
My Roommate Is Missing, Scholastic, 1983.
The Wrong Side of Love, Scholastic, 1986.

ADULT FICTION; UNDER NAME MARY CRAIG

A Candle for the Dragon, Dell, 1973.
Ten Thousand Several Doors, Hawthorn, 1973, published as *Mistress of Lost River,* Manor Books, 1976.
The Cranes of Ibycus, Hawthorn, 1974, published as *Shadows of the Past,* Manor Books, 1976.
Were He a Stranger: A Novel of Suspense, Dodd, 1978.

ADULT FICTION; UNDER PSEUDONYM ALEXIS HILL

Passion's Slave, Jove, 1979.
The Untamed Heart, Jove, 1980.

ADULT FICTION; UNDER NAME M. S. CRAIG

The Chicagoans: Dust to Diamonds, Jove, 1981.
To Play the Fox, Dodd, 1982.
Gillian's Chain: A Novel of Suspense, Dodd, 1985.
The Third Blonde: A Novel of Suspense, Dodd, 1985.
Flashpoint, Dodd, 1987.

ADULT FICTION; UNDER NAME MARY S. CRAIG

Lyon's Pride, Jove, 1983.
Pirate's Landing, Jove, 1983.
Dark Paradise, Warner Books, 1986.
The Chicagoans: Fortune's Destiny, Ace Books, 1986.

OTHER

(Under name M. F. Craig) *The Mystery at Peacock Place* (juvenile), Scholastic, 1986.

Also contributor to *Sisters in Crime* (under name M. S. Craig), edited by Marylin Wallace, Jove, 1989, and *The Courage to Grow Old* (under name Mary Shura Craig), edited by Phillip L. Berman, Ballantine, 1989. Author of column "Scrapbook from Shura 'Nuff Farm," 1959-64. Contributor of short stories and poetry to periodicals. Book reviewer, *Independent Journal,* 1973-77.

Craig's papers are housed in the Mary Craig Collection at the Acquisitions Library of the University of Oregon.

■ Adaptations

Simple Spigott was adapted as a puppet play for a three-part mini-series for Japanese public television, 1986.

■ Sidelights

Mary Shura Craig was a multifaceted writer. A quick glance at the many variations of her actual name and pseudonyms tells the story: under several variants of Craig she wrote adult mysteries and romances, while under the name Mary Francis Shura she was a well-known children's writer. Also, under two pseudonyms she wrote both adult and young adult novels. From the publication of her first book in 1960 until the posthumous publication of her last in 1992, Craig penned over fifty novels in a multitude of genres, becoming not only an award-winning children's author, but also a mystery writer of note, elected to the presidency of the Mystery Writers of America the year before her death.

Stories were bread and butter to Craig—almost literally so—from childhood. "My father was a wit and my mother a storyteller," she wrote in an entry for *Something about the Author Autobiography Series (SAAS)*. "Our family didn't so much 'eat' meals as talk and laugh its way through them." Born in Kansas, Craig moved with her family as an infant to the Pacific Northwest, but so thorough was the storytelling and description by her parents and siblings, that when she returned to her birthplace many years later, she recognized it "not from picture but from stories." Besides the family narratives there were books, read aloud to her at first by her mother and sisters. "Somehow," Craig wrote in *SAAS,* "poetry and nursery rhymes were always linked to real life.... To me the natural world was simply stiff with stories." Growing up in Portland, Oregon, Craig learned to read by the time she was four. Her older sisters, tiring of reading her *Grimm's Fairy Tales,* Kipling's *Jungle Book,* and Hawthorne's *Twice Told Tales,* taught her. "To learn to read was to master magic," she recalled for *SAAS.* "I have never lost a sense of wonder that the flat magic of ink on paper can create worlds more real and enduring than the one in which I have beds to make and teeth to brush."

From Portland, the family moved to Spokane, Washington, where Craig's father became ill. Craig, the first home from school, grew close to him during this time, making tea and toast for him. He would listen to her adventures at school until the older children came home later in the afternoon. When he died, Craig "missed him with an anguish that no one would let me express," she wrote in *SAAS,* "because I was too young to understand." Craig found solace at the library, at making up her own stories, and with a new love—drawing. Though a child of the Depression, she was "never hungrier than any other growing kid," she noted. Eight years old when she decided to be a writer, Craig never looked back.

Poetry was one of her first loves, and throughout junior high school she taught herself the forms of poetic expression, from ballads to rondelets. She continued reading voraciously and indiscriminately. Thomas Hardy was balanced by Edgar Rice Burroughs, Thackeray and Austen by Rider Haggard. Soon the family left the Pacific Northwest to return to the mother's birthplace in Missouri, and Craig had to change schools once again. Never an outstanding student, she was nonetheless an original one. When a seventh-grade teacher assigned a notebook report on nutrition, Craig did over twenty pages of verse in the metric form of Longfellow's *Evangeline.* This won her an introduction to a local writer and artist, Rose O'Neill, who encouraged her to keep on writing. Craig's first publication came at age fourteen when a poem of hers appeared in print.

Craig majored in art in college, and married in 1943. By the time the Second World War was over, she was a mother and had a freelance job writing greeting cards. While raising a family, Craig never stopped writing. Her short stories, however, "seemed to fly back to my desk as if they were homing pigeons with jet engines," she recalled for *SAAS.* She finally hit on the technique of creating the story backwards: writing the closing scene first and then going back to write the scenes leading up to it. This did the trick for her, and suddenly acceptances were arriving instead of rejections. After selling several hundred short stories, Craig wrote her first children's book. "I felt I had read about a million children's books by then .... I decided that it would be fun to write a child's book that had everything *I* liked in it, a true exercise in self-indulgence." The result was *Simple Spigott,* published in 1960, just a half year after her husband's death. The story of a little spook who comes to live with three children, the book was called a "cheerfully wacky fantasy" by a reviewer in *Christian Science Monitor,* a "delightful family story" by a *Horn Book* contributor, and "highly amusing" by a critic in the *New York Times Book Review.* The success of *Simple Spigott* encouraged Craig to continue writing children's books, and another of her early successes was *The Nearsighted Knight,* a tongue-in-cheek fairy tale of a questing knight with astigmatism. A *New York Times*

Book Review contributor commented that Craig "has a neat way with words."

Meanwhile Craig remarried and had another child while continuing her career as a children's book writer. She experimented with everything from problem themes such as the dislocations created by the mobility of Americans in *Run Away Home,* which Ethel L. Heins in *Horn Book* called "an appealing story," to modern fairy tales like *Shoefull of Shamrock* to animal stories like *Pornada,* whose porcine protagonist was "one of the most charming animal characters of this season," according to Mary Ann Wentroth in *School Library Journal.* By the 1970s, Craig also began publishing adult fiction, and her production of children's books tapered off somewhat. Mystery and suspense became a new focal point for Craig's writings, both for adults and young adults, as in *The Shop on Threnody Street, The Riddle of Raven's Gulch, The Gray Ghosts of Taylor Ridge, The Mystery at Wolf River,* which Barbara Elleman in *Booklist* noted would "intrigue readers from page one," and *Don't Call Me Toad!,* which Virginia Golodetz, writing in *School Library Journal,* characterized as a "short, fast-paced mystery story with an underlying theme of friendship."

Animals continued to be a common motif in Craig's books, as well. "I have always loved animals and been

In this fanciful tale, a knight who badly needs glasses meets a lonely dragon. (Illustration by Adrienne Adams from *The Nearsighted Knight.*)

Jane at first doesn't like Air Force brat Dinah Dobbins, but the two girls eventually become friends while searching for Dinah's runaway brother in Craig's *Don't Call Me Toad!* (Illustration by Jacqueline Rogers.)

happiest living with them about," she wrote in *SAAS.* "I always use real animals in my stories because then I know their personalities will ring true." Special favorites in the animal kingdom were goats, which Craig had around her when growing up. Goats appear in *Run Away Home* as well as in the books *Chester, Eleanor,* and *Jefferson,* which were Junior Library Guild selections. With the help of his pet goat, the eponymous protagonist of *Chester* manages to find a place for himself in his new neighborhood over the course of the seven chapters of this book—one for every day of the week. Christine McDonnell in *Horn Book* thought the writing in *Chester* was "fast-paced, clear, and fresh," and that both plot and dialogue were "humorous." Chester, McDonnell concluded, "with his fantastic family and menagerie, is an entertaining hero." *Eleanor* was the second of the three companion books, and has a female heroine—Chester's sister Eleanor—with the central problem being the construction of a school float honoring a famous athletic alumnus. In *School Library Journal* Barbara Jo McKee thought that the book was "a welcome continuation of the trials and tribulations" of the characters earlier met in *Chester,* and Ethel R. Twichell in *Horn Book* noted that the story was "cheer-

When Chester moves into Jamie's neighborhood, interesting and unpredictable events begin to happen. (Illustration by Susan Swann from *Chester*.)

ful and appealing—in the tradition of Beverly Cleary." *Jefferson,* the last of the series, revolves around money-making schemes to hold a surprise birthday party for the younger brother of Chester and Eleanor, and is a "delightful combination of realistic humor and slapstick comedy," according to Celia A. Huffman in *School Library Journal.* Craig's "natural sense of humor and colorful writing infuse this story with the same allure" that made the earlier two novels so special, noted a reviewer in *Publishers Weekly.*

In addition to writing young adult historical fiction and romances such as *Jessica, Marilee, Gabrielle, Diana,* and *Darcy* in the 1980s, Craig also wrote three novels of note for young readers: *The Search for Grissi, The Josie Gambit,* and *The Sunday Doll.* The first of these, which won a Carl Sandburg Award, is "a quiet and lovely story that works on many levels," according to Laura Bacher in *School Library Journal. The Search for Grissi* tells the story of an eleven-year-old boy's struggles to deal with his family's move from the country to the turmoil of Brooklyn and with his search for the family cat, Grissi, who has run away. A contributor in *Publishers Weekly* called it a "warm, uncontrived story." With *The Josie Gambit,* Craig used a chess metaphor to tell the story of

an unhappy young girl, Tory, who tries to use her friends Josie and Greg to get her custody changed. An exploration of both the game of chess and adolescent friendship and betrayal, *The Josie Gambit* is an "amiable story with many well drawn, contrasting relationships," noted a writer in *Kirkus Reviews.* A critic in *Bulletin of the Center for Children's Books* commented that the book had "good pace, strong characters, good dialogue, and an original plot." *The Sunday Doll,* on the other hand, tells the story of Emmy, who does not relish turning thirteen because all her friends have become so different at that age. Faced with family secrets and a mystery surrounding a faceless doll she receives as a birthday present from her aunt, Emmy tries to puzzle truth from fiction and learns to value the former by book's end. This is a "memorable novel" that discusses "serious issues," noted a *Publishers Weekly* reviewer. Roger Sutton, in *Bulletin of the Center for Children's Books,* commented that "this thirteen-isn't-so-bad-after-all story has more backbone than most and is written with more than the usual measure of intensity."

For Craig, writing was a full-time occupation. "The same early recognition that informed me that I was a writer bent my life in strange ways," Craig wrote in

Ted Lewin illustrated *The Search for Grissi,* about a boy whose attempts to find his sister's lost cat lead him to exciting discoveries.

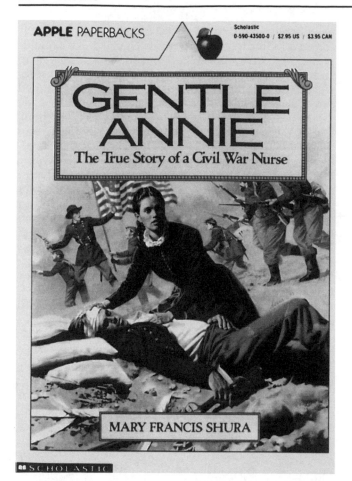

APPLE PAPERBACKS

Scholastic
0-590-43500-0 / $2.95 US / $3.95 CAN

GENTLE ANNIE
The True Story of a Civil War Nurse

MARY FRANCIS SHURA

SCHOLASTIC

In this 1991 novel, a sixteen-year-old girl from Michigan enlists in the Union Army during the Civil War.

SAAS. "I'm not very good company because I'm not at all good at accepting the judgments of other people about anything. I can't afford to. If I am to be an honest writer I have to know, not what a society thinks about something, but what rings as truth to me." Craig was a consummate storyteller for whom theme came last, growing naturally out of character and situation. "Every story is a love story," she explained in *SAAS.* "Unless your character loves something deeply enough to take uncharacteristic risks in its cause, you do not have a story. This can be anything—another human, a much loved animal, a country under threat. The point is not the object but the commitment."

Craig's real talent was her ability to find a story in everything she came into contact with. Her mysteries, animal stories, and new-kid-on-the-block problem books all reflected many of the incidents in her own childhood. "My remembered childhood was happy," she recalled in *SAAS.* "This combination of love and teasing and open communication is the kind of family background that appears over and over in my books without my planning it that way. Sometimes the mothers in my books work out of the home as my one mother did after my father's death. Sometimes they work inside the home as I almost always have." And for Craig, real fiction meant conflict.

"The writing of dynamic fiction lays on the writer the obligation to test his protagonist with every impediment that can logically fall in his path. To do otherwise is to dilute the character's triumph in the story to a weak and pallid brew."

In one of Craig's last published works, *Gentle Annie: The True Story of A Civil War Nurse,* the protagonist faces extreme challenges. The story of an actual sixteen-year-old girl who enlisted in a woman's regiment as a nurse in the civil war, *Gentle Annie* portrays a heroine who faces battle and death at every turn and who also must deal with her own fears and doubts about the value of patriotism. The book is "fictionalized history at its best," according to Mary L. Adams, writing in *Voice of Youth Advocates.*

In the end, it is this idea of testing and challenging limits that marks all of Craig's writing, both adult and juvenile. "I believe," Craig concluded in *SAAS,* "that any time human beings stretch themselves to the fullness of their possible stature, meaning rises from their story as mist rises from the face of a river, naturally, gracefully, and silently."

■ Works Cited

Adams, Mary L., review of *Gentle Annie, Voice of Youth Advocates,* June, 1991, pp. 102-103.

Bacher, Laura, review of *The Search for Grissi, School Library Journal,* May, 1985, p. 97.

Craig, Mary Francis Shura, essay in *Something About the Author Autobiography Series,* Volume 7, Gale, 1989, pp. 45-57.

Elleman, Barbara, review of *The Mystery at Wolf River, Booklist,* October 1, 1989, p. 357.

Golodetz, Virginia, review of *Don't Call Me Toad!, School Library Journal,* April, 1987, p. 104.

Heins, Ethel L., review of *Run Away Home, Horn Book,* June, 1965, p. 281.

Huffman, Celia A., review of *Jefferson, School Library Journal,* November, 1984, p. 128.

Review of *Jefferson, Publishers Weekly,* February 17, 1984, p. 89.

Review of *The Josie Gambit, Bulletin of the Center for Children's Books,* June, 1986, pp. 196-197.

Review of *The Josie Gambit, Kirkus Reviews,* July 1, 1986, p. 1018.

McDonnell, Christine, review of *Chester, Horn Book,* October, 1980, p. 522.

McKee, Barbara Jo, review of *Eleanor, School Library Journal,* April, 1983, p. 117.

Review of *The Nearsighted Knight, New York Times Book Review,* February 23, 1964, p. 22.

Review of *The Search for Grissi, Publishers Weekly,* January 25, 1985, p. 94.

Review of *Simple Spigott, Christian Science Monitor,* May 12, 1960, section B, p. 7.

Review of *Simple Spigott, Horn Book,* August, 1960, p. 291.

Review of *Simple Spigott, New York Times Book Review,* May 8, 1960, p. 29.

Review of *The Sunday Doll, Publishers Weekly,* May 13, 1988, p. 278.

Sutton, Roger, review of *The Sunday Doll, Bulletin of the Center for Children's Books,* July/August, 1988, pp. 238-239.

Twichell, Ethel R., review of *Eleanor, Horn Book,* August, 1983, p. 448.

Wentroth, Mary Ann, review of *Pornada, School Library Journal,* November, 1968, p. 90.

■ For More Information See

PERIODICALS

Bulletin of the Center for Children's Books, December, 1965, p. 68; March, 1968, p. 116; July, 1973, p. 177; October, 1975, p. 32; September, 1978, p. 18; December, 1979, p. 39; October, 1980, p. 69; February, 1982, p. 64; May, 1983, p. 178; September, 1984, p. 15; July, 1987, p. 218; May, 1990, p. 227; April, 1991, p. 205.

Horn Book, October, 1965, p. 500; August, 1972, p. 373; June, 1976, p. 292; April, 1982, p. 169; September, 1984, p. 594.

New York Times Book Review, May 9, 1965, p. 16; September 7, 1975, p. 20.

Publishers Weekly, January 1, 1973, p. 57; July 24, 1978, p. 84; February 18, 1983, p. 129; April 25, 1986, p. 82; March 13, 1987, p. 85; March 1, 1991, p. 73.

School Library Journal, May, 1975, p. 70; December, 1979, p. 89; May, 1980, p. 71; March, 1981, p. 109; January, 1982, p. 82; September, 1986, p. 139; August, 1988, p. 98; November, 1990, p. 118; May, 1991, p. 106.

Voice of Youth Advocates, April, 1985, p. 44; October, 1985, p. 264; April, 1989, p. 38.

OBITUARIES:

PERIODICALS

Detroit Free Press, January 16, 1991.
Los Angeles Times, January 18, 1991.
New York Times, January 15, 1991, section D, p. 19.
Publishers Weekly, February 8, 1991, p. 35.
School Library Journal, March, 1991, p. 106.
Washington Post, January 16, 1991.*

—Sketch by J. Sydney Jones

*   *   *

CRISPIN, A(nn) C(arol) 1950-

■ Personal

Born April 5, 1950, in Stamford, CT; daughter of George Arthur (a maritime management specialist) and Hope (a kindergarten teacher; maiden name, Hooker) Tickell; married Randy Lee Crispin (a pharmacist), May 9, 1973 (divorced); lives with significant other, Michael Capobianco; children: Jason Paul. *Education:* University of Maryland, B.A. (English literature), 1972. *Politics:* Democrat. *Religion:* "Universal."

■ Addresses

Home—Charles County, MD. *Agent*—Merrilee Heifetz, Writers House, Inc., 21 West 26th St., New York, NY 10010.

■ Career

Worked variously as a customer service representative, receptionist, technical librarian, and typist, 1972-74; U.S. Bureau of the Census, Suitland, MD, computer programmer, training specialist, and technical writer, 1974-83; writer, 1983—. Has taught writing workshops at Charles County Community College, Harrisburg Area Community College, Towson State University, and at many science-fiction and "Star Trek" conventions. Also worked as a horseback riding instructor, horse trainer, writing instructor, and swimming instructor. Steward of local union of American Federation of Government Employees. *Member:* Science Fiction Writers of America (Eastern Regional Director, 1990—).

■ Awards, Honors

Best Books for Young Adults citation, American Library Association Young Adult Services Division, for *Star-Bridge* and *Silent Songs;* Best Books for the Teen Age citation, New York Public Library, for *Serpent's Gift.*

■ Writings

FANTASY NOVELS

(With Andre Norton) *Gryphon's Eyrie,* Tor Books, 1984.
(With Norton) *Songsmith,* Tor Books, 1992.

"STAR TREK" SERIES

Yesterday's Son, Pocket Books, 1983.
Time for Yesterday, Pocket Books, 1988.
The Eyes of the Beholders, Pocket Books, 1990.
Sarek, Pocket Books, 1994.

"V" SERIES

V, Pinnacle Books, 1984.
(With Howard Weinstein) *V: East Coast Crisis,* Pinnacle Books, 1984.
(With Deborah A. Marshall) *V: Death Tide,* Pinnacle Books, 1985.

"STARBRIDGE" SERIES

StarBridge, Ace Books, 1989.
(With Kathleen O'Malley) *Silent Dances,* Ace Books, 1990.
(With Jannean Elliott) *Shadow World,* Ace Books, 1991.
(With Marshall) *Serpent's Gift,* Ace Books, 1992.
(With O'Malley) *Silent Songs,* Ace Books, 1994.

OTHER

Sylvester (movie novelization), Tor Books, 1985.

Also contributor to anthologies, including *Magic in Ithkar,* edited by Robert Adams and Norton, Volume 3, Tor Books, 1986; *Tales of the Witch World,* edited by Norton, Tor Books, Volume 1, 1987, Volume 3, 1990;

Tales from the Mos Eisley Cantina, Bantam, 1995; and *Tales from Jabba the Hutt's Palace,* Bantam, 1996.

■ Adaptations

Three of Crispin's novels have been released on audio cassette, *Yesterday's Son,* 1988, *Time for Yesterday,* 1989, and *Sarek.*

■ Work in Progress

An adult fantasy trilogy for Avon: *Storms of Destiny,* vol. 1, *Winds of Vengeance,* vol. 2, and *Flames of Chaos,* vol. 3, 1996; "Time Leaper" series of four children's books for Harper Trophy division of HarperCollins.

■ Sidelights

A. C. Crispin is the author of fifteen science fiction novels, including several additions to prominent series such as "V" and "Star Trek." Crispin also created her own series in 1989, "StarBridge," which "centers around a school for young diplomats, translators, and explorers, both alien and human, located on an asteroid far from Earth," according to the author. As Crispin explained to *SATA,* "In my science fiction I enjoy the theme of 'first contact' between humans and aliens. Communication is vital in this universe. In one way or another, all my books are about communication."

Crispin's first book, *Yesterday's Son,* features characters from the original "Star Trek" series. In this story, Mr. Spock learns that he has a son and then embarks on a mission to save him. A reviewer for *Library Journal* called the book "enjoyable reading," adding that Crispin "handles Vulcan psychology very well." *Sarek,* published in 1994, focuses on Spock's father, Ambassador Sarek. Sarek must decide whether to accept a dangerous mission to the Klingon Empire or keep a vigil at the deathbed of his human wife, Amanda. At stake is the future of the Federation. A *Publishers Weekly* review noted that Crispin "packed everything a die-hard Trekkie could want" into the book, which "should be roundly loved by its target audience." *Sarek* appeared on the *New York Times* hardcover best-seller list for five weeks.

Characters from "Star Trek: The Next Generation" take center stage in Crispin's 1990 book, *The Eyes of the Beholders.* In this story, the *Enterprise* crew is locked in a tractorbeam by a mysterious alien artifact. All the members of the crew—with the exception of the android Data—gradually become lost in private dream worlds, and Data becomes the only one who can prevent the artifact from adding the *Enterprise* to its "graveyard" of ships. Writing in *Wilson Library Bulletin,* Alan P. Mahony claimed that Crispin "brings some warmth" to the characters, though Christy Boyd of *Voice of Youth Advocates* called the book "a little stereotypical and not terribly interesting."

The five books in Crispin's "StarBridge" series revolve around a futuristic school that teaches its students the skills needed to explore other worlds and promote positive relationships between different cultures. The students at StarBridge Academy include representatives of all intelligent species in the universe—ranging from giant fungi to humans—who study science and diplomacy together. The first book in the series, *StarBridge,* is told from the perspective of sixteen-year-old Mahree Burroughs. Mahree is aboard a spaceship headed for Earth when the crew receives a weak transmission that leads them to discover an unknown race, the Simiu. Mahree is able to learn the Simiu language and make friends with them, but before long a series of conflicts between the two cultures erupts into a major crisis. Mahree and two friends then must escape to the Cooperative League of Systems to get help in resolving the situation. In a review for *Booklist,* Candace Smith praised the book's "strong theme of understanding and acceptance among races."

The second book in the series, *Silent Dances,* expands this theme to include people with disabilities. Tesa, a deaf mediator, could undergo a procedure that would enable her to hear, but instead she proves that her deafness is not a handicap. *Shadow World,* the third book in the series, focuses on Mark Kenner, whose doubts about his abilities as a mediator have convinced him to resign from the academy. Instead, he embarks on a last dangerous mission to help an alien race. The Elspind's problem is that their life span has been decreasing, so that now they only live about sixteen years. Scientists thought they had discovered a solution, but a civil war on Elseemar, the Elspind home world, caused the experiments to be destroyed. After his ship is captured by terrorists, Mark must help negotiate a truce. In the meantime, he learns that the Elspind have come to regard death very differently than humans.

Serpent's Gift, the fourth book in the series, follows the adventures of Heather Farley, an eleven-year-old girl whose telepathic powers allow her to communicate with the school's computer system. When a series of near-disasters causes school officials to suspect computer sabotage, Heather must solve the mystery in order to avoid being blamed herself. In a review for *Booklist,* Candace Smith stated that the book "combines well-rounded, likeable characters; touches of romance; the strong but subtle theme of mutual cultural respect," and interesting technological twists. *Serpent's Gift* was recognized by the New York Public Library on its annual list of Best Books for the Teen Age.

To Crispin, one of the benefits of becoming a science-fiction novelist was having the opportunity to meet and collaborate with author Andre Norton. Crispin once referred to Norton as "one of my favorite writers, and, as one of the first women to 'break into' the male-dominated science fiction field, she has also been a personal hero and an inspiration to me." Crispin worked with Norton to produce *Gryphon's Eyrie* in 1984 and *Songsmith* in 1992. "I get many ideas from visual images: mismatched words, pictures, and, often, dreams," Crispin once explained. "*Gryphon's Eyrie* came about from a dream I had about Norton's charac-

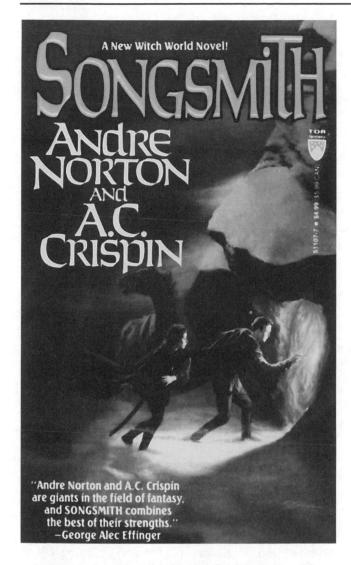

A New Witch World Novel!

SONGSMITH
ANDRE NORTON AND A.C. CRISPIN

"Andre Norton and A.C. Crispin
are giants in the field of fantasy,
and SONGSMITH combines
the best of their strengths."
—George Alec Effinger

**Andre Norton teamed with A. C. Crispin to write
Songsmith, part of Norton's popular "Witch World"
series.** (Cover illustration by Doriau.)

ters in *The Crystal Gryphon* and *Gryphon in Glory.*"
Despite the variety of her work, Crispin claimed that it
has one recurring theme: "be yourself—but don't stop
trying to be a better person."

■ **Works Cited**

Boyd, Christy, review of *The Eyes of the Beholders,*
    Voice of Youth Advocates, February, 1991, pp. 361-
    62.
Mahony, Alan P., "Live Long and Prosper," *Wilson
    Library Bulletin,* January, 1994, p. 136.
Review of *Sarek, Publishers Weekly,* January 17, 1994,
    p. 416.
Smith, Candace, review of *StarBridge, Booklist,* Septem-
    ber 1, 1989, pp. 41-42.
Smith, Candace, review of *Serpent's Gift, Booklist,* April
    15, 1992, p. 1509.
Review of *Yesterday's Son, Library Journal,* August,
    1983, p. 1507.

■ **For More Information See**

PERIODICALS

Booklist, December 1, 1990, p. 720; April 15, 1992, p.
    1509.
Chattanooga News-Free Press, September 11, 1983.
Chicago Tribune, February 18, 1994, section 7, p. 49.
Kirkus Reviews, February 1, 1994, p. 102.
Library Journal, August, 1991, p. 180.
Locus, October, 1989; June, 1990; January, 1991, p. 63.
Publishers Weekly, August 18, 1989, p. 56.
Voice of Youth Advocates, October, 1984, p. 205;
    August, 1985, p. 183; June, 1991, p. 106; August,
    1992, p. 172; August, 1994, p. 154.

                    *   *   *

CUNLIFFE, John Arthur 1933-

■ **Personal**

Born June 16, 1933, in Colne, Lancashire, England;
married Sylvia May Thompson (a musician), 1960;
children: Julian Edward. *Education:* Leeds School of
Librarianship, A.L.A., 1955; Northwest London Poly-
technic School of Librarianship, F.L.A., 1957; Charlotte
Mason College of Education, Cert. Ed., 1975.

■ **Addresses**

Office—Andre Deutsch Ltd., 105-106 Great Russell St.,
London WC1B 3LJ, England.

■ **Career**

Branch librarian, Earby, Yorkshire, England, 1951-54;
mobile librarian, Wooler, Northumberland, England,
1955-56; Decca Radar Research Laboratories, Tol-
worth, Surrey, England, deputy information officer,
1957-58; senior assistant librarian, Hendon, London,
England, 1958; Foyle's (booksellers), London, manager
of rare book department, 1958-59; regional children's
librarian, Bletchley, Buckinghamshire, England, 1959-
62; librarian in charge of work with young people,
Reading, Berkshire, England, 1962-64, and Brighton,
England, 1967-73; librarian, British Council, Belgrade,
Yugoslavia, 1964-66; education librarian, Newcastle-
upon-Tyne, England, 1966-67; Castle Park School,
Kendal, Cumbria, England, teacher, 1975-79; Manchester Education Committee, Manchester, England, teach-
er-organizer, 1979-80; Crowcroft Park School, Manchester, deputy head teacher, 1981-85; freelance writer,
1985—. *Member:* Society of Authors, National Union of
Teachers.

■ **Writings**

FOR CHILDREN

The Adventures of Lord Pip, illustrated by Robert Hales,
    Deutsch, 1970.
The Giant Who Stole the World, illustrated by Faith
    Jacques, Deutsch, 1971.

Riddles and Rhymes and Rigamaroles, illustrated by Alexy Pendle, Deutsch, 1971.
The Giant Who Swallowed the Wind, illustrated by Jacques, Deutsch, 1972.
Giant Kippernose, and Other Stories, illustrated by Fritz Wegner, Deutsch, 1972.
The Great Dragon Competition, and Other Stories, illustrated by Pendle, Deutsch, 1973.
The King's Birthday Cake, illustrated by Jacques, Deutsch, 1973.
Small Monkey Tales, illustrated by Gerry Downes, Deutsch, 1974.
The Farmer, the Rooks, and the Cherry Tree, illustrated by Prudence Seward, Deutsch, 1975.
Giant Brog and the Motorway, illustrated by Pendle, Deutsch, 1975.
Sara's Giant and the Upside-down House, illustrated by Hillary Abrahams, Deutsch, 1980.
Our Sam: The Daftest Dog in the World, illustrated by Maurice Wilson, Deutsch, 1980.
Mr. Gosling and the Runaway Chair, illustrated by William Stobbs, Deutsch, 1981.
Standing on a Strawberry and Other Poems, illustrated by David Parkins, Deutsch, 1987.
Fog Lane School and the Great Racing Car Disaster, illustrated by Andrew Tiffen, Deutsch, 1988.
The Minister's Cat, illustrated by David Parkins, Deutsch, 1989.
(With Elizabeth Lindsay and Joan Stimson) *Readaloud Stories,* Hippo, 1990.
Ted Glen's New Year Promises, illustrated by Ray Mutimer, Hippo, 1990.
Granny Dryden's Runaway Pig, illustrated by Mutimer, Hippo, 1991.
Julian and the Vacuum Cleaner, Deutsch, 1991.
Miss Hubbard's New Hat, Hippo, 1992.
Jess and the Fish, illustrated by Joan Hickson, Deutsch, 1992.
Jess Goes Hunting, illustrated by Hickson, Scholastic, 1992.
Jess's New Bed, illustrated by Hickson, Deutsch, 1992.
A Song for Jess, illustrated by Hickson, Deutsch, 1992.
Dare You Go? (poetry), Deutsch, 1992.
Tots and the Brass Band, Hippo, 1995.

"FARMER BARNES" SERIES; FOR CHILDREN

Farmer Barnes Buys a Pig, illustrated by Carol Barker, Deutsch, 1964, Lion Press, 1968.
Farmer Barnes and Bluebell, illustrated by Barker, Deutsch, 1966.
Farmer Barnes at the County Show, illustrated by Jill McDonald, Deutsch, 1966, as *Farmer Barnes at the County Fair,* Lion Press, 1969.
Farmer Barnes and the Goats, illustrated by McDonald, Deutsch, 1971.
Farmer Barnes Goes Fishing, illustrated by McDonald, Deutsch, 1972.
Farmer Barnes and the Snow Picnic, illustrated by Hickson, Deutsch, 1974.
Farmer Barnes Fells a Tree, illustrated by Hickson, Deutsch, 1977.
Farmer Barnes and the Harvest Doll, illustrated by Hickson, Deutsch, 1977.

Farmer Barnes' Guy Fawkes Day, illustrated by Hickson, Deutsch, 1978.

"POSTMAN PAT" SERIES; FOR CHILDREN

Postman Pat and the Mystery Thief, illustrated by Celia Berridge, Deutsch, 1981, Scholastic, 1993.
Postman Pat's Treasure Hunt, illustrated by Berridge, Deutsch, 1981.
Postman Pat's Secret, illustrated by Berridge, Deutsch, 1981.
Postman Pat's Rainy Day, illustrated by Berridge, Deutsch, 1982.
Postman Pat's Difficult Day, illustrated by Berridge, Deutsch, 1982.
Postman Pat's Foggy Day, illustrated by Berridge, Deutsch, 1982.
Postman Pat Takes a Message, illustrated by Berridge, Deutsch, 1982.
Postman Pat Goes Sledging, illustrated by Berridge, Deutsch, 1983.
Postman Pat's Tractor Express, illustrated by Berridge, Deutsch, 1983.
(With Ivor Wood) *Fun and Games with Postman Pat: An Activity Book,* illustrated by Hickson, Deutsch, 1983.
Postman Pat's Thirsty Day, illustrated by Berridge, Deutsch, 1983.
Postman Pat's Letters on Ice, illustrated by Berridge, Deutsch, 1984.
Postman Pat's Breezy Day, illustrated by Berridge, Deutsch, 1985.
Postman Pat to the Rescue, illustrated by Berridge, Deutsch, 1985, Scholastic, 1993.
Postman Pat Easy Readers (14 volumes), illustrated by Hickson, Deutsch, 1986-89.
Postman Pat Beginners (7 volumes), illustrated by Hickson, Deutsch, 1986-93.
Postman Pat's Summer Storybook, illustrated by Berridge, Deutsch, 1987.
Postman Pat's Winter Storybook, illustrated by Berridge, Deutsch, 1987.
The Postman Pat Fun Book, illustrated by Berridge, Deutsch, 1987.
Postman Pat's Parcel of Fun, illustrated by Stuart Trotter, Deutsch, 1987.
My Postman Pat Storytime Book, Treasure, 1987.
Postman Pat and the Letter Puzzle, illustrated by Hickson, Hippo, 1988.
Postman Pat Gets a Pet, Hippo, 1988.
Postman Pat Goes Sailing, Hippo, 1988, revised, 1993.
Postman Pat Goes to Town, Hippo, 1989.
Postman Pat's Cat-up-a-Tree Party, Hippo, 1989.
Postman Pat's Greendale Storybook, Hippo, 1989.
Postman Pat's Zodiac Storybook, illustrated by Berridge, Deutsch, 1989.
Postman Pat and the Toy Soldiers, Deutsch, 1991.
Pat and the Puzzle Parcels, illustrated by Mutimer, Hippo, 1991.
Postman Pat's Lost Hat, illustrated by Hickson and Emma Iliffe, Deutsch/National Library for Handicapped Children/National Deaf Children's Society, 1991.

(With Susannah Bradley) *Postman Pat and the Toy Soldiers Sticker Fun Book,* illustrated by Mutimer, Hippo, 1991.

Postman Pat Takes the Bus, Deutsch, 1992.

Postman Pat Wins a Prize, illustrated by Hickson, Hippo, 1992.

Postman Pat's Wild Cat Chase, illustrated by Mutimer, Deutsch, 1992.

My Favorite Postman Pat Stories, illustrated by Berridge, Dean, 1993.

Postman Pat and the Harvest Parcel, illustrated by Hickson, Hippo, 1993.

Postman Pat and the Greendale Bus, illustrated by Hickson, Hippo, 1993.

The Reverend Timms Gives a Film Show, illustrated by Mutimer, Deutsch, 1993.

Postman Pat's Market Day, illustrated by Hickson, Hippo, 1993.

Postman Pat and the Barometer, illustrated by Mutimer, Deutsch, 1994.

Postman Pat and the Tuba, illustrated by Mutimer, Scholastic, 1994.

Postman Pat and the Fly, illustrated by Mutimer, World, 1995.

Postman Pat and the Flood, illustrated by Mutimer, Hippo, 1995.

Also author of *Postman Pat and His Black and White Cat* (television series), BBC-TV, from 1981; author of *Postman Pat's Adventures,* produced in Wimbledon, England, 1987. Several titles in the "Postman Pat" series have been translated into Welsh.

"ROSIE AND JIM" SERIES; FOR CHILDREN

Rosie and Jim and the Rainbow, Deutsch, 1991.

Rosie and Jim and the Water Wizard, Deutsch, 1991.

Rosie and Jim, illustrated by Hickson, Deutsch, 1992.

Rosie and Jim and the Man in the Wind, illustrated by Berridge, Deutsch, 1992.

Fun and Games with Rosie and Jim: An Activity Book, Deutsch, 1992.

(With Anita Ganeri) *Round the Year with Rosie and Jim,* illustrated by Hickson, 1992.

Rosie and Jim and the Drink of Milk, illustrated by Berridge, Hippo, 1993.

Rosie and Jim: A Family for Ducks, illustrated by Hickson, Scholastic, 1993.

Rosie and Jim: Jim Gets Lost, illustrated by Hickson, Scholastic, 1993.

Rosie and Jim and the Snowman, illustrated by Hickson, Scholastic, 1993.

Rosie and Jim's Apple, Banana, Carrot Alphabet Book, illustrated by Berridge, Deutsch, 1993.

Rosie and Jim at the Seaside, illustrated by Hickson, Scholastic, 1993.

Rosie and Jim and the Glass Blowers, illustrated by Berridge, Deutsch, 1993.

Rosie and Jim and the Magic Sausages, illustrated by Berridge, Deutsch, 1993.

OTHER

Play Logo, Deutsch, 1984.

Contributor to *Children's Book Review.*

■ Sidelights

"John Cunliffe is a master of homely humour," Marcus Crouch states in *School Librarian.* A librarian and teacher, Cunliffe has used his sense of humor and his skills as a storyteller to compose numerous entertaining tales for children from a wide variety of age groups. His tales of giants and dragons capture young, pre-school imaginations, while unhurried life in an English village is brought very much to life for beginning readers in books featuring characters like Farmer Barnes, Our Sam, and Granny Goodberry. As a *Junior Bookshelf* critic notes, "Cunliffe is a master of the art of telling a simple story which is closely related to the realities of contemporary life." In addition, Cunliffe has authored numerous books based on the "Postman Pat" and "Rosie and Jim" television series, which are very popular with young children in England.

Busy, harried, Farmer Barnes is the main character in a series of books that focus on everyday farm life in England. Cunliffe brings the farmer and his family— wife Emily, daughter Candy, and five-year-old son Little John—to life in simple stories that deal with the kinds of realistic problems young children can readily relate to. In *Farmer Barnes and Bluebell,* chaos reigns in a small village after Bluebell decides to escape her humdrum life as a dairy cow for some excitement beyond the barn. In *Farmer Barnes Buys a Pig* Little John decides that a pig would make a fine birthday gift for his fifth birthday, so Farmer Barnes scours every hogpen for miles around, but none of the fat, squealing little piglets he brings home will do for his son. Finally, mother Emily comes through with a small, fat, pink, *quiet* piglet—perfect, because it is made of china. *Farmer Barnes Buys a Pig* is amusing to children, explains *Library Journal* reviewer Alice D. Ehlert, because they can identify with Little James's "frustration of being misunderstood in [his] wishes." A stray goat rescued by helicopter becomes the high-point in *Farmer Barnes and the Goats,* while a shopping trip to town in the Barnes family's Land Rover turns into a chilly overnight adventure in *Farmer Barnes and the Snow Picnic.* And during a festive British holiday, Little John and his sister Candy are dismayed when a flaming rocket from a much-nagged-for fireworks display hits their treehouse in *Farmer Barnes' Guy Fawkes Day.* Another low-key tragedy strikes the family farm in *Farmer Barnes Fells a Tree.* Her husband's excitement over his new chain saw gives Emily Barnes enough problems to last a week when his poorly planned attempt to cut down an overgrown tree misfires, nearly taking down the house with it.

Far from the true-to-life world of Farmer Barnes, giants and dragons roam the countryside in several of Cunliffe's other books for children. The great diversity among dragons is brought to light in *The Great Dragon Competition, and Other Stories,* a collection of ten stories that introduce young readers to the world of the fantastic in a humorous way. *Giant Kippernose, and*

In *The Great Dragon Competition and Other Stories*, Cunliffe introduces the reader to dragons both terrifying and timid. (Illustration by Alexy Pendle.)

Other Stories is a collection of stories about giants that provides "most pleasant reading—especially aloud to others," according to George Shannon in *School Library Journal.* Giants suffer problems in a big way—giant toothaches, giant spells of loneliness, and the really annoying problem of having entire towns built up on top of them while they are sleeping. Cunliffe's folksy tales are full of the kind of details that make characters like Giant Kippernose—who finally realized that people won't come near him because he never takes a bath— believable and almost human. In another story from *Giant Kippernose,* when a greedy giant pushes nearby villagers too far with his demands for food, they decide to ignore him, even when he childishly threatens to stomp their homes flat. They know that he is bluffing; but then he grumpily swallows the wind that fuels their grinding mills and pumps their water. Finally outwitted, the giant moves to the seaside, where he still receives care packages from the forgiving village. Cunliffe's brand of magic also comes into play in *Sara's Giant and the Upside-down House.* Young Sara's mother accuses Sara of turning the family home "upside down" by always making such a mess; when Sara calls on the gigantic Mr. Zub, he demonstrates what Sara's mother means—by actually flipping the house over onto its

roof. And in *The Giant Who Stole the World,* darkness and the faint smell of cheese covers the globe, and not even the world's astronomers know why, until the Astronomer Royal figures out that it has been picked out of the sky and put in the pocket of an enormous sky-giant.

Fantasy characters are a great way to let childhood imaginations grow, but most of Cunliffe's stories focus on the many things surrounding us in the real world. For example, in his *Small Monkey Tales,* published in 1974, Cunliffe invites young children to identify with a young monkey's first explorations into the world around him. The playfulness that sometimes gets the small monkey into trouble, his fear of being separated from his mother, and the natural curiosity that builds his independence are all depicted in a story that is complemented with charming pencil drawings by illustrator Gerry Downes. The tales are "told in a delightfully animated way, [and] deserve to become classics," according to a *Times Literary Supplement* reviewer. And in *Our Sam: The Daftest Dog in the World,* Cunliffe recalls his own childhood in the north of England where he used to visit his grandmother and a cocker spaniel that went by the name of "Our Sam." Each chapter finds the frisky and curious Our Sam getting in and out of so many scrapes

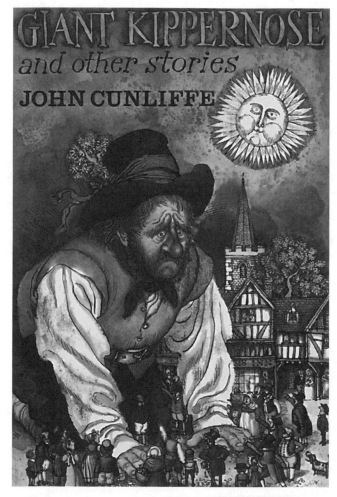

Cunliffe tells of eight very unusual giants in this 1972 collection. (Cover illustration by Fritz Wegner.)

that the reader ends up thinking he must have more lives than a cat. Our Sam becomes caught up in the excitement of a fox hunt near his yard, works his way aboard a scary Ghost Train ride at a local fair and ends up running away with one of its glow-in-the-dark skeletons, and steals the show during a local soccer match. Cunliffe includes examples of the dialogue of the northern region in *Our Sam,* and "the background is authentic, and the human characters are colourful," states a reviewer in *Junior Bookshelf.*

Colourful characters from the past abound in *The King's Birthday Cake.* The book describes Grandmother Gooseberry's efforts to send a birthday cake to the king; from a picture she had seen of him, the royal personage looks far too thin. She decides not to trust the regular mail service, so she puts her freshly baked cake in the hands of the royal cook who passes by on his way back to the palace. Grandmother's cake changes hands several more times on its hard journey; by the time the package arrives at the palace, it is deemed "nasty" and suspicious-looking. Believing that the package is a dangerous bomb of some sort, the king's guards trace the parcel's route back to Grandmother Gooseberry, who is marched to the palace where the whole matter is finally put to rights and she bakes a new cake for the king's birthday party ... and brings it to the castle herself.

If only Grandmother Gooseberry had lived in the small village of Greendale. Then she would have been able to place her cake in the capable hands of one of Cunliffe's most popular characters, Postman Pat. Cunliffe's colorful series of picture books are based on a popular British children's television show and its series of characters designed by puppeteer Ivor Wood. Intended to be read aloud to three- and four-year-old fans of the TV show, the stories take place in the small village of Greendale, where Postman Pat and his cat Jess are drawn into the goings on of everyone in the community during his daily rounds. Cunliffe's books "present an innocent, fanciful view of small-town life," Judith Elkin notes in *Twentieth-Century Children's Writers,* "where Pat is given cups of tea and cake on his rounds, collects stamps from the letters he delivers, and bats and bowls the town's cricket team to victory." In *Postman Pat's Treasure Hunt,* for example, Pat helps young Katy find Sarah-Ann, a favorite doll that she has lost. Searching for Sarah-Ann on his delivery route, Pat uncovers the whereabouts of several other items from his Greendale neighbors and finally discovers the doll in grocer Tom's Mobile Grocery truck in time to return it to Katy at her birthday party. When a heavy snowfall blankets Greendale, Pat is determined to get the mail through; after the snows prove too deep to let helpful Farmer Fogg's plow do its job, he makes a delivery on sled in *Postman Pat Goes Sledging.* Other Postman Pat books are designed for younger children and teach ABCs and 123s using the humorous predicaments of the familiar Postman Pat character. And in the "lift-the-flap" book *Postman Pat's Lost Hat,* Cunliffe's short text is supplemented by a translation into sign language, allowing deaf fans to follow the adventures of Pat and his cat Jess as they

One of Cunliffe's most popular characters is Postman Pat, who appears in a series of picture books, as well as a BBC-TV television series for children. (Illustration by Celia Berridge from *Postman Pat and the Mystery Thief.*)

search under the bed, in the bath, in a drawer, and many other places around the house, for his postal cap.

In addition to picture books and stories for young readers, Cunliffe has also written stories for older children, including *Fog Lane School and the Great Racing Car Disaster,* where three unruly students cause problems in class, and it is discovered that they have stolen the ingredients for their class project. Works of poetry by Cunliffe are included in *Standing on a Strawberry and Other Poems* and *Dare You Go?,* both containing witty verses written for middle readers to illustrate a variety of poetic styles. And in *Riddles and Rhymes and Rigmaroles* Cunliffe gathers together a group of original tall-tales, riddles, puns, and other nonsense that is popular with the six- to eight-year-old crowd. *Play Logo,* a book about computers published in 1984, has been his only turn at nonfiction. Explaining that the Logo computer language is the best way to start children out in learning about computers, he shows readers how to master Logo's steps and create basic programs that produce interesting patterns on the computer screen. Cunliffe draws upon his many years as a teacher in creating a book that teaches a useful skill and encourages experimentation among budding computer users.

■ Works Cited

Crouch, Marcus, review of *Postman Pat's Foggy Day, School Librarian,* March, 1983, p. 25.

Ehlert, Alice D., review of *Farmer Barnes Buys a Pig, Library Journal,* May 15, 1969, p. 2088.

Elkin, Judith, "John Cunliffe," in *Twentieth-Century Children's Writers,* 4th edition, edited by Laura Standley Berger, St. James Press, 1995, pp. 258-60.

Review of *Farmer Barnes' Guy Fawkes Day, Junior Bookshelf,* April, 1979, p. 93.

Review of *Our Sam: The Daftest Dog in the World, Junior Bookshelf,* October, 1980, p. 239.

Shannon, George, review of *Giant Kippernose and Other Stories, School Library Journal,* October, 1981, p. 127.

Review of *Small Monkey Tales,* "Tried and Tested," *Times Literary Supplement,* July 5, 1974, p. 722.

■ For More Information See

PERIODICALS

British Book News, spring, 1982, p. 1.

Growing Point, March, 1979, p. 3476.

Junior Bookshelf, February, 1982, p. 14; August, 1987, p. 167; June, 1989, p. 118.

School Librarian, December, 1982, p. 318; August, 1991, p. 100; February, 1993, p. 26.

School Library Journal, September, 1979, p. 107; October, 1979, p. 148; November, 1980, p. 59; August, 1981, p. 63.

Spectator, November 13, 1971, p. 700.

Times Literary Supplement, November 24, 1966, p. 1083; April 28, 1972, p. 483; November 3, 1972, p. 1333; December 6, 1974, p. 1378.*

D

DALLAS, Ruth
See MUMFORD, Ruth

* * *

de HAMEL, Joan Littledale 1924-

■ Personal

Born March 31, 1924, in London, England; emigrated to New Zealand, 1955; daughter of Humphrey Rivers (a medical practitioner) and Eleanor (Littledale) Pollock; married Francis de Hamel (a professor of medicine), April 24, 1948; children: Michael, Christopher, William, Richard, Quentin. *Education:* Lady Margaret Hall, Oxford, B.A. (with honors), 1944, M.A., 1949. *Religion:* Church of England. *Hobbies and other interests:* Art (especially French art), history, literature, education, botany, ornithology, animal behavior, oral history.

■ Addresses

Home—25 Howard St., Macandrew Bay, Dunedin, New Zealand. *Agent*—Ray Richards, 3/43 Aberdeen Rd., Castor Bay, Auckland, New Zealand; and A. P. Watt Ltd., 20 John St., London WC1N 2DL, England.

■ Career

St. Nicholas School (girls' preparatory school), Hemel Hempstead, Hertfordshire, England, assistant mistress, 1944-45; Francis Holland School, London, head of languages, 1945-48; Dunedin Teachers College, Dunedin, New Zealand, lecturer in French, 1967-79; writer. Angora goat breeder, 1985—. *Member:* New Zealand Society of Authors.

■ Awards, Honors

Esther Glen Medal, New Zealand Library Association, 1979, for *Take the Long Path;* Reed Memorial Award, 1985, for *Hemi's Pet.*

JOAN LITTLEDALE de HAMEL

■ Writings

(Self-illustrated) *X Marks the Spot,* Lutterworth, 1973.
Take the Long Path, illustrated by Gareth Floyd, Lutterworth, 1978.
Hemi's Pet, illustrated by Christine Ross, Reed Methuen, 1985, Angus & Robertson, 1985, Houghton, 1987.
The Third Eye, Viking Kestrel, 1987.
Hideaway, Puffin, 1992.

Hemi's Pet has been published in Afrikaans, Sesotho, Xhosa, and Maori. Also author of scripts, including *To Chartres in Three Hours,* produced by British Broadcasting Corp. (BBC); *Mr. Timms and Mr. Mott, The Chaubord Omelette,* and others, produced by New Zealand Broadcasting Corp. Contributor to magazines. Editor of *Polyglot.*

■ **Work in Progress**

Another book has been accepted for publication.

■ **Sidelights**

Joan Littledale de Hamel emigrated from Great Britain to New Zealand in 1955. A teacher by profession, she had written scripts for the British Broadcasting Corporation prior to her move, and capitalized on that experience in her new home by writing for radio. It wasn't until 1973, however, that de Hamel wrote her first book for young readers, *X Marks the Spot.* That book, and each of her successive works for children, is characterized by a concern for the issues currently faced by New Zealanders. From investigations of its compelling landscapes and the lives of its indigenous people, to promoting the protection of endangered species on the island and cooperation among New Zealand's diverse population, de Hamel has demonstrated a special appreciation of her adopted homeland.

X Marks the Spot tells the story of three children who are lost in the New Zealand bush following a helicopter crash. Thrilled, at first, by the landscape and the freedom their situation permits, the children are forced to confront the bush's perilous reality after losing their backpacks and supplies. With only a gun and some matches remaining, the children must make difficult decisions to survive. In the course of their adventures, the children also deal with a group of poachers who are pursuing a rare species of parrot.

The children from *X Marks the Spot* return in *The Third Eye.* The children are teenagers now, and the world around them is becoming increasingly complex. A large company is attempting to develop lands which once belonged to New Zealand's indigenous people, the Maori. A dispute arises over the rights of the Maori to determine the land's future. In the midst of this struggle, the children discover an American scientist conducting experiments on the rare tuatara lizard. The conservation issues facing the children are clouded by the facts that development will bring employment to the region, and the scientist's research is potentially a great benefit to humankind. "Young readers ... will realise that serious themes are explored within this well crafted adventure," remarked Margery Fisher in *Growing Point.*

Hideaway is a story of intrigue involving Becky and a young Russian castaway. When her parents return to England to attend to her dying grandmother, Becky moves to her uncle's goat farm. Becky is bored by life on the farm, and is disturbed by the realization that her cousin, Chloe, is hanging out with a group of delin-

quents. While Becky is puzzling over Chloe's problems, she encounters a bedraggled Russian boy who has apparently jumped from a passing ship. Becky hides the boy in a ramshackle hut, and begins a routine of bringing food to his hiding place. In addition to providing for the mysterious youth, Becky raises a young goat abandoned by its mother, and confronts Chloe's increasing rebelliousness at home. These themes are interwoven, pointed out *School Librarian* reviewer Sandra Bennett, "providing suspense until eventually all problems are resolved at the same time."

De Hamel has also authored a picture book, *Hemi's Pet,* in which a young Maori boy enters his sister in his school pet show. The other students protest, but Hemi argues that she meets the criteria for a pet: he loves her and cares for her. The judges are convinced, and Hemi is awarded the prize for most original pet. "Refreshing and warm, this is a delightful story," asserted Cathy Woodward in *School Library Journal.*

De Hamel once commented: "I wrote for myself from early childhood, for money after marriage, and sold most of it. I emigrated to New Zealand in 1955 and turned mostly to radio writing. When my fifth son was at kindergarten, I began my first full-length novel, and in 1978, at last, became a full-time writer."

A seasoned traveler, the author explained to *SATA* that her stories are the result of her own real-life adventures. "*X Marks the Spot* was based on my personal experiences, lost in the bush. At the time, this was NO JOKE, and, indeed, all my books are based on true NO JOKE events in my life. *Take the Long Path* was inspired by watching a penguin that had been savaged by a shark. *The Third Eye* came from a terrifying adventure in limestone caves. The heart-rending plight of a motherless kid goat inspired *Hideaway.*

"My books are built up from diary notes, on-the-spot jottings, and by digging deep into childhood memories, adding extras, fiddling everything around," de Hamel noted. She added that "this takes time. I am a very slow writer."

■ **Works Cited**

Bennett, Sandra, review of *Hideaway, School Librarian,* August, 1993, p. 120.
Fisher, Margery, review of *The Third Eye, Growing Point,* May, 1989, pp. 5155-63.
Woodward, Cathy, review of *Hemi's Pet, School Library Journal,* June-July, 1987, p. 81.

■ **For More Information See**

BOOKS

Gilderdale, Betty, *Introducing Twenty-one New Zealand Children's Writers,* Hodder & Stoughton, 1991, pp. 43-47.
Twentieth-Century Children's Writers, 4th edition, St. James Press, 1995, pp. 283-284.

PERIODICALS

Booklist, April 1, 1987, p. 1203.
Junior Bookshelf, December, 1978, p. 309.
Magpies, September, 1993, p. 31.
Publishers Weekly, April 10, 1987, p. 94.

*   *   *

DESIMINI, Lisa 1964-

■ Personal

Born March 21, 1964, in Brooklyn, NY; daughter of Pat (a money broker) and Vera (a medical assistant; maiden name, Klassen) Desimini. *Education:* School of Visual Arts, New York, NY, B.F.A., 1986.

■ Addresses

Home—41 Morton St., #3, New York, NY 10014.

■ Career

Children's book illustrator and writer. Teaches illustration at the School of Visual Arts, New York City.

■ Awards, Honors

Critici in Erba Honor Book, Bologna Book Fair, for *I Am Running Away Today; New York Times* Best Illustrated and American Booksellers Pick of the List citations, both for *My House.*

■ Writings

SELF-ILLUSTRATED

I Am Running Away Today, Hyperion, 1992.
Moon Soup, Hyperion, 1993.
My House, Holt, 1994.

ILLUSTRATOR

Ann Turner, *Heron Street,* HarperCollins, 1989.
Liz Rosenberg, *Adelaide and the Night Train,* Harper-
    Collins, 1989.
Christine Widman, *Housekeeper of the Wind,* Harper-
    Collins, 1990.
Nancy White Carlstrom, *Moose in the Garden,* Harper-
    Collins, 1990.
Dennis Haseley, *The Thieves' Market,* HarperCollins,
    1991.
Carlstrom, *Light: Stories of a Small Kindness,* Little,
    Brown, 1992.
Jerrie Oughton, *How the Stars Fell into the Sky: A
    Navajo Legend,* Houghton, 1993.
Liliane Atlan, *The Passersby,* translated from the French
    by Rochelle Owens, Holt, 1993.
Holly Near, *The Great Peace March,* Holt, 1993.
Carlstrom, *Fish and Flaming,* Little, Brown, 1993.
Oughton, *Magic Weaver of Rugs: A Tale of the Navajo,*
    Houghton, 1994.
Tree De Gerez, *When Bear Came Down from the Sky,*
    Viking, 1994.
Nancy Van Laan, *In a Circle Long Ago,* Knopf, 1995.

■ Work in Progress

A love story for children entitled *The Sun and the Moon* and illustrations for *Northwoods Cradle Song* by Douglas Wood for Simon and Schuster.

■ Sidelights

Lisa Desimini came to children's book illustration almost by accident. After graduating from New York's School of Visual Arts in 1986, she expected to go to work illustrating for magazines and newspapers. She told Janet Schnol of *Publishers Weekly* that even after she was referred to a Harper Junior Books editor and then given the opportunity to produce sample illustrations for Ann Turner's *Heron Street,* she still was not certain she was interested in working with children's books. She quickly found the work highly satisfying, however, and even proclaimed herself "addicted." "What I love about children's books," Desimini told Schnol, "is that I'm involved with so much—decisions about end pages, color and type. I have a great deal of freedom, especially in the layout."

Desimini's illustrations have been described as surreal and seemingly naive, and have invited comparisons to artist Henri Rousseau. In *Adelaide and the Night Train* by Liz Rosenberg, Desimini's illustrations of a night ride on a train heading toward the land of sleep echo the evocative language of the text, according to critics. Stephen Dobyns of the *New York Times Book Review* remarked that Desimini's illustrations possess "a slightly primitive cast, a magical weirdness that bears close examination.... At my house these days, when the youngest child has trouble settling down, *Adelaide and the Night Train* is the book we try first. It's as good as a glass of warm milk, and half the bother." "I like writing books that have a touch of magic," Desimini told *SATA.* "I illustrated many books for other authors before I

LISA DESIMINI

Six eggs and five kinds of purple are just some of the ingredients needed to make a fanciful meal in Desimini's self-illustrated *Moon Soup*.

started writing my own. I feel like I can truly express myself this way."

Desimini's first solo effort, *I Am Running Away Today,* is considered a lighthearted treatment of the theme of running away. At the book's opening, a cat decides to leave his home since his best friend next door is moving away, so he goes in search of a new home. The simple text is accompanied by illustrations noted for their innovation, style, and dramatic qualities. Although Zack Rogow of the *New York Times Book Review* felt that *I Am Running Away Today* "reads like a book written by someone whose training and experience have been largely in the visual arts," he praised the "playful, colorful and stylized" illustrations. Similarly, a reviewer for *Publishers Weekly* found the illustrative style a bit out of balance with the "fun and fanciful" story.

The illustrations for *Moon Soup* captured much of the critical attention bestowed upon the book. In this story, Desimini offers a fanciful recipe for soup that concludes with the main character flying off to the moon to stir and serve it. Although Ruth Semrau in the *School Library Journal* felt it had a weak story line, she noted that "shapes, lines, and colors combine to create an exciting visual experience." Ilene Cooper concluded in *Booklist:* "Desimini's fanciful art may be over the top for some, but it's hard to tear your eyes away."

Desimini's "brief text serves mainly as a springboard for stunning illustrations," remarked a reviewer in *Publishers Weekly* about *My House.* Desimini used collage with paintings, photographs, and other media to depict a house in different kinds of light and weather conditions. "For all the showiness" of the art, the review continued, "the book is reassuring" because it emphasizes the friendliness and security of the home.

■ Works Cited

Cooper, Ilene, review of *Moon Soup, Booklist,* November 1, 1993, p. 528.

Dobyns, Stephen, review of *Adelaide and the Night Train, New York Times Book Review,* April 1, 1990, p. 26.

Review of *I Am Running Away Today, Publishers Weekly,* March 16, 1992, p. 79.

Review of *My House, Publishers Weekly,* September 5, 1994, p. 110.

Rogow, Zack, "Follow the Paw Prints," *New York Times Book Review,* March 17, 1992, p. 31.

Schnol, Janet, "Flying Starts: New Faces of 1989," *Publishers Weekly,* December 22, 1989, pp. 28-29.

Semrau, Ruth, review of *Moon Soup, School Library Journal,* January, 1994, p. 88.

■ For More Information See

PERIODICALS

School Library Journal, June, 1992, p. 91.

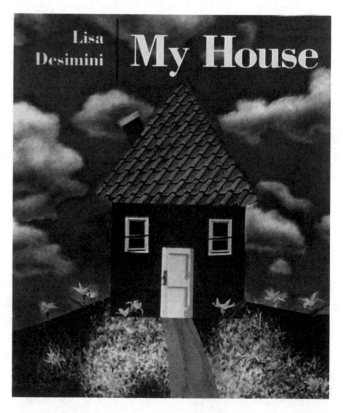

Desimini combined paint, collage, and photographs to create this visual portrait of a child's home. (Cover illustration by the author.)

LYNLEY DODD

DODD, Lynley (Stuart) 1941-

■ Personal

Born July 5, 1941, in Rotorua, New Zealand; daughter of Matthew Fotheringhan (a forester) and Elizabeth Sinclair (a secretary; maiden name, Baxter) Weeks; married Anthony Robert Fletcher Dodd, January 2, 1965; children: Matthew Fletcher, Elizabeth Anne. *Education:* Elam School of Art, diploma, 1962; further study at Auckland Teachers College, 1962.

■ Addresses

Home and office—Edward Avenue, R.D. 3, Tauranga, New Zealand.

■ Career

Queen Margaret College, Wellington, New Zealand, art mistress, 1963-68; freelance author and illustrator, 1968—. *Member:* PEN International.

■ Awards, Honors

(With Eve Sutton) Esther Glen Medal, New Zealand Library Association, 1975, for *My Cat Likes to Hide in Boxes;* Choysa Bursary for Children's Writers, New Zealand Literary Fund and Quality Packers Ltd., 1978; New Zealand Book Award for illustrations, 1981, for *Druscilla;* New Zealand Children's Picture Book of the Year Award, 1984, for *Hairy Maclary from Donaldson's Dairy,* 1986, for *Hairy Maclary's Scattercat,* and 1988,

for *Hairy Maclary's Caterwaul Caper;* Third Prize in the AIM Children's Picture Book of the Year Award, for *Hairy Maclary's Rumpus at the Vet,* 1990; The New Zealand 1990 Commemorative Medal ("in recognition of services to New Zealand"); Third Prize in the AIM Children's Picture Book of the Year Award, for *Slinky Malinki,* 1991; AIM Children's Picture Book of the Year Award, for *Hairy Maclary's Showbusiness,* 1992.

■ Writings

SELF-ILLUSTRATED; FOR CHILDREN

(With Eve Sutton) *My Cat Likes to Hide in Boxes,* Hamilton, 1973, Era, 1984.
The Nickle Nackle Tree, Hamilton, 1976, Era, 1985.
Titimus Trim, Hamilton, 1979, Hodder & Stoughton, 1979.
The Smallest Turtle, Mallinson Rendel, 1982, Gareth Stevens, 1985.
The Apple Tree, Mallinson Rendel, 1982, Gareth Stevens, 1985.
Hairy Maclary from Donaldson's Dairy, Mallinson Rendel, 1983, Gareth Stevens, 1985.
Hairy Maclary's Bone, Mallinson Rendel, 1984, Gareth Stevens, 1985.
Hairy Maclary's Scattercat, Mallinson Rendel, 1985, Gareth Stevens, 1988.
Wake Up, Bear, Mallinson Rendel, 1986, Gareth Stevens, 1986.
Hairy Maclary's Caterwaul Caper, Mallinson Rendel, 1987, Gareth Stevens, 1989.
A Dragon in a Wagon, Mallinson Rendel, 1988, Gareth Stevens, 1989.
Hairy Maclary's Rumpus at the Vet, Mallinson Rendel, 1989, Gareth Stevens, 1990.
Slinky Malinki, Mallinson Rendel, 1990, Keystone, 1990.
Find Me a Tiger, Mallinson Rendel, 1991, Gareth Stevens, 1992.
Hairy Maclary's Showbusiness, Mallinson Rendel, 1991, Keystone, 1991.
The Minister's Cat ABC, Mallinson Rendel, 1992, Gareth Stevens, 1994.
Slinky Malinki, Open the Door, Mallinson Rendel, 1993, Gareth Stevens, 1994.
Schnitzel von Krumm's Basketwork, Mallinson Rendel, 1994, Gareth Stevens, 1994.
Sniff-Snuff-Snap!, Mallinson Rendel, 1995.

ILLUSTRATOR; FOR CHILDREN

Jillian Squire, *Pussyfooting,* Millwood Press, 1978.
Clarice England, *Druscilla,* Hodder & Stoughton, 1980.

Also illustrator of several educational readers for Price Milburn, 1974-83.

■ Sidelights

Lynley Dodd told *SATA:* "I was brought up in small, isolated forestry settlements. There were few children in the neighborhood, but for those few there was unlimited space for play, and miles of pine trees in any direction provided plenty of scope for imagination. I have always had pen and drawing paper ready—most times I have had an illustrating assignment of some sort in hand. I have also done a little cartooning. At the arrival of my first baby I took on work for a correspondence school, illustrating fortnightly sets for seven- to nine-year-olds."

Dodd's work as a writer began with Eve Sutton's suggestion that they collaborate on a children's book, *My Cat Likes to Hide in Boxes,* a picture book based on Dodd's family cat. It was after this collaboration that Dodd became fascinated with picture books. She also had two small children at the time who were active readers of children's books, so she decided to try writing her own. The book that came out of this effort was *The Nickle Nackle Tree,* which a reviewer in *Publishers Weekly* called, "just the thing to lift the spirits in the bleak, lifeless winter months." This self-illustrated counting book burdens the nickle nackle tree with various kinds and quantities of birds.

"I now write as well as illustrate my own picture books," Dodd once told *SATA.* "I find being able to plan the whole book from the outset exciting and rewarding. The idea is roughed out first and fit into the format and length required. Then a 'dummy' is made, a complete miniature mock-up of the finished book. This gives the publisher a good indication of plan and serves as a working model for me when I come to do final illustrations."

Three more picture books followed *The Nickle Nackle Tree,* including *The Apple Tree* and *Titimus Trim,* the story of a man who becomes so muddled when his usual routine is interrupted that hc mows the carpet and invites the dog to tea. This book was followed by *The Smallest Turtle,* which a critic in *Junior Bookshelf* called a "delightful story . . . beautifully drawn."

The lead character in Dodd's next book is perhaps the most beloved she has created. Hairy Maclary is a small, black, scruffy terrier-type dog who inhabits a canine community that includes such friends as Hercules Morse, Muffin McLay, Bitzer Maloney, Bottomley Potts, the dachshund Schnitzel von Krumm, and the dogs' arch-enemy, the fierce tomcat Scarface Claw. *Hairy Maclary from Donaldson's Dairy* became the first in a series for which Dodd is best known around the world, and especially in her native New Zealand. Colin Mills stated in a review in *Books for Keeps* that with the combination of Dodd's text and pictures, youngsters will learn a great deal "about sound, stress, intonation and the patterning of language." The next book in the series, *Hairy Maclary's Bone,* begins happily enough with Butcher Stone bestowing his tastiest bone upon the grateful Hairy. But Hairy soon finds his bone the envy of all his canine friends. As they try to get the bone from him, he leads them on an obstacle course through the neighborhood until the competition is eliminated one by one.

In his next adventure, *Hairy Maclary's Scattercat,* Hairy is out to terrorize all the cats in the neighborhood—which he does successfully until he meets up with

Scarface Claw, who turns the tables and chases the dog home. However, in *Hairy Maclary's Caterwaul Caper,* the tough terrier and his friends save the day when Scarface gets stuck high up in a tree. The dogs' barking and yapping create such a din that Miss Plum finally comes out to investigate and rescues the unfortunate cat. Phillis Wilson noted in a review in *Booklist* that Dodd's full-page illustrations capture "the particular personality of each dog" as well as "the humor of Scarface's wounded dignity."

The series continues in *Hairy Maclary's Rumpus at the Vet,* when Hairy Maclary gets his tail nipped by a caged cockatoo in the vet's office, which precipitates a riot in the waiting room. The canny canine is the cause of another rumpus (this time at a cat show) in *Hairy Maclary's Showbusiness,* where, after overturning chairs and flustering cats and owners alike, he eventually manages to carry off the prize for Scruffiest Cat of the Show.

"Since Hairy Maclary came on the scene, books have been a full-time occupation and I seem to spend as much time answering letters as in the actual writing and illustration," Dodd commented. "I take part in the New Zealand Book Council's Writers in Schools' scheme—a worthwhile activity as it keeps me in touch with the 'consumers.' It's a two-way thing; the children are able to put a face to the name on the books and the feedback I get, plus the fun of sharing the books with large numbers of children, is stimulating and a spur to new ideas, as well as a way to keep myself on track."

Like Beatrix Potter, Dodd has been praised for creating animal characters with distinctly individual personalities, as well as for her ability to conjoin text and pictures. Two of Dodd's memorable creations from the Hairy Maclary series went on to become leading characters themselves. The dachshund is the star of *Schnitzel von Krumm's Basketwork.* Schnitzel von Krumm has slept in the same old basket all of his doggy years, and it is more than beginning to show its age. When his owners replace the basket with a stylish new one, Schnitzel goes off in search of a bed as cozy and comforting as his old one. *School Librarian* critic Carol Woolley praised the book as a "charming tale for any dog lover" and noted that its rhyme and rhythm "carry the story along swiftly."

The only feline of the Hairy Maclary cast to strike out on its own is the lithe black cat Slinky Malinki. In his first (self-titled) book, Slinky leads a secret life of crime until his loot is discovered and he reforms. In *Slinky Malinki, Open the Door,* he discovers how to open all the doors and creates mayhem when he and a parrot are left alone in the house.

Dodd's animal creations are by no means limited to Hairy Maclary and friends. Cats take the lead again in her 1992 book *The Minister's Cat ABC,* based on a traditional rhyming game. Some critics claimed the abstract adjectives were difficult concepts for young children to grasp. Others, such as Trevor Dickinson

Hairy Maclary, a black terrier who decides to antagonize the neighborhood cats, meets his match when he upsets his arch-enemy, Scarface Claw. (Illustration from *Hairy Maclary's Scattercat* by the author.)

writing in *School Librarian,* saw the demands of the vocabulary as "easily overcome through the illustrations" which made the characteristics of each cat quite clear.

Earlier works focus on animals of a less domesticated nature. In *Wake Up, Bear,* a succession of animals are unable to waken the hibernating bear—until a bee comes along and reminds him of honey. In *Find Me a Tiger,* one of Dodd's most artistically ambitious books, children have to look hard at Dodd's line and color drawings to find the cleverly camouflaged animals. A four line rhyming clue helps readers discover the hidden creatures. In a review in *Magpies,* Margaret Kelly praised the "wonderfully natural illustrations, evidence of Dodd's great knowledge of and ease with animals." Human beings do appear in Dodd's books as well, although the only one to take a leading role is Susie Fogg in *A Dragon in a Wagon.* On a walk with her dog, Sam, Susie imagines that he turns into various exciting creatures. It isn't until Susie slips and falls that she appreciates the comfort of Sam being just a dog.

"Writing for children is an exacting business," Dodd commented. "Beginning as an illustrator and only later trying my hand at writing text as well, I know only too well the truth of the saying, 'The fewer the words, the harder the job.' It's exasperating to hear, from those who should know better, 'I'd like to try writing—I think I'll start with a children's book.' One hopes the results never reach the children! (However I may have overdone the 'blood, sweat and tears' bit in my school talks, as a recent comment from a child's letter shows, 'I might just be an author when I grow up, unless I get a better job.')"

"Hard work, yes, but enormous satisfaction too. To travel halfway around the world and find a Glasgow audience of five- to seven-year-olds, muffled to the eyebrows against snow outside and draughts inside, happily chanting the results of one's labours at a desk 12,000 miles away, is to reap the reward that makes it all worthwhile."

■ **Works Cited**

Dickinson, Trevor, review of *The Minister's Cat ABC, School Librarian,* February, 1993, pp. 14-15.

Kelly, Margaret, review of *Find Me a Tiger, Magpies,* November, 1991, p. 26.

Mills, Colin, review of *Hairy Maclary from Donaldson's Dairy, Books for Keeps,* January, 1986, p. 13.

Review of *The Nickle Nackle Tree, Publishers Weekly*, January 23, 1978, p. 373.

Review of *The Smallest Turtle, Junior Bookshelf*, October, 1983, p. 206.

Wilson, Phillis, review of *Hairy Maclary's Caterwaul Caper, Booklist*, December 1, 1988, p. 646.

Woolley, Carol, review of *Schnitzel von Krumm's Basketwork, School Librarian*, November, 1994, p. 145.

■ For More Information See

PERIODICALS

Books for Keeps, November, 1993, p. 10; July, 1994, p. 6.

School Librarian, February, 1992, p. 15.

School Library Journal, August, 1991, p. 144; February, 1992, p. 15.

Times Educational Supplement, July 29, 1988, p. 21; January 7, 1994, p. 33.

DONOVAN, Mary Lee 1961-

■ Personal

Born September 18, 1961, in Pittsfield, MA; daughter of Vincent P. (an engineer) and Louise Andree (Bonin) Donovan; married Nathan Jed Santoro (a sales manager), November 14, 1992; children: Nathaniel Lee. *Education:* North Adams State College, B.A., 1983; The Center for the Study of Children's Literature, Simmons College, M.A., 1986.

■ Career

Children's book author and editor. The Children's Bookshop, Brookline, MA, salesperson, 1983-87; Houghton Mifflin Co., Boston, MA, editor, 1985-91; Candlewick Press, Cambridge, MA, editor, 1991-1995, sales manager, 1992-94. *Member:* Society for Children's Book Writers and Illustrators, Authors' Guild.

Fathers, both human and animal, tell bedtime tales to their children in this work by Mary Lee Donovan. (Illustration by Kimberly Bulcken Root from *Papa's Bedtime Story*.)

■ Writings

Papa's Bedtime Story, illustrated by Kimberly Bulcken Root, Knopf, 1993.
Snuffles Makes a Friend, Candlewick Press, 1995.

■ Work in Progress

Swamp Frolics, The Souvenir, and *Won't You Come and Play With Me?,* all picture books, and *All the Wrong Things,* a middle-grade novel.

■ Sidelights

Mary Lee Donovan's interest in children's literature began when she was an adolescent baby sitter, according to Nina Nickles in *Concord Journal.* "I really saw how children are so affected by books, how they love them and how they never seem to tire of them," Donovan told Nickles. She studied children's literature in college, earning both a bachelor's and a master's degree before entering the world of publishing. While working as a bookseller, editor, and sales manager, Donovan wrote stories for children, finally settling on a circular nonsense tale her father had told her as a child as the subject for her first publication, entitled *Papa's Bedtime Story.*

"Children's books are a wonderful mixture of beautiful language and art. It's like writing poetry, because every word has to count," Donovan told Darienne J. Hosley in a review in *Berkshire Eagle.* It took countless revisions of *Papa's Bedtime Story* over a period of nearly a decade for Donovan to achieve the high standard she set for the prose of her first book. "I would read it aloud and tape myself," she told Hosley, "then listen to it. Anywhere I faltered, anything that sounded jarring or not quite right, I'd say 'Ah, I have to work on that.'" Critics generally responded to the poetic qualities of Donovan's text, and remarked upon its calming rhythms.

In *Papa's Bedtime Story,* Donovan depicts a child begging for a bedtime story from her father, who begins to tell the story of a barn owl, whose child asks him for a story; in turn, the barn owl tells the story of a chipmunk, whose child asks him for a story—"So it goes, from one creature to another, until it finally rains and the wood frogs joyously begin to peep," wrote a reviewer in *Kirkus Reviews.* A critic in *Publishers Weekly* commented upon the "whimsical" structure of the book, and remarked that "through melodic language and inflections, [Donovan] creates a suitably soothing quality." *Horn Book* contributor Christine C. Behr dubbed *Papa's Bedtime Story* a "lovely story."

■ Works Cited

Behr, Christine C., review of *Papa's Bedtime Story, Horn Book,* fall, 1993, p. 256.
Hosley, Darienne J., "Dalton Native Turns Father's Story into Book," *Berkshire (MA) Eagle,* August 8, 1993, p. G6.
Nickles, Nina, "Children's Author Urges First-Graders to Persevere," *Concord (MA) Journal,* January 26, 1995, p. 8.
Review of *Papa's Bedtime Story, Kirkus Reviews,* February 15, 1993, p. 225.
Review of *Papa's Bedtime Story, Publishers Weekly,* March 22, 1993, p. 78.

* * *

DUPASQUIER, Philippe 1955-

■ Personal

Born September 27, 1955, in Neuchatel, Switzerland; son of Fernand (an engineer) and Christiane Dupasquier; married Sylvie Grandin (a teacher), June 16, 1979; children: Timothy, Sophie. *Education:* Attended art school in Lyon, France, 1976-79.

■ Addresses

Home—Hambledon, Spring Hill, Punnetts Town, Heathfield, East Sussex TN21 9PE, England.

■ Career

Author and illustrator of books for children. Freelance illustrator in London, England, beginning in 1979.

■ Awards, Honors

Smarties Prize and Carnegie Medal commendation, both 1989, and Oak Tree Award, Nottinghamshire Libraries, 1990, all for *Bill's New Frock.*

■ Writings

SELF-ILLUSTRATED

Dear Daddy, Andersen, 1985.
Robert and the Red Balloon, Walker, 1985.
Robert the Great, Walker, 1985.
Jack at Sea, Andersen, 1986.
Our House on the Hill, Andersen, 1987, Puffin Books, 1990.
The Great Escape, Walker, 1988.
I Can't Sleep, Andersen, 1990, Orchard Books, 1990.
A Robot Named Chip, Andersen, 1990, Viking, 1991.
My Dad, Andersen, 1991.
Follow That Chimp, Walker, 1993.
Tom's Pirate Ship, Andersen, 1993, published as *Andy's Pirate Ship,* Holt, 1994.
Paul's Present, Andersen, 1994.

"BUSY PLACES" SERIES

The Airport, Walker, 1984, published as *A Busy Day at the Airport,* 1994.
The Building Site, Walker, 1984, published as *A Busy Day at the Building Site,* 1994.
The Factory, Walker, 1984, published as *A Busy Day at the Factory,* 1994.
The Garage, Walker, 1984, published as *A Busy Day at the Garage,* 1994.

PHILIPPE DUPASQUIER

The Railway Station, Walker, 1984, published as *A Busy Day at the Railway Station,* 1994.
The Harbour, Walker, 1988, published as *A Busy Day at the Harbour,* 1994.

ILLUSTRATOR

Martin Waddell, *Going West,* Andersen, 1983.
Nigel Gray, *A Country Far Away,* Andersen, 1988.
Derek Sampson, *Follow That Pharaoh,* Methuen, 1988.
Hazel Townson, *Fireworks Galore!,* Andersen, 1988.
Anne Fine, *Bill's New Frock,* Methuen, 1989.
Tony Bradman, *The Sandal,* Viking Kestrel, 1990.
Tessa Krailing, *Whizzkid,* Paperbird, 1990.
Gillian Cross, *Gobbo the Great,* Methuen, 1991.
Fine, *The Country Pancake,* Mammoth, 1991.
Fine, *Design a Pram,* Heinemann, 1991.
Townson, *Lenny and Jake Adventures,* Red Fox, 1991.
Townson, *Hopping Mad,* Andersen, 1991.
Cross, *Save Our School!,* Dean, 1992.
Fine, *"The Chicken Gave It to Me,"* Methuen, 1992.
Mary Welfare, *Who's Afraid of Swapping Spiders?,* Mammoth, 1992.
Townson, *The Kidnap Report,* Andersen, 1992.
Michael Coleman, *Fizzy Hits the Headlines,* Orchard, 1993.
Angela Royston, *The Busy Digger,* Kingfisher, 1993.
Townson, *A Night on Smuggler's Island,* Andersen, 1993.

Jeff Brown, *Stanley's Christmas Adventure,* Methuen, 1993.
Gray, *Keep on Chomping!,* Andersen, 1993, Trafalgar Square, 1994.
Coleman, *Fizzy Steals the Show,* Orchard, 1994.
Townson, *Charlie the Champion Liar,* Methuen, 1994.
Sam McBratney, *Henry Seamouse,* Longman, 1994.

OTHER

Also illustrator of Brown, *Stanley in Space,* Mammoth; and Royston, *The Story of a Helicopter,* Kingfisher.

■ Sidelights

Artist Philippe Dupasquier has written and illustrated many children's books of his own, as well as illustrated over twenty books by prominent authors. Dupasquier, the father of two children, once commented: "Apart from my work in children's books, I would like to have more time for painting and watercolor as fine art. The family is a major theme in my books. It is also my favorite 'activity' when I am not working."

Dupasquier's first self-illustrated work, *Dear Daddy,* tells the story of little Sophie, who waits for her father to return home from a year-long sea voyage with the merchant marine. The text consists of Sophie's letters to her father describing events in her life. The pictures on the bottom half of each page show Sophie's birthday party, the delivery of a piano to her house, the growth of her baby brother's first tooth, and other occasions. The pictures on the top half of each page, meanwhile, show the details of her father's life aboard ship. The story concludes with a happy family reunion. A *Junior Bookshelf* reviewer called *Dear Daddy* "a delightful, moving little book," while Joan McGrath of *School Library Journal* predicted young readers would find it "warm and reassuring."

Our House on the Hill, Dupasquier's fourth self-illustrated book, is intended for very young children on the verge of reading. It contains no words but, like *Dear Daddy,* tells the story of a family's experiences over the course of a year using two sets of illustrations that complement one another. On each left-hand page is a birds-eye view of a house and yard during a given month. The landscape includes many small details of the season, such as hot dogs on the barbecue or laundry drying on a line. On each right-hand page is a series of small pictures that tell a story about one of the details from the previous page. In a review for *School Library Journal,* Nancy Seiner commented that Dupasquier's "lively sketches, filled in with soft watercolors, make the characters and their surroundings come to life," and claimed that families would enjoy reading the book again and again.

The Great Escape, Dupasquier's next book, is a "brilliant and breathless account of a prisoner's escape and the madcap chase after him," according to Julia Eccleshare in *Times Literary Supplement.* Told in pictures, the story follows the escaped prisoner and his police pursuers through a circus, a wedding, a museum, a hospital,

An escaped prisoner leads his pursuers on a wild chase through a museum, a hospital, a circus, and several other unlikely places in Dupasquier's self-illustrated *The Great Escape.*

a foxhunt, and a variety of other interesting places. The prisoner finally goes through a sewer that leads him back inside the prison. Susan H. Patron, writing in *School Library Journal*, stated that Dupasquier's "full-color cartoon drawings are crowded with funny details and lots of action."

Dupasquier returned to the wordless picturebook format with *I Can't Sleep*. This time, a young girl, her parents, her brother, and her cat all have trouble sleeping one night. They gather in the kitchen for a midnight snack and then wander outside to look at the stars. Finally, they all fall asleep together in one bed just in time for the sunrise. A *Publishers Weekly* reviewer praised Dupasquier's art work, noting that the "watercolors, appropriately hushed and rumpled, have a lively cinematic quality" that enhances the story and characters.

My Dad, published in 1991, is especially well-suited for "children having trouble at home," according to Beverley Mathias in *School Librarian*. In the story, a young boy thinks about all of his father's negative qualities, like not allowing the boy to do whatever he wants, or paying too much attention to the boy's sister. After a while, though, the boy also thinks of many positive things about his dad, like when his dad reads to him or takes him on outings to special places. Mathias claimed that all children feel their parents are unfair at times, and this balanced portrait of a father might help children to understand a parent's role.

Dupasquier also wrote and illustrated a series of popular books about busy places that are familiar to children. The "Busy Places" series includes six titles: *The Airport, The Building Site, The Factory, The Garage, The Harbour,* and *The Railway Station*. Each book follows the events that take place at that location during the course of a day. All of the illustrations in each book feature the same scene with new details appropriate to the time of day. For example, *The Factory* begins when the night watchman of a candy factory goes home in the morning. The story continues with the arrival of a group of schoolchildren for a tour, and includes a number of comic mishaps in candy production. The action builds and then subsides, concluding when the night watchman returns in the evening. In each book, the area surrounding the work place is also pictured and contains changing details. In a review of the series for *Times Literary Supplement*, Barbara Sherrard-Smith noted that "the pictures are full of life and human interest, stimulating children to explore, examine, discover, to discuss and be involved, and look with new eyes at the next busy place they visit."

■ Works Cited

Review of *Dear Daddy, Junior Bookshelf*, October, 1985, p. 211.

Eccleshare, Julia, "Texts and Pretexts," *Times Literary Supplement*, September 9-15, 1988, p. 1000.

Review of *I Can't Sleep, Publishers Weekly*, June 8, 1990, p. 52.

Mathias, Beverley, review of *My Dad, School Librarian,* August, 1991, p. 100.

McGrath, Joan, review of *Dear Daddy, School Library Journal,* November, 1985, p. 69.

Patron, Susan H., review of *The Great Escape, School Library Journal,* August, 1988, p. 80.

Seiner, Nancy, review of *Our House on the Hill, School Library Journal,* October, 1988, pp. 118-19.

Sherrard-Smith, Barbara, "The World Outside," *Times Literary Supplement,* June 29, 1984, p. 737.

■ For More Information See

PERIODICALS

Booklist, January 1, 1986, p. 684.

Books for Keeps, November, 1988, p. 8; January, 1996, pp. 14-15.

Junior Bookshelf, October, 1990, p. 219; April, 1993, p. 58.

Listener, November 29, 1984, p. 27; November 7, 1985, p. 32.

Publishers Weekly, February 27, 1987, p. 164.

School Library Journal, March, 1985, p. 147; October, 1987, p. 110; August, 1991, p. 145; August, 1994, p. 129.

Times Literary Supplement, October 9-15, 1987, p. 1120.

*   *   *

DUPUY, T(revor) N(evitt) 1916-1995

OBITUARY NOTICE—See index for *SATA* sketch: Born May 3, 1916, in New York, NY; committed suicide after learning he had pancreatic cancer, June 5, 1995, in Vienna, VA. Military officer, historian, educator, executive, and author. The author of more than one hundred books on military history, some written with his father, Dupuy created computer systems for use in forecasting potential battle losses in terms of people and equipment. A graduate of West Point, Dupuy began some twenty years as a career officer with the U.S. Army Artillery in 1938. During his years of service, he rose to the rank of colonel. He saw duty in Burma during World War II and served in Washington in the operations division of the War Department General Staff. Before concluding his military career, Dupuy was a professor of military science and tactics at Harvard University and was the director of military courses at Ohio State University. Following stints as a visiting professor and as a member of the International Studies Division of the Institute for Defense Analyses, he became president of T. N. Dupuy Associates. From 1983 until 1990 he was president and chair of the board of directors of Data Memory Systems, Inc. Holding the same positions for HERD-TNDA from 1990 until 1991, he became president of the Dupuy Institute, which specializes in military analysis, in 1992. Dupuy published his first book, *To the Colors,* written with his father, R. Ernest Dupuy, in 1942. Many collaborations followed, including *Brave Men and Great Captains* and *Encyclopedia of Military History.* His *How to Defeat Saddam Hussein* analyzed what war in the Persian Gulf could entail and proved fairly accurate following the conclusion of the actual conflict. He was editor-in-chief of the six-volume *Brassey's International Military and Defense Encyclopedia* and wrote the "Military Lives" series for F. Watts, profiling such leaders as Alexander the Great, Julius Caesar, and Abraham Lincoln. Several of his books were aimed at teenage audiences, including *First Book of Civil War Land Battles* and *First Book of Civil War Naval Actions.* Among Dupuy's numerous awards were the Legion of Merit and England's Distinguished Service Order.

OBITUARIES AND OTHER SOURCES:

BOOKS

Who's Who in America, 50th edition, Marquis, 1995, pp. 1016-17.

PERIODICALS

Los Angeles Times, June 9, 1995, p. A26.
New York Times, June 9, 1995, p. B11.

E

EHRENFREUND, Norbert 1921-

■ Personal

Born October 13, 1921, in Peekskill, NY; son of Leo (a knitting miller) and Henrietta (a homemaker; maiden name, Huppert) Ehrenfreund; married Mimette Wishart, October 31, 1964 (divorced, March 15, 1985); married Juliette Costigan (a medical transcriptionist), January 3, 1987; children: Zachary, Laurel. *Education:* Missouri University, B.J., 1943; Columbia University, M.A., 1950; Stanford Law School, LL.B., 1959.

■ Addresses

Home—2350 Sixth Ave., Apt. 7B, San Diego, CA 92101. *Office*—Superior Court, 220 West Broadway, San Diego, CA 92101. *Agent*—Vicky Bijur, 333 West End Ave., New York, NY 10023.

■ Career

The Stars and Stripes (newspaper), Germany, journalist, 1946-52; City of San Diego, CA, deputy district attorney, 1960-68; Defenders, Inc., San Diego, chief trial attorney, 1968-75; Superior Court, San Diego, judge, 1975—. *Military service:* U.S. Army, 1945; participated in Rhine campaign; received Bronze Star. *Member:* California Judges Association.

■ Writings

(With Lawrence Treat) *You're the Jury: Solve Twelve Real-Life Court Cases along with the Juries Who Decided Them,* H. Holt, 1992.

■ For More Information See

PERIODICALS

Booklist, July, 1992.
School Library Journal, September, 1992.

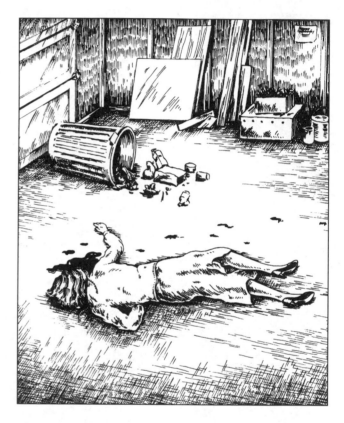

A police sketch shows the aftermath of a horrible crime in Norbert Ehrenfreund's *You're the Jury,* co-written with Lawrence Treat. (Illustration by Chris Costello.)

ENDE, Michael (Andreas Helmuth) 1929-1995

OBITUARY NOTICE—See index for *SATA* sketch: Born November 12, 1929, in Garmisch-Partenkirchen, Bavaria, Germany; died of stomach cancer, August 28, 1995, near Stuttgart, Germany. Actor, film critic, and author. A noted German writer of children's books, Ende was highly regarded for his works of fantasy, which, critics have claimed, help the reader journey into the inner world of the child. As a youth, Ende was conscripted into the German Army during World War II only to desert and allegedly join an anti-Nazi group. In 1950, he tried his hand at acting. He worked as a film critic for the Bavarian Broadcasting radio network and directed productions of the Munich Volkstheater. As a writer, Ende wrote everything from fiction to poetry. His 1960 work, translated as *Jim Button and Luke the Engine-Driver,* was published to much acclaim and received honors, including the Hans Christian Andersen Prize. Ende's *The Neverending Story,* later adapted into a film that he criticized, was also well received and achieved bestseller status. *The Neverending Story* and Ende's successful story *Momo* were written while he was in a self-imposed exile in Italy. Among his other works are *Mirror in the Mirror: A Labyrinth* and *Lirum Larum.*

OBITUARIES AND OTHER SOURCES:

BOOKS

Reginald, Robert, *Science Fiction and Fantasy Literature, 1975-1991,* Gale, 1992.

PERIODICALS

Chicago Tribune, September 3, 1995, Section 2, p. 6.
New York Times, September 1, 1995, p. D18.

*   *   *

EYERLY, Jeannette 1908-
(Jeannette Griffith, a joint pseudonym)

■ Personal

Born June 7, 1908, in Topeka, KS; daughter of Robert C. (a railroad executive) and Mabel (Young) Hyde; married Frank Rinehart Eyerly (a newspaper editor), December 6, 1932; children: Jane Kozuszek, Susan Pichler. *Education:* Attended Drake University, 1926-29; University of Iowa, A.B., 1930. *Politics:* Independent. *Religion:* Roman Catholic. *Hobbies and other interests:* Family, friends, flowers, children, reading, public libraries, playing Scrabble.

■ Addresses

Home—3524 Grand Ave., Apt. 3203, Des Moines, IA 50312. *Agent*—Curtis Brown, Inc., 10 Astor Pl., New York, NY 10003.

■ Career

Writer and lecturer. Publicity director, Des Moines Public Library, 1930-32; Des Moines Child Guidance Center, member of board of directors, 1949-54, president, 1953-54; creative writing teacher, Des Moines Adult Education Program, 1955-57. St. Joseph Academy Guild, member of board of directors, 1954-57, president, 1957. Member of acquisition committee, Des Moines Art Center, 1960-63. Polk County Mental Health Center, member of board of directors, 1968-78, president, 1977-78, 1982—. Iowa Commission for the Blind, member of board, 1977-80, chairman, 1978-79.

JEANNETTE EYERLY

Member: Authors League of America, Iowa Center of the Book of the Library of Congress (charter member).

■ Awards, Honors

Susan Glaspell Award, 1965, for *Gretchen's Hill;* Christopher Award, 1969, for *Escape from Nowhere; Radigan Cares* was selected as one of the Child Study Association's Books of the Year, 1970; *Someone to Love Me* selected "Book for Reluctant Reader", American Library Association, 1987; Polk County (Iowa) Mental Health Center was renamed "The Eyerly/Ball Community Health Services Building," 1995, in her honor.

■ Writings

NOVELS

More Than a Summer Love, Lippincott, 1962.
Drop-Out, Lippincott, 1963.
The World of Ellen March, Lippincott, 1964.
Gretchen's Hill, Lippincott, 1965.
A Girl Like Me, Lippincott, 1966.
The Girl Inside, Lippincott, 1968.
Escape from Nowhere, Lippincott, 1969.
Radigan Cares, Lippincott, 1970.
The Phaedra Complex, Lippincott, 1971.
Bonnie Jo, Go Home, Lippincott, 1972.

Goodby to Budapest: A Novel of Suspense, Lippincott, 1974.
The Leonardo Touch, Lippincott, 1976.
He's My Baby, Now, Lippincott, 1977.
See Dave Run, Lippincott, 1978.
If I Loved You Wednesday, Lippincott, 1980.
The Seeing Summer, Lippincott, 1981.
Seth and Me and Rebel Make Three, Lippincott, 1983.
Angel Baker, Thief, Lippincott, 1984.
Someone to Love Me, Lippincott, 1987.

*WITH VALERIA WINKLER GRIFFITH, UNDER JOINT
    PSEUDONYM JEANNETTE GRIFFITH*

Dearest Kate (young adult novel), Lippincott, 1961.

Also co-wrote syndicated weekly newspaper column, "Family Diary."

OTHER

(With Lee Hadley and Annabelle Irwin) *Writing Young Adult Novels,* Writer's Digest, 1988.

Also contributor to *Ladies' Home Journal, McCall's,* and other periodicals.

■ Adaptations

He's My Baby, Now was adapted as an ABC Afterschool Special titled *Schoolboy Father,* 1978; *The Seeing Summer* was adapted as a short classroom play.

■ Work in Progress

A young-adult novel, *The Education of Adams Henry;* a book of verse, *Animalographies: An ABC Book for Adults.*

■ Sidelights

In her novels for young adults, Jeannette Eyerly tackles the grittier issues teenagers face during adolescence. Since the early 1960s, Eyerly has written about teen pregnancy, abortion, suicide, mental illness, crime, alcoholism, and divorce. Many of the ideas for her novels stemmed from the troubled teens she heard about, read about, and even met during her travels.

Eyerly noted in *Something about the Author Autobiography Series* (*SAAS*) that her "lifelong preoccupation with the written word began when I was eight years old and saw my byline on a poem in the 'Children's Corner' page of the *Des Moines Capital* (Iowa). It had been submitted by my third-grade teacher without my knowledge. I was ecstatic to see my name—Jeannette Hyde, Age 8, Grade 3B, Bird School! The die was cast. I decided I wanted to be an author and that is what I became."

But becoming a writer during the Great Depression and with small children at home was not easy for her. Eyerly noted in *SAAS* that "I wrote short stories that didn't sell and articles that read like short stories that did." After World War II she tried once more "to break into the short fiction market" by submitting one of her stories to a magazine for the working press under the name of her husband, a journalist. Amazed when the story was accepted, Eyerly then "wrote with even more zeal, putting in long hours each evening after our two small daughters were in bed."

Although she soon published two more short stories, Eyerly then had difficulty selling her work. But as she explained in *SAAS,* her perseverance eventually paid off: "After talking to an older friend whose husband had died, I wrote a first-person story, 'What It Means to Be a Widow.' On its twentieth trip [as a submission] it sold to a national magazine whose editors paid the fantastic sum of $500 and requested that I write a story called 'I'm Glad I Got My Divorce.' Though happily married, I obliged, using as a framework the experiences of a friend who had divorced a worthless fellow and was struggling to raise two small children."

Eyerly used her experiences with her own family to coauthor a syndicated newspaper column called "Family Diary" with Valeria Winkler Griffith, whom she described in *SAAS* as "one of my closest friends and a highly successful fiction writer. A short story about a family—a mother, father and four children—it was syndicated and appeared weekly in twenty-five of the nation's leading newspapers." Eyerly confessed in *SAAS* that "We discontinued it after two-and-a-half years because it proved so time-consuming."

Eyerly told *SATA* that "As a mother, grandmother and great-grandmother, my books not only reflect my interest in the young, but in my involvement with my community." In addition, Eyerly's novels for young adults examine issues that are often difficult for teens to discuss with their parents and with each other. She noted in *SAAS* that her first novel for young adults, *More Than a Summer Love,* "though a romance, had a point, one in which I firmly believe: that if a boy and girl really love each other, neither will endanger the other's future by a too-early marriage."

Eyerly's next book also dealt with a serious subject: dropping out of school. "*Drop-Out* was among the first books, if not *the* first, to reflect the 'real-life' situations of young adults," Eyerly told *SATA.* She noted in *SAAS* that when writing *Drop-Out* she had a very tangible goal: "to dissuade potential dropouts by reading a good story, rather than by threats and lectures." Eyerly pointed out in *SAAS* that *Drop-Out* "is often cited as the turning point between the 'gumdrop' [novels in which the teen heroine always gets the boy of her dreams in the end] and the 'anything goes' novels of the eighties."

Eyerly's next novel, *Gretchen's Hill,* is based on her own childhood experiences in Iowa. A *Kirkus Reviews* critic wrote that the espisodes in *Gretchen's Hill* "offer the revelation that 'Mama had been irresponsible when she was little,' and seem surprisingly familiar." Beatrice M. Adam, writing in *Library Journal,* found a liveliness to the story, stating, "the most commonplace things become adventures when Gretchen does them." Unforeseen events form the plot of Eyerly's next novel, *The World of Ellen March,* about a fifteen-year-old girl whose parents go through a divorce. M. Phyllis Brine noted in *Library Journal* that *Ellen March* offered readers "rising suspense, good characterization and a reasonable conclusion."

In 1966 Eyerly tackled illegitimacy and adoption in *A Girl Like Me,* the story of Robin, who discovers that her friend, Cass, is about to give birth to an illegitimate baby. Robin, who has been tempted to have sex with her own boyfriend, then learns that she was an illegitimate child when her parents adopted her. *A Girl Like Me* was described by a contributor in *Kirkus Reviews* as "somewhat more than a do-good soap opera from one of the better writers for teenage girls," and "a quite realistic and candid story" by a reviewer in *Bulletin of the Center for Children's Books.*

Death seems to stalk the heroine of Eyerly's next novel, *The Girl Inside.* After Chris loses her mother, her father (whose death she fears she caused), and the legal guardian who takes care of her, she must learn to cope with sorrow and loss. Though a reviewer in *Bulletin of the Center for Children's Books* stated that *The Girl Inside* has the "faint air of a carefully fictionalized case history," *Horn Book* contributor Ruth Hill Viguers believed that the character of Chris was "exceptionally well drawn."

In this 1969 novel, a teenager's marijuana use has tragic consequences.

Eyerly writes about the problems of teen pregnancy in this work of realistic fiction. (Cover illustration by Ellen Raskin.)

The issue of drug use was addressed by Eyerly in *Escape from Nowhere.* Teenager Carla feels that nothing is going right in her life: she has an uncommunicative, alcoholic mother, an absent father, and problems with loneliness. She tries to escape this reality by smoking marijuana with a friend who ends up institutionalized while Carla, after being arrested, finds herself on probation. A critic in *Bulletin of the Center for Children's Books* stated that "the family situation seems contrived," adding that "the writing style sustains an insubstantial plot built around the message." Jane Manthorne, however, writing in *Horn Book,* found that *Escape to Nowhere* "sounds convincingly like Carla's confession rather than an adult's morality lesson." In 1969 *Escape from Nowhere* was awarded the Christopher Medal as the outstanding young adult novel of the year.

Moral awakening through political involvement is the basis for *Radigan Cares,* featuring high school senior Doug Radigan, who drifts through life until he becomes involved in politics to woo a fellow campaign worker. A reviewer in *Bulletin of the Center for Children's Books* found *Radigan Cares* to be a "fairly convincing depic-

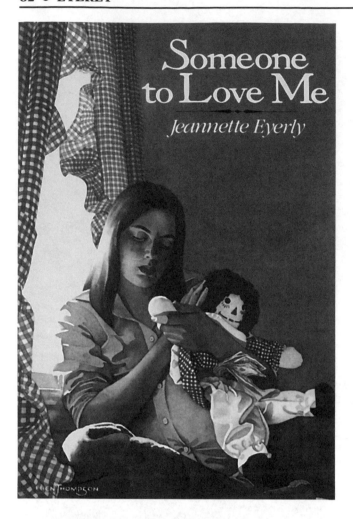

A high school sophomore's ignorance about sex leads to an unplanned pregnancy in this 1987 story.

tion of the high school student who is drawn from apathy into activism." Critic Brooke Anson, writing in *School Library Journal,* commented that "some vignettes of the mills of education carry conviction ... and the sub-plots are well-paced."

Teen pregnancy and the plight of the unwed father were themes of two of Eyerly's novels. The fatherless teenage boy Charles, who impregnates his girlfriend in *He's My Baby, Now,* decides that he does not want to sign the papers to put the infant up for adoption. A reviewer in the *Bulletin of the Center for Children's Books* observed that although the story is not entirely convincing, "it may appeal to readers since most books about premarital pregnancy focus almost exclusively on the mother," and Joan Scherer Brewer declared in *School Library Journal* that Charles's tale "is sure to twang a responsive chord in his contemporaries." A pregnant teenager's plight is detailed in *Someone to Love Me,* in which fifteen-year-old Patrice chooses to keep her baby. Cynthia J. Leibold, writing in *School Library Journal,* praised the "well constructed narrative" and "realistic actions and characteristics personified in Patrice." According to a reviewer in *Bulletin of the Center for Children's Books,* however, *Someone to Love Me* is "a

'problem novel' with a fairy-tale ending, which is presented as happy, but is in fact very sad."

In *Angel Baker, Thief,* the eponymous main character whose dysfunctional, broken family (which includes a child afflicted with cerebral palsy) cannot provide for her emotionally, steals things to give to her younger siblings. She is caught, however, and sent to disciplinary training school. Once released from that school on probation, lonely Angel longs to be accepted by an exclusive clique at her new school, but that group requires her to shoplift as an initiation rite for admission to their charmed circle. *School Library Journal* contributor Valerie A. Guarini found that the "characterization is excellent, particularly that of Angel, a teenage girl who desperately wants to be accepted by her peers." Reviewing *Angel Baker, Thief* in *Voice of Youth Advocates,* Luvada Kuhn stated, "The conflict between Angel's conscience and her need to be accepted makes for a dramatic conclusion."

Eyerly commented in *SAAS* that *The Seeing Summer,* a book for younger readers, "tells the story of the friendship between a sighted child and a blind child." Eyerly added that *The Seeing Summer* was written with the

Ten-year-old Carey learns her new friend, Jenny, is blind in *The Seeing Summer.* (Illustration by Emily Arnold McCully.)

intention of dispelling the myth that blindness is a handicap (it is, rather, a *characteristic*) and, with the proper training, a blind person can do most everything that a sighted person can do. The work was well received by critics; Debbie Barchi stated in *School Library Journal* that the information about blindness "is never presented in a patronizing or pedantic way," and a contributor in *Publishers Weekly* deemed the plot "funny" and "exciting."

Reflecting on her career, Eyerly wrote in *SAAS*, "I have sometimes wondered what it would be like to have writing as one's only occupation." She continued, "Though I've occasionally been wistful, I've never been envious. I think of myself as a wife, a mother, a grandmother, and a sister.... Add to that the roles of friend, breadmaker, volunteer worker for this or that good cause, teacher, lay psychiatrist ... the list goes on and on—and, of course, includes author, which I wanted to be all along.

"The curious thing is that had I not been all of the above, I could never have been an author at all, for in one guise or another they have been the source of what I write about."

■ Works Cited

Adam, Beatrice M., review of *Gretchen's Hill, Library Journal*, January 15, 1966, p. 424.

Anson, Brooke, review of *Radigan Cares, School Library Journal*, January 15, 1971, p. 275.

Barchi, Debbie, review of *The Seeing Summer, School Library Journal*, August, 1982, p. 115.

Brewer, Joan Scherer, review of *He's My Baby, Now, School Library Journal*, May, 1977, p. 69.

Brine, M. Phyllis, review of *The World of Ellen March, Library Journal*, January 15, 1965, p. 387.

Review of *Escape from Nowhere, Bulletin of the Center for Children's Books*, September, 1969, pp. 6-7.

Eyerly, Jeannette, essay in *Something about the Author Autobiography Series,* Volume 10, Gale, 1990, pp. 87-102.

Review of *The Girl Inside, Bulletin of the Center for Children's Books,* October, 1968, p. 25.

Review of *A Girl Like Me, Bulletin of the Center for Children's Books,* January, 1967, p. 73.

Review of *A Girl Like Me, Kirkus Reviews,* August 15, 1966, p. 841.

Review of *Gretchen's Hill, Kirkus Reviews,* September 1, 1965, p. 904.

Guarini, Valerie A., review of *Angel Baker, Thief, School Library Journal,* January, 1985, p. 84.

Review of *He's My Baby, Now, Bulletin of the Center for Children's Books,* September, 1977, p. 14.

Kuhn, Luvada, review of *Angel Baker, Thief, Voice of Youth Advocates,* February, 1985, p. 325.

Leibold, Cynthia J., review of *Someone to Love Me, School Library Journal,* April, 1987, p. 109.

Manthorne, Jane, review of *Escape from Nowhere, Horn Book,* April, 1969, p. 195.

Review of *Radigan Cares, Bulletin of the Center for Children's Books,* December, 1970, p. 58.

Review of *The Seeing Summer, Publishers Weekly,* October 23, 1991, p. 62.

Review of *Someone to Love Me, Bulletin of the Center for Children's Books,* February, 1987, p. 105.

Viguers, Ruth Hill, review of *The Girl Inside, Horn Book,* August, 1968, p. 428.

■ For More Information See

PERIODICALS

Bulletin of the Center for Children's Books, February, 1975, p. 92; December, 1984, p. 64.

Kirkus Reviews, September 1, 1972, p. 1034; July 15, 1974, p. 749; January 1, 1976, p. 12; January 15, 1981, p. 79.

Library Journal, October 15, 1971, p. 3475.

School Library Journal, October, 1978, p. 154; October, 1980, p. 154.

Voice of Youth Advocates, October, 1983, p. 200.

F

CLIFF FAULKNOR

FAULKNOR, Cliff(ord Vernon) 1913-
(Pete Williams)

■ Personal

Born March 3, 1913, in Vancouver, British Columbia, Canada; son of George Henry and Rhoda Anne Faulknor; married Elizabeth Harriette Sloan, August 21, 1943; children: Stephen Edward Vernon, Noreen Elizabeth. *Education:* University of British Columbia, B.S.A. (with honors), 1949. *Politics:* "A little right of centre." *Religion:* Protestant.

■ Addresses

Home—403-80 Point McKay Cr. N.W., Calgary, Alberta T3B 4W4, Canada.

■ Career

Affiliated with Royal Bank of Canada, beginning 1929; later worked with lumber companies, and as an assistant ranger for British Columbia Forest Service; British Columbia Department of Lands and Forests, Land Utilization Research and Survey Division, Victoria, Canada, land inspector, 1949-54; *Country Guide* (national farm monthly), Calgary, Alberta, Canada, associate editor, 1954-75; McKinnon, Allen & Associates, Calgary, accredited appraiser, 1976—; member of Alberta Land Compensation Board, 1978—. *Military service:* Canadian Army, Water Transport, 1939-45; became sergeant. *Member:* Agricultural Institute of Canada, Appraisal Institute of Canada, Writers' Union of Canada, Canadian Farm Writers' Federation, Alberta Farm Writers' Association (past president).

■ Awards, Honors

Awards from Canadian Farm Writers Federation, 1961, 1962, 1968, 1969, 1973, 1974, and 1975; Pacific Northwest Writers Conference award, 1963, for short story; Canadian Children's Book Award, Little, Brown, 1964, for *The White Calf; Pen and Plow* was named best nonfiction book by an Alberta writer, 1976; Vicky Metcalf Award, 1979, for contributions to Canadian literature.

■ Writings

FOR YOUNG ADULTS

The White Calf, illustrated by Gerald Tailfeathers, Little, Brown, 1965.
The White Peril, Little, Brown, 1966.
The In-Betweener, Little, Brown, 1967.
The Smoke Horse, McClelland & Stewart, 1968.
West to Cattle Country, McClelland & Stewart, 1975.

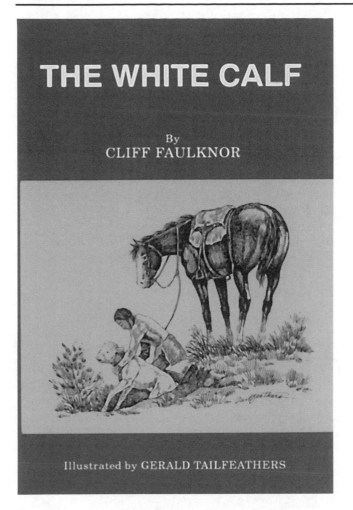

THE WHITE CALF

By
CLIFF FAULKNOR

Illustrated by GERALD TAILFEATHERS

This story of a Blackfoot Indian growing up in the mid-1800s received the Little, Brown Award and was adapted as a Canadian Broadcasting Company radio play. (Cover illustration by Gerald Tailfeathers.)

Johnny Eagleclaw, John LeBel Enterprises, 1982.

FOR ADULTS

The Romance of Beef, Public Press, 1967.
Pen and Plow, Public Press, 1976.
Turn Him Loose!, Western Producer Prairie Books, 1977.
Alberta Hereford Heritage, Advisor Graphics, 1981.

Contributor to anthologies: *Chinook Arch,* Co-op Press, 1967; *Western Profiles,* Alberta Education, 1979; *Transitions,* Alberta Education, 1979; and *The Alberta Diamond Jubilee Anthology,* Hurtig, 1979. Former author of national column for *Country Guide,* under pseudonym Pete Williams; former freelance columnist for *Victoria Times.* Also contributor of articles and short stories to numerous magazines and newspapers, including *Toronto Star Weekly, Liberty, Canadian Geographic Journal,* and *Cattlemen.*

■ Work in Progress

Dog of Destiny (juvenile).

■ Sidelights

Cliff Faulknor commented: "When I was a youth, I could idle away a whole summer's day on some beach without a twinge of conscience, just listening to the music of the waves or watching galleon-like cumulus clouds moving across the sky. Later, I was somehow inveigled into taking what is often referred to as 'higher education' and soon fell prey to the work ethic demon. In that grinding process and the various careers which followed, the boy on the beach was lost. But I found him again, or at least a part of him, when I began to write adventure stories for juveniles. I did not plan any of these stories. My daily journalistic chores gave me about all the planning I could stomach. With my juveniles, I just sat down at my typewriter and put my characters into motion. If any new ones appeared I tossed them into the pot and stirred. The characters themselves did the rest. As they went about their lives they took me with them. I recommend this as a cure to those who feel that they are growing old in heart."

Faulknor's adventure stories for young adults are noted for their action-based plots and accurate historical details. The author's best known work, the trilogy beginning with *The White Calf,* portrays the coming of age of a young Blackfoot Indian brave during the middle of the nineteenth century, just as the encroachment of whites into Indian territory begins to pose a threat to the Indians' way of life. While others of Faulknor's novels feature more contemporary settings, each offers adventure and accurate descriptions of place and culture that critics have praised.

As *The White Calf* opens, Eagle Child, age twelve, finds an orphaned albino buffalo calf, a creature so rare that tribal legend holds it as a symbol of good luck. Eagle Child spends the summer of his twelfth year learning the skills necessary to become a brave and raising the calf until the time when it can be set free to roam with the herd. Critics noted that the calf symbolizes Eagle Child's journey to manhood. Janice R. Scott said in a *Library Journal* review that the details of Blackfoot ways, including hunting buffalo and performing rituals, would likely "appeal to adventure-minded boys." A reviewer in *Times Literary Supplement* highlighted the realistic portrayal of Faulknor's Indian characters: "In a simple prose with no false note," according to the critic, Faulknor presents characters who are "alive and real," offering "exciting" descriptions of hunting, inter-tribal warfare, and performances of tribal rituals.

"The events are exciting, and the details of Blackfoot life are authentic, but [*The White Calf*] suffers a little from the presence of two heroes"—Eagle Child and his brother War Bonnet—according to John Robert Sorfleet in *Twentieth-Century Children's Writers.* Its sequel, *The White Peril,* however, offers the advantages of the earlier book, including excitement and realistic detail, claims Sorfleet, without introducing the possible problem of reader-identification presented by dual heroes. In *The White Peril,* which takes place five years after the earlier book, Eagle Child's buffalo has become a rogue killer that must be destroyed, and the increasing presence of white settlers threatens the survival of the tribe. While a critic in *Kirkus Reviews* felt that "the theme of the disintegration of the tribe is stronger than the story can support," and complained of the lack of a sympathetic central character, Sorfleet commented in *Twentieth-Century Children's Writers:* "The book contains a realistic admixture of sadness and joys, with the coming of the whites viewed from an Indian perspective."

In what Sorfleet called in *Twentieth-Century Children's Writers* "a fitting conclusion to the trilogy," *The Smoke Horse* brings Eagle Child to full manhood when he learns the quality of mercy. Faulknor relies again on the action of hunting and fighting scenes to fill out a story that Sorfleet dubbed in *Twentieth-Century Children's Writers* "well-crafted and gripping, with many flashes of Faulknor's subtle humour and adept dialogue." Of the highly-praised historical background of his adventures, Faulknor told *Twentieth-Century Children's Writers:* "As for the story setting and background information, I research this very carefully. And if I am dealing with the past, my story must be true to the history of that period, and the setting must be as it was during that period."

A title for young adults, *Johnny Eagleclaw,* is set in western Canada during the early part of the twentieth century. *Johnny Eagleclaw* presents the story of a young Indian's struggle to succeed on the rodeo circuit despite discrimination and the dangers of the work. Critics highlighted the interest of the details about life on the rodeo circuit, and, in a review that appeared in *Books in Canada,* Mary Ainslie Smith praised Faulknor's "sensitive portrayal" of his protagonist's attempts to overcome prejudice.

Faulknor once told *Twentieth-Century Children's Writers:* "I don't attempt to be very profound in any of my writings; I like to entertain and inform." It is on these grounds that many critics find his works successful. Consequently, positive reviews of Faulknor's books for young adults emphasize the excitement of his plots and his detailed depiction of life among the Indians. While he is sometimes faulted for relying on cliches of the adventure genre, other critics find his works filled with remarkable incident set against a fully realized background.

■ Works Cited

Scott, Janice R., review of *The White Calf, Library Journal,* October 15, 1965, p. 4615.

Smith, Mary Ainslie, review of *Johnny Eagleclaw, Books in Canada,* December, 1982, p. 11.

Sorfleet, John Robert, "Cliff Faulknor," *Twentieth-Century Children's Writers,* 4th edition, edited by Laura Standley Berger, St. James Press, 1995, pp. 336-37.

Review of *The White Calf,* "Wide Open Spaces," *Times Literary Supplement,* November 24, 1966, p. 1069.

Review of *The White Peril, Kirkus Reviews,* October 1, 1966, p. 1054.

■ For More Information See

PERIODICALS

Kirkus Reviews, May 15, 1965, p. 499.
Library Journal, June 15, 1967, p. 2449.
Times Literary Supplement, March 14, 1968, p. 263.

*   *   *

FISHER, Gary L. 1949-

■ Personal

Born in 1949. *Education:* University of Washington, B.S., 1973, M.Ed., 1974, Ph.D., 1982.

■ Addresses

Home—16210 Oxford Circle, Truckee, CA 96161.

■ Career

Compliance monitor/school psychologist in Issaquah, WA, 1974-81; grant coordinator in Kent, WA, 1981-82; school psychologist in Bellevue, WA, 1982-83; University of Nevada, Reno, professor in counseling and educational psychology department, 1982-93, project director of Addiction Training Center, 1993—. *Member:* National Association of School Psychologists, American Counseling Association, Nevada Association of School Psychologists (legislative contact, 1985-87), Nevada Counseling Association (treasurer, 1984-85; president-elect, 1985-86; president, 1986-87).

Written with Rhoda Woods Cummings, Fisher's *The Survival Guide for Kids with LD* offers tips to children with learning differences on how to get along at school, at home, and with friends. (Illustration by Jackie Urbanovic.)

■ Awards, Honors

Recipient of grants for research and education, including (with M. J. Bancroft) junior faculty award, University of Nevada, 1985-86, general faculty research award, University of Nevada, 1989-90, Drug Free Schools and Communities Program grant, Department of Education, 1989-91 and 1992-93, Nevada Bureau of Alcohol and Drug Abuse grant, 1991-92, Addiction Training Center Grant, Center for Substance Abuse treatment, 1993-98, and training contract with Bureau of Alcohol and Drug Abuse, 1994-95.

■ Writings

(With Rhoda Woods Cummings) *A Survival Guide for Kids with LD,* Free Spirit Publishing, 1990.
(With Cummings) *The School Survival Guide for Kids with LD,* Free Spirit Publishing, 1991.
(With Cummings) *The Survival Guide for Teenagers with LD,* Free Spirit Publishing, 1993.
(With Cummings) *The Survival Guide for Parents of LD Kids,* Free Spirit Publishing, 1995.

Contributor of scholarly articles to numerous professional journals, including *International Journal of Clinical Neuropsychology, Journal of Learning Disabilities, International Journal of Addictions,* and *Journal of Mental Health Counseling.*

■ Sidelights

Gary L. Fisher and co-author Rhoda Cummings refer to LD as "learning differences" rather than "learning disabilities." Their books offer advice to those with severe cases of attention deficit disorder and other versions of LD and to their families and friends. "The emphasis is on helping young people feel better about themselves and their ability to succeed," Nina Vande-Water said in a review of *The School Survival Guide for Kids with LD* in *Voice of Youth Advocates.* This book includes case studies, an additional bibliography of books about the subject, and a list of LD organizations.

■ Works Cited

VandeWater, Nina, review of *The School Survival Guide for Kids with LD, Voice of Youth Advocates,* October, 1990, p. 240.

■ For More Information See

PERIODICALS

Booklist, July, 1990, p. 2088.
School Library Journal, June, 1990, p. 130.*

SIMON FRENCH

FRENCH, Simon 1957-

■ Personal

Born November 26, 1957, in Sydney, Australia; son of Reginald (an electronics design draftsman) and Janette (a school librarian; maiden name, Frederick) French. *Education:* Mitchell College, Teacher's Diploma, 1979.

■ Addresses

Home—1735 East Kurrajong Rd., East Kurrajong, New South Wales 2758, Australia.

■ Career

Infants' teacher at schools in New South Wales, Australia, 1980-84, 1988—; youth worker, 1984-87. Has also worked as a library clerical assistant, a fruit picker, and in preschool child care.

■ Awards, Honors

Special mention, Australian Children's Book of the Year Awards, 1976, for *Hey, Phantom Singlet;* Australian Children's Book Award competition commendation, 1982, for *Cannily, Cannily;* Australian Children's Book of the Year, 1987, for *All We Know;* Family Award, 1991, Honour Book, Australian Children's Book Awards, 1992, and Children's Book of the Year, Bank St. School of Education, 1993, all for *Change the Locks.*

■ Writings

FOR CHILDREN

Hey, Phantom Singlet, illustrated by Alex Nicholas, Angus & Robertson, 1975.
Cannily, Cannily, Angus & Robertson, 1981.
All We Know, Angus & Robertson, 1986.
Change the Locks, Scholastic, 1991.

■ Work in Progress

A collection of short stories for ten- to fourteen-year-olds.

■ Sidelights

Simon French once commented: "The suggestion to write a book came rather jokingly from my sixth-grade teacher. As I was someone who enjoyed reading books anyway, the suggestion didn't seem all that ludicrous; and so I set to work. After a few false starts, I became enthused about recording my day-to-day school life and so began putting together a no-holds-barred account of the high school I was attending. All the kids in my class

French's 1991 novel concerns a boy named Steven whose distant memories of being abandoned as a child come to the fore during a family crisis. (Cover illustration by Derek James.)

found themselves depicted as characters in their own type of environment—rough and ready, merciless but honest. Almost the entire book was written at school—in notepads concealed inside textbooks, scribbled paragraphs at the back of exercise books. These devious methods worked incredibly well, except for the day my math teacher confiscated two whole chapters and I had to try to remember later what it was I had written.

"Thus, daily classroom humor and drama provided much live footage for the story that evolved. My suburban origins lent me a new cast of characters in addition to those at school, and chapter by chapter I pieced together the story of Matthew, whose dad is in jail, and whose mum has to work to support the family. Trying for publication was really an afterthought and of course did not prove easy. After quite a few rejections, I was lucky, and *Hey, Phantom Singlet* was published just before my seventeenth birthday. Shortly afterwards I finished high school. Being able to write away from the audience who had inspired me so much seemed very difficult for a while. With these sorts of upheavals, a second book was not an easy task.

"The politics in *Cannily, Cannily* are those of adult and peer pressure. The options open to Trevor—the child of two seasonal workers always on the move—are whether to bend to these attendant pressures and 'belong,' or to remain aloof and different, and so endure isolation and torment from the children of a conservative country town. Having been on the receiving end of peer politics, I looked at it as a significant set of experiences and ideas to put across.

"All it seems to take is a single strand of fiction to hold my ideas together, concerned as I am with reporting on real life. The challenge to me, of course, is to translate the realism and honesty to an audience, balancing the language and structure between the economical and the descriptive. My actual method of writing is not altogether studious or methodical; I do not sit down and write for an appointed time each day. Rather it is a single character or situation encountered at any time that causes me to sit with typewriter and paper, and write. I cannot offer any stunning or academic rationale as to how or why I write. My books have been written because I find it enjoyable and because I perceive a need for the type of story that children can relate to their everyday existence. My writing is about coping, interacting, and sometimes personal hardship; but it is more so about succeeding and surviving—that is the essence of growing."

■ For More Information See

PERIODICALS

Times Literary Supplement, November 20, 1981.*

*   *   *

FRYE, Sally
See MOORE, Elaine

FURLONG, Monica (Mavis) 1930-

■ Personal

Born January 17, 1930, in Harrow, Middlesex, England; daughter of Alfred Gordon and Freda (Simpson) Furlong; married William John Knights, 1953 (marriage ended, 1977); children: one son, one daughter. *Education:* Attended University College.

■ Career

Author. Reporter for several London newspapers, 1956-68; producer, British Broadcasting Corp., 1974-78. Moderator of the Movement for the Ordination of Women, 1982. *Member:* Society of Authors.

■ Awards, Honors

Voice of Youth Advocates best book nomination, 1988, for *Therese of Lisieux.*

■ Writings

FOR YOUNG ADULTS

Wise Child, Gollancz, 1987, Knopf, 1987.
A Year and a Day, Gollancz, 1990, published in the United States as *Juniper,* Random House, 1991.
Robin's Country, Hamish Hamilton, 1994, Knopf, 1995.

ADULT FICTION

The Cat's Eye, Weidenfeld & Nicholson, 1976.
Cousins, Weidenfeld & Nicholson, 1983.

POETRY

God's a Good Man and Other Poems, Mowbray 1974.

OTHER

Contemplating Now, Hodder & Stoughton, 1971, Westminster Press, 1971.
Travelling In, Hodder & Stoughton, 1971.
The End of Our Exploring, Hodder & Stoughton, 1973.
Puritan's Progress: A Study of John Bunyan, Hodder & Stoughton, 1975, Coward, 1975.
Burrswood, Focus of Healing, Hodder & Stoughton, 1978.
(Editor) *The Trial of John Bunyan and the Persecution of the Puritans,* Folio Society, 1978.
Merton: A Biography, Harper, 1980.
Christian Uncertainties, Cowley, 1982.
(Editor) *Feminine in the Church,* Society for Promoting Christian Knowledge (London), 1984.
Zen Effects: The Life of Alan Watts, Houghton, 1986.
Therese of Lisieux, Virago, 1987, Panthcon, 1987.
Dangerous Delight: Women and Power in the Church, Society for Promoting Christian Knowledge, 1991.
Bird of Paradise, Mowbray, 1995.

Also editor of *Mirror to the Church,* 1988. Contributor to *Ourselves Your Servants: The Church's Ministry,* Advisory Council for the Church's Ministry, 1967.

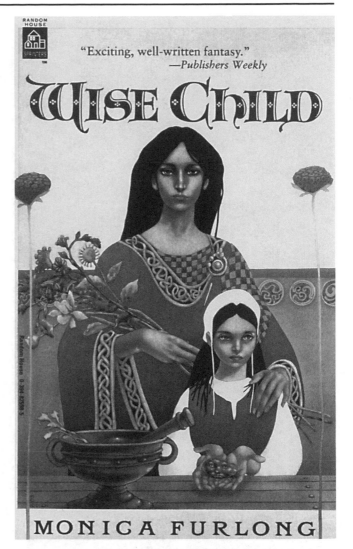

In her first fantasy for teens, Furlong weaves a magical tale of remote Scotland, where a girl named Wise Child must test her loyalties between her mother and the kindly sorceress who raised her. (Cover illustration by Leo and Diane Dillon.)

■ Sidelights

Although Monica Furlong is perhaps best known as a broadcaster and a writer of adult nonfiction—including several biographies and a number of works on philosophical, spiritual, and feminist issues—she has also written novels for both adults and young adults.

Published in 1976, Furlong's first novel, *Cat's Eye,* is a mixture of realism and mysticism and concerns a young woman's convalescence after a miscarriage and a broken marriage. *Cousins,* her 1983 work, is the story of a middle-aged sculptor who has a torrid love affair with her cousin Hugo, a theologian. In it, Furlong explores not only the first love of a mature adult, but also the life of an artist. In a review for *British Book News,* Neil Philip commented that *Cousins* is "an enjoyable and moving novel about emotional and spiritual development which promises well for Monica Furlong's future work."

MONICA FURLONG

ROBIN'S COUNTRY

Furlong makes use of the Robin Hood legend in her 1994 fantasy about a mute boy who is aided by the Saxon outlaws in his search to find his parents. (Cover illustration by Neal McPheeters.)

In *Wise Child,* Furlong wrote about a seventh-century nine-year-old, deserted by her parents, who goes to live with a witch in a small Scottish village. Juniper is a healer and an herbalist, and soon teaches Wise Child many things, including music, Latin, and sorcery. When Wise Child's mother comes to reclaim her, the girl is torn between old loyalties and new ones. But when a plague hits the village, and Juniper is accused of being the cause and sentenced to be burned at the stake, Wise Child realizes where her true loyalties lie. Although the book is set in the distant past, the emotions it displays are universal. Many of the issues facing Wise Child, such as conflict of loyalty, are easily identifiable by young readers. Fellow fantasy writer Robin McKinley remarked in the *New York Times Book Review,* "The subtle background details of life long ago are intriguing, the writing is graceful and history is never forced on the reader." Ann A. Flowers, in her *Horn Book* assessment, praised Furlong's "smooth, cool writing style."

Wise Child was followed by its prequel, *Juniper* (published in England as *A Year and a Day*). As a young girl, Juniper, who was then called Ninnoc, was sent to her irascible godmother, Euny, to be trained as a doran (wise woman) for a year and a day. The lessons are difficult and demanding. At the end of the year and the day, Ninnoc finds she must put her training to use to save her father's kingdom from his wicked sister. Barbara Hutcheson, writing for *School Library Journal,* stated that "the action is quite believable given the beliefs of the time, and our own growing knowledge of psychology, herbalism, and pre-Christian religions."

Moving from pre-Christian England to the reign of King John and the Sheriff of Nottingham, Furlong's next novel for young adults is entitled *Robin's Country.* A small, mute boy named Dummy has blocked out the traumatic events of his early life, including the destruction of his family. Apprenticed to a sadistic farmer, Dummy runs away and literally falls into Robin Hood's lair. There he is treated with kindness and soon becomes one of Robin's favorites (although Marion suspects that he might be a spy). When Robin is reunited with his rightful liege—King Richard—Dummy discovers not only his true identity (he is the king's godson), but his true voice as well. In a review for *Magpies,* Russ Merrin praised the book, calling it the "most enjoyable and credible retelling of the Robin Hood legend which I have read."

■ Works Cited

Flowers, Ann A., review of *Wise Child, Horn Book,* March/April, 1988, p. 206.

Hutcheson, Barbara, review of *Juniper, School Library Journal,* May, 1991, p. 91.

McKinley, Robin, review of *Wise Child, New York Times Book Review,* February 28, 1988.

Merrin, Russ, review of *Robin's Country, Magpies,* November, 1994, p. 33.

Philip, Neil, review of *Cousins, British Book News,* October, 1983, p. 644.

■ For More Information See

PERIODICALS

Bulletin of the Center for Children's Books, February, 1988.

Junior Bookshelf, October, 1990, pp. 242-243.

Kirkus Reviews, February 15, 1991, p. 247.

School Librarian, November, 1990, p. 158.

School Library Journal, September, 1987, p. 195.*

G

ERNEST J. GAINES

GAINES, Ernest J(ames) 1933-

■ Personal

Born January 15, 1933, in Oscar, LA (some sources cite River Lake Plantation, near New Roads, Pointe Coupee Parish, LA); son of Manuel (a laborer) and Adrienne J. (Colar) Gaines; married Dianne Saulney (an attorney), May 15, 1993. *Education:* Attended Vallejo Junior College, California; San Francisco State College (now University), B.A., 1957; graduate study at Stanford University, 1958-59.

■ Addresses

Office—Department of English, University of Southwestern Louisiana, P.O. Box 44691, Lafayette, LA 70504. *Agent*—JCA Literary Agency, Inc., 242 West 27th St., New York, NY 10001.

■ Career

Denison University, Granville, OH, writer in residence, 1971; Stanford University, Stanford, CA, writer in residence, 1981; Whittier College, CA, visiting professor, 1983, writer in residence, 1986; University of Southwestern Louisiana, Lafayette, professor of English and writer in residence, 1983—. *Military service:* U.S. Army, 1953-55. *Member:* Fellowship of Southern Writers.

■ Awards, Honors

Wallace Stegner Fellow, Stanford University, 1957; Joseph Henry Jackson Award, San Francisco Foundation, 1959, for "Comeback" (short story); National Endowment for the Arts Award, 1967; Rockefeller grant, 1970; Guggenheim fellowship, 1971; Black Academy of Arts and Letters Award, 1972; Commonwealth Club of California fiction gold medal, 1972, for *The Autobiography of Miss Jane Pittman,* and 1984, for *A Gathering of Old Men;* Louisiana Literature Award, Louisiana Library Association, 1972, for *The Autobiography of Miss Jane Pittman;* honorary doctorate of letters from Denison University, 1980, Brown University, 1985, Bard College, 1985, and Louisiana State University, 1987; award for excellence of achievement in literature, San Francisco Arts Commission, 1983; D.H.L., Whittier College, 1986; literary award, American Academy and Institute of Arts and Letters, 1987; John D. and Catherine T. MacArthur Foundation fellowship, 1993; National Book Critics Circle Award for fiction, 1994, for *A Lesson before Dying.*

■ Writings

FICTION

Catherine Carmier, Atheneum, 1964.

Of Love and Dust, Dial, 1967.

Bloodline (short stories), Dial, 1968.

A Long Day in November (for children; originally published in *Bloodline*), illustrated by Don Bolognese, Dial, 1971.

The Autobiography of Miss Jane Pittman, Dial, 1971.

In My Father's House, Knopf, 1978.

A Gathering of Old Men, Knopf, 1983.

The Sky Is Gray (story; originally published in *Bloodline*), Creative Education (Mankato, MN), 1993.

A Lesson before Dying, Knopf, 1993.

A collection of Gaines's manuscripts is maintained at the Dupree Library, University of Southwestern Louisiana, Lafayette.

■ Adaptations

The Autobiography of Miss Jane Pittman was made into an Emmy-winning television movie by Columbia Broadcasting System (CBS-TV), 1974; the story "The Sky Is Gray" was filmed for public television, 1980; *A Gathering of Old Men* was made into a television movie, CBS-TV, 1987. *A Lesson before Dying* is available on cassette and has been optioned for a television movie.

■ Sidelights

Through a series of acclaimed novels and short stories, including his best-known work, *The Autobiography of Miss Jane Pittman,* Ernest J. Gaines has brought to life the history, culture, and people of his childhood home in Louisiana for countless readers. As a teenager in the late 1940s, Gaines moved with his family to California from rural Louisiana. His new home was much more integrated than the South, and Gaines found new opportunities available to him, the most important of which was the public library. "When we moved to California I was lonely, so I went to the library and began to read a lot of fiction," Gaines told Paul Desruisseaux in the *New York Times Book Review.* "But the books I read did not have my people in them, no Southern blacks, Louisiana blacks. Or if they did it was by white writers who did not interpret things the way I would have. So I started writing about my people."

Born in 1933 on a plantation in Oscar, Louisiana, Gaines was working in the fields by the time he was nine. Although this curtailed his schooling, he still found enrichment through the stories told by family and friends. One relative in particular proved an inspiration: his Great-Aunt Augusteen Jefferson, who cared for Gaines and his siblings even though she had been disabled since birth. Unable to walk, Gaines's aunt crawled to get around; she cooked, cleaned, and even tended the garden. "Anytime someone asks me who had the greatest influence on me as an artist or a man, I say she had," Gaines said in an *Essence* interview. Aunt Augusteen was later to serve as the inspiration for Gaines's most memorable character, the resilient and spirited former slave, Miss Jane Pittman.

After moving to California, Gaines graduated from high school and attended junior college before joining the army. During this time, he continued reading widely and began writing his own fiction, using the works of Russian novelists such as Ivan Turgenev and Leo Tolstoy as his models for how to write about country people. By the time he graduated from San Francisco State College in 1957, he had published his first story, won a creative writing fellowship to attend Stanford University, and found an agent to represent him. He began writing novels on the advice of a critic who said they were more marketable than stories, and in 1964 he published his first book, *Catherine Carmier.* This novel about an educated young black man who returns to his Louisiana home and rekindles a doomed romance with a Creole woman was the first of Gaines's books to be set in the fictional area of Bayonne, Louisiana. His next book, *Of Love and Dust,* explored plantation life more fully through a series of interracial romances and conflicts set in the 1940s.

Gaines's first two novels were successful enough for him to publish a short story collection, *Bloodline,* in 1968. The author made minor revisions to one of these stories, *A Long Day in November,* and published it as a book for children in 1971. The story begins on a chilly fall morning when six-year-old Sonny's parents are arguing; his mother leaves angrily, and his father spends the day searching for a way to win her back. Sonny narrates the tale of this difficult day, which includes an embarrassing incident at school. "Sonny's observations, fantasies and problems are very real," Marilyn Sachs states in the *New York Times Book Review.* The critic praises Gaines for his "wonderfully funny" portrayal of a poor black family, adding that he "includes those small, human details that so many authors neglect."

Book World contributor Digby B. Whitman similarly observes that "people, talk, and action are wholly credible" in *A Long Day in November,* adding that "the simple, halting language makes for extraordinary realism and tenderness." While Mary M. Burns believes that it will take a "sophisticated" reader to grasp the "subtle nuances of characterization, the skilled uses of contrast, and the superbly realized setting," she notes in her *Horn Book* review that mature readers will find "a well-wrought story which is very real and touchingly human." A *Publishers Weekly* contributor likewise remarks that the book may be more appealing to adults than children, but concludes that "there is no reason why older readers could not enjoy this truly remarkable story."

The year that Gaines produced *A Long Year in November* was also the year he brought out his breakthrough novel, *The Autobiography of Miss Jane Pittman,* a book which *Iowa Review* contributor Jerry H. Bryant calls "one of the finest novels written since World War II in America and a distinguished contribution to our national literature." In the novel, Miss Jane relates the story of her life, from the time she is freed from slavery as a young girl to her participation in a civil rights demonstration when she is 110 years old. Her experiences echo the history of African Americans in the South, a history Gaines heard firsthand from his Great-Aunt Augusteen and others. When people came to visit his aunt, the author related to Desruisseaux, "I'd be there to serve them icewater, or coffee. There was no radio, no television, so people *talked* about everything, even things that had happened 70 years earlier. I learned about storytelling by listening to these people talk." He continued, "The idea behind 'Miss Jane Pittman' was based on things I'd heard as a child, and from the life I come from, the plantation."

"*The Autobiography of Miss Jane Pittman* is history rewritten and sifted through the mind of a talented novelist," Addison Gayle, Jr. writes in *The Way of the New World: The Black Novel in America.* In recollections taped by a young historian, Miss Jane tells of the arrival of Union troops to her Louisiana home; her emancipation and trip northward, when most of her fellow travellers are murdered by Klansmen; her settling down on a Louisiana plantation, her marriage, and her adoption of the orphan Ned; Ned's return home after a Northern education, when he is assassinated for challenging white racism; and her joining the modern civil rights movement after another bright, outspoken young man is killed for what he believes. "Never mind that Miss Jane Pittman is fictitious, and that her 'autobiography,' offered up in the form of taped reminiscences, is artifice," Josh Greenfeld asserts in *Life.* "The effect is stunning." This success is due to Gaines's skill with dialect and language, as Bryant claims: "So successful is he in *becoming* Miss Jane Pittman, that when we talk about her story, we do not think of Gaines as her creator, but as her recording 'editor.'"

What distinguishes Gaines's story of black persecution from similar novels, according to many critics, is the restrained manner in which he tells it. "Gaines does not avoid having Jane report white atrocities, but he does not allow her to use the propagandistic and sociological stridency that characterizes so many earlier novels," Bryant observes. In *Miss Jane Pittman,* fellow novelist Alice Walker writes in the *New York Times Book Review,* "racists are dangerous, unstable, vicious individuals, but never that alone. They are people, fully realized in Gaines's fiction." "Gaines does not make the revolution happen by surreal rhetoric," Melvin Maddocks similarly remarks in his *Time* review. "He simply watches, a patient artist, a patient man, and it happens for him." Nevertheless, Gayle states, in Miss Jane's story "is symbolized the odyssey of a race of people; through her eyes is revealed the grandeur of a people's journey through history."

Other novels examine historical themes in a similarly subtle fashion. As Larry McMurtry writes in the *New York Times Book Review,* "it is the force of Mr. Gaines's character and intelligence, operating through this deceptively quiet style, that makes his fiction compelling."

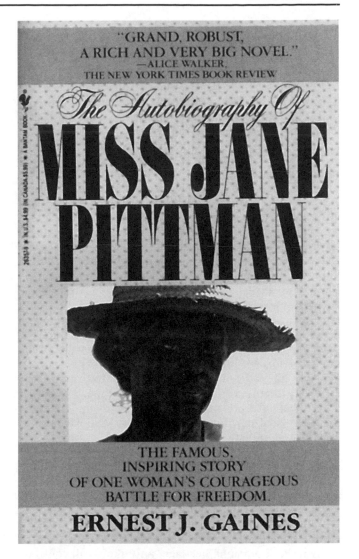

"GRAND, ROBUST, A RICH AND VERY BIG NOVEL."
—ALICE WALKER,
THE NEW YORK TIMES BOOK REVIEW

The Autobiography Of
MISS JANE PITTMAN

THE FAMOUS,
INSPIRING STORY
OF ONE WOMAN'S COURAGEOUS
BATTLE FOR FREEDOM.

ERNEST J. GAINES

Gaines' award-winning 1971 novel is an epic story of a heroic woman's tumultuous life, which spans the years from the Civil War to the Civil Rights Movement.

Gaines's 1978 novel *In My Father's House,* for instance, "will attract ... those readers interested in the nonviolent vs. violent activism question," Ellen Lippmann writes in *School Library Journal.* The novel follows the chaos created in the life of Reverend Philip Martin, a local civil rights leader, when the illegitimate son he abandoned thirty years before unexpectedly turns up. Not only does Gaines look at the conflicting approaches toward gaining civil rights, but also, as McMurtry summarizes it, "the profoundly destructive consequences ... of a father's abandonment of his children."

Similarly, the results of a lifetime of enduring racism are portrayed in *A Gathering of Old Men.* When a white man is found shot in a black man's yard, nineteen elderly black men and a young white woman all claim responsibility for the murder in order to foil the coming lynch mob. Each of the men relates his reasons for wanting the murdered man dead; Gaines's "portraits of the aged men taking a stand against their oppressors— some of them for the first time in their long lives—are beautiful and painful," Gregory Maguire writes in *Horn*

Book. One of the strengths of the book, according to *Voice of Youth Advocates* contributor Penny Parker, is Gaines's ability to bring the reader into the story and the minds of the characters "without losing interest in the events, nor even suspecting what will occur." While the book has a contemporary setting, the critic concludes, as Gaines reveals his characters' stories "we are swept into a maelstrom that began many, many years before."

A 1940s setting is the basis for another examination of race and injustice, a novel a *Publishers Weekly* critic says "may be [Gaines's] crowning achievement." In *A Lesson before Dying,* a barely literate young black man is an unwitting participant in and only survivor of a robbery of a white store owner. Despite his defense attorney's claims that executing the young man for the shopkeeper's murder would be tantamount to killing a "hog," Jefferson is condemned to death. Outraged by the portrayal of her godson as an animal, Miss Emma convinces teacher Grant Wiggins to prepare Jefferson to die like a man. Despite Wiggins's reluctance—both Jefferson's ignorance and the white system's condescension make him uncomfortable—he inspires the young man to succeed through the writing of a journal. Praising the author's unusual ability to capture the everyday manners and prejudice of the time, *Time* critic R. Z. Sheppard adds that few writers "have [Gaines's] dramatic instinct for conveying the malevolence of racism and injustice without the usual accompanying self-righteousness." "As in his earlier novels, Gaines evokes a sense of reality through rich detail and believable characters," Carolyn E. Gecan states in *School Library Journal,* concluding that students who want "thought-provoking reading will enjoy" this novel.

Gaines has said that he sees no end to the inspiration he finds in his Louisiana heritage, and likely will continue to write about the American South. "Before Alex Haley called it *Roots,* I was trying to do something like that, to write about our past, where we come from," Gaines told Mary Ellen Doyle in *Melus.* He further explained, "I'm trying to write about a people I feel are worth writing about, to make the world aware of them, make them aware of themselves." In addition, the author revealed that "my aim in literature is to develop character, not only the character in the book, but my character as well as yours, so that if you pick up the book, you will see something you feel is true, something not seen before, that will help develop your character from that day forward."

■ Works Cited

Bryant, Jerry H., "From Death to Life: The Fiction of Ernest J. Gaines," *Iowa Review,* winter, 1972, pp. 106-20.

Burns, Mary M., review of *A Long Day in November, Horn Book,* April, 1972, p. 153.

Desruisseaux, Paul, "Ernest Gaines: A Conversation," *New York Times Book Review,* June 11, 1978, pp. 13, 44-45.

Gaines, Ernest, interview with Mary Ellen Doyle in *Melus,* summer, 1984, pp. 59-81.

Gaines, Ernest, interview in *Essence,* August, 1993, p. 52.

Gayle, Addison, Jr., *The Way of the New World: The Black Novel in America,* Doubleday, 1975, pp. 294-300.

Gecan, Carolyn E., review of *A Lesson before Dying, School Library Journal,* July, 1993, p. 110.

Greenfeld, Josh, review of *The Autobiography of Miss Jane Pittman, Life,* April 30, 1971, p. 18.

Review of *A Lesson before Dying, Publishers Weekly,* March 1, 1993, p. 38.

Lippmann, Ellen, review of *In My Father's House, School Library Journal,* November, 1978, p. 81.

Review of *A Long Day in November, Publishers Weekly,* August 23, 1971, p. 81.

Maddocks, Melvin, "Root and Branch," *Time,* May 10, 1971, pp. K13-17.

Maguire, Gregory, review of *A Gathering of Old Men, Horn Book,* December, 1983, pp. 739-40.

McMurtry, Larry, "Reverend Martin's Son," *New York Times Book Review,* June 11, 1978, p. 13.

Parker, Penny, review of *A Gathering of Old Men, Voice of Youth Advocates,* April, 1984, p. 30.

Sachs, Marilyn, review of *A Long Day in November, New York Times Book Review,* February 13, 1972, p. 8.

Sheppard, R. Z., "An A-Plus in Humanity," *Time,* March 29, 1993, pp. 65-66.

Walker, Alice, review of *The Autobiography of Miss Jane Pittman, New York Times Book Review,* May 23, 1971, pp. 6, 12.

Whitman, Digby B., review of *A Long Day in November, Book World,* November 7, 1971, Part II, p. 6.

■ For More Information See

BOOKS

Beavers, Herman, *Wrestling Angels into Song: The Fictions of Ernest J. Gaines and James Alan Mc-Pherson,* University of Pennsylvania Press, 1994.

Concise Dictionary of American Literary Biography, Volume 6: *Broadening Views, 1968-1988,* Gale, 1989.

Contemporary Literary Criticism, Gale, Volume 3, 1975; Volume 11, 1979; Volume 18, 1981.

Dictionary of Literary Biography, Gale, Volume 2: *American Novelists since World War II,* 1978, Volume 33: *Afro-American Fiction Writers after 1955,* 1984.

Dictionary of Literary Biography Yearbook: 1980, Gale, 1981.

Estes, David C., editor, *Critical Reflections on the Fiction of Ernest J. Gaines,* University of Georgia Press, 1994.

O'Brien, John, editor, *Interview with Black Writers,* Liveright, 1973.

Simpson, Anne K., *A Gathering of Gaines: The Man and the Writer,* University of Southwestern Louisiana, Center for Louisiana Studies, 1991.

Twentieth-Century Young Adult Writers, 1st edition, St. James Press, 1995.

Wooton, Carl, and Marcia Gaudet, editors, *Porch Talk with Ernest Gaines: Conversations on the Writer's Craft,* Louisiana State University Press, 1990.

PERIODICALS

Bulletin of the Center for Children's Books, February, 1972, p. 91.
Horn Book, October, 1978, p. 546.
Kliatt, spring, 1984, p. 8.
Los Angeles Times Book Review, May 30, 1993, p. 11.
Publishers Weekly, March 8, 1971, p. 64; May 24, 1993, pp. 62, 64.
New Statesman, September 2, 1973, pp. 205-6.
New York Times Book Review, October 30, 1983, p. 15; August 8, 1993, p. 21.
Saturday Review, May 1, 1971, p. 40.
Voice of Youth Advocates, October, 1993, p. 216.
Washington Post Book World, March 28, 1993, p. 3.

OTHER

Louisiana Stories: Ernest Gaines (television documentary), WHMM-TV, 1993.*

—*Sketch by Diane Telgen*

MARY W. GEHMAN

GEHMAN, Mary W. 1923-

■ Personal

Born September 25, 1923, in Berks County, PA; daughter of Henry and Anna (Weber) Gehman. *Education:* Eastern Mennonite University, B.S., 1958; Kutztown University, M.Ed., 1969. *Religion:* Mennonite/Protestant. *Hobbies and other interests:* Reading, listening to music, writing, tutoring in English as a second language.

■ Addresses

Home—Route 2, Box 181, Reinholds, PA 17569.

■ Career

Gehmans Mennonite School, Denver, PA, elementary teacher, 1954-1957, 1976-79; elementary teacher and teacher of English as a second language with Eastern Mennonite Missions to Somalia, 1958-76; Cocalico School District, Denver, teacher of English as a second language, 1979-83; teacher of English as a second language in missions to Somalia, 1983-87, 1990. Volunteer tutor of English as a second language, Berks Literacy Council, 1991—. Member, Friends of the Reading-Berks Public Libraries. *Member:* Berks Literacy Council.

■ Writings

Abdi and the Elephants, Herald Press, 1995.

Contributor of articles to periodicals.

*   *   *

GLENN, Patricia Brown 1953-

■ Personal

Born May 14, 1953, in Kansas City, MO; daughter of Maynard H. (an investor) and Virginia L. (a volunteer/philanthropist; maiden name, Lippert) Brown; married Christopher Armand Glenn (an oil and gas executive), September 9, 1978; children: Eliot Armand, Virginia Brown. *Education:* Attended Connecticut College, 1971-73, and University of Michigan/Sarah Lawrence, Florence, Italy, 1974; Williams College, B.A. (art history; cum laude), 1975; University of Chicago, M.A. (art history), 1984. *Religion:* Jewish. *Hobbies and other interests:* Horseback riding, coaching youth sports, photography.

■ Addresses

Home—638 West 67th St., Kansas City, MO 64113.

■ Career

Landmarks Commission, Kansas City, MO, research historian, 1978-79; Historic Kansas City Foundation, Kansas City, survey coordinator and architectural histo-

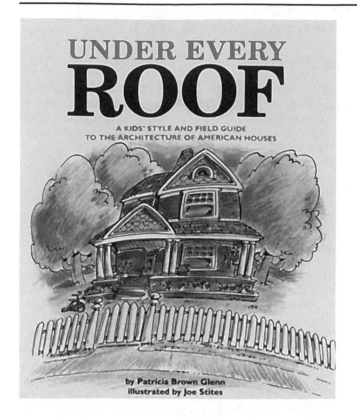

Glenn wrote this book to teach youngsters the history of American architecture. (Cover illustration by Joe Stites.)

rian, 1979-81, director of research and education, 1981-83, member of board of directors, 1992-94; Ottawa University, Kansas City, member of adjunct faculty, 1981-83; University of Missouri, Kansas City, member of adjunct faculty, 1983, 1985-90; currently full-time writer, researcher, and lecturer. Consultant in art education and architectural history, 1983—. Member, Kansas City Municipal Arts commission, 1985-92; member, Junior League of Kansas City; board member of parents association, Pembroke-Hill School, 1992—. *Member:* American Institute of Architects, Society of Architectural Historians, Williams College Society of Alumni, Mission Valley Hunt Club, Shotokan Karate Association.

■ Awards, Honors

Honorable Mention, Thorpe Menn Book Award, American Association of University Women, 1994, for *Under Every Roof: A Kid's Style and Field Guide to the Architecture of American Houses;* Distinguished Young Alumni Service Award, Pembroke-Hill School, 1994.

■ Writings

Under Every Roof: A Kid's Style and Field Guide to the Architecture of American Houses, illustrated by Joe Stites, Preservation Press of the National Trust for Historic Preservation (Washington, DC), 1993.

From the Ground Up: Architects at Work in America, Preservation Press of the National Trust for Historic Preservation, 1996.

Art critic, *Forum Magazine* (Kansas City), 1992—; editor, *Historic Kansas City Foundation Gazette,* 1981-83, and *HARK: Newsletter of the Mission Valley Hunt,* 1994—. Author of several editions of *Historic Kansas City Foundation Possum Trotters* newsletter, 1981-83.

■ Sidelights

Patricia Brown Glenn told *SATA* how she came to write her first book: "Art has been a large part of my life since my first art history class in high school. I always thought I would end up as a curator of European decorative arts or sculpture in a museum. After graduate school, there were no jobs available in my field in my hometown, so I took a job with the local historical society. I had worked for the Landmarks Commission for two years prior to that. What I needed to know about architecture I learned on the job conducting architectural surveys and writing national register nominations. Graduate school didn't prepare me for vernacular styles, bungalows, American four square, and the like. It was definitely a 'seat of the pants' kind of experience.

"*Under Every Roof* is a direct outgrowth of that experience. I learned by really looking at the architecture, considering its location and function and building on my knowledge of styles.

"One of the best things about writing this book was talking to so many different people about their homes. I include house museum directors in this group because they consider the properties they manage to be their own. One man and I were on the phone together for one hour talking about his historic house, family, politics, and future dreams. And I paid for the call! People are a large part of what makes the house. They certainly make a house a home. Everyone needs a place to live and work. This type of art has come to have the greatest appeal for me because it is a social and aesthetic phenomenon. Not exclusive at all, but by its very nature inclusive and accessible.

"In closing, I remember that while I was working on my masters in art history at the University of Chicago, I used to go out of my way to walk past the Robie House on the way to class. I used to run my hands along the wall next to the sidewalk marveling at the absolute purity and beauty of its design. I guess even then, before I was aware, architecture had a hold on me."

■ For More Information See

PERIODICALS

Booklist, July, 1994, p. 1939.
School Library Journal, June, 1994, p. 137.
Washington Post Book World, December 5, 1993, p. 24.

GRIFFITH, Jeannette
See EYERLY, Jeannette

* * *

GRIFFITHS, Helen 1939-
(Helen Santos)

■ Personal

Born May 8, 1939, in London, England; daughter of Mary Christine (Selwood) Griffiths; married Pedro Santos de la Cal (a hotel manager), October 17, 1959 (died June 21, 1973); children: Elena, Cristina, Sara. *Education:* Attended Balham and Tooting College of Commerce, London, 1953-56.

■ Career

Novelist and freelance writer. Cowgirl on farm in Bedfordshire, England, 1956; Blackstock Engineering, Cockfosters, Hertfordshire, secretary, 1957-58; Selfridges department store, London, employee in record section, 1958-59; Oliver and Boyd Ltd., London, publishers, secretary, 1959-60; teacher of English as a foreign language, Madrid, 1973-76; parish church secretary, Bath, 1984—.

■ Awards, Honors

Highly commended by Carnegie Medal Award, 1966, for *The Wild Horse of Santander;* Child Study Association book list mention, 1968, for *Stallion of the Sands;* Silver Pencil Award, Holland, 1978, for *Witch Fear.*

■ Writings

JUVENILE

Horse in the Clouds, illustrated by Edward Osmond, Hutchinson, 1957, Holt, Rinehart, 1958.
Wild and Free, illustrated by Edward Osmond, Hutchinson, 1958.
Moonlight, illustrated by Edward Osmond, Hutchinson, 1959.
Africano, Hutchinson, 1961.
The Wild Heart, illustrated by Victor Ambrus, Hutchinson, 1963, Doubleday, 1964.
The Greyhound, illustrated by Victor Ambrus, Hutchinson, 1964, Doubleday, 1966.
The Wild Horse of Santander, illustrated by Victor Ambrus, Hutchinson, 1966, Doubleday, 1967.
Leon, illustrated by Victor Ambrus, Hutchinson, 1967, Doubleday, 1968.
Stallion of the Sands, illustrated by Victor Ambrus, Hutchinson, 1968, Lothrop, 1970.
Moshie Cat: The True Adventures of a Mallorquin Kitten, illustrated by Shirley Hughes, Hutchinson, 1969, Holiday House, 1970.
Patch, illustrated by Maurice Wilson, Hutchinson, 1970.
Federico, illustrated by Shirley Hughes, Hutchinson, 1971.

Russian Blue, illustrated by Victor Ambrus, Hutchinson, 1973, Holiday House, 1973.
Just a Dog, illustrated by Victor Ambrus, Hutchinson, 1974, Holiday House, 1975.
Witch Fear, illustrated by Victor Ambrus, Hutchinson, 1975, published as *The Mysterious Appearance of Agnes,* Holiday House, 1975.
Pablo, illustrated by Victor Ambrus, Hutchinson, 1977, published as *Running Wild,* Holiday House, 1977.
The Kershaw Dogs, illustrated by Douglas Hall, Hutchinson, 1978, published as *Grip: A Dog Story,* Holiday House, 1978.
The Last Summer: Spain 1936, illustrated by Victor Ambrus, Hutchinson, 1979, Holiday House, 1979.
Blackface Stallion, illustrated by Victor Ambrus, Hutchinson, 1980, Holiday House, 1980.
Dancing Horses, Hutchinson, 1981, Holiday House, 1982.
Hari's Pigeon, Hutchinson, 1982.
Jesus, as Told by Mark, illustrated by Jenny Kisler, Scripture Union, 1983.
Rafa's Dog, Hutchinson, 1983, Holiday House, 1983.
(Under name Helen Santos) *Caleb's Lamb,* Scripture Union, 1984.
The Dog at the Window, Hutchinson, 1984, Holiday House, 1984.
(Under name Helen Santos) *If Only,* Scripture Union, 1987.

FOR ADULTS

The Dark Swallows, Hutchinson, 1966, Knopf, 1967.

■ Adaptations

The Wild Heart was serialized by the BBC.

HELEN GRIFFITHS

■ Sidelights

Helen Griffiths, like many authors, began at an early age to write down her thoughts and impressions. Unlike most, however, she began publishing at age seventeen. That first book, *Horse in the Clouds,* was "all about horses and gauchos," as she described it in an entry in *Something about the Author Autobiography Series* (*SAAS*), and it set the tone for nearly two dozen books to follow: compassionate animal stories set in foreign lands. Her twin passions—animals and things Spanish—set the course for much of her life, as well, for she married a Spaniard and lived for many years in Spain. Griffiths' central "kindling theme," according to Naomi Lewis in *Twentieth-Century Children's Writers,* is "the lot of animals—those especially linked with man—in a predatory human world." It is this central theme that runs thread-like through her work, and always allied with the animal is some very special child who forges the link between animal and human. Her books feature dogs and cats and even a pigeon, but it is horses that predominate, reflecting her own interests and fantasies when Griffiths herself was growing up.

Hers were not the easiest of times to grow up. Born in London in 1939, Griffiths predated the onset of World War II by only a few months. "By the time I was four months old," Griffiths recalled in *SAAS,* "Britain was at war with Germany and, as invasion was expected at any moment, children were sent away from London to be out of danger." Griffiths and her brother were among these evacuees, and she spent the war years and several years after in the care of foster parents in Yorkshire. 'Aunty', her foster parent, became her mother for the next ten years. The living was simple in the industrial town of Hebden Bridge where they were sent, but their foster parents were musical and loving, and all about were the moors and open farmland. "If I had to sum up my childhood in one word," Griffiths wrote in *SAAS,* "it would be 'freedom.' When I look back on those years, I find it hard to believe that we were allowed to roam so far and wide."

It was during these early years that Griffiths was filled with a deep love for landscape and for the animals that worked the farms and fields. She watched the village blacksmith shoeing the huge Shire work horses and went on expeditions on the moors in search of wild ponies. The first book she bought was *Black Beauty.* "It didn't have any pictures in it," Griffiths explained, "but I read it and reread it and reread it, in all some twenty-five times." Love of real horses as well as love of the literary representation of them came at an early age. Other books Griffiths treasured when she was young included *Tales from the Arabian Nights,* the tales of Hans Christian Andersen and the Grimm Brothers, and *Wuthering Heights,* which was also a favorite for repeated readings.

This Yorkshire childhood ended when Griffiths was eleven: her Aunty suddenly died of cancer and Griffiths and her brother went back to London to live with their mother. "I must have been at just the right age to make

that transition from a small village to what was then the biggest city in the world," Griffiths recalled in *SAAS.* Though she missed the moors of Yorkshire, Griffiths had new fields to explore: the zoo, Madame Tussaud's Wax Museum, and the rich and colorful life of the streets of the city. There were horses still—dairy carts were pulled by horses into the 1950s and cavalry horses passed her front door.

Griffiths, who had been writing since age five, now began seriously to organize her impressions, to gather them into stories. "I was always writing things," she noted in *SAAS,* "keeping notes, creating my own magazines and, as I got older, writing serial stories to entertain my friends at school." The winner of the Matthew Arnold Memorial Prize, presented every three years to a London schoolgirl, Griffiths chose as her prize the *Oxford Dictionary.* A near miss at having a story of hers broadcast on the BBC further helped to convince Griffiths that she would some day become a published author, writing about things she knew best: animals and the countryside. By this time her brother was working on a farm and she visited him during holidays, working with the animals and growing to love them, but unsentimentally. "I was inclined to look upon animals as being similar to humans," she wrote in *SAAS,* "able to reason and think and feel much as we do. When you live in close working proximity with them you discover that this isn't true. Of course they have feeling and can be as clever and cunning as any person, but they don't reason as we do, and neither do they suffer as we do. They have no self-awareness. We can impose behaviour patterns on them and, to a certain extent, 'humanise' some of the more intelligent animals, but when we do this we degrade them. The best kind of animal is one that is being itself." This understanding would inform all of Griffiths' writing.

Griffiths decided that instead of working toward university entrance, she would work on a farm. She left school at fifteen to work as a cowgirl in Bedfordshire, and it was then she also began to write *Horse in the Clouds.* With the milking starting at six in the morning, Griffiths had to squeeze writing in whenever she could. "My ambition was to write the kind of horse story I'd always wanted to read. I tried to put into it just about everything I'd always wanted to find in a horse story, but never had." At the time she was wild about Argentina, for no explainable reason. But she read everything she could get her hands on about the country and put it all into this horse book so that it was brimming with energy and lore and information. Meanwhile, Griffiths had left the farm and taken a secretarial job and when the publishers Hutchinson accepted and published the book, she became something of a celebrity for her extreme youth. "There were interviews on BBC television and radio," she recalled in *SAAS,* "fan letters, and seventy-five pounds, an incredible sum of money when I was earning three pounds a week as an office junior."

Three more books quickly followed, "best forgotten," according to Griffiths, but more importantly, she married, had a child, and moved to Spain, all in that order. Her husband had come to England learning the hotel business and she was convinced by friends to trade English lessons for Spanish. Thus began a love that grew into marriage and a fifteen-year sojourn in Spain. With her husband away much of the time, Griffiths was thrown into Spanish life and threw herself into writing, as well. The result was *The Wild Heart,* which critics consider among her best horse stories, set in Argentina, as was *Horse in the Clouds,* and in the last century. One of Griffiths' most popular books, it has seen many translations and was serialized on the BBC.

With *The Greyhound,* Griffiths began to mine some of the experiences of her London youth, playing in the bomb craters of the city. This book tells the story of young Jamie and the dog Silver which he buys from an old man in need. But soon Jamie, a child of the slums, is in debt, as well, keeping the dog in a bomb site and forced to help a gang of hoodlums with petty crime. A happy ending finally ensues, but the reviewer for the *New Yorker* still felt the book was "far from being a conventional dog story." Griffiths' one foray into adult fiction, *The Dark Swallows,* followed, and then came the award-winning *The Wild Horse of Santander,* an "absorbing story," according to the *Times Literary Supplement.* Here Griffiths explores more fully her theme of the wild animal spirit that cannot be broken or tamed by man. A young Spanish boy, temporarily blind after an illness, receives a foal from his father. The boy is dependent on the horse in this turn-around plot, while the animal remains wild.

Spain was the setting for many of Griffiths' novels, both contemporary and historical. In several books she delved into the Civil War years. In *Leon,* Griffiths created a "memorable story of the relationship between dog and man," according to Virginia Haviland, writing in *Horn Book.* Ten years later she returned to the historical epoch of the Spanish Civil War, this time taking on the challenge of writing a sympathetic treatment of somebody on the Franco side of the conflict. The result was *The Last Summer: Spain 1936,* a story of a young boy whose father is killed by the revolutionary soldiers and who must ride on his favorite mare to the safety of his mother. Ethel L. Heins, in *Horn Book,* noted that Griffiths' "profound knowledge of Spain and her love of animals" are everywhere evident in this "moving, sensitively told story." A reviewer for *Publishers Weekly* concluded that *The Last Summer* was an "engrossing adventure."

Griffiths also periodically returned to Argentina in her writings, a land she had never visited, but one so accurately drawn that when her books were published in that country she received fan mail telling her how well she had captured the sense of place. *Stallion of the Sands,* though criticized for its lengthy opening told from the horse's point of view, is also "an exciting adventure story," according to Mary E. Ballou writing in *Library Journal.* Young Aurelio sets out to find his long-missing gaucho father and proves himself to be a gaucho in the process. The strength of the book,

according to *Kirkus Reviews,* is in "the embrace of 19th century life on the pampas."

Griffiths turned her hand to cat stories with *Moshie Cat,* a story patterned after the family's own cat when they were living on Majorca. "Here is a book for the true cat lover," commented Lavinia Russ in *Publishers Weekly.* This was followed up by another cat book, *Russian Blue,* in which the cat in question is a rare breed which wanders away from her wealthy home and into the life of a poor little boy. Bluey, the boy calls the cat, and confounds the vet who wants to put the animal to sleep after it has been run over and its back legs paralyzed. A reviewer for *Times Literary Supplement* noted that Griffiths did not take the easy way out by simply turning her story into a fairy tale. Griffiths, according to this reviewer, has "a pleasantly rational approach to life," and her book is a "strong mainstay of children's fiction." With *Just a Dog,* Griffiths once again used a family pet to tell her story. Shadow was a Madrid mutt that adopted the Griffiths family and provided the inspiration for a story of a stray and its four pups. Following the dog through both good and bad times,

Although she had never been to Argentina, Griffiths successfully recreated this setting in her story of a boy who wants to be a gaucho and the wild albino stallion who is instrumental in his quest. (Cover illustration by Victor Ambrus.)

Griffiths creates, as Susan Sprague noted in *School Library Journal,* "an exciting, unsentimentalized animal story."

By the early 1970s Griffiths had become a well respected children's author, turning out a book a year, and balancing the obligations of wife and mother of three with her work. She had a simple formula: "I decided without any difficulty," Griffiths recalled in *SAAS,* "that my husband was worth more than any amount of books and, as the children came along, they were worth more than books, too. From the very beginning there was no conflict because there was no competition. I gave my attention to writing only when everything else had been done." But all this changed in 1973 when her husband was killed in an automobile accident. She was now the provider for all and in addition to her writing, became an instructor in English as a Second Language, giving lessons in Madrid. Adversity suited her: Griffiths wrote in the following hard years two of her most popular books, *The Mysterious Appearance of Agnes* and *Running Wild.* The first, originally published in England as *Witch Fear,* was a complete departure for Griffiths: a story told without an animal protagonist. Set in the sixteenth century, the book tells the story of a young autistic girl who wanders out of the forest one day and is adopted by a childless couple. Later the girl is taken for a witch but in the process of proving her innocence, she also begins to heal the trauma leading to her autism. A "powerful story," noted Paul Heins in *Horn Book,* and Elizabeth Jane Howard in *New Statesman* agreed, concluding that Griffiths had "true imaginative power." The book also won the Silver Pencil Award from Holland upon translation into Dutch. *Running Wild,* on the other hand, returns to Griffiths' main concerns:

After a lost, autistic child wanders into the lives of a childless couple in sixteenth-century Germany, she is accused of witchcraft in *The Mysterious Appearance of Agnes.* (Illustration by Victor Ambrus.)

Spain and animals. Here lonely Pablo is forced to abandon a litter of puppies and they subsequently go wild, attacking local farm animals. Published as *Pablo* in England, the book brings home the powerful message of—as Paul Heins in *Horn Book* put it—the "great disparity between nature's way and man's way."

Griffiths and her family moved to England in 1976, setting up house in Bath, and there the author continued writing books largely concerned with animals and their relationship to the human world. *Grip: A Dog Story* was not only about an animal but about the Yorkshire Griffiths remembered from her childhood. One exception to these stories was *Blackface Stallion,* written at the request of one of her daughters and told solely from the horse's point of view without any humans in it. "It wasn't an easy book to write," Griffiths noted in *SAAS.* "I really wanted to get across the nature of the wild horse, just as it must be. So much nonsense is written about horses in the field of fiction; so much is sentimental and unreal; and I wanted to get away from that." And she succeeded, according to Kate M. Flanagan in *Horn Book:* "Terse vivid writing illuminates the spirit that is the animals' key to survival."

In a book that tested the "loyalty of her animal-lover fans," as *Publishers Weekly* put it, Griffiths explored the

Grip: A Dog Story tells how young Dudley is torn between love for his father and his gentle dog, Grip, whom his father wishes to train to become a vicious champion fighter. (Illustration by Douglas Hall.)

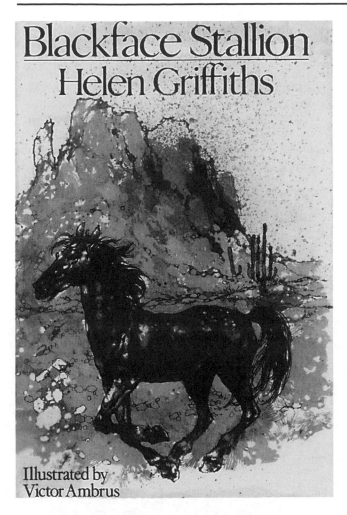

Blackface Stallion
Helen Griffiths

Illustrated by
Victor Ambrus

In this 1980 book, told completely from a horse's point of view, Griffiths follows Blackface as he grows from a colt to the leader of a herd of wild horses. (Cover illustration by Victor Ambrus.)

world of bullfighting in *Dancing Horses*. Set in Spain after the Civil War, this coming-of-age story traces the dreams of a stableboy who wants to train an unruly Andalusian for bullfighting on horseback. Charlene Strickland, writing in *School Library Journal*, noted that the book contained "fast-paced action," and Karen M. Klockner in *Horn Book* commended the book as "gracefully written."

From horses, Griffiths set out to find a new animal to write about and found it in *Hari's Pigeon*, in preparation for the writing of which she kept a pigeon in a spare bedroom for several months to study its activities and movements. The story of a young Anglo-Indian adjusting to a new life and school, the book is told in diary form and with, as a *Junior Bookshelf* contributor noted, "sympathy and insight." In addition to two further dog books, *Rafa's Dog* and *The Dog at the Window*, Griffiths' more current books have also included religious themes, reflecting her own renewed interest and commitment to Christianity. A strong believer in prayer, Griffiths had the entire plot of *Rafa's Dog* flash into her mind after praying for a new story to come to her. "I've

never had, either before or since, a whole plot for a book," Griffiths noted in her *SAAS* entry.

Whether God-inspired or not, the plots Griffiths has come up with over the years have entertained decades of readers. Her first book, *Horse in the Clouds*, written when Griffiths was a school girl herself, continues to enthrall. "My youngest daughter, Sara," Griffiths wrote in *SAAS*, "had the distinct embarrassment at her last school, when she was about sixteen, of being told by her English teacher how she had wept over *Horse in the Clouds* as a fourteen-year-old!" In the end, it is this connection—whether it be weeping or insight—that Griffiths has sought in her works. She once told *SATA* that she had a very straightforward intention with her books: "I love animals, I have an instinctive feeling for them, so that it is only natural that I should combine my love of writing with my love of animals to produce books about them. I hope that my books in some small way help children to understand and appreciate animals too."

■ **Works Cited**

Ballou, Mary E., review of *Stallion of the Sands, Library Journal,* January 15, 1971, p. 268.

Review of *Dancing Horses, Publishers Weekly,* June 18, 1982, p. 74.

Flanagan, Kate M., review of *Blackface Stallion, Horn Book,* December, 1980, p. 649.

Review of *The Greyhound, New Yorker,* December 17, 1966, p. 223.

Griffiths, Helen, essay in *Something about the Author Autobiography Series,* Volume 5, Gale, 1988, pp. 147-60.

Review of *Hari's Pigeon, Junior Bookshelf,* April, 1983, p. 81.

Haviland, Virginia, review of *Leon, Horn Book,* April, 1968, p. 177.

Heins, Ethel L., review of *The Last Summer: Spain 1936, Horn Book,* April, 1980, p. 173.

Heins, Paul, review of *The Mysterious Appearance of Agnes, Horn Book,* February, 1976, p. 50.

Heins, Paul, review of *Running Wild, Horn Book,* April, 1978, pp. 165-66.

Howard, Elizabeth Jane, review of *Witch Fear, New Statesman,* November 7, 1975, p. 583.

Klockner, Karen M., review of *Dancing Horses, Horn Book,* August, 1982, p. 403.

Review of *The Last Summer: Spain 1936, Publishers Weekly,* December 3, 1979, p. 51.

Lewis, Naomi, "Helen Griffiths," *Twentieth-Century Children's Writers,* St. James Press, 1995, pp. 417-18.

Russ, Lavinia, review of *Moshie Cat: The True Adventures of a Mallorquin Kitten, Publishers Weekly,* September 28, 1970, p. 80.

Review of *Russian Blue, Times Literary Supplement,* June 15, 1973, p. 684.

Sprague, Susan, review of *Just a Dog, School Library Journal,* September, 1975, p. 103.

Review of *Stallion of the Sands, Kirkus Reviews,* October 15, 1970, p. 1162.

Strickland, Charlene, "Equine Fiction in the 1980s," *School Library Journal,* August, 1986, pp. 36-37.

Review of *The Wild Horse of Santander, Times Literary Supplement,* November 24, 1966, p. 1091.

■ For More Information See

PERIODICALS

Booklist, September 15, 1966, p. 119; March 15, 1968, p. 867; March 1, 1971, p. 558; April 1, 1971, p. 663; September 1, 1975, p. 40; January 1, 1976, p. 626; February 1, 1978, p. 924; December 1, 1978, p. 616; January 1, 1980, p. 667; November 15, 1980, p. 459; February 1, 1984, p. 813.

Bulletin of the Center for Children's Books, September, 1975, p. 9; April, 1976, p. 124; April, 1984, p. 147.

Horn Book, October, 1967, p. 593; February, 1979, p. 61; February, 1984, p. 53; January, 1985, p. 50.

School Library Journal, December, 1975, p. 67; January, 1978, p. 89; January, 1979, p. 61; December, 1979, p. 91; February, 1984, p. 70; February, 1985, p. 84.

Times Literary Supplement, November 24, 1966, p. 1091; November 30, 1967, p. 1157; October 3, 1968, p. 1110; June 26, 1969, p. 700; April 2, 1971, p. 391; December 5, 1975, p. 1450.*

—Sketch by J. Sydney Jones

H–I

HADLEY, Lee 1934-1995
(Hadley Irwin, a joint pseudonym)

OBITUARY NOTICE—See index for *SATA* sketch: Born October 10, 1934, in Earlham, IA; died of cancer, August 22, 1995, in Madrid (one source says Des Moines), IA. Educator, copywriter, and author. Hadley, who wrote young adult fiction under the pseudonym Hadley Irwin with Ann Irwin, penned more than one dozen acclaimed novels dealing with contemporary social issues such as racism, substance abuse, and suicide. Their 1985 *Abbey, My Love* dealt with incest and was the first such work of its kind written for younger audiences. Hadley began her career as a copywriter for the Younkers of Des Moines department store in 1955. After stints as a high school teacher in De Soto, Iowa, and Monmouth, New Jersey, she served as an instructor in English at Ocean County Community College from 1965 until 1968. Hadley joined the Iowa State University faculty in 1969 and eventually became a full professor. At Iowa she met Irwin and they began their writing collaboration in 1979. Their other novels include *What About Grandma?*, winner of the Best Young Adult Book Award from the American Library Association, *We Are Mesquakie, We Are One*, which was named a Jane Addams Peace Association Honor Book, and *So Long at the Fair*. Their tentatively titled *Sarah with an H* is set for 1996 publication.

OBITUARIES AND OTHER SOURCES:

PERIODICALS

New York Times, August 26, 1995, p. 9.
Washington Post, August 25, 1995, p. C6.

*   *   *

HAMILTON, Buzz
See HEMMING, Roy (G.)

ROSMARIE HAUSHERR

HAUSHERR, Rosmarie 1943-

■ Personal

Born June 25, 1943, in Muri, Switzerland; emigrated to the United States in 1969; divorced.

■ Addresses

Home—145 West 17th St., New York, NY 10011.

■ Career

Freelance photographer in New York and Vermont, 1972—.

■ Awards, Honors

International Photo Prize, Amsterdam, 1969; photography grant, Solothurn, Switzerland, 1969; photography grant, Swiss National Council of the Arts, 1970, 1971.

■ Writings

FOR CHILDREN; AND PHOTOGRAPHER

My First Kitten, Macmillan, 1985.
My First Puppy, Macmillan, 1986.
The One-Room School at Squabble Hollow, Macmillan, 1988.
Children and the AIDS Virus: A Book for Children, Parents, and Teachers, Clarion, 1989.
The City Girl Who Went to the Sea, Macmillan, 1990.
What Instrument Is This?, Scholastic, 1992.
What Food Is This?, Scholastic, 1994.

FOR CHILDREN; PHOTOGRAPHER

Joanne E. Bernstein and Stephen V. Gullo, *When People Die,* Dutton, 1977.
Mary Milgram, *Brothers Are All the Same,* Dutton, 1978.
Ron Roy, *Move Over, Wheelchairs Coming!,* Clarion, 1985.
Marilyn Gelfand, *My Great-Grandpa Joe,* Macmillan, 1986.
Roy, *Whose Hat Is That?,* Clarion, 1987.
Roy, *Whose Shoes Are These?,* Clarion, 1988.
Christopher J. Goedecke, *The Wind Warrior: The Training of a Karate Champion,* Macmillan, 1992.
Goedecke, *Smart Moves: A Kid's Guide to Self-defense,* Simon & Schuster, 1995.

FOR ADULTS; PHOTOGRAPHER

M. J. Jones, *The Sundial Book,* Hawthorn, 1978.
Jean Yueh, *The Great Taste of Chinese Cooking,* Times Inc., 1979.
Michael Litchfield, *The Complete House Renovation,* J. Wiley, 1980.
Litchfield, *Salvaged Treasures,* Van Nostrand, 1982.
Vicki Cobb, *Brave in the Attempt,* Pinwheel, 1983.
Donald L. Fennimore, *Knopf Collector's Guild to American Antiques, Silver and Pewter,* Knopf, 1992.

■ Sidelights

Rosmarie Hausherr told *SATA:* "The writing process, in comparison to photography, is calmer, less nerve-wrecking. I usually go into 'hiding.' My last two books, *What Instrument Is This?* and *What Food Is This?,* were written in the back of a small library, in Peacham, Vermont. I start working on my texts after the photographs have been taken. My pictures and my research material provide inspiration and information. I enjoy this intense work. The design of my books is of great importance to me. I dummy my manuscripts, determine the flow of text and pictures, crop the photographs, and work closely with designers and art directors.

"Since a few years ago I have been visiting elementary schools in several states as an author. My programs are tailored to students in kindergarten through grade six. From my presentations, which are based on my books, students learn about photography and writing. I share with them the joys and frustrations an author experiences along the creative path. Younger children get to see photos and writing samples, older ones are treated to exciting slide shows. Inspired by my presentations, teachers often follow up by building nonfiction writing into their curriculum. And they encourage their students to illustrate their texts with either their own photographs, or with copies of pictures from books or magazines. School visits are energizing. I always learn from my young readers."

Born and raised in Switzerland, Hausherr was educated as a photo-journalist in her homeland before emigrating to the United States as a young woman. Hausherr's photographs have illustrated several books for adults, as well as numerous children's books, and have garnered high praise for their appeal to young readers. Having started out as a photographer, Hausherr began writing the texts for her own children's books in the early 1980s. Primarily nonfiction, Hausherr's books have been favorably reviewed for their effective formats and clear, simple, and informative prose, as well as for their inclusion of minorities and children with physical disabilities.

Hausherr's first picture books for children, *My First Puppy* and *My First Kitten,* follow a young child through the steps of acquiring and caring for a pet. In *My First Puppy,* Jenny chooses a poodle, and photos show her learning how to feed and train her dog. In *My First Kitten,* Adam raises a kitten, teaching it to use a litterbox and taking it to the veterinarian. Lillian N. Gerhardt, a reviewer in *School Library Journal,* found Hausherr's sentimental depiction of cat ownership "cloying," and concluded: "The world awaits a really straightforward book on kitten care." However, Ilene Cooper averred in her review in *Booklist* that "this photo-essay offers readers much more than sweet poses." A review of *My First Puppy* by Florence M. Brems in *School Library Journal* highlighted the usefulness of the information presented for both parents and children, and dubbed this work "an excellent introduction to the responsibilities and joys of owning a dog."

In *The One-Room School at Squabble Hollow,* Hausherr presents "a detailed, affectionate, accurate, upbeat portrait" of a school in Vermont that, before it closed in 1986, combined traditional and modern values and methods, according to a reviewer in *Kirkus Reviews.* Illustrated with photos that range from the beginning of the school year to Halloween, the book shows the children receiving individualized instruction as well as learning cooperation, as the older children help the younger and all the students share in taking care of the

Hausherr shot the photos for Christopher J. Goedecke's *The Wind Warrior: The Training of a Karate Champion*, which follows one student's training regimen for a martial arts tournament.

school. A critic in *Booklist* called *The One-Room School at Squabble Hollow* a "well-photographed, smoothly written documentary."

Hausherr's next book, *Children and the AIDS Virus: A Book for Children, Parents, and Teachers* combines information about Acquired Immunodeficiency Syndrome aimed at the picture-book audience, with more detailed explanations in smaller type for older children and adults, and concludes with the stories of some children who have AIDS. Reviewers found that Hausherr successfully manages to reassure children while communicating some of the frightening realities of this disease. Critics disagreed about the effectiveness of the author's mixed format, however. While *School Library Journal* reviewer Anne Osborn felt that the text aimed at picture-book readers "is too difficult for the intended audience," Ellen Mandel wrote in *Booklist* that "with thoughtfully composed black-and-white photos attractively placed throughout, Hausherr's text forthrightly and nonthreateningly fosters schoolchildren's under-

standing of AIDS." And while Osborn concluded in *School Library Journal* that *Children and the AIDS Virus* is "for adults working with children rather than for children themselves," the critic in *Publishers Weekly* found it to be successful "in reaching and reassuring its target audience."

In 1977, Alicia, a ten-year-old New Yorker, spent a summer with relatives who live in a remote fishing village in Newfoundland, Canada. Hausherr's next book, *The City Girl Who Went to the Sea,* documents that visit with black-and-white photographs "that complement a warm, sensitive text," according to Linda Callaghan, a reviewer in *Booklist*. Critics noted Alicia's fascination with the people of the village and their traditional occupations, including making fishnets, quilts, and brooms by hand. Although *School Library Journal* critic Maggie McEwen felt "the book fails to provide a clear sense of place" and contained "stilted writing and poor transitions," critic Callaghan praised

The City Girl Who Went to the Sea as "a portrait of Newfoundland life that reads like a novel."

What Food Is This? and *What Instrument Is This?*, two of Hausherr's subsequent books, share a format that relies on questions and answers and numerous photographs in both color and black-and-white. Critics praised these picture books for their inclusiveness and entertaining method of teaching children about the foods they eat and musical instruments. In *What Food Is This?* Hausherr poses a question accompanied by a photograph of a child with the food in question, followed by a short discussion. The book features items from all the major food groups and includes a food pyramid, glossary of terms, and tips on nutrition directed to parents. Although Stephanie Zvirin called this a "very appealing looking book" in a review in *Booklist,* she also felt that it was best used with adult supervision. A critic in *Kirkus Reviews,* on the other hand, called *What Food Is This?* "a thoughtfully structured book that is particularly outstanding for its photos" and for teaching children how to reach conclusions from material that is logically structured.

What Instrument Is This? also garnered positive reactions to its appealing and gently humorous photographs, as well as for its effective, informative text. *Booklist* critic Kay Weisman commented: "An attractive and useful addition to most libraries, [*What Instrument Is This?*] will be popular with music students and browsers alike." A critic in *Kirkus Reviews* singled out Hausherr's photos for special praise, and dubbed the effect of the whole "inspiring."

Hausherr's photographs illustrate *The Wind Warrior: The Training of a Karate Champion,* by Christopher J. Goedecke, which reviewer Weisman in *Booklist* found to be "a well-written, nonsensationalized presentation about karate." The book follows Nick, a young adolescent, as he trains for a state tournament, learns the various forms, practices regularly, and finally competes in the karate tournament. Although *School Library Journal* reviewer Cathryn A. Camper recommended that students interested in karate "would be best off observing or attending a class or two, to see what it's really about," a critic in *Kirkus Reviews* wrote that "the look of karate, as well as some of its excitement, are nicely captured" in *The Wind Warrior.*

Hausherr is a photographer whose children's books are widely considered entertaining as well as informative. Critics have praised her delicate handling of difficult material in her book on children and AIDS, and her appealing presentation of information on owning pets, playing musical instruments, and selecting nutritious food in other works. Hausherr has garnered positive responses to the clarity and simplicity of her narratives. In addition, her illustrative photographs have been universally admired.

■ Works Cited

Brems, Florence M., review of *My First Puppy, School Library Journal,* March, 1987.

Callaghan, Linda, review of *The City Girl Who Went to the Sea, Booklist,* January 1, 1991.

Camper, Cathryn A., review of *The Wind Warrior, School Library Journal,* July, 1992.

Review of *Children and the AIDS Virus: A Book for Children, Parents, and Teachers, Publishers Weekly,* June 9, 1989.

Cooper, Ilene, review of *My First Kitten, Booklist,* January 1, 1986, p. 685.

Gerhardt, Lillian N., review of *My First Kitten, School Library Journal,* January, 1986.

Mandel, Ellen, review of *Children and the AIDS Virus, Booklist,* July, 1989.

McEwen, Maggie, review of *The City Girl Who Went to the Sea, School Library Journal,* March, 1991.

Review of *The One-Room School at Squabble Hollow, Booklist,* June 1, 1988.

Review of *The One-Room School at Squabble Hollow, Kirkus Reviews,* April 1, 1988, p. 538.

Osborn, Anne, review of *Children and the AIDS Virus, School Library Journal,* July, 1989.

Weisman, Kay, review of *The Wind Warrior, Booklist,* June 1, 1992.

Weisman, Kay, review of *What Instrument Is This?, Booklist,* May, 1994.

Review of *What Food Is This?, Kirkus Reviews,* February 15, 1994.

Review of *What Instrument Is This?, Kirkus Reviews,* November 15, 1992.

Review of *The Wind Warrior, Kirkus Reviews,* May 1, 1992.

Zvirin, Stephanie, review of *What Food Is This?, Booklist,* April 15, 1994.

■ For More Information See

PERIODICALS

Booklist, January 1, 1987, p. 709.
Bulletin of the Center for Children's Books, June, 1989, p. 251.
Horn Book, March, 1987, p. 221.
School Library Journal, August, 1988, p. 88; January, 1993.

—*Sketch by Mary Gillis*

*   *   *

HELMER, Diana Star 1962-

■ Personal

Born June 11, 1962, in Redwood Falls, MN; married Thomas S. Owens (an author), April 7, 1982. *Education:* Iowa State University, B.A., 1986. *Politics:* "Primarily Rational (which is probably a dichotomy), with a fair amount of Bleeding-Heart Liberal." *Religion:* Agnostic. *Hobbies and other interests:* Ballet, portrait drawing, reading ("though I don't seem to care for most of the

Diana Star Helmer and her husband Thomas S. Owens

books that grown-ups are supposed to like"), long walks, playing classical piano ("which includes Beethoven and Irving Berlin"), origami, and recording stories for the Marshalltown Public Library's Dial-a-Story.

Addresses

Office—1001 West Boone St., Marshalltown, IA 50158-2412. *Agent*—Barbara Kouts, P.O. Box 558, Bellport, NY 11713.

Career

Writer and journalist. Contributed arts features and reviews to Iowa State *Daily,* Ames *Tribune,* and Des Moines *Register* while attending Iowa State University; Tacoma *News Tribune,* Tacoma, WA, feature writer, for five years; regular contributor to *Legends* magazine for five years; wrote features for workers in the food service industry for one year; wrote for one year at *Sports Collectors' Digest.* Has also taught piano, directed children's theater, and taught ballet and preschool. Storyteller with husband Tom Owens, performing together and recording original stories for Dial-a-Story for the Marshalltown (Iowa) Public Library. *Member:* Society of Children's Books Writers and Illustrators, National Storytelling Association.

Awards, Honors

Books for the Teen Age citation, New York Public Library, 1994, for *Belles of the Ballpark.*

Writings

The Snow Queen (play; adapted from the story by Hans Christian Andersen), produced in Marshalltown, IA, 1979, revised version produced 1995.

If Mama Ain't Happy . . . (play for teens), produced in Marshalltown, IA, 1993.
Belles of the Ballpark, Millbrook Press, 1993.
(With husband, Thomas S. Owens) *Inside Collectible Card Games,* Millbrook Press, 1996.

Articles, features, and reviews have appeared in *U.S. Art, Totally Kids, Elysian Fields,* and *Baseball America.*

■ Work in Progress

"I like all kinds of writing and stories, so I have picture books I'm thinking hard about, and easy readers (which I like because they can be funny), and nonfiction about people and nonfiction about animals, and a novel that I guess is a fantasy. I want to rewrite *Mama* as a novel, so that people can read it whenever they want to, instead of waiting for thirty people to put on a show."

■ Sidelights

Diana Star Helmer told *SATA:* "I was surprised that my first book was a work of nonfiction. I grew up loving books, nonfiction as well as fiction, but I always thought that fiction was somehow more important. I dreamed of writing fiction someday.

"I still want to write stories that come from my head. But I no longer believe that is most important. Nonfiction is our memories. Fiction is our dreams. We need both, because memories and dreams make us exactly who we are.

"Perhaps I thought fiction was best because, when you are seven or eleven, you have more power to dream than to do. When you get to be fifteen or seventeen, you begin to be able to test your dreams. Sometimes the doing is better than dreaming. Sometimes, it is worse. So then you dream of something else, so you can do that, too. That is all that growing up is. If you are lucky, you never get all the way there.

"That is why I love nonfiction now, just as much as fiction. Nonfiction is the doing. When I write a true story for a newspaper or a book, the people who lived the stories invite me into their worlds. There are so many worlds I would never have discovered all alone! *Belles of the Ballpark* is an example. When I first heard of 'The Ladies' League,' there were no books or movies on the subject—just memories in old newspapers and in peoples' hearts. I helped the people who lived an amazing story tell that story, and that is an honor for me. And I learned about a world I hadn't known, the world of America before I was born, and how people thought, and how they treated each other. I understand my own world so much better now.

"I think the whole world is nothing but stories. With stories, pieces of me can find pieces of you that each of us needs to find. In a story, the way things sound or look won't frighten you so much, because you can say, 'It's only a story.' And so you'll stay, and you'll listen. And that's when a story becomes more than a story, when somebody really listens."

In *Belles of the Ballpark,* Helmer recounts the history of the All-American Girls Professional Baseball League, an idea born during World War II, when many of the best and most popular male baseball players were fighting in the war. Philip Wrigley, owner of the Chicago Cubs baseball team, started the league to ensure the continuance of professional baseball during the war. Women from the United States and Canada were auditioned, selected, trained, groomed, and paid to play what eventually came to bear a close resemblance to professional baseball played by men, though at first a larger ball and shorter basepaths were used, and the game was pitched underhand. The league was popular for more than a decade, but because of lack of money and competition from women's softball leagues, the All-American Girls Professional Baseball League ceased to exist in 1954.

Inevitably compared to the popular 1992 feature film on the same subject, *A League of Their Own,* Helmer's *Belles of the Ballpark* received mixed reviews. While some critics found the strict chronological account lacked flair, *Bulletin of the Center for Children's Books* writer Roger Sutton called Helmer's narrative "an informative overview" of the league's history. Although *Voice of Youth Advocates* reviewer Carol Buchanan felt the book could have used more of "the vivid descriptions and personal anecdotes that make the people and events come alive," she concluded that she "very definitely would purchase this book" in order to provide students with information on "this captivating episode in our history."

■ Works Cited

Buchanan, Carol, review of *Belles of the Ballpark, Voice of Youth Advocates,* June, 1993, p. 113.
Sutton, Roger, review of *Belles of the Ballpark, Bulletin of the Center for Children's Books,* May, 1993, p. 282.

*   *   *

HEMMING, Roy (G.) 1928-1995
(Buzz Hamilton)

OBITUARY NOTICE—See index for *SATA* sketch: Born May 27, 1928, in Hamden, CT; died of multiple myeloma, September 13, 1995, in New York City, NY. Journalist, critic, author. Hemming devoted his career to the written word, first as a reporter and later as news editor and music columnist. Beginning work at the *New Haven Journal-Courier* as a reporter in 1947, he held various writing jobs before joining Scholastic Magazines in 1954. Hemming stayed with Scholastic for more than twenty years, serving in stints as news editor, record reviewer, editor of *World Week,* executive editor of *Senior Scholastic,* and editor-at-large. In 1975, he assumed the duties of editor-in-chief of *Retirement Living.* Hemming contributed articles and reviews to *Stereo*

Review, Opera News, and *Gramophone* magazines— sometimes under the pseudonym Buzz Hamilton—and authored a number of books, including *Movies on Video, The Melody Lingers on: The Great American Songwriters and Their Movie Musicals, Discovering the Great Singers of Classic Pop,* and *Discovering Great Music on CDs, LPs and Tapes.*

OBITUARIES AND OTHER SOURCES:

BOOKS

Who's Who in America, 50th edition, Marquis, 1995.
PERIODICALS
New York Times, September 13, 1995, p. B8.

*   *   *

HERRIOT, James 1916-1995

■ Personal

Given name, James Alfred Wight; born October 3, 1916, in Sunderland, County Tyne and Werr, England; died February 23, 1995, of prostate cancer, in Thirsk, Yorkshire, England; son of James Henry (a musician) and Hannah (a professional singer; maiden name, Bell) Wight; married Joan Catherine Danbury, November 5, 1941; children: James, Rosemary Page. *Education:*

JAMES HERRIOT

Glasgow Veterinary College, M.R.C.V.S., 1938. *Religion:* Protestant. *Hobbies and other interests:* Music, walking with his dog.

■ Career

Sinclair & Wight, Thirsk, Yorkshire, England, partner and general practitioner in veterinary medicine, 1938-c. 1992; writer, 1966-95. *Military service:* Royal Air Force, 1943-45. *Member:* British Veterinary Association (honorary member), Royal College of Veterinary Surgeons (fellow).

■ Awards, Honors

Best Young Adult Book citations, American Library Association, 1974, for *All Things Bright and Beautiful,* and 1975, for *All Creatures Great and Small;* Order of the British Empire, 1979; D.Litt., Watt University, Scotland, 1979; honorary D.Vsc., Liverpool University, 1984; James Herriot Award established by Humane Society of America.

■ Writings

If Only They Could Talk (also see below), M. Joseph, 1970.

It Shouldn't Happen to a Vet (also see below), M. Joseph, 1972.

All Creatures Great and Small (contains *If Only They Could Talk* and *It Shouldn't Happen to a Vet*), St. Martin's, 1972.

Let Sleeping Vets Lie (also see below), M. Joseph, 1973.

Vet in Harness (also see below), M. Joseph, 1974.

All Things Bright and Beautiful (contains *Let Sleeping Vets Lie* and *Vet in Harness*), St. Martin's, 1974.

Vets Might Fly (also see below), M. Joseph, 1976.

Vet in a Spin (also see below), M. Joseph, 1977.

All Things Wise and Wonderful (contains *Vets Might Fly* and *Vet in a Spin*), St. Martin's, 1977.

James Herriot's Yorkshire, illustrated with photographs by Derry Brabbs, St. Martin's, 1979.

(With others) *Animals Tame and Wild,* Sterling, 1979, published as *Animal Stories: Tame and Wild,* 1985.

The Lord God Made Them All, St. Martin's, 1981.

The Best of James Herriot, St. Martin's, 1983.

James Herriot's Dog Stories, illustrated by Victor G. Ambrus, St. Martin's, 1986.

Every Living Thing, St. Martin's, 1992.

James Herriot's Cat Stories, illustrated by Lesley Holmes, St. Martin's, 1994.

Also author of *James Herriot's Yorkshire Calendar.*

FOR CHILDREN

Moses the Kitten, illustrated by Peter Barrett, St. Martin's, 1984.

Only One Woof, illustrated by Barrett, St. Martin's, 1985.

The Christmas Day Kitten, illustrated by Ruth Brown, St. Martin's, 1986.

Bonny's Big Day, illustrated by Brown, St. Martin's, 1987.

Blossom Comes Home, illustrated by Brown, St. Martin's, 1988.

The Market Square Dog, illustrated by Brown, St. Martin's, 1990.

Oscar, Cat-about-Town, illustrated by Brown, M. Joseph, 1990.

Smudge, the Little Lost Lamb, illustrated by Brown, St. Martin's, 1991.

James Herriot's Treasury for Children, St. Martin's, 1992.

■ Adaptations

All Creatures Great and Small was filmed by EMI Production, 1975, was presented on the *Hallmark Hall of Fame,* NBC-TV, 1975, adapted as a television series by BBC-TV, 1978, and shown on PBS-TV, 1979, and recorded on audio cassette by Listen for Pleasure, 1980; *All Things Bright and Beautiful* was filmed by BBC-TV, 1979 (also released as *It Shouldn't Happen to a Vet*), and recorded as an audio cassette by Listen for Pleasure, 1980; audio cassette versions were recorded by Cassette Book for *All Things Wise and Wonderful,* and by Listen for Pleasure for *The Lord God Made Them All,* 1982; Listen for Pleasure also released an audio cassette entitled *Stories from the Herriot Collection.*

■ Sidelights

James Herriot was not just a simple country veterinarian, as he liked to call himself. His story collections, *All*

Lisa Harrow (left) and Simon Ward starred in the 1975 NBC-TV version of Herriot's *All Creatures Great and Small.*

The warm and joyful sequel to THE LORD GOD MADE THEM ALL

Every Living Thing
James Herriot

In 1992 Herriot brought his readers up to date on his life in the Yorkshire countryside in his last lengthy work.

Creatures Great and Small (1972) and *All Things Bright and Beautiful* (1975), made Herriot famous in England and the United States; readers and critics alike appreciated the joy he found in his hard work, laughed at his humorous anecdotes, marveled at the curative practices he explained, and relaxed with his descriptions of the English countryside. In Herriot's later years, to the delight of children and adults alike, he transformed some of his most endearing vignettes into picture book stories. Although these tales are short and uncomplicated, their emotional content is vintage Herriot: they exude love, humor, and, at times, elicit tears.

Herriot rejected the idea that his work was extraordinary. He once reflected to William Foster in *Scotsman,* "I know some writers dream of best sellerdom and the best table in the restaurants and all that, but not me. I just had this compulsion to write down what it was like to be a vet in those funny old days in the 1930s before I forgot. If I could find a publisher and my stories amused a few people well, that was the summit of my ambition." In his opinion, Herriot told David Taylor of *Radio Times,* Americans "read ... all kinds of weighty, humanitarian, sociological meanings" into his work that

he couldn't see and didn't have time to wonder about. "I'm much too busy being a vet."

Herriot grew up in Hillhead, a small town near Glasgow, Scotland. He once told *SATA:* "I had what I can only describe as an idyllic childhood, because, although I grew up in the big city of Glasgow, my home was only a few miles from the beauties of Loch Lomond and the Scottish hills. I spent much of my childhood and adolescence walking along with my dog, camping and climbing among the highlands of Scotland so that at an early age three things were implanted in my character: a love of animals, reading and the countryside."

Herriot was just thirteen years old when he decided to become a veterinarian. By the time he received a degree from Glasgow Veterinary School, however, England was in the midst of the Great Depression. He was fortunate to find a job as an assistant vet in North Yorkshire, England. Although Herriot had always assumed he would be a small-animal surgeon and own his own modern office, this job involved house calls to treat horses, cows, pigs, and other livestock. It was not long before Herriot realized he loved what he did, and soon he revised his high-tech vision of what his ideal career path should be.

He wrote in *All Creatures Great and Small,* "Maybe it was something to do with the incredible sweetness of the air which still took me by surprise when I stepped out into the old wild garden at Skeldale House every morning. Or perhaps the daily piquancy of life in the graceful old house with my gifted but mercurial boss, Siegfried, and his reluctant student brother, Tristan. Or it could be that it was just the realization that treating cows and pigs and sheep and horses had a fascination I had never even suspected; and this brought with it a new concept of myself as a tiny wheel in the great machine of British agriculture. There was a kind of solid satisfaction in that."

Herriot was made a partner in the Yorkshire practice and married Joan Catherine Danbury (known as Helen in his books) on the same day in 1941. The couple lived together in the house Herriot called Skeldale House in his books, where Herriot was disturbed at all times of the night to tend sick animals. Herriot's rigorous practice and his happy life with his new wife were interrupted when he was called, at twenty-seven years of age, into active duty with the Royal Air Force (RAF) in 1943. After reporting to the Lords Cricket Ground at St. John's Wood in London for his initial training, Herriot was posted to Scarborough, Yorkshire, not too far from home. He was able to visit home when his son, James, was born in 1944.

Herriot was sent to flying school in Windsor and was then posted to Manchester. A subsequent operation made him unfit to fly, and he returned home to Yorkshire for good. Herriot had time to reflect on his career, and decided he was happy as a country vet. He wrote in *All Things Bright and Beautiful,* "I had no regrets, the life which had been forced on me by circumstances had turned out to be a thing of magical fulfillment. It came to me with a flooding certainty that I would rather spend my days driving over the unfenced roads of the high country than stooping over that operating table."

It was not until Herriot was fifty years old that he began to write. He once told Foster of *Scotsman*, "The life of a country vet was dirty, uncomfortable, sometimes dangerous. It was terribly hard work and I loved it. I felt vaguely that I ought to write about it and every day for 25 years I told my wife of something funny that had happened and said I was keeping it for the book. She usually said, 'Yes, dear' to humour me but one day, when I was fifty, she said: 'Who are you kidding? Vets of fifty don't write first books.' Well, that did it. I stormed out and bought some paper and taught myself to type.

"Then I started to put it all down and the story didn't work. All I managed to pick out on the machine was a very amateur school essay. So I spent a year or two learning my craft, as real writers say. I read *How to Be a Writer* and *Teach Yourself to Write* and I bombarded newspapers, magazines and the BBC with unreadable short stories. They came back, every one, without a word of comment. Not even 'You show promise.'" Herriot began to study and learn from his favorite writers, like Charles Dickens, Arthur Conan Doyle, Ernest Hemingway, and J. D. Salinger, and kept on writing.

Although Herriot was still working as a vet, he wrote when he found time, sometimes in front of the television. He wrote his first book in 18 months. *If Only They Could Talk* (1970) was published under the name James Herriot because Herriot thought it would be akin to advertising to publish under his own name. He had to choose a pseudonym. "I was sitting in front of the TV tapping out one of my stories and there was this fellow James Herriot playing such a good game of soccer for Birmingham that I just took his name," Herriot explained to Arturo F. Gonzalez in *Saturday Review*.

Although his first book sold only 1,200 copies, his second, *It Shouldn't Happen to a Vet* (1972) was bound with the first in the volume *All Creatures Great and Small* (1972) and published in the United States. This book was a best-seller and an immediate success. *All Creatures Great and Small* recalls moments from Herriot's career: assisting in the birth of calves, relieving Tricki Woo (an obese Pekingese dog pampered by her owner), and diagnosing and treating the ailments of other dogs, cats, cows, horses, pigs, and sheep. Herriot also describes the people he worked with, including his boss, Siegfried Farnon, and his boss's brother, Tristan. According to Nelson Bryant of *New York Times Book Review*, the book "shines with love of life" and "there is humor everywhere."

All Things Bright and Beautiful (1974), a compilation of Herriot's next two books, provides new stories about treating animals as well as tales of his courtship of Helen. Tristan's exploits are related with humor. As

Moses the Kitten **is the charming tale of a cat who is saved from freezing by a farm family and nursed back to health.** (Illustration by Peter Barrett.)

Edward Weeks of *Atlantic Monthly* observed, the "laughter and fidelity in the writing arise from the fact that Dr. Herriot loves his work." Eugene J. Linehan of *Best Sellers* asserted that even those who don't like children, pets, and animals will like *All Things Bright and Beautiful*: "It's a joy."

Herriot began *All Things Wise and Wonderful* (1977) with his training in the RAF at the beginning of World War II. The focus of this book is on Herriot's homesickness, memories, and desires, not his RAF duties; the vet misses his wife, family, practice, and the Yorkshire countryside, and recalls events and moments of times at home with flashbacks. At the end of the book, Herriot has received his discharge and is happily marching home. Although Richard R. Lingeman of *New York Times Book Review* concluded that *All Things Wise and Wonderful* is "ingratiating," he sensed "formula creeping into the stories."

With *The Lord God Made Them All* (1981) Herriot takes up a new narrative "as if the others had never ended, the same way old friends meet again and talk, at once forgetting they have been apart," wrote Lola D. Gillebaard in *Los Angeles Times Book Review*. After writing *The Lord God Made Them All*, Herriot insisted that he would never write another "big" book. He had grandchildren to visit, gardens to tend, and walks to take. He also wanted to mitigate his popularity: since two of his books had been adapted as motion pictures and one had been transformed into a BBC television series in the

1970s, desperate fans found him despite his attempts to lead them astray on Yorkshire's winding roads. Herriot needed to rest. He did not write another large book until *Every Living Thing*, published in 1992.

Fortunately for fans of all ages, Herriot began to adapt some of the stories he'd told in his books for adults as stories for children. *Moses the Kitten* (1984) is based on an anecdote in *Vet in Harness*. Moses is a small black kitten rescued by Dr. Herriot from icy death among the frozen rushes of a pond. Herriot gives the kitten to a farm family, who warm it in an oven and allow it to live with the pigs in their barn. Bertha, a sow, nurses and cares for Moses like one of her own. Although Bertha's piglets grow up and leave her, she and Moses become fast friends. "Patience, kindness and caring are the dominant themes here," wrote Mary Lou Budd of *School Library Journal*.

Another stray cat figures in *The Christmas Day Kitten* (1986); based on a tale from *All Things Wise and Wonderful*, the book tells how Debbie, a roving female cat, refuses to live with kind Mrs. Pickering. Nevertheless, Mrs. Pickering continues to offer love and food to the cat when she calls. Early one Christmas morning, Debbie arrives sick and dying at Mrs. Pickering's home, carrying a tiny kitten. While Dr. Herriot cannot save Debbie, the kitten grows up to be Mrs. Pickering's beloved pet, Buster. According to Ann A. Flowers of *Horn Book, The Christmas Day Kitten* is "warm, compassionate, and very suitable for the season."

A young girl rescues a lamb and returns it to its mother in Herriot's 1991 children's story *Smudge, the Little Lost Lamb*. (Illustration by Ruth Brown.)

Dogs have also starred in Herriot's books for children. Gyp and Sweep are sheep dog siblings parted as puppies in *Only One Woof* (1985). Gyp lives with the Wilkins, his mother's owners, and Sweep is a sheepherder on another farm. Gyp never barks until, at a sheep dog competition with his owners, he recognizes the winner of the competition as Sweep and barks once to say hello. The "woof" is the only one of his life. Ethel R. Twichell of *Horn Book* commented that Herriot's "affection and respect for animals warm the tale; yet the story avoids cuteness and sentimentality."

Another special dog story, *The Market Square Dog* (1990), "tugs at the heartstrings as only a Herriot tale can," in the words of a *Publishers Weekly* critic. In this story, Herriot notices a dog begging for food from vendors in the market. He tries to help the dog, but it runs away. Days later, a policeman brings the injured dog to the vet, who saves him. The dog is finally adopted by the policeman and his family.

Farm animals and their special relationship with their masters have also inspired Herriot's books for children. Although his carthorses have worked for twelve years, farmer John Skipton takes Herriot's advice to enter his carthorse Dolly in the pet show in *Bonny's Big Day* (1987). Skipton's love and care revives the horse enough to win first prize in the family pet category. Tom S. Hurlburt of *School Library Journal* wrote that readers "are bound to be moved ... as Herriot again shows the deep feelings" animals and humans share. According to *Horn Book*'s Karen Jameyson, the "curmudgeonliness, humor, and down-to-earth qualities of the community shine right through."

Similarly, when the aging bovine heroine of *Blossom Comes Home* (1988) can no longer produce large quantities of milk, Mr. Dakin hands her over to the cattle drover. Blossom however, has a mind of her own and escapes from the drover's herd. Upon her surprising arrival back home, Mr. Dakin decides to let the determined cow stay to feed calves. *School Library Journal*'s Eldon Younce proclaimed that "Herriot has again done a superb job of describing one of his many experiences."

Herriot's last two picture books feature wanderers. The feline protagonist of *Oscar, Cat-about-Town* (1990) is a stray who seems to find the village's social events, especially soccer matches, fascinating. Herriot makes friends with the stray only to learn that he has a home and a loving owner. *Smudge, the Little Lost Lamb* (1991), tells the story of a little lamb who manages to escape under Farmer Cobb's fence. When the hungry lamb tries to return home, a dog and bull frighten him. A little girl finds the lamb in the midst of a blizzard, and takes him home for a drink of warm milk. The next day, she returns Smudge to his mother. Karen Hutt wrote in *Booklist* that young children would "appreciate" *Smudge, the Little Lost Lamb*, "especially because Smudge is rescued by a child."

Children may also enjoy Herriot's compilations of stories about dogs and cats. *James Herriot's Dog Stories*

Although Dr. Herriot can't save Mrs. Pickering's cat, her kitten Debbie becomes a beloved pet in *The Christmas Day Kitten*. (Illustration by Ruth Brown.)

(1986) is a collection of many of Herriot's dog stories from *All Creatures Great and Small* and *All Things Bright and Beautiful,* along with some stories which have never been published in the United States. The fifty stories discuss Herriot's own dogs, how he cured dogs with various ailments and injuries, and how the dogs reacted to treatment. According to a *Kirkus Reviews* critic, the stories "bear witness to [Herriot's] own good character and sensibility." Mary Wadsworth Sucher of *School Library Journal* asserted that many of the stories will "bring a smile or a tear to the eyes of dog lovers."

James Herriot's Cat Stories, written after Herriot's retirement as a veterinarian, offers new stories. As Michele Slung of *New York Times Book Review* noted, this book features a "large cast of mostly impassive furry creatures who never for an instant question the devotion they inspire or the havoc they create." Children familiar with Herriot's picture books about cats will recognize the story of Moses, the black kitten found almost frozen and adopted by a sow, as well as the story of Debbie, who brought a kitten home to Mrs. Ainsworth before the cat died on Christmas day. There's a story about a cat living in a candy store, and another about a cat living in a tarpaulin house. Herriot also tells about Olly and Ginny, his own cats, who refused to live indoors. "A must for Herriot followers and cat lovers alike," concluded a *Kirkus Reviews* critic.

When *Every Living Thing* was published in 1992, Herriot fans were finally provided with updated information about Herriot's personal life. Herriot even discussed his struggle against an infection that left him feverish and depressed. A *Kirkus Reviews* critic asserted that *Every Living Thing* was a "smashingly good sequel to the beloved veterinarian's earlier memoirs, and well worth the ten-year-wait since *The Lord God Made Them All.*" *Every Living Thing* was Herriot's last original book.

In the winter of 1995, Herriot died at home in England, leaving his son James, who worked in the same practice Herriot had entered in 1938, and his daughter, Rosemary, a doctor. Before he died, Herriot insisted that he had everything he wanted. "If you get married and have kids, that's the main thing, isn't it?" he asked *Life* magazine. "And I've lived in this beautiful district, having the great pleasure of being associated with animals. Oh aye, it's been a marvelous life."

■ Works Cited

Bryant, Nelson, "A Place Where the Wind Blows Clean," *New York Times Book Review*, February 18, 1973, p. 10.

Budd, Mary Lou, review of *Moses the Kitten, School Library Journal*, December, 1984, p. 71.

Review of *Every Living Thing, Kirkus Reviews*, July 1, 1992, p. 827.

Flowers, Ann A., review of *The Christmas Day Kitten, Horn Book*, January/February, 1987, p. 46.

Foster, William, "James Herriot Talking to William Foster," *Scotsman*, October 16, 1981.

Gillebaard, Lola D., review of *The Lord God Made Them All, Los Angeles Times Book Review*, June 7, 1981, p. 4.

Gonzalez, Arturo F., interview with James Herriot, *Saturday Review*, May/June, 1986.

Herriot, James, *All Creatures Great and Small*, St. Martin's, 1972.

Herriot, James, *All Things Bright and Beautiful*, Pan, 1978.

Herriot, James, remarks in "*Life* Visits Herriot Country," *Life*, March, 1988.

Hurlburt, Tom S., review of *Bonny's Big Day, School Library Journal*, May, 1988, p. 91.

Hutt, Karen, review of *Smudge, the Little Lost Lamb, Booklist*, January 15, 1992, p. 951.

Review of *James Herriot's Cat Stories, Kirkus Reviews*, July 1, 1994, p. 903.

Review of *James Herriot's Dog Stories, Kirkus Reviews*, May 1, 1986, pp. 695-96.

Jameyson, Karen, review of *Bonny's Big Day, Horn Book*, January/February, 1988, p. 54.

Linehan, Eugene J., review of *All Things Bright and Beautiful, Best Sellers*, October 1, 1974, pp. 304-05.

Lingeman, Richard R., "Animal Doctor," *New York Times Book Review*, September 18, 1977, p. 13.

Review of *The Market Square Dog, Publishers Weekly*, October 13, 1989, p. 51.

Slung, Michelle, "Hairballs and Havoc," *New York Times Book Review*, September 11, 1994, p. 12.

Sucher, Mary Wadsworth, review of *Dog Stories, School Library Journal*, September, 1986, p. 154.

Taylor, David, "It Could Only Happen to a Vet," *Radio Times*, January, 1978.

Twichell, Ethel R., review of *Only One Woof, Horn Book*, March/April, 1986, p. 192.

Weeks, Edward, review of *All Things Bright and Beautiful, Atlantic Monthly*, October, 1974, pp. 114-15.

Younce, Eldon, review of *Blossom Comes Home, School Library Journal*, August, 1989, p. 136.

■ For More Information See

BOOKS

Contemporary Literary Criticism, Volume 12, Gale, 1980, pp. 282-84.

PERIODICALS

Bulletin of the Center for Children's Books, February, 1985, p. 107.
Detroit Free Press, February 24, 1995.
Junior Bookshelf, December, 1990, p. 266.
Library Journal, August, 1994, p. 112.
London Times, July 23, 1976.
National Observer, December 28, 1974.
New York Times, December 14, 1972; September 24, 1974.
People, March 18, 1985.
School Library Journal, December, 1986, p. 88.
Smithsonian, November, 1974.
Washington Post Book World, December 8, 1974; December 5, 1976; May 25, 1988, p. 4.*

—*Sketch by R. Garcia-Johnson*

* * *

HILL, Alexis
See CRAIG, Mary (Francis) Shura

* * *

HILL, Meredith
See CRAIG, Mary (Francis) Shura

* * *

HUANG, Benrei 1959-

■ Personal

Born December 2, 1959, in Taipei, Taiwan, Republic of China; daughter of Fung-Hao and Chiou-Kuei Ni; married Shida Kuo (a sculptor), July 7, 1985. *Education:* National Taiwan Normal University School, B.F.A., 1982; School of Visual Arts, M.F.A., 1992.

■ Addresses

Home and office—28 East 4th St., Apt. 6E, New York, NY 10003-7004. *Agent*—Publishers' Graphics, Inc., 251 Greenwood Ave., Bethel, CT 06801.

■ Career

Self-employed illustrator in Los Angeles, CA, 1986-89, and New York City, 1989—.

■ Writings

SELF-ILLUSTRATED

The Kite, Grolier, 1988.
Surprise, Grolier, 1988.
Boo! Guess Who!, Random House, 1989.
A Very Special Baby, David C. Cook, 1989.
Friends Everywhere (six-book series), Western, 1991.
Hot Spot, Macmillan, 1991.
Random House Calendar for Kids, 1992, Random House, 1992.
Mrs. Sato's Hens, Scott, Foresman, 1992.
Where Is Baby Pig?, Macmillan, 1992.
The Teeny Tiny Woman, Grosset & Dunlap, 1993.
Jack and the Beanstalk, Grosset & Dunlap, 1994.

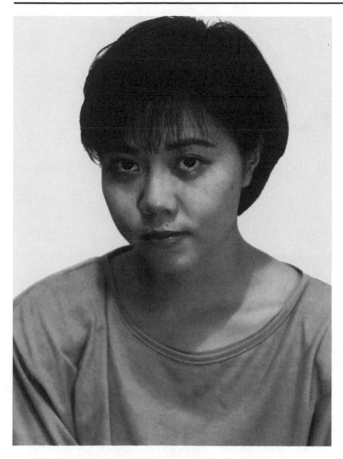

BENREI HUANG

Jonah and the Whale, Random House, 1994.
Little Slam Dunker, Random House, 1995.

Also author and illustrator of *Where Can a Hippo Hide?,* 1995.

"POP-UP" SERIES

Pop-Up Monster Party, Grosset & Dunlap, 1992.
Pop-Up Merry Christmas, Grosset & Dunlap, 1992.
Pop-Up Santa's Workshop, Grosset & Dunlap, 1992.
Pop-Up Spooky Night, Grosset & Dunlap, 1992.

ILLUSTRATOR

Fran Manushkin, *Let's Go Riding in Our Strollers,* Hyperion, 1993.
Mary Louise Cuneo, *What Can a Giant Do?,* HarperCollins, 1994.
Pam Munoz Ryan, *One Hundred Is a Family,* Hyperion, 1994.
Bonny Becker, *The Quiet Way Home,* Holt, 1995.
Lu Xun, *Diary of a Madman,* Grimm Press, 1995.
Lao Shur, *Mr. Jodpurs,* Grimm Press, 1995.

Also creator of three-dimensional illustrations in box form for *Diary of a Madman,* 1992.

■ Work in Progress

Three Musicians, I Hate Haircuts, and *Suma—The City Cat.*

■ Sidelights

Benrei Huang told *SATA:* "I was born and raised in Taipei, Taiwan, where I finished my B.F.A. degree in painting. I tried to find unique language and symbols to paint what I learned from my environment and my concerned contemporaries. After graduating from college I became an art teacher in a junior high school for a while. I felt that I was learning again from those growing children.

"In 1986 I came to the States to live with my family. I found thousands and thousands of beautifully illustrated books that I never saw before. This led me to become a children's book illustrator. To further my skill and knowledge in this professional field, I also attended the School of Visual Arts in New York City to study in a graduate program in illustration.

"I used to think that illustrating children's books was purely an enjoyable experience and pleasure. That might be the reason that most of my books were warm stories or poems and had sweet characters. But as the years went by and I illustrated more and tried to create my own stories, I discovered more and more that illustration was about the combination of images that enables the artist to express his or her own understanding of life. Illustrators turn the things that touch them into an art form, even if the end result is not so enjoyable and pleasant.

"*Diary of a Madman* is my first book that has a not-so-happy story and a not-so-satisfying ending. Some of my other stories also deal with not-so-perfect characters, even annoying ones. But they all have something in common. They are all true human beings with a lot of shortcomings but real feelings—just like everybody."

■ For More Information See

PERIODICALS

Los Angeles Times Book Review, December 4, 1994, p. 36.
New York Times Book Review, January 1, 1995, p. 15.
Publishers Weekly, September 7, 1992, pp. 57-9.

*   *   *

IRWIN, Hadley
  See HADLEY, Lee

J–K

JACQUES, Robin 1920-1995

OBITUARY NOTICE—See index for *SATA* sketch: Born March 27, 1920, in London, England; died March 18, 1995. Art director, educator, and illustrator. A prolific illustrator of children's books, Jacques provided the art for some one hundred books. Orphaned as a child, he taught himself to be an artist and began working in an advertising agency in his teens. He became a freelance illustrator in 1945 and also served stints as art editor of *Strand* magazine and art director for the Central Office of Information. A contributor to various magazines, Jacques began teaching at the Harrow College of Art in 1973 and at the Canterbury Art College and Wimbledon Art College in 1975. Among the books he illustrated were twenty-five collections authored by Ruth Manning-Sanders. His work was featured in volumes such as *Fairy Tales with a Twist, Around the World in Eighty Days, Favorite Tales of Hans Christian Andersen, Dr. Wortley's School,* and *Portrait of a Lady.* His work was also featured in various exhibitions.

OBITUARIES AND OTHER SOURCES:

BOOKS

Who's Who, St. Martin's, 1995.

PERIODICALS

Junior Bookshelf, June, 1995, pp. 89-91.

* * *

KALLEN, Stuart A(rnold) 1955-

■ Personal

Born August 24, 1955, in Cleveland, OH; son of Edward Samuel (a salesperson) and Ruth (a secretary) Kallen; married Marlene Boekhoff. *Education:* Attended Ohio University. *Politics:* "Frankly, I'm appalled." *Religion:* Jewish. *Hobbies and other interests:* Playing music, art photography, travel, cooking, reading, humor.

■ Addresses

Home—4601 30th Ave. South, Minneapolis, MN 55406. *Agent*—Jeremy Solomon, First Books, 2040 North Milwaukee, Chicago, IL 60647.

■ Career

Freelance writer and musician.

■ Awards, Honors

Mid-American Publishers Association award, for *Recycle It! Once Is Not Enough.*

■ Writings

Recycle It! Once Is Not Enough, Abdo & Daughters, 1990.

"THE HISTORY OF ROCK 'N ROLL" SERIES

Roots of Rock, two volumes, Abdo & Daughters, 1989.
Renaissance of Rock, two volumes, Abdo & Daughters, 1989.
Revolution of Rock, Abdo & Daughters, 1989.
Retrospect of Rock, Abdo & Daughters, 1989.

"THE BUILDING OF A NATION" SERIES

Newcomers to America, 1400-1650, Abdo & Daughters, 1990.
Life in the 13 Colonies, 1650-1750, Abdo & Daughters, 1990.
The Road to Freedom, 1750-1783, Abdo & Daughters, 1990.
A Nation United, 1780-1850, Abdo & Daughters, 1990.
A Nation Divided, 1850-1900, Abdo & Daughters, 1990.
A Modern Nation, 1900-1990, Abdo & Daughters, 1990.

"BLACK HISTORY AND THE CIVIL RIGHTS MOVEMENT" SERIES

The Lost Kingdoms of Africa, Abdo & Daughters, 1990.
Days of Slavery, Abdo & Daughters, 1990.
The Civil War and Reconstruction, Abdo & Daughters, 1990.

The Twentieth Century and the Harlem Renaissance, Abdo & Daughters, 1990.

The Civil Rights Movement, Abdo & Daughters, 1990.

The Struggle into the 1990s, Abdo & Daughters, 1990.

"GHASTLY GHOST STORIES" SERIES

How to Catch a Ghost, Abdo & Daughters, 1991.

(And illustrator) *Haunted Hangouts of the Undead,* Abdo & Daughters, 1991.

Phantoms of the Rich and Famous, Abdo & Daughters, 1991.

Vampires, Werewolves, and Zombies, Abdo & Daughters, 1991.

Monsters, Dinosaurs, and Beasts, Abdo & Daughters, 1991.

Ghosts of the Seven Seas, Abdo & Daughters, 1991.

World of the Bizarre, Abdo & Daughters, 1991.

Witches, Magic, and Spells, Abdo & Daughters, 1991.

"THE WORLD RECORD LIBRARY" SERIES

Human Oddities, Abdo & Daughters, 1991.

Spectacular Sports Records, Abdo & Daughters, 1991.

Incredible Animals, Abdo & Daughters, 1991.

Awesome Entertainment Records, Abdo & Daughters, 1991.

Super Structures, Abdo & Daughters, 1991.

Amazing Human Feats, Abdo & Daughters, 1991.

"THE SECOND REVOLUTION" SERIES

Princes, Peasants, and Revolution, Abdo & Daughters, 1992.

The Rise of Lenin, Abdo & Daughters, 1992.

Stalin: Man of Steel, Abdo & Daughters, 1992.

Khrushchev: The Coldest War, Abdo & Daughters, 1992.

Brezhnev: Before the Dawn, Abdo & Daughters, 1992.

Gorbachev-Yeltsin: The Fall of Communism, Abdo & Daughters, 1992.

"THE FABULOUS FUN LIBRARY" SERIES

Ridiculous Riddles (Giggles, Gags, and Groaners), illustrated by Terry Boles, Abdo & Daughters, 1992.

Tricky Tricks (Simple Magic Tricks), Abdo & Daughters, 1992.

Mad Scientist Experiments (Safe, Simple Science Experiments), Abdo & Daughters, 1992.

Math-a-magical Fun (Fun with Numbers), Abdo & Daughters, 1992.

Puzzling Puzzles (Brain Teasers), Abdo & Daughters, 1992.

Silly Stories (Funny, Short Stories), Abdo & Daughters, 1992.

Funny Answers to Foolish Questions, Abdo & Daughters, 1992.

The Giant Joke Book, Abdo & Daughters, 1992.

"TARGET EARTH" SERIES

If the Clouds Could Talk, Abdo & Daughters, 1993.

If Trees Could Talk, Abdo & Daughters, 1993.

If the Sky Could Talk, Abdo & Daughters, 1993.

If the Waters Could Talk, Abdo & Daughters, 1993.

If Animals Could Talk, Abdo & Daughters, 1993.

Eco-Games, Abdo & Daughters, 1993.

Precious Creatures A-Z, Abdo & Daughters, 1993.

Eco-Fairs and Carnivals, Abdo & Daughters, 1993.

Earth Keepers, Abdo & Daughters, 1993.

Eco-Arts & Crafts, Abdo & Daughters, 1993.

"I HAVE A DREAM" SERIES

Maya Angelou: Woman of Words, Deeds, and Dreams, Abdo & Daughters, 1993.

Arthur Ashe: Champion of Dreams and Motion, Abdo & Daughters, 1993.

Martin Luther King Jr.: A Man and His Dream, Abdo & Daughters, 1993.

Thurgood Marshall: A Dream of Justice for All, Abdo & Daughters, 1993.

"FAMOUS ILLUSTRATED SPEECHES AND DOCUMENTS" SERIES

The Statue of Liberty: The New Colossus, Abdo & Daughters, 1994.

The Gettysburg Address, Abdo & Daughters, 1994.

Pledge of Allegiance, Abdo & Daughters, 1994.

Star-Spangled Banner, Abdo & Daughters, 1994.

Declaration of Independence, Abdo & Daughters, 1994.

"IF THE DINOSAURS COULD TALK ..." SERIES

Brontosaurus, illustrated by Kristen Copham, Abdo & Daughters, 1994.

Stegosaurus, illustrated by Kristen Copham, Abdo & Daughters, 1994.

Tyrannosaurus Rex, illustrated by Kristen Copham, Abdo & Daughters, 1994.

Pterandon, illustrated by Kristen Copham, Abdo & Daughters, 1994.

Plesiosaurus, illustrated by Kristen Copham, Abdo & Daughters, 1994.

Triceratops, illustrated by Kristen Copham, Abdo & Daughters, 1994.

"THE HOLOCAUST" SERIES

The History of Hatred: 70 A.D. to 1932, Abdo & Daughters, 1994.

The Nazis Seize Power: 1933-1939, Abdo & Daughters, 1994.

The Holocaust: 1940-1944, Abdo & Daughters, 1994.

The Faces of Resistance, Abdo & Daughters, 1994.

Bearing Witness: Liberation and the Nuremberg Trials, Abdo & Daughters, 1994.

Holocausts in Other Lands, Abdo & Daughters, 1994.

FOR ADULTS

Beer Here: A Traveler's Guide to American Brewpubs & Microbreweries, Citadel Press, 1995.

Also author of numerous articles for magazines.

■ Work in Progress

The Book of Love, a self-help book, and writing CD-Roms and children's videos.

■ Sidelights

Prolific children's author Stuart A. Kallen, with dozens of books for young readers to his credit, has allowed his curiosity as a writer to lead him to gather information about a variety of topics, from history to science to fun and games. One case in particular, Kallen's award-winning *Recycle It! Once Is Not Enough,* which identifies ways to reduce waste, piqued his writer's curiosity more than usual; further study led Kallen to write a ten-book series, "Target Earth," which focuses on ecology and the natural world.

In his "The History of Rock 'n' Roll" series, Kallen offers a chronological look at the story of rock music. The sounds of the 1950s are represented in the two-volume *Roots of Rock.* The two volumes of *Renaissance of Rock,* covering the 1960s, are separated into American music and the sounds of the British Invasion. The music of the 1970s is discussed in *Revolution of Rock,* and Kallen closes his series with *Retrospect of Rock,* a look at the nostalgic influences that shaped much of the popular rock and roll of the 1980s.

World history is another subject to which Kallen has devoted dozens of books. The history of the United States is encapsulated in "The Building of a Nation," a collection of six books that covers the American experience from the age of exploration and colonialism through the Revolutionary and Civil War periods to the twentieth century. The history of African Americans is covered in even greater detail in "Black History and the Civil Rights Movement," a six-volume series. And Kallen's "I Have a Dream" books contain biographies of notable black Americans such as civil rights activist Martin Luther King, Jr., author Maya Angelou, tennis player Arthur Ashe, and Supreme Court Justice Thurgood Marshall.

Kallen's curiosity has also led him to examine conflicts on distant shores, as in *The Nazis Seize Power: 1933-39* and *Bearing Witness: Liberation and the Nuremberg Trials,* two of the books in his series describing the torments endured by Jews during the Holocaust of World War II. The volumes in "The Second Revolution" series allow readers to explore the rise and fall of yet another world power, the Communist empire of the former Soviet Union, from its prerevolutionary days as Mother Russia through the Cold War era to the present.

In addition to his many volumes of nonfiction, Kallen has written a number of books in a much lighter vein. *Witches, Magic and Spells, Haunted Hangouts of the Undead,* and *Phantoms of the Rich and Famous* are just a few of the titles in Kallen's "Ghastly Ghost Stories" series. And the books he has compiled for his "The Fabulous Fun Library" series provide young readers with a host of ideas for fun and games that include brain teasers, magic tricks, riddles, jokes, math games, and simple science experiments.

A writer who tries to project his great enthusiasm for learning beyond the pages of his books, Kallen has strong feelings about his readers. "I believe there are only three solutions to the problem facing America today," he told *SATA.* "Education, education, and education. But learning must be exciting and fun. I believe in piquing a reader's curiosity with humor to generate interest in the topic at hand. I was not the greatest student back in the 1960s, but books have been some of my best friends since childhood. I read the 'Lord of the Rings' trilogy in sixth grade, all the while getting low marks in English class. As my list of published works can attest, one is never too old to keep learning and growing. Writing is a gift, but it is also one that needs to be nurtured and fed with an open book and an open mind."

■ For More Information See

PERIODICALS

School Library Journal, May, 1993; February, 1995; March, 1995; April, 1995.*

*   *   *

KEENE, Ann T(odd) 1940-

■ Personal

Born May 10, 1940, in Chicago, IL; daughter of William L. L. McCaghey (an electrical engineer) and Helen G. Keene (a librarian); married Thomas J. Bartunek (a broadcasting executive), November 23, 1974; children: Charles; (adopted) Lisa, Rebecca, Nathaniel. *Education:* Attended Swarthmore College; Indiana University, B.A., M.A., doctoral candidate in American studies. *Hobbies and other interests:* Music, gardening, hiking, photography.

ANN T. KEENE

■ Addresses

Office—Edit, Etc., Westport, CT 06880.

■ Career

Bloomington Montessori Association, Bloomington, IN, founder, 1968; Bloomington Montessori School, Bloomington, cofounder, 1969; Indiana University, Bloomington, instructor/adjunct professor, 1974-79; *Business Horizons* (magazine), Bloomington, managing editor, 1977-79; President's Select Commission on Immigration, Washington, DC, chief writer/editor, 1979-81; George Mason University, Fairfax, VA, adjunct professor of writing, 1982-83; E. P. Dutton, New York City, managing editor, 1984-85; freelance writer and editor, 1986—. *Member:* Authors Guild, Mensa, Appalachian Mountain Club.

■ Writings

NONFICTION; FOR YOUNG ADULTS

Earthkeepers: Observers and Protectors of Nature, Oxford University Press, 1993.
Willa Cather, Simon & Schuster/J. Messner, 1994.
Racism, Raintree, 1995.
Peacemakers: Winners of the Nobel Peace Prize, Oxford University Press, 1996.

OTHER

(Editor) *Encyclopedia of Psychoactive Drugs,* revised edition, Chelsea House, 1992.

Also contributor to *Young Oxford History of Women in the United States,* Oxford University Press, 1994; contributor to *Twentieth-Century British Literature, Twentieth-Century American Literature,* and *The New Moulton's Encyclopedia,* all published by Chelsea House.

■ Work in Progress

A novel for adults set in the first half of the twentieth century; a young-adult biography of Nathaniel Hawthorne; researching animal rights and protection, conservation, the history of science, and the history of blacks in America, especially issues of assimilation and "race passing."

■ Sidelights

Ann T. Keene has written four nonfiction books for young adults, as well as edited or contributed to several adult reference books. Her first young-adult book, *Earthkeepers: Observers and Protectors of Nature,* published in 1993, consists of forty-six short biographies of prominent "earthkeepers" who have contributed to preserving the earth through their work as scientists, naturalists, and conservationists. The biographies are arranged in four chronological chapters, each covering a different era in the environmental movement. The book begins in the 1700s with a profile of pioneering botanist John Bartram, who travelled across North America collecting plants and created the first botanical garden

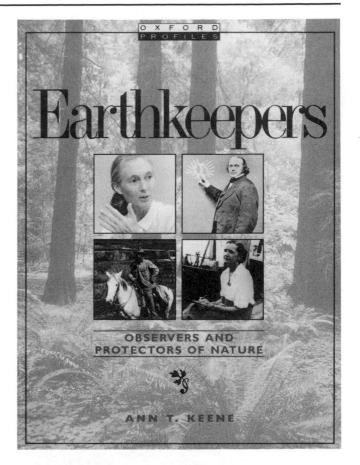

Scientists, naturalists, and conservationists who have helped protect the world's environment are profiled in Keene's 1993 work.

in the colonial United States. The book goes on to discuss the work of Sierra Club founder John Muir as he established the first national parks in the late 1800s and concludes by profiling leaders of the green movement in the late twentieth century. Each section begins with some background information about the time period. The book also includes a glossary, an index, a list of books for further reading, information on organizations that promote conservation and nature study, and numerous photographs. In a review in *Voice of Youth Advocates,* Joyce Hamilton called *Earthkeepers* "an admirable, well-organized overview of naturalists who have left their imprint on the natural world," adding that "the author's many anecdotes about the earthkeepers' personal lives provide interesting reading." Ellen Dibner echoed these sentiments in a review in *School Library Journal,* claiming that *Earthkeepers* is an "accessible and enjoyable foray into the lives of people dedicated to preserving our national world."

Keene has also written the young adult study *Willa Cather,* which *School Library Journal* contributor Judy R. Johnston calls "an insightful biography" of the author of *My Antonia* and *O Pioneers!* Keene examines Cather's background as a journalist in the East during the early part of the century, and the restlessness she exhibited in both her life and her books. Keene does address the issue of Cather's sexuality, and concludes that Cather, who often assumed a male identity and had several important relationships with women, was lesbian "in *orientation*." Nevertheless, the focus of her book is on "Willa Cather the writer," Susan Ware observes in the *New York Times Book Review,* "and her book will appeal to those who want to understand Cather's place within the pantheon of writers ... who shaped American literature." As Johnston concludes, Keene's biography is "an interesting and worthwhile look" into Cather's life and work.

■ Works Cited

Dibner, Ellen, review of *Earthkeepers, School Library Journal,* August, 1994, pp. 163-64.

Hamilton, Joyce, review of *Earthkeepers, Voice of Youth Advocates,* February, 1994, p. 397.

Johnston, Judy R., review of *Willa Cather, School Library Journal,* November, 1994.

Ware, Susan, review of *Willa Cather, New York Times Book Review,* May 7, 1995.

■ For More Information See

PERIODICALS

Booklist, June 1, 1994, p. 1874.
Horn Book Guide, spring, 1994, p. 161.
Voice of Youth Advocates, December, 1995, p. 320.

* * *

KENNEDY, Joseph Charles 1929-
(X. J. Kennedy)

■ Personal

Born August 21, 1929, in Dover, NJ; son of Joseph Francis (a timekeeper and paymaster) and Agnes (a public-health nurse; maiden name, Rauter) Kennedy; married Dorothy Mintzlaff (a writer), January 31, 1962; children: Kathleen Anna, David Ian, Matthew Devin, Daniel Joseph, Joshua Quentin. *Education:* Seton Hall University, B.Sc., 1950; Columbia University, M.A., 1951; University of Paris, certificat, 1956; University of Michigan, graduate student, 1956-62.

■ Addresses

Home and office—4 Fern Way, Bedford, MA 01730. *Agent*—Curtis Brown Ltd., 10 Astor Pl., New York, NY 10003.

■ Career

University of Michigan, Ann Arbor, teaching fellow, 1956-60, instructor in English, 1960-62; Women's College of University of North Carolina (now University of North Carolina at Greensboro), lecturer in English, 1962-63; Tufts University, Medford, MA, assistant professor, 1963-67, associate professor, 1967-73, professor of English, 1973-79; freelance writer, 1979—. Visiting lecturer at Wellesley College, 1964, and University of California at Irvine, 1966-67; Bruern fellow in

JOSEPH CHARLES KENNEDY

American civilization at the University of Leeds, 1974-75. Judge of National Council on Arts poetry book selections, 1969, 1970. *Military service:* U.S. Navy, 1951-55, journalist second class. *Member:* Poetry Society of America, Modern Language Association, National Council of Teachers of English, PEN, Authors Guild, John Barton Wolgamot Society, Phi Beta Kappa.

■ Awards, Honors

Avery Hopwood Awards, University of Michigan, 1959, for poetry and essay; Bread Loaf fellowship in poetry, 1960; Bess Hokin Prize, *Poetry* magazine, 1961; Lamont Award, Academy of American Poets, 1961, for *Nude Descending a Staircase: Poems, Song, a Ballad;* grant, National Council on the Arts and Humanities, 1967-68; Shelley Memorial Award, 1970; Guggenheim fellowship, 1973-74; Golden Rose Trophy, New England Poetry Club, 1974; Outstanding Book of the Year citation, *New York Times Book Review,* November, 1975, for *One Winter Night in August;* Teachers' Choice Book, National Council of Teachers of English (NCTE), and book of the year citation, *School Library Journal,* both 1983, both for *Knock at a Star: A Child's Introduction to Poetry;* Best Children's Books of the Year citation, Library of Congress, and award for Finest Fantasy, Ethical Culture School, both 1983, for *The Owlstone Crown; Los Angeles Times* book award for poetry, 1985, for *Cross Ties: Selected Poems;* American Library Association Notable Book citation, 1986, Notable Children's Trade Book for the Language Arts, NCTE, and William Allen White nomination, both 1988, all for *The Forgetful Wishing Well: Poems for Young People;* Notable Children's Trade Book for the Language Arts, NCTE, 1986, for *Brats;* Best of the New Books citation, *Learning 90* magazine, 1989, for *Ghastlies, Goops and Pincushions: Nonsense Verse;* Michael Braude Award for Light Verse, American Academy and

Institute of Arts and Letters, 1989; Best Children's Books of the Year citation, Bank Street College, for *The Kite that Braved Old Orchard Beach,* 1991; 100 Best Books of the Year citation, New York Public Library, Editors' Choice citation, *Booklist,* Children's Choice citation, International Reading Association and Children's Book Council, all 1991, all for *Fresh Brats;* ten notable children's books of the year citation, *New York Times Book Review,* Fanfare list, *Horn Book,* best book, *School Library Journal,* Notable Book citation, American Library Association, Award for Excellence in Children's Literature, *Parenting* magazine, California Children's Media Award, and 100 Best Books of the Year citation, New York Public Library, all 1992, and ABC Children's Booksellers' Choice book, 1993, all for *Talking Like the Rain: A First Book of Poems;* 100 Best Books of the Year citation, New York Public Library and Christian Children's Book Award, 1992, for *The Beasts of Bethlehem;* Award for Excellence in Children's Literature, *Parenting* magazine, 1993, for *Drat These Brats!.* L.H.D., Lawrence University, 1988.

■ Writings

FOR CHILDREN; UNDER PSEUDONYM X. J. KENNEDY

One Winter Night in August and Other Nonsense Jingles, illustrated by David McPhail, McElderry Books/Atheneum, 1975.

The Phantom Ice Cream Man: More Nonsense Verse, illustrated by D. McPhail, McElderry Books/Atheneum, 1979.

Did Adam Name the Vinegarroon? (verse), illustrated by Heidi Johanna Selig, Godine, 1982.

(Compiler with wife, Dorothy M. Kennedy) *Knock at a Star: A Child's Introduction to Poetry,* illustrated by Karen Ann Weinhaus, Little, Brown, 1982.

The Owlstone Crown (novel), illustrated by Michele Chessare, McElderry Books/Atheneum, 1983.

The Forgetful Wishing Well: Poems for Young People, illustrated by Monica Incisa, McElderry Books/Atheneum, 1985.

Brats (comic verse), illustrated by James Watts, McElderry Books/Atheneum, 1986.

Ghastlies, Goops and Pincushions: Nonsense Verse, illustrated by Ron Barrett, McElderry Books/Macmillan, 1989.

Fresh Brats (comic verse), illustrated by J. Watts, McElderry Books/Macmillan, 1990.

The Kite That Braved Old Orchard Beach: Year-Round Poems for Young People, illustrated by Marian Young, McElderry Books/Macmillan, 1991.

(Compiler with D. M. Kennedy) *Talking Like the Rain: A First Book of Poems,* illustrated by Jane Dyer, Little, Brown, 1992.

The Beasts of Bethlehem (verse), illustrated by Michael McCurdy, McElderry Books/Macmillan, 1993.

Drat These Brats! (comic verse), illustrated by J. Watts, McElderry Books/Macmillan, 1993.

Uncle Switch (verse), McElderry Books/Simon & Schuster, in press.

ADULT POETRY; UNDER PSEUDONYM X. J. KENNEDY

Nude Descending a Staircase: Poems, Song, a Ballad, Doubleday, 1961.

Growing into Love, Doubleday, 1969.

Bulsh, Burning Deck, 1970.

Breaking and Entering, Oxford University Press, 1971.

Emily Dickinson in Southern California, Godine, 1974.

Celebrations after the Death of John Brennan, Penmaen, 1974.

(With James Camp and Keith Waldrop) *Three Tenors, One Vehicle,* Open Places, 1975.

(Translator from the French) *French Leave: Translations,* Robert L. Barth, 1983.

Missing Link, Scheidt Head, 1983.

Hangover Mass, Bits Press, 1984.

Cross Ties: Selected Poems, University of Georgia Press, 1985.

Winter Thunder, Robert L. Barth, 1990.

Dark Horses: New Poems, Johns Hopkins University Press, 1992.

Jimmy Harlow, Salmon Run Press, 1994.

ANTHOLOGIES AND TEXTBOOKS; UNDER PSEUDONYM X. J. KENNEDY

(Editor with Camp) *Mark Twain's Frontier: A Textbook of Primary Source Materials Research and Writing,* Holt, 1963.

An Introduction to Poetry, Little, Brown, 1966, 8th edition (with Dana Gioia), HarperCollins, 1993.

(Editor with Camp and Waldrop) *Pegasus Descending: A Book of the Best Bad Verse,* Macmillan, 1971.

(Editor) *Messages: A Thematic Anthology of Poetry,* Little, Brown, 1973.

An Introduction to Fiction, Little, Brown, 1976, 6th edition (with Gioia), HarperCollins, 1995.

Literature: An Introduction to Fiction, Poetry, and Drama, Little, Brown, 1976, 6th edition (with Gioia), HarperCollins, 1995.

(Editor) *Tygers of Wrath: Poems of Hate, Anger and Invective,* University of Georgia Press, 1981.

(With D. M. Kennedy) *The Bedford Reader,* St. Martin's, 1982, 4th edition (also with Jane E. Aaron), 1991, abridged edition as *The Brief Bedford Reader,* 1994.

(With D. M. Kennedy) *The Bedford Guide for College Writers,* St. Martin's, 1987, 3rd edition (also with Sylvia A. Holliday), 1993, 4th edition (also with D. M. Kennedy and Holliday), 1996.

OTHER

Poetry editor, *Paris Review,* 1961-64; coeditor and publisher, with D. M. Kennedy, *Counter/Measure,* 1971-74; contributor of verse to *Cricket, Allsorts, Atlantic, Children's Digest, Nation, New Yorker, Poetry,* and *Times Literary Supplement.*

■ Adaptations

Spoken recording, *Is Seeing Believing,* Poets' Audio Center, 1985; Kennedy's poems have also been heard on the *Today* show and on Garrison Keillor's *Prairie Home Companion* and *The Writer's Almanac* on National Public Radio.

■ Work in Progress

The Eagle as Wide as the World, a sequel to *The Owlstone Crown.*

■ Sidelights

Joseph Kennedy, better known to his readers by the pseudonym X. J. Kennedy, is a self-confessed "schizophrenic" as regards his writings. In an entry for *Contemporary Authors Autobiography Series* (*CAAS*) Kennedy noted that "I write for three separate audiences: children, college students (who use textbooks), and that small band of people who still read poetry." But there is unity in all of Kennedy's writings—underlying it is a love of poetry and meter, a playfulness verging on the absurd, and a fervent regard for the possibilities of language. That "small band" of adults who still read poetry may very well be swelled by Kennedy's verse for children—both nonsensical and serious. By using verse to speak to middle graders, Kennedy is certainly creating a new audience for poetry of all forms.

The Kennedy universe is engaging, humorous and full of chaos; a place where spaghetti can be used for shoelaces, where a great-great-grandmother sleeps in a tree house and torpedoes pour out of a gravy boat. While Kennedy's nonsense verse—in which strange animals are often set in domestic situations—reflects the absurdity of modern life, his more serious children's poems investigate themes from loss to loneliness and aching desire. Kennedy described himself in *CAAS* as "a metrical, riming poet, a traditionalist in shape if not in matter."

The shape of his own life was forged through many influences, the first of which was his "working-class, white-collar proletarian growing up." Born in Dover, New Jersey, just before the stock market crash of 1929, Kennedy was an only child. "Although our three-person family survived the Depression without going hungry," Kennedy recalled for *CAAS,* "luxuries were rare." Kennedy's father worked as a timekeeper and paymaster for the local boiler works. A simple, unassuming man, the elder Kennedy taught his son an early appreciation for poetry, reciting verses he had learned during his own schooldays. "On large family occasions, such as anniversaries," Kennedy recalled, "my father would himself write a celebratory doggerel ode." Kennedy also became familiar at an early age with the work of Wallace Stevens, Gerard Manley Hopkins, and Emily Dickinson from an anthology of modern poetry found in the family bookshelves.

A retiring youth, Kennedy was bookish rather than athletic. "At baseball I was a loss," he commented in *CAAS.* "Always the one picked last when a gym class divided into teams." He was a scribbler from toddler on, content to sit in his high chair for hours on end with a pencil and paper. By early puberty his scribbling had turned into a magazine with a circulation of one—his mother. In junior high and high school he began drawing his own comics in the *Marvel Comics* vein, and sold them to his classmates at a nickel a pop. By the time he was thirteen, Kennedy had found a new passion: the pulp magazines. Of all the sorts of stories assembled there, he loved science fiction the best. At first he tried to copy the style of these writers, submitting his own stories to the magazines, but soon found that he was better at writing to the readers' letter sections and soon became a "letter hack," his epistles published in several pulp fiction magazines. This interest in science fiction informed much of Kennedy's teenage years: He made friendships with other aficionados in the New York-New Jersey area and published two fanzines with limited local readership.

Upon graduation from high school, Kennedy was surprised to have his parents tell him he would be going on to college. "I had always assumed myself destined for the work force like just about everybody else in town," he wrote in *CAAS.* He was sent to nearby Seton Hall College and spent the next four years amidst the crowds of returning veterans going to school on the G.I. Bill. One summer without a job, Kennedy managed to sell two science fiction stories for $50 apiece, a treasure at the time. Still, his interest in science fiction was already waning, replaced by a love for poetry. After graduation and an unsuccessful attempt at high school English teaching, Kennedy enrolled for a year of graduate studies at Columbia University. Columbia was a "new horizon" as compared to the conservative Seton Hall. Here Kennedy could attend lectures by luminaries such as Bertrand Russell and Lionel Trilling, and come face to face with the realities of mid-20th century America.

After his year at Columbia, Kennedy enlisted in the U.S. Navy, and as luck would have it, was sent to Naval Journalist School in Illinois. "The next four years taught me more than college," Kennedy noted in *CAAS.* "Finding time on my hands, I began to write verse in earnest. In fact, during most of my naval career, my work load was so slight that I could spend most of my time writing what I wanted to, and that was just fine with the navy." There were also cruises—to the Caribbean, to Scotland and Holland, and a five-month trip to the Mediterranean where Kennedy found himself "displaced from the tame, comfortable existence" he had known. Travel was a revelation for him. And on board he produced a daily newspaper that was gobbled up by a crew starved for any entertainment. "It was a wonderful situation for a writer," Kennedy recalled in *CAAS.* "I have never in later life had a sense of writing for such an immediate, eager audience."

It was toward the end of his stretch in the navy that Kennedy first sold his poetry, placing two pieces in the *New Yorker.* It was then also that he hit on the use of a pseudonym. Tired of being ribbed about being a relation of Joseph Kennedy, the ambassador to England and father of the future president, John F. Kennedy, he added an X onto his name and became X. J. Kennedy, writer. After discharge from the navy, Kennedy availed himself of the G.I. Bill and attended the Sorbonne in Paris for a year, meeting other poets and editors in the expatriate colony, such as Cid Corman who helped Kennedy not only with his verses but also in understanding the sacrifices inherent in choosing the life of a poet. On Corman's advice, Kennedy applied to and was accepted by the University of Michigan. Hired as a teaching assistant during his doctorate studies, Kennedy stayed in Ann Arbor for six years, making friends with the poets James Camp and Keith Waldrop, both of whom he would later collaborate with on a volume of poetry and poetry anthologies, and most importantly, meeting his future wife, Dorothy Mintzlaff, another aspiring writer. In 1959 he won one of the university's prestigious Hopwood Awards, which ultimately led to his first volume of poetry, *Nude Descending a Staircase,* published by Doubleday. This volume, in turn, won the Lamont Award of the Academy of American Poets, "a kind of rookie-of-the-year prize," Kennedy noted in *CAAS.*

The following year Kennedy married and left Ann Arbor without finishing his doctorate. "I decided not to pose as the scholar I wasn't, but to try to teach on nothing but my credentials as a writer." Such a decision worked out amazingly well. Within two years he was brought to Tufts University, where he remained until 1979, and where he set out on a career of writing textbooks as well

A child's purple dragon makes a fearsome friend in the poem "My Dragon," from the 1979 collection *The Phantom Ice Cream Man.* (Illustration by David McPhail.)

Uncle Ike creates unusual mechanical beasts in "Mechanical Menagerie," from Kennedy's first poetry collection for children, *One Winter's Night in August* (Illustration by David McPhail.)

as teaching. Throughout these next years Kennedy continued to produce poetry of note, winning prestigious prizes and garnering a devoted readership. There was also family life—five children soon filled their house. He and his wife collaborated on textbooks and even started a poetry magazine, *Counter/Measure: A Magazine of Rime, Meter, & Song,* "a promising new literary magazine," according to the *New Republic.* Over the years Kennedy also began writing private poetry for his own children, pieces that he stuck away in a drawer after reading a few times. It wasn't until he received a letter from a California poet and anthologist for children requesting poems for children such as two that appeared in his *Nude Descending a Staircase* that Kennedy realized he might have a new readership. He sent off some humorous poems to the anthologist, who in turn showed them to the children's book editor Margaret McElderry, and that was the beginning of Kennedy's third audience.

In 1975, Kennedy brought out *One Winter Night in August and Other Nonsense Jingles* and the reception was warm. "[*One Winter Night* is] both skillful and funny," wrote Samuel French Morse in a *Horn Book* review. Silly alliterative verses such as "With walloping tails, the whales off Wales / Whack waves to wicked whitecaps" amused not only youthful readers but critics such as one at *Kirkus Reviews,* who declared Kennedy's "bite-sized nonsense rhymes" to be of "munchy perfection." No one was more surprised than Kennedy himself about the popularity of this first children's book of verse. "It startled and cheered me to find anyone inviting work that rimed and scanned," Kennedy recalled in *CAAS.* "In later days, as a visitor to schoolrooms, I have found that kids don't know that poetry in

In addition to his own verses, Kennedy has collected whimsical poems for children—such as Edward Lear's rhyme about a very big bird published in *Knock at a Star*—with his wife, Dorothy. (Illustration by Karen Ann Weinhaus.)

America is now written mostly in open forms, don't mind verse with a metrical bounce to it, don't even care what's fashionable."

Kennedy followed up this collection with *The Phantom Ice Cream Man: More Nonsense Verse* in 1979, the very year he quit his tenured position at Tufts to go full-time as a freelance writer. "A fresh, original celebration of absurdity," is how Mary M. Burns, writing in *Horn Book,* described the volume. Such playful and metaphoric verses as "If combs could brush their teeth, / If a needle's eye shed tears, / If bottles craned their necks, / If corn pricked up its ears ... " made Donald Hall comment in the *New York Times Book Review* that Kennedy displayed "a joy of rhythm here, a joy of rhyme." Kennedy experimented with alphabetical form in *Did Adam Name the Vinegarroon?,* a bestiary from a to z with such colorful descriptions as this alliterative rhyme for the mammoth: "A hairy mountain ten feet tall / With peepers moist and misty, / It stood as solid as a wall, / Its twin tusks long and twisty." Alicia Ostriker, in the *New York Times Book Review,* noted that Kennedy's alphabet book was "a lively example of its type," and Burns noted in *Horn Book* that it "is an engaging gathering of creatures ... elegantly and thoughtfully planned."

Together with his wife, Kennedy next put together an anthology of children's poetry, *Knock at a Star: A*

Child's Introduction to Poetry, with entries from William Blake to Bob Dylan. Kennedy explained in *CAAS* that he was trying "to show that kids, who like to look closely at interesting creatures, machines, and things, will look closely at poems as well." Largely successful in this endeavor, Kennedy and his book won excellent reviews. "Charming, delightful, witty, a treasure of a book," commented a *Washington Post Book World* reviewer, and Steven Ratiner, writing in the *Christian Science Monitor,* thought the book was "an ideal place to start" an introduction to poetry.

A departure for Kennedy was his 1983 *Owlstone Crown,* juvenile fiction that was his first attempt at the novel. The book took him ten years to write, and as he told *SATA,* it "just may be the least contemptible thing I have done, besides being a father." The book is a mixture of detective novel and sci-fi, "a delightful children's fantasy," according to Richard Mathews in *Fantasy Review,* that is "rich with amusing detail and poetic imagery," as Anne Connor noted in *School Library Journal.*

Returning to poetry once again with *The Forgetful Wishing Well: Poems for Young People,* Kennedy explored more serious themes, such as loss and growing up, as in "Growing Pains": "I take my plastic rocket ship / To bed, now that I'm older. / My wooly bear is packed away, / Why do nights feel colder?" "His poems sing," commented Kathleen D. Whalin in a *School Library Journal* review of the book. "Kennedy's verse is always unassumingly elegant," noted a *Kirkus Reviews* writer, and Mary M. Burns, in *Horn Book,* concluded that "these are poems to delight the ear and stimulate the imagination."

If *The Forgetful Wishing Well* explored themes other than the silly, Kennedy's three ensuing books dealing with brats are an evocation of the absurd, celebrations

Kennedy celebrates naughty children in his 1986 collection, *Brats.* (Illustration by James Watts.)

The BEASTS of
BETHLEHEM

verse by X. J. Kennedy
drawings by Michael McCurdy

According to legend, animals can speak on Christmas Eve, and Kennedy uses this idea to his advantage in his 1992 award-winning book of poems. (Cover illustration by Michael McCurdy.)

of mischievous children told largely in rhymed quatrains and iambic tetrameter couplets. *Brats, Fresh Brats,* and *Drat These Brats!* explore the world of rapscallions with startling results: "On a factory tour, / Will Gossage, / Watching folks make bratwurst sausage, / Jumped into the meat feet-first. / Brats are bad, but Will's the wurst." Or continuing on the meat theme, there is the impish Sue in *Brats* who sticks a pig to the ceiling with glue: "Uncle, gawking, spilled his cup. / 'Wow!' he cried. 'Has pork gone up!'" The trio of prankish books contain "irrepressibly rhymed verses," according to Betsy Hearne in *Bulletin of the Center for Children's Books.* "Kennedy's humor is sufficiently outrageous to be rib-tickling, rather than frightening," commented Peter Neumeyer in *New York Times Book Review.*

In the midst of these brats books, Kennedy explored further comic verse with *Ghastlies, Goops and Pincushions: Nonsense Verse,* a sort of brats companion piece of unwanted individuals and crazy antics. *The Kite That Braved Old Orchard Beach: Year-Round Poems for Young People* is similar to *The Forgetful Wishing Well* in its use of simple language to evoke imagery; it is also

less rollicking and more reflective about such themes as family, friends, and growing up. Kennedy also collaborated with his wife again in the 1992 anthology, *Talking Like the Rain: A First Book of Poems.* With the 1993 *The Beasts of Bethlehem,* nineteen poems portraying animals gathered around the baby Jesus in the stable, Kennedy "crowned his rich career," according to Hearne of *Bulletin of the Center for Children's Books.* The verses have the "musicality of carols," noted Hearne, and a *School Library Journal* reviewer agreed, commenting favorably on Kennedy's "small quiet verses."

Kennedy has never been an ivory tower poet. "To survive as a poet in America today means hitting the reading trail," he wrote in *CAAS.* A veteran of more than 200 readings in the U.S. and England, Kennedy has also appeared on radio and television and in grade schools, where he takes his duty seriously even though it is disguised in the form of nonsense verse. "In approaching children with poems in our hands," he once wrote in an article for *Horn Book,* "I think it helps to begin by recognizing the child as a person with an intellect." Never one to talk down to his audience or shy away from big words, Kennedy is also a champion of meter and rhyme in poetry as well as of analysis. "I believe that the form of a poem is worth noticing and that it will sometimes evade the child's gaze unless it is pointed out," he noted in his *Horn Book* article. "I'm not just a versifier," Kennedy told *SATA,* adding that his works "don't try to persuade children that everything is sweetness and light. Such a view, as even infants know, is pure malarkey. The face of a world, however imaginary, has to have a few warts, if a child is going to believe in it; and it must wear an occasional look of foolishness or consternation. It also needs, I suspect, a bit of poetry, and a dash of incredible beauty and enchantment, if possible."

■ Works Cited

Review of *The Beasts of Bethlehem, School Library Journal,* October, 1992, p. 42.

Burns, Mary M., review of *The Phantom Ice Cream Man: More Nonsense Verse, Horn Book,* August, 1979, p. 433.

Burns, Mary M., review of *Did Adam Name the Vinegarroon?, Horn Book,* December, 1982, p. 664.

Burns, Mary M., review of *The Forgetful Wishing Well: Poems for Young People, Horn Book,* July-August, 1985, p. 460.

Connor, Anne, review of *The Owlstone Crown, School Library Journal,* January, 1984, p. 78.

Review of *Counter/Measure, New Republic,* December 4, 1971, p. 35.

Review of *The Forgetful Wishing Well: Poems for Young People, Kirkus Reviews,* May 15, 1985, pp. J38-J39.

Hall, Donald, review of *The Phantom Ice Cream Man: More Nonsense Verse, New York Times Book Review,* April 29, 1979, p. 25.

Hearne, Betsy, review of *Fresh Brats, Bulletin of the Center for Children's Books,* March, 1990, p. 165.

Hearne, Betsy, review of *The Beasts of Bethlehem,* *Bulletin of the Center for Children's Books,* December, 1992, p. 103.

Kennedy, X. J., *One Winter Night in August and Other Nonsense Jingles,* McElderry Books/Atheneum, 1975.

Kennedy, X. J., *The Phantom Ice Cream Man: More Nonsense Verse,* McElderry Books/Atheneum, 1979.

Kennedy, X. J., "Go and Get Your Candle Lit," *Horn Book,* June, 1981, pp. 273-79.

Kennedy, X. J., *Did Adam Name the Vinegarroon?,* Godine, 1982.

Kennedy, X. J., *The Forgetful Wishing Well: Poems for Young People,* McElderry Books/Atheneum, 1985.

Kennedy, X. J., *Brats,* McElderry Books/Atheneum, 1986.

Kennedy, X. J., essay in *Contemporary Authors Autobiography Series,* Volume 9, Gale, 1989, pp. 73-88.

Kennedy, X. J., *Drat These Brats!,* McElderry Books/Macmillan, 1993.

Review of *Knock at a Star: A Child's Introduction to Poetry, Washington Post Book World,* November 10, 1985, p. 12.

Mathews, Richard, review of *The Owlstone Crown, Fantasy Review,* August, 1984, p. 48.

Morse, Samuel French, review of *One Winter Night in August and Other Nonsense Jingles, Horn Book,* February, 1976, p. 67.

Neumeyer, Peter, review of *Brats, New York Times Book Review,* October 5, 1986, p. 30.

Review of *One Winter Night in August and Other Nonsense Jingles, Kirkus Reviews,* April 1, 1975, p. 380.

Ostriker, Alicia, "Tulip, Julep, Sloshes, Galoshes," *New York Times Book Review,* November 14, 1982, p. 45.

Ratiner, Steven, "Rhyme and Imagery to Capture Kids," *Christian Science Monitor,* June 29, 1983, p. 9.

Whalin, Kathleen D., review of *The Forgetful Wishing Well: Poems for Young People, School Library Journal,* May, 1985, p. 90.

■ For More Information See

BOOKS

Children's Literature Review, Volume 27, Gale, 1992, pp. 96-103.

Dictionary of Literary Biography, Volume 5: *American Poets Since World War II,* Part 1: A-K, Gale, 1980, pp. 394-397.

Janeczko, Paul, editor, *Poetspeak: In Their Work, about Their Work,* Bradbury Press, 1983.

Twentieth Century Children's Writers, 4th edition, St. James Press, 1995, pp. 514-16.

PERIODICALS

Horn Book, September, 1989, p. 633; July, 1992, p. 460; March, 1994, p. 213.

Kirkus Reviews, May 1, 1969, p. 547; May 15, 1979, p. 577; August 1, 1982, p. 870; November 1, 1983, p. J192; February 1, 1989, p. 210; May 1, 1990, p. 659; February 1, 1991, p. 175; March 15, 1992, p. 395; November 1, 1993, p. 1393.

Publishers Weekly, August 27, 1982, p. 358; December 9, 1983, p. 50; May 31, 1985, p. 57; November 9, 1992, p. 79.

School Library Journal, November, 1975, p. 79; May, 1979, p. 63; December, 1982, p. 65; August, 1986, p. 94; December, 1989, p. 108; July, 1990, p. 85; July, 1991, p. 82; June, 1992, p. 108; June, 1993, p. 145; March, 1994, p. 230.

—*Sketch by J. Sydney Jones*

*   *   *

KENNEDY, X. J.
See KENNEDY, Joseph Charles

*   *   *

KLAVENESS, Jan O'Donnell 1939-

■ Personal

Name is pronounced *Klav*-e-ness; born March 19, 1939, in York, PA; daughter of Robert E. (an air conditioning/refrigeration engineer) and Cecelia A. (a homemaker; maiden name, Pearce) Miller; married Charles R. O'Donnell (a professor; died, 1979); married Charles A. Klaveness (a journalist), October 17, 1981; children: Elizabeth A. O'Donnell Lamberini, Paul Robert O'Donnell. *Education:* University of Michigan, B.A. (with honors). *Politics:* Liberal. *Religion:* Episcopalian. *Hobbies and other interests:* Gardening, canoeing, traveling, reading, and attending the ballet.

■ Addresses

Home and office—41 Vliet Dr., Belle Mead, NJ 08502. *Agent*—Jean V. Naggar, 216 East 75th St., New York, NY 10021.

■ Career

Children's book writer. University of Michigan, Ann Arbor, MI, assistant director of student organizations, 1963-65; Hofstra University, Hempstead, NY, assistant director of financial aid, 1979-82. Mentor, Hillsborough Gifted and Talented Program, Hillsborough School District. *Member:* Authors Guild, Authors League of America, Society for Children's Book Writers and Illustrators.

■ Awards, Honors

Minor Hopwood Award, University of Michigan, 1958; nominations for Edgar Award, Mystery Writers of America, Young Hoosier Book Award, Mark Twain Award Master List, and Dorothy Canfield Fisher Book Award, and Children's Book of the Year citation, Child Study Association Children's Book Committee, all 1984, all for *The Griffin Legacy;* Young Adult Choice, International Reading Association, 1987, and New York

JAN O'DONNELL KLAVENESS

Public Library annual list, Books for the Teen Age, both for *Ghost Island;* New York Public Library annual list, Books for the Teen Age, for *Keeper of the Light.*

■ Writings

A Funny Girl Like Me, Scholastic, 1980.
The Griffin Legacy, Macmillan, 1983.
Ghost Island, Macmillan, 1985.
Keeper of the Light, Morrow, 1990.
Beyond the Cellar Door, Scholastic, 1991.

■ Work in Progress

Where Do the Birds Go, a picture book completed in 1994; *Oh! Susannah,* a chapter book, completed in 1994; a mystery for mid-level readers; and a fantasy for mid-level readers.

■ Sidelights

Jan O'Donnell Klaveness told *SATA:* "In one of my earliest memories I am curled in the window seat of my room with a book open on my lap. I have not yet learned to read, so I am making up stories about the pictures I see on the page. Today, when I open that same book, I find a double exposure of written and the remembered tales. That insatiable love of stories, and a memory that is, according to my family, more vivid than accurate, made me a storyteller.

"But without the library in Wheaton, Illinois, where I grew up, and my grandmother's pea soup, I might never have become a writer. An author's visit to the library revealed to me the astonishing fact that not all writers were dead. Living human beings wrote books. And if they could do it, I thought at the age of nine, so, perhaps, could I. That same year my grandmother slipped in a spill of pea soup and broke her leg. But when she arrived to stay with us while it healed, she was in no condition to bake the plum cakes and muffins I anticipated. Instead she gave me a more important nourishment—she gave me stories that not only rooted me to my past and anchored me in a knowledge of where I came from and who I was, but also provided a wealth of material that I draw upon in my work today.

"I wrote poetry until I was in college, when a professor told me to stop writing derivative Keats and start writing original prose. I not only took his advice, I married him. Until his death in 1979, a year before my first book was published, he was my best critic and strongest supporter. Proving lightning can strike twice, I'm now married to a journalist who offers me not only unconditional enthusiasm and encouragement, but clear-eyed editing as well.

"When my daughter and son were young, I began writing children's stories. My first book recalled the pain of moving to a new community—something my family had done frequently while I was growing up. *The Griffin Legacy* drew upon local history as well as family stories to solve a two-hundred-year-old mystery. The book gave me a way to preserve the historic house on Constitution Hill in Massachusetts that had been destroyed by fire in 1962."

The mystery at the center of *The Griffin Legacy* is set during the American Revolution. In "a deft blend of fantasy and realism," according to *Bulletin of the Center for Children's Books,* Klaveness depicts the story of Amy's visit to her family home in Massachusetts, where the ghosts of her ancestors enlist her aid in setting right the wrongs committed nearly two centuries before. In addition, neighbor twins Ben and Betsy inform Amy of a local legend concerning silver treasure buried on the family estate. Critics highlighted the interest of the colonial era in their positive reviews of *The Griffin Legacy.* "Elements in the book could inspire an intellectually gifted student to study old colonial houses or Revolutionary War events," remarked Josephine Raburn in *School Library Journal.* Others emphasized the book's satisfying mystery. Anne Frost in *Voice of Youth Advocates* called *The Griffin Legacy* "an outstanding ghost story, with just the right amount of excitement for junior high and middle school readers."

When Delia, the protagonist of Klaveness's next novel, *Ghost Island,* returns with her mother and stepfather to the island in Canada where she and her mother frequently vacationed with her father before his death, she finds the place much altered for the worse. Devoid of the usual tourists, the island seems deserted except for a few locals who behave strangely. Smugglers, a kidnapping, and several deaths occur before the book's conclusion, but "the strong characters, with their compelling emotions, keep the pace of the story moving," wrote Nancy A. Gifford in *School Library Journal.*

As in *The Griffin Legacy,* Klaveness incorporates a detailed historical subplot into a modern-day mystery in *Keeper of the Light,* in which sixteen-year-old Ian travels to North Carolina to claim an inheritance from his recently deceased grandmother, whom he had never met because of a family feud. Upon his arrival at the family estate, he meets his grandmother's sinister housekeeper and her terrified daughter and, as he researches his grandmother's life, begins to realize that he may be in danger. Although Hazel Rochman of *Booklist* predicted that young adult readers would solve the mystery long before Klaveness's protagonist, Bruce Anne Shook in *School Library Journal* called *Keeper of the Light* "a solid, suspenseful mystery that moves along swiftly from start to finish," and singled out the author's accurate depiction of the North Carolina setting for special praise.

With the publication of Klaveness's next work, *Beyond the Cellar Door, Kirkus Reviews* called the "past's influence on the present" Klaveness's "accustomed theme." In this work, Jeff and Megan's grandfather comes to live with their family, crowding the house and arousing varying emotions in those around him. The children escape the tense situation at home by exploring an empty Victorian house nearby that undergoes mysterious repairs each time they return. While the reviewer for *Kirkus Reviews* preferred the family drama centered on the grandfather to the mystery about the house, Vee V. Garry called the whole "exciting, mysterious and thrilling!" in a review in *Children's Book Review Service.* Tatiana Castleton in *School Library Journal* agreed, characterizing *Beyond the Cellar Door* as a "nice mix of adventure, suspense, humor, and the ambiance of summertime in a small town."

"Like my grandmother," Klaveness told *SATA,* "I try to tell stories that offer hope—stories in which people and truth prevail. I try to tell good stories, thought-provoking stories that engage the reader. I believe that the best stories come out of the pain and joy of the writer's experience. When they succeed, those stories touch their readers, bringing recognition and understanding, and the strength to live on."

■ Works Cited

Review of *Beyond the Cellar Door, Kirkus Reviews,* July 15, 1991, p. 932.
Castleton, Tatiana, review of *Beyond the Cellar Door, School Library Journal,* September, 1991, pp. 254-55.
Frost, Anne, review of *The Griffin Legacy, Voice of Youth Advocates,* April, 1984, p. 32.
Garry, Vee V., review of *Beyond the Cellar Door, Children's Book Review Service,* September, 1991, p. 10.
Gifford, Nancy A., review of *Ghost Island, School Library Journal,* September, 1985, p. 146.

Review of *The Griffin Legacy, Bulletin of the Center for Children's Books,* February, 1984.
Raburn, Josephine, "Ghost Stories," *School Library Journal,* November, 1984, pp. 25-27.
Rochman, Hazel, review of *Keeper of the Light, Booklist,* December 1, 1990.
Shook, Bruce Anne, review of *Keeper of the Light, School Library Journal,* October, 1990.

■ For More Information See

PERIODICALS

Horn Book, July/August, 1985, p. 454.

*   *   *

KNAAK, Richard A. 1961-

■ Personal

Surname is pronounced "Nack"; born May 28, 1961, in Chicago, IL; son of James Richard and Anna Maria Knaak. *Education:* University of Illinois at Urbana-Champaign, B.A., 1984.

■ Addresses

Home and office—P.O. Box 8151, Bartlett, IL 60103. *Agent*—Peekner Literary Agency, 3418 Shelton Ave., Bethlehem, PA 18017.

■ Career

Writer. *Member:* Science Fiction Writers of America.

■ Writings

The Legend of Huma, TSR, Inc., 1988.
Firedrake, Warner/Questar, 1989.
Kaz, The Minotaur, TSR, Inc., 1990.
The Crystal Dragon, Warner/Questar, 1993.
King of the Grey, Warner/Questar, 1993.
The Dragon Crown, Warner/Questar, 1994.
Frostwing, Warner/Questar, 1995.
The Janus Mask, Warner/Questar, 1995.

"DRAGONREALM" SERIES

Ice Dragon, Warner/Questar, 1990.
Shadow Steed, Warner/Questar, 1990.
Wolfhelm, Warner/Questar, 1990.

"ORIGIN OF DRAGONREALM" SERIES

The Shrouded Realm, Warner/Questar, 1991.
Children of the Drake, Warner/Questar, 1991.

Also author of short stories.

■ Work in Progress

Jackalhead, a science fantasy; *Gifts of the Drunn,* science fiction.

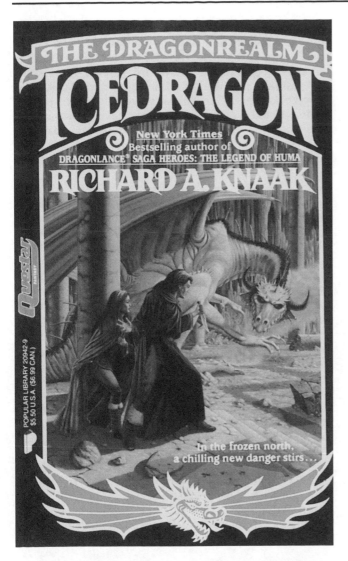

Knaak is the author of many fantasy novels, including this 1989 adventure about a young warrior who must fight the shape-shifting Dragon Kings.

■ Sidelights

"I began writing when I was young, after I realized that I didn't have the patience to learn to draw but could put a decent story together," Richard A. Knaak once wrote. "My imagination has always been a strong part of me. I started reading mysteries but soon discovered science fiction and fantasy; I've been hooked since.

"If there is any theme running through my work, it is that one should never give up. There is always hope. You are the one who generally determines your own success or failure. This represents my personal view as well as my own experience. Many people hope to sell someday. I went out and found my first sale and things have moved smoothly since then. In a nutshell, your only limits are the ones you form in your own mind.

"On another note, it is essential that we support the space program before we run out of resources and time."*

KOSHKIN, Alexander (A.) 1952-

■ Personal

Born July 24, 1952, in Moscow, Russia; son of Arnold (an aviation engineer) and Ludmila (a teacher; maiden name, Chudaeva) Koshkin; married A. Arkhipova, November 12, 1977 (marriage ended, 1982); married Tatiana Vorontzova (a physician), June 1, 1985; children: (first marriage) Kamil; (second marriage) Filipp. *Education:* Moscow Surikov Art College, 1970-76. *Religion:* Christian Orthodox.

■ Addresses

Home—Apt. 13, B52 Metalurgov St., Moscow, Russia 111399.

■ Career

Illustrator, 1973—. State Committee of Publishing, Russia, member of "Best Book of the Year" annual contest jury. *Member:* Coordinate Council of Agency for Authors Rights Reservations (VAAP).

■ Awards, Honors

1st Degree, XXIII All Russian Contest, 1982; Bronze Medal, Leipzig, Germany, 1982; Best Cover, Melody Records, 1991.

■ Illustrator

Elizabeth Warner, *Heroes, Monsters and Other Worlds from Russian Mythology,* edited by Peter Lowe, Eurobook, 1985.

J. V. Goethe, *The Pupil of Magician,* edited by Lowe, Eurobook, 1986.

Elizabeth Winthrop, *Vasilissa the Beautiful: A Russian Folktale,* HarperCollins, 1991.

Brothers Grimm, *Hansel and Gretel, Little Red-Cap, The Musicians of Bremen,* World Book, 1992.

Mary Stolz, *Say Something,* revised edition, HarperCollins, 1993.

Shirley Climo, reteller, *Stolen Thunder: A Norse Myth,* Clarion, 1994.

Climo, reteller, *Atalanta's Race: A Greek Myth,* Clarion, 1995.

Katherine Paterson, *The Angel and the Donkey,* Clarion, 1996.

Works illustrated include Kitchinova V. Lifshitz, "Forest Not without Kind Animals," in *Sceneries for Children's Theater,* 1978; *Aladdin's Magic Lamp,* 1978; *The Thunder Rumbles on the Mountains,* 1979; Leo Tolstoy, *Golden Key: The Adventures of Buratino,* 1981; V. Zhukovsky, *Ballads,* 1981; V. Odocvsky, *Snuff Box City,* 1981; *Battle on the Kalinov Bridge,* 1982; Zhukovsky, *Flowers of Dream,* 1984; *The Master of the Sea: Eskimo Tales,* 1986; *Zhirenshe the Wise and Karanash the Beauty,* 1987. Also illustrator of Rudyard Kipling, *The Jungle Book,* Lewis Carroll, *Alice in Wonderland,* A. A. Milne, *Winnie-the-Pooh,* J. M. Barrie, *Peter Pan,* and

ALEXANDER KOSHKIN

Alexander Block, *Twelve,* all for the Library of the World, Literature for Children series, 1979.

Other published works include illustrations for books for Politizdat (Moscow), 1978; S. Mikhalkov, *Dream with Continuation* (Moscow), 1984; *Suite: The Prince's Toys Andante Quasi Passacagli E Toccata,* by Nikita Koshkin, edited by Gendai Guitar (Tokyo), 1985; *A Thousand and One Nights,* Haus (Moscow), 1988; Grimm, *Los Cuentos Mas Bonitos,* and *Le Fiabe Piu' Belle,* Happy Books (Milan), 1990; Antoine Saint-Exupery, *The Little Prince,* Golden Cocky (Moscow), 1994.

■ Sidelights

Alexander Koshkin is a Russian artist whose paintings, rendered in diverse styles, have appeared in American picture books since the late 1980s. Koshkin told *SATA* that he has been "really interested" in books since he was just three years old. As a child and young adult, he studied art, but was "bored" by the "Soviet educational system" and the "endless portraits" he had to paint; he preferred to paint the "unreal, fantastic world." Koshkin explained that book illustration attracted him because "it is a synthetic kind of art" which requires "connecting text and visual image."

Early in his career, Koshkin illustrated a number of stories and books published in the former Soviet Union and Europe. In 1988, he traveled to the United States to serve as a panelist at the Third Annual U.S.-Soviet Symposium on Children's Literature and the Arts in New York City. Later, an executive editor with Harper Junior Books, Nina Ignatowicz, gave Koshkin the opportunity to share his elaborate fairy-tale paintings with American readers by illustrating Elizabeth Winthrop's retelling of an old Russian folktale, *Vasilissa the Beautiful* (1991).

Vasilissa the Beautiful begins as Vasilissa's mother is dying. She gives Vasilissa a doll, and tells her that the doll will assist her whenever she needs help. Vasilissa's father marries again, and like Cinderella, she finds herself living with a nasty stepmother and two spiteful stepsisters. They send Vasilissa into the forest to get a light from Baba Yaga, hoping that the girl will be killed by the witch. With the help of the doll, however, Vasilissa manages to escape Baba Yaga and capture her light. When the girl returns home, the light kills everyone but Vasilissa. An old woman cares for the girl, and Vasilissa eventually marries the Tsar.

Koshkin presents the characters of *Vasilissa the Beautiful* in detailed, patterned clothing from seventeenth-century Russia. According to Deborah Abbott of *Booklist,* the illustrations of Baba Yaga's house, based on chicken legs and with a "path lit by glowing eyes from toothy skulls," are "particularly effective." Although she lamented the fact that the tempera paintings are "erratically sandwiched between solid pages of print," Denise Anton Wright of *School Library Journal* thought that the artist's "dramatic" work complemented the "somber tone" of the story.

In *Stolen Thunder: A Norse Myth* (1994), retold by Shirley Climo, Thrym, the Frost King, steals Thor's thunder-making hammer, Mjolnir. Thor blames Loki, a prankster, for the theft. To prove his claim of innocence, Loki flies to Thrym's land in a falcon suit. Thrym refuses to give Thor his hammer unless Freya, the goddess of love, marries him. Loki returns to Thor, and comes up with the suggestion that they trick Thrym: Thor must shave his beard, disguise himself as Freya, and regain his hammer. When the Frost King attempts to kiss his bride before the ceremony, Thor grabs the hammer, sheds his disguise, and strikes Thrym with a bolt of thunder.

Critics have lauded Koshkin's illustrations for *Stolen Thunder.* As Wright noted in *School Library Journal,* the acrylic-wash illustrations, bordered with various motifs, are influenced by various cultures and styles. According to Wright, they "possess a luxuriousness that is somehow appropriate for this story." "The artwork is alternately ethereal and solid," wrote a *Publishers Weekly* critic. A *Kirkus Reviews* critic noted that Koshkin emphasizes the humor of the story "with the intensity of his character's expressions," and Deborah Abbott of *Booklist* explained that his paintings "heighten both the distinctive characters and fast-moving plot."

Koshkin provided illustrations for Climo's text again in *Atalanta's Race* (1995). Climo's retelling of the ancient Greek story begins as Atalanta is rejected by her father at her birth because she is a girl. Atalanta survives with the help of a bear and a hunter and grows into a strong young woman. When her father realizes that she possesses astounding athletic abilities, he welcomes Atalanta home again. He plans to marry Atalanta to a young man so that she will bear him a grandson, and promises her hand in marriage to any man who can beat her in a foot race. One suitor, Melanion, finds Atalanta a tough competitor despite the fact that she is attracted to him. Atalanta and Melanion fall in love, but because Atalanta forgets to honor Aphrodite for her help, the goddess turns her into a lioness. According to a critic for *Publishers Weekly*, Koshkin's neo-classic paintings for *Atalanta's Race*, framed with classical architectural details, "amplify the drama" of the story. Patricia Dooley in *School Library Journal* appreciated the "gorgeous double-spread endpapers" and the presentation of Aphrodite; she concluded that among the many retellings of the story of Atalanta, "none surpasses this one."

Say Something (1993) provides an example of Koshkin's illustrations for nontraditional tales. Mary Stolz's text of *Say Something* was originally published in 1968 with different illustrations; Koshkin's color, double-page paintings bring it a new look. In *Say Something*, a boy goes fishing with his father, and urges him to "say something" about each of the natural things he points out. The boy's father responds with sweet words describing the grass, the sky, a brook, the wind, and a cave. According to Leone McDermott in *Booklist*, the artist uses "color and proportion" to create "an intimate, childlike perspective." Susan Scheps in *School Library Journal* also noted the "childlike quality" of the "realistic color paintings."

■ Works Cited

Abbott, Deborah, review of *Vasilissa the Beautiful*, *Booklist*, May 1, 1991.

Abbott, Deborah, review of *Stolen Thunder*, *Booklist*, May 1, 1994.

Review of *Atalanta's Race*, *Publishers Weekly*, April 10, 1995.

Dooley, Patricia, review of *Atalanta's Race*, *School Library Journal*, April, 1995.

McDermott, Leone, review of *Say Something*, *Booklist*, January 15, 1993.

Scheps, Susan, review of *Say Something*, *School Library Journal*, April, 1993.

Review of *Stolen Thunder*, *Kirkus Reviews*, March 1, 1994.

Review of *Stolen Thunder*, *Publishers Weekly*, March 7, 1994.

Wright, Denise Anton, review of *Vasilissa the Beautiful*, *School Library Journal*, June, 1991.

Wright, Denise Anton, review of *Stolen Thunder*, *School Library Journal*, July, 1994.

■ For More Information See

PERIODICALS
Publishers Weekly, November 25, 1988, p. 39.

*   *   *

KRAKAUER, Hoong Yee Lee 1955-

■ Personal

Born March 23, 1955, in New York, NY; daughter of Koung Shin (a civil engineer) and Ming Hwa (a teacher) Lee; married Seth Anthony Krakauer (a social worker), September 8, 1985; children: Mikki Lee Krakauer (daughter), Remy Lee Krakauer (son). *Education:* Oberlin College, B.A., 1976; Manhattan School of Music, M.A., 1979.

■ Addresses

Home—446 Beach 124 St., Rockaway Park, NY 11694. *Agent*—Edythea Ginis Selman, 14 Washington Pl., New York, NY 10003.

■ Career

Author and illustrator.

■ Writings

(Self-illustrated) *Rabbit Mooncakes*, Little, Brown, 1994.

HOONG YEE LEE KRAKAUER

Also author and illustrator of *One Chinese Dragon*, 1995.

■ Sidelights

Hoong Yee Lee Krakauer told *SATA:* "I was born into a family of Manchurian generals, concubines, poets, and gamblers. Chinese, a richly visual language of pictograms and symbols, was my mother language. But English, acquired from TV cartoons and the schoolyards of New York, quickly became my language as well. Now, years later, I am married to a nice Jewish boy from Rockaway Beach, and Yiddish fills the ears of my children. There are many memories to enjoy, many stories to share. Writing and illustrating not only gives dimension and vitality to the twists and stories in my life, the very act of writing, seeing words and images flow from my pen onto blank sheets of paper, always fills me with a sense of discovery and wonder."

Krakauer's debut book for children, *Rabbit Mooncakes,* is drawn from her own experience growing up in a Chinese immigrant family. Centered around the family's celebration of the Harvest Moon Festival, which is similar to the American Thanksgiving, the book tells the story of two young sisters who try to avoid playing the piano during the festivities. Hoong Wei, the younger sister, is convinced that she will make a mistake and be embarrassed in front of her relatives. She is even more distressed because her older sister, Hoong Lee, always plays flawlessly. The story follows the girls over the course of the day as they play and help prepare food. When the time comes to play music, however, Hoong Wei convinces Hoong Lee to hide in a tree. The family begins singing without their accompaniment, and the girls finally decide to join in the fun. Even though Hoong Wei does make a mistake, her mother just sings louder to cover it up, and the whole family congratulates her when she is finished. Both sisters receive a treat of traditional mooncakes as their reward. A *Publishers Weekly* critic praised Krakauer's "appealing depiction of Chinese American life," adding that her illustrations "reflect a comfortable mix of Eastern and Western cultures." Although *School Library Journal* reviewer Margaret A. Chang commented that Krakauer's cartoonlike figures are "drawn without volume or substance, and the art overall lacks a unifying style," a contributor in *Kirkus Reviews* claimed that the "lively, freely drawn illustrations" added to the cultural flavor of the text.

■ Works Cited

Chang, Margaret A., review of *Rabbit Mooncakes, School Library Journal,* July, 1994, p. 79.
Review of *Rabbit Mooncakes, Kirkus Reviews,* May 15, 1994, p. 701.
Review of *Rabbit Mooncakes, Publishers Weekly,* May 16, 1994, p. 63.*

KRISHER, Trudy (B.) 1946-

■ Personal

Born December 22, 1946, in Macon, GA; daughter of Whitley Herron (in business) and Lois (a homemaker; maiden name, Drane) Butner; children: Laura, Kathryn, Mark. *Education:* College of William and Mary, B.A., 1968; Trenton State College, M.Ed., 1972. *Politics:* Democrat. *Religion:* Unitarian.

■ Addresses

Agent—Jane Jordan Browne, Multimedia Product Development, 410 South Michigan Ave., Suite 724, Chicago, IL 60605-1465.

■ Career

University of Dayton, Dayton, OH, assistant professor and campus writing center coordinator, 1985—. *Member:* Miami Valley Literacy Council (member of board of directors), Miami Valley Unitarian Fellowship.

■ Awards, Honors

Miami Valley Cultural Alliance Arts Award, 1994; Honor Book selection, Parents' Choice, 1994, Best Book

TRUDY KRISHER

for Young Adults selection, American Library Association, 1994, Best Young Adult Novel award, International Reading Association (IRA), 1995, and Jefferson Cup Honor Book, Virginia Library Association, 1995, all for *Spite Fences;* Cuffie Award for Most Promising New Author, *Publishers Weekly,* 1994.

■ Writings

Kathy's Hats: A Story of Hope, illustrated by Nadine Bernard Westcott, Albert Whitman, 1992.
Spite Fences, Delacorte, 1994.
Writing for a Reader, Prentice-Hall, 1995.

■ Work in Progress

Kinship, a novel "to be read as a companion piece to *Spite Fences.*"

■ Sidelights

Trudy Krisher's first two books for children and young adults have established her reputation as a talented writer who does not hesitate to explore sensitive issues. *Kathy's Hats: A Story of Hope* portrays the courage of a child battling cancer, and *Spite Fences* presents a young white woman's difficult attempt to stand up for civil rights in the southern United States during the early 1960s. This latter book earned Krisher critical recognition in 1994, and she won the Cuffie Award from *Publishers Weekly* for 1994's most promising new author.

Krisher told *SATA* that "my father, through his love of history, taught me to value the telling detail, and my mother, through her concern for the welfare of others, taught me the gift of compassion. My own love of literature has taught me the value of true and honest work." In addition, Krisher's life struggles have served her writing well. Her first book, *Kathy's Hats* (1992), was inspired by her daughter Kathy's battle with cancer.

Kathy's Hats begins as Kathy discusses her fondness for hats: she wore a hat when she was a baby and still wears them during the winter and the summer and at Easter. Yet when Kathy is diagnosed with cancer and her chemotherapy treatments make her hair fall out, Kathy's perspective on hats changes. Her treatments are difficult and painful; she especially dislikes the long needles the nurses use to inject her medicine. Having to wear hats is another aspect of her cancer treatment which Kathy resents. Finally, Kathy's mother explains that the young girl can think of her hats as thinking caps which can help her fight her disease. Kathy finds this advice helpful and changes her attitude about hats. By the time the children in her class enjoy a favorite hat party with Kathy, she is far along the road to recovery.

According to Krisher, *Kathy's Hats* affirms "the courage and creativity" she has witnessed in young children with cancer. Some reviewers appreciated the positive tone of the book, its realistic portrayal of cancer treatment, and the bright illustrations that accompany Krisher's text. A

Kirkus Reviews critic appreciated the story as a "straightforward and upbeat picture of a child coping with cancer," and Ilene Cooper in *Booklist* concluded that *Kathy's Hats* is a "good piece of bibliotherapy" which may be useful in the classroom.

Krisher told *SATA* that her next book, *Spite Fences,* "marks a young girl's evolving social consciousness, and it has its roots in my childhood in the Jim Crow South at the beginning of the modern civil rights movement." Life for thirteen-year-old Magnolia "Maggie" Pugh has never been blissful. Her father is withdrawn, and her emotionally and physically abusive mother cares only about helping Maggie's little sister, Gardenia, win a beauty pageant. Yet events in the summer of 1960 in Kinship, Georgia, add to Maggie's troubles.

First, her friend Zeke, a black man who has listened to Maggie's concerns and even given her a camera, is arrested after he uses a restroom designated for white people. Later, while Maggie is high up in a tree, she witnesses a terrible scene. A group of men which includes one of her neighbors strips Zeke, humiliates him, and beats him mercilessly. Although she would like to help Zeke, Maggie stays in the tree, and after the incident she is afraid to tell anyone what she has seen. To make matters worse, Virgil Boggs, one of Zeke's attackers, maliciously harasses Maggie and her little sister. At one point in the story, Virgil almost rapes Maggie.

Maggie's life begins to change when Zeke finds Maggie a job as a housekeeper for a highly educated black man who has moved to Kinship. George Hardy, a lawyer, teaches Maggie about the civil rights movement. She gradually gains respect for him and begins to fight for civil rights herself. Maggie even tells Mr. Hardy about

When Kathy's hair begins to fall out because of her chemotherapy treatments, she uses her favorite hats and a little imagination to lift her spirits. (Illustration by Nadine Bernard Westcott from *Kathy's Hats*.)

Zeke's beating. Maggie's parents are upset about her friendship with Mr. Hardy and his friends, and the townspeople of Kinship ostracize her. Despite this lack of support, Maggie manages to overcome the ignorance and cruelty surrounding her, and she uses the camera Zeke gave her to understand and communicate the white community's abuse of the black. According to a critic in *Publishers Weekly,* Maggie's "final triumph is a tribute to all who have suffered for justice."

Krisher's *Spite Fences* has been lauded by critics. A contributor in *Kirkus Reviews* commented that with the "stunning narrative and achingly real characters, Maggie's pain and redemption are brought to vivid life." "To read" *Spite Fences,* wrote Margaret Cole in *School Library Journal,* "is to climb inside the narrator's skin, share her emotions, and gain the wisdom she acquires." Frances Bradburn in *Booklist* described the book as "a superbly crafted first novel" and "a masterful, sobering display." About the writing of *Spite Fences,* Krisher explains that the novel allowed her to "explore the fences that divide and create the bridges that unite."

Krisher told *SATA* that she loves writing. "I am happiest when I am dreaming about, planning, working out, sharing, or revising a piece of writing. Writing enables me to put the events in my life and those of my characters into perspective. It enables me to deepen my compassion for others and to probe the mystery of the human condition." Krisher further commented, "I believe that my strengths as a writer are an eye for detail, a compassion for the joys, pains, struggles, and dreams of other human beings, and an uncompromising honesty. I hope to continue to write books that promote the highest values of which we as human beings are capable."

When she is not writing, Krisher helps others develop writing skills. She works as an assistant professor and writing center coordinator at the University of Dayton, Ohio, and is the author of a textbook for college students, *Writing for a Reader.*

■ Works Cited

Bradburn, Frances, review of *Spite Fences, Booklist,* December 1, 1994, p. 666.

Cole, Margaret, review of *Spite Fences, School Library Journal,* November, 1994, p. 121.

Cooper, Ilene, review of *Kathy's Hats, Booklist,* October 1, 1992, p. 336.

Review of *Kathy's Hats, Kirkus Reviews,* September 1, 1992.

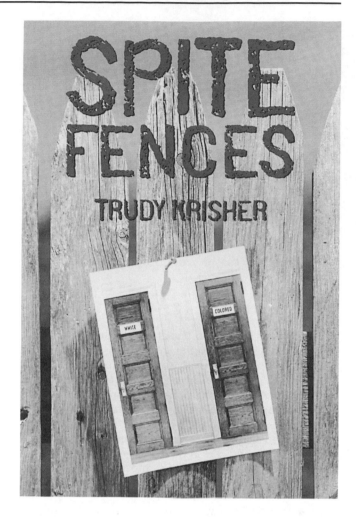

In her award-winning 1994 young adult book, Krisher tells of a young girl's awakening to racial injustice in 1960s Georgia. (Cover illustration by Will Ryan.)

Review of *Spite Fences, Kirkus Reviews,* December 15, 1994.

Review of *Spite Fences, Publishers Weekly,* November 14, 1994, p. 70.

■ For More Information See

PERIODICALS

Bulletin of the Center for Children's Books, October, 1992, p. 46.

Horn Book Guide, spring, 1993, p. 36.

Voice of Youth Advocates, October, 1994, p. 209.

L

LAUTURE, Denize 1946-

■ Personal

Born May 11, 1946, in Haiti; emigrated to the United States in 1968; son of Lhomond and Viergenie (a farmer; maiden name, Prevot) Lauture; children: Charles, Conrad. *Education:* City College of New York, B.A., 1977, M.S., 1981. *Politics:* Socialist.

■ Addresses

Office—St. Thomas Aquinas College, Rd 340, Sparkill, NY 10976.

■ Career

St. Thomas Aquinas College, Sparkill, NY, assistant professor of French and Haitian culture, 1980—. Performance poet; consultant on Haitian culture and language; children's book writer, 1980—. *Member:* Poets and Writers, Poetry Society of America, Alliance Francaise, American Association of Teachers of French.

■ Awards, Honors

Images Award nominee, National Association for the Advancement of Colored People, 1993, for *Father and Son;* Award for Excellence, St. Thomas Aquinas College, Board of Trustees, 1994.

■ Writings

The Blues of the Lightning Metamorphosis (poetry; in Creole), Bohio Press, 1987.
When the Denizen Weeps (poetry), Bronx Press, 1989.
Father and Son (picture book), illustrated by Jonathan Green, Putnam, 1993.
Running the Road to ABC (picture book), illustrated by Reynold Ruffins, Simon & Schuster, 1996.

Contributor to numerous periodicals, including *African Commentary, Black American Literature Forum, Callaloo, Litoral,* and *Presence Africaine.*

Lauture captures the special relationship between a father and son in the 1993 picture book *Father and Son.* (Illustration by Jonathan Green.)

■ Work in Progress

The Cactus Legend, prose and poetry in English, French, and Creole, and research in Haitian culture and supra-creativity.

■ Sidelights

The firstborn of thirteen peasant children, Denize Lauture migrated from Haiti to the United States in 1968. He was twenty-two years old and did not have a high school diploma. He worked as a welder in Harlem

135

and attended evening classes at the City College of New York, and in 1977 he earned a B.A. in sociology. He received his M.S. in bilingual education four years later.

Lauture has become known for his lyrical and tender evocations of life. His picture book *Father and Son* garnered special attention for its quietly joyous depiction of the relationship between fathers and sons as experienced while performing ordinary daily tasks. Critics emphasized the beauty and simplicity of Lauture's text-poem in enthusiastic reviews of his premiere children's book.

Publishers Weekly called *Father and Son* "an auspicious debut" picture book for Lauture and illustrator Jonathan Green. The text, a brief free-verse poem, shows a father and son working, playing, and going to church near their seaside home in the Carolinas in what *Kirkus Reviews* described as "a lovely evocation of a companionable and spiritual relationship at its best." Several critics highlighted the distinctive Gullah culture that forms the poem's backdrop, and the universal nature of the close relationship that is the poem's main subject. "Lauture's simple, eloquent poetry superbly conveys the joy and satisfaction in routine tasks and day-to-day life shared with familial love and pride," wrote Brenda Mitchell-Powell in *Multicultural Review*. "Young children will delight in reading, or having this book read to them," Sally Williams Cook concluded in her review in the *Associated Press Special Features*.

Lauture also describes himself as "an excellent multilingual performance poet" who has given readings at such places as the United Nations, the American Museum of Natural History, the Poetry Society of America, the New York Public Library, Gracie Mansion, as well as many colleges, universities, and reading centers.

"The main source of my children's books is my childhood in rural Haiti," Lauture told *SATA*. "I decided to write children's books because I understood that, to save the world in its course toward destruction, concerned writers must reach the children's minds and hearts."

■ Works Cited

Cook, Sally Williams, review of *Father and Son, Associated Press Special Features*, February 26, 1993.
Review of *Father and Son, Kirkus Reviews*, December 15, 1992.
Review of *Father and Son, Publishers Weekly*, December 14, 1992.
Mitchell-Powell, Brenda, review of *Father and Son, Multicultural Review*, vol. 2, no. 1, pp. 73-74.

■ For More Information See

PERIODICALS

Miami Herald, February 12, 1993.
Orange County Register, January 31, 1993.
School Library Journal, February, 1993.

LEITNER, Isabella 1924-

■ Personal

Born May 28, 1924, in Kisvarda, Hungary; married Irving A. Leitner in 1956; children: two sons.

■ Addresses

Home—101 West 90th Street, Apt. 18E, New York, NY 10024.

■ Career

Writer; lecturer on the Holocaust. Board member of Juvenile Diabetes Foundation.

■ Awards, Honors

Wonder Woman Foundation Awards finalist, 1983; *Fragments of Isabella* was nominated for the Pulitzer Prize and received a Best Books for Young Adults citation, American Library Association.

■ Writings

Fragments of Isabella, Crowell, 1978.
(With Irving A. Leitner) *Saving the Fragments: From Auschwitz to New York,* New American Library, 1985.

ISABELLA LEITNER

The Big Lie: A True Story (for children), illustrated by Judy Pederson, Scholastic, 1992.

(With I. Leitner) *Isabella: From Auschwitz to Freedom,* Anchor Books/Doubleday, 1994.

■ Adaptations

Fragments of Isabella was recorded on tape by the author for Caedmon, adapted for the stage at the Abbey Theatre in Dublin, Ireland, and made into a film by director Ronan O'Leary, 1989.

■ Sidelights

Isabella Leitner was born in Krisvada, a small town in Hungary. On May 28, 1944, Leitner, her mother, four sisters, brother, and all other Jews from Kisvarda were taken by cattle car to Auschwitz in southern Poland, site of the largest Nazi concentration camp during World War II. Though Leitner was not chosen for execution, her youngest sister and her mother were murdered on the day of arrival, and her eldest sister later died after an attempted escape.

Isabella and her two surviving sisters escaped during a death march to Bergen-Belsen and were liberated by Russian soldiers. The three sisters were the first survivors of Auschwitz to reach the United States, arriving on May 8, 1945, the very day the war in Europe ended. They were reunited with their father, who had come across at the outbreak of World War II in an unsuccessful attempt to obtain exit visas for his family, and also received word that their brother had survived.

Leitner's first book, *Fragments of Isabella,* a memoir of her ordeal, won international acclaim and was nominated for a Pulitzer Prize. Mary Silva Cosgrove, reviewing the work in *Horn Book,* praised its "terse, eloquent simplicity," and Isabel Forgang in the New York *Daily News* called it a "slender, moving volume that's all the more powerful for Leitner's positive attitude toward living despite the torture and death all around." A one-woman show adapted from the work was first presented by the Abbey Theater in Dublin and later produced in Vienna on the fiftieth anniversary of *Kristallnacht,* or the "Night of Broken Glass," an organized pogrom (riot) that occurred in November 1938 in which the Nazis destroyed synagogues and Jewish-owned businesses, arrested Jewish men, and even murdered some individuals.

Leitner's second book, *Saving the Fragments: From Auschwitz to New York,* tells the story of her liberation from the concentration camp, her journey to America, and her struggle to become human again. In order to be reunited with her father in New York, Leitner had to walk across Germany, take a packed train to Odessa, and cross the ocean in a merchant marine ship. Her joy, and even disbelief, at her new freedom, is tinged with her sorrow and concern for missing family members. In a review in *School Library Journal,* Pam Spencer wrote: "The upbeat style of [Leitner's] writing assures readers of her desire to put the past behind her and get on with

her life." In 1994, Leitner's two books were combined, with additional material, to form *Isabella: From Auschwitz to Freedom.*

Leitner retold her tragic story for young children in *The Big Lie: A True Story.* "Because children are the makers of the future, I want to inspire them to live full and productive lives and work for a brand new way of life where human beings do not nurture hatred and destroy other human beings," Leitner once said. A reviewer in *Booklist* commented that "the telling has the elemental power of the best children's literature, in which the simplicity is poetic and speaks volumes."

■ Works Cited

Review of *The Big Lie: A True Story, Booklist,* February 1, 1993, p. 982.

Cosgrove, Mary Silva, review of *Fragments of Isabella: A Memoir of Auschwitz, Horn Book,* August, 1979, pp. 460-61.

Forgang, Isabel, "Holocaust Retold from Experience," New York *Daily News,* April 17, 1988.

Leitner, Isabella, press release from Scholastic, 1992.

Spencer, Pam, review of *Saving the Fragments: from Auschwitz to New York, School Library Journal,* August, 1986, p. 114.

■ For More Information See

PERIODICALS

Kirkus Reviews, July 15, 1985, p. 702.

New York Times Book Review, November 6, 1994, p. 40.

People, June 24, 1985.

Publishers Weekly, September 6, 1985, p. 61; June 6, 1994, p. 63.

Reading Teacher, February, 1994, p. 410.

*   *   *

LERNER, Carol 1927-

■ Personal

Born July 6, 1927, in Chicago, IL; daughter of Edwin August (in sales) and Elsie (Harders) Drath; married Ralph Lerner (a teacher), October 30, 1954; children: Joshua, Jesse. *Education:* University of Chicago, B.A., 1950, M.A., 1954. *Hobbies and other interests:* Film, gardening.

■ Addresses

Office—c/o William Morrow & Company, Inc., 1350 Avenue of the Americas, New York, NY 10019.

■ Career

Writer and illustrator, 1977—. *Exhibitions:* Exhibitor in one-person shows at Morton Arboretum, Lisle, IL, 1977; Chicago Botanic Garden, Glencoe, IL, 1984; Fernwood Nature Center, Niles, MI, 1984; Arnold

CAROL LERNER

Arboretum of Harvard University, Jamaica Plain, MA, 1985; National Arboretum, Washington, DC, 1986; Callaway Gardens, Pine Mountain, GA, 1986; Cantigny, Wheaton, IL, 1987; Art Institute of Chicago Junior Museum, Chicago, IL, 1990; and Arlington Heights Memorial Library, Arlington Heights, IL, 1990.

Exhibitor in group shows at Forest Foundation of DuPage County, IL, 1975; 5th International Exhibition, Hunt Institute for Botanical Documentation, Pittsburgh, PA, 1983; Yeshiva University Museum, New York City, 1983-84; Museum of Science and Industry, Chicago, 1984; Guild of Natural Science Illustrators National Exhibit, National Museum of Natural History, Washington, DC, 1986; Illinois State Museum, Lockport Gallery, Lockport, IL, 1988-89, and Springfield, IL, 1989; Chicago Public Library Cultural Center, Chicago, 1989; and Freeport Art Museum and Cultural Center, Freeport, IL, 1995. *Member:* Society of Children's Book Writers and Illustrators, Children's Reading Roundtable, Society of Midland Authors.

■ **Awards, Honors**

Outstanding Science Books for Children citations, National Science Teachers Association and Children's Book Council, 1977, for *Peeper, First Voice of Spring,* 1980, for *Green Darner: The Story of a Dragonfly,* 1983, for *The 100-Year-Old Cactus,* and also for *Dumb Cane and Daffodils: Poisonous Plants in the House and Garden* and *Cactus;* Special Artistic award, Friends of American Writers, 1979, for *On the Forest Edge;* Notable Children's Book selection, American Library

Association (ALA), 1980, Ambassador of Honor Book, English-Speaking Union of the United States, Outstanding Science Books for Children citation, 1980, and William Allen White Children's Book Award Master List, 1982-83, all for *Seasons of the Tallgrass Prairie;* ALA Notable Children's Book selection, and Outstanding Science Trade Books for Children citation, both 1982, both for *A Biblical Garden;* Carl Sandburg Award, Friends of the Chicago Public Library, 1984, and ALA Notable Book selection, both for *Pitcher Plants: The Elegant Insect Traps;* Outstanding Science Trade Book for Children citation, ALA Notable Book selection, and Children's Book of the Year selection, Library of Congress, 1984, all for *Tree Flowers;* Outstanding Science Trade Book for Children citation, Children's Book of the Year selection, Child Study Association, and Choice selection, Cooperative Children's Book Center, 1987, all for *A Forest Year;* Outstanding Science Trade Book for Children citation, and Cooperative Children's Book Center Choice selection, 1988, both for *Moonseed and Mistletoe: A Book of Poisonous Wild Plants;* Outstanding Science Trade Book for Children citation, and New York Academy of Science Honor Book, 1989, both for *Plant Families;* annual award, Children's Reading Round Table, 1994, for contributions to children's literature.

■ **Writings**

SELF-ILLUSTRATED BOOKS FOR JUVENILES

On the Forest Edge, Morrow, 1978.
Flowers of a Woodland Spring, Morrow, 1979.
Seasons of the Tallgrass Prairie, Morrow, 1980.
(Author with husband, Ralph Lerner) *A Biblical Garden,* Morrow, 1982.
Pitcher Plants: The Elegant Insect Traps, Morrow, 1983.
A Forest Year, Morrow, 1987.
Moonseed and Mistletoe: A Book of Poisonous Wild Plants, Morrow, 1988.
Plant Families, Morrow, 1989.
Dumb Cane and Daffodils: Poisonous Plants in the House and Garden, Morrow, 1990.
A Desert Year, Morrow, 1991.
Cactus, Morrow, 1992.
Plants That Make You Sniffle and Sneeze, Morrow, 1993.
Backyard Birds of Winter, Morrow, 1994.
Backyard Birds of Summer, Morrow, 1996.

ILLUSTRATOR

Glenda Daniel, *Dune Country: A Hiker's Guide to the Indiana Dunes* (for adults), Swallow Press, 1977, revised edition, Ohio University Press, 1984.
Robert M. McClung, *Peeper, First Voice of Spring,* Morrow, 1977.
McClung, *Green Darner: The Story of a Dragonfly,* Morrow, 1980.
Daniel and Jerry Sullivan, *A Sierra Club Naturalist's Guide to the North Woods of Michigan, Wisconsin, and Minnesota* (for adults), Sierra Club, 1981.
McClung, *Sphinx: The Story of a Caterpillar,* Morrow, 1981.

Anita Holmes, *The 100-Year-Old Cactus,* Four Winds, 1983.

Millicent E. Selsam, *Tree Flowers,* Morrow, 1984.

■ **Sidelights**

Carol Lerner began to write and illustrate books about plants for children in part because she noticed a lack of quality books on the subject. After nearly twenty years, the publication of several books, and the reception of numerous awards, Lerner has emerged, as Barbara C. Scotto noted in *Appraisal: Children's Science Books,* as "one of our foremost writers and illustrators of books on botany for children." Lerner's books are known for their clear organization, substantive content, lucid text, and accurate, multi-perspective illustrations. While some critics have appreciated the scientific precision and elegant detail of Lerner's black-and-white drawings and watercolor paintings, others have applauded them as works of art; according to *Horn Book*'s Margaret A. Bush, her "lovely botanical paintings and drawings are always appealing."

In addition, as Maeve Visser Knoth of *Horn Book* observed, Lerner's works demonstrate "a respect for her audience." This respect is reflected in the tone of Lerner's text, in her choice of subject matter, and in the care she takes in researching and editing her work to ensure that it is correct and up-to-date. Lerner once explained this respect to *SATA:* "I think of my audience as being the same kind of children that my own kids were—children who respond to the beauty and variety of the natural world and who have a serious curiosity about the plant world and the creatures that inhabit it."

Lerner did not expect to become a writer and illustrator; growing up on the northwest side of Chicago during the Great Depression, she went through high school thinking she would be a secretary. After graduating and finding a job with a small firm, she visited a friend at the University of Chicago. As she wrote in her *Something about the Author Autobiography Series* (*SAAS*) entry, everything she "heard and saw that day was dazzling. I had already begun to realize that I was not going to find self-fulfillment with a steno pad. Now I discovered where I wanted to be."

Lerner worked, saved money, and took math and science courses at night for the next year, and finally matriculated at the University of Chicago. With a combination of financial aid and part-time and temporary jobs, she managed to fund her education. When she graduated from college, Lerner did not know what she wanted to do. She worked as a social worker for a year, saved money for a tour of Europe, and embarked upon a four-month journey. She then returned to the University of Chicago to earn her master's degree in history, but the study of history fell short of her expectations.

After completing her master's degree program, Lerner traveled to Europe once again. This time, she went to visit her boyfriend, Ralph Lerner, who had been drafted after the Korean War, and found a job as a clerical worker for the U.S. Air Force in France. The couple married in Paris; they lived in Germany and England and traveled through western Europe, Yugoslavia, and Greece. In 1956, the Lerners returned to Chicago.

Lerner began to take a serious interest in nature, and in botany in particular. The Lerners' cottage on Lake Michigan was surrounded by pockets of wild vegetation, which Lerner and her two boys happily explored. Lerner's children, she told *SATA,* "were endlessly fascinated by everything that moved and grew." Lerner decided to study the flora and fauna she had been exploring and enrolled in courses at the Morton Arboretum. "After some years of those classes," she explained to *SATA,* "I was emboldened to try their botanical illustration course. I had no prior art training, but the teacher stoutly maintained that she could teach anyone to draw. For the next three years I continued in her classes, working hard to prove she was no liar."

Through her art classes and the collection of prints owned by the Morton Arboretum, Lerner wrote in *SAAS,* she "began to realize the multitude of methods the illustrator can employ to explain as well as depict . . . . [The subject] can be shown from any perspective, whole or exploded into its component parts . . . . The illustration can always choose to present the *typical,* the example that shows the relevant features most clearly." Lerner also "found pen and ink especially congenial."

When, as she remarked to *SATA,* Lerner finally "felt ready to do something with the things" she had learned, she decided to try "to become established as a free-lance natural history illustrator, but approaches to educational publishers in the Chicago area failed to bring in many assignments. Then I decided to shift my focus to children's nature and science books, thinking they would offer more scope and opportunity for the kind of illustration I wanted to do." Lerner began to look into the nature and science books available for children at the time. She elaborated in *SAAS,* "I was struck by the relative scarcity of children's nonfiction books about plant life . . . . I thought that many inherently interesting plant subjects had not been treated adequately in children's books and that botanical illustration—with its ability to dissect and combine—was the ideal tool to use in presenting these subjects."

Lerner spent months of research on the prairie, wrote a text, and began submitting it to publishers. After the original manuscript for *Seasons of the Tallgrass Prairie* (1980) was rejected sixteen times, Lerner put it away and began a new project. With writer Glenda Daniel, she conducted fieldwork at the National Lakeshore and the Indiana Dunes State Park and illustrated *Dune Country: A Hiker's Guide to the Indiana Dunes.* Later, after a rejection from Morrow for a book on spring peepers (little tree frogs) she was asked to illustrate a book by Robert McClung on the same topic: *Peeper, First Voice of Spring* (1977). In a review of *Peeper* in *Booklist,* Denise M. Wilms appreciated the "beauty and precision" of Lerner's illustrations and asserted that *Peeper* "sets a striking standard for illustration."

Lerner soon began to work on a new subject that, she commented in *SAAS*, "had been ignored by other juvenile writers ... a habitat that most people are unaware of, though it is one of enormous importance to the survival of our remaining rural wildlife." The favorable reception of *Peeper* had given her "a foot in the publisher's door," and her manuscript for *On the Forest Edge* was accepted.

On the Forest Edge (1978), according to Anne Boes in *School Library Journal*, is a "sensitive, ecological portrait" of life in the ecotone, or "in-between habitat" where the forest meets the field. After defining the meaning of ecosystem and ecotone, Lerner explains how the ecotone is a place of tension and change. She describes the mammals, birds, insects, and plants that find a home there. While a critic for *Kirkus Reviews* lamented the author's "species-by-species treatment," Denise M. Wilms of *Booklist* commented that the book was "smoothly written," and described Lerner's illustrations as "incisive, pristine spreads."

Lerner's next book, *Flowers of a Woodland Spring* (1979) focuses on the ephemeral wildflowers that bloom and produce seeds in early spring. As she commented in

Although many of her books are about plants, Lerner also writes about animals in such books as 1991's *A Desert Year*. (Illustration by the author.)

SAAS, she "had been intrigued by the display of the early-spring wildflowers" that shriveled and disappeared in just a short time near the Lerner country cottage. In *Flowers of a Woodland Spring,* Lerner explains how these ephemeral blossoms—including toothworts, Dutchman's breeches, spring beauty, wild leeks, and trout lilies—complete their annual cycle by the time the forest trees leaf out and deprive them of sunlight.

As Lerner's illustrations clearly demonstrate, a complex system of rhizomes, corms, bulbs, and tubers allows the flowers to complete their cycle and live underground until the next spring. Barbara Peklo Serling in *School Library Journal* remarked that Lerner "captures" the "delicate radiance" of the ephemerals in her black-and-white and watercolor illustrations. Zena Sutherland in *Bulletin of the Center for Children's Books* concluded that *Flowers of a Woodland Spring* is a "good book for budding botanists."

With the publication of two of her own books, Lerner revised and submitted *Seasons of the Tallgrass Prairie* to her editor at Morrow, and it was accepted. In *Seasons of the Tallgrass Prairie,* as Steve Matthews of *School Library Journal* observed, Lerner "illuminates the intricate relationships" that enable the survival of the prairie. After providing what Matthews calls an "alluring description" of the prairie, Lerner showcases the native American plants that inhabit the prairie season by season. The focus in Lerner's illustrations is not just on the parts of the grasses and flowers seen above ground, but on the underground root systems as well. Lerner discusses the role of the prairie plants in enriching the soil and explains how fire contributes to the maintenance of the prairie ecosystem. Sutherland in *Bulletin of the Center for Children's Books* appreciated Lerner's "meticulously detailed, fine-line drawings."

Lerner teamed up with her husband to create *A Biblical Garden* (1982) after he noticed a newspaper article about a biblical garden in Israel. This book required trips to the library, gardens, greenhouses, and the herbarium collection in Chicago's Field Museum. It features Ralph Lerner's translations of verses of the Hebrew Bible and Carol Lerner's descriptions of the plants these verses mention. Lerner presents twenty plants, including the fig tree, papyrus, olive, coriander, castor bean, barley, cedar, pomegranate, lentil, and myrtle. These are identified by their English, Hebrew, and scientific Latin names and rendered in colored paintings and black-and-white drawings that a *Publishers Weekly* critic characterized as "lovely" and "exquisite."

When Lerner and her family lived in North Carolina for a year, she discovered the nearby North Carolina Botanical Garden and its collection of native carnivorous plants. She began to work on a book about one genus of these plants, the pitcher plants, or *Sarracenia.* As Lerner explains in this work, *Pitcher Plants: The Elegant Insect Traps* (1983), these plants live in deficient soil and trap insects to meet their nutritional needs. She describes and illustrates the plants' structure and the various species, and explains how the plant attracts, traps, and digests insects. Various perspectives of the plants, especially cross-sections, provide clarity.

In *Pitcher Plants,* Lerner also discusses the ways certain insects have adapted to live with the plant and even take advantage of it. Some species find shelter within the pitchers and appropriate the pitcher plants' victims for themselves. Sarah Gagne of *Horn Book* appreciated Lerner's "exquisite watercolor paintings" and "attractive" line drawings. According to *School Library Journal* contributor Margaret Bush, Lerner's "elegant presentation" will evoke "respect and curiosity" from its readers. To help satisfy this interest, Lerner provides a list of botanic gardens and greenhouses in the United States that feature carnivorous plants. She also includes a glossary and index.

Researching *A Forest Year* (1987) presented Lerner with an enormous task. This book provides information on the mammals, birds, reptiles and amphibians, insects, and plants of an Eastern U.S. forest and describes the seasonal adaptations typical of each. Lerner organizes the book by season, and uses a double-page spread for each group in each season. At least one page per section is devoted to text which is, according to Kathleen Odean in *School Library Journal,* "gracefully-written." The illustrations, as *School Library Journal's* Bush noted, "fill whole pages and some double-spread half-pages

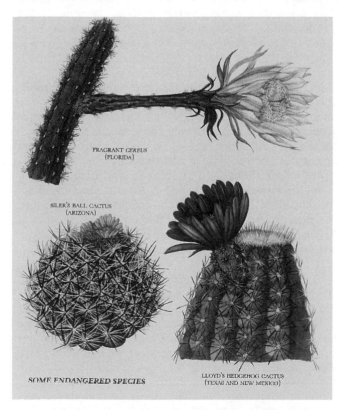

FRAGRANT CEREUS (FLORIDA)

SILER'S BALL CACTUS (ARIZONA)

SOME ENDANGERED SPECIES

LLOYD'S HEDGEHOG CACTUS (TEXAS AND NEW MEXICO)

Lerner uses her talent with watercolors and extensive knowledge of botany to describe some of the fifteen hundred varieties of a distinctive desert plant in 1992's *Cactus.*

with beautifully composed detail" and are enhanced with magnified drawings of smaller forms of life. This book also includes a glossary and index.

Like *A Forest Year, A Desert Year* (1991) is organized by seasons and describes the seasonal adaptations of the animals and plants living in the habitat. Mammals, birds, reptiles and amphibians, arthropods, and plants in the southwestern United States are portrayed in watercolor paintings. As a critic in *Kirkus Reviews* noted, "Size and scale are not given" and "scientific names appear only in the index." In *School Library Journal,* Ruth M. McConnell described *A Desert Year* as a "useful survey" and a "discussion starter on the other intriguing topics it mentions." Those intrigued with a *Desert Year* may appreciate *Cactus* (1994) which Matthews of *School Library Journal* called a "succinct and lovely volume" that "schools and public libraries will welcome."

A friend's inability to distinguish raspberry and wild strawberry plants from poison ivy inspired Lerner to write the first of she called her "most conventional books." She recalled in *SAAS,* "When I looked among the juveniles for books that dealt specifically with poisonous plants, I saw that none of them had good, clear illustrations that could be used for identifying the species under discussion. Since this is my forte, I set about to make one, and it was published as *Moonseed and Mistletoe: A Book of Poisonous Wild Plants*" (1988).

Moonseed and Mistletoe features many wild plants common to the United States and Canada which can make people sick. In five chapters, Lerner discusses skin-irritating plants like poison ivy and poison oak, poisonous berries, dangerous flowers, trees, and bushes, and poisonous plants used for decorative purposes, like holly and mistletoe. Lerner provides a color painting for each chapter and embellishes the text with black-and-white drawings where appropriate. Lerner explains how these plants have been used by people historically and the dangers of attempting to consume them. As Betsy Hearne in *Bulletin of the Center for Children's Books* commented, *Moonseed and Mistletoe* "will intrigue children as well as benefit them."

As Lerner worked on *Moonseed and Mistletoe,* she "realized that children today are far more likely to come into contact with troublesome domestic plants than with wild ones." So, in *Dumb Cane and Daffodils: Poisonous Plants in the House and Garden* (1990) Lerner discusses domesticated yet potentially harmful plants like crocus, amaryllis, delphinium, English ivy, foxgloves, and hyacinths. Four chapters treat garden flowers, shrubs and vines, vegetables, and houseplants, and, as in *Moonseed and Mistletoe,* fine line drawings in the text are featured in addition to full-page color paintings. Lerner explains that some parts of plants with edible fruits or vegetables, the perfumes of some flowers, and the berries of some houseplants are poisonous. As Bush noted in *Horn Book,* although Lerner does not include "explanations of the poisonous substances and their functions in the plants," she provides "other interesting bits of material." *School Library Journal* writer Matthews concluded that the book "performs a service" to gardeners while "reaffirming a love" for nature's "beautiful creations."

Plants That Make You Sniffle and Sneeze (1993) relates how some of nature's creations can cause those with allergies extreme discomfort. Through her illustrations and text, Lerner focuses on the source of trouble for hay fever sufferers: pollen from flowers on trees, bushes, grasses, and weeds. Wind-spread pollen is released at various times during the growing season. Lerner explains pollen's role in the reproduction of plants and provides suggestions for those with allergies on how to avoid it. Hearne in *Bulletin of the Center for Children's Books* commented that *Plants that Make You Sniffle and Sneeze* is "clean, clear, and well organized," and Bush in *Horn Book* concluded that the book is "lovely in spite of its subject" and described it as an "astute presentation."

Lerner commented in her *SAAS* entry that she "had wanted to" work on *Plant Families* (1989) "for years." "Botanists have described over three hundred different families.... Knowing even a handful of these botanical families and the characteristics that distinguish them brings a degree of order to the multitude of different species we see around us." *Plant Families,* which presents twelve botanical families (including buttercup, mustard, pink, mint, pea, rose, parsley, composite, lily, arum, grass, and orchid), is, in the words of *Voice of Youth Advocate*'s JoEllen Broome, an "intelligent, infor-

Allergy sufferers can benefit by reading Lerner's 1993 book, which describes many of the culprits that cause hay fever and how best to avoid them. (Cover illustration by the author.)

CAROLINA WREN

In *Backyard Birds of Winter* Lerner describes and illustrates over forty species of North American birds—and explains how best to attract them to one's backyard.

mative botanical guide" as well as "a work of art." Lerner's color illustrations of a species of each family, which include life-sized pictures of the plant as well as detailed and enlarged labeled drawings of smaller parts, face each page of text. She includes both the common and scientific names of the species, as well as the pronunciation of the scientific name. Lerner also encourages readers to carefully identify, classify, and collect plants.

Backyard Birds of Winter departed from the botanical focus of most of Lerner's books. It presents forty-five species of birds most likely to be seen at backyard feeders in the United States and Canada. Each bird is shown in full color, drawn to scale, with a map for species of limited winter distribution. The book gives information about food preferences and makes suggestions for successful bird feeding. An introductory chapter describes the strategies that enable birds to survive the rigors of winter. Carolyn Phelan of *Booklist* called it "a beautiful as well as a practical way to learn about wildlife that even city children can observe."

As Lerner's career as writer and illustrator blossomed, she continued to illustrate books for other authors. She wrote in *SAAS* that such assignments are "enjoyable" as a "change of pace." Her black-and-white drawings for *Green Darner: The Story of a Dragonfly* (1980) won her praise. Martha T. Kane of *Appraisal: Children's Science Books* noted that "even a very young child could 'read' the story" with Lerner's illustrations, and Susanne S. Sullivan commented in the same issue that the artist's "details" are "as fine and fragile as the dragonfly itself." *Sphinx: The Story of a Caterpillar,* also by McClung, tells the story of the tomato hornworm. According to A. H. Drummond, Jr. in *Appraisal,* Lerner's black-and-white drawings are "excellent in every respect." Barbara

L. Greer in *School Library Journal* likewise stated that Lerner's illustrations "at times ... border on fine art." Lerner's illustrations for Anita Holmes's *The 100-Year-Old Cactus* (1983), in the words of *School Library Journal*'s Lisa Brooks Williams, capture "the spirit of desert life."

Lerner continues to write, illustrate, and spend summers at the Lerner cottage with her husband, where she tends a large and expanding garden. She wrote in her *SAAS* autobiography, "I have a list of subjects I would like to turn into a book some day ... having arrived so tardily at a truly absorbing occupation, I mean to stay with it. There's no point in stopping when you're having a good time."

■ Works Cited

Review of *A Biblical Garden, Publishers Weekly,* April 9, 1982, p. 50.

Boes, Anne, review of *On the Forest Edge, School Library Journal,* November, 1978, p. 65.

Broome, JoEllen, review of *Plant Families, Voice of Youth Advocates,* October, 1989, p. 236.

Bush, Margaret, review of *Pitcher Plants, School Library Journal,* April, 1983, p. 115.

Bush, Margaret A., review of *A Forest Year, Horn Book,* May-June, 1987, pp. 357-58.

Bush, Margaret A., review of *Moonseed and Mistletoe, Horn Book,* May-June, 1988, p. 372.

Bush, Margaret A., review of *Dumb Cane and Daffodils: Poisonous Plants in the House and Garden, Horn Book,* March-April, 1990, p. 221.

Bush, Margaret A., review of *Plants That Make You Sniffle and Sneeze, Horn Book,* January-February, 1994, pp. 89-90.

Review of *A Desert Year, Kirkus Reviews,* July, 1991, p. 858.

Drummond, A. H., Jr., review of *Sphinx, Appraisal: Science Books for Young People,* winter, 1982, p. 43.

Gagne, Sarah, review of *Pitcher Plants, Horn Book,* June, 1983, pp. 333-334.

Greer, Barbara L., review of *Sphinx, School Library Journal,* January, 1982, pp. 67-8.

Hearne, Betsy, review of *Moonseed and Mistletoe, Bulletin of the Center for Children's Books,* March, 1988, pp. 140-41.

Hearne, Betsy, review of *Plants That Make You Sniffle and Sneeze, Bulletin of the Center for Children's Books,* October, 1993, p. 50.

Kane, Martha T., review of *Green Darner, Appraisal: Children's Science Books,* fall, 1980, p. 46.

Knoth, Maeve Visser, review of *Cactus, Horn Book,* January-February, 1993, p. 104.

Lerner, Carol, autobiography in *Something about the Author Autobiography* Series, Volume 12, Gale, 1991, pp. 215-231.

Matthews, Steve, review of *Seasons of the Tallgrass Prairie, School Library Journal,* February, 1981, p. 68.

Matthews, Steve, review of *Dumb Cane and Daffodils, School Library Journal,* September, 1990, pp. 242-43.

Matthews, Steve, review of *Cactus, School Library Journal,* December, 1992, p. 123.

McConnell, Ruth M., review of *A Desert Year, School Library Journal,* November, 1991, p. 130.

Odean, Kathleen, review of *A Forest Year, School Library Journal,* August, 1987, p. 86.

Review of *On the Forest Edge, Kirkus Reviews,* September 15, 1978, p. 1018.

Phelan, Carolyn, review of *Backyard Birds of Winter, Booklist,* November 15, 1994.

Scotto, Barbara C., review of *Dumb Cane and Daffodils, Appraisal: Science Books for Young People,* autumn, 1990, pp. 26-8.

Serling, Barbara Peklo, review of *Flowers of a Woodland Spring, School Library Journal,* January, 1980, p. 57.

Sullivan, Susanne S., review of *Green Darner, Appraisal: Children's Science Books,* fall, 1980, p. 46.

Sutherland, Zena, review of *Flowers of a Woodland Spring, Bulletin of the Center for Children's Books,* October, 1979, p. 31.

Sutherland, Zena, review of *Seasons of the Tallgrass Prairie, Bulletin of the Center for Children's Books,* November, 1980, p. 57.

Williams, Lisa Brooks, review of *The 100-Year-Old Cactus, School Library Journal,* November, 1983, pp. 64-5.

Wilms, Denise M., review of *Peeper, First Voice of Spring, Booklist,* November 1, 1977, p. 479.

Wilms, Denise M., review of *On the Forest Edge, Booklist,* September 15, 1978, pp. 221-22.

■ For More Information See

BOOKS

Children's Literature Review, Volume 34, Gale, 1995, pp. 120-139.

PERIODICALS

Booklist, October 1, 1979, p. 279.

Bulletin of the Center for Children's Books, May, 1987, p. 172; April, 1989, pp. 199-200.

Horn Book, September/October, 1991, p. 612.

Kirkus Reviews, August 15, 1977, p. 854; January 15, 1990, p. 106.

School Library Journal, May, 1989, p. 120; January, 1994, p. 124.

—Sketch by R. Garcia-Johnson

* * *

LEVENKRON, Steven 1941-

■ Personal

Born March 25, 1941, in New York, NY; son of Joseph A. (a paperhanger) and Florence (a salesperson; maiden name, Shader) Levenkron; married Abby Rosen (a therapist), May 25, 1963; children: Rachel, Gabrielle. *Education:* Queens College of the City of New York, B.A., 1963; Brooklyn College of the City of New York, M.S., 1969.

■ Addresses

Office—16 East 79th Street, New York, NY 10021. *Agent*—George Wieser, Wieser and Wieser, Inc., 79 Valley View, Chappaqua, NY 10514.

■ Career

Social studies teacher at secondary schools, New York City, 1963-68; guidance counselor at secondary schools, New York City, 1968-74; part-time private practice of psychotherapy, 1972-74; Montefiore Hospital and Medical Center, Bronx, NY, visiting psychotherapist, 1975—; Center for the Study of Anorexia, New York City, clinical consultant, 1981—. *Member:* National Association of Anorexia Nervosa and Associated Disorders (member of advisory board), American Personnel and Guidance Association, American Orthopsychiatric Association.

■ Awards, Honors

The Best Little Girl in the World was named best book for young adults by the American Library Association, 1978-79; annual award from the National Association of Anorexia Nervosa and Associated Disorders, 1981, for bringing anorexia nervosa to public attention.

■ Writings

NOVELS FOR YOUNG ADULTS

The Best Little Girl in the World, Contemporary Books, 1978.
Kessa, Popular Library, 1986.

NONFICTION FOR ADULTS

Treating and Overcoming Anorexia Nervosa, Scribner, 1982.

■ Adaptations

The Best Little Girl in the World was adapted as a film for television.

■ Sidelights

One of the world's foremost authorities on anorexia nervosa, Steven Levenkron is a psychotherapist whose specialty is treating people suffering from this devastating, self-inflicted malady, a disease in which a person starves him- or herself in an attempt to be thinner. As defined by an article in *Los Angeles Times,* anorexia nervosa is a "hysterical aversion to food, leading to severe weight loss and malnutrition." While the remedy for anorexia nervosa is simple—just eat—that is the last thing persons suffering from this disease can bring themselves to do. Instead, they will resort to every kind of deceit to keep from eating.

Statistics show that the mortality rate for those suffering from anorexia nervosa is the highest of any psychiatric disorder. Once rare, this eating disorder is thought to afflict more than 100,000 people in the United States,

Revealing a young girl's darkest fantasies and the triumphant story of her return to the sunlight of reality.

The bestselling novel about the obsession that kills— ANOREXIA NERVOSA

OVER 1/2 MILLION COPIES IN PRINT

The Best Little Girl In The World

Steven Levenkron

In his first novel, Levenkron addresses the serious issue of anorexia nervosa through the eyes of a teenaged girl who suffers from the eating disorder.

almost all of them white, middle-class women under the age of twenty-five. Anorexia nervosa can lead to complications like infection, heart failure, irreversible hypoglycemia, and ultimately death. Levenkron's young adult novel, *The Best Little Girl in the World,* was the first to bring this excruciating disease and its dangers to the public's awareness.

Levenkron based *The Best Little Girl in the World* on his work with anorexics, most of whom are teenage girls. In it, he describes the experiences of Francesca, a fictional anorexic teen, who began dieting in an attempt to qualify for a very prestigious ballet camp. As her health deteriorates from not eating, Francesca's thinking becomes muddled because of malnutrition. Her family is distraught. Finally Francesca's physicians hospitalize her in an attempt to keep her alive. It is only when she forms a trusting relationship with her psychotherapist that Francesca has a chance of surviving. At the same time her family is forced to examine and change the way they have treated Francesca, Francesca herself must change the way she has viewed and valued herself. Her anorexia nervosa was motivated by her need for attention and approval. Ultimately, therapy for Francesca and her whole family is the only way the teenager can save herself. Writing in *Publishers Weekly,* Barbara A. Bannon referred to Levenkron as "an impassioned and skillful author" who used a method "more powerful than dry facts" to raise public awareness. The book was made into a television movie.

In 1986 Levenkron published *Kessa,* the sequel to *The Best Little Girl,* continuing the story of Francesca. Although it is a sequel, Linda Polomski suggested in *School Library Journal* that Kessa "can be read independently." Called a "thoughtful sequel" by *Voice of Youth Advocates* reviewer Evie Wilson, *Kessa* follows Francesca through her ongoing battle to save herself and her attempts to keep a friend from falling prey to the same disease. *Kessa* "may help some YAs to understand the pressures and insecurities of their own lives while also providing a good read," Wilson wrote in *Voice of Youth Advocates.* However, a critic in *Publishers Weekly* did not share Wilson's enthusiasm for *Kessa,* reporting that "the story is difficult to follow [and] the transitions are not smooth."

Levenkron explains the symptoms of anorexia nervosa and how he treats his patients in *Treating and Overcoming Anorexia Nervosa. Voice of Youth Advocates* reviewer Susan Levine stated that Levenkron writes with "clarity and compassion." Although Priscilla Johnson concluded in *School Library Journal* that *Treating and Overcoming* was "a clear, concise guide" she then stated that "the lack of a bibliography and/or more footnotes limits the use of this book as a source for further study." In spite of this criticism, psychotherapist Levenkron has done much to raise the public's awareness about anorexia nervosa.

■ Works Cited

Bannon, Barbara A., review of *The Best Little Girl in the World, Publishers Weekly,* July 17, 1978, p. 163.

Johnson, Priscilla, review of *Treating and Overcoming Anorexia Nervosa, School Library Journal,* December, 1982, pp. 89-90.

Review of *Kessa, Publishers Weekly,* December 6, 1985, p. 73.

Levine, Susan, review of *Treating and Overcoming Anorexia Nervosa, Voice of Youth Advocates,* October, 1983, p. 234.

Los Angeles Times, August 24, 1979.

Polomski, Linda, review of *Kessa, School Library Journal,* March, 1986, p. 177.

Wilson, Evie, review of *Kessa, Voice of Youth Advocates,* August/October, 1986, p. 146.

■ For More Information See

PERIODICALS

Kirkus Reviews, July 15, 1978, p. 767.
School Library Journal, March, 1979, p. 152.*

LI, Xiao Jun 1952-

■ Personal

Born February 7, 1952, in Huhehaote, China; son of Xi-Wei Li and Feng-Ying Liu; married Wei Sun (an illustrator), August 8, 1985; children: Fei. *Education:* College of Fine Arts, China, B.A. (studio art), 1979.

■ Addresses

Home—1850 Hanover Dr., #131, Davis, CA 95616.

■ Career

Illustrator. China Children's Publishing House, Beijing, China, art director, 1979-88; University of California, Davis, visiting scholar in the art department, 1988-90; T. S. Post, Inc., Davis, designer, 1991-1994; Howard & Neilson Sculpture Design, Davis, CA, sculptor, 1991—. *Member:* Society of Children's Book Writers and Illustrators, Chinese Artists Association, China Artists Association (China).

■ Awards, Honors

Silver medal, Sixth National Exhibition of Fine Arts, Beijing, China; Sixth Noma Concours for Children's Picture Book Illustrations, Tokyo, Japan.

■ Illustrator

The Old Wolf's Cave, Inner Mongolia Publishing House, c. 1972.
Cherry, China Children's Publishing House, 1987.
Suho and His White Horse, China Children's Publishing House, 1988.
Love in Snow, China People's Art Press, 1989.

XIAO JUN LI

The Long March to the Fourth of June, translated by E. J. Griffiths, Duckworth, 1990.

Long Hair Sister, Komine Shoten Publishing House, 1992.

Frank P. Araujo, *Nekane, the Lamina & the Bear: A Tale of the Basque Pyrenees,* Rayve Productions, 1993.

Araujo, *The Perfect Orange,* Rayve Productions, 1994.

■ Work in Progress

Preparing illustrations for *Dragon Water,* a picture book written by Frank P. Araujo, and *The Abacus Contests and Other Stories.*

■ Sidelights

"My first illustrated book, *The Old Wolf's Cave,* was published by the Inner Mongolia Publishing House when I was 20," Xiao Jun Li told *SATA.* "I had begun work at age 17 doing graphic arts on a newspaper during the terrible days of China's Cultural Revolution. It was during that time I realized that others could enjoy my work.

"Once in a bookstore in Inner Mongolia, I saw a couple of boys looking at my book. There were few children's books available in China in those days and they did not have enough money between them to buy the book. I gave them enough for the book and it pleased me beyond words to know they would get pleasure from my work.

"My love for illustrating children's books is complex. I want to be free to express what I feel, rather than be compelled to create something someone else wants. A child's world is full of discovery and wonder, and free from political propaganda and petty economic interests. I feel liberated by giving the child in myself the freedom to express feelings and perceptions artistically. And today, I still find myself in that child's world of discovery and wonder."

■ For More Information See

PERIODICALS

Booklist, February 1, 1994, p. 1007.

Bulletin of the Center for Children's Books, March, 1994, p. 214.

Five Owls, March, 1994, p. 86.

Publishers Weekly, December 13, 1993, p. 70.

School Library Journal, May, 1994, p. 106.

Times Educational Supplement, February 16, 1990, p. 26.

Times Literary Supplement, March 23, 1990, p. 304.

M

MACDONALD, Caroline 1948-

■ Personal

Born October 1, 1948, in Taranaki, New Zealand.

■ Addresses

Home—P.O. Box 4189, Hamilton, New Zealand. *Agent*—Margaret Conolly, Curtis Brown, 27 Union St., Council, Paddington, New South Wales 2021, Australia.

■ Career

Writer of novels and short stories for young adults and children. Deakin University, Geelong, Australia, editor of teaching materials, 1984-88.

■ Awards, Honors

New Zealand Literary Fund Choysa bursary, 1983; Esther Glen Medal, New Zealand Library Association, 1984; New Zealand Children's Book of the Year award, 1985; Children's Book Council of Australia Book of the Year, older honor, 1989.

■ Writings

Elephant Rock, Hodder & Stoughton (Auckland), 1984.
Visitors, illustrated by Garry Meeson, Hodder & Stoughton, 1984.
Yellow Boarding House, Oxford University Press (Auckland), 1985.
Joseph's Boat, illustrated by Chris Gaskin, Hodder & Stoughton, 1988.
Earthgames, illustrated by Chris Johnson and Rowena Cory, Rigby (Melbourne), 1988.
The Lake at the End of the World, Hodder & Stoughton, 1988, Dial, 1989.
Speaking to Miranda, Hodder & Stoughton, 1991, HarperCollins, 1992.
Hostilities: Nine Bizarre Stories, Omnibus Books (Norwood, South Australia), 1991, Scholastic, 1994.
Eye Witness, Hodder & Stoughton, 1992.

Secret Lives, Ashton Scholastic (Melbourne), 1993, Simon & Schuster, 1995.

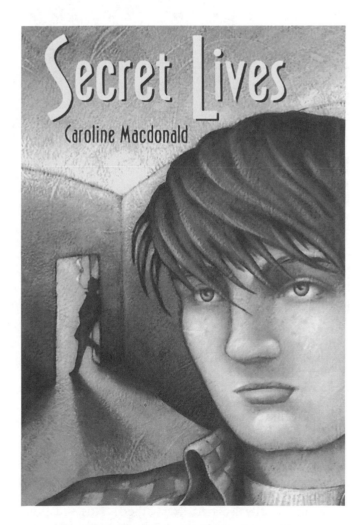

In one of Macdonald's recent books for teens, young Ian is led into trouble with the law and his family by mysterious Gideon, who has an evil and irresistible power over him. (Cover illustration by Janet Atkinson.)

HOSTILITIES
Nine Bizarre Stories

CAROLINE MACDONALD

The horror tales in this collection are not traditional ghost stories, but they nevertheless have the power to frighten readers in unexpected and subtle ways. (Cover illustration by Eric Dinyer.)

■ Sidelights

New Zealand author Caroline Macdonald once told *Twentieth-Century Children's Writers:* "Future fiction, science fiction, the supernatural and the mystical are the thematic areas I'm interested in. I like to suggest there's a strange edge to be found in a mundane world. I enjoy forming characters who are for some reason removed from the usual processes of conditioning."

Macdonald's fiction for older children and young adults is frequently classified as science fiction or horror and often features young people who are lonely and physically or emotionally isolated from others. This situation "renders them more sensitive to the unusual," remarked Betty Gilderdale in *Twentieth-Century Children's Writers,* and Macdonald exploits this situation by introducing her characters to visitors from outer space, time travel, and other uncommon, and sometimes frightening, occurrences. Though she has been compared to Stephen King and R. L. Stine for the horrifying or merely unsettling elements in many of her stories and novels, some critics find Macdonald's fiction more

thought-provoking and better composed than that of either of these more famous writers.

Elephant Rock, Macdonald's first novel, shares with several of her other works an examination of a difficult parent-child relationship. In this work, a twelve-year-old's grief over her mother's impending death from cancer is alleviated somewhat when she is able to travel back in time and experience her mother's youth. While acknowledging the book's "inevitably sad" conclusion, Gilderdale recommended *Elephant Rock,* remarking: "The reader will grow through experiencing it." At the center of Macdonald's next book, *Visitors,* is a boy whose parents have given him everything but their time and attention, and a girl whose physical handicaps have made her especially adept at working with computers. Together the two encounter aliens from outer space trapped on Earth for hundreds of years by their inability to communicate with humans, and they eventually help the visitors return to their home. "In addition to investing fantasy with a compelling life of its own," Gilderdale commented, "Macdonald demonstrates considerable scientific acumen" in her depiction of how the children help the visitors.

Lacking the science fiction element, *Yellow Boarding House,* Macdonald's third novel for young adults, focuses on the evolving relationship between a mother and daughter from New Zealand as the daughter strives to assume the greater responsibilities associated with growing up. Set in contemporary Australia, this novel depicts their mutual struggle to survive in a new country after the girl's father fails to return from a trip. A picture book, *Joseph's Boat,* followed *Yellow Boarding House* with another realistic portrayal of an isolated parent and child struggling to communicate with each other.

In *The Lake at the End of the World* Macdonald returned to science fiction with a story set in a future in which the earth has been made uninhabitable by pollution. A lake in New Zealand provides the only livable environment for humans, and two groups of people, a community that lives in underground caves and a family that lives nearby, unknowingly share its bounty until a chance meeting between a teenage boy from the community and Diana, the daughter of the family, introduces the two groups. "The book unobtrusively asks large questions about power, the direction of agricultural management, and industrial pollution," Gilderdale noted.

Macdonald has also written a collection of short tales, entitled *Hostilities: Nine Bizarre Stories,* that highlights the horrific side of the author's imagination. "A delicately macabre ambience infuses these tales," wrote a contributor in *Kirkus Reviews,* and a *Publishers Weekly* reviewer compared them to *The Twilight Zone,* the classic television program of the 1960s. Two of the stories are set in the future, and several employ Macdonald's characteristic device of using isolated teenagers who encounter unusual situations that "arouse feelings that range from sticky unease to gut-wrenching terror," according to a reviewer in *Voice of Youth Advocates.*

Some critics noted the presence of Australian slang expressions but felt that they would not spoil an American adolescent's appreciation of the stories, which were praised as well-written and, in the words of *Booklist* reviewer Chris Sherman, "satisfyingly creepy."

Macdonald is the author of several novels, short stories, and picture books that successfully mesh acute portrayals of child and adolescent relationships with adults and encounters with supernatural or futuristic phenomenon. Often set in the author's native New Zealand and Australia, Macdonald's stories commonly pit an isolated character against unusual and sometimes frightening circumstances. Although she is usually considered a science fiction writer, Macdonald has garnered praise for the accuracy and depth of the human relationships she depicts, as well as for the subtlety and craft of her stories' construction.

■ Works Cited

Gilderdale, Betty, "Caroline Macdonald," *Twentieth-Century Children's Writers*, St. James, 1995, pp. 610-11.
Review of *Hostilities, Kirkus Reviews*, January 1, 1994.
Review of *Hostilities, Publishers Weekly*, December 13, 1993.
Review of *Hostilities, Voice of Youth Advocates*, October, 1994.
Macdonald, Caroline, comments in *Twentieth-Century Children's Writers*, St. James, 1995, p. 610.
Sherman, Chris, review of *Hostilities, Booklist*, January 15, 1994.

■ For More Information See

PERIODICALS

School Library Journal, March, 1994.*

*   *   *

MALI, Jane Lawrence 1937-1995

OBITUARY NOTICE—See index for *SATA* sketch: Born June 2, 1937, in New York, NY; died of cancer, October 2, 1995, in Norfolk, CT. Author. A writer of children's books in collaboration with Alison Cragin Herzig, Mali also achieved recognition for her contributions to conservation and education. Mali worked with the Collegiate School in Manhattan, New York, to establish scholarships for children of nursery school age—one of the first programs of its kind. She also set up a child care class for boys. With Herzig, Mali prepared a documentary-style book based on this course which was entitled *Oh, Boy! Babies!* The winner of the American Book Award in 1981, the work was also honored by the Children's Book Council. Mali worked on environmental issues and contributed to a nature preserve in Connecticut. Her other collaborations with Herzig include *A Season of Secrets, Thaddeus,* and *The Ten-Speed Babysitter.*

OBITUARIES AND OTHER SOURCES:

PERIODICALS

New York Times, October 7, 1995, p. 10.

*   *   *

MARGOLIS, Richard J(ules) 1929-1991

■ Personal

Born June 30, 1929, in St. Paul, MN; died of heart failure, April 22, 1991, in New Haven, CT; son of Harry Sterling (a rabbi) and Clara (Brunner) Margolis; married Diane Rothbard (a sociologist), April 3, 1954; children: Harry Sterling, Philip Eliot. *Education:* University of Minnesota, B.A., 1952, M.A., 1953.

■ Career

Worked as a reporter for the Chicago City News Bureau; *Brooklyn Heights Press,* Brooklyn, NY, editor and publisher, 1956-60; Lerner Newspapers, Chicago, IL, editorial director, 1960-62; freelance writer, 1962-91. Taught writing course at State University of New York. National chairman, Rural Housing Alliance; founding chairman, Rural America, Inc.; consultant at various times to Ford Foundation, Stern Fund, U.S. Civil Rights Commission, U.S. Office of Economic Opportunity, U.S. Bureau of Indian Affairs, and other government and private agencies. Member of library board, Wilton, CT.

■ Awards, Honors

George Polk Memorial Award for achievement in journalism, 1959; National Editorial Association Award for editorial writing, 1962; Junior Library Guild selection, 1972, for *Wish Again, Big Bear;* Christopher Award, 1985, for *Secrets of a Small Brother.*

■ Writings

FOR CHILDREN

Only the Moon and Me (poetry), photographs by Marcia Kay Keegan, Lippincott, 1968.
Looking for a Place (poetry), illustrated by Ilse Koehn, Lippincott, 1969.
The Upside-Down King, illustrated by Lee Lorenz, Windmill Books, 1971.
Wish Again, Big Bear, illustrated by Robert Lopshire, Macmillan, 1972.
Homer the Hunter (fable), illustrated by Leonard Kessler, Macmillan, 1972.
Big Bear to the Rescue, illustrated by Lopshire, Greenwillow Books, 1975.
Big Bear, Spare That Tree, illustrated by Jack Kent, Greenwillow Books, 1980.
Secrets of a Small Brother (poetry), illustrated by Donald Carrick, Macmillan, 1984.

FOR ADULTS

Something to Build On (nonfiction), American Friends Service Committee, 1966.

At the Crossroads: An Inquiry into Rural Post Offices and the Communities They Serve, U.S. Postal Rate Commission, 1980.

Homes of the Brave, Rural America for the Farmworker Housing Coalition, 1981.

Risking Old Age in America, Westview Press, 1989.

Editor of *Change.* Contributor of articles and reviews to *Harper's, New Republic, Life, New Leader, Redbook, New York Times Magazine, Nation, Washington Monthly,* and many other periodicals.

■ Sidelights

The children's books written by journalist Richard J. Margolis include poetry collections (one of which won the Christopher Award), fables, and other animal tales. The poems found in Margolis's collections use both rhyme and free verse to depict various objects and events from a child's viewpoint, and his animal stories and fables end with lessons and morals for his young readers to learn. In addition to his children's writings, Margolis spent the majority of his career as a freelance journalist, perhaps best known for his social issues column in *New Leader* magazine. Similar issues are covered in his adult writings, including the problems faced by such minorities as Native Americans, migrant farm workers, and the elderly.

Following graduation from the University of Minnesota, Margolis acquired his first job as a reporter for the Chicago City News Bureau. "During my first two weeks," he remembered in *Junior Library Guild,* "I found myself covering a prison riot, the collapse of a hotel building, and an FBI dope raid. I had the illusion that life was a chain of public emergencies." A couple years later, Margolis moved to New York, working in advertising and promotion for a variety of magazines. Then, in 1956, he purchased the *Brooklyn Heights Press,* becoming the editor and publisher of this weekly newspaper, which was the first weekly to win the George Polk Memorial Award for excellence in journalism.

All of this journalism experience enabled Margolis to become a freelance writer, and eventually the author of both adult and children's books. The poetry collections *Only the Moon and Me* and *Looking for a Place* were the first two children's books Margolis published. The poems in *Only the Moon and Me* deal with issues and events that children wonder about, including night and the things that adults do. *Looking for a Place* has more of a structured progression, starting with a poem in which a man on the street and a boy in a window are alienated from each other as the man looks for a place to live. The rest of the poems are all set in the city and follow the man through his search.

In *Only the Moon and Me,* observed *Library Journal* contributor Sarah Ann Long, Margolis communicated "his truths in an appealing child-like manner." Review-

Big Bear appears in three stories of friendship, including *Big Bear, Spare That Tree,* in which he has a change of heart about chopping down a tree that has a bird's nest in it. (Illustration by Jack Kent.)

ing the collection *Looking for a Place,* a *Bulletin for the Center of Children's Books* contributor remarked that the poems "reflect the inner city patterns and the thoughts of its residents." And Madeleine L'Engle stated in the *New York Times Book Review* that *Looking for a Place* is a "powerful book."

The inspiration behind Margolis's children's poetry can be found in his own two children. He once explained to *SATA:* "I began writing children's poetry when my two sons started talking back to me in uncanny ways. The things they said made me remember the things *I* had said when I was a child. So much of my poetry is based on the plain talk of children. I believe that poetry is the art of saying something important in a way that people won't forget. (It doesn't have to be Significant; it simply must mean a lot to the poet.)"

Following his successful beginning with poetry, Margolis turned to writing stories and fables. The author once related to *SATA* that these books "are simple ideas that occur to me from time to time, usually early in the morning. They are mostly about friendship and how hard it is to come by." Friendship is exactly the thing Big Bear is searching for in the three books which feature him: *Wish Again, Big Bear; Big Bear to the Rescue;* and *Big Bear, Spare That Tree.*

Wish Again, Big Bear begins with Big Bear catching a clever fish, who offers him three wishes for his freedom. By the time he realizes that the fish is not really a wish fish, though, Big Bear is unable to eat him because he is now a friend. In his second adventure, *Big Bear to the Rescue,* Big Bear sees Mr. Mole lying at the bottom of the well and immediately sets out to rescue him, not realizing that Mr. Mole is merely sleeping. Asking for help, Big Bear turns out to be the only unselfish one as all the other animals refuse to help unless they get something in return. Finally, Big Bear comes up against Blue Jay and her unhatched eggs in *Big Bear, Spare That Tree.* Chopping down a tree for firewood, Big Bear is determined to continue despite the fact that Blue Jay's nest and eggs will fall. As the tree begins to drop, though, Big Bear catches it and carries the nest and new babies to safety.

Wish Again, Big Bear "is slightly slapstick, with gentleness in its humor," pointed out a *New York Times Book Review* contributor. Finding *Big Bear to the Rescue* to be humorous also, Mary M. Burns wrote in *Horn Book* that the book contains "an accumulation of funny swaps" as the "blundering bruin" attempts his friend's rescue. *Horn Book* reviewer Ethel L. Heins asserted that *Big Bear, Spare That Tree* "is given originality, interest, and humor by the protagonists' sprightly repartee."

Margolis returned to verse for his last children's book, *Secrets of a Small Brother,* which won the Christopher Award in 1985. This collection covers everything involved with being a little brother. The big brother dominates the little brother in the first half of the poems, making fun of him and teasing him, and teaching him dirty words to say to their mother. At the same time, the little brother laments hand-me-down clothes and having to do everything second. The poems near the end of collection show the two brothers developing a bond, with the older teaching the younger to ride his bike, and saving him when he falls into a lake.

In *Secrets of a Small Brother* "charming and pointed poems capture the experience of being a younger brother," related Ilene Cooper in *Booklist.* James Fallows similarly contended in the *New York Times Book Review:* "As a former big brother, I found the poems poignant and affecting." Ellen D. Warwick, writing in *School Library Journal,* also found the poems to be "honest and insightful.... Often the poems surprise in a quiet, understated way." Warwick went on to add: "Margolis does fine things with words."

■ Works Cited

Burns, Mary M., review of *Big Bear to the Rescue, Horn Book,* February, 1976, p. 46.

Cooper, Ilene, review of *Secrets of a Small Brother, Booklist,* October 1, 1984, p. 250.

Fallows, James, review of *Secrets of a Small Brother, New York Times Book Review,* February 10, 1985, p. 20.

Margolis returned to poetry in his last children's book, ***Secrets of a Small Brother,*** which won the 1985 Christopher Award. (Illustration by Donald Carrick.)

Heins, Ethel L., review of *Big Bear, Spare That Tree, Horn Book,* August, 1980, p. 401.

L'Engle, Madeleine, review of *Looking for a Place, New York Times Book Review,* December 14, 1969, p. 34.

Long, Sarah Ann, review of *Only the Moon and Me, Library Journal,* June 15, 1969, p. 2497.

Review of *Looking for a Place, Bulletin of the Center for Children's Books,* April, 1970, p. 130.

Margolis, Richard J., comments in *Junior Library Guild,* September, 1975.

Warwick, Ellen D., review of *Secrets of a Small Brother, School Library Journal,* March, 1985, p. 156.

Review of *Wish Again, Big Bear, New York Times Book Review,* March 10, 1974.

■ For More Information See

PERIODICALS

Kirkus Reviews, January 1, 1972, p. 2939; February 15, 1972, p. 192; August 15, 1972, p. 938; May 1, 1980, p. 582.

Library Journal, May 15, 1970, p. 1912; September 15, 1972, p. 2939; December, 1989, p. 151.

New York Times Book Review, November 5, 1972; January 21, 1990, p. 36.

Publishers Weekly, March 24, 1969, p. 54; September 7, 1984, p. 79.

School Library Journal, December, 1975, p. 64; May, 1980, p. 81.
Times Literary Supplement, March 29, 1974, p. 330.

OBITUARIES:

PERIODICALS

New York Times, April 23, 1991.
Washington Post, April 25, 1991.*

* * *

McFARLANE, Sheryl P. 1954-

■ Personal

Born January 20, 1954, in Pembroke, Ontario, Canada; daughter of Patrick Martin (a hardrock miner) and Constance Vivian (a clerk; maiden name, Brunette) McFarlane; married John Anthony Hewitt (a vocational rehabilitation consultant), September 27, 1977; children: Ali, Cloe, Katie. *Education:* University of British Columbia, Bachelor of Education, 1985, children's literature courses, 1986. *Hobbies and other interests:* Reading, gardening, kayaking, hiking, biking and travel.

■ Addresses

Home—168 Beechwood Ave., Victoria, British Columbia, Canada V8S 3W5.

SHERYL P. McFARLANE

■ Career

Children's book author, 1989—. Hosts readings, book talks, and writing workshops at libraries, schools, and festivals. Has also worked in child care, 1972-78; managed Job Corp work program at Agriculture Canada, and served as research technician for Agriculture Canada and U.B.C. in Department of Animal Resource Ecology, 1978-84; directed school tours, Arts, Science and Technology Center, Vancouver, and taught gifted students science through enrichment program at U.B.C., 1985-86. *Member:* Writers' Union of Canada, Canadian Society of Authors, Illustrators and Performers (CANSCAIP), Children's Writers and Illustrators of British Columbia (CWILL BC), Federation of British Columbia Writers, Canadian Children's Book Centre, Vancouver and Victoria Children's Literature Roundtables, British Columbia College of Teachers.

■ Awards, Honors

Ira Dilworth Prize for most promising student of Canadian literature, 1985; Canadian Children's Book Centre "Our Choice Award," 1992, for *Jessie's Island,* and 1994, for *Moonsnail Song* and *Waiting for the Whales;* IODE Nation Chapter Book Award, and Canadian National Library Notable Book, 1994, both for *Waiting for the Whales;* B.C. Cultural Services Grant.

■ Writings

PICTURE BOOKS

Waiting for the Whales, Orca, 1991, Philomel, 1992.
Jessie's Island, Orca, 1992.
Eagle Dreams, Orca, 1994, Philomel, 1995.
Tides of Change, Orca, 1995.
Going to the Fair, Orca, 1996.

POETRY

Moonsnail Song, Orca, 1994.

■ Work in Progress

Shades of Grey.

■ Sidelights

Sheryl P. McFarlane told *SATA* that "I was never the sort of kid you'd imagine becoming a writer when they grew up. I didn't even read much until I hit my teens. I was too busy building forts in the cottonwood trees that lined the irrigation ditches, playing hide-and-seek in the orange groves and cotton fields, playing pick-up baseball in the park, and building skateboards out of discarded baby carriage wheels and scrap wood.

"Junior high opened up a whole new and unexpected world for me," she continued. "For the first time I stepped beyond the boundaries of my small world and I loved it. I travelled to distant places, met fascinating people and lived in a multitude of pasts and a wealth of possible futures. While it never occurred to me that I

A young girl finds comfort and reassurance after her grandfather's death when the whales return to her coastal home in McFarlane's *Waiting for the Whales.* (Illustration by Ron Lightburn.)

could create such worlds myself, it did spark my interest in travel."

After graduating from high school, McFarlane traveled about North America, met her husband in the Ottawa Valley, and in 1974 moved with him to the west coast, where she became a teacher. After the birth of her second daughter, McFarlane decided to change careers. She explained her career change to *SATA,* saying, "I wanted to transport readers in the same way that I had been as a young teen. I wanted to be a writer!" But becoming a published writer was not easy for McFarlane. "It took me countless hours of writing and rewriting, and enough rejections to wallpaper a bedroom before my career took off with *Waiting for the Whales.* Looking back, though, I'm glad some of my earlier work was rejected. I feel proud that *Waiting for the Whales* was my first book."

Students who attend McFarlane's writing workshops or her lectures at schools often ask her where she gets her ideas for her books. "I tell them that there is no shortage of ideas," McFarlane said. "I have file folders full of ideas. I get them from newspapers, the radio, things that have happened to me or to someone I know. Sometimes a story idea comes from jut a visual image. *Waiting for the Whales* began as a prose poem after a close friend died. But it wasn't a story about one person's death," she explained. "Rather, it was a framework to make sense of all the deaths that I and my family have had to

work through in the last several years. For me, the important thing was writing from my own heart about the things that mattered most to me."

When asked about her writing habits, McFarlane told *SATA,* "When I write, I tend to eat, breathe and dream the story I'm working on. It's not unusual for me to forget to make dinner, or jump up at two A.M. and scribble in the notebook I keep beside my bed. It's fortunate that my husband and children help with the meals and are all sound sleepers!"

■ For More Information See

PERIODICALS

Booklist, May 15, 1993, p. 1696.
Publishers Weekly, March 15, 1993, p. 86.
Quill & Quire, March 1994, p. 84; September 1994, p. 69.
School Library Journal, June 1993, p. 83.

*   *   *

MENDELSON, Steven T. 1958-1995

■ Personal

Born in 1958 in Chicago, IL; died of complications related to AIDS, February 11, 1995. *Education:* Attended Rhode Island School of Design.

■ Career

Washington Post, Washington, D.C., staff illustrator, c. 1978; writer and illustrator, c. 1980-95.

■ Writings

(And illustrator) *Stupid Emilien,* Stewart, Tabori & Chang, 1991.
(Reteller and illustrator) *The Emperor's New Clothes* (based on the story by Hans Christian Andersen), Stewart, Tabori & Chang, 1992.

Also illustrator of four volumes of political commentary by Art Buchwald.

■ Work in Progress

Was illustrating a version of *The Sorcerer's Apprentice* at the time of his death.

■ Sidelights

Steven T. Mendelson's career began when he served as a staff illustrator for the *Washington Post* during the late 1970s. By the next decade, Mendelson's work had found a place in four volumes of political commentary authored by popular syndicated political columnist Art Buchwald.

Stupid Emilien, Mendelson's first book for children, was published in 1991 to critical praise. His whimsical

Animals take over the roles of the characters in Mendelson's self-illustrated retelling of _The Emperor's New Clothes._

illustrations, featuring a richly drawn zoo of animal characters, bring to life a foolish Russian peasant named Emilien and his efforts to marry the daughter of the king of Russia. In 1992 Mendelson followed the success of _Stupid Emilien_ with _The Emperor's New Clothes._ His retelling of this classic children's story features a witty text and rich, fanciful artwork. Noting that the work is "both fun and hard-hitting," a _Publishers Weekly_ reviewer added that "the final scenes of the near naked gorilla are a delight." Mendelson was preparing to follow his second book with an illustrated version of _The Sorcerer's Apprentice_ at the time of his death.

■ Works Cited

Review of _The Emperor's New Clothes, Publishers Weekly,_ October 5, 1992.

■ For More Information See

PERIODICALS

School Library Journal, December, 1992.

OBITUARIES AND OTHER SOURCES:

PERIODICALS

Publishers Weekly, March 6, 1995, p. 29.*

MOORE, Elaine 1944-
(Sally Frye)

■ Personal

Born May 31, 1944, in St. Louis, MO; daughter of F. Robert (a U.S. State Department intelligence research officer) and Kathryn (a ceramicist; maiden name, Lammert) Berg; married Robert "Mike" Moore (chief financial officer of a construction company), April 5, 1974; children: Devon, Amy. _Education:_ Attended St. Mary's Academy, 1962; took graduate-level courses in creative writing and writing for children at George Mason University, under author Susan Shreve. _Religion:_ Catholic. _Hobbies and other interests:_ Collecting purple hats and characters from children's books.

■ Addresses

Home—702 Seneca Rd., Great Falls, VA 22066. _Electronic mail_—(America Online) ElainM@aol.com.

■ Career

Novelist and lecturer, 1985—. Worked variously as a secretary and administrative assistant in law offices and at a school for children with learning disabilities; has taught creative writing in adult education courses; writer in residence at over fifty elementary schools throughout the United States each year. _Member:_ International Reading Association, Authors' Guild, Poets & Writers, Inc., Virginia State Reading Association, Washington Children's Book Guild (corresponding secretary, 1994-95).

■ Awards, Honors

Top ten picture books of the year citation, _Christian Science Monitor,_ 1985, "Pick of the Lists" citation, American Booksellers Association, _Pennywhistle Press_ citation, Gannett, and selection as a work to represent intergenerational relationships between American women and children and to be presented as a gift to Russian women and children, Congressional Peace Links Group, 1989, all for _Grandma's House;_ Wisconsin's Cooperative Children's Book Center Award, 1988, and International Reading Association/Children's Book Center (IRA-CBC) Children's Choice Award, 1988, for _Grandma's Promise;_ Children's Choice Award, IRA/CBC, 1989 for _Mixed-Up Sam;_ recipient of the Jenny McKean Moore Fellowship for fiction writing at George Washington University, 1978, and of grants from Virginia Commission of the Arts, School Partnership Program in St. Louis, Humanities Project, Writers-in-Virginia Program, Poets & Writers, and Foundation for the Advanced Education in the Sciences.

■ Writings

PICTURE BOOKS

(Under pseudonym Sally Frye) _God's Day, Today and Everyday,_ illustrated by Erin Leigh, Concordia, 1980.

Grandma's House, illustrated by Elise Primavera, Lothrop, 1985.
What Is a Family?, illustrated by Patricia Mattozzi, Concordia, 1987.
Jesus Had a Family Just Like Me, illustrated by Michelle Dorenkamp, Concordia, 1987.
Grandma's Promise, illustrated by Primavera, Lothrop, 1988.
Mixed-Up Sam, illustrated by Joe Boddy, Milliken, 1989.
Deep River, illustrated by Henri Sorensen, Simon & Schuster, 1994.
Grandma's Garden, illustrated by Dan Andreasen, Lothrop, 1994.
Good Morning, City, illustrated by William Low, BridgeWater, 1995.
Grammy, Do You Love Me?, illustrated by Kathy Wilburn, Longmeadow, 1995.
Grandma's Smile, illustrated by Andreasen, Lothrop, 1995.
Roly Poly Puppies, illustrated by Jacqueline Rogers, Scholastic, in press.

Grandma's House was translated into Japanese as *Obah-chan no Ie,* Holp, 1985.

NOVELS FOR YOUNG READERS

Sarah with an "H", Scholastic, 1992.
The Substitute Teacher from Mars, Troll, 1994.
Who Let Girls in the Boys' Locker Room?, Troll, 1994.
I'd Rather Be Eaten by Sharks, Scholastic, 1995.
The Peanut Butter Trap, Troll, 1996.
Help! There's a Mastodon in My Living Room, Troll, in press.

OTHER

Also contributor of adult short fiction to various magazines and publications, including *Reading Teacher, Virginia Country,* and *Christian Science Monitor.*

■ Work in Progress

Chocolate Daze, for Troll, 1997; research on the 1950s for a novel and for a collection of poems, essays, and anecdotes about the process of writing.

■ Sidelights

Elaine Moore is a prolific author of books for children, writing picture books for very young children and novels for elementary to junior high readers. Moore helps children learn to write their own stories by visiting schools throughout the United States, while wearing her trademark purple writer's hat. In addition to helping classroom authors with their writing, Moore collaborates with them on her own projects, sharing with them the actual joys, challenges, and difficulties professional writers have writing, rewriting, and editing manuscripts for publication. One of Moore's methods of good writing which she teaches students is her "Pizza Game," a recipe that incorporates the elements necessary for a successful story.

ELAINE MOORE

Moore, who has always written for children, began writing stories when she was very young. "I think I always wrote. When I was four, I used a paint brush, then crayons, and on to fat pencils, skinny pencils, fountain pens, ball points, typewriters," she told *SATA.* "Now I use a computer. No matter what instrument I use, I try to use my heart. The good stuff really comes from the heart." By the time she was in seventh grade, Moore discovered that her writing could affect other people, especially her younger sister. "My mother gave me the worst job in the world—baby-sitting my younger sister," Moore said to *SATA.* "My little sister never got punished for the trouble she caused. Finally, I discovered I could keep my sister completely under my control if I wrote exciting stories for her that had chapters with cliffhanger endings. But I would only read them out loud to her on Friday nights and only if she was very good to me for an entire week. Oh, what power! My sister cleaned my room. She picked up my laundry. She even gave me her Oreo cookies. I had sweet chocolate power!"

But Moore admits that writing is hard work—even for a professional writer. "I struggle with my writing!" she confessed to *SATA.* "A sentence is a minor miracle. A paragraph is cause for celebration. One thing I've learned is to turn difficult jobs into games. For me

Summer is a joyful time of year when Kim gets to spend time with her grandmother in Moore's first book in the series, *Grandma's House.* (Illustration by Elise Primavera.)

writing is like a jigsaw puzzle. Sometimes I'm frustrated because I can't find the missing pieces, but once I'm finished, I forget the frustrations. Then it's on to the next story, and the next, and the next . . . . I think I must be hooked. I love stringing words together. I like the sounds and the twisting and turning of ideas. I love how well-placed words make me feel; how they make me think. I share my stacks of drafts with classroom authors and talk about the difficult revision process, showing them how editors mark up an 'almost perfect' manuscript with notes and suggestions on almost every page.

"I am probably the world's most distractible person. Writing is so enormously difficult for me that I'm always tempted to do something else instead. When my daughters were teenagers, they kept interrupting my writing time and I kept losing my temper. What we needed was a signal, so I began wearing a purple hat. At first everyone laughed, but not any more. My purple writer's hat works. When I visit schools and conventions, I always take my purple writer's hat along." The

purple writer's hat has become such a trademark of Moore's that students often appear at her workshops wearing their own writers' hats.

The effects of Moore's purple writer's hat can be found in her award-winning picture books. In *Grandma's House,* the first of Moore's season-specific quartet, Kim spends the summer with her grandmother, "a vigorous, youthful figure in jeans and workshirt," according to Lucy Rollin in *Record.* Grandmother and granddaughter celebrate their "half birthday" and together pick a succession of fruit, competing with critters for every one, from early summer strawberries, which rabbits nibble on, to mid-summer peaches devoured by crows, and finally to end-of-summer plums—most of which the squirrels eat. The overall impression readers "will gain from the book is one of warmth and sharing, an echo of the closeness between the little girl and the older woman," wrote Kathie Meizner in *School Library Journal.* Rollin reported in *Record* that *Grandma's*

House "combines the inevitable passage of time with a sense of renewal."

Moore's second volume of this seasonal series describes Kim's winter visit in *Grandma's Promise.* Whether bedding down beside a glowing wood-burning stove during a blizzard that knocks out the electricity or smearing peanut butter on pine cones for the birds, Kim's grandmother is not stereotypical. A reviewer in the *New Advocate* stated that the promise mentioned in the title is that "no matter how big [Kim] grows, she is always welcome back" at Grandma's place. Writing in *Reading Today,* Barbara N. Kupetz stated that discussing books such as *Grandma's Promise* "help children to avoid making assumptions based on stereotypes, and to see everyone—including the elderly—as they really are."

The spring book in this series, *Grandma's Garden,* "teems with information about gardening and plants," according to Kay Weisman in *Booklist.* Kim helps her grandmother plant a vegetable garden and then replant it after a thunderstorm washes it away. Kim's autumn dilemma arises when she takes her giant pumpkin (which she's grown from seed) to a jack-o'-lantern carving contest in *Grandma's Smile.* Kim is so fond of her pumpkin that she does not want to change it in any way. Finally, her grandmother explains that the pumpkin offers Kim many gifts of change: pulp for pies, seeds for snacks, and then a shell just perfect for carving. Readers will be surprised to see what Kim carves into her beloved pumpkin!

There are surprises in *Mixed-Up Sam* too: a boy's dog purrs and his cat barks happily in an upside-down, inside-out house until his Aunt Edna arrives and tries to put them all on television. Another book with a surprise ending is Moore's *Deep River,* a story about young Jess's first fly-fishing trip with her grandfather. In her review in the *School Library Journal,* Caroline Parr writes that the "details of the fishing expedition and of Jess's fears add depth to the story." A critic in *Publishers Weekly*

Kim and her grandmother once again share special moments as they prepare and plant a garden. (Illustration by Dan Andreasen from *Grandma's Garden.*)

said that Jess's actual catch takes "a back seat to Moore's languid descriptive passages and reassuring dialogue."

Far from the stillness of trout streams, the hustle and bustle of the city awakening is celebrated in Moore's nonfiction prose poem for all ages, *Good Morning, City*. In this picture book illustrated by William Low, the early risers who bake the bagels, deliver newspapers, clean the streets, and keep the subways running bring the city to life. Two of Moore's earliest books, *What Is a Family?* and *Jesus Had a Family Just Like Me*, are "excellent for home or church libraries," wrote Sandy Christopherson in *Lutheran Libraries*. *What Is A Family?* explores the many kinds and sizes of families that exist today. *Jesus Had a Family Just Like Me* shows young children the similarities between their families and that of Jesus Christ.

Grammy, Do You Love Me? is a story about a little bunny who plays a game with his grandmother to see how much she loves him. Puppies are featured in *Roly Poly Puppies*, a counting book for very young readers, which Moore wrote about several Australian shepherd puppies who suddenly appeared in her yard one day after escaping from their own home.

Escaping is what Joy would like to do in *I'd Rather Be Eaten by Sharks* when she has to stand up in front of the class and make an oral report. In this hilarious volume (which forms an integrated language arts program with its teacher's study guide) Moore gives public speaking tips for children. Just getting to school while parents are away can be a real challenge for children, especially if the person staying with them is as unconventional as Sarah and Zac's Aunt Mary, who wears mismatched socks to match her mood. It is not until Aunt Mary writes a letter to the children's teacher excusing them for being late that Sarah really starts to worry in *Sarah with an "H"*.

In another novel about school situations, Moore collaborated on *The Substitute Teacher from Mars* with some of her classroom authors. Older readers will identify with the pranks a sixth grade class pulls on a succession of substitute teachers as the kids attempt to make *The Guinness Book of Records* for having the most substitute teachers in a single year. The class is headed for infamy until the substitute teacher from Mars appears. In *Who Let Girls in the Boys' Locker Room?*, chaos of a different kind breaks out at school when petite Michelle and two of her sixth-grade girlfriends try out for and make the formerly all-boys' basketball team. There are rivalries between girls, boys, girls and boys, and brothers and sisters in this action-packed novel. But, the differences between boys and girls reach new heights—or lows—in *The Peanut Butter Trap*, when Frank McCormick puts bubble gum in Crystal's braids. It is peanut butter to the rescue, until the sandwich spread is used to trap Frank to make him eat his words ... and other things.

Another boy's trouble with words—on paper, this time—lead him into one of Moore's most outrageous

adventure novels, *Help! There's a Mastodon in My Living Room*. Jason is supposed to be reading his assigned book list, not watching television. What happens when he disobeys can best be described as an ecological time-travel nightmare that involves a wooly mammoth and the king of rock 'n' roll.

Whether her subject matter is families, children's difficulty accepting change, or Elvis Presley, Moore's picture books for very young children and novels for young readers are prime examples of the writing strategies she teaches children in her writer-in-residence programs. As Moore told Sandra Jontz-Merrifield in *Potomac News*, "My goal always is that the child should get the best book possible. That's why I do it. It can't be for the money, because you don't get very much. Turning kids into writers—that's my goal."

■ Works Cited

Christopherson, Sandy, review of *Jesus Had a Family Just Like Me* and *What Is a Family?*, *Lutheran Libraries*, spring, 1988, p. 69.

Review of *Deep River*, *Publishers Weekly*, May 9, 1994, p. 72.

Review of *Grandma's Promise*, *New Advocate*, winter, 1989, p. 56.

Jontz-Merrifield, Sandra, "Children's Author Finds Fulfillment in Classroom," *Potomac News*, October 7, 1994.

Kupetz, Barbara N., "Young and Old Together: Bridging the Gap with Books," *Reading Today*, June/July, 1994.

Meizner, Kathie, review of *Grandma's House*, *School Library Journal*, September, 1985, p. 122.

Parr, Caroline, review of *Deep River*, *School Library Journal*, August, 1994, p. 141.

Rollin, Lucy, "Picture Book Gives Subject of Summer at Grandma's Special Poignancy," *Record* (Columbia, SC), March 6, 1986.

Weisman, Kay, review of *Grandma's Garden*, *Booklist*, June 1, 1994, p. 1842.

■ For More Information See

PERIODICALS

Kirkus Reviews, May 1, 1994, p. 634.
Potomac News, October, 1993, pp. C1, C4.
St. Louis Post-Dispatch, August 25, 1985.
School Library Journal, April, 1988, p. 82; May, 1994, p. 100.
Trout, summer, 1994, p. 62.

—*Sketch by Mel Wathen*

*   *   *

MULLER, (Lester) Robin 1953-

■ Personal

Born October 30, 1953, in Toronto, Ontario, Canada; son of Frederick Walter and Sara Ada (Thomas) Muller.

ROBIN MULLER

Education: Algonquin College, 1979; attended George Brown College, 1982.

■ Addresses

Home—26 Wardell St., Toronto, Ontario, Canada.

■ Career

Fine artist, editorial illustrator, and set designer. University of Toronto, Fine Art Department, Toronto, Ontario, studio coordinator, 1977-83; Graph Em, Toronto, art director, 1984. *Member:* Canadian Writers Union, Canadian Society of Children's Authors, Illustrators, and Performers (CANSCAIP).

■ Awards, Honors

Toronto Art Directors Award, 1982, and Silver Birch Award, Ontario Library Association, 1995, both for *Mollie Whuppie and the Giant;* New York Art Directors Award, 1984, for "Carrion Comfort"; Best Children's Book of the Year Award, I.O.D.E. (International Order of the Daughters of the Empire), 1985, and Alcuin Award for excellence in book design, 1986, both for *The Sorcerer's Apprentice;* Ezra Jack Keats Memorial Silver Medal, 1986, for various works; Governor General's

Award for illustration, 1989, for *The Magic Paintbrush;* Studio Magazine Award, 1991, and Canadian Library Association Notable Book citation, 1992, both for *The Nightwood.*

■ Writings

RETELLER OF FOLKTALES; SELF-ILLUSTRATED

Mollie Whuppie and the Giant, Scholastic, 1982.
Tatterhood, Scholastic, 1984.
The Sorcerer's Apprentice, Kids Can Press, 1985.
The Lucky Old Woman, Kids Can Press, 1987.
Little Kay, Scholastic, 1988.
The Magic Paintbrush, Doubleday (Canada), 1989, Viking, 1992.
The Nightwood, Doubleday, 1991.

OTHER

Hickory Dickory Dock, illustrated by Suzanne Dureanceau, Scholastic, 1992.
(Self-illustrated) *Row, Row, Row Your Boat,* North Winds/Scholastic, 1993.
(Self-illustrated) *Little Wonder,* North Winds/Scholastic, 1994.

■ Sidelights

Robin Muller's talent lies in being able to take old folktales and retell or adapt them so that they are clear, interesting and relevant to twentieth-century readers. Almost of all of the stories Muller chooses have heroes and heroines who are young, feisty, brave, and smart. Faced with obstacles and limitations, they each find ways to turn negatives into positives and come out a better person as well. "Like all good adaptors of traditional narratives," Jon C. Stott commented in *Twentieth-Century Children's Writers,* "Robin Muller discovers the contemporary relevance of old motifs and tale types, and in the timeless essences of the stories, themes that speak to young readers of the late twentieth century."

The first of these heroines is Mollie Whuppie, the youngest of three sisters abandoned in the woods, whose story is told in *Mollie Whuppie and the Giant.* In text that Anne Gilmore described in *Quill & Quire* as "elegant" with "simple yet evocative similes," Muller tells how Mollie succeeds at three demanding tests of courage before she can destroy the giant. Gilmore also praised the black and white illustrations as being "rich in detail" and "startlingly effective," while Mary Ainslie Smith noted in *Books in Canada* that Muller's artwork had "all the details just right."

The heroine in Muller's *Tatterhood* is less immediately likable. She's wild and mischievous, rides a goat and wears outrageous clothing, and suffers in comparison to her beautiful, lovable sister Belinda. But when a witch removes Belinda's head and replaces it with that of a calf, Tatterhood comes to the rescue. When the two girls flee they, of course, meet two young princes, one of whom is immediately smitten with Belinda. When the other, Galen, admires Tatterhood's courage, she is transformed into a lovely maiden. In *Canadian Children's Literature,* Murray J. Evans admired Muller's skill at portraying expressive faces, especially "Galen's astonished visage at Tatterhood's transformation, with her back as yet to the reader, until the page turns to reveal the beautiful face which we saw Galen seeing."

In what is perhaps an autobiographical touch, the young hero of *The Sorcerer's Apprentice* is named Robin. This is not the tale made so famous by the Disney movie *Fantasia.* Instead, it is the story of a hungry, homeless young boy apprenticed to a wicked magician. Robin is determined to learn good spells to countermand his master's evil schemes. He is helped by a white dove, who turns out in the end to be an enchanted princess. Ellen Mandel, writing for *Booklist,* noted the "masterfully phrased text in this magical retelling of a fanciful classic," and Ronald A. Van De Voorde, in his *School Library Journal* review, praised the "realistically drawn" illustrations in blues, browns, and yellows as "dramatic, detailed, and effective." Muller explained the technique he used for the effective illustrations in *The Sorcerer's Apprentice:* "I splattered the paper with a dusting of black ink flicked off of a toothbrush and modeled it into a background, foreground, and middle ground with the use of an exacto knife. I then used pencil crayons for color, rubbing the color in with tissue paper."

The only one of Muller's books to have an elderly heroine, *The Lucky Old Woman* was called a "refreshing change" from the typical fairy tale by Andy Butcher in a *Books for Your Children* review, explaining that in this tale "mild manners, rather than muscle and might, earn the best." An old woman who makes her living running errands for wealthier folk one day runs into Grumpleteaser, a malevolent gnome. Although he teases and tricks the old woman continuously, he is finally worn down by her simplicity and goodness. Mary Ainslie Smith praised the "lively" story in *Books in Canada,* and called Muller's elderly protagonist "a sympathetic creation."

Coming back to younger heroines, Muller created *Little Kay,* a fairy tale with decidedly modern overtones. One day, a sultan sends a message to all the townsfolk that every household is to send a son to the palace for a year's knightly service. A magician with only three daughters fears the sultan's retribution. But Little Kay persuades her father to let her go to the sultan disguised as a boy. The suspicious sultan tries several times to unmask Little Kay, but each time she proves braver and stronger than the boys. She is finally discovered, however, and her family is about to be punished when she uses her wit and agility to save the land from a fearsome ogre. Susan Perren, writing in *Books for Young People,* described Muller's language as "simple, forceful, and funny," and hailed the "simply wonderful" illustrations. *Books in Canada* contributor Linda Granfield similarly found the illustrations "glorious, filled with textures and swirls of colour, moving from silhouette to patterned borders and back," and concluded that this artwork,

when added to the action-filled and humorous text, creates "a refreshing and amusing look" at equality.

The essence of art and artists is the theme of Muller's *The Magic Paintbrush.* Based on an old Chinese tale, it is the story of Nib, a talented young artist who rescues an old wizard, and, as a reward, is given a paintbrush that will make his paintings real. When the king hears of Nib's talent, he wants the boy to make him even more powerful than he already is. Nib outsmarts the king with his clever use of the paintbrush (he sends the king and his newly painted navy out to sea in a storm), then throws away the brush because he realizes the best pictures are "the ones you make with your heart." While she found the text "too complicated," *School Library Journal* contributor Shirley Wilton observed that the "richly detailed and sophisticated" artwork, full of details and references to classic artists, will appeal to both adults and children.

The Nightwood is a retelling of one of the oldest Scottish folktales, that of Tamlynne. One evening, Elaine, the daughter of the Earl of March, journeys into the forbidden Nightwood. There she plucks a single red rose that summons the young knight Tamlynne, who is doomed to be sacrificed unless the love of a mortal can save him. Elaine stands fast during the fight for his soul, and because of her love, Tamlynne becomes mortal. In a review for *Canadian Children's Literature,* Terri L. Lyons commented that "the story literally pulsates with suspense and foreboding, but, as with every good folktale, all is right with the world in the end." She added that Muller's unique illustrations of the faery dance, filled with evil creatures who look out of the page right at the reader, are "eerie and deliciously disconcerting."

Muller has also retold two of the most familiar of all children's rhymes: *Row, Row, Row Your Boat* and *Hickory, Dickory, Dock.* In the latter, a nattily dressed gentleman cat is throwing a party. When a debonair masked mouse and other unexpected guests arrive, chaos ensues. In Muller's interpretation of *Row, Row, Row Your Boat,* the song has been expanded and provided with a plot in which a badger dreams of being a sailor and sets out for his adventure in a rowboat. Muller, who drew the illustrations on bond paper with colored pencils, has dressed all his characters in Edwardian garb and, according to Granfield in *Quill & Quire,* "taken a monotonous childhood tune and given it new life."

"I draw my inspirations from folk and fairy tales," Muller once commented. "These stories are often the first introduction a child has to the world at large, to his or her own heritage, and the importance of history...."

"Being an author/illustrator is a full-time endeavor; the majority of that time is spent on the illustrations, for which I set high standards. The reader is rewarded with a high quality picture that pulls them into the story and leaves them lingering on the page...."

In *Row, Row, Row Your Boat,* Muller takes a popular children's song and turns it into a rollicking adventure. (Illustration by the author.)

"I believe there should be a richness to children's illustration," Muller concluded, "something that will embroider the imaginations of young readers."

■ Works Cited

Butcher, Andy, review of *The Lucky Old Woman, Books for Your Children,* spring, 1988, p. 7.

Evans, Murray J., "Middle Ages for Young Ages," *Canadian Children's Literature,* Number 39/40, 1985, pp. 145-48.

Gilmore, Anne, review of *Mollie Whuppie and the Giant, Quill & Quire,* February, 1983, pp. 35-36.

Granfield, Linda, review of *Little Kay, Books in Canada,* April, 1989, p. 37.

Granfield, Linda, review of *Row, Row, Row Your Boat, Quill & Quire,* September, 1993, p. 68.

Lyons, Terri L., review of *The Nightwood, Canadian Children's Literature,* Number 73, 1994, p. 88-89.

Mandel, Ellen, review of *The Sorcerer's Apprentice, Booklist,* January 17, 1987, p. 787.

Muller, Robin, *The Magic Paintbrush,* Doubleday (Canada), 1989.

Perren, Susan, "Feisty Young Heroines' Offbeat Adventures," *Books for Young People,* February, 1989, p. 9.

Smith, Mary Ainslie, review of *Mollie Whuppie and the Giant, Books in Canada,* December, 1982, p. 9.

Smith, Mary Ainslie, review of *The Lucky Old Woman, Books in Canada,* December, 1987, p. 14.

Stott, Jon C., "Robin Muller," *Twentieth-Century Children's Writers,* 4th edition, St. James Press, 1995, p. 687.

Van De Voorde, Ronald A., review of *The Sorcerer's Apprentice, School Library Journal,* February, 1987, p. 72.

Wilton, Shirley, review of *The Magic Paintbrush, School Library Journal,* July, 1990, p. 78.

For More Information See

PERIODICALS

Booklist, May 1, 1994, p. 1609.
Books in Canada, April, 1992, pp. 44-45.
Canadian Children's Literature, Number 57/58, 1990, pp. 116-117; Number 63, 1991, pp. 83-87.
Junior Bookshelf, February, 1987, p. 22.
Quill & Quire, February, 1985, pp. 10, 12, 14; September, 1994, p. 69.
School Library Journal, May, 1994, p. 109.

* * *

MUMFORD, Ruth 1919-
(Ruth Dallas)

Personal

Born September 29, 1919, in Invercargill, New Zealand; daughter of Francis Sydney (in business) and Minnie Jane (Johnson) Mumford. *Education:* Attended Southland Technical College, Invercargill, New Zealand.

Addresses

Home—448 Leith St., Dunedin, New Zealand.

Career

Poet and children's writer. Began to write as a child for the children's page of the *Southland Daily News* (now *Southland Times*), 1932. *Member:* PEN (New Zealand).

Awards, Honors

New Zealand Literary Fund achievement award, 1963, for *The Turning Wheel;* Robert Burns Fellow at the University of Otago, 1968; New Zealand Book Award in poetry, 1977, for *Steps of the Sun;* Buckland Literature Award, 1977, for *Song for a Guitar and Other Songs;* D.Litt., University of Otago, 1978.

Writings

CHILDREN'S FICTION; UNDER PSEUDONYM RUTH DALLAS

Ragamuffin Scarecrow, illustrated by Els Noordhof, University of Otago Bibliography Room, 1969.
The Children in the Bush, illustrated by Peter Campbell, Methuen, 1969.
A Dog Called Wig, illustrated by Edward Mortelmans, Methuen, 1970.
The Wild Boy in the Bush, illustrated by Peter Campbell, Methuen, 1971.
The Big Flood in the Bush, illustrated by Peter Campbell, Methuen, 1972, Scholastic, 1974.
The House on the Cliffs, illustrated by Gavin Rowe, Methuen, 1975.
Shining Rivers, illustrated by Gareth Floyd, Methuen, 1979.
Holiday Time in the Bush, illustrated by Gary Hebley, Methuen, 1983.

CHILDREN'S NONFICTION; UNDER PSEUDONYM RUTH DALLAS

Sawmilling Yesterday, illustrated by Juliet Peter, Department of Education (Wellington, New Zealand), 1958.
Curved Horizon: An Autobiography, University of Otago Press, 1991.

POETRY; UNDER PSEUDONYM RUTH DALLAS

Country Road and Other Poems 1947-1952, Caxton Press, 1953.
The Turning Wheel, Caxton Press, 1961.
Experiment in Form, University of Otago Bibliography Room, 1964.
Day Book: Poems of a Year, Caxton Press, 1966.
Shadow Show, Caxton Press, 1968.
Walking on the Snow, Caxton Press, 1976.
Song for a Guitar and Other Songs, edited by Charles Brasch, University of Otago Press, 1976.
Steps of the Sun, Caxton Press, 1979.
Collected Poems, University of Otago Press, 1987.

Contributor to *An Anthology of Twentieth Century New Zealand Poetry,* edited by Vincent O'Sullivan, Oxford University Press, 1970, and *Ten Modern New Zealand Poets,* Longman, 1974. Contributor to literary quarterlies, including *Landfall, Meanjin,* and *Islands,* and to school journals.

Dallas's manuscripts are collected in the Hocken Library at the University of Otago, Dunedin, New Zealand.

Sidelights

Author and poet Ruth Mumford, who writes under the pseudonym Ruth Dallas, is well-known for her commitment to the children's literature of New Zealand. Dallas is a native New Zealander and was raised on the southern tip of South Island. Development was sparse in that area of New Zealand, and Dallas's family enjoyed the solitude. The only books Dallas had, however, were about people who lived in large European cities she had never seen. To Dallas's extreme disappointment, there were no books for young readers depicting the rough natural beauty of New Zealand or describing the lives of New Zealanders. She decided that when she grew up she would write books about children in New Zealand.

Dallas has since written widely for children, and in particular, about her childhood during the European settlement of New Zealand. Her grandparents and great-grandparents were early settlers, and the stories they handed down served as the basis and inspiration for her books.

In *The Wild Boy in The Bush,* three adventuresome youngsters discover the bones of a moa (an extinct flightless bird), a cave which seems to be the ideal hideout, and, most surprisingly, a wild boy who is living alone in the bush. "By letting an eight-year-old tell the tale, [Dallas] tunes right in, both vocabulary-wise and fictionally, to the wavelength of younger readers," remarked Alice Andrews in *Books and Bookmen.* In *Holiday Time in the Bush* Dallas describes the pioneer children's preparations for Christmas. The book is "full of typical happenings of an ordinary family, and this is what makes the story such an acceptable read," noted a *Junior Bookshelf* reviewer.

Dallas set *Shining Rivers* in the 1860s, during New Zealand's gold rush. Johnie and his parents have set out for New Zealand from Great Britain, but Johnie's father dies en route, and Johnie has to go to work as soon as he and his mother land. He finds work in a bakery, but succumbs to the lure of gold and begins prospecting. Johnie meets with both success and failure in the goldfields before returning home to begin life as a farmer. Johnie is a "boy trying to cope with a man's world and managing to do so remarkably well," observed a *Junior Bookshelf* reviewer. Margery Fisher in *Growing Point* found Dallas's depiction of the New Zealand landscape evocative, but concluded that the story and characters were less than convincing.

■ Works Cited

Andrews, Alice, "Child's-eye View," *Books and Bookmen,* December, 1971, p. R14.
Fisher, Margery, "Steam and Elbow-Grease," *Growing Point,* January, 1980, pp. 3619-24.
Review of *Holiday Time in the Bush, Junior Bookshelf,* August, 1983, p. 161.
Review of *Shining Rivers, Junior Bookshelf,* April, 1980, p. 80.

■ For More Information See

PERIODICALS

Growing Point, May, 1983, pp. 4072-76.
School Librarian, March, 1980, p. 54.*

N

NAUGHTON, Bill
See NAUGHTON, William John (Francis)

* * *

NAUGHTON, William John (Francis)
1910-1992
(Bill Naughton)

■ Personal

Born June 12, 1910, in Ballyhaunis, County Mayo, Ireland; died January 9, 1992, on the Isle of Man, United Kingdom; son of Thomas (a coal miner) and Maria (Fleming) Naughton; married Ernestine Pirolt. *Education:* Attended St. Peter and St. Paul School, Bolton, Lancashire, England. *Religion:* Catholic.

■ Career

Writer and playwright. Worked as a laborer, truck driver, weaver, coal bagger and bleacher before becoming a playwright in the 1950s. *Wartime service:* Civil Defense driver in London, England, during World War II.

■ Awards, Honors

Screenwriters Guild awards, 1967 and 1968; Prix Italia, 1974, for *The Mystery;* Children's Rights Workshop Other Award, 1978, for *The Goalkeeper's Revenge.*

■ Writings

CHILDREN'S FICTION; UNDER NAME BILL NAUGHTON

Pony Boy, Pilot Press, 1946.

The Goalkeeper's Revenge and Other Stories, illustrated by Dick De Wilde, Harrap, 1961.

The Goalkeeper's Revenge [and] *Spit Nolan,* illustrated by Trevor Stubley, Macmillan (London), 1974.

A Dog Called Nelson, illustrated by Charles Mozley, Dent, 1976.

WILLIAM JOHN NAUGHTON

My Pal Spadger, illustrated by Mozley, Dent, 1977.

Split Nolan, illustrated by Kate Brennan Hall, Creative Education, 1988.

ADULT AUTOBIOGRAPHY; UNDER NAME BILL NAUGHTON

A Roof Over Your Head, Pilot Press, 1945.

On the Pig's Back: An Autobiographical Excursion, Oxford University Press, 1987.

Saintly Billy: A Catholic Boyhood, Oxford University Press, 1988.

NOVELS FOR ADULTS; UNDER NAME BILL NAUGHTON

Rafe Granite, Pilot Press, 1947.

One Small Boy, MacGibbon & Kee (London), 1957.

Alfie, MacGibbon & Kee, 1966, Ballantine, 1966.

Alfie, Darling, MacGibbon & Kee, 1970, Simon & Schuster, 1971.

SHORT STORIES FOR ADULTS; UNDER NAME BILL NAUGHTON

Late Night on Watling Street and Other Stories, MacGibbon & Kee, 1959, Ballantine, 1966.

The Bees Have Stopped Working and Other Stories, Wheaton, 1976.

PLAYS; UNDER NAME BILL NAUGHTON

My Flesh, My Blood (two-act comedy; first broadcast in 1957; revised version first produced as *Spring and Port Wine* in Birmingham, England, 1964, and at the West End, 1965; also produced as *Keep It in the Family* on Broadway at Plymouth Theatre, Septem-

ber 27, 1967), Samuel French, 1959, published as *Spring and Port Wine,* 1967.

June Evening (first broadcast in 1958; produced in Birmingham, 1966), Samuel French, 1973.

She'll Make Trouble (first broadcast in 1958), published in *Worth a Hearing: A Collection of Radio Plays,* edited by Alfred Bradley, Blackie & Son, 1967.

All in Good Time (first televised in 1961 as *Honeymoon Postponed;* produced in London, 1963, and New York City, 1965), Samuel French, 1964.

Alfie (three-act; first broadcast in 1962 as *Alfie Elkins and His Little Life;* produced as *Alfie* in London, 1963, New York, 1964), Samuel French, 1963.

He Was Gone When We Got There, music by Leonard Salzedo, first produced in London, 1966.

Annie and Fanny, first produced in Bolton, Lancashire, England, at Octagon Theatre, 1967.

Lighthearted Intercourse, first produced in Liverpool, England, at Liverpool Playhouse, December 1, 1971.

(With others) *A Special Occasion: Three Plays* (includes *A Special Occasion,* first broadcast as a radio play, 1982), Longman, 1988.

Also author of radio plays: *Timothy,* 1956, *My Flesh, My Blood,* 1957, *She'll Make Trouble,* 1958, *June*

Michael Caine starred in the 1966 movie, *Alfie,* Naughton's adaptation of his humorous play about a cockney Don Juan which became his best-known work.

Evening, 1958, *Late Night on Watling Street*, 1959, *The Long Carry*, 1959, *Seeing a Beauty Queen Home*, 1960, *On the Run*, 1960, *Wigan to Rome*, 1960, *'30-'60*, 1960, *Jackie Crowe*, 1962, *November Day*, 1963, and *The Mystery*, 1973. Author of television plays: *Nathaniel Titlark* (series), 1957, *Starr and Company* (series), 1958, (with Allan Prior) *Yorky* (series), 1960-61, *Looking for Frankie*, 1961, *Honeymoon Postponed*, 1961, *Somewhere for the Night*, 1962, and *It's Your Move*, 1967.

SCREENPLAYS; UNDER NAME BILL NAUGHTON

Alfie (adaptation of Naughton's play of the same title), Paramount, 1966.
(With Roy Boulting and Jeffrey Dell) *The Family Way* (adaptation of Naughton's play *All in Good Time*), Warner Brothers, 1967.
Spring and Port Wine (adaptation of Naughton's play of the same title), Warner-Pathe, 1970.

■ Sidelights

Best known to adults for *Alfie*, William John Naughton, who wrote under the name Bill Naughton, was a British playwright, novelist, short story writer and memoirist whose autobiographical and semi-autobiographical books are of particular interest to young adult readers. His tremendous output of plays for the stage, screen, television and radio is noteworthy, especially since Naughton began writing plays for radio and the theater only when he was in his forties, after a varied career as a laborer, truck driver, coal bagger and weaver. No matter what the medium, most of Naughton's work is based on his life, primarily his childhood in poverty and his experiences as a young man in working-class Lancashire, England, during the Great Depression. Reviewers have celebrated the author's talent for presenting children and young adults realistically in terms of their families and peers.

Throughout his career, Naughton wrote about the people, places and times that he knew best—those he had grown up with, first in a hamlet in Ireland and then in the small coal mining town of Bolton in the county of Lancashire in England. When Naughton was four years old, many members of the family moved to England and shared a crowded home in Bolton, where Naughton's father and uncles found employment in the "pits" or the "colliers," as the coal mines were called.

Naughton's memoir based on his earliest recollections of his childhood, *Saintly Billy: A Catholic Boyhood*, focuses on how the demands of work and the socioeconomic conditions of the time shaped the life of his family and the people around him. Naughton himself responded by becoming intensely involved with the Roman Catholic church after his family moved to England. Although not every young adult reader may have shared Naughton's fascination with a religion or its rituals, it is easy to identify with Naughton's description of himself as a child staring longingly into a store window at the calendars of religious festivals which he could not afford, no matter how hard he saved for them. The days and events highlighted on the date books

represented special times to be anticipated; as the author explained in *Saintly Billy*, these calendars "offered an annual string of feast-days and celebrations which brought an excitement and purpose to a [child's] life lacking incentives." "Ending this book is like waking from a peculiarly vivid dream," Dervla Murphy commented in the *Times Literary Supplement*. "The reader seems really to have been living in Bolton's slums in the 1920s, experiencing all the tensions and humiliations of extreme poverty, but also being amused and sustained by the wit and generosity of one's neighbors."

Naughton's first novel based on his boyhood was *Pony Boy*, the nickname used in England during the 1930s for delivery boys who drove pony carts around London. In 1966, a *Times Literary Supplement* critic wrote that this 1946 novel presented "a world where the adolescent's chief problem was worth rather than leisure." The two leading characters, Ginger and Corky, get and then manage to lose their jobs as pony boys. Jobless, the boys hitch a ride to Liverpool where they hope to be hired as hands on an ocean-going vessel. When that scheme fails, they return home safely. The *Times Literary Supplement* critic wrote that although *Pony Boy* "is episodic, dated, sentimental, even crude at times ... Naughton's characters and dialogue bang off the page with a force and life that none of the other more polished books can match. He catches too the wild swinging of adolescent mood."

Many of Naughton's other works of fiction for children are based on his own childhood experiences or those of the people around him. *The Goalkeeper's Revenge and Other Stories*, published in 1961, focuses on delinquency. (This book was reissued in 1974 with *Spit Nolan*.) In 1971 a *Times Literary Supplement* reviewer commented that in this work, "accomplished dialogue and a keen sense of youthful delinquency lull the reader past a succession of Mr. Naughton's urban folk heroes." Although *Books and Bookmen* contributor Auberon Waugh felt that Naughton's work *A Dog Called Nelson* "has little incident, no tension, too much whimsy and moves too slowly," he also confessed, "I quite liked it."

Naughton's 1977 venture into fiction for children, *My Pal Spadger*, fared better with the critics. In this novel Naughton writes about a boyhood friendship. "With a fine sense of what will appeal to young readers, he begins the collection of short incidents centering on Spadger, calm, resourceful, imaginative, so different in every way from the other boys, with an account of the time his small brother fell into the earth closet [the privy]," wrote a reviewer for *Junior Bookshelf*. The book is full of harsh reality leavened with fun. The book "evokes an authentic picture of urban childhood," Tim Hopkins decreed in *New Statesman*.

■ Works Cited

Review of *The Goalkeeper's Revenge and Other Stories*, *Times Literary Supplement*, December 3, 1971, p. 1512.

Hopkins, Tim, "Matters of Form," *New Statesman*, May 19, 1978, p. 683.

Murphy, Dervla, "Faith Among the Ashpits," *Times Literary Supplement*, April 1-7, 1988, p. 351.

Review of *My Pal Spadger, Junior Bookshelf*, June 1977, p. 181.

Naughton, Bill, *Saintly Billy: A Catholic Boyhood*, Oxford University Press, 1988.

Review of *Pony Boy, Times Literary Supplement*, November 24, 1966, p. 1085.

Waugh, Auberon, review of *A Dog Called Nelson, Books and Bookmen*, December 1976, p. 76.

■ For More Information See

BOOKS

Dictionary of Literary Biography, Volume 13: *British Dramatists since World War II*, Gale, 1982.

Twentieth-Century Children's Writers, fourth edition, St. James Press, 1995, pp. 691-692.

PERIODICALS

Books, March 1988, p. 20.

New Statesman and Society, July 7, 1989, pp. 42-3.*

—*Sketch by Mary Lawrence Wathen*

*   *   *

LILITH NORMAN

NORMAN, Lilith 1927-

■ Personal

Given name is pronounced "*Lie*-lith"; born November 27, 1927, in Sydney, New South Wales, Australia. *Education:* Studied with Library Association of Australia. *Politics:* "Small 'l' liberal, left of center." *Hobbies and other interests:* Animals, films, opera, conservation, reading, food, and "what makes people tick."

■ Addresses

Home—21 Rhodes Ave., Naremburn, New South Wales 2065, Australia. *Agent*—Margaret Connelly & Associates, 37 Ormond St., Paddington, New South Wales 2021, Australia.

■ Career

Newtown Municipal Library, Sydney, Australia, library assistant, 1947-49; Bonnington Hotel, London, England, telephonist, 1950-51; Angus & Robertson Books, Sydney, book shop assistant, 1951-53; Balmain District Hospital, Sydney, nursing trainee, 1953-56; City of Sydney Public Library, Sydney, library assistant, 1956-58, research officer, 1958-66, children's librarian, 1966-70; New South Wales Department of Education, *School Magazine*, Sydney, assistant editor, 1970-76, editor, 1976-78; full-time writer, 1978—. *Member:* Library Association of Australia (branch councillor, 1969-70; president of Children's Libraries Section, New South Wales Division, 1969-71), Australian Society of Au-

thors, Children's Book Council of New South Wales (treasurer, 1968-70).

■ Awards, Honors

Commendation from Children's Book Council Australian Book Awards, 1971, for *Climb a Lonely Hill;* Queen's Silver Jubilee Medal, 1977; IBBY Honour Book, Australia, 1980, for *A Dream of Seas.*

■ Writings

FOR CHILDREN

Climb a Lonely Hill, Collins, 1970, Walck, 1972.

The Shape of Three, Collins, 1971, Walck, 1972.

The Flame Takers, Collins, 1973.

Mocking-Bird Man (reader), illustrated by Astra Lacis, Hodder & Stoughton, 1977.

A Dream of Seas, illustrated by Edwina Bell, Collins, 1978.

My Simple Little Brother, illustrated by David Rae, Collins, 1979.

The Hex, Nelson Educational, 1989.

The Laurel & Hardy Kids, Random House, 1989.

The Paddock: A Story in Praise of the Earth (picture book), illustrated by Robert Roennfeldt, Random House, 1992.

Aphanasy (picture book), illustrated by Maxim Svetlanov, Random House, 1994.

The Beetle (picture book; retelling of a Hans Christian
   Andersen tale), illustrated by Maxim Svetlanov,
   Random House, 1995.

FOR ADULTS

*The Brown and Yellow: Sydney Girls' High School 1883-
   1983,* Oxford University Press, 1983.

NONFICTION

The City of Sydney: Official Guide, Sydney City Council,
   1959.
Facts about Sydney, Sydney City Council, 1959.
Asia: A Select Reading List, Sydney City Council, 1959.
Some Notes on the Early Land Grants at Potts Point,
   Sydney City Council, 1959.
A History of the City of Sydney Public Library, Sydney
   City Council, 1960.
Notes on the Glebe, Sydney City Council, 1960.
Historical Notes on Paddington, Sydney City Council,
   1961.
Historical Notes on Newtown, Sydney City Council,
   1962.

OTHER

Also author of episode for television series, *Catch
Kandy,* 1973. Contributor to *Reading Time* and *School
Magazine.* Editor, *Felis,* Journal of Siamese Cat Society
of New South Wales, 1965-69.

■ Sidelights

An author of diverse books ranging from realistic
adventure to fantasy and, more recently, lyrical picture
books, Lilith Norman creates works for children that are
consistent in their love for the author's native Australian landscape and their realistic young protagonists. A
librarian by profession, Norman did not begin writing
for children until she was in her forties. "I managed to
avoid becoming a writer for quite a long time, mainly, I
think, because it seemed like very hard work for a very
speculative result," she said in *Twentieth-Century Children's Writers.* "It wasn't until I started working as a
children's librarian that I realized *these* were the books I
wanted to write.... I like to write about ordinary
children trying to cope, for I believe that most of us can
cope with whatever is thrown at us, *if we really have
to*—otherwise we'd all be living in caves still."

Norman's first two novels, *Climb a Lonely Hill* and *The
Shape of Three,* depict just these types of children. The
former work is an adventure tale set in the Australian
outback. Young Jack and Sue Clarke are stranded in
inhospitable country when the truck they are riding in
with their uncle crashes and their uncle dies. With little
food and water to help them survive until they can be
rescued, they have to risk a trek into the distant hills to
find a waterhole. What follows is a realistic depiction of
their grueling journey under the unrelenting desert sun
and eventual rescue. Though critics didn't find the
premise of the story particularly original, and one
Booklist critic called the conclusion "contrived," reviewers admired the novel for its skillful characterization and faithful rendering of the Australian outback. As

**Stranded in the Australian bush after an accident kills
their uncle, Jack and his sister struggle for survival in
this 1970 adventure commended by Australia's
Children's Book Council.**

one *Times Literary Supplement* contributor commented, Norman is able to draw the reader into the story
because "the children are real children, frail and recognizable; one cares about their fate." The critic concluded, "The book will be a sad experience for soft-hearted
readers and yet a worthwhile one, for it is an honest
book."

With her second novel, *The Shape of Three,* Norman
examines a different type of challenge in an inhospitable
environment. In this case, a newborn twin is accidental-
ly switched with the boy of another mother while they're
at the hospital. Bruce is sent home to become the only
child of the wealthy Protestant Cunningham family,
while Shane is taken home with Bruce's twin brother,
Greg, to the large Catholic Herbert family. Greg and
Shane are raised together as fraternal twins, and all
seems well until Greg and Bruce meet and discover their
remarkable similarity in appearance. When their mothers learn of this—and blood tests prove who the real
twins are—they insist that Bruce and Shane be switched
back again, which results in both boys being miserable,
since they are not used to the new families that have
been forced upon them. Only after much emotional

suffering is it finally decided that the boys should be returned again to the families they have known since birth. Critical reaction to *The Shape of Three* was mixed. A reviewer in *Bulletin of the Center for Children's Books* felt that the "characterization and dialogue are adroit," and that Norman's comparisons of Catholic and Protestant households is well done, but added that the "book's weakness is that it smacks of the documentary approach to a case history."

After her first two books, Norman began to venture into the genre of fantasy. *The Flame Takers* is an unusual blend of reality and fantasy about the talented Malory family—the parents are actors and their son is a musician—who are subjected to the wicked machinations of a sadistic schoolmaster and the mysterious "flame takers" who destroy people's talent, and then helped by a rotund German chess aficionado. In a way that is not really explained in the story, the schoolmaster and the flame takers seek to extinguish the family's flame of talent and turn them into uninspired, materialistic, card-carrying members of the bourgeoisie, but are thwarted by the German and by the boy's sister who, having no particular talents, is able to stand up to the flame takers. "Put like this," one critic in *Times*

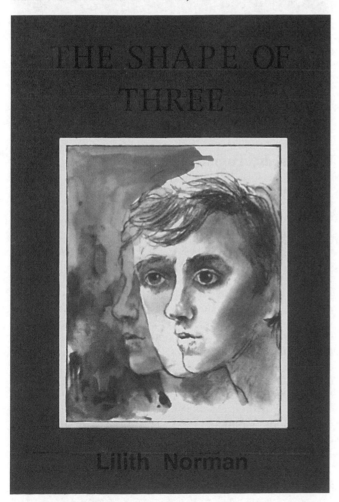

Imagine Greg Herbert's astonishment when, after already having a fraternal twin brother Shane, he runs into his exact double.

Literary Supplement remarked, "it sounds ridiculous but it is in fact a powerful and exciting allegory."

Norman once again blends fantasy and reality in *A Dream of Seas.* Taking a much more lyrical approach to the genre than in her previous novel, Norman writes about a young Australian boy nicknamed "Seasie," whose father has recently drowned. His mother takes him to live near Bondi Beach, where Seasie becomes obsessed with the sea (thus his nickname). The story of his growing interest in the sea is paralleled by the tale of a young seal's maturation from pup to young adult. As the novel progresses, Seasie's existence among humans becomes more like a dream, while the life of the sea becomes increasingly real. Boy and seal's lives draw closer together, and when Seasie's mother remarries and becomes pregnant his final ties to human civilization are broken; he embraces the ocean and becomes one with the seal. The story shows "how a boy achieves independence and a separate identity," Margery Fisher pointed out in *Growing Point.* As the boy matures, so does the seal, so that the ending "seems an inevitable if fantastic climax to a perfectly rational story."

Norman's love for the Australian landscape, which can be seen throughout her works, is especially poignant in her picture book, *The Paddock: A Story in Praise of the Earth.* Focusing on a particular plot of land in Australia, the author follows its history from original formation, through the age of dinosaurs, to the first human settlements, and finally its death from industrial usage, but the ending implies that the land will be reborn again after mankind leaves. Calling this picture book a "hymn to the resilience and dominance of the land," a *Publishers Weekly* critic felt that Norman's "dense imagery will likely be beyond the book's intended audience." On the other hand, a *Junior Bookshelf* reviewer praised the "beautifully composed text" adding that "today's children will understand what it is saying."

As Betty Gilderdale observed in *Twentieth-Century Children's Writers,* Norman's books tend to be interested in "the effect of environment on character." Whether she is writing about the influences and challenges of the natural environment on her young protagonists, or the effects of family and other social pressures, her themes have often been related in at least some way to this subject. The author, however, does not like to analyze her books, believing instead that they should be self-explanatory. As she once commented, "It seems to me that a book should speak directly to the reader. If I have anything worth saying it is there, in my books, in a far more entertaining and accessible (I hope) way than a pretentious self-analysis would provide."

■ Works Cited

Review of *Climb a Lonely Hill, Booklist,* September 15, 1972, p. 101.
Review of *Climb a Lonely Hill,* "Enduring All Things," *Times Literary Supplement,* October 30, 1970, pp. 1266-67.

Fisher, Margery, "Neighbourhood Tales," *Growing Point*, July, 1979, pp. 3539-42.

Review of *The Flame Takers*, "Haunted Houses," *Times Literary Supplement*, July 5, 1974, p. 717.

Gilderdale, Betty, "Lilith Norman," *Twentieth-Century Children's Writers*, fourth edition, St. James, 1995, pp. 707-9.

Review of *The Paddock: A Story in Praise of the Earth*, *Junior Bookshelf*, April, 1993, p. 61.

Review of *The Paddock: A Story in Praise of the Earth*, *Publishers Weekly*, March 29, 1993, p. 55.

Review of *The Shape of Three*, *Bulletin of the Center for Children's Books*, February, 1973, p. 96.

■ For More Information See

BOOKS

Saxby, H. M., *A History of Australian Children's Literature, 1941-1970*, Wentworth Books, 1971.

PERIODICALS

Booklist, January 1, 1973, p. 450.
Horn Book Guide, fall, 1993, p. 270.
Junior Bookshelf, June, 1979, p. 171.
Kirkus Reviews, March 1, 1993, p. 303.
Library Journal, September 15, 1972, p. 2965; March 15, 1973, p. 1015.
Publishers Weekly, January 1, 1973, p. 57.
School Librarian, August, 1993, p. 104.
Times Literary Supplement, December 3, 1971, p. 1516.

—*Sketch by Janet L. Hile*

* * *

NYE, Naomi Shihab 1952-

■ Personal

Maiden name is pronounced "*shee*-hab"; born March 12, 1952, in St. Louis, MO; daughter of Aziz (a journalist) and Miriam (a Montessori teacher; maiden name, Allwardt) Shihab; married Michael Nye (a photographer and lawyer), September 2, 1978; children: Madison Cloudfeather (son). *Education:* Trinity University, B.A. (summa cum laude) in English and world religions, 1974. *Politics:* Independent. *Religion:* Independent. *Hobbies and other interests:* Reading, cooking, bicycling, traveling, collecting old postcards.

■ Addresses

Home and office—806 South Main Ave., San Antonio, TX 78204.

■ Career

Poet and writer of children's books. Worked full time in the Texas Commission on the Arts Writers in the Schools project, 1974-86; has been a visiting writer or writer in residence through numerous arts programs and schools in Texas, Wyoming, Maine, California, and Alaska; teacher at the University of California, Berke-

NAOMI SHIHAB NYE

ley, the University of Hawaii at Manoa, and the University of Texas at Austin. Member of the Friends of the Library in San Antonio and the King William Downtown Neighborhood Association. *Member:* Texas Institute of Letters, Phi Beta Kappa.

■ Awards, Honors

Voertman Poetry Prize, Texas Institute of Letters, 1980, for *Different Ways to Pray;* Pushcart Prizes, 1982, 1984; Voertman Prize, Texas Institute of Letters, and Notable Book, American Library Association (ALA), both 1982, and National Poetry Series selection, all for *Hugging the Jukebox;* Lavan Award, Academy of American Poets, and co-winner, Charity Randall Citation for Spoken Poetry, International Poetry Forum, both 1988; Jane Addams Children's Book Award, and Honorary Book for Christians and Jews, National Association for Christians and Jews, both 1992, both for *This Same Sky: A Collection of Poems from around the World;* Best Book citation, *School Library Journal*, 1994, Pick of the List citation, American Booksellers Association, 1994, Notable Children's Trade Book in the Field of Social Studies citation, National Council for Social Studies and Children's Book Council, 1995, and Jane Addams Children's Book Award for picture book, 1995, all for *Sitti's Secrets*.

■ Writings

FOR CHILDREN

(Editor) *This Same Sky: A Collection of Poems from around the World*, Four Winds Press, 1992.

POEMS BY
NAOMI SHIHAB NYE

RED SUITCASE

In this anthology for adults, the Arab-American poet writes of childhood and loss, wonder and war, and the many mysteries of life with freshness and compassion. (Cover illustration by Beck Whitehead.)

Sitti's Secrets (picture book), illustrated by Nancy Carpenter, Four Winds Press, 1994.
Benito's Dream Bottle (picture book), illustrated by Yu Cha Pak, Simon & Schuster, 1995.
(Editor) *The Tree Is Older Than You Are: Bilingual Poems and Stories from Mexico,* Simon & Schuster, 1995.

POETRY FOR ADULTS

Tattooed Feet, Texas Portfolio, 1977.
Eye-to-Eye, Texas Portfolio, 1978.
Different Ways to Pray, Breitenbush, 1980.
On the Edge of the Sky, Iguana, 1981.
Hugging the Jukebox, Dutton, 1982.
Yellow Glove, Breitenbush, 1987.
Invisible, Trilobite, 1987.
Mint, State Street Press, 1992.
Red Suitcase, BOA Editions Ltd., 1994.
Words under the Words: Selected Poems, Far Corner Books/Eighth Mountain, 1995.

Also author of "Twenty Other Worlds," in *Texas Poets in Concert: A Quartet,* edited by Richard B. Sale, University of North Texas Press, 1990.

RECORDINGS

Rutabaga-Roo (children's songs), Flying Cat, 1979.
Lullaby Raft (folk songs), Flying Cat, 1981.
The Spoken Page (poetry), International Poetry Forum, 1988.

■ Work in Progress

I Feel Jumpy around You, a book of gender poems edited with Paul Janeczko, for Simon & Schuster; *Lullaby Raft,* a picture book, illustrated by Vivienne Flesher, for Simon & Schuster; *Habibi,* a novel for teenagers, for Simon & Schuster.

■ Sidelights

Naomi Shihab Nye is a poet of note who has turned her hand to children's books—both poetry anthologies and picture books—which in one way or another deal with the idea of connections. "I see that as one of the primary themes to all my work," Nye told *Something about the Author* (*SATA*) in an interview. "Connections between times and people and cultures." Not a simple tip of the hat toward fashionable multiculturalism, Nye's work has been built on a bedrock of such simple connections as the everyday life of people around the world, or of ancestry played out in primary daily tasks. Never one to write with a thesaurus rather than her heart, Nye employs a "direct, unadorned vocabulary," according to Pat Monaghan in a *Booklist* review of *Red Suitcase,* that conveys both depth and mystery. "I write poems and stories out of daily life," Nye told *SATA,* "with lots of invention thrown in. I believe we can revise our lives by writing. We can invent and explore new connections through language."

The idea of connections between peoples is fundamental to Nye's own personal life. The daughter of a Palestinian immigrant and an American, Nye was brought up in two worlds. "I felt I had an ideal childhood," Nye told *SATA* in her interview. "I grew up in a mixed neighborhood in St. Louis, in a home very nurturing for self-expression. I had the sense of people speaking up for themselves very early on. My father was a spectacular teller of Middle Eastern folk tales. My brother and I always went to sleep with my father's folk tales and my mother's lullabies." Nye's father was a journalist and her mother a fine arts graduate in painting, so there was never any lack of verbal or visual stimuli. "But I don't remember books being an obsession in our home like they are for me now," Nye said. "I have twenty books stacked up by my bed at all times and I get very nervous when I enter someone's house and no books are visible. I read incessantly and obsessively."

At about age five Nye encountered the poet Carl Sandburg, first on TV and then a bit later, when she learned to read, through his poems. "I began writing as a child of six, fascinated by the power of words on the page to make us look differently at our lives, to help us see and connect. Early on I was introduced to the works of not only Sandburg, but also Margaret Wise Brown, Emily Dickinson, William Blake in his *Songs of Inno-*

cence, and Louisa May Alcott. Reading gave me the passionate urge to write." By the age of seven, Nye had published her first poem in the publication *Wee Wisdom.* "I had a second grade teacher who was a strong advocate of memorizing poetry and writing it ourselves. She nurtured the seed that was already growing. I also remember that the library was my great friend as a child. It still is. But then it was truly the heart of my life and I was always searching out new places to submit my poetry." Throughout her school years Nye continued publishing her works, first in children's magazines and then later in publications such as *Seventeen.*

Her childhood was not all books, though. "I guess I was a fairly normal kid and did the usual things with friends: skating in the winter and going to movies. But I always knew I had a private place to go to, an interior haven that was all mine, partly as a Palestinian American and partly as an interested observer of the world. I never felt prejudice; my father was a respected man in the community—a charismatic, handsome type. People were naturally drawn to him. But still I felt that I could be in the middle of the circle of our neighborhood, so to speak, or step back and watch the circle and wonder about it. The writer's ability to detach and witness. I do remember how troubled I was as a child that there were no black students in my school. St. Louis was a mixed community, but the lines were drawn. Black students went to their schools and we went to ours. I always wondered about that. Why was my father acceptable, yet black kids wouldn't be? Now, of course, that neighborhood is thoroughly integrated. But back then I wondered how different you could be and still be accepted."

In high school Nye moved with her family to Jerusalem and it was the first time she met her father's family. The move was a revelation for her, a confirmation of what she had long suspected: that though separated by space and time, there is a real connection between all peoples. She attended high school first in Ramallah, and then at St. Tarkmanchatz in the old city of Jerusalem. "The lessons were taught in Arabic, Armenian, and English," Nye recalled for *SATA,* "so I just sat back and waited for the teachers' English lessons to come on." Her father was editing the *Jerusalem Times* and Nye wrote a column on teen matters for that same daily's English-language newspaper. The Six-Day War cut short the family's stay, and they returned to the United States, settling in San Antonio, Texas, where Nye still resides.

"I finished high school in Texas," Nye said in her interview. "And I was always proud of the fact that I did so without ever having attended a football game. I guess you have to be from Texas to understand what an accomplishment that is." Known as something of a renegade in high school, Nye was still devoted to reading and writing. "I passionately consumed the writings of Thoreau in high school," she recalled. "In college I was very attracted to the Beat writers like [Jack] Kerouac, [Gregory] Corso, and [Gary] Snyder. The writers of the Twenties were very appealing, too, especially Gertrude Stein. But my strongest influence was and is William Stafford. I started reading him in

high school, but never formally studied under him. In fact, I didn't meet him until the late 1970s, but his work and life remain a powerful inspiration for me today." Nye attended Trinity University in San Antonio, living at home all four years. She continued writing and publishing throughout her college years, "but I never called myself a writer until I graduated from college," she told *SATA.*

Upon graduation, Nye found work in the Texas Writers in the Schools project, whereby writers would go into the schools to work directly with the children. "For the next dozen years or so," Nye explained, "I was the busiest visiting writer around. I worked full time at it, every day of the week in different schools all around the state." Meanwhile she was also establishing a name for herself as a poet with a distinctive voice, publishing chapbooks and collections of poetry. In 1982, her second full-length collection, *Hugging the Jukebox,* was chosen for the National Poetry Series, and Nye gained national publication. Her poems deal with the everyday aspects of life and with the harsh realities as well: death and missed opportunities. "Nye observes the business of living and the continuity among all the world's inhabitants, whether separated by oceans or time," wrote Jane L. Tanner in the *Dictionary of Literary Biography.* "She lives in Texas but is regional only insofar as she has a strong sense of place wherever she happens to be." Nye also garnered prestigious awards and was invited as a visiting instructor to colleges and schools around the country. "Basically," Nye told *SATA,* "I have made a permanent job out of being an itinerant visitor. I've never had benefits and all that, and don't want them. I feel more free this way."

Nye was married in 1978 to a lawyer and budding photographer who has since become a photographer and sometime-lawyer, and in 1986 their son Madison was born. "It was then I really began to look around for other ways to make a living so that I would not be in the schools full time," Nye said in her interview. She turned her hand to a wide variety of writing styles, but it was not until the early 1990s that she got into children's writing. "I had done an earlier album of children's songs," Nye explained, "now out of print. And I always felt that my poetry was for all ages. In fact some of my collections are used in high schools around the country. I've always been attracted to texts for children, whether poetry or prose. I think adults need them as much as children do sometimes, for clarity and focus. One of the delights of having our son was that it was now legitimate for me to return to that part of the library I so loved when I was young. I never felt there had to be a huge division between adult and children's literature. We often underestimate what kids can understand. Working with so many students in schools over the years, that is one thing I learned—don't underestimate."

So when editor Virginia Duncan contacted Nye for possible children's book ideas, Nye found the offer appealing. Having a child herself as well as having worked with children for so many years made it seem like a natural next step to create her own children's books. "I was always looking for crossover texts," Nye said, "for the books that would appeal to fifth graders as well as college-age readers. Finally I had the opportunity to try to make some myself. In my own writing, I did not see it as such a stretch to be understood by both audiences. My style is both simple and understandable. I always felt revulsion for the cutesie sorts of children's books. I had no desire to be condescending." But the first several ideas Nye came up with were rejected. Finally an idea for an anthology of poems grew quite naturally out of her work in the schools. "It was during the Gulf War," Nye recalled for *SATA*, "and the country was pulsing with hatred for Arabs. It was a scary time for me, and I wanted to bring the war down to the human level for the children I was working with. So I found some poems by Iraqi poets and had the kids read them and let them see that these people were no different than we were. They had the same daily needs, the same inner lives. It was a very powerful experience and the teachers wanted more. They wanted an international anthology to share with their students. That's when I got the idea for *This Same Sky*."

Nye's itinerant life served her well in compiling this collection, for she had contacts with writers all around the world. "I basically sat down and wrote letters all over the place requesting submissions," Nye said. "What resulted was an international anthology that has gone through several printings and has been used in schools all around the country. That makes me very happy." Nye gathered together 129 poets from 68 countries to celebrate the natural world and its human and animal inhabitants in *This Same Sky: A Collection of Poems from around the World*. "The book as a whole reflects the universality of human concerns across cultures," commented Jim Morgan in *Voice of Youth Advocates*. According to Morgan, "the most striking aspect of this collection, and the book's greatest potential appeal to adolescents, is the sense of real human life behind the words." The poets speak directly, not in some idealized manner, and the work "would definitely be a strong multicultural contribution" to a school's poetry collection, Morgan concluded. Mary M. Burns in *Horn Book* thought *This Same Sky* "should prove invaluable for intercultural education as well as for pure pleasure."

Sitti's Secrets, also written during the Gulf War, was Nye's second children's offering, this time a picture book. "I was very close to my paternal grandmother, despite the fact that she lived so far away," Nye explained to *SATA*. "I was intrigued that when you have a loved one on the other side of the world, it is hard to look at that world as divided. There is a link between people, between all people, and that's what I wanted to write about when I began this story of a 'sitti' or grandmother." Nye tells the story of a young Arab American girl, Mona, who goes to visit her grandmother in Palestine. The child and grandmother do not speak the same language and at first must communicate through Mona's father, but soon they begin to use their own language as Mona watches her grandmother go through her daily routines of making flat bread and watching the men pick lentils. There are differences and commonalities, but returning to the United States, Mona takes her love for her sitti with her and writes to the president of the United States to ask for peace between people. "The author writes a compassionate story in poetic, rich language," noted Maeve Visser Knoth in *Horn Book*. Knoth also commented on the use of illustration to further the effect of connections between cultures, as when Mona says "that her grandmother's voice 'danced as high as the whistles of birds,'" and the Arabic letters on the page slowly turn into birds. This is a book, concluded Knoth, "about the love of a family separated by space but united in spirit." Betsy Hearne, in *Bulletin of the Center for Children's Books,* thought that "the setting is unusual and the details vividly realized," and Luann Toth, in *School Library Journal,* wrote that *Sitti's Secrets* "serves as a thoughtful, loving affirmation of the bonds that transcend language barriers, time zones, and national borders."

Despite the distance between Palestine and Texas, Mona and her grandmother Sitti find that once they have met and lived together, nothing can separate them again. (Illustration by Nancy Carpenter from *Sitti's Secrets.*)

"What pleases me most about the book," Nye said to *SATA*, "is how universally it seems to have worked for children. When I am with kids in the schools after reading the book, they talk about their own relatives who are far away. They'll say they have a grandmother in another country. She's actually in Montana, but the concept of country is relative. What's important is that the story has translated the emotion of missing someone, acknowledging their own details, and feeling connected despite distance."

Nye's son Madison was the inspiration for her next picture book, *Benito's Dream Bottle*. "When Madison was two," Nye explained, "he began telling about a dream bottle that stretched from his stomach to his chest. He really believed in that bottle and would talk about it every morning. I loved the idea of dreams being something we carry around with us and that we fill up and empty, fill up and empty." In the book, Benito is concerned that his grandmother's dream bottle is empty, and he helps her to concentrate on images and to think hard about "stoplights blinking and trees shivering in the wind and telephone answering machines full of voices." Finally his grandmother dreams again—of her grandson, "who took her by the hand and led her outside. He showed her how to cook leaves inside a broken toaster oven."

Both picture books won praise not only for the text, but also for the art work (by Nancy Carpenter in *Sitti's Secrets* and Yu Cha Pak in *Benito's Dream Bottle*). "I was blessed in both of my first two picture books to have spectacular illustrators," Nye told *SATA*. For her next children's book, however, Nye returned to anthologies, compiling poems, stories, and paintings from Mexico in the bilingual *The Tree Is Older Than You Are: Bilingual Poems and Stories from Mexico*. "I've travelled in Mexico quite a lot and love the culture. And living in San Antonio I am in the midst of Mexican American culture. I've noticed there are quite a few books dealing with latino or latina culture in the U.S. but too few that represent Mexican culture on its own terms. That's what I hoped to do with *The Tree Is Older Than You Are*."

Nye is in the process of editing another anthology with Paul Janeczko, a book of gender poems, *I Feel Jumpy around You*. "The poems are arranged thematically," Nye explained to *SATA*, "with a male and a female

Benito finds a way to help Grandma dream again, through memories, questions, and imaginings, in this intriguing picture book. (Illustration by Yu Cha Pak from *Benito's Dream Bottle*.)

viewpoint, either parallel or contrasting, on the same subject or theme on facing pages. It's an attempt at showing the connections and contrasts we have across gender much as the earlier anthologies show it across cultures." Nye is also returning to picture books with another project in the works, *Lullaby Raft*, taken from a song of the same title she wrote and recorded in 1981. And all the while she is also writing her own poetry. Additionally, Nye has taken part in two television series to be aired by PBS: a Bill Moyers production, *Language of Life*, and another about poets around the country, *United States of Poetry*. Nye's is an energetic life and to squeeze all the projects in she gets up at four in the morning to start her work day. "Those are the best hours," she said, "the early morning when everyone else is still asleep. I believe in abundance: write a lot and if you're lucky, you'll like *something*. I never work to a real schedule unless I have a deadline to make. Usually I just let whatever needs to come, come, whether it is poetry or children's stories. I keep notebooks and refer to them for images or opening lines, but writing is an ongoing process. You're doing it even when you're not sitting down with pen and paper in front of you. You're thinking it, seeing it, hearing it in your mind. Recently I've been experimenting with William Stafford's technique of lying down on the couch to write poems. Just writing as freely as possible and letting directions evolve."

Nye's years of working with children in the schools have given her a natural sense of audience. "I don't really think of audience when I write," she explained. "But I do know instinctively what appeals to students of different ages, what works with them. And it is so rewarding writing for children. They are still linked to that essential world of childhood where everything is possible. It is the most exquisite world if one is favored with good circumstances. If not, writing may be a crucial tool for expression. Words have magic for children. They are less tired of things. I hope for a certain receptivity in younger readers that is sometimes harder to find in adults. And the amazing thing is that it is still there, in spite of television.

"Ultimately I look at writing as a form of discovery," Nye told *SATA*. "I hope my words reach out to the reader and they can say yes to them. 'Yes, I have felt that way before.' I personally feel close to what other people are saying and their words broaden my life. They give comfort that we are not, and never have been, alone out here. I always tell young writers how important the link is between reading and writing. You just cannot be a good writer without reading, reading. It's a way of sharing. I didn't set out to publish to prove something. It

was simply a way to connect with unseen friends out there. I felt the writers I read were my personal friends, and I still feel that way. That's the effect I'm trying to achieve with my own work. To connect."

■ Works Cited

Burns, Mary M., review of *This Same Sky: A Collection of Poems from around the World, Horn Book,* March/April, 1993, p. 215.

Hearne, Betsy, review of *Sitti's Secrets, Bulletin of the Center for Children's Books,* March, 1994, p. 228.

Knoth, Maeve Visser, review of *Sitti's Secrets, Horn Book,* May/June, 1994, pp. 317-318.

Monaghan, Pat, review of *Red Suitcase, Booklist,* October 15, 1994, p. 395.

Morgan, Jim, review of *This Same Sky: A Collection of Poems from around the World, Voice of Youth Advocates,* April, 1993, p. 59.

Nye, Naomi Shihab, *Sitti's Secrets,* Four Winds Press, 1994.

Nye, Naomi Shihab, *Benito's Dream Bottle,* Simon & Schuster, 1995.

Nye, Naomi Shihab, interview with J. Sydney Jones for *Something about the Author,* conducted May 25, 1995.

Tanner, Jane L., "Naomi Shihab Nye," *Dictionary of Literary Biography,* Volume 120: *American Poets Since World War II,* Gale, 1992, p. 223.

Toth, Luann, review of *Sitti's Secrets, School Library Journal,* June, 1994, p. 112.

■ For More Information See

BOOKS

Spaar, Lisa Russ, introduction to *Texas Poets in Concert: A Quartet,* University of North Texas Press, 1990, p. 2.

PERIODICALS

Booklist, March 15, 1993, p. 1338; March 15, 1994, p. 1374.

Bulletin of the Center for Children's Books, November, 1995, p. 101.

Kirkus Reviews, February 15, 1994, p. 231.

New York Times Book Review, April 11, 1993, p. 30.

Publishers Weekly, April 24, 1995, p. 71.

School Library Journal, December, 1992, p. 139; October, 1995, p. 150.

Swamp Root, spring, 1989, pp. 83-93.

Voice of Youth Advocates, December, 1995, p. 333.

—Sketch by J. Sydney Jones

O

OLDFIELD, Pamela 1931-

■ Personal

Born in 1931, in London, England; children: one son and one daughter.

■ Addresses

Home—Kent, England. *Agent*—c/o Blackie Children's Books, 7 Leicester Place, London WC2H 7BP, England.

■ Career

Has worked as a teacher and secretary.

■ Writings

FOR CHILDREN

Melanie Brown Goes to School, illustrated by Carolyn Dinan, Faber, 1970.

Melanie Brown Climbs a Tree, illustrated by Dinan, Faber, 1972.

The Adventures of Sarah and Theodore Bodgitt, Brockhampton Press, 1974.

The Halloween Pumpkin, illustrated by Ferelith Eccles Williams, Hodder and Stoughton, 1974, Children's Press, 1976.

Melanie Brown and the Jar of Sweets, illustrated by Dinan, Faber, 1974.

Simon's Extra Gran, illustrated by Derek Lucas, Knight, 1974, Children's Press, 1976.

A Witch in the Summer House, illustrated by Susan Hunter, Hodder and Stoughton, 1976.

The Terribly Plain Princess and Other Stories, illustrated by Glenys Ambrus, Hodder and Stoughton, 1977.

Katy and Dom, illustrated by Jane Paton, Angus and Robertson, 1978.

Children of the Plague, illustrated by Janet Duchesne, Hamish Hamilton, 1979.

The Princess Well-I-May, illustrated by Ambrus, Hodder and Stoughton, 1979.

The Rising of the Wain, illustrated by Thelma Lambert, Abelard, 1980.

The Riverside Cat, illustrated by Charlotte Voake, Hamish Hamilton, 1980.

Cloppity, illustrated by Linda Birch, Hamish Hamilton, 1981.

Parkin's Storm, illustrated by Peter Westcott, Abelard, 1982.

Tommy Dobbie and the Witch-Next-Door, illustrated by Ambrus, Hodder and Stoughton, 1983.

(Editor) *Helter-Skelter: Stories for Six-Year-Olds,* illustrated by Birch, Blackie, 1983.

Ghost Stories, illustrated by Gavin Rowe, Blackie, 1984.

(Editor) *Hurdy Gurdy,* illustrated by Birch, Blackie, 1984, published as *Merry-Go-Round: Stories for Seven-Year-Olds,* Knight, 1985.

Barnaby and Bell and the Birthday Cake, illustrated by Jenny Williams, Piccadilly, 1985.

Barnaby and Bell and the Lost Button, illustrated by Williams, Piccadilly, 1985.

The Christmas Ghost, illustrated by Vanessa Julian-Ottie, Blackie, 1985.

Ginger's Nine Lives, illustrated by Birch, Blackie, 1986.

Toby and the Donkey, illustrated by Birch, Methuen, 1986.

(Editor) *Roller Coaster,* illustrated by Birch, Blackie, 1986.

The Ghosts of Bellering Oast, illustrated by Julian-Ottie, Blackie, 1987.

Spine Chillers, illustrated by Colin Robinson, Blackie, 1987.

Sam, Sue and Cinderella, illustrated by Jenny Williams, Methuen, 1989.

Bomb Alert, Armada, 1989.

Secret Persuader, Armada, 1989.

A Shaggy Dog Story, Blackie, 1990.

A Ginger Cat and a Shaggy Dog, Puffin, 1992.

Cat with No Name, illustrated by Birch, *Blackie,* 1994.

"GUMBY GANG" SERIES; PUBLISHED BY BLACKIE

The Adventures of the Gumby Gang, illustrated by Lesley Smith, 1978.

The Gumby Gang Again, illustrated by Smith, 1978.

More about the Gumby Gang, illustrated by Smith, 1979.

Stories from Ancient Greece, a collection of retellings by Oldfield for primary school-age children, includes many classic tales such as "Theseus and the Minotaur." (Illustration by Nick Harris)

The Gumby Gang Strikes Again, illustrated by Smith, 1980.
The Gumby Gang on Holiday, illustrated by Smith, 1983.
The Return of the Gumby Gang, illustrated by Kate Rodgers, 1986.

NONFICTION

Stories from Ancient Greece (retellings), illustrated by Nick Harris, Doubleday, 1988.
The Mill Pond Ghost and Other Stories, Lions, 1991.
The Haunting of Wayne Briggs and Other Spinechilling Stories, Lions, 1993.
(With others) *The Marvellous Magical Storybook,* Dean, 1993.

FOR ADULTS

Green Harvest, Century Hutchinson, 1983.
Summer Song, Century Hutchinson, 1984, Ulverscroft, 1993.
Golden Talley, Century Hutchinson, 1985.
The Gooding Girl, Century Hutchinson, 1985.
The Stationmaster's Daughter, Century Hutchinson, 1986.
Lily Golightly, Century Hutchinson, 1987.
Turn of the Tide, Century Hutchinson, 1988.
A Dutiful Wife, Joseph, 1989.
Sweet Sally Lunn, Joseph, 1990.
The Halliday Girls, Joseph, 1991, Ulverscroft, 1993.
Long Dark Summer, Joseph, 1992, Ulverscroft, 1993.

Passionate Exile, Joseph, 1993.
An Embarrassment of Riches, Ulverscroft, 1994.
String of Blue Beads, G.K. Hall, 1995.

"THE HERON" SAGA

The Rich Earth, Futura, 1980, Ulverscroft, 1994.
This Ravaged Land, Futura, 1980.
After the Storm, Futura, 1981.
White Water, Futura, 1982.

OTHER

Author of "The Willerbys and the Burglar" series, illustrated by Shirley Bellwood, published by Blackie.

■ Sidelights

Melanie Brown Goes to School is one of three stories that Pamela Oldfield wrote about the enthusiastic and energetic Melanie. The books are aimed at four to six year olds. Melanie experiences many comic disasters as she learns by experience. A critic in *Children's Literature in Education* described the book as "written in simple, rhythmic prose with very natural, unforced repetitions: it is very readable." Valerie Brinkley-Willsher wrote in *Twentieth-Century Children's Writers* that Oldfield's "assured knowledge of the primary school age group for which she writes leads to confident handling of her always appropriate themes."

■ Works Cited

Review of *Melanie Brown Goes to School, Children's Literature in Education,* summer, 1982.
Valerie Brinkley-Willsher, "Pamela Oldfield," *Twentieth-Century Children's Writers,* 4th edition, St. James, 1995, pp. 720-21.*

*   *   *

OWENS, Thomas S(heldon) 1960-
(Tom Owens)

■ Personal

Born October 20, 1960, in Los Angeles, CA; son of Ernest T. (a machinist and minister) and Jeanette M. (a secretary; maiden name, Walton) Owens; married Diana Star Helmer (a children's book author), April 7, 1982. *Education:* Iowa State University, B.A. (journalism), 1986. *Politics:* Democrat. *Religion:* Christian. *Hobbies and other interests:* Walking, gardening, cooking.

■ Addresses

Home and office—1001 West Boone St., Marshalltown, IA 50158-2412. *Agent*—Barbara Kouts, P.O. Box 558, Bellport, NY 11713.

■ Career

Freelance writer and author-in-the-schools, 1988—. *Marshalltown Times-Republican,* Marshalltown, IA, reporter, 1979-80; *Iowa State Daily,* staff writer, 1980-84; *Des Moines Register,* Des Moines, IA, sports correspondent, 1984-86; co-editor of *Sports Collectors Digest,* 1987-88. Co-author and reader for "Dial-a-Story," Marshalltown Public Library, IA. *Member:* Society of Children's Book Writers and Illustrators, National Storytelling Association, Society for American Baseball Research.

■ Awards, Honors

Collecting Baseball Cards was named a New York Public Library "Book for the Teen Age," 1994.

■ Writings

(Under name Tom Owens) *Complete Book of Baseball Cards,* Publications International, 1988.
(Under name Tom Owens) *Collecting Sports Autographs,* Bonus Books, 1989.
Greatest Baseball Players of All Time, Publications International, 1990.
Official Baseball Card Price Guide, Publications International, 1990.
(Under name Tom Owens, with David Craft) *Redbirds Revisited: Great Stories and Memories from St. Louis Cardinals* (oral histories; for adults), Bonus Books, 1990.
Collecting Baseball Cards, Millbrook Press, 1993.
Collecting Comic Books: A Young Person's Guide, Millbrook Press, 1995.
(With wife, Diana Star Helmer) *Collectible Card Games: Play It Your Way,* Millbrook Press, 1996.
Beyond Baseball Cards, Millbrook Press, 1996.
Remember When Baseball Was . . . , Michael Friedman, 1996.
The Great Catchers, for Michael Friedman, in press.
Beyond Comic Books, Millbrook Press, in press.
Autograph Hounds: Collecting Famous Signatures, Millbrook Press, in press.

Contributor of articles to periodicals, including *Legends Sports Memorabilia, USA Today Baseball Weekly,* and *Trading Cards,* and to official team publications of the Los Angeles Dodgers, San Francisco Giants, St. Louis Cardinals, Houston Astros, Seattle Mariners, Baltimore Orioles, and California Angels.

■ Work in Progress

Research on the life and career of puppeteer Bil Baird.

■ Sidelights

"If you ever saw me protesting on a street corner or waving a sign at TV news cameras, chances are my message would be 'Equal Rights for Nonfiction,'" Thomas S. Owens told *SATA.* "I grew up reading more newspapers and biographies than any other types of stories. I believed that truth was stranger, and mostly more exciting, than fiction that kids were supposed to read.

THOMAS S. OWENS

"I earned a journalism degree in college and worked for newspapers and magazines. Writing articles and features was fun, but I hated knowing that, within a week, my creations could become kitty-litter box liners. Even more, I wondered just how much adults appreciated what I wrote. Most of the reader letters I got while working at *Sports Collectors Digest* were from hobbyists age fourteen or under.

"That's when I decided to write books for young people, starting with how-to books about collecting autographs and baseball cards. Writing books for young people is fun, because my wife, Diana Helmer, has the same job. We go to libraries together to do research, and we read and edit what the other one writes. The first book we wrote together was *Collectible Card Games: Play It Your Way.* We've collaborated on several works of fiction, too, which we want to see published.

"Students we meet during school visits seem surprised that I think they could write better books for young people than some adults. It's true! Adults may think juvenile literature will make them rich and famous, or will allow them to brainwash children into being polite, vegetable-eating robots. Kids, however, are better at keeping writing simple. They write to be scary or funny or sad, and they write the kind of stories they'd like to read. Some adults, though, try to write what they think will please a publisher, instead of pleasing themselves.

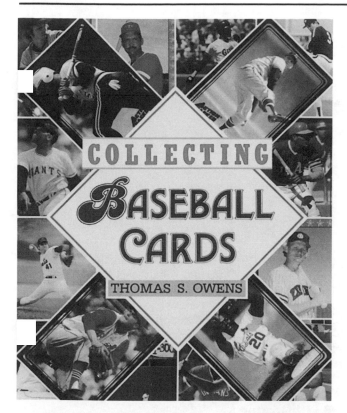

Selected as a New York Public Library "Book for the Teen Age" in 1994, this book will be sought after by baseball card collectors, beginners and die-hards alike.

Most kids know that, if you're bored with what you're writing, the readers will be, too."

This philosophy helped Owens to write several practical guides for young hobbyists, including *Collecting Baseball Cards* and *Collecting Sports Autographs*. In *Collecting Baseball Cards*, Owens provides a brief history, then covers strategies for finding and making good purchases, protecting valuable cards, and organizing a collection. For example, Owens suggests methods of developing sets, such as rookie cards, star cards, or cards containing errors. The last chapter of the book includes numerous addresses for major league baseball teams and sports card collecting organizations and publications. *Collecting Baseball Cards* also contains many color photographs of cards to illustrate important aspects of the hobby. *School Library Journal* reviewer Tom S. Hurlburt recommended the book for "youngsters who want to get started or novices looking for ways to improve upon or give focus to their collections."

Owens covered similar territory in *Collecting Sports Autographs*, which Wes Lukowsky, writing in *Booklist*, called a "wonderful introduction to an ever-growing hobby." The book includes advice on how to obtain autographs, both in person and by mail, as well as how to determine an autograph's value and how to protect a collection. Owens also examines the controversial phenomenon of celebrities receiving payment for their autographs at sports memorabilia and hobby shows. He provides added interest for the reader, as Lukowsky remarked in *Booklist*, by using anecdotes from his own collecting experiences. Like Owens's previous book, *Collecting Sports Autographs* concludes with a chapter of addresses for relevant organizations and periodicals.

■ Works Cited

Hurlburt, Tom S., review of *Collecting Baseball Cards*, *School Library Journal*, June, 1993, p. 122.
Lukowsky, Wes, review of *Collecting Sports Autographs*, *Booklist*, May 1, 1989, p. 1504.

■ For More Information See

PERIODICALS

Booklist, August, 1993, p. 2056.
School Library Journal, January, 1996, p. 121.
Small Press, October, 1989, p. 72.
Voice of Youth Advocates, December, 1993, p. 324.

* * *

OWENS, Tom
See OWENS, Thomas S(heldon)

P

DAWN PETERSON

PETERSON, Dawn 1934-

■ Personal

Born November 5, 1934, in Cape Girardeau, MO; daughter of Joseph R. (a building contractor) and Agnes (a homemaker and poet; maiden name, Butler) Gerhardt; married Edward E. Peterson, January 10, 1962

(divorced, 1979); children: Heather Curtis, Holly Peterson. *Education:* Attended Southeast Missouri State University, Washington University, and Arts Student League; studied portraiture with S. Edward Oppenheim. *Politics:* Independent. *Religion:* Episcopalian.

■ Career

Illustrator.

■ Illustrator

Evariste Bernier, *Baxter Bear and Moses Moose,* Down East Books, 1990.
Kate Rowinski, *L. L. Bear's Island Adventure,* Down East Books, 1992.
Kate Rowinski, *Elie Bear and the Fly-Away Fly,* Down East Books, 1993.
Emily Chetkowski, *Mabel Takes the Ferry,* Heritage Printing and Publishing, 1995.

■ Sidelights

"I began drawing when I was a small child, recording family events and drawing our many pets," Dawn Peterson told *SATA.* "When I was in elementary school, I sold drawings to classmates for a very small fee!

"While growing up in Missouri, my sisters and I were outdoors most of the time, exploring the lovely woods near our home and climbing trees that I wouldn't venture into today! All of this helped me to develop a life-long love of nature, which is reflected in the illustration that I most enjoy doing today.

"While in my senior year of high school I had a wonderful art teacher who arranged for me to become an apprentice to an art director at a local newspaper/ publisher. There, I learned the skills needed to become a graphic artist, while continuing my studies.

"I have worked and studied in California, Missouri, and New York, taking classes in painting, portraiture, and sculpture. At present I work mostly in watercolor, doing book and magazine illustration. I live on the Maine Coast with my three cats, where, in addition to illustration, I enjoy birding, baking, and listening to classical music. I also look forward to visits with my two daughters, son-in-law, and two small grandsons."*

* * *

PLATT, Kin 1911-

■ Personal

Born December 8, 1911, in New York, NY; son of Daniel (a singer) and Etta (Hochberg) Platt; married twice (divorced); children: Christopher. *Hobbies and other interests:* Golf, juggling, piano.

■ Addresses

Home—3163 Sawtelle Blvd., Los Angeles, CA 90066. *Agent*—Marilyn E. Marlow, Curtis Brown Inc., 10 Astor Pl., New York, NY 10003.

■ Career

Cartoonist, caricaturist, comedy and fiction writer. Theatrical caricaturist for various New York newspapers, including the *Brooklyn Daily Eagle* and *Village Voice,* and for the *Los Angeles Times,* early 1930s; radio comedy writer for Jack Benny, Stoopnagle & Budd, Burns & Allen, Ken Murray, and the *National Biscuit Comedy Hour* of 1936, beginning mid-1930s; writer of animated cartoons for Disney and Hanna-Barbera, beginning late 1930s, and creator of Supermouse for

KIN PLATT

comic books; New York Herald Tribune Syndicate, New York City, cartoonist (writer and illustrator) of comic strips "Mr. and Mrs.," 1947-63, and "The Duke and the Duchess," 1950-54; book author, both adult and young adult, 1961—. *Military service:* U.S. Army Air Force, 1943-46, served in Air Transport Command in China-Burma-India theater; became corporal; received Bronze Star, China Star, two Combat Stars. *Member:* Authors Guild, Authors League of America, Mystery Writers of America.

■ Awards, Honors

Edgar Allan Poe Award for best juvenile mystery, Mystery Writers of America, 1967, for *Sinbad and Me;* Edgar Allan Poe Award runner-up, 1970, for *The Mystery of the Witch Who Wouldn't;* Distinguished Book of the Year award, Southern California Council on Literature for Children and Young People, 1974, for *Chloris and the Creeps;* Notable Book citation, American Library Association, 1975, for *Headman;* award for outstanding contribution to children's literature, Central Missouri State University, 1986.

■ Writings

FOR CHILDREN AND YOUNG ADULTS

Big Max, illustrated by Robert Lopshire, Harper, 1965.
The Boy Who Could Make Himself Disappear, Chilton, 1971.
Hey, Dummy, Chilton, 1971.
Chloris and the Creeps, Chilton, 1973.
(Editor) Jack London, *The Call of the Wild,* illustrated by Fred Carrillo, Pendulum Press, 1973.
(Editor) Robert Louis Stevenson, *Dr. Jekyll and Mr. Hyde,* illustrated by Nestor Redondo, Pendulum Press, 1973.
(Editor) Arthur Conan Doyle, *The Great Adventures of Sherlock Holmes,* Pendulum Press, 1974.
(Editor) Robert Louis Stevenson, *Kidnapped,* Pendulum Press, 1974.
Chloris and the Freaks, Bradbury, 1975.
Headman, Greenwillow, 1975.
Big Max and the Mystery of the Missing Moose, illustrated by Robert Lopshire, Harper, 1975, Harper/Trophy, 1983.
The Terrible Love Life of Dudley Cornflower, Bradbury, 1976.
Run for Your Life, photographs by Chuck Freedman, F. Watts, 1977.
Chloris and the Weirdos, Bradbury, 1978.
The Doomsday Gang, Greenwillow, 1978.
Dracula, Go Home, illustrated by Frank Mayo, F. Watts, 1979.
The Ape Inside Me, Crowell, 1980.
Flames Going Out, Methuen, 1980.
Brogg's Brain, Crowell, 1981.
Frank and Stein and Me, F. Watts, 1982.
Crocker, Lippincott, 1983.
(Self-illustrated) *Darwin and the Great Beasts,* Greenwillow, 1992.

"STEVE FORRESTER" YOUNG ADULT MYSTERIES

The Blue Man, Harper, 1961.
Sinbad and Me, Chilton, 1966.
The Mystery of the Witch Who Wouldn't, Chilton, 1969.
The Ghost of Hellsfire Street, Delacorte, 1980.

"MAX ROPER" ADULT MYSTERIES

The Pushbutton Butterfly, Random House, 1970.
The Kissing Gourami, Random House, 1970.
The Princess Stakes Murder, Random House, 1973.
The Giant Kill, Random House, 1974,
Match Point for Murder, Random House, 1975.
The Body Beautiful Murder, Random House, 1976.
The Screwball King Murder, Random House, 1978.

FOR ADULTS

Dead as They Come (mystery), Random House, 1972.
A Pride of Women (suspense), Robert Hale, 1974.
Murder in Rosslare (mystery), Walker, 1986.

Also author of an unpublished musical, *Let Freedom Ring,* written during World War II.

■ Adaptations

The Boy Who Could Make Himself Disappear was co-produced as a film by Hanna-Barbera under the title *Baxter* in 1973; *Big Max* was adapted for audiocassette, Listening Library, 1986.

■ Work in Progress

My Sound Gone, The Baddest Thing, Tending to Witches, and *A Puzzle for Thoreau.*

■ Sidelights

Kin Platt's long and varied career began with the drawing of theatrical caricatures in the 1930s. In a way he has dealt in caricature ever since, even in his fiction for young adults that spans the spectrum from old-fashioned adventure yarns to introspective studies of deeply troubled kids. These stories are caricatures not in a negative sense; Platt takes extreme, end-of-the-line cases as his starting point, eschewing comfortable, typical, and familiar protagonists or situations for his fiction. "I would like to see less genteel supervised attitudes toward books for children," Platt once told *SATA,* "and more imaginative approaches welcomed." And in an interview with Kathleen J. Edgar for *Authors & Artists for Young Adults* (*AAYA*), Platt elaborated on the motivation that makes him keep breaking boundaries: "Publishers have been afraid of the kind of books I've wanted to do.... I didn't want to keep doing ordinary books. I always felt that I had to stay ahead of everybody else, in my own mind at least.... I don't write to make money: I write because the story has to be told." In books as varied as rousing mysteries such as *Sinbad and Me* to gritty tales of gang violence like *Headman* to stories of emotional turmoil such as *The Boy Who Could Make Himself Disappear,* Platt has followed his own dictum and has created a body of work

that has expanded the boundaries of what constitutes young adult fiction.

It was a role Platt seemed tailor-made for. Born in New York City, there was nothing comfortable or traditional about his own childhood. He is the first to say that he had a difficult youth, running away from home at age seven, and he was always pushing the bounds of the acceptable. By ten, he was drawing all the time, copying cartoons and dreaming of having his own syndicated comic strip one day. He was also involved in sports, both running and baseball. And to fill any empty hours, he read voraciously and indiscriminately, up to five books per day. "I think boys read more in those days," he wrote in an essay for *Something about the Author Autobiography Series* (*SAAS*), "before books became pretentious, hardcovered and high-priced, and pigeon-holed into age categories." He read adventure stories: Tom Swift, the Hardy Boys, and the Rover Boys among others. Then later came Jack London, Charles Lamb, Rabelais, Cervantes, and Freud. He simply read and gave no thought to whether it was so-called "good literature" he was reading or not.

Platt finished high school at age nineteen and there was no thought nor money for college. "To my mind," he wrote in *SAAS,* "it was a waste of time and I had to make my living by drawing." For the next decade, Platt drew caricatures of contemporary theater and screen stars, and then included political cartoons, as well. His caricature of Hitler in the *Brooklyn Daily Eagle* was one of the first anti-Hitler cartoons in U.S. newspapers. He also found work in advertising, where cartoon strips were then used, and began writing comedy scripts. It was one of these scripts that started his career in radio comedy. Some of his early scripts were adapted for use by both Jack Benny and the comedy team of Stoopnagle and Budd, and in 1936 he drove to Hollywood to throw himself full-heartedly into radio. It was not exactly a match made in heaven.

"It didn't take long to discover that although I had an auspicious beginning writing multiple shows," Platt commented in *SAAS,* "radio comedy for a mass audience of forty million nightly was not to my liking, nor was it my strength." Platt's humor, droll and offbeat, was not what radio comedy of the day was built on. Radio comedians wanted one-liners, and the more tried and proven the jokes were by other comics, the better. Platt also had problems working in tandem with a group of other writers. The one show he felt comfortable with was *The National Biscuit Comedy Hour,* where he met and made the lasting friendship of young Mary Martin, later of *Peter Pan* and Broadway fame. Soon he left the fast lane of writing for three comedy shows at the same time and went to work in the story departments of Disney and MGM shorts unit, where he continued honing his storytelling skills. These were the golden years of animated cartoons and writing stories. "I was to return to that crazy imaginary world many more times," he wrote in his *SAAS* entry, "doing hundreds of feature-lengths and shorts, some award-winning." Later credits in animated cartoons included writing credits on the

Topcat series, *The Flintstones, Jonny Quest,* and *The Jetsons.* Meantime, the prolific Platt was also drawing and writing comic books, creating the superheroes Captain Future and Supermouse. In the midst of all this hectic activity, Platt also married and moved back to New York.

By 1943, however, he was in uniform, drafted along with millions of others around the globe for World War II. Classified as an entertainment specialist, Platt spent most of the war in the Far East working on a newspaper, *Hump Express,* and writing and drawing a weekly cartoon strip depicting scantily clad women—the GI's favorite visual art. He also wrote a musical and had a traveling troupe that entertained GIs in China and Burma. He did not take to the regimented life of a soldier any better than he did to writing teams in Hollywood, writing his own orders when he felt like it, but by the end of the war he had been awarded the Bronze Star and was one of the lucky early group of soldiers to be discharged. Back in New York, he had a life to start over, and was lucky enough to take over the well-established syndicated cartoon strip "Mr. and Mrs.," a job he kept for seventeen years. He also tried his hand at his own strip, "The Duke and Duchess," which stayed in syndication for five years and got him into a bit of hot water with his editor when he decided to take on the communist-baiting senator Joe McCarthy.

Even before the end of "Mr. and Mrs.," however, Platt was already moving to a new career. He had by 1960 written hundreds of radio scripts and animated cartoons, as well as literally thousands of comic book stories, and was again living in California. He was ready for a change; ready to concentrate on one story at a time. Ready to begin a new career as a book author. His first book, *The Blue Man,* was the first of what became the popular series of "Steve Forrester" mysteries. From the outset, Platt challenged publishing precepts about what constitutes a young adult title. He wanted to create fiction for young readers that was as fresh, exciting, and unpretentious as the stuff he read as a youth. And, with this very first book, dealing with the hunt for a blue-bodied alien that the young protagonist thinks killed his uncle, Platt encountered what would become a familiar experience with much of his young adult fiction: controversy over his appropriateness and his use of so-called adult themes, situations, and language in his books. In particular, *The Blue Man* has Steve Forrester packing a rifle and taking the law into his own hands; that, in addition to the ungrammatical vernacular that the hero uses, convinced reviewer Miriam S. Mathes in *School Library Journal* that "the book cannot be recommended for purchase." Other reviewers disagreed; *New York Times Book Review* contributor Robert Berkvist, for instance, called the protagonist "a sort of whole-wheat Holden Caulfield," indirectly comparing Platt's work to another offbeat classic, J. D. Salinger's *Catcher in the Rye.*

Undaunted by critics and librarians who Platt felt made his first book difficult to find, he brought out his second title, *Big Max,* in 1965. Written for a younger audience, this detective yarn features a sleuth who travels through the air by blowing into his umbrella. "Spontaneous fun," Virginia Haviland of *Horn Book* called the book. "Easy to read, easy to laugh at," likewise commented a *Kirkus Reviews* critic. Platt next turned his hand to Steve Forrester once again, writing a second mystery, this time with his own son Chris in mind. An adventure story about a boy and his bulldog named Sinbad, *Sinbad and Me* has enough plot twists and subplots to keep young readers turning pages: there is the story of the dog, then also one of pirate treasure. There are secret panels, codes, caves, gamblers, a haunted house, an unsolved murder, and invisible ink. Add a quirky protagonist—a kid who has flunked science, but is an expert in old houses and antiques—and humor and it adds up to a recipe for success. The book, however, was turned down by his publishers. "They wanted excessive cuts," Platt recalled in *SAAS.* "It was too long, they said. I said no way, this is going to be the best book of the year!" Platt found a new publisher at Chilton Company and proved his own prophecy correct: the Mystery Writers of America gave *Sinbad and Me* the award for best juvenile mystery of 1967. "This is a funny book," wrote Phyllis Cohen in *Young Readers Review.* "So few mysteries are genuinely funny, that this one stands out like a beacon!" Other critics concurred: "A delightful book for the mystery-loving young reader," noted *Best Sellers,* while *School Library Journal* contributor Sarah Law Kennerly termed it "refreshingly funny."

Platt sold his next five books to Chilton Company, establishing his career as a writer for younger readers. But it was far from easy sailing. "*The Boy Who Could Make Himself Disappear* was turned down by my own agent at the time," Platt wrote in his *SAAS* entry. "She said nobody would want to read about a rotten American mother." The story of young Roger Baxter, who is trapped in a dysfunctional family—divorced parents and a mother who abuses him—may not be happy times reading, but it touches a nerve. Roger, suffering from a severe speech impediment and a hostile mother, finally learns how to cope through the help of friends and a therapist. Filmed as a movie under the title *Baxter,* the book also won critical attention on both ends of the scale: *Kirkus Reviews* thought it not worthy of recommendation, while Zena Sutherland of *Bulletin of the Center for Children's Books* thought that Roger's tale was "brilliantly told," and John Gillespie, writing in *School Library Journal,* noted that the book "will remain with thoughtful young people long after it is read." Another book of note that Platt wrote in the 1960s was *The Mystery of the Witch Who Wouldn't,* a further installment in the adventures of Steve Forrester.

The 1970s saw Platt turn his hand to adult as well as juvenile fiction, creating the Max Roper series in the former while still exploring such taboo subjects as mental retardation and adolescent sexuality in the latter. *Hey, Dummy* is the story of Neil Comstock, who slowly begins to feel protective of Alan, a retarded boy who has just moved into the neighborhood. Circumstances eventually force Neil to run off with Alan, with whom he increasingly identifies, even to the extent of taking over the "Dummy's" speech pattern. "A perceptive treatment of a child's sensitivity," commented Sutherland in *Bulletin of the Center for Children's Books*.

Platt also focused on divorce and the effects it has on children in a set of three books with a protagonist named Chloris. Partly inspired by his second marriage to a woman with a daughter who resented him, Platt investigated the hostility that the fictional Chloris feels for the men in her divorced mother's life. *Chloris and the Creeps* sees her attempting to disrupt her mother's marriage to Fidel Mancha, and in *Chloris and the Freaks* she succeeds. *Chloris and the Weirdos* takes off from that point, with the mother starting to date again and Chloris's reaction to these new men, or weirdos as she calls them. Once again, Sutherland of *Bulletin of the Center for Children's Books* championed Platt, finding *Chloris and the Creeps* a "moving and realistic story" in spite of some stylistic problems. And C. Nordhielm Wooldridge, in *School Library Journal*, thought that the third book in the series, *Chloris and the Weirdos*, "should appeal widely to young adult readers" both for its humor and mature issues.

Teenager Monty Davis struggles to hold on to his sense of humor and self, despite pressure to become the fastest miler at Emerson High. (Cover illustration by Fred Marcellino.)

In *The Terrible Love Life of Dudley Cornflower*, Platt tackled adolescent sexuality, and this book once again aroused controversy. "Judy Blume and others could write of a girl's concern for her budding breasts and her period," Platt wrote in *SAAS*, "but you could not write about a young boy's preoccupation with his erections." The storm eventually died down, but not Platt's indignation. "Reviewers and librarians have often attacked my books. Some are overprotective of children and their exposure to the real world. I like children too, and have never thought facts about life and their consequences should be avoided for the age groups most needing this information." Platt wrote of harsh consequences to gang violence in *Headman* and *The Doomsday Gang*, both of which deal with realistic situations and use realistic street language. A "taut and very tough novel about growing up dead in the white, black and Chicano ghettos of Los Angeles," is how Robert Berkvist described *Headman* in *New York Times Book Review*. "Provocative and engrossing," added Jack Forman in *School Library Journal*. The second gang novel, *The Doomsday Gang*, about a teen group dealing drugs, examines the futility of gang life—a theme still topical almost two decades after the book was written. Meanwhile, Platt was also publishing adult detective novels throughout the 1970s, a productive decade in which the author saw 20 of his books published.

Troubled teens figure in two further titles from the early 1980s: *Flames Going Out*, the story of a sixteen-year-old girl for whom a burning match symbolizes her life's ebbing, and *The Ape Inside Me*, about a disturbed fifteen-year-old trying to gain control of his temper. "Painfully poignant" is how Claire M. Dyson, writing in *Best Sellers*, described the latter book, and *Booklist* found it to be a "simply written, positive story." *Flames Going Out* had a more mixed reception with reviewers. Forman, in *School Library Journal*, felt that "the stark realism of Platt's gang stories ... doesn't work here," but Patty Campbell of *Wilson Library Bulletin*, while she had reservations about sexism in the text, thought the book "surpassed anything" Platt had written in years.

The 1980s were not kind years in terms of publication for Platt. His output continued, but he increasingly had difficulties finding publishers. "What makes a book or author controversial?" Platt asked in *SAAS*. "Dealing with a current topic that the guardians consider too risky to discuss. All my good books were so categorized, and I've done a dozen since that were turned down for the same kind of attack on the injustices and frauds I see." He did publish a story about a reluctant sportsman, *Brogg's Brain*, and the spoof *Frank and Stein and Me*, as well as a teen romance, *Crocker*, but for the prolific Platt, the 1980s were slow going.

"All in all," Platt wrote in *SAAS*, "you do the best you can at the moment.... When I'm doing a book, using all my concentration and powers, I feel fulfilled. It's the best in me, the best I can do at the time.... A book comes at you sneakily, in strange ways. It is formless and incomplete and hums in your head. It demands attention and doesn't care if you are sleeping, or shaving, or eating, or making love—it will not go away."

And neither did Platt go away. *Darwin and the Great Beasts*, a picture book written and illustrated by Platt, was published in 1992, his first children's publication in almost a decade. Young Darwin is transported back in time when his school class visits the La Brea Tar Pits, and he meets up with some of the animals who died in the pit. "This book brims with information about subjects of perennial fascination to youngsters," a reviewer in *Publishers Weekly* noted. Platt also got to realize a long-standing dream: to both write and illustrate a book of his own.

Regardless of the controversy surrounding much of his best writing, Platt remains at heart a writer doing a writer's job: putting down black on white. "The most satisfactory aspect of my writing career, long as it has been, is not the output, the great quantity of books for different age groups," Platt commented in *SAAS*, "although that has been a constant personal measure of my existence. Rather, it is the simple matter of reaching the minds of some children, getting them to react and think. Some have learned for the first time the great pleasure of reading books. For those reluctant readers, I provided the spark and excitement needed to get them glued to the page."

■ Works Cited

Review of *The Ape Inside Me, Booklist*, January 1, 1980, p. 662.

Berkvist, Robert, review of *The Blue Man, New York Times Book Review*, September 24, 1961, p. 40.

Berkvist, Robert, review of *Headman, New York Times Book Review*, December 14, 1975, p. 8.

Review of *Big Max, Kirkus Reviews*, August 1, 1965, p. 750.

Review of *The Boy Who Could Make Himself Disappear, Kirkus Reviews*, May 15, 1968, p. 556.

Campbell, Patty, review of *Flames Going Out, Wilson Library Bulletin*, February, 1981, pp. 454-55.

Cohen, Phyllis, review of *Sinbad and Me, Young Readers Review*, October, 1966, pp. 1-2.

Review of *Darwin and the Great Beasts, Publishers Weekly*, June 15, 1992, p. 103.

Dyson, Claire M., review of *The Ape Inside Me, Best Sellers*, February, 1980, p. 410.

Forman, Jack, review of *Headman, School Library Journal*, December, 1975, p. 61.

Forman, Jack, review of *Flames Going Out, School Library Journal*, December, 1980, pp. 63-64.

Gillespie, John, review of *The Boy Who Could Make Himself Disappear, School Library Journal*, October, 1968, p. 172.

Haviland, Virginia, review of *Big Max, Horn Book*, October, 1965, p. 498.

Kennerly, Sarah Law, review of *Sinbad and Me, School Library Journal*, December, 1966, p. 71.

Mathes, Miriam S., review of *The Blue Man, School Library Journal*, November, 1961, p. 54.

Platt, Kin, interview with Kathleen J. Edgar in *Authors & Artists for Young Adults*, Volume 11, Gale, 1993, pp. 161-72.

Platt, Kin, essay in *Something about the Author Autobiography Series*, Volume 17, Gale, 1994, pp. 275-96.

Review of *Sinbad and Me, Best Sellers*, October 1, 1966, p. 251.

Sutherland, Zena, review of *The Boy Who Could Make Himself Disappear, Bulletin of the Center for Children's Books*, September, 1968, pp. 14-15.

Sutherland, Zena, review of *Hey, Dummy, Bulletin of the Center for Children's Books*, June, 1972, p. 162.

Sutherland, Zena, review of *Chloris and the Creeps, Bulletin of the Center for Children's Books*, January, 1974, p. 84.

Wooldridge, C. Nordhielm, review of *Chloris and the Weirdos, School Library Journal*, November, 1978, p. 67.

■ For More Information See

BOOKS

Contemporary Literary Criticism, Volume 26, Gale, 1983, pp. 348-56.

PERIODICALS

Booklist, April 15, 1992, p. 1529.

Bulletin of the Center for Children's Books, January, 1978, p. 85; December, 1978, p. 70; March, 1979, p. 124; September, 1979, p. 16; May, 1980, pp. 180-81; November, 1980, p. 62; October, 1981, pp. 35-36; January, 1984, p. 95.

Kirkus Reviews, September 1, 1969, p. 939; December 1, 1969, p. 1291; November 15, 1971, p. 1213; February 15, 1973, p. 188; July 15, 1975, p. 783; October, 1, 1977, p. 1048; March 1, 1978, p. 269; December 1, 1978, p. 1308; February 1, 1980, p. 136; March 1, 1986, pp. 347-48.

Library Journal, September 1, 1972, p. 2758; February 1, 1973, p. 438.

New York Times Book Review, March 1, 1970, p. 45; January 3, 1971, p. 10; July 30, 1972, p. 22; November 16, 1975, pp. 50, 52; August 10, 1986, p. 23.

Publishers Weekly, December 29, 1969, p. 61; October, 19, 1970, p. 46-47; December 18, 1972, p. 34; June 14, 1976, p. 103; April 3, 1978, p. 70; October 28, 1983, p. 70.

School Library Journal, December, 1969, p. 64; December, 1977, pp. 58, 65; May, 1979, p. 82; November, 1979, p. 92; January, 1983, p. 87; January, 1984, p. 88; June, 1992, p. 124.

Voice of Youth Advocates, April, 1981, p. 35; December, 1981, p. 34; February, 1984, p. 340; June, 1988, p. 74.

—Sketch by J. Sydney Jones

PRINCE, Alison (Mary) 1931-

■ Personal

Born March 26, 1931, in Beckenham, Kent, England; daughter of Charles (a bank official) and Louise (David) Prince; married Goronwy Siriol Parry (a teacher), December 26, 1957 (separated); children: Samantha, Andrew, Benjamin. *Education:* Slade School of Fine Art, London, diploma in fine art, 1952; Goldsmiths' College, London, art teachers' certificate, 1954. *Politics:* Green. *Religion:* Agnostic. *Hobbies and other interests:* Films, music, art, children, schools, animals.

■ Addresses

Home—Burnfoot House, Whiting Bay, Isle of Arran KA27 8QL, Scotland.

■ Career

Author and illustrator. Elliott Comprehensive School, London, England, head of art department, 1954-58; adult education art teacher in Bromley, Kent, England, beginning 1960; Jordanhill College of Education, Glasgow, Scotland, fellow in creative writing, 1988. *Member:* International PEN, Society of Authors, Royal Society of Painter-Etchers and Engravers.

■ Awards, Honors

Best books for young adults citation, American Library Association, 1980, for *The Turkey's Nest.*

■ Writings

SELF-ILLUSTRATED CHILDREN'S BOOKS

The House on the Common, Methuen, 1969, Farrar, Straus, 1970.
The Red Alfa, Methuen, 1971, published as *The Red Jaguar,* Atheneum, 1972.
(With Jane Hickson) *Whosaurus? Dinosaurus!* (nonfiction), Studio Vista, 1975.
Who Wants Pets?, Methuen, 1980.
The Type One Super Robot, Deutsch, 1986, Four Winds Press, 1988.
How's Business, Deutsch, 1987, Four Winds Press, 1988.
The Blue Moon Day, Deutsch, 1988.

FICTION FOR CHILDREN

Joe and the Horse, and Other Short Stories about Joe from "Watch with Mother," British Broadcasting Corp., 1969.
(With Joan Hickson) *Joe and the Nursery School,* British Broadcasting Corp., 1972.
(With Hickson) *Joe Moves House,* British Broadcasting Corp., 1972.
(With Chris Connor) *Ben's Fish,* illustrated by Connor, Benn, 1972.
The Doubting Kind, Methuen, 1975, Morrow, 1977, published in two volumes as *A Friend in Need* and *All Who Love Us,* Macmillan, 1977.

The Night I Sold My Boots (young adult), Heinemann, 1979.
The Turkey's Nest, Methuen, 1979, Morrow, 1980, published as *Willow Farm,* Ace, 1980.
Haunted Children (stories), illustrated by Michael Bragg, Methuen, 1982.
The Sinister Airfield, illustrated by Edward Mortelmans, Methuen, 1982, Morrow, 1983.
Goodbye Summer, Methuen, 1983.
Night Landings, illustrated by Mortelmans, Methuen, 1983, Morrow, 1984.
The Ghost Within (stories), Methuen, 1984.
The Others, Methuen, 1984.
Scramble!, illustrated by Anne Knight, Methuen, 1984.
A Job for Merv, illustrated by David Higham, Deutsch, 1986.
Nick's October, Methuen, 1986.
A Haunting Refrain (stories), Methuen, 1988.
A Dog Called You, Pan Macmillan, 1993.
Merv on the Road, Young Piper, 1993.
The Sherwood Hero, Macmillan, 1995.

"MILL GREEN" SERIES; FOR CHILDREN

Mill Green on Fire, Armada, 1982.
Mill Green on Stage, Armada, 1982.
A Spy at Mill Green, Armada, 1983.
Hands Off, Mill Green!, Armada, 1984.
Rock On, Mill Green, Armada, 1985.

ILLUSTRATOR

(With Samantha Parry) Audrey Coppard, *Don't Panic!,* Heinemann, 1975.
Audrey Coppard, *Keeping Time,* Heinemann, 1976.

ALISON PRINCE

Audrey Coppard, *Get Well Soon,* Heinemann, 1978.
Jane Allen and Mary Danby, *Hello to Ponies,* Heinemann, 1979.
Jane Allen and Mary Danby, *Hello to Riding,* Heinemann, 1980.

Also illustrator of *Let's Explore Mathematics* and *Jessica on Her Own.*

OTHER

The Joe Annual, Polystyle Publications, 1968-71.
The Good Pets Guide, Armada, 1981.
(Self-illustrated) *The Necessary Goat* (essays), Taranis, 1992.
(Editor with Cicely Gill) *A Book of Arran Poetry,* illustrated by Saji Gill, Arran Theatre and Arts Trust, 1993.
On Arran, Argyll Publications, 1994.
Kenneth Grahame: An Innocent in the Wild Wood, Allison & Busby, 1994.
Having Been in the City (poems), Taranis, 1994.
The Witching Tree (adult novel), Allison & Busby, 1996.

Also author of television plays for children, including *Joe* series, 1968-71; *War Stories,* 1970 (part of *Jackanory* series); *Trumpton,* 1970; and scripts for *Watch with Mother* series. Author of adult radio play, *Ellie Bagg's Account,* 1984. Author of regular column, "On the Green," for *Arran Banner;* contributor to *Times Educational Supplement.*

■ **Work in Progress**

A biography of Hans Christian Andersen; a second adult novel.

■ **Sidelights**

In over thirty children's books that range from picture stories to young adult novels, Alison Prince has demonstrated that she is "a writer of great versatility," according to *Twentieth-Century Children's Writers* contributor Valerie Bierman. Since the 1969 publication of her first book, the first of a series of stories also produced on television, Prince has sampled genres that include mysteries, science fiction, ghost stories, historical fiction, school stories, and contemporary "problem" novels; she has even illustrated several of her works. Also the author of adult works, including a newspaper column and a biography of *The Wind in the Willows* creator Kenneth Grahame, Prince once told *SATA:* "Writing for me is something which happens all the time."

In one of her earliest works, *The House on the Common,* Prince recreates the wartime England of her childhood. The year is 1943, and young Jane and Derek are convinced that their new neighbors, an elderly couple who speak German, are potential enemy spies who need to be watched. The two learn a lesson about jumping to conclusions when they embarrass themselves during a nighttime "patrol" and discover the Liepmanns are Jewish refugees. A *Kirkus Reviews* critic praises the

Written with twenty-one British schoolchildren, this novel tells of evacuee Howard Grainger, who learns to cope with hostility, prejudice, and the risks of World War II London. (Cover illustration by Toby Gowing.)

depth of Prince's portrayal of the time, noting that within "the facade of a conventional mystery ... [and] family story is the long and the short of people in wartime."

The author returned to the World War II era for an unusual literary experiment, in which she collaborated with 21 schoolchildren in developing the plot and characters for a novel. 1988's *How's Business* takes place in the Lincolnshire countryside, where young Howard Grainger—who goes by the name How—has left his friends and successful trading business in London to live with an aunt and uncle during the war. An outsider because he is an evacuee, How's only friend is Anna, also an outcast because of her German background. When his mother stops sending him letters, How returns to London, where he discovers his home has been destroyed by bombs and his mother has been hospitalized. *Bulletin of the Center for Children's Books* critic Zena Sutherland finds the "all-problems-solved" ending too unrealistic, but notes that "the period details, wartime atmosphere, and writing style are effective" and How's return to London is "exciting and credible." Louise L. Sherman likewise observes in *School Library*

Journal that "Prince excels in recreating the historical period," and adds that the characters, even the minor ones, "are convincing and well-drawn."

While Prince often includes some type of puzzle in her books—such as the background of the Liepmanns in *The House on the Common* or the identity of a button thief in *The Red Jaguar*—she has also written pure mystery stories filled with suspense. In *The Sinister Airfield,* for instance, Harrie, her brother Ian, and their new friend Neil are exploring the woods near a reputedly "haunted" airport when they discover a dead body that disappears before they can return with the police. The children's persistence in investigating the airfield leads them to a gang of rustlers, and during an adventurous night chase the criminals are caught. While "less ambitious" than Prince's other novels, a *Kirkus Reviews* writer remarks that *The Sinister Airfield* is "a straightforward mystery with adeptly tuned suspense and more than the usual texture." *School Library Journal* writer Drew Stevenson similarly hails the story as "a good solid mystery with a touch of the macabre for spice and a wild climax."

The three friends return in *Night Landings* and "have lost none of their grit" in this story of smugglers and kidnapping, Stevenson observes. This time mysterious nighttime activity at the airstrip alerts Harrie, and when she discovers a boy hiding in a nearby barn the young sleuths have another riddle to solve. "This has just as much action as the first book, but is better structured," Sutherland notes in the *Bulletin of the Center for Children's Books,* adding praise for the book's "firmly drawn" characters and "brisk" pace. As Stevenson concludes, the ending "is as wild as anyone could want," and *Night Landings* provides readers with "good fun all the way around."

Suspense of a higher order is found in several of Prince's collections of ghost stories—"a genre in which Prince has had considerable success," according to Bierman. In the nine stories of *Haunted Children,* for example, ghosts ranging from the friendly to the sinister confront ordinary children; by using a "rather low-keyed style," Margery Fisher remarks in *Growing Point,* Prince "throws into relief the sensational, supernatural moments rising from everyday circumstances." The eight stories of *The Ghost Within* all feature a usually lonely, isolated child whose supernatural encounter triggers, or is triggered by, an internal conflict; the stories again demonstrate the author's "knack of being able to juxtapose convincingly the banal and the bizarre," according to *School Librarian* contributor Robert Dunbar. The tales in *A Haunting Refrain* are less chilling, dealing with voyages through time and the mixture of past and present. While Prince's use of detail and narrative skill create a believable present, D. A. Young writes in *Junior Bookshelf,* "she manipulates the transition into the past so smoothly that it seems the most natural thing in the world." Whatever the degree of horror she uses, the hallmark of Prince's ghost stories is their believability. As A. Thatcher concludes in a *Junior Bookshelf* review of *Haunted Children,* "Alison Prince is

a master of suspense writing, able to create out of simple everyday occurrences a menacing atmosphere in which anything can happen."

Less menacing but just as thoughtful is Prince's science fiction novel *The Others,* which is set in a post-nuclear society where people's bodies are genetically engineered to fit their occupations and their minds are given implants to prevent unsocial behavior. Ergo, whose thumb and forefinger have been given sharp edges for gardening, discovers and eventually joins an underground movement that teaches him about forbidden things like books and feelings. As Ergo assumes the dangerous life of a dissenter, he learns more about his restrictive society; nevertheless, "human strengths and weaknesses play the major part in keeping the story moving," Young notes in *Junior Bookshelf.* The critic praises the author for "fleshing out" her fictional society, as well as for creating characters that are "drawn in depth." A completely different approach to science fiction distinguishes *The Type One Super Robot,* a humorous story about a housekeeping robot that has its hands full babysitting a young boy. As young Humbert tests Manders's skills with unusual activities such as kite-building, the pair's "comic antics should

In Prince's self-illustrated *The Red Jaguar,* Robbie's loyalty to his friend Kevin, with whom he shares an enthusiasm for cars, is put to the test.

Humbert is sent to Uncle Bellamy with his own household robot, who manages to be more headache than help in Prince's self-illustrated *The Type One Super Robot.*

keep readers chuckling," a *Kirkus Reviews* critic declares, adding that "Manders has unusual charm, even for a robot."

Not all of Prince's books contain elements of adventure or the supernatural, however. Her "Mill Green" series follows the amusing incidents and everyday happenings at a traditional British school. Like the very popular "Grange Hill" books, another British series about school life, Prince's cycle is "authentic in its hierarchies and power struggles, and ... alive and alert in style," Fisher notes in a *Growing Point* review of *Mill Green on Fire.* Some of the author's picture books also deal with commonplace experiences. *Merv on the Road,* for instance, shows a handyman and his employer both learning to drive a car, with hilarious complications. Jean Needham remarks in *School Librarian* that Prince's pictures "ably demonstrate the eccentricities of the main characters" in this "funny" book.

It is Prince's young adult novels, however, that "are perhaps the most accurately observed," Bierman claims, with "language, sexuality, and unconventional lifestyles [that] are accurately and perceptively described." In addition, the critic relates, Prince's "dialogue is honest, fresh, and often humorous, and controversial subjects such as pregnancy are handled in a sympathetic and straightforward manner." *The Doubting Kind,* for instance, follows two fifteen-year-olds through a particularly difficult week in their lives. Fanny has a crush on the leader of her theatre group, but he has feelings for one of her teachers instead; Fanny's friend Bobbie has just lost her father in a car accident and has run off to a religious cult to avoid dealing with her alcoholic mother. While Sutherland, writing in the *Bulletin of the Center for Children's Books,* faults the "lack of a strong story line," she nevertheless observes that readers will appreciate the true-to-life characters and writing that is "casual and brisk, sophisticated in its candor." In taking her characters through the turmoil of adolescence, Prince shows "a good deal of understanding" of teenage life, Graham Hammond says in *Children's Literature in Education,* and examines her themes "with wit, pace, insight, and responsibility." Best of all, the critic concludes, "Prince pays her readers the compliment of showing rather than preaching, of looking at a question all round and not rushing into judgments."

In 1979 Prince published both *The Night I Sold My Boots,* a romance told from the boy's point of view, and *The Turkey's Nest,* a story of a teen's unexpected pregnancy. In the former, Ken's story of how he moves from London to the country and learns to adjust with the help of a free-spirited older girl is "right on the wavelength of mid-teenage readers," Thatcher states in *Junior Bookshelf.* In *The Turkey's Nest,* Kate also makes a journey to the country; there she plans to have her baby, although her boyfriend, who has reconciled with his dying wife, wants Kate to have an abortion. While the resolution to Kate's problems is "a bit pat," Sutherland remarks in recommending the book, Prince's writing "is smooth, the characters sturdy if a bit stock, and the pace even." *Horn Book* critic Ethel L. Heins likewise finds the novel's ending "somewhat too neat," but praises the "nicely individualized" characters and the "cool objectivity that matches the unusual, dispassionate tone of the book."

Prince took two novels to explore the turbulent relationship of a pair of working-class teens, one from each individual's point of view. In *Goodbye Summer,* Sasha is working at her first job—a dead-end position as a clerk in a shoe shop—when she meets Nick, a mechanic who is a bit of a bad boy. As her attachment to Nick develops, she also gains insight into her parents' lives and improves her relationship with them as well. While *Times Literary Supplement* writer Nicholas Tucker calls Prince "a good writer ... [whose] sentences have an authority that normally makes it easy for readers to sit back and let the story take over," he asserts that Nick's powerful attraction for someone "so clearly his superior" weakens the believability of the story line. *Junior Bookshelf* critic R. Baines, on the other hand, notes that for the most part *Goodbye Summer* "is a realistic and interesting novel." Nick's side of the story is explored in *Nick's October:* his strained relationship with his parents; his search for a meaningful job; and his fear of being caught in a routine. Nick's tale of his feelings of rebellion is "distinguished from others ... by its affectionate and humorous realism," Caroline Heaton comments in *British Book News*. Taken together, the books reveal "the uncertainty and insecurity of young people and explore their fears with friends and parents," Bierman concludes. "They also portray the pressures of parental manipulation—all refreshingly realistic."

Prince once explained to *SATA* how she develops her books: "Sitting down at a typewriter is just the last stage of a process which has usually been going on for weeks, or often months. The tantalizing beginnings of stories are everywhere; in a turn of phrase, a funny anecdote, a casual incident. Yet none of these things are in themselves a story, any more than flour and eggs and milk are pancakes. They need rearranging and altering before they start to form an interesting plot, and even after that there is a lot of careful development to do before the characters and the things which happen to them are really convincing.

"A story won't always 'come' through aggressive hard work. When the raw materials are all there, it needs to be shut away in the mysterious subconscious workings of the mind, rather as an egg starts to live in the dark warmth under a hen. Periodically one can, so to speak, 'take it out' and see how it is getting on. When it is ready to enter the 'finished writing' stage then the job seems fascinating and not difficult. If it is mind-bafflingly hard, then it's not ready.

"Running a small farm fits in well with writing. The routine work of caring for animals gives me exercise and fresh air as well as constant interest and, most importantly, it does not interfere with the mental process of writing. In fact, many of the knottiest plot problems seem to solve themselves while I am peacefully milking my Jersey cow!"

■ Works Cited

Baines, R., review of *Goodbye Summer, Junior Bookshelf,* June, 1984, p. 149.

Bierman, Valerie, "Alison Prince," in *Twentieth-Century Children's Writers,* 4th edition, St. James Press, 1995, pp. 778-79.

Dunbar, Robert, review of *The Ghost Within, School Librarian,* June, 1985, p. 163.

Fisher, Margery, review of *Mill Green on Fire, Growing Point,* September, 1982, p. 3946.

Fisher, Margery, review of *Haunted Children, Growing Point,* November, 1982, p. 3986.

Hammond, Graham, review of *The Doubting Kind, Children's Literature in Education,* summer, 1982, pp. 61-62.

Heaton, Caroline, review of *Nick's October, British Book News,* March, 1987, p. 33.

Heins, Ethel L., review of *The Turkey's Nest, Horn Book,* June, 1980, p. 308.

Review of *The House on the Common, Kirkus Reviews,* May 1, 1970, p. 508.

Needham, Jean, review of *Merv on the Road, School Librarian,* August, 1993, p. 111.

Sherman, Louise L., review of *How's Business, School Library Journal,* September, 1988, p. 185.

Review of *The Sinister Airfield, Kirkus Reviews,* February 15, 1983, p. 185.

Stevenson, Drew, review of *The Sinister Airfield, School Library Journal,* May, 1983, p. 93.

Stevenson, Drew, review of *Night Landings, School Library Journal,* May, 1984, p. 102.

Sutherland, Zena, review of *The Doubting Kind, Bulletin of the Center for Children's Books,* April, 1978, p. 133.

Sutherland, Zena, review of *The Turkey's Nest, Bulletin of the Center for Children's Books,* June, 1980, p. 199.

Sutherland, Zena, review of *Night Landings, Bulletin of the Center for Children's Books,* May, 1984, pp. 172-73.

Sutherland, Zena, review of *How's Business, Bulletin of the Center for Children's Books,* October, 1988, pp. 50-51.

Thatcher, A., review of *The Night I Sold My Boots, Junior Bookshelf,* June, 1980, p. 146.

Thatcher, A., review of *Haunted Children, Junior Bookshelf,* February, 1983, p. 47.

Tucker, Nicholas, "Stretching Sympathies," *Times Literary Supplement,* November 25, 1983.

Review of *The Type One Super Robot, Kirkus Reviews,* March 15, 1988, p. 457.

Young, D. A., review of *The Others, Junior Bookshelf,* October, 1986, p. 193.

Young, D. A., review of *A Haunting Refrain, Junior Bookshelf,* December, 1988, pp. 309-10.

■ For More Information See

PERIODICALS

Books for Keeps, May, 1986, p. 22.

Bulletin of the Center for Children's Books, May, 1983, p. 175; June, 1988, p. 215.

Junior Bookshelf, February, 1985, p. 45; April, 1987, pp. 98-99.

Kirkus Reviews, October 15, 1972, p. 1191.

Library Journal, November 15, 1972, p. 3808.

School Librarian, March, 1984, p. 74.

School Library Journal, December, 1977, p. 55.

Times Literary Supplement, December 3, 1971, p. 1517.

Voice of Youth Advocates, December, 1988, p. 241.

—Sketch by Diane Telgen

R

RAMANUJAN, A(ttipat) K(rishnaswami) 1929-1993

■ Personal

Surname pronounced "Ray-*may*-nu-jan"; born March 16, 1929, in Mysore, India; died of heart failure, July 13, 1993, in Chicago, IL; son of Attipat Asuri (a professor) and Seshammal Krishnaswami; married Molly A. Daniels (a writer), June 7, 1962 (divorced, 1971), remarried, 1976 (divorced, 1989); children: Krittika (daughter), Krishnaswami (son). *Education:* Mysore University, B.A. (with honors), 1949, M.A., 1950; Deccan College, received graduate degrees in 1958 and 1959; Indiana University, Ph.D., 1963. *Politics:* "Non-political." *Religion:* Hindu (Brahmin).

■ Career

Lecturer in English at colleges in India, 1950-58, including University of Baroda, 1957-58; University of Chicago, Chicago, IL, research associate in Tamil, 1961, assistant professsor of linguistics (Tamil and Dravidian languages), 1962-65, associate professor, 1966-68, professor of linguistics and Dravidian studies, 1968-93, professor on committee on social thought, 1972-93, chairman of department of South Asian languages and civilizations, 1980-85, William E. Colvin Professor, 1983-93. Visiting professor, University of Wisconsin, 1965 and 1971, University of California at Berkeley, 1966 and 1973, University of Michigan, 1970, and Carleton College, 1978 and 1982; guest lecturer at Oxford University, Harvard University, and the Ecole des Hautes Etudes in Paris.

■ Awards, Honors

Fulbright travel fellowship and Smith-Mundt fellowship for study in the United States, 1959-60; faculty research fellowship, American Institute of Indian Studies, 1963-64; fellow, Indiana School of Letters, 1963; Poetry Society recommendation, 1964, for *The Striders;* Tamil Writers' Association Award, 1969; Fulbright fellowship, 1969; American Council of Learned Societies fellow-ship, 1973; National Book Award nomination, 1974, for *Speaking of Siva;* National Endowment for the Humanities fellowships, 1976 and 1982; received the honorary title of Padma Shri from the Government of India, 1976, for his work in the fields of literature and languages; MacArthur Prize fellowship, 1983-89.

■ Writings

(With Edward C. Dimock Jr. and others) *The Literatures of India: An Introduction,* University of Chicago Press, 1975.
Mattobbana Atmakate (novel), [Dharwar], 1978.
(With Stuart Blackburn) *Another Harmony: New Essays on the Folklore of India,* University of California Press, 1986.
(Editor and translator) *Folktales from India: A Selection of Oral Tales from Twenty-two Languages* (for young readers), illustrated by Jenny Vandeventer, Pantheon, 1991.
(Editor with Vinay Dharwadker) *The Oxford Anthology of Modern Indian Poetry,* Oxford University Press, 1994.
(Editor and translator with V. Narayana Rao and David Shulman) *When God Is a Customer: Telugu Courtesan Songs by Ksetrayya and Others,* University of California Press, 1994.
Collected Essays, Oxford University Press, 1996.

POETRY

Proverbs (in Kannada), Karnatak University (Dharwar, India), 1955.
Fifteen Poems from a Classical Tamil Anthology, Writer's Workshop (Calcutta, India), 1965.
The Striders, Oxford University Press, 1966.
No Lotus in the Navel (in Kannada), Manohar Granthmala (Dharwar), 1969.
Relations, Oxford University Press, 1971.
Selected Poems, Oxford University Press, 1976.
And Other Poems (in Kannada), [Dharwar], 1977.
Second Sight, Oxford University Press, 1986.

Ramanujan's poems have also been published in over sixty anthologies and have appeared in Indian, British, and American periodicals.

TRANSLATOR

Shouri Ramanujan (pseudonym of wife, Molly Ramanujan) *Haladi Meenu* (translated into Kannada from her book, *The Yellow Fish*), Manohar Granthmala, 1966.

The Interior Landscape: Love Poems from a Classical Tamil Anthology, Indiana University Press, 1967.

(With Michael Garman and Rajeev Taranath) M. Gopalakrishna Adiga, *The Song of the Earth and Other Poems,* Writer's Workshop, 1968.

(With others) *Selected Poems of G. Sankara Kurup,* Dialogue Calcutta, c. 1969.

Speaking of Siva, Penguin, 1973.

U. R. Anantha Murthy, *Samskara: A Rite for a Dead Man* (novel; translated from Kannada), Oxford University Press, 1976.

Hymns for the Drowning: Poems for Visnu by Nammalvar, Princeton University Press, 1981.

Poems of Love and War: From the Eight Anthologies and the Ten Long Poems of Classical Tamil, Princeton University Press, 1985.

This diverse collection of over one hundred Indian folktales is further enhanced with A. K. Ramanujan's introduction and explanatory notes.

Based on ancient Tamil poetry, Ramanujan's distinguished translation introduces modern western readers to Indian classics outside the Sanskrit tradition. (Cover illustration by Meera Dayal Deshaprabhu.)

■ Sidelights

A respected poet and scholar, A. K. Ramanujan used his prodigious knowledge of Indian culture to bring together a collection of folktales suitable for teenage readers entitled *Folktales from India: A Selection of Oral Tales from Twenty-two Languages.* A collection of over one hundred tales springing from a variety of sources in the diverse Indian society, this valuable anthology is a "scholarly but very readable introduction to India and its variety of languages and cultural traditions," according to *Voice of Youth Advocates* contributor Jane Chandra.

Born in Mysore, India, in 1929, Ramanujan first gained an interest in folklore and the Indian oral tradition as a child listening to his grandmother tell stories at family meals. Largely responsible for introducing the West to Tamil literature—thus disposing of the narrow view of Sanskrit being the only important language of Indian culture—Ramanujan first became interested in Tamil when he stumbled upon a collection of first-century poems written in that ancient language. "This little event had a dramatic effect on his consciousness and his writing," according to his former wife, Molly A. Daniels. She also told *SATA,* "It led not only to the publication of four major works, *The Interior Landscape, Speaking of Siva, Poems of Love and War,* and *Hymns for the Drowning,* but also altered permanently the perception in the West of the Indian literary map."

■ Works Cited

Chandra, Jane, review of *Folktales from India: A Selection of Oral Tales from Twenty-two Languages, Voice of Youth Advocates,* August, 1992, p. 186.

■ For More Information See

BOOKS

King, Bruce Alvin, *Three Indian Poets: Nissim Ezekiel, A. K. Ramanujan, Dom Moraes,* Oxford University Press, 1991.
Kurup, P. K. J., *Contemporary Indian Poetry in English: With Special Reference to the Poetry of Nissim Ezekiel, Kamala Das, A. K. Ramanujan, and R. Parthasarathy,* Atlantic Publishers & Distributors (New Delhi, India), 1991.

PERIODICALS

Choice, July, 1986, p. 1684.
Library Journal, October 1, 1967, p. 3427; May 15, 1972, p. 1814; February 1, 1992, p. 100.
New York Times Book Review, November 20, 1965.
Poetry, March, 1967.
Publishers Weekly, August, 1967, p. 52; December 13, 1991, p. 46.
School Library Journal, July, 1992, p. 100.
Times Literary Supplement, February 3, 1978, p. 136.

OBITUARIES:

PERIODICALS

Chicago Tribune, July 15, 1993, Section 3, p. 11; July 18, 1993, Section 6, p. 2.
New York Times, July 16, 1993, p. D20.
Washington Post, July 16, 1993, p. B4.*

*   *   *

REY, Margret (Elisabeth) 1906-

■ Personal

Born May 16, 1906, in Hamburg, Germany; came to the United States in 1940; naturalized citizen, 1946; daughter of Felix and Gertrude (maiden name, Rosenfeld) Waldstein; married Hans Augusto Rey (a writer and illustrator), 1935 (died, 1977). *Education:* Attended Bauhaus, 1927, Dusseldorf Academy of Art, 1928-29, and University of Munich, 1930-31. *Politics:* Democrat.

MARGRET REY

■ Addresses

Home and office—14 Hilliard St., Cambridge, MA 02138-4922. *Agent*—A. P. Watt Ltd., 20 John St., London, WC1N 2DR England.

■ Career

Reporter and advertising copywriter in Berlin, Germany, 1928-29; held one-woman shows of watercolors in Berlin, 1929-34; photographer in London, England, Hamburg, Germany, and Rio de Janeiro, Brazil, 1930-35; freelance writer in Paris, France, 1936-40, New York City, 1940-63, and Cambridge, MA, 1963—; writer of children's books, 1937—; script consultant, Montreal, Quebec, Canada, 1977-83; Brandeis University, Waltham, MA, adjunct instructor in creative writing, 1978-84. Member of board of directors, Phillips Brooks House, Harvard University, Cambridge, MA, 1989—; founder and trustee of the Curious George Foundation, Cambridge, MA, 1991—. *Member:* World Wildlife Fund, Smithsonian Institution, Museum of Fine Arts, Audubon Society, Defenders of Wildlife.

■ Awards, Honors

Best Illustrated Children's Books of the Year citation, *New York Times,* 1957, for *Curious George;* Children's Book Award, Child Study Association of America, 1966, for *Curious George Goes to the Hospital.*

■ Writings

ALL ILLUSTRATED BY HUSBAND, H. A. REY

Pretzel, Harper, 1944.
Spotty, Harper, 1945.
Pretzel and the Puppies, Harper, 1946.
Billy's Picture, Harper, 1948.

WITH H. A. REY; ILLUSTRATED BY H. A. REY

How the Flying Fishes Came into Being, Chatto & Windus, 1938.
Raffy and the Nine Monkeys, Chatto & Windus, 1939, published as *Cecily G. and the Nine Monkeys*, Houghton, 1942.
Anybody at Home? (verse), Chatto & Windus, 1939, Houghton, 1943.
How Do You Get There?, Houghton, 1941.
Elizabite: The Adventures of a Carnivorous Plant, Harper, 1942.
Tit for Tat (verse), Harper, 1942.
Where's My Baby? (verse), Houghton, 1943.
Feed the Animals (verse), Houghton, 1944.
Mary Had a Little Lamb, Penguin, 1951.
See the Circus (verse), Houghton, 1956.

"CURIOUS GEORGE" SERIES (ALL TITLES PUBLISHED IN ENGLAND AS "ZOZO" SERIES); COAUTHORED AND ILLUSTRATED BY H. A. REY

Curious George, Houghton, 1941.
Curious George Takes a Job, Houghton, 1947.
Curious George Rides a Bike, Houghton, 1952.
Curious George Gets a Medal, Houghton, 1957.
Curious George Flies a Kite, Houghton, 1958.
Curious George Learns the Alphabet, Houghton, 1963.
Curious George Goes to the Hospital, Houghton, 1966.

EDITOR WITH ALLAN J. SHALLECK; BASED ON "CURIOUS GEORGE" FILM SERIES

Curious George and the Dump Truck, Houghton, 1984.
Curious George Goes to the Circus, Houghton, 1984.
Curious George Goes to the Aquarium, Houghton, 1984.
Curious George Goes Sledding, Houghton, 1984.
Curious George Goes Hiking, Houghton, 1985.
Curious George and the Pizza, Houghton, 1985.
Curious George at the Fire Station, Houghton, 1985.
Curious George Visits the Zoo, Houghton, 1985.
Curious George Walks the Pets, Houghton, 1986.
Curious George Plays Baseball, Houghton, 1986.
Curious George Goes to a Costume Party, Houghton, 1986.
Curious George at the Ballet, Houghton, 1986.
Curious George Visits the Police Station, Houghton, 1987.
Curious George Goes Fishing, Houghton, 1987.
Curious George at the Laundromat, Houghton, 1987.
Curious George at the Airport, Houghton, 1987.
Curious George at the Beach, Houghton, 1988.
Curious George at the Railroad Station, Houghton, 1988.
Curious George Goes to a Restaurant, Houghton, 1988.
Curious George Visits an Amusement Park, Houghton, 1988.
Curious George and the Dinosaur, Houghton, 1989.
Curious George Goes to an Ice Cream Shop, Houghton, 1989.
Curious George Goes to School, Houghton, 1989.
Curious George Goes to the Dentist, Houghton, 1989.
Curious George Bakes a Cake, Houghton, 1990.
Curious George Goes Camping, Houghton, 1990.
Curious George Goes to an Air Show, Houghton, 1990.
Curious George Goes to a Toy Store, Houghton, 1990.

OTHER

Contributor, with H. A. Rey, of the "Zozo Page for Children," *Good Housekeeping*, 1951. The Reys' works have been translated into numerous languages.

■ Adaptations

Weston Woods Studios made *Curious George Rides a Bike* into both a motion picture with teaching guide, 1958, and a filmstrip with text, 1960; Teaching Resources Films made filmstrip-record sets from *Curious George*, *Curious George Flies a Kite*, *Curious George Gets a Medal*, *Curious George Goes to the Hospital*, and *Curious George Takes a Job*, all 1971. *Curious George and Other Stories about Curious George* and *Curious George Learns the Alphabet and Other Stories about Curious George*, both read by Julie Harris, were released by Caedmon Records, 1972-73. A television series based on the "Curious George" books has also been produced; the musical play *Curious George*, music by Timothy Brown and book and lyrics by Thomas Toce, has toured with Theatreworks/USA.

■ Work in Progress

Curious George films for television.

■ Sidelights

Part of the European migration of World War II that landed world-famous scientists and artists on American shores, Margret Rey and her husband H. A. Rey arrived in America in 1940 with a suitcase full of manuscripts and a great deal of hope. A husband and wife team in children's books, the Reys also brought with them a Central European tradition, valuing education and cosmopolitan traditions. They set about creating classic picture books—especially the "Curious George" series—that display, according to James E. Higgins in *Twentieth-Century Children's Writers*, "endless inventiveness."

Born in Hamburg, Germany, in the early years of the twentieth century, Rey was not one to be kept down by traditional expectations of what a young woman should be. A painter and photographer, she learned her art not only at the Dusseldorf Academy of Art, but also at the avant garde Bauhaus in Dessau. The heady days of Weimar Germany, when experimentation was in the air, led to several exhibits of Rey's watercolor works in Berlin. Soon, however, her photography led her out of Germany to London and Rio de Janeiro, Brazil. She worked variously as a reporter and also as an advertising copy writer, and when she met H. A. Rey in Rio de

In their *Curious George Flies a Kite*, first published in 1958, the Reys used a new simpler format to tell about the irrepressible monkey. (Illustration by H. A. Rey.)

Janeiro in 1935, she convinced him to become her partner in founding the first advertising firm in Brazil. At the time, H. A. Rey, who had been drawing since he was a youth in Hamburg but who could not afford art school, was selling bathtubs for a living. The partnership soon became a marriage, and the two moved to Paris, where they began collaborating on book projects.

"In Paris, we did our first children's book," Rey recalled in an entry for *Authors and Illustrators of Children's Books: Writings on Their Lives and Works*. "It came about by accident: H. A. had done a few humorous drawings of a giraffe for a Paris periodical. An editor at Gallimard, the French publishing house, saw them and called us up to ask whether we could not make a children's book out of them. We did and this became our first book, *Cecily G. and the Nine Monkeys,* one of the nine became George, incidentally." But the birth of the mischievous, curious George in his own series was still several years away. Rey, an artist in her own right, left the illustrating to her husband in this collaboration, and concentrated on the text. And with the lonely giraffe, Cecily, who offers to share her house with a monkey family, the Reys hit on a formula for success that would see them through the rest of their books for children: "An unforced humor which is irresistible," as Anne T. Eaton described it in the *New York Times Book Review*. It was not just the humor that was so effective

in this first book, Eaton noted, but also the carefully worked out details of the story that made the absurd so "entirely logical and credible." It was this ability to turn the absurd into the credible which would prove so invaluable in the Curious George books.

But as the Reys were enjoying their first success in children's books, the political world around them was tumbling out of control. By 1939 Europe was at war; Germany invaded France in 1940, and the Reys had no choice but to flee. "In June, 1940," Rey wrote in *Authors and Illustrators of Children's Books,* "on a rainy morning before dawn, a few hours before the Nazis entered, we left Paris on bicycles, with nothing but warm coats and our manuscripts (*Curious George* among them) tied to the baggage racks, and started pedaling south. We finally made it to Lisbon, by train, having sold our bicycles to customs officials at the French-Spanish border. After a brief interlude in Rio de Janeiro, our migrations came to an end one clear, crisp October morning in 1940, when we saw the Statue of Liberty rise above the harbor of New York and landed in the U.S.A."

Although strangers in a new country, the Reys were not without resources. They rented an apartment in Greenwich Village and pounded the pavement until they found a publisher interested in their work. It took only a week for *Curious George* to be accepted by Houghton Mifflin. What is still more amazing is that the book itself, written during dark times, was so full of light and good cheer. From the opening lines describing George, the reader is taken into a world at once simple and quite plausible: "He lived with his friend, the man with the yellow hat. He was a good little monkey, but he was always curious." It is this curiosity that becomes the operative word for the George books—a sense of

The mischievous Curious George finds himself in another predicament in Rey's *Curious George and the Dinosaur.* (Illustration by H. A. Rey.)

In addition to the _Curious George_ books, the Reys collaborated on stories like _Pretzel,_ about a very long dachshund who found his shape both a hindrance and an asset in love. (Illustration by H. A. Rey.)

innocent childish wonder that leads the little monkey into all sorts of mischief.

Best of all, children can identify with the impish monkey. "George is a kind of release for children," noted Margot Dukler in _Elementary English._ "While they themselves cannot do the things he does, they can 'be' George, in a safe and acceptable way." When George flies off on a balloon or decides to use a garden hose to clean the floor, children can vicariously be part of that innocent mischief. Dukler also points out how the man in the yellow hat—always there when George needs him but never reproachful—is an adult combination of "mother-father-guardian angel." While some critics were disparaging of the similarity of the Curious George books to the format of the comic book, others praised the Reys. "The story has a breathless pace," remarked Lillian H. Smith in _The Unreluctant Years: A Critical Approach to Children's Literature._ "The simplicity and brevity of the telling is rhythmic and dramatic ... told in words carefully chosen for their speed, animation, and sound.... No wonder little children return again and again to _Curious George._" As Eaton summed it up in the _New York Times Book Review,_ "_Curious George_ is an ideal picture book for the 3-to-5-year-old.... We shall hope for other such lively picture books from [the Reys'] brush and pen."

Eaton and an army of children got that wish. Curious George over the years became something of an institution in children's literature, though it took six years for the second installment of his adventures to appear. "Each book took a long time," Rey explained in a _People_ article commemorating Curious George's fiftieth birthday. "All my life I spent standing behind [H. A.] at his desk. I made all the movements George makes." The couple would frequently debate the plot, from beginning to ending, as well as the content of the imaginatively detailed illustrations. "When we had one book finished," the author continued, "I'd vow, 'Never again.'" Nevertheless, the Reys produced seven of the Curious George stories together. With the early picture books, only H. A. Rey's name appeared on the title page, but they were most definitely collaborative works, H. A. doing the illustrations and Margret Rey writing the text. Both would come up with story ideas.

With _Pretzel_ and _Spotty,_ however, the books were written solely by Margret Rey and then illustrated by her husband. These stories, published toward the end of World War II, can both be looked at as cautionary tales about tolerance for people's differences. _Pretzel_ concerns the courtship of an exceptionally long dachshund who is rejected because of his freakish length. But in the end it is his long body that comes in handy when Pretzel is able to save Greta, his doggy sweetheart, by pulling her out of a deep box. The book ends on a happy, tolerant note: "How good that Pretzel was so long!" Siddie Joe Johnson, writing in *Library Journal,* thought that *Pretzel* was the type of book that "the very young child or the very sophisticated adult will like."

Spotty, "a delightful picture book for any age from three up" according to a reviewer for *Virginia Kirkus' Bookshop Service,* tells another tale of goodwill and fellowship. A brown-and-white bunny, Spotty, leaves home after being teased by his pink-and-white brethren to find a new and welcome home with other brown-and-white bunnies. To his surprise, however, he soon discovers a pink-and-white bunny—an outsider—who is just as miserable as he was in his former home. Their friendship provides an end to their loneliness—and a lesson in tolerance.

Another perennial favorite Rey collaboration outside of the Curious George series is *Elizabite: The Adventures of a Carnivorous Plant,* "a unique creation," according to Ellen Lewis Buell in the *New York Times Book Review.* The picture book provides "a bright spot of hilarity in a darkened world," Buell concluded. This book presents "the strangest character yet to be celebrated in a picture book," noted a critic for the *New Yorker,* and May Lamberton Becker commented in *New York Herald Tribune Books* that the adventures of this ferocious flower are "funny in the hearty slapstick way children enjoy."

The second in the Curious George series, *Curious George Takes a Job,* appeared in 1947, and over the next twenty years the Reys turned out five more stories of the inquisitive monkey. All follow the same successful formula: the likeable and innocent main character— part monkey, part child—gets into all sorts of trouble, described by engaging text and boldly colorful illustrations. And always there is the one constant that children look for in the books—the man with the yellow hat, the kind of adult, according to Higgins in *Twentieth-Century Children's Writers,* that children "most admire and respect." Readership grew with each new title. Reviewing *Curious George Takes a Job* in the *New York Herald Tribune Weekly Book Review,* Becker commented on its "rippling fun and absurd color-pictures." The playful antics of the 1952 *Curious George Rides a Bike* prompted Katherine T. Kinkead to say in the *New Yorker* that "George's ultimate triumph this time is magnificent." And *Curious George Gets a Medal* provides "plenty of unexpected fun to keep the children turning the pages," Buell noted in the *New York Times Book Review.*

With 1958's *Curious George Flies a Kite,* Rey changed the textual format somewhat, simplifying it so that the books could be read by a child, but the husband and wife collaborations, except for *Elizabite,* never steered away from a focus on an amiable animal. "Not all our children's books are about George," Rey noted in *Authors and Illustrators of Children's Books,* "but they are all about animals. We both love them, and one of the first things we do when we come to a new town is visit

Causing characteristic pandemonium, here is the lively monkey in the last of the original Curious George books, *Curious George Goes to the Hospital.* (Illustration by H. A. Rey.)

the Zoo." The Reys had various animal companions throughout the years, from turtles and other reptiles to dogs—particularly cocker spaniels—to monkeys during their stay in Brazil.

The last of the original Curious George books appeared in 1966, *Curious George Goes to the Hospital.* As usual, the little main character is up to a lot of monkey business even when going to the hospital for surgery himself. "As a book that prepares the child for the hospital this new 'Curious George' is one of the best," noted George A. Woods in the *New York Times Book Review.* "About the most useful book you will be ordering for a long time," a *Publishers Weekly* critic concurred.

With the death of her husband in 1977, Rey stopped writing children's books, but her connection to Curious George goes on. As coeditor of some thirty new titles based on the Curious George animated film series, Rey has ensured that the antics George gets up to and the lessons he learns in each new title fit the original intention of the books. Critics have generally agreed that textually the books work, though the illustrations, adapted from the films, leave something to be desired. "Fans will be happy to know that curious George is still curious, and as appealing as ever," wrote Anne L. Okie in *School Library Journal*, reviewing the first four titles in the adapted series. However, the critic found the illustrations to be "blurred and grainy."

In addition to editing the new series of Curious George books, Rey taught writing for a time at Brandeis University, a task she enjoyed "enormously," as she once commented. She is also the founder and trustee of the Curious George Foundation, and it is with that at once gregarious and naive primate—part comedian, part child—that Rey's name, as well as her husband's, will long be associated.

■ Works Cited

Becker, May Lamberton, "Fun and Laughter for the Little Children," *New York Herald Tribune Books*, May 10, 1942, p. 17.

Becker, May Lamberton, review of *Curious George Takes a Job, New York Herald Tribune Weekly Book Review*, November 23, 1947, p. 8.

Buell, Ellen Lewis, review of *Elizabite: The Adventures of a Carnivorous Plant, New York Times Book Review*, April 26, 1942, p. 8.

Buell, Ellen Lewis, review of *Curious George Gets a Medal, New York Times Book Review*, September 15, 1957, p. 30.

Review of *Curious George Goes to the Hospital, Publishers Weekly*, January 31, 1966, p. 100.

Dukler, Margot, "Five Popular Children's Authors," *Elementary English*, January, 1958, pp. 3-11.

Eaton, Anne T., review of *Curious George, New York Times Book Review*, October 26, 1941, p. 10.

Eaton, Anne T., review of *Cecily G. and the Nine Monkeys, New York Times Book Review*, November 15, 1942, p. 36.

Review of *Elizabite: The Adventures of a Carnivorous Plant, New Yorker*, May 23, 1942, p. 56.

Higgins, James E., "H. A. and Margret Rey," *Twentieth-Century Children's Authors*, 4th edition, edited by Laura Standley Berger, St. James Press, 1995, pp. 803-4.

Johnson, Siddie Joe, review of *Pretzel, Library Journal*, December 15, 1944, p. 1104.

Kinkead, Katherine T., review of *Curious George Rides a Bike, The New Yorker*, December 6, 1952, p. 191.

Okie, Anne L., review of *Curious George and the Dump Truck, School Library Journal*, February, 1985, p. 62.

Rey, Margret, *Pretzel*, Harper, 1944.

Rey, Margret, "Curious George and His Literary Mama, Margret Rey, Celebrate a Half-Century of Monkeyshines," *People*, June 1, 1987.

Rey, Margret, and H. A. Rey, *Curious George*, Houghton, 1941.

Rey, Margret, and H. A. Rey, "Margret and H. A. Rey," *Authors and Illustrators of Children's Books: Writings on Their Lives and Works*, edited by Miriam Hoffman and Eva Samuels, Bowker, 1972, pp. 359-63.

Smith, Lillian H., "Picture Books," *The Unreluctant Years: A Critical Approach to Children's Literature*, American Library Association, 1953, pp. 114-29.

Review of *Spotty, Virginia Kirkus' Bookshop Service*, November 1, 1945, p. 491.

Woods, George A., review of *Curious George Goes to the Hospital, New York Times Book Review*, March 20, 1966, p. 26.

■ For More Information See

BOOKS

Bader, Barbara, *American Picture Books from Noah's Ark to the Beast Within*, Macmillan, 1976, pp. 199-211, 241-64.

Children's Literature Review, Volume 5, Gale, 1983, pp. 188-200.

Fisher, Margery, *Who's Who in Children's Books: A Treasury of the Familiar Characters of Childhood*, Holt, Rinehart, 1975, p. 77.

MacCann, Donnarae, and Olga Richard, *Their Child's First Books: A Critical Study of Pictures and Texts*, H. W. Wilson, 1973, pp. 95-106.

Norby, Shirley, and Gregory Ryan, *Famous Children's Authors*, Denison, 1988, pp. 49-50.

PERIODICALS

Horn Book, November-December, 1941, p. 460; April, 1963, p. 169; July, 1989, p. 42; July, 1990, p. 59.

New York Times Book Review, November 11, 1944, p. 10; January 6, 1946, p. 8; November 10, 1946, p. 42; September 21, 1947, p. 37; October 12, 1952, p. 26; November 2, 1958, p. 52; May 12, 1963, pp. 4-5.

School Library Journal, February, 1987, p. 74.; April, 1988, p. 88; April, 1990, p. 95; January, 1991, p. 37.

Times Literary Supplement, November 30, 1967, p. 1152.*

—Sketch by J. Sydney Jones

*   *   *

ROCKLIN, Joanne 1946-

■ Personal

Born March 7, 1946, in Montreal, Quebec, Canada; daughter of Hyman (a businessman) and Adele (a special education teacher; maiden name, Sandler) Rocklin; married Robert A. Silverberg (a physician), 1968 (divorced, 1982); married Gerald Nelson (a realtor), August 14, 1988; children: (first marriage): Michael, Eric. *Education:* McGill University, B.A. (with great distinction), 1967, teaching diploma, 1968; California School of Professional Psychology, M.A., 1981, Ph.D., 1984. *Politics:* Democrat. *Religion:* Jewish. *Hobbies and other interests:* Cooking, baking, all kinds of music, swimming, walking, reading, movies, plays, cats.

■ Addresses

Home—1830 Westholme Ave., Los Angeles, CA 90025. *Electronic mail*—(America Online) Purrsonl@aol.com. *Agent*—Ruth Cohen, P.O. Box 7626, Menlo Park, CA 94025.

JOANNE ROCKLIN

■ Career

Author. Devonshire Elementary School, Montreal, Quebec, Canada, teacher, 1968-72; Burbank Child Guidance Clinic, Burbank, CA, psychotherapist, 1984-87; Omega Center for Mental Health, Woodland Hills, CA, psychotherapist, 1984-92; West Valley Center for Educational Therapy, Canoga Park, CA, psychodiagnostic assessor, 1987. Lecturer on writing for children at schools, libraries, and writers' and teachers' conferences; instructor for The Learning Annex; writer in residence, University of Southern California Writing Project, 1995. *Member:* International Reading Association, Society of Children's Book Writers and Illustrators, Authors Guild, Association of Booksellers for Children, American Psychological Association, California Reading Association, Southern California Council on Literature for Children and Young People, Los Angeles Reading Association.

■ Awards, Honors

University Scholarship, McGill University, 1967; Governor General's Medal for the Art of Teaching, 1968; California Graduate State Fellowships, 1980-81, 1981-82, 1983-84; Best Books citation, New York Public Library, 1987, for *Feeling Great;* Outstanding Work of Fiction for Children citation, Southern California Council on Literature for Children and Young People, 1989, for *Dear Baby;* Children's Book of the Year citation, Bank Street College of Education, c. 1992, for *Discovering Martha.*

■ Writings

(With Nancy Levinson) *Getting High in Natural Ways: An Infobook for Young People of All Ages* (nonfiction), Borgo Press, 1986, reprinted as *Feeling Great: Reaching out to Life, Reaching in to Yourself—without Drugs,* Hunter House, 1992.
Sonia Begonia, illustrated by Julie Downing, Macmillan, 1986.
Dear Baby, illustrated by Eileen McKeating, Macmillan, 1988.
Jace the Ace, illustrated by Diane deGroat, Macmillan, 1990.
Discovering Martha, illustrated by McKeating, Macmillan, 1991.
Musical Chairs and Dancing Bears (picture book), illustrated by Laure de Matharel, Holt, 1993.
Three Smart Pals (first reader), illustrated by Denise Brunkus, Scholastic, 1994.
How Much Is that Guinea Pig in the Window? (first reader), illustrated by Meredith Johnson, Scholastic, 1995.
The Case of the Missing Birthday Party (first reader), Scholastic, 1996.

Contributor of articles to *L.A. Parent Magazine, Baltimore Child, Minnesota Parent, Chicago Parent,* and other parenting publications.

■ Work in Progress

"A humorous middle grade novel written in the form of a girl's journal to her teacher illustrating her growing love for poetry and understanding of the world, to be published by Scholastic."

■ Sidelights

Joanne Rocklin told *SATA:* "I was born in Montreal, Canada and have always lived within walking distance of a library. As soon as I learned to hold a pencil I began writing poems, stories, and diaries. I loved reading my own stories and library books to my two younger sisters. My favorite books when I was growing up were *Anne of Green Gables* by L. M. Montgomery and everything written by Beverly Cleary. As a matter of fact, I would *still* include them among my favorites.

"When I was ten years old I wrote a poem about Humpty Dumpty potato chips (my favorite brand at the time; I think you can only buy them in Canada) and mailed the poem to the Humpty Dumpty company. A huge barrel of potato chips was delivered to my doorstep! Was I excited! That was the first time I was ever 'paid' for my writing.

"However, the real reward of writing is the tremendous joy it brings to me. I love being alone in my room with my word processor, my cat, and a new idea. Most of the details of my books are grounded in my everyday life. The feelings and themes, however, come from my childhood (for example, the loneliness of the outsider and the importance of friendship and communication in overcoming this loneliness).

"My first book, the middle grade novel *Sonia Begonia,* grew out of a wonderful UCLA Extension class taught by author Eve Bunting. The Society of Children's Book Writers and Illustrators has also been a tremendous source of support and information.

"I love to read and write, but I also love to talk—especially about writing. I will never fully understand the writing process—it is incredibly mysterious! Many of my ideas seem to arrive out of nowhere. In the end, as I tell children in the schools I visit, you have to discover what works best for you, but sometimes it is helpful and inspiring to hear what works for other writers.

"What works for me: writing 'I remember' at the top of a page and free-associating about my childhood; realizing that my first, rough draft is going to be awful, but that this is perfectly alright! Good ideas happen when I allow myself to be untidy and free during the discovery process. One idea will lead to another one and I often have to return to the beginning and add a scribble or two, which adds to the messiness. And sometimes I write the end of a book before the middle just to find out

Sonia Begley, alias Sonia Begonia, begins a business of her own and learns the hard way what it takes to be both successful and happy in *Sonia Begonia.* (Illustration by Julie Downing.)

what's going to happen; 'fooling myself'—telling myself that it is quite enough to write only one paragraph a day. I usually end up writing more than that and feel very proud that I have surpassed my goal!"

Rocklin's novels for middle grade readers are considered lighthearted treatments of the problems children have making friends and being part of a family. Critics highlight her humorous depiction of realistic, likeable characters in reviews that emphasize her positive resolution of ordinary problems. Rocklin has also written a picture book, a first-reader, and, with Nancy Levinson, a book about alternatives to drugs for young adults.

In *Sonia Begonia,* the title character feels left out of the family business of selling women's lingerie, and decides to give up the ordinary job of babysitting to create Sonia's Safety Sentinel Service (S.S.S.S.). The idea is to help protect her vacationing neighbors' homes from the rash of burglaries that has recently cropped up in the area. Unfortunately, due to Sonia's loose tongue, S.S.S.S. actually helps target which homes can be easily burgled, and Sonia and her friend Jason set themselves the task of trying to catch the robbers. Reviewers especially admired the energy and optimism of Rocklin's protagonist. "Young readers will immediately warm up to the heroine in this lighthearted first novel," remarked Kristiana Gregory in the *Los Angeles Times Book Review.* While Betsy Hearne of the *Bulletin of the Center for Children's Books* found Rocklin's conclusion "a bit muddled and unconvincing," Katharine Bruner added in *School Library Journal:* "All in all, a nice light tale revolving around wholesome, sensitive characters."

Rocklin's next novel for this age group, *Dear Baby,* is an award-winning treatment of the awkward feelings of a pre-adolescent toward a new sibling. Set as a journal or letter to the unborn child, *Dear Baby* depicts Farla's feelings about the new addition to the family, her mother's new husband, his great-aunt who has come to live with them, and the changes in her grandmother, who stops cooking and gets a boyfriend. "The minor false starts and wrong turns as the family adjusts ring true," according to Sally T. Margolis, who reviewed *Dear Baby* for *School Library Journal.* This is "a well-balanced look at a common problem," Margolis concluded.

Rocklin treats the problem of being the new kid in town in *Jace the Ace.* Fifth-grader Jason, who has just moved to Los Angeles with his family, decides to impress his new schoolmates by pretending to be a counterintelligence spy and a photojournalist. These grandiose plans backfire, but Jason's "imaginative attempts to find friends ... in a new home will generate an empathetic response among readers," according to Roger Sutton in the *Bulletin of the Center for Children's Books.* Although *School Library Journal* contributor Judie Porter called *Jace the Ace* "didactic," she felt that Jason's self-dramatizing would "elicit smiles of recognition" among young readers. "The feelgood ending," according to a *Kirkus Reviews* writer, "is sure to please."

Martha, the title character in Rocklin's next novel for the middle grades, *Discovering Martha,* shares with the protagonist of *Jace the Ace* a tendency to talk about herself in ways that potential friends do not like. Martha starred in two television commercials at the age of four, but as a sixth-grader is waiting in vain to be rediscovered by Hollywood. When a guitar arrives in the mail one day, free for a six-week trial period, Martha secretly learns how to play the instrument and finds her life transformed until the guitar must be returned. Martha is "a believable underdog worth rooting for," averred Deborah Stevenson in the *Bulletin of the Center for Children's Books.* While *School Library Journal* contributor Jane Marino complained that Rocklin's failure to resolve Martha's "overwhelming number of problems" would frustrate her readers, *Publishers Weekly* asserted that the author "poignantly captures the dreams and fears of her audience through this spunky, honest heroine."

Using the game of musical chairs, Rocklin's picture book *Musical Chairs and Dancing Bears* teaches the concept of simple subtraction. The author starts with ten bears dancing around nine chairs, then nine bears and eight chairs, and so forth, each time with a different musical theme. While Louise L. Sherman, a critic for *School Library Journal,* felt that children would "get much more enjoyment from playing musical chairs than from reading this book," *Publishers Weekly* dubbed Rocklin's idea "ingenious."

Rocklin is also the coauthor, with Nancy Levinson, of *Feeling Great: Reaching out to Life, Reaching in to Yourself—without Drugs* (once titled *Getting High in Natural Ways: An Infobook for Young People of All Ages*)—an inspirational book for adolescents and those who work with them. *Feeling Great* suggests exercise, meditation, and time spent with friends and alone as drug-free alternative ways of feeling good.

■ Works Cited

Bruner, Katharine, review of *Sonia Begonia, School Library Journal,* May, 1986, p. 97.

Review of *Discovering Martha, Publishers Weekly,* November 15, 1991, p. 73.

Gregory, Kristiana, review of *Sonia Begonia, Los Angeles Times Book Review,* July 27, 1986, p. 9.

Hearne, Betsy, review of *Sonia Begonia, Bulletin of the Center for Children's Books,* September, 1986, p. 17.

Review of *Jace the Ace, Kirkus Reviews,* August 15, 1990, pp. 1172-73.

Margolis, Sally T., review of *Dear Baby, School Library Journal,* June, 1988, p. 106.

Marino, Jane, review of *Discovering Martha, School Library Journal,* December, 1991, p. 118.

Review of *Musical Chairs and Dancing Bears, Publishers Weekly,* August 9, 1993, p. 476.

Porter, Judie, review of *Jace the Ace, School Library Journal,* December, 1990, pp. 106, 111.

Sherman, Louise L., review of *Musical Chairs and Dancing Bears, School Library Journal,* March, 1994, p. 208.

A newcomer to town and a camera buff, Jason Caputo begins fifth grade as *Jace the Ace,* photojournalist on a case, until the truth comes out. (Illustration by Diane de Groat.)

Stevenson, Deborah, review of *Discovering Martha, Bulletin of the Center for Children's Books,* November, 1991, pp. 73-4.

Sutton, Roger, review of *Jace the Ace, Bulletin of the Center for Children's Books,* December, 1990, pp. 98-9.

*   *   *

ROGASKY, Barbara 1933-

■ Personal

Born April 9, 1933, in Wilmington, DE; daughter of Charles (a grocer) and Ida (Rubin) Rogasky. *Education:* Attended University of Delaware, 1950-55. *Politics:* Independent. *Religion:* Jewish. *Hobbies and other interests:* Music, photography.

■ Addresses

Home—P.O. Box 34, Academy Rd., Thetford Hill, VT 05074. *Agent*—George Nicholson, Sterlinglora Literistic Inc., 65 Bleecker St., New York, NY 10012.

■ Career

Full-time children's books writer and photographer, 1980—. Has held various editorial positions with publishers in New York City, including Macmillan Publishing Co. and Harcourt Brace Jovanovich, 1955-77; part-time freelance editorial consultant, editor, and writer, 1955-79; Pyramid Books, New York City, editor, production editor, managing editor, 1966-74; Harcourt and Jove Books, New York City, senior acquisitions editor and director of special publications, 1974-77. *Member:* New England Business Association, League of New Hampshire Craftsmen.

■ Awards, Honors

In 1988 *Smoke and Ashes: The Story of the Holocaust* was named an American Library Association (ALA) notable children's book, a best nonfiction book for young adults by *Publishers Weekly,* one of the best books of the year by *School Library Journal* and the ALA Young Adult Services Division, and the most outstanding book in secondary social studies by the Society of School Librarians International; "Best of the Best" listing, *School Library Journal,* 1994, for *Smoke and Ashes: The Story of the Holocaust; Winter Poems* was named an ALA notable children's book, 1994; Present Tense/Joel H. Cavior Award for children's literature, American Jewish Committee, for *Smoke and Ashes: The Story of the Holocaust.*

■ Writings

FOR CHILDREN

(Reteller) Brothers Grimm, *Rapunzel,* illustrated by Trina Schart Hyman, Holiday House, 1982.
(Reteller) Brothers Grimm, *The Water of Life,* illustrated by Hyman, Holiday House, 1986.
Smoke and Ashes: The Story of the Holocaust (nonfiction), Holiday House, 1988.
(Photographer) Myra Cohn Livingston, *Light and Shadow,* Holiday House, 1992.
(Compiler and editor) *Winter Poems,* illustrated by Hyman, Scholastic, 1994.
The Golem: A Version, illustrated by Hyman, Holiday House, 1996.

Also contributor to history books for children, including *From Sea to Shining Sea,* compiled by Amy L. Cohn, Scholastic, 1993; and *Young Reader's Companion to American History,* edited by John A. Garraty, Houghton, 1994.

■ Work in Progress

A history of U.S. immigration, tentatively titled *Tenement Book,* for Scholastic; photographs for a collection of Myra Cohn Livingston's poems, tentatively titled *Cloud Poems;* researching a multi-volume history of Jews for teenagers; updating and revising *Smoke and Ashes;* compiling selections for *Fall Poems,* illustrator undecided; *Dybbuk and Gilgul* (working title), new versions of ancient Jewish legends.

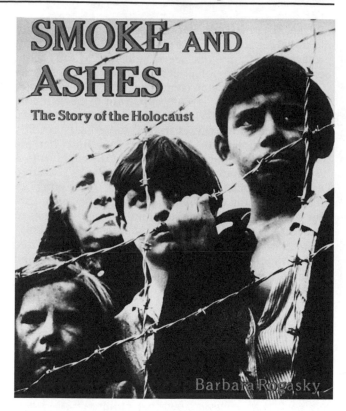

Barbara Rogasky's well-documented and profusely illustrated summary of the causes, events, and legacies of the Holocaust was chosen as an ALA notable children's book in 1988.

■ Sidelights

Barbara Rogasky's interests in children's literature include history, poetry, and fairy tales. She told *SATA,* "I was born and raised in Wilmington, Delaware, where I spent most of my time being the typical eyeglasses-wearing, braces-hooked, pigtail-encumbered outsider. I was blessed with an older sister who introduced me to good literature and magnificent music. I was also more than blessed by a few—very few—great teachers throughout my school years who encouraged and stimulated me and made me believe that a life in and with the world was possible, after all.

"I moved to what then seemed the Mecca [of publishing,] ... New York City, right after college. In publishing, which I simply fell into, I worked over the years ranging from 'gopher,' proofreader, production editor, [and] managing editor, to department head and senior acquisitions editor. When the need for sanity became paramount, and [New York City] life seemed on the edge of apocalypse, I moved to New England in 1978. Freelancing full time (which, over the years, had been only part time), I was editorial consultant, content editor, rewriter, [and] 'ghost' for just about every major publisher and many minor ones. Work included much fiction, and nonfiction ranging from fishing guides and cookbooks, to Japanese architecture and biblical history.

"Starting with the retelling of *Rapunzel*, much to my thorough enjoyment—not to mention great surprise—I seem to have found my niche as a writer and photographer of books for children and young adults.

"*Smoke and Ashes: The Story of the Holocaust* will arguably remain the most lasting book of my career. Years after its publication, it remains in print and in use in classrooms and libraries around the country. It is a history of the development of perhaps history's greatest horror, told objectively if not dispassionately. The voices throughout are not only those of the victims, but also those of the perpetrators. Here they are, ranging from Hitler to the lowliest soldier, describing what they will do, what they are doing, what they have already done. In the midst of today's climate of ignorance and the growing clamor to deny the very existence of the Holocaust, the words of the murderers themselves form the barest undeniable truth."

Winning numerous honors, *Smoke and Ashes* was widely praised by critics who admired Rogasky's starkly honest treatment of her subject. Noting what a "formidable literary obligation" it was for the author to write a book about the Holocaust for young readers, Ari L. Goldman said in a *New York Times Book Review* article that Rogasky "rises to both the challenge and the obligation . . . . Aided by a powerful collection of photographs—most of them taken by the Nazi SS and German newspaper photographers—Ms. Rogasky tells the story without dramatizing, moralizing, sensationalizing or even judging." *Voice of Youth Advocates* critic Laura L. Lent further declared that Rogasky's book is more comprehensive than Elie Wiesel's *Night* and is written in language that is more accessible to young readers than Leon Poliakov's *Harvest of Hate*. "I believe any adolescent with even a marginal interest in the Holocaust will find this book fascinating," Lent concluded.

In addition to her interest in history in general and Jewish history in particular, Rogasky has a great love of poetry. She collected twenty-five poems related to the season for *Winter Poems*, sources both ancient and modern. "*Winter Poems* is a perfect combination of some of the things I call most important to me," Rogasky told *SATA*. "It is that unique combination of *language*, and a language that can be *music*, used to convey *images* that can be revealed no other way. Trina Hyman's art reflects that and goes its own wondrous way as well."

■ Works Cited

Goldman, Ari L., review of *Smoke and Ashes: The Story of the Holocaust, New York Times Book Review*, November 6, 1988, p. 37.

Lent, Laura L., review of *Smoke and Ashes: The Story of the Holocaust, Voice of Youth Advocates*, December, 1988, p. 254.

■ For More Information See

PERIODICALS

Bulletin of the Center for Children's Books, July, 1982, p. 206; November, 1986, p. 49; June, 1988, p. 215.
Five Owls, March, 1988, p. 62; September, 1988, p. 6.
Horn Book, February, 1983, p. 38; March, 1987, p. 229; September, 1988, p. 647; January, 1989, p. 31; November, 1994, p. 761.
Kirkus Reviews, September 15, 1986, p. 1449; May 15, 1988, p. 765.
New York Times Book Review, January 2, 1983, p. 19.
Publishers Weekly, July 16, 1982, p. 78; August 22, 1986, p. 97; January 9, 1987, p. 52; May 13, 1988, p. 276; January 6, 1989, p. 52; April 26, 1991, p. 60; November 1, 1991, p. 82; October 31, 1994, p. 63.
School Library Journal, May, 1982, p. 62; November, 1986, p. 83; June, 1988, p. 128; December, 1994, p. 26.

*   *   *

ROSEN, Michael J(oel) 1954-

■ Personal

Born September 20, 1954, in Columbus, OH; son of Marvin and Nona (Mindell) Rosen. *Education:* Attended Kent State University, 1972-73; Ohio State University, B.S., 1976, graduate study, 1976-77; attended St. George's School of Medicine, Grenada, West Indies, 1978; Columbia University, M.F.A., 1981. *Hobbies and other interests:* Animals and their welfare, gardening, cooking.

■ Addresses

Home—1623 Clifton Ave., Columbus, OH 43203. *Office*—The Thurber House, 77 Jefferson Ave., Columbus, OH 43215. *Agent*—Gouverneur and Co., 10 Bleecker St., No. 4A, New York, NY 10012.

■ Career

Ohio State University, Columbus, instructor, 1978-84, lecturer, 1983, 1985; free-lance illustrator and designer, 1981—; The Thurber House, Columbus, literary director, 1982—, and program director. Youth services director, program coordinator, and administrator of children's services for Leo Yassenoff Jewish Center, 1973-78; assistant at Bread Loaf Writers Conference, 1977-79; design consultant to Jefferson Center for Learning and the Arts, 1982—; founder and director of The Company of Animals Fund, 1990—. Member of board of directors, Share Our Strength, 1993—; ongoing involvement as teacher and guest artist at schools, young author conferences, and teacher workshops. *Member:* International PEN (American Center), Poetry Society of America, Academy of American Poets.

MICHAEL J. ROSEN

■ **Awards, Honors**

Ohio Arts Council fellow, 1979, 1981, 1985, and 1987; Ingram Merrill fellow, 1982-83 and 1989; National Endowment for the Arts fellow, 1984; Gustav Davison Award, Poetry Society of America, 1985, for "The Map of Emotions"; Ohioana Library Award for poetry and Ohio Poetry Day Award, both 1985, for *A Drink at the Mirage;* grants from Jefferson Center for Learning and the Arts, 1988 and 1989; National Jewish Book Award for children's picture book, Living the Dream Award, and Indiana Author's Day Award, all 1993, for *Elijah's Angel: A Story for Chanukah and Christmas.*

■ **Writings**

FOR CHILDREN

(Self-illustrated) *Fifty Odd Jobs: A Wild and Wacky Rhyming Guide to One-of-a-Kind Careers,* Willowisp Press, 1988.

The Kids' Book of Fishing, Workman Publishing, 1991.

(Editor) *Home: A Collaboration of Thirty Distinguished Authors and Illustrators of Children's Books to Aid the Homeless,* HarperCollins, 1992.

Elijah's Angel: A Story for Chanukah and Christmas, illustrated by Aminah Brenda Lynn Robinson, Harcourt, 1992.

(Self-illustrated) *Kids' Best Dog Book,* Workman Publishing, 1993.

(Editor) *SPEAK!: Children's Book Illustrators Brag about Their Dogs,* Harcourt, 1993.

All Eyes on the Pond, illustrated by Tom Leonard, Hyperion, 1994.

(And editor) *The Greatest Table: A Banquet to Fight Against Hunger,* Harcourt, 1994.

Bonesy and Isabel, illustrated by James Ransome, Harcourt, 1995.

A School for Pompey Walker, illustrated by Robinson, Harcourt, 1995.

(Editor) *Purr ... Children's Book Illustrators Brag about Their Cats,* Harcourt, 1996.

(Editor and illustrator) *Food Fight: Poets Join the Fight against Hunger with Poems to Their Favorite Foods,* Harcourt, 1996.

Bubbe's Wishbones, illustrated by John Thompson, Blue Sky Books, 1996.

Fishing with Dad, illustrated by Will Shively, Artisan, 1996.

OTHER

(With Rosemary O. Joyce and Donn F. Vickers) *Of Thurber and Columbustown,* Thurber House, 1984.

A Drink at the Mirage (poems), Princeton University Press, 1985.

(Editor) *Collecting Himself: James Thurber on Writing and Writers, Humor, and Himself,* Harper, 1989.

(Editor) *The Company of Dogs: Twenty-one Stories by Contemporary Masters,* Doubleday, 1990.

(Editor) *The Company of Cats: Twenty Contemporary Stories of Family Cats,* Doubleday, 1992.

(Editor) *The Company of Animals: Twenty Stories of Alliance and Encounter,* Doubleday, 1993.

(Editor) *People Have More Fun Than Anybody: A James Thurber Centennial Collection,* Harcourt, 1994.

(Editor) *Dog People: Portraits of Canine Companionship,* Artisan, 1995.

Penn: The Stories of Gordon Penn (poetry), University of South Carolina Press, 1996.

Work represented in anthologies, including *Townships,* edited by Michael Martone, University of Iowa Press; *Literature: Options for Reading and Writing,* edited by Donald Daiker, Harper, 1984; *A Place of Sense: Eight Essays in Search of the Midwest,* edited by Michael Martone, University of Iowa Press, 1988; *The Direction of Poetry,* edited by Robert Richman, Houghton, 1988; *Louder than Words,* edited by William Shore, Vintage Books, 1990; and *The Best Poems of 1994,* edited by David Lehman, Knopf, 1995. Contributor of articles, poems, stories, illustrations, and reviews to magazines, including *New Yorker, Paris Review, Atlantic Monthly, Salmagundi, Prairie Schooner, House and Garden, Gourmet,* and *New York Times Book Review. High Plains Literary Review,* associate poetry editor, 1987-89, poetry editor, 1990—; columnist for *Canine Press* (an Ohio newspaper).

■ **Work in Progress**

The Walkers of Hawthorn Park, for Harcourt; *The Remembering Movies* and *Exceptional Matthew and the Dolphins,* two chapter books; picture books.

■ Sidelights

Michael J. Rosen is a poet, anthologist, and children's author best known for his award-winning picture book *Elijah's Angel: A Story for Chanukah and Christmas.* Though he does not define himself as a traditional hunger activist, he has also published numerous works in support of the anti-hunger movement, as well as on behalf of animal welfare efforts.

Rosen told *SATA:* "When I was a kid—and even twenty years ago—I wondered if I could earn a living by writing and drawing. It took me years to realize that what I liked most about these arts was the very fact that they were hard for me. But until my late twenties, I assumed that writing and art were about doing something perfectly. There were two ways to do things: either perfectly or wrong.

"I didn't realize that art included a little imperfection— the crazily individual ways that our own personalities and abilities mix up everything. Now I know that we need to describe our world in every possible way, with every sort of language. Sure, some artists use realistic lines (that's the kind of talent I thought I had to have and just didn't) and create art that closely matches its subject. But other talents are better at capturing the spirit, humor, confusion, or feeling of their subjects— and they do this without trying for an exact and realistic imitation. So as I became confident enough to appreciate the things I learned to do, I found what you'd have

Written by MICHAEL J. ROSEN
Illustrated by AMINAH BRENDA LYNN ROBINSON

Rosen's prize-winning picture book *Elijah's Angel* tells about the unique relationship between a nine-year-old Jewish boy and an African American octogenarian. (Cover illustration by Aminah Brenda Lynn Robinson.)

to call a style: all the things a person can do, along with all the other things a person cannot do.

"I can't say enough about the people who gave me that confidence to follow my interests. Parents, mentors, teachers, friends—I was fortunate to have many people offer encouragement. I had an immediate audience for nearly anything I tried. And this meant that I could give myself permission to continue these pursuits that, honestly, no one asked me to pursue.

"I have always enjoyed working in a variety of forms. The things I care about, the stories and characters that intrigue me, the data and stuff and detail and irony of this world—I can't catch all this in a single form. Sometimes it requires a net, sometimes a jar, sometimes two cupped hands, and sometimes just the lids of two closed eyes. Some subjects need a poem's tight control and its welcome ambiguity. Others need a character's voice to search out the insider's point of view. Yet other times, I need to unfold a plot to find a subject."

Rosen's 1992 picture book *Elijah's Angel,* which *New York Times Book Review* contributor Ari L. Goldman called "a surprise and a delight," explores the friendship between nine-year-old Michael, who is Jewish, and the eighty-year-old African American woodcarver Elijah Pierce. Rosen received the 1993 National Jewish Book Award for this work; in his acceptance speech, reprinted in *Horn Book,* he identified the catalyst for the story as "a single precipitating, unsettling experience—the day my friend Elijah Pierce gave me a Christian symbol as a gift for Hanukkah."

In *Elijah's Angel,* the gift that Michael receives from Elijah is a hand-carved angel. Although he has been hoping to buy one of his friend's works of art, Michael is uncomfortable with this particular gift because "graven images" are forbidden in Judaism. "What was I going to do?" he worries. "I did want the angel, because it was carved by my friend Elijah, but what would my parents say?" When his parents explain that an angel can mean different things to different people, however, Michael begins to feel better. His mother remarks, "What I think it means is that Elijah cares about you. I think that's what he wants it to mean to you. It's an angel of friendship. And doesn't friendship mean the same thing in every religion?" With his parents' help, Michael is able to appreciate the angel, and decides to give Elijah the Chanukah menorah he made in school. As Goldman summarized, "The narrator learns that people may be Christian or Jewish, but that angels are for everyone." *Horn Book* critic Rudine Sims Bishop added that this seasonal story "is special enough to read at any time."

Rosen described his childhood impressions of Elijah Pierce's shop in his acceptance speech: "I entered the barbershop all wonder and curiosity, spellbound by the ever-changing display—chaos, really—of free-standing carvings and wall reliefs." Despite the many differences between himself and Pierce, Rosen noted that Elijah's artwork "provided a comfortable vehicle for the conversations we shared"—conversations which led to a unique friendship. As the character Michael muses: "Even though Elijah talks about Jesus and the Bible more than anyone I've ever met, I never thought about being the only visitor who wasn't a good Christian. I also didn't think about being seventy-five years younger or a different color from the other people at Elijah's. I just thought that Elijah and I were friends."

"In all my work—whether for kids or for adults—I try to address some of the issues that matter most to me ... but sideways," Rosen told *SATA.* "I can't begin head-on, just writing about a cause or a problem. Even though I try to talk about human predicaments like divorce or misunderstanding, and human wrongs—toward animals, the earth, or one another—I need to start with a single image, one odd turn of events, or a peculiar remark.

"So when kids pose their perennial question, 'Where do you get your ideas?' I try to convince them of two things. The first is that writers aren't blessed with more or better ideas than anyone else. We don't receive 'poetic' ideas while the rest of the public suffers along with pedestrian ones. We all get both varieties, the good and bad notions. Sure, writers practice enough so that they are less likely to spend time on the unfruitful ones. But the operant distinction is that a writer's necessary, passionate resolve ensures that no worthy idea is ever lost to the moment's passing and the mayhem of good intentions.

"When I think about the valiant and lofty ideas and themes that uncomfortably fit under the rubric of 'social responsibility,' I realize that although I may address such topics as citizen or teacher or in some other role as public exemplar, I do not directly invite them into the writing of a story. Again, trying to begin a story with Poverty or Death as the sole motivating idea would get me nowhere. The topics are so harrowing, complex, daunting that they overwhelm the imagination. I end up feeling, 'Who am I to think I have anything to say about that?' So, instead, I begin with a few circumstances that are troubling or uncategorical—meaning, their topics don't begin with capital letters and aren't so obvious that they intimidate me. I bring them together on the page so that, as in a chemical reaction, they create a reaction ... in me, and I do hope, in a reader."

Among Rosen's efforts to combat hunger is his 1994 "accordion" book *The Greatest Table: A Banquet to Fight Against Hunger.* Illustrated with works donated in support of the cause, his text deals with the theme of food being shared. "From bountiful banquets to solitary feasts there is something here to engage everyone, be it a family gathering, a bustling cafe, or a schoolroom lunch," Marcia Hupp noted in *School Library Journal.* "As books-with-a-mission go," she continued, "this is as worthy as any, affirming, uplifting, and—unfortunately—always timely."

"When I undertook my first collaborative project, *Home,* I hardly thought of myself as a hunger activist," Rosen explained to *SATA.* "Even now, after *The Great-*

est Table and *Food Fight* and my other involvements with Share Our Strength, one of the nation's largest private hunger relief organizations, I have not yet accepted the term for myself. I do know a little more about the issues surrounding domestic hunger and a lot more about the SOS-supported programs across the nation that work toward preventing and alleviating hunger. I haven't become someone who stages protests, maintains vigilant letter-writing campaigns with members of Congress, debates passionately, donates hours helping cook or transport food at local shelters, or performs many of the other roles I am grateful others do. My work for SOS has been confined to using my own talents as a writer and editor (and board member) to work with other talented individuals, very few of whom previously identified themselves as hunger activists. The genius of this agency has not only been to help those people enduring the exigencies of poverty, but also to help others cultivate their own personal varieties of social contribution. It basically taught me to let go of the inadequacy, paralysis, inarticulateness, and sheepishness that I felt when facing the conglomeration of causes all demanding attention, and to find instead some pride, confidence, joy, and genuine energy in the development of my own working version of moral citizenship.

"Emboldened by my involvement with SOS, I initiated an animal welfare project, beginning with the editing of the anthology *The Company of Dogs.* The profits from

An unusual gathering of sixteen well-known children's book illustrators were inspired by Rosen's poem to donate their artwork to combat hunger.

that book, as from five subsequent anthologies—*The Company of Cats, The Company of Animals, Dog People, SPEAK!,* and *Purr ...* —have been directed into a fund established by the books' royalties. More than two hundred people have donated work so that these books have provided grants to dozens of organizations nationwide to aid those individuals whose health, age, or finances compromise their ability to keep their companion animals. Once again, hardly a person in this group of creative professionals is an animal rights activist, elevating this cause above all others. Yet most contributors have appreciated the chance to have a modest effort multiplied as part of this concerted, compassionate work."

■ Works Cited

Bishop, Rudine Sims, "Books from Parallel Cultures: A 'Throw of Threes' from 1992," *Horn Book,* July, 1993, pp. 433-38.

Goldman, Ari L., review of *Elijah's Angel: A Story for Chanukah and Christmas, New York Times Book Review,* December 13, 1992, p. 35.

Hupp, Marcia, review of *The Greatest Table: A Banquet to Fight Against Hunger, School Library Journal,* April, 1995, p. 128.

Rosen, Michael J., *Elijah's Angel: A Story for Chanukah and Christmas,* Harcourt, 1992.

Rosen, Michael J., National Jewish Book Award acceptance speech, *Horn Book,* November, 1993, pp. 714-16.

■ For More Information See

PERIODICALS

Booklist, May 15, 1992, p. 1684; August, 1992, p. 2013; September 1, 1993, p. 66; September 15, 1993, p. 126; May 1, 1994, p. 1604.

Bulletin of the Center for Children's Books, November, 1992, p. 86; January, 1996, p. 170.

Choice, June, 1985, p. 1496.

Five Owls, March, 1992, pp. 69, 73; November, 1992, p. 43; November, 1993, p. 34.

Horn Book, May, 1992, p. 333; November, 1992, p. 712.

Kirkus Reviews, June 1, 1992, p. 724; October 15, 1992, p. 1315.

Language Arts, November, 1992, p. 540; January, 1994, p. 56; March, 1994, pp. 214, 217.

Los Angeles Times Book Review, October 20, 1990, p. 2; July 17, 1994, p. 9.

New York Times Book Review, April 7, 1985, p. 12.

Publishers Weekly, March 16, 1992, p. 65; May 18, 1992, p. 68; September 7, 1992, p. 62; August 30, 1993, p. 94; May 30, 1994, p. 56; September 12, 1994, p. 93.

School Library Journal, April, 1992, p. 109; October, 1992, p. 44; October, 1993, p. 146; July, 1994, p. 97; June, 1995, pp. 94-95; November, 1995, p. 81.

Voice of Youth Advocates, April, 1991, p. 52.

Washington Post Book World, May 10, 1992, p. 14; October 10, 1993, p. 11.

S–T

DAVID SALTZMAN

SALTZMAN, David (Charles Laertes) 1967-1990

■ Personal

Born March 13, 1967, in Los Angeles, CA; died from Hodgkin's disease, March 2, 1990; son of Joe (a professor and journalist) and Barbara (an editor and journalist) Saltzman. *Education:* Yale University, B.A. (English and art; magna cum laude), 1989.

■ Addresses

Home—c/o Barbara Saltzman, The Jester Co., Inc., P.O. Box 817, Malaga Cove Plaza, Palos Verdes Estates, CA 90274.

■ Career

Children's author, illustrator, poet, and cartoonist.

■ Awards, Honors

David Everett Chantler Award, 1989, Yale University, for "the senior who throughout his college career best exemplified the qualities of courage and strength of character and high moral purpose."

■ Writings

(Self-illustrated) *The Jester Has Lost His Jingle* (picture book), The Jester Co., 1995.

■ Adaptations

Plush toy versions of the Jester & Pharley are planned for release in 1996 by The Jester Co.

■ Work in Progress

Another picture book, *The Rainmaker,* and a journal of Saltzman's experiences after being diagnosed with Hodgkin's disease entitled *Soaring—The Journals of David Charles Laertes Saltzman,* both to be published by The Jester Co.

■ Sidelights

A talented writer and artist from an early age, David Saltzman had a dream of becoming a successful children's book author. Tragically, his life was cut short by Hodgkin's disease, a form of cancer that affects the lymphatic system, and he died before he ever saw one of his books in print. Five years after his death in 1990, his parents managed to start their own company and publish Saltzman's first book, *The Jester Has Lost His Jingle,* themselves. Their efforts were not only a labor of love, but also a mission to see that a worthwhile piece of children's literature would find its way into the hands of those for whom it was meant.

David Saltzman first began creating cartoons as a student at the Chadwick School in Palos Verdes, California, where he wrote a comic strip parodying school life called "The Chadwick Chronicles." He also drew editorial cartoons on local, national, and international issues for a *Los Angeles Times* publication distributed to Southern California high schools. In addition to all this, he was the editor of the school's yearbook and a recipient of the Citizenship and Drama Awards. Graduating from high school, David attended Yale University, where his talent was noted by students and teachers alike, some of whom called him "the next Garry Trudeau," comparing him to the Yale alumnus and creator of the cartoon strip *Doonesbury.* At Yale David began a weekly cartoon strip called "Pops," which was about a fictitious Yale professor. The strip was so successful that Saltzman created and sold "Pops" aca-

demic calendars. He also drew weekly editorial cartoons for the *Yale Daily News* and the *Yale Herald.*

But Saltzman, who was an avid fan of Maurice Sendak, wanted to be a children's book author not an editorial cartoonist, so he set up a makeshift studio in his parents' garage to make this dream a reality. The idea for his jester character first came to Saltzman when he was taking a summer course in Greece. He walked into one of his classes, cracked a joke, and nobody laughed. Though he admitted to himself his witticism wasn't the most hilarious ever told, he was surprised that it hadn't elicited at least a mild guffaw. Sitting down at his desk, he began to doodle, drawing a man with three triangles atop his head, which evolved into a jester's hat—and so his character, the Jester, was born.

As a senior at Yale, David received the news that he had been diagnosed with Hodgkin's disease. As anyone might, his first reaction was to sit down at the foot of a tree and cry. But then David was visited by his Jester, who encouraged him to laugh instead of cry. That was when he became determined to complete *The Jester Has Lost His Jingle.* Told in rhyme, *The Jester* is the story of a court jester and his friendly talking scepter, Pharley, who are banished from their kingdom when they fail to

The Jester was beside himself. He grinned a great big grin.

He hugged and thanked the little girl, and kissed her on the chin.

After learning that the people of the world have lost their sense of humor, the Jester and his sidekick Pharley find it again in an unexpected place. (Illustration by the author from *The Jester Has Lost His Jingle.*)

make the king laugh. At first, the Jester blames himself, thinking that he must have lost his touch, but Pharley convinces him that it's not his fault at all. The problem is that people have lost their sense of humor; so the Jester and Pharley set off into the wide world to find humor again. Journeying into a modern city, the Jester encounters an entire population of grumpy, moody, unhappy people, all of whom think the world is such a miserable place that there is no reason to laugh. But the Jester and Pharley refuse to give up. They are rewarded for their efforts when they visit a little girl in a hospital who is suffering from a brain tumor. The Jester goes into his act, and the girl's resulting laughter spreads throughout the hospital, the city, and the world. The Jester and Pharley have rediscovered laughter at last.

Before David died, his family promised that his dream would become a reality and *The Jester* would be published. David's mother, Barbara Saltzman, a long-time editor for the *Los Angeles Times,* and his brother, Michael, who has worked as an executive producer for the television sitcom *Murphy Brown,* especially devoted their time to this labor of love. But the agents and publishers they presented the book to either rejected it outright—rhyming stories aren't marketable, some explained—or wanted to cut the story down from 64 to 32 pages, an offer that wasn't acceptable to the Saltzmans. "We wanted to publish the book ourselves to ensure that it would be printed with the quality of a fine-arts volume and that it will always remain in print and be made available to the children David wanted to reach," Barbara Saltzman told *SATA.*

Using the money from a home equity loan that had originally been taken out to pay for David's bone marrow transplant (an operation that proved unsuccessful), the Saltzmans established their own publishing house, The Jester Co., Inc., and proceeded to produce the book on their own. At first, Barbara and Michael did the work themselves, while David's father, Joe, assuaged his grief by concentrating on his job as a professor of documentary film making. "Looking at David's pictures was just too painful for him," Barbara Saltzman said in a *Good Housekeeping* article by Ellen Seidman. "But for Michael and me, our way of dealing was to make sure we brought the Jester alive." When the book was ready to go to press at last, however, David's father was finally ready to make the trip to Hong Kong, where they had hired a printer. "That was a turning point," Barbara told Seidman. "He wanted to be part of the final realization."

The Saltzmans printed thirty thousand copies of the book and stored them in their garage, where they had built a climate-controlled room. As part of their promise to David, the Saltzmans also made ten thousand copies of *The Jester* available through the David Saltzman Fund/Parents Against Cancer Donor Program, which gives free copies to children who have been diagnosed with cancer. Distributed to stores across the country, *The Jester* soon became so popular that book shops have had trouble keeping copies on their shelves. As of early 1996, there were over two hundred thousand copies in print, with no end to demand in sight.

Though *The Jester Has Lost His Jingle* might technically be considered a privately printed book, it has begun to receive critical reactions from book reviewers and other professionals. Although one critic, Barbara Kiefer, complained in *School Library Journal* that the story's rhyme "is uneven in meter and awkwardly constructed" and that the narration never explains the transition from a medieval castle to a modern-day city, others have found much to praise in Saltzman's book. For example, award-winning animator and Senior Critic at the Yale School of Art, Faith Hubley, stated in a Jester Co. publicity release, "The Jester and Pharley are extraordinary characters, at once poignant and humorous." And Maurice Sendak himself made this statement in the afterword to *The Jester:* "That [David] managed through his harrowing ordeal to produce a picture book so brimming with promise and strength, so full of high spirits, sheer courage and humor is nothing short of a miracle."

But perhaps the most worthwhile praise comes from the young readers of the book themselves. As David's father related in a *University of Southern California Chronicle* article by Robert Wynne, "A speech pathologist in Bethesda, Md., told us that an 8-year-old boy who experienced trauma and couldn't speak is now reading the book out loud. People who are sick call me at home and say they read the book before they go to sleep, and it tells them life is worth living. I have never heard that type of reaction before. It makes me feel fantastic."

■ Works Cited

Hubley, Faith, in *Praise for The Jester Has Lost His Jingle* (publicity release), The Jester Co., Inc., 1995.

Kiefer, Barbara, review of *The Jester Has Lost His Jingle, School Library Journal,* October, 1995, pp. 116-17.

Seidman, Ellen, "GH Profiles," *Good Housekeeping,* October, 1995, p. 26.

Wynne, Robert "A Quest to Save Laughter," *University of Southern California Chronicle,* September 18, 1995, pp. 3, 5.

■ For More Information See

PERIODICALS

Boston Globe, November 27, 1995, p. 33.
Chicago Sun-Times, June 27, 1995.
Detroit Free Press, January 16, 1996, Section D, pp. 1, 4.
Hartford Courant, November 19, 1995, p. G3.
Los Angeles Times, June 18, 1995.
New York Times, December 6, 1995.
People, December 18, 1995, p. 136.
Philadelphia Inquirer Magazine, January 2, 1996, p. 1.
Publishers Weekly, October 9, 1995, p. 29; October 23, 1995, p. 67.
Small Press, March/April, 1996, p. 14.
USA Today, January 18, 1996.
Yale Bulletin & Calendar, November 20, 1995, p. 1.

OBITUARIES:

PERIODICALS

Los Angeles Times, March 22, 1990.

[Sketch reviewed by mother, Barbara Saltzman]

*   *   *

SANTOS, Helen
See GRIFFITHS, Helen

*   *   *

SARTON, (Eleanor) May 1912-1995

OBITUARY NOTICE—See index for *SATA* sketch: Originally named Eleanore Marie Sarton; born May 3, 1912, in Wondelgem, Belgium; brought to the United States, 1916; naturalized U.S. citizen, 1924; died of breast cancer, July 16, 1995, in York, ME. Actor, educator, lecturer, and author. A prolific writer of poetry, novels, scripts, children's stories, and nonfiction, Sarton penned works that delved into the concepts of love and individuality. She was lauded for her feminist writings, although the public's enthusiasm toward her work far outweighed that of literary critics. As she was beginning to write poetry seriously, Sarton also tried her hand at acting with Eva Le Gallienne's Civic Repertory Theatre in New York City. When the Associated Actors Theatre, which she founded and directed, disbanded, Sarton began the first of a series of jobs as a teacher. These would include stints at Stuart School, Harvard University, and Wellesley College. She began to publish in the late 1930s, penning poetry collections, including *Encounter in April* and *Inner Landscape,* and novels, including *The Single Hound.* Sarton also began lecturing, speaking before the Bread Loaf Writers' Conference and the Boulder Writers' Conference. Among her other books of verse are *The Lion and the Rose, A Private Mythology, Coming into Eighty,* and her 1988 collection, *The Silence Now: New and Uncollected Earlier Poems.* Her novels included *Faithful Are the Wounds* and *Mrs. Stevens Hears the Mermaids Singing.* The latter work, which concerned a lesbian relationship, signalled Sarton's admission that she, too, was homosexual. The author of a published play and several scripts, she also wrote journals which treated the topic of aging, including *After the Stroke* and *Encore: A Journal of the 80th Year.* Her numerous awards include eighteen honorary degrees. A work describing her eighty-second year is in press.

OBITUARIES AND OTHER SOURCES:

BOOKS

Writers Directory, St. James Press, 1994.

PERIODICALS

Chicago Tribune, July 23, 1995, section 2, p. 3.
Chicago Tribune, July 20, 1995, section 3, p. 11.
New York Times, July 18, 1995, P. B7.
Washington Post, July 7, 1995, p. B4.

SASSO, Sandy Eisenberg 1947-

■ Personal

Born January 29, 1947, in Philadelphia, PA; daughter of Irving (an insurance agent) and Freda (a homemaker; maiden name, Plotnick) Eisenberg; married Dennis C. Sasso (a rabbi); children: David, Debora. *Education:* Temple University, B.A., 1969, M.A., 1972; Reconstructionist Rabbinical College, rabbi, 1974. *Politics:* Democrat. *Religion:* Judaism.

■ Addresses

Home—1919 Huckleberry Ct., Indianapolis, IN 46260. *Office*—Congregation Beth-El Zedeck, 600 West 70th St., Indianapolis, IN 46260.

■ Career

Jewish Reconstructionist Foundation, New York City, research associate, 1974-76; Manhattan Reconstructionist Havurah, New York City, rabbi, 1974-77; Congregation Beth-El Zedeck, Indianapolis, IN, rabbi, 1977—. Lecturer in religious studies, Department of Religion, Butler University, 1996. Member of Gleaners Food Bank, 1989-93, president, 1992-93; member of IUPUI governing board, Friends of Women's Studies, 1989—; member of Greater Indianapolis Progress Committee, 1992-94; member of advisory board, National Chil-

SANDY EISENBERG SASSO

dren's Film Festival, 1995; member of board, Indianapolis Children's Choir, 1995. Lecturer on renewal of spirituality, the discovery of the religious imagination of children, and women and religion. *Member:* Reconstructionist Rabbinical Association (president, 1989-91), Planned Parenthood (member of board, 1992-94).

■ Awards, Honors

But God Remembered: Stories of Women from Creation to the Promised Land was named a *Publishers Weekly* Best Book in Religion, 1995; D.H.L., DePauw University; Children's Books of Distinction award finalist, *Hungry Mind Review,* for *In God's Name;* Special Merit Award, Vermont Book Publication Association, for *God's Paintbrush.*

■ Writings

FOR CHILDREN

God's Paintbrush, illustrated by Annette Compton, Jewish Lights Publishing, 1992.
In God's Name, illustrated by Phoebe Stone, Jewish Lights Publishing, 1994.
But God Remembered: Stories of Women from Creation to the Promised Land, Jewish Lights Publishing, 1995.

FOR ADULTS

Call Them Builders: A Resource Booklet about Jewish Attitudes and Practices on Birth and Family Life, Reconstructionist Federation of Congregations and Havurot, 1977.
(With Sue Levi Elwell) *Jewish Women,* Alternatives in Religious Education, 1983, revised edition, 1986.

Contributor to *According to Scripture,* World YWCA, 1972; *Putting God on the Guest List,* Jewish Lights Publishing, 1992; *Women and Religious Ritual: An Interdisciplinary Investigation,* edited by Dr. Lesley A. Northrup, Pastoral Press, 1993; and *Lifecycles: Jewish Women on Life Passages and Personal Milestones,* edited by Rabbi Debra Ornstein. Contributor to periodicals, including *Youth Magazine, Response Magazine, Moment, Menorah, Davka, Reconstructionist,* and *Raayanot.*

■ Sidelights

Sandy Eisenberg Sasso has written books for children that celebrate the child's curiosity about religious matters and encourage recognition and acceptance of differences among people in their conceptions of God. Beginning with her first book for children, *God's Paintbrush,* the author explores the nature of God in terms that are "well within a child's frame of reference," according to a reviewer in *Publishers Weekly,* and asks readers to question themselves about, for example, whether God can cry and how to be a friend to God. Although some reviewers find Sasso's books inappropriately anthropomorphic in their descriptions of the God, others praise the joyous and uplifting quality of her works. Her works have garnered positive attention from

In God's Name **is a multicultural, nondenominational tribute to the diversity and unity of all people and their belief in one God, poetically written by Sasso.** (Illustration by Phoebe Stone.)

critics who find her explorations of the concept of God appropriate for children's sensibilities and evocative of the issues and concerns that affect them. She has also been praised for the multicultural focus and poetic rhythms of her prose.

Sasso's first book for children, *God's Paintbrush,* presents short essays on a variety of experiences common to children and poses related spiritual questions for adults and children to discuss together. Some critics have found the amount of text and the great variety of issues raised in the book overwhelming, and the verdict on the book's usefulness has been mixed. *School Library Journal* contributor Susan Kaminow remarked that "perhaps [the book] would be useful in religious classes," and a critic in the *Jewish World News* stated, "This is just the kind of book to stimulate questions between the reader and his or her audience...." But the reviewer in *Publishers Weekly* felt that *God's Paintbrush* "presents an anthropomorphic view of God that may not fit in with some readers' beliefs." On the other hand, William Craig in *Valley News* enthusiastically praised Sasso's approach to exploring children's conceptions of the divine, commenting: "*God's Paintbrush* ... is a children's book of rare worth and meaning. It respects and stimulates kids' thoughts about God, questioning and deepening their relationship with a God of their own understanding."

In God's Name presents a story which explains why there are many different names for God by showing that each person finds in God a reflection of what he or she most values in the world. Hence, some call God "healer," others "giver of light," and others "protector." Although the people in Sasso's story are first puzzled and then angry when they learn of others' names for their God, they eventually come to understand that each name points to a different aspect of the same God. "This book glories in the thought that there is one true nondenominational God who fulfills each description offered," remarked P. Finn McManamy in the *Vermont Times.*

In God's Name was generally treated to favorable reviews, some of which highlighted the book's multicultural focus and universal applicability. Mary Wade Atteberry singled out Sasso's prose for special praise in her review in the *Indianapolis Star:* "The spare and poetic text, rich in metaphor, is impressive in its simplicity.... Sasso has taken a concept and deftly developed a story children can absorb." While a contributor in *Kirkus Reviews* found *In God's Name* "a little too earnest," McManamy emphasized the poetry of Sasso's story: "I was immediately taken by ... the smooth, deliberate cadences of the story," she commented. Atteberry added: "It is always pleasant to find a story that suggests the possibility of peace and unity among people—even when it is a children's book."

Sasso's next work, a picture book for older children titled *But God Remembered: Stories of Women from Creation to the Promised Land,* presents a collection of midrash, that is, an enlargement of stories from the Bible that appear incomplete. The four stories in *But God Remembered* focus on women whose contributions are mentioned only in passing, including Lilith, the first woman in the Garden of Eden; Serach, a singer of psalms; Bityah, who scooped the infant Moses from the Nile; and the five daughters of Zelophehad, a group of strong-willed individuals who take their property claims argument directly to God. A *Booklist* critic commended the author's choice of tales, writing, "Although part of the book lies in its strong feminist voice, Sasso also tells good stories." In the *Indianapolis Jewish Post and Opinion,* Anne Shelburne Jones observed, "It is the words, and the space between Rabbi Sasso's words, that make room for the reader to live for a while in another time, a time that informs and shapes our time, more than we can know."

Sasso told *SATA,* "I have always admired the art of storytelling, marvelling how a good story grabs hold of an audience in a way no lecture or sermon can. As a rabbi I became the storyteller at family worship in my congregation and began to write my own stories. I fell in love with the sound of letters, the rhythm of words and their power to invoke laughter, tears, hope. The beliefs about which I theorized in sermons, I began to write as stories.

"I write stories that honor our children's religious imagination. We do not give children enough credit for thinking about God and thinking profoundly. I wanted to give children a language to speak about what they care most deeply, a story about God in which they all see themselves reflected. So much of children's religious literature teaches how people are different in their beliefs. I wanted a book which celebrated those differ- ences but also recognized that difference doesn't mean superiority or inferiority. If good words can inspire, so they can teach great tolerance and respect.

"I also write to reclaim the names and stories of women, to help children and adults hear another voice. So many words, so many visions have been lost. Beneath the ruins of layers of civilizations lie the oral traditions that never found their way between the hard covers of a book. Research wedded to imagination can reconstruct them for a new generation.

"I write to teach and for joy. It is a great privilege, awesome responsibility, and pure delight."

■ Works Cited

Atteberry, Mary Wade, review of *In God's Name, Indianapolis Star,* December 1, 1994, p. E8.

Review of *But God Remembered: Stories of Women from Creation to the Promised Land, Booklist,* September 1, 1995.

Craig, William, review of *God's Paintbrush, Valley News,* December 11, 1992.

Review of *God's Paintbrush, Jewish World News,* May, 1993.

Review of *God's Paintbrush, Publishers Weekly,* December 14, 1992.

Review of *In God's Name, Kirkus Reviews,* December 15, 1994.

Jones, Anne Shelburne, review of *But God Remembered: Stories of Women from Creation to the Promised Land, Indianapolis Jewish Post and Opinion,* July 19, 1995.

Kaminow, Susan, review of *God's Paintbrush, School Library Journal,* June, 1993.

McManamy, P. Finn, review of *In God's Name, Vermont Times,* November 23, 1994.

* * *

SCARIANO, Margaret M. 1924-

■ Personal

Born March 19, 1924, in Sunday Creek, MT; daughter of Austin B. (a prison warden and railroad commissioner) and Lucille (a homemaker; maiden name, Burt) Middleton; married Franklin A. Scariano (a financial consultant), September 3, 1945; children: Richard R., Ralph M., Ronald J., Lisa Scariano Frahm, Frank. *Education:* Attended University of Montana; Fresno State College, B.A., 1971; Illinois State University, M.S., 1973.

■ Addresses

Home—California.

MARGARET M. SCARIANO

■ Career

Writer. Teacher of creative writing and in General Equivalency Diploma (GED) program, Indian Valley College, Novato, CA.

■ Writings

YOUNG ADULT FICTION

Bigfoot and the Timberland Mystery, Baker Book House (Grand Rapids, MI), 1982.
Too Young to Know (romance), Berkley Publishing Group, 1983.

YOUNG ADULT NONFICTION

(With Edward F. Dolan) *Cuba and the United States: Troubled Neighbors,* Franklin Watts, 1987.
The Picture Life of Corazon Aquino, Franklin Watts, 1987.
(With Edward F. Dolan) *The Police in American Society,* Franklin Watts, 1988.
(With Edward F. Dolan) *Nuclear Waste: The 10,000 Year Challenge,* Franklin Watts, 1990.
Dr. Ruth Westheimer, Enslow Publishers, 1992.
(With Edward F. Dolan) *Guns in the United States,* Franklin Watts, 1994.
(With Edward F. Dolan) *Illiteracy in America,* Franklin Watts, 1995.
(With Edward F. Dolan) *Secretaries of State,* Franklin Watts, 1995.

FICTION FOR REMEDIAL READERS; ALL PUBLISHED BY ACADEMIC THERAPY PUBLICATIONS (NOVATO, CA)

The Winchester Connection, 1982.
Deputy at Wild Card, 1982.
To Catch a Mugger, 1982.
Horse Power, 1984.
A Load of Danger, 1984.
Wild Wind, 1984.
Burning of the Big Top, 1984.
Crash at Sea, 1984.
Box Girl, 1984.
A New Leaf, 1984.
The Set-Up, 1984.
High Adventures, 1984.
Summer Strike-Out, illustrated by Matthew Gouig, 1988.

FOR ADULTS

(With Temple Grandin) *Emergence: Labeled Autistic* (nonfiction), Academic Therapy Publications, 1986.
Island Mystery (gothic romance), Harlequin, 1987.

Coauthors Scariano and Ed Dolan deal with the probable causes, effects, and possible solutions to problems in education in this informative work.

■ Sidelights

Margaret M. Scariano told *SATA:* "I was born in Sunday Creek, Montana, and grew up in Montana State Prison where my father was the warden. I attended (more a guest appearance) the University of Montana at Missoula and married during World War II. As an adult, I received a B.A. from Fresno State University and an M.S. from Illinois State University. I have taught classes in the GED program and creative writing in the Adult Education Department at Indian Valley College in Novato, California.

"Having enjoyed rearing four sons and a daughter, my husband and I now enjoy semi-retirement—my husband still works part-time as a financial consultant and I work full time on my writing. Our life is full and rewarding with family, friends, and work."

■ For More Information See

PERIODICALS

Booklist, June 15, 1982, p. 1365; January 15, 1988, p. 868; March 15, 1991; September 15, 1992, p. 136; January 15, 1995.
Bulletin of the Center for Children's Books, January, 1984, pp. 96-97.
Horn Book Guide, fall, 1992, p. 330.
Library Journal, May 15, 1986.
School Library Journal, February, 1984, p. 84; February, 1988, pp. 81-2; April, 1989; February, 1991; September, 1992.
Voice of Youth Advocates, October, 1992, p. 257.

*   *   *

SEED, Cecile Eugenie 1930-
(Jenny Seed)

■ Personal

Born May 18, 1930, in Cape Town, South Africa; daughter of Ivan Washington (a draftsman) and Bessie (Dickerson) Booysen; married Edward Robert Seed (a railway employee), October 30, 1953; children: Anne, Dick, Alan, Robbie. *Religion:* Christian. *Hobbies and other interests:* Tennis, bowling, reading, entertaining, church work.

■ Addresses

Home—10 Pioneer Cres., Northdene, Kwa Zulu-Natal, Natal, 4093, South Africa.

■ Career

Roads Department, Town Planning Department, Pietarmaritzburg, South Africa, draftsman, 1947-53. Freelance writer, 1965—.

CECILE EUGENIE SEED

■ Awards, Honors

M. E. R. Award for Children's Literature in South Africa, 1987, for *Place Among the Stones.*

■ Writings

FICTION; UNDER PSEUDONYM JENNY SEED

The Dancing Mule, illustrated by Joan Sirr, Nelson, 1964.
The Always-Late Train, illustrated by Pieter de Weerdt, Nasionale Boekhandel, 1965.
Small House, Big Garden, illustrated by Lynette Hemmant, Hamish Hamilton, 1965.
Peter the Gardener, illustrated by Mary Russon, Hamish Hamilton, 1966.
Tombi's Song, illustrated by Dugald MacDougall, Hamish Hamilton, 1966, published as *Ntombi's Song,* illustrated by Anno Berry, Beacon Press, 1989.
To the Rescue, illustrated by Constance Marshall, Hamish Hamilton, 1966.
Stop Those Children!, illustrated by Mary Russon, Hamish Hamilton, 1966.
Timothy and Tinker, illustrated by Lynette Hemmant, Hamish Hamilton, 1967.
The River Man, illustrated by Dugald MacDougall, Hamish Hamilton, 1968.
The Voice of the Great Elephant, illustrated by Trevor Stubley, Hamish Hamilton, 1968, Pantheon, 1969.
Canvas City, illustrated by Lynette Hemmant, Hamish Hamilton, 1968.
The Red Dust Soldiers, illustrated by Andrew Sier, Heinemann, 1968.

Prince of the Bay, illustrated by Trevor Stubley, Hamish Hamilton, 1970, published as *Vengeance of the Zulu King,* Pantheon, 1971.
The Great Thirst, illustrated by Trevor Stubley, Hamish Hamilton, 1971, Bradbury Press, 1973.
The Broken Spear, illustrated by Trevor Stubley, Hamish Hamilton, 1972.
Warriors on the Hills, illustrated by Pat Ludlow, Abelard Schuman, 1975.
The Unknown Land, illustrated by Jael Jordan, Heinemann, 1976.
Strangers in the Land, illustrated by Trevor Stubley, Hamish Hamilton, 1977.
The Year One, illustrated by Susan Sansome, Hamish Hamilton, 1981.
The Policeman's Button, illustrated by Joy Pritchard, Human & Rousseau, 1981.
Gold Dust, illustrated by Bill le Fever, Hamish Hamilton, 1982.
The New Fire, illustrated by Mario Sickle, Human & Rousseau, 1983.
The 59 Cats, illustrated by Alida Carpenter, Daan Retief, 1983.
The Shell, illustrated by Ann Walton, Daan Retief, 1983.
The Sad Cat, illustrated by Marlize Groenewald, Daan Retief, 1984.
The Karoo Hen, illustrated by A. Venter, Daan Retief, 1984.
The Disappearing Rabbit, illustrated by Ann Walton, Daan Retief, 1984.
Big Boy's Work, illustrated by Paula Collins, Daan Retief, 1984.
The Spy Hill, illustrated by Nelda Vermaak, Human & Rousseau, 1984.
The Lost Prince, illustrated by Ann Walton, Daan Retief, 1985.
Day of the Dragon, illustrated by Paula Collins, Daan Retief, 1985.
Bouncy Lizzie, illustrated by Esther Boshoff, Daan Retief, 1985.
The Strange Blackbird, illustrated by Hettie Saaiman, Daan Retief, 1986.
The Far-Away Valley, illustrated by Joan Rankin, Daan Retief, 1987.
The Christmas Bells, illustrated by Hettie Saaiman, Daan Retief, 1987.
Place among the Stones, illustrated by Helmut Starcke, Tafelberg, 1987.
The Station-Master's Hen, illustrated by Elizabeth de Villiers, Human & Rousseau, 1987.
The Corner Cat, illustrated by Elizabeth de Villiers, Human & Rousseau, 1987.
Hurry, Hurry, Sibusiso, illustrated by Cornelia Holm, Daan Retief, 1988.
The Big Pumpkin, illustrated by Anno Berry, Human & Rousseau, 1989.
Stowaway to Nowhere, Tafelberg, 1990.
Nobody's Cat, illustrated by Alida Bothma, Human & Rousseau, 1990.
The Wind's Song, illustrated by Joan Rankin, Daan Retief, 1991.
The Hungry People, Tafelberg, 1992.

Old Grandfather Mantis, Tafelberg, 1992.
A Time to Scatter Stones, Macmillan, 1993.
Eyes of a Toad, Macmillan, 1993.
Run, Run, White Hen, Oxford University Press, 1994.
Lucky Boy, Excellentia Publishers, 1995.

FOLKTALES; UNDER PSEUDONYM JENNY SEED

Kulumi the Brave: A Zulu Tale, illustrated by Trevor Stubley, Hamish Hamilton, World, 1970.
The Sly Green Lizard (Zulu folktale), illustrated by Graham Humphreys, Hamish Hamilton, 1973.
The Bushman's Dream: African Tales of the Creation, illustrated by Bernard Brett, Hamish Hamilton, 1974, Bradbury Press, 1975.

OTHER

Many of Seed's children's stories have been republished in Canada, England, Zimbabwe, New Zealand, and Australia.

■ Adaptations

Some of Seed's children's stories have been adapted for broadcasts in countries around the world.

■ Work in Progress

The Strange Large Egg, for Gecko Books.

■ Sidelights

Cecile Eugenie Seed, who writes under the pseudonym Jenny Seed, has provided children of all countries with insight into South African and African culture with her original stories, her retellings of African folktales, and her historical novels. Most of Seed's work has been devoted to these historical novels, which portray the experiences and emotions of young characters (indigenous as well as immigrant) as they cope with historical situations and events. Seed once told *SATA* that she began to write such works for children around the time that she discovered that her own children's history homework was dull and emphasized "facts and dates." Seed "began to delve into old books" in the Durban reference library and "the past became real" to her. She "found that it was not boring at all but tremendously exciting and filled with real and interesting people just waiting to be put into books."

Seed's 1971 book *The Great Thirst,* one of her many historical novels set in the nineteenth century, chronicles the development of a conflict between the Nama Hottentots and the Hereros in West Africa in the 1830s. At the same time, Seed's narrative relates the story of a Nama boy named Garib. The trouble begins when the Hereros, displaced from their own land by a drought, attempt to force the Nama from their grazing lands so that their own cattle may feed. Garib's father is killed by one of the Hereros; the boy is expected to gain revenge in an attack on the Hereros. Instead of succeeding in his plans, Garib is captured. It is not until Jonker Afrikaner arrives with Namas of another region and European weapons that Garib is freed from slavery. Garib serves

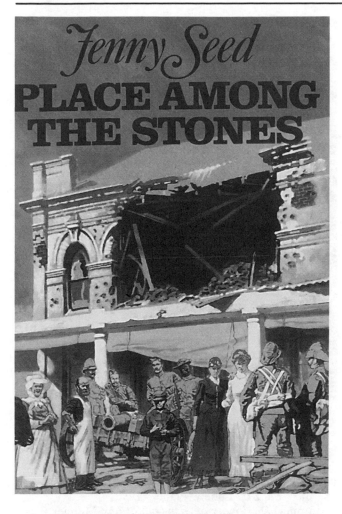

South African folktale reteller and history buff Seed's many works include this award-winning historical novel. (Cover illustration by Helmut Starcke.)

as Jonker Afrikaner's aide for a while, but later grows tired of the conflict and sets out on his own. A reviewer for *Bulletin of the Center for Children's Books* found that the characters of *The Great Thirst* possess "vitality" and that "tribal cultures" in the book are "described with dignity." Paul Heins, a critic for *Horn Book,* concluded that Seed's "historical data," "well-sustained narrative," and the "spiritual development of the protagonist" are all "skillfully interwoven."

Many of Seed's novels recall how settlers in South Africa struggled to survive in harsh climates already inhabited by inhospitable groups of people. *The Unknown Land* follows the Boers when they leave the Cape colony after it is annexed by Great Britain. Pieter, the young hero of this book, is present at a battle in which the Boers (armed with muskets) defeat the Matabele warriors who occupy the territory the Boers desire. In *Strangers in the Land* Seed describes the alienation and confusion of the immigrants from Great Britain who come to live in South Africa after the annexation. Mathew Thompson must help his family, formerly traders in London, adjust to life as Cape Colony farmers. Similarly, in *The Year One* eight-year-old Alice finds Natal a strange place; when her parents' settlement plans fall through, they

must quickly sell their furniture and find employment if they are to survive.

Seed once explained to *SATA* that she began writing stories for young people only after she had married and had four children of her own. Nevertheless, she recalled, she had always been interested in writing as a child growing up in Cape Town, South Africa. "My father was a writer when he was younger, and as a small child I can remember rummaging through his cupboard drawers when I was allowed to play in his room, sorting through piles of his old manuscripts. And then, too, my mother was an excellent reader of stories. My sister Jewel and I would keep her busy with stories until her poor voice was reduced to a croak. It was not surprising then that from the age of about eight I too became interested in the written word and used to enjoy trying to compose little verses."

Seed's retellings of folktales in *Kulumi the Brave: a Zulu Tale* and *The Bushman's Dream: African Tales of the Creation* demonstrate her talent for adapting myths and legends which originally developed orally. In *Kulumi the Brave,* Kulumi's father, a king, believes that his young son will grow up to defeat and unseat him; he banishes the boy from his kingdom. Seed's book tells how Kulumi thrives despite this treatment—he bravely faces a dragon, learns to use magic, and successfully challenges an ogress in order to claim his bride. According to Gertrude B. Herman, writing for *Library Journal,* "The use of Zulu words is authentic." Stories by W. H. I. Bleek and Lucy C. Lloyd appear in Seed's *The Bushman's Dream.* A critic for *Horn Book* welcomed this "well-told ... material" about the magic Old Mantis, keeper of the Dream during the time the world was in the process of creation.

Tombi's Song, first published in 1968, provides an example of Seed's original fiction for young children. This story follows a six-year-old Zulu girl as she runs an errand for her mother. Tombi tries to be brave as she travels from her home through the forest to the store, but her neighbors have frightened her with tales of a monster. She manages to buy the sugar her mother wants, but spills it when a bus roars by and startles her. Tombi begins to sing a song her mother taught her, and then she begins to dance; in appreciation, a white woman gives Tombi a coin which enables the girl to buy another bag of sugar. Lillian N. Gerhardt asserted in *School Library Journal* that the story "promote[s] at least four attitudes that derogate Negro races" and is not just a story of a small girl on an errand. A critic for *Kirkus Reviews* observed that *Tombi's Song* "may be marred for many readers by a semblance of colonial paternalism." The 1989 version of the book, published as *Ntombi's Song,* features illustrations that present a black tourist couple giving the girl the coin. A critic for *Publishers Weekly* described *Ntombi's Song* as "a warm and lovely story of a small triumph," and another critic for *Kirkus Reviews* found it to be a "happy, long, well-knit story."

■ Works Cited

Review of *The Bushman's Dream, Horn Book,* December, 1975, p. 590.
Gerhardt, Lillian N., review of *Tombi's Song, Library Journal,* July, 1968, p. 2731.
Review of *The Great Thirst, Bulletin of the Center for Children's Books,* May, 1975, p. 155.
Heins, Paul, review of *The Great Thirst, Horn Book,* April, 1975, pp. 154-55.
Herman, Gertrude B., review of *Kulumi the Brave: A Zulu Tale, Library Journal,* May 15, 1971, p. 1806.
Review of *Ntombi's Song, Kirkus Reviews,* August 1, 1989, p. 1167.
Review of *Ntombi's Song, Publishers Weekly,* July 28, 1989, p. 220.
Review of *Tombi's Song, Kirkus Reviews,* March 1, 1968, p. 262.

■ For More Information See

PERIODICALS

Junior Bookshelf, February, 1983, p. 49.
Kirkus Reviews, December 1, 1969, p. 1259.
School Library Journal, November, 1989, p. 94.
Times Literary Supplement, December 11, 1970, p. 1460; November 3, 1972, p. 1320; April 6, 1973, p. 383.

* * *

SEED, Jenny
See SEED, Cecile Eugenie

* * *

SHEEHAN, Sean 1951-

■ Personal

Born October 27, 1951, in London, England; son of Michael (a transport worker) and Eileen (a nurse; maiden name, Neary) Sheehan; married Patricia Levy (a teacher), 1987; children: Joseph Levy Sheehan, Danny Levy Sheehan. *Education:* Swansea University, B.A. (honors), 1973; Oxford University, P.G.C.E., 1975. *Politics:* Libertarian socialist. *Religion:* None. *Hobbies and other interests:* Gardening, fishing.

■ Addresses

Home—Raferigeen, Kilcrohane, Bantry, County Cork, Ireland.

■ Career

English teacher, at a school in Newcastle upon Tyne, England, 1975-80; English teacher, at a school in London, England, 1980-85; English teacher, at a school in Singapore, 1986-91; freelance writer, 1992—.

SEAN SHEEHAN

■ Writings

(With Tony Wheeler and John Murray) *Ireland: Travel Survival Kit,* Lonely Planet, 1992.
(Compiler) *Dictionary of Irish Quotations,* Mercier Press (Ireland), 1993.
(With Patrick Murray and Geraldine Skelly) *Limelight,* Educational Company of Ireland, 1993.
(With others) *Western Europe: Shoestring Guide,* Lonely Planet, 1994.
(Compiler) *The Sayings of James Joyce,* Duckworth (London), 1995.

"CULTURES OF THE WORLD" SERIES

Austria, illustrated by Kelvin Sim, Marshall Cavendish, 1992.
Jamaica, Marshall Cavendish, 1993.
Pakistan, Marshall Cavendish, 1993.
Turkey, Marshall Cavendish, 1993.
Zimbabwe, Marshall Cavendish, 1993.
Cuba, Marshall Cavendish, 1994.
Romania, Marshall Cavendish, 1994.
Cambodia, Marshall Cavendish, 1995.

■ Work in Progress

The Blue Guide to Malaysia and Singapore, Dent (London) and Norton (U.S.), 1996; an encyclopedia of Ireland—a research interest, no publisher as yet.

■ Sidelights

"I was born and brought up in London, but—genetically at least—I am Irish," Sean Sheehan told *SATA.* "Both my parents came to England in the late 1930s looking for work, but they never attempted to lose their Irish backgrounds and traditions. I myself now use an Irish passport and I find it difficult to think of myself as English. This, of course, is a contradiction because—having spent nearly all my life living and working in England—I'm obviously English whether I like it or not.

"Perhaps it's this underlying problem with a sense of identity that has nurtured and motivated my interest in travel and writing.

"To compound my sense of ambivalence, I feel very unsure about the value of writing about travel. Tourism, whether conducted in an armchair with colourful books about foreign places or actively pursued through foreign travel, is not something I always feel happy about promoting. I am becoming more interested in the past—especially Ireland's past, hence my interest in the idea of an encyclopedia of Ireland."

*   *   *

SHOUP, Barbara 1947-

■ Personal

Born May 4, 1947, in Hammond, IN; daughter of Richard (a payroll clerk) and Gladys (a department store clerk; maiden name, Farmer) White; married Steven V. Shoup (an attorney), January 29, 1967; children: Jennifer, Katherine. *Education:* Indiana University, B.S., 1972, M.S., 1976. *Hobbies and other interests:* Travel, art.

■ Addresses

Home and office—6012 North Broadway, Indianapolis, IN 46220. *Agent*—Mary Evans, Inc., 242 East 5th St., New York, NY 10003.

■ Career

Learning Unlimited, North Central High School, Indianapolis, IN, community programs coordinator, 1975-78; Indiana University, Bloomington, IN, associate instructor in creative writing, 1979; Indianapolis Museum of Art, Indianapolis, school programs coordinator, 1980; Broad Ripple High School Center for the Humanities and the Performing Arts, Indianapolis, writer in residence, 1982—; Prelude Academy, Indianapolis Children's Museum and Penrod Society, Indianapolis, coordinator, 1985—. Member, Indiana Arts Commission Grants Panels, 1983-86; fiction judge, Society of Midland Authors and National Society for Arts and Letters, 1988. *Member:* Authors Guild, Indiana Teachers of Writing, Indiana Writers' Center, Midland Society of Writers.

■ Awards, Honors

Best Book in Field, Association for Experiential Education, 1980, for *Living and Learning for Credit;* Master

BARBARA SHOUP

Artists fellowship, Indiana Arts Commission and the National Endowment for the Arts, 1990; Butler University Writers' Studio Literary fellowship, 1990-91, 1994; Pushcart Prize nomination, 1994; Notable Young Adult Book citation, *Bulletin for the Center for Children's Books,* 1994, and Best Books for Young Adults citation, American Library Association, 1995, both for *Wish You Were Here.*

■ Writings

NOVELS

Night Watch, Harper, 1982.
Wish You Were Here, Hyperion Books for Children, 1994.

OTHER

Living and Learning for Credit, Phi Delta Kappa, 1978.
(With Joan G. Schine and Diane Harrington) *New Roles for Early Adolescents in Schools and Communities,* National Commission on Resources for Youth, 1981.
(With Freddi Stevens-Jacobi) *Learning Unlimited: A Model for Options Education,* Washington Township Schools, 1981.

Contributing editor, *Arts Insight,* 1984, and *Other Voices,* 1991—. Contributor to periodicals, including *Mississippi Valley Review, Crazy Quilt, Persuasions: The Journal of the Jane Austen Society of North America, Hurricane Alice, Other Voices, Louisville Review, Rhino, Artful Dodge,* and *New York Times.*

■ Work in Progress

Everything You Want, an adult novel about a family who wins a $15 million lottery; *Stranded in Harmony,* a young adult novel about the relationship between a teenage boy and a woman who was involved in political acts of the sixties.

■ Sidelights

Barbara Shoup told *SATA,* "I wanted to be a writer from the time I understood what a book was. As soon as I learned how to form the alphabet, I began to write stories in a special blue notebook. I was eleven when I attempted my first novel, the story of a black slave girl journeying north by Underground Railroad. I came home every day after school and worked diligently, secretly until I got the story told. Certainly fame and fortune were imminent—or so I thought until we got to the unit on the Civil War in Social Studies and I learned that the slave railroad was not a subway train that ran from Atlanta to New York City, as I'd imagined it to be. I was so mortified by my mistake that I gave up writing for nearly twenty years. When I began again, it was because one of my high school students asked me whether teaching was what I had always meant to do with my life...."

"Teaching has played an important part in my writing and my sense of myself as a writer ever since. I am infinitely fascinated by the lives of my young writers, inspired by the earnestness and courage with which the best of them approach their work. In my twelve years as writer in residence at Broad Ripple High School's Center for the Humanities, I've collected a wealth of insight about the lives of my students and their families. I've unearthed wonderful details that just cry out to be put into stories; some found their way into *Wish You Were Here.*

"Jackson Watt, the main character in the book, is exactly the kind of teenager I love. He's earnest and funny. He desperately tries to understand things. He's a much, much better person than he believes himself to be. What I find most compelling about him, however, is the grief he feels about his parents' divorce and how the divorce complicates the large and small problems of his adolescent life. I think that it is in the way Jackson wrestles with the ongoing effects of the divorce that he most poignantly represents so many real teenagers of his generation and offers some useful insights into their lives."

■ For More Information See

PERIODICALS

Kirkus Reviews, August 1, 1982, p. 898.
Library Journal, October 1, 1982, p. 1896.
Publishers Weekly, July 30, 1982, p. 63.

* * *

SHURA, Mary Francis
See CRAIG, Mary (Francis) Shura

* * *

SLEIGH, Barbara 1906-1982

■ Personal

Born January 9, 1906, in Acock's Green, Worcestershire, England; died February 13, 1982; daughter of Bernard (an artist) and Stella (Phillip) Sleigh; married David Davis (head of BBC *Children's Hour*), January 29, 1936; children: Anthony, Hilary, Fabia. *Education:* Attended West Bromwich School of Art, Birmingham, England, 1922-25; Clapham High School Art Teacher's Training College, London, England, diploma, 1928. *Religion:* Church of England.

■ Career

Smethwick High School, Staffordshire, England, art teacher, 1928-30; Goldsmiths' College, London, England, lecturer, 1930-33; British Broadcasting Corporation, London, assistant on radio program *Children's Hour,* 1933-36; writer for children.

■ Writings

FOR CHILDREN

Carbonel, illustrated by V. H. Drummond, Parrish (London), 1955, Bobbs-Merrill, 1958.
Patchwork Quilt, illustrated by Mary Shillabeer, Parrish, 1956.
The Singing Wreath and Other Stories, illustrated by Julia Comper, Parrish, 1957.
The Seven Days, illustrated by Susan Einzig, Parrish, 1958, Meredith, 1968.
The Kingdom of Carbonel, illustrated by D. M. Leonard, Parrish, 1958, Bobbs-Merrill, 1960.
No One Must Know, illustrated by Jillian Willett, Collins, 1962, Bobbs-Merrill, 1963.
North of Nowhere: Stories and Legends from Many Lands, illustrated by Victor Ambrus, Collins, 1964, Coward-McCann, 1966.
Jessamy, illustrated by Philip Gough, Bobbs-Merrill, 1967.
Pen, Penny, Tuppence, illustrated by Meg Stevens, Hamish Hamilton, 1968.
The Snowball, illustrated by Patricia Drew, Brockhampton Press, 1969.
West of Widdershins: A Gallimaufry of Stories Brewed in Her Own Cauldron, illustrated by Victor Ambrus,

Collins, 1971, published as *Stirabout Stories,* Bobbs-Merrill, 1972.

Ninety-Nine Dragons, illustrated by Gunvor Edwards, Brockhampton Press, 1974.

Funny Peculiar: An Anthology, illustrated by Jennie Garratt, David & Charles, 1974.

Charlie Chumbles, illustrated by Frank Franus, Hodder & Stoughton, 1977.

Grimblegraw and the Wuthering Witch, illustrated by Glenys Ambrus, Hodder & Stoughton, 1978, revised edition, Penguin (London), 1979.

Carbonel and Calidor, illustrated by Charles Front, Kestrel, 1978.

Winged Magic: Legends and Stories from Many Lands Concerning Things That Fly, illustrated by John Patience, Hodder & Stoughton, 1979.

(Editor) *Broomsticks and Beasticles: Stories and Verse about Witches and Strange Creatures,* illustrated by John Patience, Hodder & Stoughton, 1981.

(Editor) Kenneth Grahame, *The Wind in the Willows,* illustrated by Philip Mendoza, Hodder & Stoughton, 1983.

Also author of radio plays, stories, and talks for children, for the British Broadcasting Corporation.

FOR ADULTS

The Smell of Privet (autobiography), Hutchinson, 1971.

■ **Sidelights**

Barbara Sleigh was well known in her native England as an author and editor of children's fantasy fiction, her most famous works being those about the character of Carbonel, King of the Cats, who appears in *Carbonel, The Kingdom of Carbonel,* and *Carbonel and Calidor.* Beginning her career as a teacher and later a storyteller on the BBC's *Children's Hour,* Sleigh didn't start writing until later in her life, and even then she was never very prolific. Beloved for her short stories as much as for her longer works, Sleigh created magical characters that have been compared to those in the finest tradition of children's literature. As one *Junior Bookshelf* critic stated in a review of *Carbonel and Calidor,* "There is a Nesbit quality about Miss Sleigh's writing as there is in her manipulation of magic.... Miss Sleigh is the least prolific of writers, but her books are always well worth waiting for."

Quickly gaining fans with the publication of *Carbonel* in 1955, Sleigh "added a splendidly individual contribution to the long line of fictional felines," according to Geoffrey Trease in the *Times Literary Supplement.* In this first story, the author introduces her famed character as a kitten who is rescued by two children named Rosemary and John from a witch named Mrs. Cantrip. As it turns out, Carbonel is no ordinary cat: he is a king with whom the children can communicate through the use of a magic ring. In addition to the anthropomorphic world of Carbonel and his fellow felines into which Rosemary and John are drawn, there is also much in these books about witchcraft and its colorful practition-

ers, in particular the "idiosyncratic Mrs. Cantrip," whom Trease called an "unforgettable creation."

After *Carbonel* and *The Kingdom of Carbonel,* Sleigh did not return to this world of witches and intelligent cats for another twenty years, until her 1978 publication of *Carbonel and Calidor.* The central character in this story is actually Calidor, Carbonel's son and heir to the throne. Trouble arises when Carbonel falls in love with Dumpsie—a bright and feisty commoner who lives in the dump—and refuses to take Princess Melissa's paw in marriage. Melissa's mother, Queen Grissana, takes umbrage to this and enlists the help of two witches to wreak her revenge. "Barbara Sleigh laces adventure with humour and has a casually expert way of twisting everyday settings and events into something bizarre and wholly entertaining," said Margery Fisher in her *Growing Point* assessment of the tale.

In addition to her Carbonel stories, Sleigh's lighthearted style of fantasy can be found in shorter works like *Ninety-Nine Dragons* and *Grimblegraw and the Wuthering Witch,* as well as in her short stories, many of which appear in *West of Widdershins: A Gallimaufry of Stories Brewed in Her Own Cauldron,* which was published in the United States as *Stirabout Stories.* In *Ninety-Nine Dragons,* Ben and Beth have a problem when the fifty sheep that Beth has been counting to help her go to sleep are threatened by the dragons that Ben has been dreaming about. *Grimblegraw and the Wuthering Witch* is about a giant who kidnaps people to do his housework because his eyes have been turned into Catherine wheels (wheels that have spikes projecting from the rims) by a wicked witch and how Prince Benedict and Princess Yolanda intervene. "This stylish tale looks back to Andrew Lang's comic tales of a fairy court as it unwinds," remarked Fisher in another *Growing Point* article.

Sleigh once commented, "My own pleasure in storytelling stems from the time when I was a small girl. My father, who among other artistic activities designed stained glass windows, would often use me as a model for an infant angel, or perhaps a young St. John the Baptist. To stop me fidgeting, he would tell me tales which kept me riveted. I write stories in the hope that I may pass on some of this same delight to children today." In a *Twentieth-Century Children's Writers* entry, she further explained why she chose to write fantasy stories: "I largely write fantasy, but, I hope, of a down-to-earth kind, avoiding mere whimsy. I feel strongly this leads young readers to wider horizons, and later to imaginative adult reading."

■ **Works Cited**

Review of *Carbonel and Calidor, Junior Bookshelf,* August, 1978, p. 195.

Fisher, Margery, "A Place for Magic," *Growing Point,* July, 1978, pp. 3354-58.

Fisher, Margery, "Animal Humours," *Growing Point,* January, 1979, pp. 3435-39.

Sleigh, Barbara, comments in *Twentieth-Century Children's Writers*, 4th edition, edited by Laura Standley Berger, St. James Press, 1995, pp. 880-81.

Trease, Geoffrey, review of *The Kingdom of Carbonel*, *Times Literary Supplement*, November 25, 1983.

■ **For More Information See**

PERIODICALS

Bulletin of the Center for Children's Books, October, 1967; December, 1969, p. 65; November, 1972, p. 49.

Growing Point, October, 1975, p. 2729; November, 1977, p. 3211.

Junior Bookshelf, February, 1975, pp. 50-51; April, 1978, pp. 93, 195; April, 1980, p. 74; February, 1982, p. 30.

Kirkus Reviews, April 1, 1967, p. 416; October 1, 1968, p. 1165; August 15, 1972, p. 941.

Library Journal, May 15, 1967, p. 2024.

New Statesman, October 22, 1971, pp. 559-60; December 4, 1981, p. 18.

Times Educational Supplement, November 20, 1981, p. 34.

Times Literary Supplement, October 22, 1971, p. 1321; December 8, 1972, p. 1499; November 23, 1973, p. 1438; December 6, 1974, p. 1384; July 7, 1978, p. 765.

* * *

SMOLINSKI, Dick 1932-

■ **Personal**

Born October 11, 1932, in Bristol, CT; son of Chester and Bernice (Markowski) Smolinski; married Teresa Williams, February 9, 1952 (deceased, 1965); married Joanne Baldassari (a medical social worker), October 28, 1978; children: Susan Smolinski Halagan, Richard Jr. *Education:* Attended University of Hartford and Paier School of Art. *Religion:* "Raised Catholic." *Hobbies and other interests:* American history.

■ **Addresses**

Home and office—3 Pine St., Columbia, CT 06237. *Agent*—Bookmakers, Ltd., Taos, NM.

■ **Career**

Did layout work for art directors at various agencies and studios, 1958-77; freelance illustrator, 1977—. *Military service:* U.S. Air Force, 1951-53; cartoonist for base newspaper at Sampson Air Force Base, Geneva, NY.

■ **Illustrator**

Catherine E. Chambers, *Frontier Dream: Life on the Great Plains,* Troll Associates, 1984.

Catherine E. Chambers, *Frontier Village: A Town Is Born,* Troll Associates, 1984.

DICK SMOLINSKI

Catherine E. Chambers, *Wagons West: Off to Oregon,* Troll Associates, 1984.

Rae Bains, *Abraham Lincoln,* Troll Associates, 1985.

Rae Bains, *Babe Ruth,* Troll Associates, 1985.

Rae Bains, *Christopher Columbus,* Troll Associates, 1985.

Rae Bains, *Louis Pasteur,* Troll Associates, 1985.

Louis Sabin, *Johnny Appleseed,* Troll Associates, 1985.

Louis Sabin, *Paul Bunyan,* Troll Associates, 1985.

Laurence Santrey, *Prehistoric People,* Troll Associates, 1985.

Roy Wandelmaier, *Secret of the Old Museum,* Troll Associates, 1985.

Laurence Santrey, *John Adams, Brave Patriot,* Troll Associates, 1986.

Rae Bains, *Robert E. Lee, Brave Leader,* Troll Associates, 1986.

Ski Michaels, *Mystery of the Missing Fuzzy,* Troll Associates, 1986.

Louis Sabin, *Andrew Jackson, Frontier Patriot,* Troll Associates, 1986.

Kira Daniel, *Home Builder,* Troll Associates, 1989.

Margaret Holland, *Martin Luther King, Jr.,* Worthington Press, 1990.

Daughters of St. Paul staff, *I Pray with Jesus,* Pauline Books & Media, 1991.

Margaret Holland, *Abraham Lincoln,* Worthington Press, 1991.

Margaret Holland, *Christopher Columbus,* Worthington Press, 1992.

Margaret Holland, *Mother Teresa,* Worthington Press, 1992.

Tracey E. Dils, *George Washington: Country Boy, Country Gentleman,* Worthington Press, 1992.

Children's Way of the Cross, Pauline Books & Media, 1992.

Keith Elliot Greenberg, *Nolan Ryan: Ageless Superstar,* Rourke Enterprises, 1993.

Keith Elliot Greenberg, *Bill Bowerman and Phil Knight: Building the Nike Empire,* Blackbird Press, 1994.

Laurie Rozakis, *Bill Hanna and Joe Barbera: Yabba-Dabba-Doo!,* Blackbirch Press, 1994.

The Greedy Man in the Moon, Riverbank Press, 1994.

Benjamin Franklin, Worthington Press, 1994.

Jon Zonderman, *A Colonial Printer,* Rourke Book Co., 1994.

Jon Zonderman, *A Whaling Captain,* Rourke Book Co., 1994.

Also illustrator of six books on Indian tribes for Rourke Publications, 1994.

■ Sidelights

Dick Smolinski told *SATA* that he is "generally 'on the board' daily from 11:00 a.m. to 11:00 p.m., then I unwind watching old movies (30s and 40s are favorites) till 2:00 a.m. next morning. Aside from vacations and trips (mainly Hutchinson Island in Florida) I have maintained this routine since becoming a freelancer in 1977. The work I get is varied and challenging, ranging from a black and white spot to a 40-inch by 70-inch oil."

■ For More Information See

PERIODICALS

School Library Journal, March, 1986.

* * *

STOPS, Sue 1936-

■ Personal

Born December 3, 1936, in Coventry, England; daughter of Clifford (a personnel officer) and Connie (Grimsley) Harris; married John Stops (an artist), August 1, 1959; children: William, Emma. *Education:* Attended Newton Park College of Education, 1956-58; *Politics:* "Middle of the road." *Hobbies and other interests:* Theater, puppets, natural history.

■ Addresses

Home—9 Freeland Pl., Hotwells, Bristol BS8 4NP, England. *Office*—Westbury Park Primary, Bayswater Ave., Bristol, England.

SUE STOPS

Career

Teacher in primary and secondary schools in Bristol, England, 1960-95. Serves on management committees for Hope Center (a community arts center), Abbeyfield (an extra-care home for frail elderly people), and The Puppet Place (a networking organization bringing puppets and audiences together). *Member:* National Union of Teachers.

Writings

Dulcie Dando, illustrated by Debi Gliori, Andre Deutsch, 1990, published in the United States as *Dulcie Dando, Soccer Star,* Holt, 1992.
Sally Moves South, Scholastic, 1994.
Mystery in the Peaks, Scholastic, 1994.

Also author of *Dulcie Dando Disco Dancer,* illustrated by Gliori, published by Andre Deutsch; and *Maurice,* illustrated by Marc Vyvyan Jones, published by Spindlewood.

Work in Progress

A lighthearted/serious book about reading and books for emergent readers for Scholastic; research on how children learn to read.

Sidelights

"I have worked as a teacher for many years, mainly with infants and also as a literacy tutor for the county of Avon," Sue Stops told *SATA.* "I had the good fortune to spend time at Bristol University devising ways of bringing books to children. From this developed BOOKSAMAZING, an annual performance designed to show children that reading is a brilliant way to spend time. We've brought some of the best authors and illustrators to Bristol, my city. We've toured and even presented a hands-on science/book event, EUREKA, which reached thousands of children in our area. It's all been great fun! I've ventured late into writing, but I enjoy it enormously. I'm learning all the time and I can't wait to retire so that I can spend more time both writing and visiting schools to share my pleasure in children's books."

*   *   *

TATE, Joan 1922-

Personal

Born September 23, 1922, in Tonbridge, Kent, England; married, 1945; children: two daughters, one son.

Addresses

Home—7 College Hill, Shrewsbury SY1 1LZ, England.

JOAN TATE

Career

Freelance writer, translator, and publisher's reader. *Member:* PEN International, Amnesty International, Swedish English Literary Translators' Association (SELTA).

Writings

FICTION FOR CHILDREN

Coal Hoppy, illustrated by J. Yunge-Bateman, Heinemann, 1964.
The Crane, illustrated by Richard Wilson, Heinemann, 1964.
Jenny, illustrated by Charles Keeping, Heinemann, 1964.
Lucy, illustrated by Richard Wilson, Heinemann, 1964.
The Next-Doors, illustrated by Charles Keeping, Heinemann, 1964, Scholastic, 1976.
Picture Charlie, illustrated by Laszlo Acs, Heinemann, 1964.
The Rabbit Boy, illustrated by Hugh Marshall, Heinemann, 1964.
The Silver Grill, illustrated by Hugh Marshall, Heinemann, 1964, Scholastic, 1976.
Bill, illustrated by George Tuckwell, Heinemann, 1966.
The Holiday, illustrated by Leo Walmsley, Heinemann, 1966.
Mrs. Jenny, illustrated by Charles Keeping, Heinemann, 1966.
Tad, illustrated by Leo Walmsley, Heinemann, 1966.
The Tree, illustrated by George Tuckwell, Heinemann, 1966, published as *Tina and David,* Nelson, 1973.
Bits and Pieces, illustrated by Quentin Blake, Heinemann, 1967.
The Circus and Other Stories, illustrated by Timothy Jacques, Heinemann, 1967.
The Great Birds, Almqvist & Wiksell, 1967, Blackie, 1976.

Letters to Chris, illustrated by Mary Russon, Heinemann, 1967.
Luke's Garden, illustrated by Quentin Blake, Heinemann, 1967, Hodder, 1976, published as *Luke's Garden and Gramp: Two Short Novels,* Harper, 1981.
The New House, Almqvist & Wiksell, 1967, Pelham, 1976.
The Old Car, Almqvist & Wiksell, 1967.
Polly, Almqvist & Wiksell, 1967, Cassell, 1976.
The Soap Box, Almqvist & Wiksell, 1967.
The Train, Almqvist & Wiksell, 1967.
Wild Martin and the Crow, illustrated by Richard Kennedy, Heinemann, 1967.
Sam and Me, Macmillan, 1968, Coward McCann, 1969.
The Ball, illustrated by Mary Dinsdale, John Dyke, and Prudence Seward, Macmillan, 1969.
The Caravan, Almqvist & Wiksell, 1969.
The Cheapjack Man, illustrated by Richard Rose, Jenny Williams, and Mary Dinsdale, Macmillan, 1969.
Clipper, Macmillan, 1969, published as *Ring on My Finger,* 1971, Scholastic, 1976.
Edward and the Uncles, Almqvist & Wiksell, 1969.
The Gobblydock, illustrated by Richard Rose, Jenny Williams, and Mary Dinsdale, Macmillan, 1969.
The Letter, Almqvist & Wiksell, 1969.
The Lollipop Man, illustrated by Mary Dinsdale, John Dyke, and Prudence Seward, Macmillan, 1969.
The Nest, illustrated by Prudence Seward, Macmillan, 1969.
Out of the Sun, Heinemann, 1969.
Puddle's Tiger, Almqvist & Wiksell, 1969.
The Secret, Almqvist & Wiksell, 1969.
The Treehouse, illustrated by Mary Dinsdale, Macmillan, 1969.
Whizz Kid, Macmillan, 1969, published as *Not the Usual Kind of Girl,* Scholastic, 1974, published as *Clee and Nibs,* Penguin, 1990.
Gramp, illustrated by Robert Geary, Chatto Boyd and Oliver, 1971, revised edition, Pelham, 1979, published as *Luke's Garden and Gramp: Two Short Novels,* Harper, 1981.
The Long Road Home, Heinemann, 1971.
Wild Boy, illustrated by Trevor Stubley, Chatto Boyd and Oliver, 1972, Harper, 1973.
Wump Day, illustrated by John Storey, Heinemann, 1972.
Ben and Annie, illustrated by Mary Dinsdale, Brockhampton Press, 1973, Doubleday, 1974.
Dad's Camel, illustrated by Margaret Power, Heinemann, 1973, new edition, Red Fox/Anderson Press, 1991.
Dinah, Almqvist & Wiksell, 1973.
Grandpa and My Sister Bee, illustrated by Leslie Wood, Brockhampton Press, 1973, Children's Press, 1976.
Jock and the Rock Cakes, illustrated by Carolyn Dinan, Brockhampton Press, 1973, Children's Press, 1976.
Journal for One, Almqvist & Wiksell, 1973.
The Man Who Rang the Bell, Almqvist & Wiksell, 1973.
The Match, Almqvist & Wiksell, 1973.
Night Out, Almqvist & Wiksell, 1973.
Taxi!, Schoeningh, 1973.
Dirty Dan, Almqvist & Wiksell, 1974.

Ginger Mick, Heinemann, 1974, revised edition, Longman, 1975.
The Runners, illustrated by Douglas Phillips, David and Charles, 1974, revised edition, Longman, 1977.
Sunday's Trumpet, Almqvist & Wiksell, 1974.
The Thinking Box, Almqvist and Wiksell, 1974.
Zena, Almqvist & Wiksell, 1974.
Your Dog, Pelham, 1975.
Billoggs, illustrated by Trevor Stubley, Pelham, 1976.
Crow and the Brown Boy, illustrated by Gay Galsworthy, Cassell, 1976.
The House That Jack Built, Pelham, 1976.
Polly and the Barrow Boy, illustrated by Gay Galsworthy, Cassell, 1976.
Turn Again, Whittington, Pelham, 1976.
You Can't Explain Everything, Longman, 1976.
See You and Other Stories, Longman, 1977.
See How They Run, Pelham, 1978.
Cat Country, Ram, 1979.
Jumping Jo the Joker, illustrated by Maggie Dawson, Macmillan, 1984.

NONFICTION AND FABLES FOR CHILDREN

Going Up, three volumes, Almqvist & Wiksell, 1969-74.
Your Town, illustrated by Virginia Smith, David and Charles, 1972.
How Do You Do?, three volumes, Schoeningh, 1973-76.
The Living River, illustrated by David Harris, Dent, 1974.
Disco Books (contains *Big Fish, Tom's Trip, The Day I Got the Sack, Girl in the Window, Supermarket, Gren, Day Off, Moped*), eight volumes, illustrated by Gay Galsworthy, Jill Cox, and George Craig, Cassell, 1975.
Your Dog, illustrated by Babette Cole, Pelham, 1975.
On Your Own 1-2, two volumes, Wheaton, 1977-78.
Frankie Flies, Macmillan, 1980.
Club Books (contains *The Jimjob, The Totter Man, Trip to Liverpool, New Shoes*), four volumes, illustrated by George Craig and Jill Cox, Cassell, 1981.
(With M. Wiese) *How to Go Shopping,* Hirschgraben, 1982.
(With M. Wiese) *How to Get Help,* Hirschgraben, 1983.
(With M. Wiese) *How to Eat Out,* Hirschgraben, 1983.
The Fox and the Stork and Other Fables (fables from Aesop), illustrated by Svend Otto S., Pelham, 1985.
Avalanche!, illustrated by Svend Otto S., Pelham, 1987.
The Donkey and the Dog (fable from Aesop), illustrated by Svend Otto S., Pelham, 1987.
Twenty Tales of Aesop, illustrated by Svend Otto S., Pelham, 1987.

OTHER

Contributor of poems and short stories to anthologies. Also translator of more than seventy books for children by Gunnel Beckman, Astrid Lindgren, Svend Otto S., Gun and Ingvar Bjork, Irmelin Sandman Lilius, and others. Also translator of over sixty books from the Swedish, Danish, and Norwegian for adults, including works by Maj Sjowall and Per Wahloo, Maria Lang, Elisabeth Soderstrom, Carl Nylander, Ingmar Bergman, P. C. Jersild, Britt Ekland, and Thomas Dinesen.

Tate's work has been translated into several languages. A collection of her manuscripts is housed in the Kerlan Collection, University of Minnesota, Minneapolis.

■ Adaptations

Gramp was adapted for BBC radio in 1971.

■ Work in Progress

A series of nonfiction books on the theater arts, including *Shadow Theater of Thailand, Shadow Theater of China, Shadow Theater of Indonesia, Shadow Theater of the Middle East, Shadow Theater of India,* and *Shadow Theater of Malaysia.* Two children's fiction titles, *Catspoon and Fiddle* and *Jimmy.*

■ Sidelights

Joan Tate is best known for her short novels written for adolescents. Employing such themes as early marriage, kidnapping, runaways, and contemporary urban life, Tate appeals to the twelve to sixteen age group with stories that hit home. A typical Tate book is "topical, full of snappy dialogue, and [has] a plot that is relevant and interesting to teenagers," according to Jean Russell in *Twentieth-Century Children's Writers.* Tate, who is fluent in Swedish, has also written young adult titles in simple English for second language readers in Sweden, Norway, Denmark, Finland, and Germany, and she is a translator of books for both children and adults. Add to this a full complement of books for younger readers, several young adult nonfiction works, retellings from Aesop, and the fact that Tate began writing at about age forty, and it is clear that the author has had a very busy writing career.

In many ways Tate has managed to pack a lot into her life. Born in England in 1922, she was an early and avid reader. "I have been reading since I was four," she once told *SATA,* "always indiscriminately, but gradually discovering that there is always something new to be learnt about human kind." Writing came early, as well, first in the form of letters. "Letters are talking on paper, not usually works of great literature," she wrote in an essay for the *Something about the Author Autobiography Series (SAAS).* "We always had to write thank you letters when we were children. If you were away at school, in my day you had to write home every Sunday, a boring chore, so I used to jot down every day what I had done that day and then filled pages and pages every Sunday with what I had done, and occasionally what I thought about what I had done. My parents endured the letters without comment or complaint." Her school years in the 1930s brought her into contact with children of several nationalities whose families had fled the civil war in Spain or the Nazi ascendancy in Germany. Tate attended a university in Sweden, where she was cut off from communications home after the outbreak of World War II, and she remained in that neutral country until 1942. It was during this period that she became proficient in Swedish. "When survival is at the top of your agenda," she wrote in *SAAS,* "you learn a language very well and it becomes part of you. When you are stuck, while young, in a foreign country, you learn to be independent very quickly, as there is no one else to help you. Swedes are kindly, civilized people and they helped as best they could, but in the end you are out there on your own."

Tate was finally able to return to Britain, but she never lost the independence she learned in Sweden. In England she married and had three children, and when the last of them were in school she began working and writing again. Her early writing included broadcasts for the BBC. "Writing for radio ... is also talking on paper," Tate said in *SAAS,* "but you have to talk succinctly, and it is no use launching into long and beautiful descriptions of glorious landscapes which your audience can't see. So broadcasting ... taught me to write simply and clearly, not to waffle, and preferably to write so that the listener could see in his or her mind the picture of what I was saying." As well as broadcasting, Tate turned her hand to journalism. Journalism, Tate noted in *SAAS,* is much the same as writing stories. "There is a beginning and end to any article or any book review, just as there is a beginning and an end to any story. The only difference is that you have to *invent* the story, whereas in journalism and broadcasting and articles, you are usually dealing in facts, the truth as you see it, if you can get anywhere near it. Story-writing is another kind of truth. If it isn't 'true' and if the reader senses that, he or she will not go on reading it."

This was a dictum Tate carried with her into another form of writing. She described her works in *SAAS* as stories "for young people who were no longer children, who hadn't started reading when they were four, who had never read a whole book, who had no books at home and whose parents never or rarely went into a library or a bookshop." These were more like long short stories than actual novels, packaged in paperback with illustrated covers. The themes were relevant to the intended audience. These readers "wanted books about the real life they actually lived themselves," Tate wrote in *SAAS,* "not stories about bunny rabbits or squirrels going shopping or improbable 'adventure' stories." Tate wrote about their lives, about young people who "went dancing, drove cars, got into trouble, got out of trouble, wept or laughed or hurt themselves, stories with a beginning, middle, but very rarely a conclusive end." She avoided moralizing, as well as the usual genres such as thrillers. Beginning in 1964, she published nineteen such short novels, dealing with everything from noisy neighbors in *The Next-Doors* to the life of a young West Indian girl in *Jenny* and *Mrs. Jenny.* The 1966 work *Tina and David,* published in England as *The Tree,* is indicative of the sort of sensitive interaction between teenage protagonists that Tate became known for. Eighteen-year-old David is painfully shy of girls, so shy that he literally can't talk to them. But when he runs into a former classmate, Tina, with whom he used to exchange notes in school, he finds a new strategy to communicate. One day Tina discovers a note left by David in a tree by her usual bus stop. From this fragile beginning, the two form a real friendship that soon blossoms into love, and when the tree is cut down Tina is saddened, but David realizes they no longer need it. A reviewer in the *Bulletin of the Center for Children's Books* concluded that Tate's sensitivity in handling the relationship was "affective and realistic."

Tate's early books were so successful in reaching their audience that she was asked by a Swedish publisher to write the same sort of books for second language readers in Sweden as well. *The Great Birds,* published first in Stockholm and then a decade later in England, tells the story of the loner Mark who has a phobia about airplanes until meeting—through a shared hobby of bird watching—a pilot from a nearby air base and taking an unexpected flight. The theme of this book, noted Margery Fisher in *Growing Point,* "is developed with the shrewd sympathy typical of Joan Tate's writing."

Tate's inspirations come from many sources: She kept a file of story ideas culled from the newspapers or from personal experience and scribbled onto scraps of paper. "'Girl imprisoned for stealing baby' said one [scrap of paper]," Tate recalled in *SAAS.* "I remember the sense of outrage at any young girl being sent to prison (which actually happened many years ago) and wondering first

A beautiful friendship between young Ben and wheelchair-bound Annie is destroyed through an adult's insensitivity.

what made her steal a child, and secondly what kind of system did we, a civilized country, have that didn't find out what made her do it and try to help her? So I invented a story about a girl who stole a baby, which was eventually called *Sam and Me.* It was short, succinct, in relatively simple language." The kidnapping theme gave the book a dramatic punch, according to a critic in the *Bulletin of the Center for Children's Books,* but it is the self-analysis by the main character, Jo, and "her realization that she has been docile, childlike, and sexually apathetic that is the crux of the story."

Searching for another topic, Tate would dip her hand into the story file. "'Boy who grows roses' said another scrap of paper," Tate wrote in *SAAS.* "I can't remember where that came from, but it grew into a kind of allegory, a kind of Christ story, called *Luke's Garden,* a story about a boy who was different and everyone was either scared of him or disliked him just *because* he was different." This difference eventually leads to his death. "Tate's poignant descriptions ... will touch all readers," noted Beverly B. Youree in *Voice of Youth Advocates.* Another story featuring a young boy with a loving heart, though without such a tragic ending, is *Gramp.* The grandfather of the title becomes withdrawn to the point of deep depression when his family moves to a cramped apartment where there is no room for his treasured workshop and tools. His young grandson, Simon, comes to the rescue, finally finding a space for the tools and giving his grandfather a reason to live once again. "Tate writes with gentle tone and sharp insight," noted a *Bulletin of the Center for Children's Books* reviewer. The grandfather was drawn, a critic in *Times Literary Supplement* commented, "with loving preciseness of detail, like a child's Holbein."

"Another grubby piece of paper I remember said 'Living on the moor,'" Tate recalled in *SAAS.* Out of this bit of information grew first a short story for Swedish readers and then a novel, *Wild Boy,* "about two older boys, one from the small Yorkshire town who knew the moors and had known them since childhood like the back of his hand, the other the smart guy, the sharp-witted, runaway, street-wise London boy, who tried living alone on the moor with disastrous results." When the Yorkshire boy discovers the runaway on the moor, he helps him out, reversing the usual roles of who is clever and who is not. "A gracefully written story," noted a contributor in *Bulletin of the Center for Children's Books.* Virginia Haviland, writing in *Horn Book,* commented on "the skillful prose which conveys the atmosphere of the open moors and the boys' intimate understanding of each other."

Another favorite of Tate's realistic young adult novels is *Whizz Kid,* published in the United States as *Not the Usual Kind of Girl,* a "kind of love story," as Tate described it in *SAAS.* "Actually, the story is about what happens when the girl's boyfriend gets out of the car for a moment to relieve himself on the way back from a football match and completely disappears. The story is told in two halves, first her view of what happened, and then, secondly, his." It was a story popular enough with readers to be published in Danish, Norwegian, and French, with a main character, Clee, who is "wonderfully crisp and unique," according to a *Times Literary Supplement* reviewer. Another story about a boy and girl, *Ben and Annie,* is about two young people who live in the same apartment house. Annie is thirteen and confined to a wheelchair, and Ben, who is two years younger, communicates with her via two tin cans connected by string and later by a second-hand intercom rigged up by Ben's father. Ben takes Annie for outings to the park and shopping, but when Ben and a friend playfully push Annie down a hill, this is misunderstood by an onlooker. Thinking that the boys are somehow torturing the girl, this adult reports the incident to Annie's parents who end the friendship. Written in the present tense and with large blocks of dialogue, the story has "a strong feeling of immediacy," Paul Heins noted in *Horn Book,* concluding that the book was a "story skillful for its condensation and powerful for its presentation of the emotions of childhood." A contributor in *Bulletin of the Center for Children's Books* concurred, calling *Ben and Annie* a "short and poignant story." And a *Publishers Weekly* reviewer praised Tate for the fact that she didn't "prettify the ending.... The reader's sense of loss ... is acute."

Usually eschewing genre formats in her writing, Tate has written three books that could be loosely termed mysteries for children. Nursery rhyme titles link these books: *See How They Run; Turn Again, Whittington;* and *The House That Jack Built.* But the books were not the typical Agatha Christie fare of whodunit in that "the *only* person who knew what was going on was the *reader,*" Tate explained in *SAAS.* The characters in the books had to slog through the mystery while the reader all the while knew what was happening. "Joan Tate's adventure stories combine dash and pace with a precision that makes them almost like activated maps," commented Fisher in a *Growing Point* review of *See How They Run,* and a contributor in the *Times Literary Supplement* found *Turn Again, Whittington* to be a "well constructed, humorous, lively, interesting thriller."

In the field of books for five- to seven-year-olds who are just beginning to read, Tate has also made a mark with such fanciful stories as *Grandpa and My Sister Bee, Jock and the Rock Cakes,* and *Dad's Camel.* In the first of these, a "gently humorous" story according to a *Times Literary Supplement* reviewer, little Bee helps her grandfather plant a row of weeds; the second takes a look at young Jock's disastrous attempts at baking. *Dad's Camel* is the light-hearted story of a father who brings a camel back from the pub after having won it in a bet.

In addition to these fictional pieces for young adults and children, Tate has also worked in nonfiction and with translations of fables by Aesop. Her nonfiction includes explanations of city government in *Your Town,* and the habits and behaviors of dogs in *Your Dog,* which a critic for *Junior Bookshelf* described as a book "well researched, clearly presented without sentimentality and with authority." With *The Living River,* Tate considered

environmental matters by describing waterways: their sources and courses, wildlife dependent on rivers, and man's development of them. "This is a compact, practical book which could be used in the classroom for reference or as a basis for discussion," noted Fisher in a *Growing Point* review. A *Junior Bookshelf* critic concluded that the book was "ordered, concise, full of interest, and markedly up to date." Tate, with the popular Danish illustrator Svend Otto S., has translated fables from Aesop, including *The Fox and the Stork and Other Fables,* which *Growing Point*'s Fisher has termed "a cheerful, engaging look" at the world of Aesop. She has also done the same with well-known tales by Hans Christian Andersen.

Tate's career has spanned four decades and over a hundred original publications, including a long list of translations. But for the author, this is all in a day's work. "In reality," she wrote in *SAAS,* "I am quite an ordinary person who spends almost every day in working hours banging away on a machine in a small room in a small house in a small market town in an agricultural area of England near Wales, and the post office does quite well out of me." Of her more recent work, Tate told *SATA,* "Nowadays I am largely occupied with translations of Scandinavian literature, of which there is a great deal, and today it is beginning to be noticed everywhere outside Scandinavia. It's a good life."

■ Works Cited

Review of *Ben and Annie, Publishers Weekly,* August 5, 1974, p. 58.

Review of *Ben and Annie, Bulletin of the Center for Children's Books,* November, 1974, p. 55.

Fisher, Margery, review of *The Living River, Growing Point,* March, 1975, p. 2578.

Fisher, Margery, review of *The Great Birds, Growing Point,* March, 1977, p. 3060.

Fisher, Margery, review of *See How They Run, Growing Point,* January, 1979, p. 3443.

Fisher, Margery, review of *The Fox and the Stork and Other Fables, Growing Point,* January, 1986, p. 4549.

Review of *Gramp, Times Literary Supplement,* July 2, 1971, p. 775.

Review of *Grandpa and My Sister Bee, Times Literary Supplement,* September 28, 1973, p. 1127.

Haviland, Virginia, review of *Wild Boy, Horn Book,* December, 1973, p. 596.

Heins, Paul, review of *Ben and Annie, Horn Book,* December, 1974, p. 694.

Review of *The Living River, Junior Bookshelf,* April, 1975, p. 137.

Review of *Luke's Garden and Gramp: Two Short Novels, Bulletin of the Center for Children's Books,* October, 1981, p. 38.

Russell, Jean, "Tate, Joan," *Twentieth-Century Children's Writers,* edited by Laura Standley Berger, St. James Press, 1995, pp. 938-40.

Review of *Sam and Me, Bulletin of the Center for Children's Books,* April, 1970, p. 135.

Tate, Joan, essay in *Something about the Author Autobiography Series,* Volume 20, Gale, 1995, pp. 269-77.

Review of *Tina and David, Bulletin of the Center for Children's Books,* May, 1974, p. 151.

Review of *Turn Again, Whittington, Times Literary Supplement,* November 21, 1980, p. 1324.

Review of *Whizz Kid, Times Literary Supplement,* December 8, 1972, p. 1497.

Review of *Wild Boy, Bulletin of the Center for Children's Books,* February, 1974, p. 102.

Review of *Your Dog, Junior Bookshelf,* April, 1976, p. 109.

Youree, Beverly B., review of *Luke's Garden and Gramp: Two Short Novels, Voice of Youth Advocates,* October, 1981, p. 38.

■ For More Information See

PERIODICALS

Growing Point, March, 1975, p. 2579; July, 1976, p. 2919; November, 1976, p. 2988; September, 1987, p. 4872.

Horn Book, October, 1981, p. 545.

Kirkus Reviews, February 1, 1969, p. 108; September 1, 1973, p. 973; September 15, 1973, p. 1045; July 15, 1974, p. 744; February 1, 1982, p. 137.

Library Journal, October 15, 1969, p. 3836; January 15, 1974, p. 219; May 15, 1974, p. 1478.

School Library Journal, September, 1976, p. 97; September, 1981, p. 142.

Times Literary Supplement, March 14, 1968, p. 258; April 2, 1971, p. 385; December 3, 1971, p. 1512; April 28, 1972, p. 481; November 3, 1972, p. 1335; April 6, 1973, p. 387; September 28, 1973, p. 1123; December 6, 1974, p. 1373; November 21, 1980, p. 1324.

—Sketch by J. Sydney Jones

W

CAROLYN KOTT WASHBURNE

WASHBURNE, Carolyn Kott 1944-

■ Personal

Born February 9, 1944, in Indianapolis, IN; daughter of Roland Wilson (an insurance executive) and Shirley Ruth (a homemaker; maiden name, Williamson) Kott; divorced; children: Jessie Washburne-Harris, Charles Roland Spring. *Education:* Wellesley College, B.A., 1965; University of Pennsylvania School of Social Work, M.S.W., 1971.

■ Addresses

Home—1909 East Menlo Blvd., Shorewood, WI 53211-2519. *Office*—Washburne Literary Services, 4465 North Oakland Ave., Milwaukee, WI 53211-1662.

■ Career

Women in Transition, Inc., Philadelphia, PA, co-director, 1971-76; University of Wisconsin—Milwaukee School of Social Welfare, social worker, 1976-83; freelance writer, editor, and public relations consultant, Milwaukee, 1983—.

■ Writings

(With others) *Women in Transition,* Scribner, 1975.
(With Jennifer Baker Fleming) *For Better, for Worse: A Feminist Handbook on Marriage and Other Options,* Scribner, 1977.
A Multicultural Portrait of Colonial Life, Marshall Cavendish, 1994.
The 1930s, Marshall Cavendish, 1994.
Italian Americans, Marshall Cavendish, 1995.

Contributor of articles to periodicals, including *New York Times, Ms., Mademoiselle, Utne Reader, Harper's Bazaar, Chicago Tribune, Milwaukee Magazine,* and *Wisconsin Magazine.*

■ Sidelights

A full-time writer who has published several nonfiction books that reflect her interest in various aspects of the women's and civil rights movements, Carolyn Kott Washburne spent her early professional career as a social worker. She served as editor of her high school newspaper and then turned to social activism during and after college.

In 1971 Washburne and several other women founded Women in Transition, Inc., a counseling program for divorcing and battered women in the Philadelphia area.

The program provided her with the opportunity to utilize her writing and editing skills on *Women in Transition,* a manual intended to provide program participants with advice and information on surviving divorce. The publisher Charles Scribner's Sons approached the leaders of the group and asked if they would be interested in revising the manual for national distribution. After *Women in Transition* was revised and published, Washburne's second book, authored with Jennifer Baker Fleming, was *For Better, for Worse: A Feminist Handbook on Marriage and Other Options,* which provides a feminist perspective on marriage. Several chapters from *For Better, for Worse* were subsequently excerpted by magazines, a development that encouraged Washburne to continue her writing efforts.

Family life and the demands of her job in a child welfare program, however, made it difficult for Washburne to devote significant hours to her writing. "Although her articles had appeared in *Ms., Mademoiselle, Harper's Bazaar,* and *Modern Bride,* among others," noted a biographical statement Washburne supplied to *SATA,* "she wasn't selling enough to quit her job. Working full time and taking care of her family, Carolyn was forced to squeeze in her writing at night and on weekends." Washburne's determination to succeed as a writer, though, eventually led her to turn to a full-time freelancing career in 1983. By cultivating relationships with editors and honing her writing and copyediting skills, Washburne soon had a thriving business that enabled her to support herself and her two children. Those early years, she noted in the biographical statement, taught her the value of writing to meet deadlines and writing about unfamiliar topics.

Washburne's work has included a wide range of freelance assignments. An editor of consumer and professional books, she has also written public relations materials and taught college courses in nonfiction writing at the University of Wisconsin—Milwaukee. In addition, Washburne has published several other books, including *A Multicultural Portrait of Colonial Life,* a 1994 title intended for middle school and high school audiences. The book examines the influences of women, Native Americans, and African Americans on U.S. colonial life. *School Library Journal* reviewer Janice C. Hayes noted that "the narrative is presented in an interesting and convincing manner," although she cautioned that "the sentences are long and often complex." In 1995 Washburne wrote *Italian Americans,* another nonfiction work.

Washburne's biographical statement noted that "she sometimes tires of working alone, with its isolation and need for constant self-motivation. Yet she realizes that freedom and flexibility of being her own boss are well worth the trade-off." As Washburne admitted, "I'm addicted to freelancing."

■ Works Cited

Hayes, Janice C., review of *A Multicultural Portrait of Colonial Life, School Library Journal,* April, 1994, p. 167.

Washburne, Carolyn Kott, "Meet Your WDS Instructor" (biographical note), c. 1991.

* * *

WEISS, Nicki 1954-

■ Personal

Born January 25, 1954, in New York, NY; daughter of Harry (a textile importer) and Lyla (a sculptress; maiden name, Gutman) Weiss. *Education:* Union College, B.A., 1976; Bank Street College of Education, M.S., 1996.

■ Addresses

Home—New York, NY; and Jerusalem, Israel.

■ Career

Scheck-Rosenblum Textiles, Inc., New York City, textile designer, 1977-79; freelance textile designer, 1979-

NICKI WEISS

81; children's author and illustrator, 1981—; Walden School, New York City, pre-school teacher, 1983-84; kindergarten teacher in New York City Public Schools, 1993—. Visiting author in schools and libraries, 1983—.

■ Writings

SELF-ILLUSTRATED

Menj!, Greenwillow, 1981.
Waiting, Greenwillow, 1981.
Chuckie, Greenwillow, 1982.
Hank and Oogie, Greenwillow, 1982.
Maude and Sally, Greenwillow, 1983.
Weekend at Muskrat Lake, Greenwillow, 1984.
Battle Day at Camp Delmont, Greenwillow, 1985.
Princess Pearl, Greenwillow, 1986.
A Family Story, Greenwillow, 1987.
If You're Happy and You Know It, Greenwillow, 1987.
Barney Is Big, Greenwillow, 1988.
Where Does the Brown Bear Go?, Greenwillow, 1989.
Sun Sand Sea Sail, Greenwillow, 1989.
Dog Boy Cap Skate, Greenwillow, 1989.
An Egg Is an Egg, Putnam, 1990.
Surprise Box, Putnam, 1991.
On a Hot, Hot Day, Putnam, 1992.
The First Night of Hanukkah, Grosset & Dunlap, 1992.
Stone Men, Greenwillow, 1993.

■ Work in Progress

A large sculpture.

■ Sidelights

It is through the combination of words, illustrations, and overall design that Nicki Weiss creates her self-illustrated picture and juvenile books, which range from lively, fun tales to sensitive, warm stories. The driving force behind many of these stories, though, is change. The young characters in such books as Hank and Oogie, Maude and Sally, and Barney Is Big bravely face such new situations as the first day of school and an entire summer without a best friend. And in other stories Weiss focuses on the ever-changing family as the relationships within it grow and develop. In the end, these changes give Weiss's characters the strength and courage to face future challenges.

Weiss herself underwent a period of change before she eventually became an author and illustrator of children's books. Despite early signs of artistic talent, Weiss, unlike everyone else around her, did not think she would be an artist. So, after graduating from college, she began her own textile design firm before finally realizing that she craved something more creative. Weiss soon found this creativity and a new career in the form of children's books.

Among Weiss's first books is the picture book Waiting, which focuses on a simple situation and brings it to life. Using pastel colors, Weiss depicts a young child, Anna-lee, as she waits in the yard for her mother's return from the store. Eagerly waiting, Annalee mistakes many things for her mother's return, including a good smell, singing birds, and the tickle of a ladybug on her leg. "Illustrations and text combine as an eloquent, credible portrayal that will be welcomed," asserts Carolyn Noah in School Library Journal. And a Kirkus Reviews contributor concludes that the "still, boundless setting is ... a metaphor for the stop-time endlessness of Annalee's wait. One small idea, wholly realized."

A larger idea encompassing a longer time period is the basis for Weiss's first book dealing with change—Hank and Oogie. Published in 1982, this story begins with Hank's first birthday, for which he is given Oogie, a stuffed hippo. Hank takes Oogie everywhere until he turns five and begins kindergarten. There he learns that his classmates don't think much of kids who still play with stuffed animals, so thereafter Hank leaves Oogie at home. "Weiss treats with sensitivity and humor the need for children to adjust to changes wrought by the years," writes a Publishers Weekly contributor, adding that Hank and Oogie is "animated by beguiling pictures in harmonious colors."

Another pair of best friends populates Maude and Sally and its 1985 sequel, Battle Day at Camp Delmont. In the first, Maude and Sally spend all their time together until Sally goes off to camp one summer without Maude. As the summer wears on, it becomes evident to Maude that Sally has new friends at camp. Maude initially does not want a new friend because it will be different, but with her mother's encouragement she gives it a try and ends up with two best friends. Both Sally and Maude make it to camp at Battle Day at Camp Delmont. Their friendship is put to the test, though, when they are on opposing teams during field day competitions. Peggy Forehand, writing in School Library Journal, points out that in Maude and Sally "Weiss sensitively portrays the warmth and fun of friendships with all the insecurities that youngsters experience in relationships."

Family relationships and the changes within the family structure are related in the two stories featuring young Pearl—Weekend at Muskrat Lake and Princess Pearl. Spending a weekend with her family in the first story, Pearl shares an activity with each member of her family; she swims with her mother, picks blueberries with her older sister, and fishes with her father. "The overall feeling" of Weekend at Muskrat Lake "is that of reassurance and quiet joy at togetherness in a peaceful and beautiful setting," as Robin Fenn Elbot describes it in School Library Journal. Things are not as calm at the family's real home in Princess Pearl. Sibling rivalry between Pearl and her older sister Rosemary is at its peak as Rosemary takes every opportunity to torment her younger sister. But when one of Pearl's friends comes over and bullies her, Rosemary is the first to her rescue. Ann A. Flowers writes in Horn Book that "the gratifying conclusion" of Princess Pearl "will be both salutary and satisfactory to many a young reader."

The relationship between two more sisters, and the generations that follow them, is the focus of Weiss's

1987 work *A Family Story*. Rachel and Annie have a special relationship that grows as they do, and flows over when they each have daughters of their own. And these daughters, Louise and Jane, carry on the unique bond of their mothers. "This is a warm, loving look at the rare and wonderful relationships between big girls and little girls, made especially nice by placing it in the context of family," observes *School Library Journal* contributor Lucy Young Clem. And a *Publishers Weekly* reviewer relates that *A Family Story* "celebrates love in this softspoken and endearing telling."

A younger audience is reached in the simpler picture books *Where Does the Brown Bear Go?, Sun Sand Sea Sail,* a.. ¹ *Dog Boy Cap Skate*. In these stories Weiss uses repetition, rhyme, and single words in combination with her illustrations. The lullaby *Where Does the Brown Bear Go?* asks where a variety of animals go when night comes, answering the questions on the last few pages with a picture of a bed full of stuffed animals and a young child asleep. Praising Weiss's use of rhythm and rhyme, Elizabeth S. Watson concludes in *Horn Book* that *Where Does the Brown Bear Go?* is "an exquisite book to end a young one's day." *Dog Boy Cap Skate* and *Sun Sand Sea Sail* use one-word captions to tell lively, humorous tales, including that of a young boy learning to ice skate and a family trip to the beach. "Readers will marvel at the vast images conjured by so few words in these two picture books," maintains a *Publishers Weekly* reviewer.

A variety of images are also employed in Weiss's 1992 description of the seasons, found in *On a Hot, Hot Day*. Set in an inner-city Hispanic neighborhood, this story portrays a mother's love for her son while it describes the passing seasons through the activities the pair partake in, ending with the mother putting her young son to bed. Once again, Weiss utilizes rhyme in the words of the story, which are enhanced by her pencil and watercolor illustrations. "The verse is simple, endearing, and predictable, allowing listeners to connect immediately," states Liza Bliss in *School Library Journal*. *On a Hot, Hot Day* is "an unassuming and reassuring domestic slice of life overflowing with a mother's love for her child," concludes *Horn Book* contributor Ellen Fader.

In a 1993 picture book, Weiss tells a traditional fairy tale within her own story. *Stone Men* begins with Arnie asking his grandmother to tell him a story he's never heard before. Grandmother does just this, telling the tale of a courageous peddler. The peddler Isaac travels from town to town selling his merchandise, lessening his loneliness by building a man out of stone as he leaves each village. When he hears a band of soldiers plotting to rob and ransack a village on his route, he quickly tries to warn the townspeople. Unable to wake them, he instead constructs an army of stone men that scare away the soldiers in the early dawn. "The language is direct and dramatic, giving the story the cadence of a family tale passed from one generation to the next," describes *School Library Journal* contributor Joy Fleishhacker. And a *Publishers Weekly* reviewer similarly concludes:

"Economy in prose and art produces a picture book with the power and pungency of the finest folk tales."

■ Works Cited

Bliss, Liza, review of *On a Hot, Hot Day, School Library Journal,* July, 1992, pp. 65-66.

Clem, Lucy Young, review of *A Family Story, School Library Journal,* June/July, 1987, p. 91.

Review of *Dog Boy Cap Skate* and *Sun Sand Sea Sail, Publishers Weekly,* July 28, 1989, p. 218.

Elbot, Robin Fenn, review of *Weekend at Muskrat Lake, School Library Journal,* December, 1984, p. 78.

Fader, Ellen, review of *On a Hot, Hot Day, Horn Book,* May/June, 1992, p. 335.

Review of *A Family Story, Publishers Weekly,* March 20, 1987, p. 78.

Fleishhacker, Joy, review of *Stone Men, School Library Journal,* July, 1993, pp. 73-74.

Flowers, Ann A., review of *Princess Pearl, Horn Book,* September/October, 1986, p. 584.

Forehand, Peggy, review of *Maude and Sally, School Library Journal,* May, 1983, pp. 67-68.

Review of *Hank and Oogie, Publishers Weekly,* July 2, 1982, p. 55.

Noah, Carolyn, review of *Waiting, School Library Journal,* September, 1981, p. 116.

Review of *Stone Men, Publishers Weekly,* February 1, 1993, p. 94.

Review of *Waiting, Kirkus Reviews,* August 15, 1981, p. 1008.

Watson, Elizabeth S., review of *Where Does the Brown Bear Go?, Horn Book,* May/June, 1989, p. 366.

■ For More Information See

PERIODICALS

Booklist, September 1, 1988, p. 86; November 1, 1990, p. 532; October 1, 1992, pp. 339-40.

Bulletin of the Center for Children's Books, October, 1981, p. 39; February, 1982, p. 119; July/August, 1983, p. 221; February, 1988, p. 127; November, 1990, p. 73.

Horn Book, October, 1982, p. 514; August, 1983, p. 438; September/October, 1984, pp. 586-87.

Kirkus Reviews, March 15, 1981, pp. 355-56; May 15, 1985, p. J-29; May 15, 1986, p. 789; August 1, 1989, p. 1170; June 1, 1991, p. 738; February 15, 1993, p. 236.

New York Times Book Review, April 25, 1982, p. 48.

Publishers Weekly, October 9, 1987, p. 86; February 10, 1989, p. 68.

School Library Journal, May, 1981, p. 82; March, 1982, p. 141; October, 1982; September, 1985, p. 128; August, 1986, p. 88; November, 1987, pp. 101-02; December, 1988, p. 95; March, 1989, p. 171; December, 1989, p. 91; October, 1990, pp. 103-04; November, 1991, pp. 108-09; October, 1992, p. 45.

WHEELER, Jill 1964-

■ Personal

Born March 12, 1964, in Sibley, IA; daughter of Norman J. (a farmer) and Carol L. (a homemaker; maiden name, Bensch) Wheeler; married Paul D. Libra (an auditor), September 5, 1987; children: Anna G. *Education:* South Dakota State University, B.A., 1986. *Politics:* Independent. *Religion:* United Methodist. *Hobbies and other interests:* Motorcycle riding, cooking, Jungian psychology.

■ Addresses

Home and office—13025 Court Pl., Burnsville, MN 55337.

■ Career

Owner of Wheeler & Grace (marketing communications consulting), 1995—. *Member:* International Association of Business Communicators (board of directors, Minnesota Chapter, 1992-94).

■ Writings

NONFICTION; ALL PUBLISHED BY ABDO & DAUGHTERS

Lost in London, 1988.
Bound for Boston, 1989.
The Story of Crazy Horse, 1989.
The Story of Geronimo, 1989.
The Story of Hiawatha, 1989.
The Story of Pontiac, 1989.
The Story of Sequoyah, 1989.
The Story of Sitting Bull, 1989.
Corazon Aquino, 1991.
Earth Day Every Day, 1991.
Earth Moves: Get There with Energy to Spare, 1991.
The Food We Eat, 1991.
Healthy Earth, Healthy Bodies, 1991.
Nancy R. Reagan, 1991.
The People We Live With, 1991.
The Throw-Away Generation, 1991.
A. A. Milne: Creator of Winnie the Pooh, 1992.
Coretta Scott King, 1992.
Dr. Seuss, 1992.
Laura Ingalls Wilder, 1992.
Michael Landon, 1992.
Mother Teresa, 1992.
Princess Caroline, 1992.
Raisa Gorbachev, 1992.
Beastly Neighbors, 1993.
Branch Out: A Book about Land, 1993.
Earth Kids, 1993.
Every Drop Counts: A Book about Water, 1993.
For the Birds: A Book about Air, 1993.
The Midwest and the Heartland, 1994.
The Northeast, 1994.
The Pacific West, 1994.
The Southeast and Gulf States, 1994.
The West, 1994.

JILL WHEELER

■ Work in Progress

Biographies of Heather Whitestone and Tiger Woods, for Abdo & Daughters, 1995.

■ Sidelights

Jill Wheeler is a very prolific author of nonfiction biographies, regional descriptions, and ecology books for children. In addition to her writing, she owns her own marketing communications consulting firm. Wheeler's biographies for children range from those of historically well-known Native Americans such as Geronimo, Chief Crazy Horse, Hiawatha, and Chief Sitting Bull to black American leader Coretta Scott King, politician Corazon Aquino of the Philippines, author Laura Ingalls Wilder, humanitarian Mother Teresa, and media stars like Princess Caroline. Some of the crucial subjects Wheeler has written about in her ecology books are air quality, global warming, pesticides, renewable energy issues, land conservation, and refuse recycling.

When asked to describe how she is able to write about so many different subjects, Wheeler told *SATA,* "I approach writing with the belief that there's something of interest in everything and everyone on the planet. It's the writer's job to find out what that is and share the excitement with readers. I also believe books remain the widest and most easily opened doors to a better understanding of the world around us. Life is too short to see and experience all the world has to offer, yet books allow us to cheat and catch a glimpse of that wonder."

Wheeler suggested that "Everyone should write something—even if it's never published. The words you commit to paper will be a gift to yourself, regardless of whatever else happens."

* * *

WICKENS, Elaine

■ Personal

Born in West Virginia. *Education:* Sarah Lawrence College, B.A., 1952; Columbia University, Teachers College, M.A., 1957; Anthropology Film Center, received degree, 1977.

Addresses

Office—Bank Street College of Education, 610 West 112th St., New York, NY 10025-1120.

Career

Elementary school teacher, Reece School for Emotionally Disturbed Children, 1952-55; Mental Retardation Project, Teachers College, Columbia University, New York City, teacher and research assistant, 1959-60; Bank Street College of Education, New York City, worked in a variety of capacities, including elementary school teacher, researcher, graduate school faculty member, M.A. student advisor, director of Bank Street College/Parsons School of Design Masters Program, media coordinator of Bank Street College/Simon Rodriguez University, director of Bank Street College/Ryle School Project, media specialist in mainstreaming programs with local educators, nonprint documenter with Teacher Corps Project, consultant to Yonkers museum/school project, and field representative/consultant across the country, 1960—.

Awards, Honors

Child Development Center (New York City), teacher fellowship, 1957-59.

Writings

Anna Day and the O-Ring, Alyson, 1994.

Contributor to *Science and Children, Young Children, Bank Street Publications,* and *Teachers College Record.*

PHOTOGRAPHER

Calvin Cannon, *What I Like to Do,* Coward, McCann, 1971.
Calvin Cannon, *Kirt's New House,* Coward, McCann, 1972.
Ada Graham and Frank Graham Jr., *Let's Discover Birds in Our World,* Golden Press, 1974.

Also photographer for "Doc and Me," *Wake Sleeping Book,* Houghton, 1972.

OTHER

Films, filmstrips, and videos include *Experiences pre escolares en Caracas,* 1978; *Working Together; I Am a Teacher Aide; One Family, One Home Visitor and Learning; Reading: Working with Individual Children; My First Year of Teaching in an Open Classroom; Charts: Children Take Responsibility through Use of Charts;* and *No Longer Separate.*

■ Sidelights

Elaine Wickens told *SATA,* "I grew up in a small town in West Virginia, which had one river, two mountains, and a train that went through the middle of town. I liked being a part of that town, roaming the mountains and swimming in the river. I first began taking pictures of it to send to my brothers during the Second World War. Upon graduation from college, I began a career in teaching. I am currently on the faculty of Bank Street College of Education, where I am developing curriculum materials and working with teachers.

"Being committed to the importance of the home and the school in a child's life, I wanted a way to show this importance, not just say it. I wanted to encourage teachers to find out about the skills a child develops at home so that they can build on those skills when teaching at school."

■ For More Information See

PERIODICALS
School Library Journal, August, 1994.

* * *

WILLEY, Margaret 1950-

■ Personal

Born November 5, 1950, in Chicago, IL; daughter of Foster (an artist) and Barbara (Pistorius) Willey; married Richard Joanisse, 1980; children: one daughter. *Education:* Grand Valley State College, Allendale, Michigan, B.Ph., B.A., 1975; Bowling Green State University, Ohio, M.F.A., 1979.

■ Addresses

Home—431 Grant, Grand Haven, MI 49417.

■ Career

Writer.

■ Awards, Honors

American Library Association best books for young adults listings, 1983, for *The Bigger Book of Lydia,* 1986, for *Finding David Dolores,* 1988, for *If Not for You,* and 1990, for *Saving Lenny;* Creative Artist Grant, Michigan Arts Council, 1984, 1988, and 1995; Recommended Books for Reluctant YA Readers selection,

MARGARET WILLEY

Young Adult Services Division, 1989, for *If Not For You;* Best of the Best for Children listing, American Library Association, 1993, for *David Dolores.*

■ Writings

FOR YOUNG ADULTS

The Bigger Book of Lydia, Harper, 1983.
Finding David Dolores, Harper, 1986.
If Not for You, Harper, 1988.
Saving Lenny, Bantam, 1990.
The Melinda Zone, Bantam, 1993.
Facing the Music, Delacorte, 1996.

Also author of short stories published in *Redbook, Good Housekeeping,* and literary journals.

■ Sidelights

"The success of Margaret Willey's books for young adults is due at least in part to her skill at presenting totally believable characters who must struggle to resolve their problems in her coming-of-age dilemmas," remarked Jan Tyler in *Twentieth-Century Young Adult Writers.* "Hers are distinctly drawn personalities with a wide range of conflicts: problems with parents; troubles with boyfriends; breeches of loyalty between best friends; school woes; and particularly, always, the struggle to find and to be oneself."

Willey published her first novel for teenagers, *The Bigger Book of Lydia,* in 1983. The plot introduces a double conflict: Lydia wishes she wasn't so tiny, and Michelle wishes she wasn't so large. Nasty schoolyard nicknames hurt Lydia deeply, for she believes herself to be strong and independent. Due to her embarrassment and lack of support from teachers, she begins to withdraw from her classmates. With caution, lonely

Michelle befriends Lydia, and, as trust enters the friendship, Michelle reveals to Lydia her problem with anorexia nervosa. The two friends work together to solve their predicaments.

Willey followed *The Bigger Book of Lydia* with other novels addressing serious issues, including *The Melinda Zone,* which is about a fourteen-year-old girl's personal struggles with her parents' divorce. "Diverse though the works and characters of this ... ALA Best Book awardee certainly are," concluded Tyler, "it is easy to recognize a common thread: the attempt of the protagonist to strike a balance in the chaotic blend of relationships that so often characterizes adolescence."

■ Works Cited

Tyler, Jan, "Margaret Willey," *Twentieth-Century Young Adult Writers,* St. James Press, 1994, pp. 708-9.

Torn between the conflicting demands of her divorced parents, it takes a summer away and a new relationship for fifteen-year-old Melinda to resolve the situation.

For More Information See

PERIODICALS

Booklist, January 15, 1993.
Kirkus Reviews, November 1, 1983, p. 210; January 1, 1993, p. 69.
Publisher's Weekly, December 9, 1983, p. 50; January 18, 1993.
School Library Journal, December 1983, p. 78; March 1993, p. 224.
Voice of Youth Advocates, April, 1984, p. 36.

*   *   *

WILLIAMS, Pete
See FAULKNOR, Cliff(ord Vernon)

*   *   *

WOODRUFF, Noah 1977-

Personal

Born February 27, 1977; son of David (a chemical engineer) and Elvira (an author; maiden name, Pirozzi) Woodruff.

Addresses

Home—P.O. Box 24, Martins Creek, PA 18063.

Career

Student and illustrator.

Illustrator

(With brother, Jess Woodruff) Elvira Woodruff, *Dear Napoleon, I Know You're Dead, But . . .*, Holiday House, 1992.

Sidelights

Noah Woodruff told *SATA,* "As a high school senior I look at the whole idea of being an illustrator as a dream come true. My mom got me started and got me to illustrate one of her books. I've been influenced by such great authors as Isaac Asimov, Robert Heinlein, J. R. R. Tolkien, and David Eddings."

For More Information See

PERIODICALS

Booklist, December 15, 1992.
School Library Journal, October 1992.

WYLLIE, Stephen

■ Personal

Born in England. *Education:* Attended Royal Academy of Dramatic Arts.

■ Addresses

Office—c/o Sadie Fields Productions, 3D Westpoint, 36/37 Warple Way, London W3 OR6, England.

■ Career

Writer.

■ Awards, Honors

Redbook's top ten children's picture books citations, 1985, for *There Was an Old Woman,* and 1987, for *Monkey's Crazy Hotel.*

■ Writings

There Was an Old Woman, illustrated by Maureen Roffey, Harper, 1985, Methuen (London), 1985.
(With Anni Axworthy) *The Great Race,* Methuen, 1986, HarperCollins, 1987.
Monkey's Crazy Hotel, illustrated by Maureen Roffey, Harper, 1987, Methuen, 1987.
(With Anni Axworthy) *Topsy-turvy: A Mix-the-Tab Book,* Hamilton (London), 1988.
Snappity Snap!, illustrated by Maureen Roffey, Harper, 1989, Macmillan (London), 1989.
(With Anni Axworthy) *A House for White Rabbit: A Tab-and-Slot Book,* Hamish Hamilton (London), 1990.
Dinner with Fox: A 3-Dimensional Picture Book, illustrated by Korky Paul, Dial, 1990.
Ghost Train: A Spooky Hologram Book, illustrated by Brian Lee, Dial, 1992, Orchard (London), 1992.
The Incredible Cloud Machine, Gollancz (London), 1992.
The Red Dragon: A 3-D Picture Book with Press-out Disguises, illustrated by Jonathan Allen, Dial, 1993, Tango (London), 1993.
The War of the Wizards: A Magical Hologram Book, illustrated by Julek Heller, Dial, 1994, published in England as *The Two Wizards: A Magical Hologram Book,* Tango, 1994.
Bear Buys a Car: A 3-D Picture Book, illustrated by Jonathan Allen, Dial, 1995.
The Wizards' Revenge, illustrated by Julek Heller, Dial, in press.

■ For More Information See

PERIODICALS

Books for Your Children, autumn, 1992, p. 2; spring, 1994, p. 16.
Horn Book Guide, spring, 1993, p. 51; spring, 1994, p. 61.
Kirkus Reviews, October 15, 1993, p. 1340.

Y-Z

KEN YOUNG

YOUNG, Ken 1956-

■ Personal

Born October 31, 1956, in Baton Rouge, LA; son of Peter B. (in public relations) and JoAnne (Hinson) Young; married Deborah Kurtz (an editor), July 5, 1990; children: Emily, Joshua. *Education:* Auburn University, B.S., 1979; University of Alabama, M.B.A., 1981. *Hobbies and other interests:* Tennis.

■ Addresses

Home—5 Glen Dr., Plainview, NY 11803.

■ Career

Has worked for Sports Illustrated and CBS Sports.

■ Writings

NONFICTION

Cy Young Award Winners, Walker & Company, 1994.

Contributor of articles to *Sports Illustrated, People, The Sporting News,* and *Sports Illustrated for Kids.*

■ Sidelights

Ken Young's interest in sports began when he was a boy. "I've had a passion for sports since I was a small child," he confessed to *SATA.* "Working for *Sports Illustrated* (*SI*) and CBS Sports was like a dream come true. I first began writing while at *SI,* which continues to showcase some of the best sports writing in the world."

The juxtaposition of the good and bad in as public a spectacle as sports fascinates Ken Young. "There is great drama in sports," he told *SATA.* "I'm not just referring to the games. The struggle of the individual to overcome a variety of obstacles is what continually captures my interest."

■ For More Information See

PERIODICALS

School Library Journal, August, 1994.
Voice of Youth Advocates, April, 1995.

ZELDIS, Malcah 1931-

■ Personal

Born September 22, 1931, in New York, NY; daughter of Morris and Tania (Guttman) Brightman; married Chayym Zeldis, 1950 (divorced, 1974); children: David, Yona Zeldis McDonough. *Religion:* Jewish. *Hobbies and other interests:* Opera, ballet.

■ Addresses

Home—80 North Moore St., Apt. 30-L, New York, NY 10013.

■ Career

Artist. Member of the Museum of American Folk Art. *Exhibitions:* Exhibitor in numerous group exhibits, including "Muffled Voices: Folk Artists in Contemporary America," Museum of American Folk Art, New York City, and a solo exhibition, "Malcah Zeldis: American Self-Taught Artist," Museum of American Folk Art, 1988; paintings held in sixteen museum collections, including the permanent collections of the Museum of American Folk Art, New York, NY, the Smithsonian Institution, Washington, DC, and the American Museum, Bath, England, and various private collections.

■ Awards, Honors

Award from Memorial Foundation for Jewish Culture, 1981.

MALCAH ZELDIS

■ Illustrator

Mary Ann Hoberman, *A Fine Fat Pig, and Other Animal Poems,* HarperCollins, 1991.
Edith Kunhardt, *Honest Abe,* Greenwillow, 1993.
Yona Zeldis McDonough, *Eve and Her Sisters: Women of the Old Testament,* Greenwillow, 1994.
Rosemary L. Bray, *Martin Luther King,* Greenwillow, 1995.

Also illustrator of George Shannon's *Spring: A Haiku Story.*

■ Work in Progress

Illustrating a biography of Nelson Mandela; paintings of Biblical subjects.

■ Sidelights

The paintings of Malcah Zeldis, which grace such picture books as *Honest Abe* by Edith Kunhardt and Rosemary L. Bray's *Martin Luther King,* have been celebrated by folk art experts for their vivid colors, primitive representation, careful composition, and busy, detailed backgrounds. Some children may be surprised to learn that this internationally renowned artist did not develop her unique style under the influence of formal training or study. Instead, Zeldis taught herself how to paint the people, memories, ideas and events that were important to her.

Like her evocative paintings held in private collections and museums such as the Smithsonian Museum of Art in New York City, Zeldis' paintings for children present the profound with a seemingly "naive" or childlike portrayal of historical and literary figures and personalities. While some critics have wondered if children will appreciate Zeldis' primitive works, which are often unrealistic in color and shape, many have asserted that her paintings allow children insight into difficult, sensitive, or heretofore neglected topics and issues.

Zeldis was born in New York City and raised in Detroit. There her father, a blue-collar worker, painted whenever he found the time. Zeldis left the United States for Israel when she was just eighteen years old. She explored her Jewish heritage, lived on a kibbutz, and began her own family, which later relocated to New York. It was not until the mid-1970s, after Zeldis and her husband divorced, that she began to paint seriously and zealously. Just over a decade later, Zeldis' works received recognition by folk art critics. One of these critics, Henry Niemann, curated a show for the Museum of American Folk Art in New York in 1988 to introduce the general public to Zeldis' particular talent. According to a press release from the museum, the sixty paintings in this exhibit provide a sample of the range of subjects explored by Zeldis. Zeldis has recalled her past with family portraits like *My Wedding* and her Jewish heritage with *Family Seder* and renderings of scenes from the Old Testament. Zeldis has painted portraits of Martin Luther King, Abraham Lincoln, and Alexander

Zeldis used gouache and a folk-art style to illustrate Rosemary L. Bray's *Martin Luther King,* a biography made all the more accessible to young readers by the artist's colorful renderings.

Solzhenitsyn, all freedom fighters who inspired her. Finally, Zeldis has recorded her personal responses to events that rocked the world with *The Holocaust* and *Hiroshima.* As the museum press release explained, the "all-encompassing narrative" of these paintings "dramatically reveals the universal horror" these events have evoked.

Zeldis made her first contribution to children's literature by illustrating Mary Ann Hoberman's book of fourteen animal poems, *A Fine Fat Pig,* in 1991. The art for each poem, according to Barbara Chatton in *School Library Journal,* "reflects the content and humor" of the poetry while emphasizing the "unique features" of the animals.

Edith Kunhardt's *Honest Abe* demonstrates Zeldis' affinity for painting historical figures with bold colors against vivid patterns while providing children with a memorable history lesson. Abraham Lincoln appears on each page of this picture book in paintings that, in the words of a *Publishers Weekly* critic, seem "unpolished but genuinely American, much like the man they commemorate." In the opinion of *Booklist* writer Carolyn Phelan, *Honest Abe* is suitable for reading aloud: "this is the one teachers will be asking for come February."

Zeldis developed *Eve and Her Sisters* in collaboration with her daughter, Yona Zeldis McDonough. This picture book recalls the women's Jewish heritage while emphasizing the role of women in the Old Testament of the Bible. *Eve and Her Sisters* features the stories of fourteen women including Eve, Sarah, Rachel, Ruth, Deborah, Hagar, Esther, and the Queen of Sheba. While critics lauded McDonough's text, Patricia Dooley in *School Library Journal* concluded that the style of Zeldis' full-page paintings of the women "might appeal more to sophisticated viewers." Noting that the women in the paintings "look alike," Ilene Cooper also commented in *Booklist* that Zeldis' "bright, bubblegum colors" result in illustrations that are "full of energy."

A *Publishers Weekly* critic commented that Zeldis' rendering of the renowned African American leader in Rosemary L. Bray's *Martin Luther King* "may persuade those already familiar with his story to see it in a new light." Zeldis' "eye-catching, full-page gouache paintings," as *School Library Journal* critic Martha Rosen described them, complement Bray's detailed presentation of Dr. King's childhood, adult struggles, death, and legacy. Rosen appreciated a painting of an enlarged King in jail, "guarded by small scale policemen."

■ Works Cited

Chatton, Barbara, review of *A Fine Fat Pig, School Library Journal,* April, 1991.

Cooper, Ilene, review of *Eve and Her Sisters, Booklist,* May 15, 1994.

Dooley, Patricia, review of *Eve and Her Sisters, School Library Journal,* May, 1994.

Review of *Honest Abe, Publishers Weekly,* December 28, 1992.

Review of *Martin Luther King, Publishers Weekly,* November 28, 1994.

Museum of American Folk Art Presents 'Malcah Zeldis: American Self-Taught Artist' (press release), Museum of American Folk Art, 1988.

Phelan, Carolyn, review of *Honest Abe, Booklist,* December 1, 1992.

Rosen, Martha, review of *Martin Luther King, School Library Journal,* February, 1995.

■ For More Information See

PERIODICALS

Booklist, February 15, 1995.

Kirkus Reviews, December 15, 1992; February 15, 1995.

Publishers Weekly, April 18, 1994.

*   *   *

ZEPHANIAH, Benjamin (Obadiah Iqbal) 1958-

■ Personal

Born April 15, 1958, in Birmingham, England; son of Oswald (a post office manager) and Valerie (a nurse; maiden name, Eubanks) Springer; married Amina Iqbal

BENJAMIN ZEPHANIAH

Zephaniah (a theater administrator), March 17, 1990. *Education:* Attended Ward End Hall Comprehensive School and Broadway Comprehensive School.

■ Addresses

Agent—Sandra Boyce Management, 1 Kingsway House, Albion Rd., London N16 0TA, England.

■ Career

Poet, playwright, and performing artist. Africa Arts Collective, Liverpool, England, writer in residence, 1989. Actor in films and television programs, including *Didn't You Kill My Brother?, Farendg,* and *Dread Poets Society.* President, SHOP (self-help organization for ex-prisoners); chairperson, Hackney Empire Theatre, and Umoja Housing Co-Op; patron, Irie Dance Company, Tom Allen Centre, Market Nursery–Hackney, Newham Young People's Theatre Scheme, Chinese Women's Refuge Group, Music Works–Brixton, and Newcastle One Work Association.

■ Awards, Honors

British Broadcasting Corporation Young Playwrights Festival award, 1988, for *Hurricane Dub.*

■ Writings

FOR CHILDREN

Talking Turkeys (poetry), Penguin, 1994.

POETRY

Pen Rhythm, Page One Books, 1980.
The Dread Affair, Arena, 1985.
In a Liverpool, Africa Arts Collective, 1988.
Rasta Time in Palestine, Shakti, 1990.
City Psalms, Bloodaxe Books, 1992.

PLAYS

Playing the Right Tune (stage play), produced at Theatre East, London, 1985.
Job Rocking (stage play), produced at Riverside Studios, 1987.
Hurricane Dub (radio play), British Broadcasting Corporation, c. 1988.
Streetwise (stage play), produced at Temba, 1990.
Delirium (stage play), produced at Union Dance Company, 1990.
The Trial of Mickey Tekka (stage play), produced at the Hay-on-Wye Literature Festival, 1991.
Dread Poets Society (teleplay), British Broadcasting Corporation, 1991.

Also contributor to numerous television and radio programs for the British Broadcasting Corporation, Menton Films, After Image, Thames TV, Tyne Tees, Yorkshire-TV, and World Service.

RECORDINGS

Dub Ranting, The Cartel, 1982.
Rasta, The Cartel, 1983.
Big Boys Don't Make Girls Cry, The Cartel, 1984.
(With The Wailers) *Free South Africa,* The Cartel, 1986.
Us and Dem, Island/Mango, 1990.
Crisis, Workers Playtime, 1992.
Back to Roots, Acid Jazz, 1995.

■ Work in Progress

A history of the presence of slaves in the British Isles for the British Broadcasting Corporation, for television and also in book form.

■ Sidelights

Although he was born in Birmingham, England, Benjamin Zephaniah spent much of his childhood in Jamaica, giving him a multiracial experience that has shaped his work as a poet, playwright, musician, and actor. Reminiscent at times of rasta or rap music, Zephaniah's poetry bypasses the formality of written verse to find its rhythms in the everyday speech of ordinary people. Having produced several plays, records, books, and even a television film, Zephaniah brought out his first volume of poetry for children in 1994. Like the author's other work, the poems in *Talking Turkeys* recall the oral tradition in their use of rhythm and language, and cover subjects of freedom, peace, love, and politics. As D. A. Young of *Junior Bookshelf* notes, Zephaniah's "wit is devastating and his well aimed shafts of satire rarely miss their mark," making *Talking Turkeys* "jolly good fun."

Zephaniah once commented: "My mission: to popularize poetry. Many working class people in Britain and worldwide believe that poetry is an art of the middle class. To redress this, I make a great effort to perform anywhere on the planet, always try to keep my publications to a low purchase price and write around issues that concern working class people. Very concerned about the idea of a New World Order: Who ordered it?"

■ Works Cited

Young, D. A., review of *Talking Turkeys, Junior Bookshelf,* February, 1995, p. 47.

■ For More Information See

BOOKS

Contemporary Poets, St. James Press, 1991.